Cases in Business Strategy & Policy

Joseph C. Latona
College of Business Administration
The University of Akron

K. Mark Weaver
College of Commerce and Business Administration
University of Alabama

Ronald M. Zigli
College of Business
Appalachian State University

Anthony M. Akel
College of Business Administration
C. W. Post Center of Long Island University

Published by

G05 **SOUTH-WESTERN PUBLISHING CO.**

CINCINNATI   WEST CHICAGO, ILL.   DALLAS   PELHAM MANOR, N.Y.   PALO ALTO, CALIF.

Preface

CASES IN BUSINESS STRATEGY & POLICY contains a repertoire of cases which were submitted by or solicited from colleagues throughout the country. It was inspired by a previously published casebook entitled *Application of Decision Sciences in Organizations: A Case Approach.* Many of the included cases were extracted from that textbook. Still other cases were developed at subsequent workshops conducted at a series of annual meetings of the American Institute for Decision Sciences. All cases have been pretested in the classroom. In most instances the real organizational name has been used; however, a few cases have been disguised at the request of the contributing organization.

This casebook may be used as the primary text supplemented by in-class materials or as a complement to another strategic management or business policy textbook. A variety of cases are included. Some of these may be analyzed by students having little or no background in the specific area while others are more challenging, requiring an extensive background in the topic area gained through either personal experience or previous course work.

The book is divided into seven major sections. The first six sections focus on vital environments or functional areas and are designed to develop analytical and diagnostic skills. The last section consists of seven comprehensive and integrative cases challenging the student to apply those skills. There are 37 cases in all which vary in complexity, type of organization, focus, and organizational size. A variety of organizational types are illustrated, ranging from educational institutions to highly technical manufacturing firms. Organizational size ranges from the small entrepreneurial firm to the huge multinational conglomerate. All major functional areas of business are covered, and a number of excellent international and comprehensive cases have been included.

Section I introduces the impact of the environment on strategy and policy formulation. Several cases highlight selected relevant issues in the environment. For example, deregulation and its effects on the trucking industry are presented. Other issues include acquisition strategy, the effects of federal regulations, and the social responsibility of organizations.

Section II focuses on human resource management in organizations. It begins with an Australian subsidiary of an American oil company, which must find a way to accommodate changes relative to the characteristics or profile of its employees and customers in an entirely different and unfamiliar culture. The remaining cases introduce a variety of topics including employee reaction to job enrichment, resistance to change, organizational conflict, manpower planning, the consequences of developing technology and production more rapidly than human resources, interpersonal conflict, overlapping lines of authority, and ambiguous definition of responsibility in a not-for-profit organization.

Section III addresses a series of classical marketing questions. It begins with a fast-food company faced with the need to develop an effective promotional strategy and an accurate, timely, forecasting system. The next case moves from the development of a forecasting system to problems encountered when such a system is implemented in a maladroit manner. Other topics in this section include the appropriate use of consultants, resistance to technological change, the misuse of quantitative forecasting systems, and the consequences of an advanced stage of marketing myopia relative to forecasting, budgeting, and advertising policy.

Production and operations management is the subject of Section IV. A variety of organizations are presented, some with serious operational problems and others with specific, "down-to-earth," pragmatic shop-floor questions. Also covered are model buildings, the efficacy of models for solving production and inventory control problems, logistics, and other management science techniques.

The financial function of organizations is examined in Section V. A variety of topics including cost structures, pricing methods, liquidity, budgeting, financial forecasting, standard cost systems, and variance analysis are presented. Questions are raised about the efficacy and acceptance of each of these financial decision tools and cycles by those people that must implement them. Section V then shifts the focus from internal financial efficiency to external financial effectiveness. Financing company growth through the use of equity, debt, and/or retained earnings is addressed in one case, and the assessment of several projects relative to long-run return on investment is the issue in another.

Section VI is entitled "Policy Issues in International Business." As the name implies, international business is the subject of this section. A number of small and large firms operating in the world market are presented. The impact of culture, economics, and politics on multinational firms are some of the topics introduced. Multinational competition, variegated investment opportunities, employee compensation in other countries, world distribution systems, and different legal environments are some of the specific topics covered in this section. The vulnerability of U.S. firms doing business abroad is exemplified in one case where a U.S. company becomes embroiled in a myriad of difficulties promulgated by change in a foreign government and its commensurate shift in regulatory policy. Government decrees, unilateral decisions by foreign firms, and possible litigation at home are just some of the problems presented.

Section VII concludes the casebook and consists of seven comprehensive cases covering a broad range of issues and functional areas. By the time the reader has reached this section, he or she should have developed all the needed skills and competencies to fully evaluate each case. These cases are deliberately sequenced and reflect varying degrees of complexity.

We would like to express our gratitude to the authors of the included cases and for the assistance and cooperation extended to us by the American Institute for Decision Sciences.

Joseph C. Latona ● K. Mark Weaver ● Ronald M. Zigli ● Anthony M. Akel

Contents

DYNAMIC ENVIRONMENT OF BUSINESS STRATEGY AND POLICY

Executives must understand the dynamic environment in which firms operate to properly evaluate alternative courses of action. The need for corporate strategies and policies to cope with changing conditions faced by all functional units requires constant review and appraisal of corporate policies. Previous implicit strategies begin to break down as change and growth occur in a firm. The need for explicit strategy statements is a result of increasing needs for coordination in this dynamic environment.

The *McLean Trucking Company* case requires a review of the planning process so the firm will have a sound footing for anticipating future changes. The case illustrates the consequences of multiple changes in the operating environment faced by the firm. Deregulation, changing labor conditions, and a depressed economy are only part of the changing conditions. McLean must consider: (1) how the firm can convert these situations into opportunities; (2) what impacts deregulation will have on the firm; (3) the industry; and (4) where McLean will be in relation to the industry in the next five years. Analysts of the operating and financial functions within this complex environment can provide a fruitful experience.

Environmental impact and managerial style can also interact to determine opportunities and limitations in the strategic planning process. The *Chrysler Corporation* case requires analysis of the total environment facing the firm at various points in its history and how the various management styles and values of the chief executive influenced strategic decisions. Strategy formulation in less than an ideal environment can be explored in this case.

In the *American Express Company* case, an abortive attempt to take over the diversified publishing house of McGraw-Hill, Inc. is presented. Numerous defenses by McGraw are offered for review. The corporation primarily analyzes and illustrates the basic dimensions of a conglomerate takeover bid in the media industry. Issues from corporate acquisition criteria to the role of federal regulations are available for analysis.

The *Oximeron Manufacturing Company* case shifts the focus of top management from basic regulatory and operating limitations to the more nebulous areas of social policy formulations. Pressures on corporations to be "socially responsible" citizens is a continuous force for change. This case examines the evolution from passive to active involvement in solutions to the problems facing the community *and* the firm. A basic process of identifying "social needs" and formulating a response to them is introduced. Then a change in the game, an arrest of an executive's son, drastically altered the firm's approach to dealing with a "not-so-nice" social issue. Analysis of the corporate procedures to cope with the problems provides an opportunity to look inside a firm.

The last case in this section is the *Braniff International Corporation* case—a classic example of an ill-considered response to deregulation. This case provides an opportunity to glimpse a business failure in the making and then to conduct a postmortem on the interlocking events leading up to that failure.

The development of acceptable responses to the dynamic environment firms face in decision making is a key factor in the long run for growth and survival of the firm. The cases in this section offer a wide range of situations for analysis.

The McLean Trucking Company*

Amory Mellen, president and chief executive officer of the McLean Trucking Company, was concerned with several significant developments which had impacted the company's operations over the past few months. It was apparent to him that current planning had to be reviewed and updated so McLean would have a firm footing from which to anticipate future changes.

McLean Trucking was the fourth largest Class I motor freight common carrier of general commodities in the United States.[1] The company employed more than 13,000 persons and served 42 states, the District of Columbia, and the Canadian province of British Columbia. McLean operated 206 terminals to service its fleet of 14,000 tractors, trailers, and local delivery trucks. The company was primarily engaged in the transportation of less-than-truckload (LTL) and truckload (TL) freight. Over 70 percent of the company's operating revenue came from LTL shipments (shipments weighing less than 10,000 pounds).

McLean operated a division for specialized freight called PaceSetter Transportation. This division utilized owner-operated flatbed, reefer, van, and container equipment to transport volume commodities nationwide. McLean was also the parent company to four wholly-owned subsidiaries: Houston Trailer & Truck Body, Inc., Modern Automotive Services, Inc., Salem Contract Carrier, Inc., and Malja Corporation.

When President Jimmy Carter signed into law the Motor Carrier Act of 1980 (MCA), the federal government completed its move toward deregulation of the trucking industry (see Appendix I). Bennett Whitlock, Jr., the president of the American Trucking Associations (an industry trade group representing the larger trucking firms), commented that the consumer needed "reregulation," not deregulation.[2] The American Trucking Associations (ATA) was opposed to the 1980 MCA.

Fuel prices increased 85 percent in 1979, and another 30 percent in 1980. This increase was forcing McLean to rethink its route structure and equipment design to improve fuel economy. Recent litigation in both state and federal courts was having an impact on which states would allow length and weight restrictions on vehicles to be relaxed. A work stoppage by the Teamsters'

---

*This case was prepared by Don Powell and Sexton Adams, North Texas State University, and Adelaide Griffin, Texas Woman's University, with the intention of providing a basis for class discussion rather than illustrating either effective or ineffective management of a business situation.

Union (organized labor's representative in the trucking industry) occurred in April of 1979. As a result, significant wage concessions were made and private carriers gained a large portion of the market share. As Mr. Mellen reflected over these events, "It is obvious there has never been a greater need for effective management." A ten-year summary of operations for McLean is presented in Exhibit 1.

CORPORATE HISTORY

McLean Trucking began operations in North Carolina in 1934. It has grown since that time through mergers with other trucking firms, purchase of the operating rights held by other firms, and by obtaining new route authorization from the Interstate Commerce Commission (ICC). A summary of the important events in McLean's history is found in Exhibit 2.[3]

The first of McLean's wholly-owned subsidiaries was Houston Trailer & Truck Body, Inc. This unit repaired and rebuilt aluminum and stainless steel tankers and trailers. Many of these units were used in the McLean Fleet. Houston Trailer was one of the largest suppliers of heavy-duty trailer parts in the Southwest.

The second subsidiary was Modern Automotive Services, Inc., of Winston-Salem. Modern Automotive was the maintenance arm of McLean, doing preventive maintenance, major overhauls, repairs, and rebuilds of power units. The firm also operated a tire recapping plant for tires used in the McLean fleet. Purchasing and procurement duties were handled by Modern for the entire McLean Company.

The third subsidiary was Salem Contract Carrier, Inc., which operated as a contract carrier serving the K mart Corporation. It was based in Charlotte, North Carolina, where K mart had a major distribution facility, and handled K mart movements to points in 24 states. This unit was formed in an effort to take advantage of industry deregulation. Contract business provided a guaranteed amount of freight at a prearranged price. According to Lynn Perucca, the sales manager for McLean in Carrollton, Texas, Salem had proved to be a profitable unit.[4] McLean could be expected to expand its contract operations.

The fourth subsidiary was the Malja Corporation, which was a real estate holding company for terminals and other properties throughout the McLean system. Malja was responsible for locating and acquiring terminal space, including the construction of new facilities. In fast growing markets, some of these facilities were acquired through lease agreements, and Malja acted as the lessee. The large maintenance base and parts warehouse of Modern Automotive Services was held for them by Malja.

MANAGEMENT

The top management and directors of McLean are listed in Exhibit 3. The board of directors met monthly to discuss operating results and corporate policy and direction.

It had been the policy of McLean to stress achievement in its management team and to use a college recruitment program to obtain persons who could quickly develop into qualified managers. Trainees hired under this program began their career loading freight in a terminal. After a few weeks they would drive over-the-road trucks for a few months—developing an understanding of the McLean system, where it was, and how it worked. Other typical assignments in the first year of employment included working as a dispatcher, bookkeeper, and loading supervisor. This training and variety of job assignments gave upper management a good appraisal of the trainees' potentials. Personnel hired under this program were expected to advance beyond first level supervisory positions.

Management took pride in the fact that almost all of McLean's executives were college graduates. They believed that this was unique in the trucking industry, although consistent with the innovativeness and complexity of McLean.

OPERATIONS

The organization chart in Exhibit 4 shows that McLean had adopted a geographically divisionalized structure for its trucking operations. Five geographic divisions were each headed by a vice president. The sixth division was PaceSetter Transportation, and it was also headed by a unique vice president.

Each of the division vice presidents had numerous district managers reporting to them. The district managers were in control of local operations. An integrated computer system, utilizing an IBM 370 mainframe and central processor, speeded the communication and control process. All of the 206 freight terminals were linked to the main computer in Winston-Salem with an input/output printer. Full period WATS and regular telephone lines tied the system together.

The district managers were provided daily operations summaries through the computer. This data organized such items as fuel and maintenance expense, payroll costs, sales, cash flow, and return on investment. Variances from budget were calculated and highlighted for comparison.

Reporting to the district managers were the safety managers, sales managers, and terminal managers. The local sales representatives reported to the sales managers. The terminal managers, who were responsible for the movement of freight into, out of, and within a terminal, supervised drivers, dockworkers, dispatchers, and local supervisory personnel. Safety managers were responsible for administering safety procedures within the district.

The organization chart also shows that the other functional areas were individually headed by vice presidents, who reported to executive vice presidents. McLean's primary business was hauling freight. Other operations provided support to the trucking operation. National accounts, for example, were handled by sales personnel from the corporate office as well as local sales representatives.

Exhibit 1   **Ten-Year Summary**

	1980	1979	1978
Summary of Operations			
(In thousands except for per share items)			
Operating revenues			
Carrier	$598,352	$483,751	$431,812
Refinery....................................	121,945	71,712	58,431
Other	4,592	3,897	3,453
Total	724,889	559,360	493,696
Operating expenses	725,826	541,372	465,742
Interest expense	8,158	5,959	4,220
Income (loss) before income taxes			
Carrier	(8,368)	9,010	22,290
Refinery....................................	(575)	2,959	1,696
Other	1,098	781	570
Total	(7,845)	12,750	24,556
Income tax expense (benefit)	(5,414)	4,630	9,140
Net income (loss)	(2,432)	8,120	15,416
Net income (loss) per common share[1]	(.43)	1.44	2.74
Cash dividends per common share[1]	.64	.64	.58
Selected Financial Data			
(In thousands except for per share items)			
Earnings (loss) retained in the business for the			
year..	$ (6,034)	$ 4,518	$ 12,152
Current assets.................................	122,686	99,570	74,145
Tangible property cost..........................	271,509	261,042	212,658
Current liabilities..............................	81,251	72,730	54,354
Long-term debt	111,468	93,956	54,129
Working capital	41,434	26,840	19,791
Shareholders' equity	102,950	108,984	104,458
Book value per common share[1]	18.29	19.36	18.56
Selecting Operating Data			
(Exclusive of noncarrier revenue and expenses)			
Revenue per mile	$2.32	$1.99	$1.85
Revenue per 100 pounds........................	$6.72	$4.62	$4.20
Pounds billed (in millions)	8,903	10,468	10,280
Number of shipments (in thousands)..............	6,514	5,601	5,583
Average weight per shipment (lbs.)	1,367	1,869	1,841
Average load (lbs.)	27,663	29,404	29,269
Ton miles of intercity freight carried (in millions)	3,570	3,576	3,413
Intercity miles traveled (in thousands)............	258,116	243,252	233,217
Average haul (miles)...........................	802	683	664
Number of employees at end of year	13,767	13,636	11,428
Average carrier revenue per employee............	$43,463	$40,648[3]	$37,785
Average ton miles per carrier employee	259,323	300,507[3]	298,652

[1]All "per common share" data have been adjusted to reflect two-for-one stock splits effective January 14, 1972, and July 1, 1976.

[2]Acquired Winston Refining Co. (formerly Fort Worth Refining Company) October 1, 1973.

[3]Based on average number of carrier employees.

1977	1976	1975	1974[2]	1973	1972	1971
$375,096	$319,708	$266,132	$277,515	$232,952	$194,226	$169,363
58,975	49,959	52,594	31,657			
3,120	2,034	1,643	1,750	1,110	867	672
437,191	371,701	320,369	310,922	234,062	195,093	170,035
407,738	341,922	299,894	286,200	213,358	176,728	155,782
2,849	2,927	4,181	3,729	2,291	2,199	2,463
24,646	24,767	15,325	20,878	18,722	16,176	11,791
2,280	2,198	1,748	704			
500	368	351	314	184	146	124
27,426	27,333	17,424	21,896	18,906	16,322	11,915
12,125	12,367	7,433	10,338	8,673	7,711	5,886
15,301	14,967	9,991	11,558	10,233	8,612	6,029
2.73	2.68	1.79	2.07	1.84	1.55	1.09
.46	.415	.36	.345	.30	.30	.25
$ 12,727	$ 12,651	$ 7,983	$ 9,634	$ 8,561	$ 6,940	$ 4,638
57,877	58,773	50,150	51,208	35,579	33,909	27,287
179,344	160,202	139,703	124,508	107,512	95,372	91,102
47,076	50,568	36,354	40,345	24,580	25,833	18,382
33,319	34,741	43,910	39,618	33,117	30,561	34,967
10,801	8,205	13,796	10,862	11,000	8,076	8,905
92,207	78,860	66,135	58,151	48,490	39,930	32,972
16.40	14.13	11.86	10.43	8.70	7.16	5.92
$1.73	$1.56	$1.47	$1.33	$1.19	$1.11	$1.02
$3.98	$3.70	$3.43	$3.01	$2.83	$2.78	$2.57
9,415	8,635	7,700	9,220	8,243	6,979	6,591
5,752	5,196	4,753	5,284	5,142	4,720	4,755
1,637	1,662	1,635	1,745	1,603	1,479	1,386
28,526	27,012	26,940	27,339	25,264	23,963	24,136
3,087	2,766	2,434	2,843	2,480	2,089	2,006
216,438	204,776	180,670	207,970	196,330	174,320	166,270
656	641	626	617	602	599	609
10,519	10,167	9,295	10,127	9,600	8,635	8,343
$35,700	$31,400	$28,600	$27,800	$24,200	$22,600	$20,400
293,500	272,000	261,800	285,000	256,700	241,900	240,500

Exhibit 2   **Important Events in McLean's History**

1934   Founded March 10 in North Carolina.

1943   Established general offices in Winston-Salem, North Carolina, June 7.

1945   Purchased operating authority of American Trucking Company, November 1.

1947   Purchased operating authority of Pee Dee Express, Inc., October 31.

1948   Purchased operating authority of Simpson Motor Lines, Inc., April 2.

1951   Purchased operating authority of Fleetway Motor Freight, Inc., November 9.

1952   Acquired Modern Automotive Services, Inc. as a wholly-owned subsidiary (maintenance).

1953   Organized Malja Corporation as wholly-owned subsidiary (real estate).

1957   Merged Carolina Motor Express Lines, Inc., (CMX) July 1, following operating under temporary authority since February 18, 1952.

1958   Trading in McLean Trucking Company common stock on the New York Stock Exchange began January 6—first in the industry on the "Big Board."

        Merged Service, Incorporated, May 16, following operation under temporary authority since June 26, 1956.

1963   Merged Hayes Freight Lines, Inc., December 31, following operation under temporary authority since July 16, 1958.

1966   Merged Chicago Express, Inc., (CXI) December 31, following operation under temporary authority since December 13, 1962.

1968   Purchased and merged Daily Transport, Inc., June 1.

        Purchased operating authority of Almar's Express Inc., June 24.

1969   Purchased Young-Hall-West Equipment Corp., Houston, Texas, September 30, and merged its principal operating subsidiary, Herrin Transportation Company, October 1.

1970   Purchased operating authority of Harrison Motor Express, January 30, following operation under temporary authority since October 1, 1968.

        Purchased operating authority of Murray's Fast Express, Inc., April 27, following operation under temporary authority since November 24, 1969.

1971   Purchased operating authority of Boston and Maine Transportation Company, Inc., October 31, following operation under leased rights since May 14.

1973   Organized Winston Refining Co. as a wholly-owned subsidiary, and merged Fort Worth Refining Company, Forth Worth, Texas, into Winston Refining Co., November 1. Fort Worth Refining Company was purchased October 1.

1974   Purchased partial operating authority of Valley Express, Inc., Schofield, Wisconsin, May 23, extending service to Milwaukee, Wisconsin.

1977	Purchased operating authority of South Texas Motor Lines, Inc., March 15, following operation under temporary authority since June 18, 1976.
	Merged Topeka Motor Freight, Inc., July 31. Commenced operating under temporary authority October 1, 1972.
	Purchased Wolverine Express, Inc., of Muskegon, Michigan, October 1, extending service to a major portion of Michigan.
1978	Merged Crescent Motor Lines of Spartanburg, South Carolina, August 15. Crescent had been operated as a wholly-owned subsidiary since May 1.
	Occupied new corporate headquarters building in Winston-Salem beginning November 6. It had been under construction since May 1976.
1979	Purchased certain operating rights of ET & WNC Transportation Company, February 20, following operation under temporary authority since November 15, 1977.
	Received temporary authority from the Interstate Commerce Commission May 1 to lease the operating authority of O.N.C. Freight Systems, the general commodity motor freight business of ROCOR International of Palo Alto, California.
	Following I.C.C. temporary approval, organized Salem Contract Carrier, Inc., August 16, 1979, as a wholly-owned subsidiary to provide specialized contract carrier service.
	Sold operating authority and equipment of Herrin Petroleum Transport Equipment Corp., September 26, 1979, to Sunbelt Transport, Inc., of Dallas, Texas.
	Merged Wolverine Express, Inc., December 31, 1979, after operating it as a wholly-owned subsidiary since October 1, 1977.
1980	Received initial I.C.C. decision May 16, 1980, pertaining to the grant of permanent authority to acquire the assets of O.N.C. Freight Systems.
	Reorganized Special Commodities Division as PaceSetter Transportation and moved its headquarters June 16, 1980, from Hammond, Indiana, to Winston-Salem, North Carolina.
	Sold Winston Refining Co. on October 31, 1980.
1981	Received authority from the I.C.C. to serve all points in Alabama and Mississippi.

Exhibit 3

Executive Officers and Directors
(Year Elected)

*Paul P. Davis (1948)
   Chairman of the Board
   Chairman of the Executive Committee
   Joined the company in 1943
   Elected president in 1955
   Elected to present office in 1970

*Amory Mellen, Jr. (1968)
   President and Chief Executive Officer
   Member of the Executive Committee
   Joined the company in 1951
   Elected president in 1970
   Elected Chief Executive Officer in 1976

*Fred C. Bauer (1971)
   Executive Vice President/Marketing
   Member of the Executive Committee
   Joined the company in 1951
   Elected to present office in 1974

*Joe B. Eldridge (1974)
   Executive Vice President/Administration
   Treasurer
   Member of the Executive Committee
   Joined the company in 1952
   Elected to present office in 1974

*David J. Wanchick (1979)
   Executive Vice President/Field Operations
   Joined the company in 1979
   Elected to present office in 1979

Alvin M. Bodford
   Vice President/Comptroller
   Joined the company in 1973
   Elected to present office in 1978

Edwin R. Brenegar, Jr.
   Vice President/Personnel
   Joined the company in 1949
   Elected to present office in 1974

Wilton W. Broadwell
   Vice President/Western Division
   Joined the company in 1953
   Elected to present office in 1979

Alton Z. Canady
   Vice President/Transportation
   Joined the company in 1950
   Elected to present office in 1977

S. Vernon Cartner
   Vice President/Traffic
   Joined the company in 1949
   Elected to present office in 1979

P. Michael Davis
   Vice President/Eastern Division
   Joined the company in 1962
   Elected to present office in 1979

T. Michael Guthrie
   Vice President/Claims Prevention
   Joined the company in 1974
   Elected to present office in 1980

*Claude M. Hamrick (1975)
   Vice President/General Counsel
   Secretary
   Joined the company in 1977
   Elected to present office in 1977

C. R. Jones
   Vice President/Labor Relations
   Joined the company in 1975
   Elected to present office in 1976

Floyd L. Morris
   Vice President/Maintenance
   Joined the company in 1961
   Elected to present office in 1978

*Member of the Board of Directors.

John R. Morris
   Vice President/Midwestern Division
   Joined the company in 1963
   Elected to present office in 1979

James C. Ratcliff
   Vice President/Sales
   Joined the company in 1948
   Elected to present office in 1974

Myron W. Sexton
   Vice President/Southern Division
   Joined the company in 1953
   Elected to present office in 1976

Gordon M. Sisk, Jr.
   Vice President/PaceSetter Transportation
   (Special Commodities Division)
   Joined the company in 1956
   Elected to present office in 1980

Charles W. Staley
   Vice President/Real Estate
   Joined the company in 1952
   Elected to present office in 1961

Robert H. Sykes
   Vice President/Southwestern Division
   Joined the company in 1963
   Elected to present office in 1976

*James K. Glenn (1971)
   General Partner, Quality Oil Company,
      Winston-Salem, North Carolina
   Member of the Executive Commitee
   Member of the Audit Committee

*J. Berkley Ingram, Jr. (1977)
   Vice Chairman of the Board, Massachusetts
      Mutual Life Insurance Company,
      Springfield, Massachusetts
   Chairman of the Audit Committee

*Dalton L. McMichael (1979)
   Chairman of the Board
   Chief Executive Officer and Treasurer,
      MacField Texturing Inc., Madison, North
      Carolina

*Claude H. Wells, Jr. (1955)
   Retired Vice President/Operations
   McLean Trucking Company
   Member of the Audit Committee

Exhibit 4

Organization Chart
McLean Trucking Company

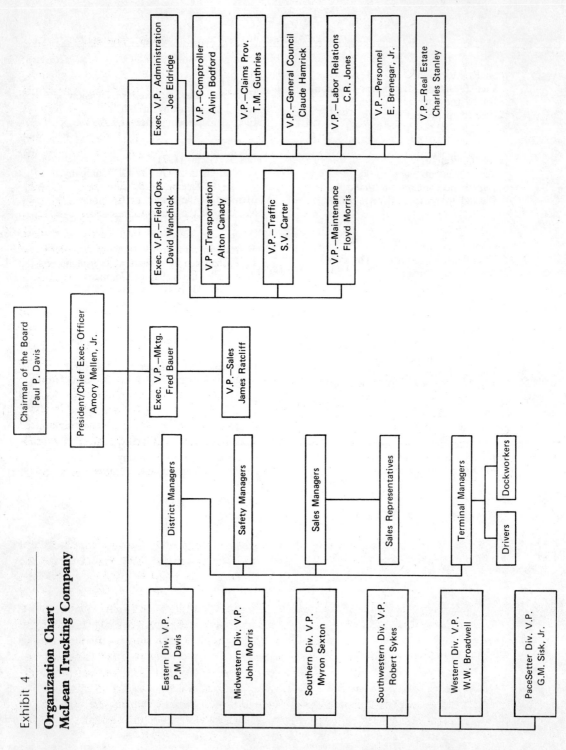

Chairman of the Board
Paul P. Davis

President/Chief Exec. Officer
Amory Mellen, Jr.

Exec. V.P.—Mktg.
Fred Bauer

V.P.—Sales
James Ratcliff

Exec. V.P.—Field Ops.
David Wanchick

V.P.—Transportation
Alton Canady

V.P.—Traffic
S.V. Carter

V.P.—Maintenance
Floyd Morris

Exec. V.P. Administration
Joe Eldridge

V.P.—Comptroller
Alvin Bodford

V.P.—Claims Prov.
T.M. Guthries

V.P.—General Council
Claude Hamrick

V.P.—Labor Relations
C.R. Jones

V.P.—Personnel
E. Brenegar, Jr.

V.P.—Real Estate
Charles Stanley

District Managers

Safety Managers

Sales Managers

Sales Representatives

Terminal Managers

Drivers

Dockworkers

Eastern Div. V.P.
P.M. Davis

Midwestern Div. V.P.
John Morris

Southern Div. V.P.
Myron Sexton

Southwestern Div. V.P.
Robert Sykes

Western Div. V.P.
W.W. Broadwell

PaceSetter Div. V.P.
G.M. Sisk, Jr.

THE McLEAN FLEET

McLean purchased equipment through special order. The fleet was large enough that the company felt this could be done economically. The budgeting system which was assisted by the computer, helped in the equipment planning process. When the the decision was made to purchase units, the bid routine began. McLean would specify how many units were needed, and what particular equipment was needed. The trucks would be custom made for McLean, with the particular engines, transmissions, axles, and other features desired. Specification sheets were sent to all truck manufacturers, with requests for bids.

McLean had purchased many makes of trucks over the years. General Motors Corporation (GMC) had received the majority of McLean's business. GMC was also one of McLean's largest shippers. Mr. Niendorhf, district manager for Texas and Louisiana, noted in an interview that Caterpillar diesel engines were being used almost exclusively now because of their excellent fuel economy and longevity. Company statistics showed that a $1.0 million annual savings in fuel expense was achieved for every one-tenth of a gallon improvement in fleet fuel mileage ratings.

The trailer fleet consisted mainly of 40 and 45-foot trailers. McLean did have some 27-foot "pup" units which could be operated as doubles, but because the route structure had been based historically in the South and East, it was deemed infeasible to maintain a large fleet. Mr. Perucca, the Carrollton sales manager, explained that it could become an operations nightmare to manage a fleet with short and long units intermixed. It was not economical to haul pup units individually over long distances as opposed to 40-foot units. It was a burdensome task to monitor short and long unit activities. With the relaxing of length laws in some states, it was now feasible to begin using more pup trailers.

Trailers typically had a depreciable life of ten years. Power units would normally last for five to seven years.

THE COMPUTER SYSTEM

McLean used its computer as a sophisticated tool in moving freight. It kept up with each bill of lading (the document which in effect was an order for McLean's services) currently in the system, and could be used on a real-time basis to locate shipments. If a customer called wanting to know when his delivery would arrive, it could be located within seconds and advice given. This system also knew at any given time what driver was driving the truck the shipment was in, and whether or not it was on a dock somewhere. Department of Transportation regulations required a driver to work no more than ten consecutive hours without an eight-hour rest period. The computer helped monitor each driver in this regard; other personnel data was also maintained for administrative functions. A mileage and maintenance history was kept on all units in the fleet. A report was printed daily showing which units were due for an oil change, preventive maintenance, or major overhaul.

Management believed that the integrated computer system, which it called its Management Information System, helped McLean grow to its present size. McLean delivered over 100,000 shipments weekly, and it was felt that the activity needed to coordinate and control this would be ineffective without the computer. It was also used for accounting and record keeping in many other phases of the business, such as payroll, planning, and tracking operating results. Each district manager was provided a daily report on the profit margin earned by revenue breakdown in that territory.

THE TERMINAL NETWORK

Moving the thousands of pieces of freight that entered the system daily was the most complex task of trucking companies. The management of McLean believed that most Class I and II carriers were basically homogenous in the eyes of the shipper, except for one factor: service. McLean had built its operations strategy by providing more service to each customer. Frequently, this translates into being first and fastest in getting a shipment from its origin to its destination.

Local Terminals

McLean used a network concept in routing freight in which local terminals were clustered around 16 larger terminals known as break-bulk terminals. In essence, the local terminals fed freight into their break-bulk terminal, which consolidated freight for shipment to other break-bulk facilities—where the process reversed.

The individual local terminals had local trucks operating out of them which made pickups and deliveries in their assigned community. A dispatcher was in touch via two-way radio with each driver to tell the driver to make a pickup at a particular shipper if the truck would not otherwise be stopping there. The local trucks, which could be either a tractor-trailer combination or one piece "bobtail" unit, returned every evening to their local terminal with freight moving to any point in the world.

The freight was taken off the trucks, and each individual shipment was weighed. The number of pieces on the bill of lading turned in by the driver was checked, and the weight was posted to it. Tariffs provided different rates for many classes of goods. So an accurate description of the particular goods in the shipment was placed on the bill of lading, along with the appropriate charges based upon length of haul and special handling required. This information was fed into the computer system, which printed a final bill of lading for the shipment, and prepared an invoice for payment to the correct party. Not all shipments were paid for by the shipper.

The next step in processing the freight was to get it loaded onto the appropriate truck for shipment out. McLean used a cross-dock operation in most of its terminals. A group of local trucks, which had assigned routes, were parked each evening at their assigned door. A dockworker was assigned to handle a group of three to five doors, depending upon the normal volume of freight coming across. The dockworker for door set "A," for example, would take freight off the trucks parked at door set "A," weigh it, and place it on a cart labeled by destination. This dockworker was also responsible for loading the trucks at this same door set.

If the "A" dockworker was idle but the dockworker at door set "B" was busy, "A" would come over and help "B." This helped to utilize each dockworker fully. McLean had used constant motion conveyor systems in the past, which required a dockworker to be present at an assigned door at all times. It was felt by management that some dockworkers were only utilized productively for four to six hours out of the eight-hour day.

The cross-dock method provided that as the freight was moved off a truck and weighed, it moved to the appropriate truck which was bound for the break-bulk terminal. This truck would be parked directly across from the local truck, normally.

As freight came in from the break-bulk terminal for local delivery, the same procedure was followed, except there was no need to weigh the goods.

Break-Bulk Terminals

As many trucks as were necessary would be moved each night from the local terminals to their assigned break-bulk terminals. All freight, unless it would be delivered out of the same terminal which made the pickup, moved in this fashion. A cluster of local terminals fed their freight into their break-bulk terminal, and received their freight to deliver from their break-bulk terminal.

The freight moved through each break-bulk facility in much the same way it moved through a local terminal. It was off-loaded from a truck, and loaded onto another, which would be bound for the break-bulk terminal serving the final destination. The over-the-road units would be "cubed out" (loaded fully), and moved to their destination break-bulk terminal. In the event the distance from one break-bulk point to another was longer than a ten-hour trip, a relief driver would meet the originating driver at a predetermined checkpoint. Two-man driver teams were formerly used, but in those cases one man was inactive at any given time.

Management believed there were two advantages to the break-bulk method of operation, combined with the relief-driver system. First, with average highway operation costs of $1 per mile, it was very important to move as much freight on each unit as possible. Secondly, this arrangement kept equipment and freight moving. Each break-bulk point operated a maintenance base to service trucks as they moved in and out for routine and preventive items. Records of maintenance were fed into the computer system.

MARKETING

McLean considered itself to be an aggressive marketer of its services. Sales representatives called on established accounts and sought new ones on a regular basis. During a sales call, the salesperson established what person at the shipper actually decided which freight line would be used. In some cases, a traffic manager was responsible for the decision, but often it was a shipping clerk who made the choice. The sales effort keyed on the appropriate person. Items such as calendars, note pads, coffee mugs, and terminal directories were used as sales tools.

A nationwide advertising campaign supplemented these personal contact efforts. Ads were placed in a variety of business and industry periodicals. Direct mail was also used to promote special programs. Discount rates were offered to some cities in an effort to balance the flow of shipments from and to any break-bulk pair. McLean had closely controlled this program.

Another promotional effort was the "diamond back" service offered between certain break-bulk pairs. Those pairs that had a very high volume of traffic were advertised through direct mail for their quick delivery time. This commitment could be made due to the high volume.

Substantial changes happened to the character of the business in 1980. The average weight of each shipment had decreased to 1,369 pounds—the lowest in ten years. The record high had been set in 1979 at 1,869 pounds. The number of shipments, however, was up to 6.5 million in 1980, a new high which helped offset the lower average shipment weight. The average distance of each haul had been steadily increasing the last nine years, going up ten to twenty miles per year. A large jump was recognized in 1980—from 683 miles in 1979 to 802 in 1980.[5] The longer, lighter hauls were more characteristic of McLean.

McLean was the first of the Class I common carriers to set up a separate contract division (Salem Transportation, Inc.), although Yellow Freight and Carolina Freight were two other Class I common carriers that had followed suit.[6] McLean's plans were to continue expanding the contract operation. *The Value Line Investment Survey* in January 1981 stated that one of the major reasons TL business had been depressed for common carriers was because of the aggressiveness of some independent, specialized contract carriers. As one manager noted, McLean was going after this business.

FINANCIAL REVIEW

Operating revenue in 1980 was up 29.6 percent over that for 1979, but McLean suffered a loss of $2.4 million, as shown in Exhibit 7. This loss equated to a loss of $0.43 per share—the first loss in the company's modern history.[7] Exhibits 5 through 11 show financial data for the fiscal years 1979 and 1980.

On October 31, 1980, McLean sold one of its wholly-owned subsidiaries, The Winston Refining Company. This unit was not included as one of the four current subsidiaries. McLean had owned Winston since 1973. The decision to sell the refinery was made primarily for two reasons: (1) to get out of the petroleum industry, and (2) to get rid of a significant drain on financial resources. Winston operated at a loss of $575,000 in 1980. The sale of Winston enabled McLean to reduce short-term debt by $3.0 million and long-term debt by $15.0 million.

Exhibit 5

McLean Trucking Company
Highlights for the Fiscal Years Ended June 30

	1980	1979
Operating revenues	$724,888,627	$559,360,342
Income (loss) before income taxes....	$(7,845,432)	$12,749,781
Net income (loss)...................	$(2,431,832)	$8,119,781
Net income (loss) per common share	$(0.43)	$1.44
Shares of common stock outstanding	5,628,492	5,628,492
Cash dividends on common shares ...	$3,602,235	$3,602,235
Dividends per common share	$0.64	$0.64
Operating ratio (carrier only)	100.33%	97.20%

OPERATING REVENUE (millions of $)	NET INCOME (millions of $)	WORKING CAPITOL (millions of $)
'80 — 725	'80 (2.4)	'80 — 41.4
79 — 559	79 — 8.1	79 — 26.8
78 — 494	78 — 15.4	78 — 19.8
77 — 437	77 — 15.3	77 — 10.8
76 — 372	76 — 15.0	76 — 8.2
75 — 320	75 — 10.0	75 — 13.8
74 — 311	74 — 11.6	74 — 10.9
73 — 234	73 — 10.2	73 — 11.0
72 — 195	72 — 8.6	72 — 8.1
71 — 170	71 — 6.0	71 — 8.9

Exhibit 6

McLean Trucking Company
Distribution of the 1980 Revenue Dollar

Wages, salaries, and employee benefits		
Drivers	$0.290	
Terminal employees	0.206	
Sales and traffic force	0.018	
Maintenance employees	0.042	
General office force	0.015	
Refinery employees	0.003	
Officers..	0.002	$0.576
Operation and maintenance		0.371
Operating taxes and licenses		0.023
Depreciation		0.031
Interest and other deductions		0.010
Income taxes		(0.008)
Shareholders' equity { Cash dividends	0.005	
{ Decrease in retained earnings ...	(0.008)	(0.003)
Total...		$1.00

Exhibit 7

McLean Trucking Company
Comparative Consolidated Income Statements
(In thousands of dollars)

	Year ended June 30			Percentage increase (decrease) from previous year		Common size information		
	1980	1979	1978	1980	1979	1980	1979	1978
Total operating revenue	$724,889	$559,360	$493,696	29.6	13.3	100%	100%	100%
Wages, salaries, & benefits	409,341	328,763	287,054	24.5	14.5	56%	59%	58%
Operations & maintenance	110,334	75,957	63,262	43.5	20	15%	14%	13%
Operating taxes & licenses	16,796	14,576	13,862	15.2	5.2	2%	3%	3%
Insurance	16,016	13,882	11,003	15.4	26.2	2%	2%	2%
Communications & utilities	8,261	6,376	5,950	29.6	7.2	1%	1%	1%
Depreciation	21,330	17,571	14,913	21.4	17.8	3%	3%	3%
Rent & purchased transportation	18,265	13,074	10,470	39.7	24.9	3%	2%	2%
Total operating expenses	$600,343	$470,199	$406,514	30	15.7	83%	84%	82%
Cost of sales	125,484	71,172	59,228	76.3	20.2	17%	13%	12%
Net operating income	(938)	17,989	27,954	(105)	(35.7)	---	3%	6%
Other income	1,493	961	994	55.4	(3.3)	---	---	---
Interest expense	8,158	5,969	4,220	36.7	36.7	1%	1%	1%
Other deductions	242	241	172	0	40	---	---	---
Income taxes	(5,414)	4,620	9,140	(216.9)	(49.3)	---	1%	2%
Net income	$ (2,431)	$ 8,120	$ 15,416	(130)	(47.32)	---	1.5%	3%
Retained earnings, beg. of year	104,475	99,957	87,805					
Dividends	3,602	3,602	3,264					
Retained earnings, end of year	$ 98,442	$104,475	$ 99,957					

Exhibit 8

McLean Trucking Company
Comparative Consolidated Balance Sheets (In thousands of dollars)

	Year ended June 30			Percentage increase (decrease) from previous year		Common size information		
ASSETS	1980	1979	1978	1980	1979	1980	1979	1978
Current assets:								
Cash	$ 16,592	$ 9,490	$ 13,042	74.8	(27)	5%	3%	6%
Accounts receivable	59,305	56,603	36,387	4.8	55.5	20%	20%	17%
Prepayments	15,203	16,156	13,989	(5.8)	15.5	5%	6%	6%
Inventory	24,985	12,628	10,106	97.9	25	8%	4%	5%
Other current assets	6,601	4,692	621	40.6	656	2%	2%	0.3%
Total current assets	$122,686	$ 99,569	$ 74,145	23.2	34.3	40%	35%	34%
Operating property	271,509	261,042	212,658	4	22.8	90%	92%	96%
Less depreciation	106,171	90,849	77,304	16.9	17.5	(35%)	(32%)	(35%)
Net property	$165,338	$170,193	$135,354	(2.9)	25.7	55%	60%	61%
Intangible property (net)	12,220	12,002	9,838	1.8	22	4%	4%	4%
Other assets	2,951	1,628	2,206	81.3	(26.2)	1%	1%	1%
Total assets	$303,195	$283,392	$221,543	7	27.9	100%	100%	100%

LIABILITIES AND STOCKHOLDERS' EQUITY

	1980	1979	1978	1980	1979	1980	1979	1978
Liabilities:								
Notes payable	$ 2,000	$ —	$ —	—	—	1%	—	—
Accounts payable	24,222	21,682	15,130	11.7	43.3	8%	8%	7%
Accrued payroll, taxes, etc.	15,284	15,372	14,053	(0.6)	9.4	5%	5%	6%
Bonuses & other accruals	18,383	16,633	12,283	10.5	35.4	6%	6%	6%
Federal & state taxes	—		1,295			—		0.6%
Dividends payable	901	901	816			0.2%	0.3%	0.4%
Long-term debt due in one year	5,606	5,392	1,693	4	218.5	2%	2%	1%
Other liabilities	14,855	12,750	9,084			5%	4%	4%
Total liabilities	$ 81,251	$ 72,730	$ 54,354	11.7	33.8	27%	25%	25%
Long-term debt	105,862	88,564	52,437	19.5	68.9	35%	31%	23%
Deferred federal & state income tax	10,307	10,759	8,332	(4.2)	29.1	3%	4%	4%
Other reserves	2,825	2,355	1,962	20	20	1%	1%	1%
Common stock	2,814	2,814	2,814			1%	1%	1%
Premium on stock	1,696	1,696	1,687			0.5%	0.6%	0.8%
Retained earnings	98,440	104,474	99,957	(5.8)	4.5	32%	37%	45%
Total liabilities and stockholders' equity	$303,195	$283,392	$221,543	7	27.9	100%	100%	100%

McLean Trucking Company
Statement of Changes in Consolidated Financial Position
For the Years Ended June 30

Exhibit 9

	1980	1979	Percentage increase (decrease) from '79 to '80
ADDITIONS			
Net income (loss) for the year	$ (2,431,832)	$ 8,119,781	(70%)
Charges to operations not requiring outlay of working capital:			
Depreciation	22,391,629	18,872,858	19%
Provision for deferred income taxes	(453,343)	2,426,819	(81%)
Amortization and other	604,684	620,044	(2%)
Total from operations	20,111,138	30,039,502	(33%)
Execution of long-term debt	30,893,000	36,437,000	(15%)
Proceeds from disposition of tangible property—less gains of $446,831 in 1980 and $742,606 in 1979	6,070,898	2,185,194	178%
Total additions	$57,075,036	$68,661,696	(17%)
DEDUCTIONS			
Purchase of tangible property	20,725,099	22,896,045	(9%)
Net assets of business in 1979 exclusive of working capital deficit	3,087,000	18,990,000	(84%)
Reduction of long-term debt	13,594,665	16,542,939	(18%)
Cash dividends on common shares	3,602,235	3,602,235	0
Other deductions (additions)—net	1,471,208	(418,141)	450%
Total deductions	$42,480,207	$61,613,078	(31%)
INCREASE IN WORKING CAPITAL	$14,594,829	$ 7,048,618	107%
CONSOLIDATED WORKING CAPITAL—AT BEGINNING OF YEAR	26,839,661	19,791,043	36%
CONSOLIDATED WORKING CAPITAL—AT END OF YEAR.	$41,434,490	$26,839,661	36%
CHANGES IN COMPONENTS OF WORKING CAPITAL			
Increase (decrease) in current assets:			
Cash and short-term investments	$ 7,102,469	$ (3,551,938)	(300%)
Accounts receivable	2,701,656	20,216,702	(87%)
Recoverable federal and state income taxes	2,021,269	3,768,161	(46%)
Prepayments	(952,178)	2,165,971	(56%)
Inventories and other current assets	12,243,022	2,825,642	333%
	$23,116,238	$25,424,538	(9%)
Increase (decrease) in current liabilities:			
Note payable	$ 2,000,000	$ -0-	0
Trade accounts payable	2,540,307	6,551,188	(61%)
Accrued payrolls, payroll taxes, and others	(87,469)	1,318,741	(93%)
Accrued vacation pay	1,749,958	4,349,652	(60%)
Accrued federal and state income taxes	-0-	(1,295,283)	0
Current maturities of long-term debt	213,425	3,699,642	(94%)
Other current liabilities	2,105,188	3,751,980	(44%)
	$ 8,521,409	$18,375,920	(54%)
INCREASE IN WORKING CAPITAL	$14,594,829	$ 7,048,618	107%

Exhibit 10

McLean Trucking Company and Subsidiaries
Statements of Consolidated Operations
(Unaudited)

	Three Months Ended December 31		Six Months Ended December 31	
	1980	1979	1980	1979
CONTINUING OPERATIONS				
Operating revenues	$148,638,398	$150,725,165	$298,872,242	$303,428,092
Operating expenses	149,966,905	155,084,650	296,217,487	304,486,458
Operating income (loss)	(1,328,507)	(4,359,485)	2,654,755	(1,058,366)
Other income and deductions—net	2,146,599	1,785,226	3,958,647	3,115,067
Income (loss) before income taxes	(3,475,106)	(6,144,711)	(1,303,892)	(4,173,433)
Provision for income taxes	(1,433,600)	(1,866,100)	(482,400)	(1,203,600)
Income (loss) from continuing operations	(2,041,506)	(4,278,611)	(821,492)	(2,969,833)
DISCONTINUED OPERATIONS				
Loss of Winston Refining Co., less income taxes	(1,293,107)	(389,740)	(2,060,106)	(632,131)
Gain on sale of Winston Refining Co., less income taxes	4,214,283	—	4,214,283	—
Income (loss) from discontinued operations	2,921,176	(389,740)	2,154,177	(632,131)
INCOME (LOSS) BEFORE EXTRAORDINARY CHARGE	879,670	(4,668,351)	1,332,685	(3,601,964)
EXTRAORDINARY CHARGE				
Write-off of interstate operating rights	(11,703,199)	—	(11,703,199)	—
NET INCOME (LOSS)	$(10,823,529)	$ (4,668,351)	$(10,370,514)	$ (3,601,964)
INCOME (LOSS) PER SHARE				
Continuing operations	$ (.36)	$(.76)	$ (.14)	$(.53)
Discontinued operations	.52	(.07)	.38	(.11)
Extraordinary charge	(2.08)	—	(2.08)	—
Net income (loss)	$(1.92)	$(.83)	$(1.84)	$(.64)

Exhibit 11

McLean Trucking Company
Condensed Consolidated Balance Sheets (Unaudited)

ASSETS	December 31, 1980	December 31, 1979*
Current assets	$ 80,024,142	$105,432,311
Tangible property—net	142,135,554	166,680,720
Operating rights and other assets	7,820,996	14,608,588
Total........................	$229,980,692	$286,721,619
LIABILITIES AND SHAREHOLDERS' EQUITY		
Current liabilities	$ 52,463,760	$ 80,784,339
Long-term debt	72,794,306	91,066,840
Other noncurrent liabilities	13,043,449	11,289,205
Shareholders' equity	91,679,177	103,581,235
Total........................	$229,980,692	$286,721,619

*Note: Winston Refining Co., a wholly-owned subsidiary, was sold effective October 31, 1980. At December 31, 1979, the assets and liabilities of the refinery are included in their normal account classifications.

McLean had revolving credit through a group of commercial banks where a $50.0 million line of credit was available at the prime rate in effect at the time the money was borrowed. An agreement existed with the banks for this credit. McLean had agreed in this covenant to refrain from retiring capital stock, to restrict dividends, and to incur no more than $50.0 million in long-term debt.[8] McLean had increased its debt under this agreement from $23.0 million in 1979 to $41.0 million in 1980, and thus had a $9.0 million leeway left.

Overall, McLean followed a fairly conservative line of accounting policies. Revenue was recognized on the date the shipment was picked up from the shipper. Inventory was accounted for on the average-cost method, and depreciation of tangible property was accounted for on the straight-line basis. Costs of truck maintenance and repairs were expensed as they were incurred, unless the repairs were actually improvements over the original condition of the equipment, in which case the costs were capitalized and subsequently depreciated.

The operating rights granted McLean by the ICC had been amortized over a 40-year period, as with most intangibles. Because of deregulation, the value of these rights was written off during the second quarter of fiscal 1981, which ended December 31, 1980. The rights were deemed worthless by the company because of the 1980 MCA. This write-off resulted in a net loss of $10.8 million or $1.92 per share.[9]

A review of McLean's current balance sheet showed increases in cash and long-term debt for 1980. McLean had to lay off 3,000 employees in the third quarter of 1980 because high labor costs and small shipment net volume made the previous force level unnecessary.

McLean reduced some of its operating loss in 1980 by taking advantage of the Investment Tax Credit and by capitalizing interest costs on construction. This produced a net benefit of $7.4 million.

THE OUTLOOK

The trucking industry closely tracked economic activity. Consequently, truck traffic dropped in early 1981, and seemed unlikely to score a significant rebound until perhaps the second half of 1981, by which time the economy would again be supporting rising freight tonnage. Earnings of trucking companies could have been bottoming, as cost reductions came in line with reduced business and weak pricing in the wake of deregulation.[10]

Economic indicators continued to show a slow rise from the recession of early 1980. However, the strong areas of the economy had been services, electronics, and communications—not automotive, steel, and manufactured products.[11] The future of the common carrier was tied to the economy in general, but certainly to the manufacturing industries. As Mr. Mellen noted in the 1980 annual report, "Frankly, we do not expect a return to our historical profit margins until there is an improvement in the economy."[12] McLean had set a goal to return to profitability in fiscal 1981.

Drake Sheahan and Stewart Dougall, Inc., a consulting firm that specialized in the transportation industry, issued a forecast in early 1981 regarding rates and costs. This forecast is presented in Exhibit 12.

Exhibit 12   **Trucking Cost and Rate Forecast**

| ITEM | Percentage Increase | | | | | |
	1980	1981	1982	1983	1984	1985
Labor cost	11	13	12	13	13	8
Fuel cost	35	13	10	10	12	12
Materials & supplies	11	11	10	10	12	12
Depreciation	8	5	5	5	5	5
Miscellaneous	9	10	8	9	9	9

| | Percentage of Costs by Functional Area | | | |
| | TL | | LTL | |
	1978	1985	1978	1985
Labor cost	44.9	44.7	76.3	77.7
Fuel cost	11.8	18.0	2.9	4.5
Materials & supplies	16.7	16.9	5.0	5.3
Depreciation	11.2	7.3	5.7	3.7
Miscellaneous	15.4	13.1	10.1	8.8
	100.0	100.0	100.0	100.0

| Rate Increase Forecast [Percentage] | | |
	TL	LTL
1980	14	12
Annual Average through 1985	11	11
Cumulative increase through 1985	92	89

Source: *Handling and Shipping Management*, January, 1981.

The highway system was a factor in future plans, also. The Interstate Highway System was virtually complete, and few roads were planned. This meant no relief from congested roads was expected on federally funded and managed roads. Relief in the form of new roads, expansions, and alternate routes would have to come from the states.

The highway funds to maintain the road system were encountering squeezes that might get worse. Less driving overall, caused by higher gasoline costs, were resulting in lower gasoline tax revenues. Truckers, however, did not reduce driving due to fuel costs and were thought by many to cause much of the deterioration of the highway system. Higher taxes were an alternative to such deterioration, with perhaps more of the burden on the trucking industry.

Deregulation of the trucking industry was expected by many industry experts to contribute to an industry "shakeout."[13] Mergers, new entries, and rerouting were expected in large amounts since industry analysts predicted "As many as 20 percent of the trucking firms in the country will be out of business by 1981 year end."[14] While some companies were dreading the new rules, the new entrants were anticipating the future as more favorable. Industry analysts expected profitability to permanently suffer, with rate increases to follow after the rate cutting of the "shakeout" period. McLean's management was uncertain whether their profits would be any more affected than their competitors.

Two trends had shown up which might have a serious effect on common carriers to expand their contract business, or for some, to begin it. D. H. Karel of Cleo Wrap, a contract carrier, felt that contract carriage would be "The name of the game in the near future . . . More contract rates between common carrier and the shipper."[15] Another aspect of the contract business was the private carrier. It was possible for these carriers to carry common freight on backhauls. This right had been limited to regulated common carriers prior to the 1980 MCA. Extension of this right to private carriers was being fought by the Regular Common Carrier Conference of the American Trucking Associations and the Teamsters' Union in court. Appeals were pending. The near future appeared to be turbulent as opposed to the last decade.

APPENDIX I   **The Trucking Industry**

STRUCTURE OF THE TRUCKING INDUSTRY

There are over 14 million trucks operating on the highways of the United States, belonging to over 40,000 trucking firms. The complexity of the industry is illustrated by the fact that there are over 20 billion pairs of origination and destination points between the 60,000 communities served by the trucks. The average shipment weighs less than a ton, and 60 percent of all shipments are less than 500 pounds.[1]

---

1. *Congressional Digest,* November 2, 1979, p. 225.

The motor carrier industry can be categorized into a number of different classes:

Local or intercity. A motor carrier is classified as local if at least half of its business is conducted in metropolitan or commercial zone operations. If this is not the case, it is classified as intercity.

Private or For-Hire. Private carriers are those shippers, manufacturers, merchants, and others who use their own vehicles or leased trucks under their direct control for moving their own goods. Private carriers are subject to safety, equipment, and hours of service rules set by the United States Department of Transportation (DOT). For-hire carriers are those trucking companies providing transportation of freight owned by another party. Interstate carriers are regulated by the Interstate Commerce Commission (ICC). Intrastate and local carriers are regulated by state and local agencies.

For-Hire Categories.

1. Common carriers transport, at published rates, a given type of freight between points which they have authority to serve.

2. Contract carriers operate under continuing contracts with one or more shippers. They must secure an operating permit from the ICC.

3. Exempt carriers operate in stipulated types of commodities or operations, such as transporting unmanufactured agricultural commodities. They are not regulated by the ICC, but are subject to the same DOT regulations that private carriers are subject to.

General or specialized. General freight carriers haul a wide variety of packaged goods called general commodities. However, their operating rights exclude certain freight categories, including bulk commodities, household goods, heavy and dangerous materials, and other items requiring special handling equipment. The special freight items are handled by specialized carriers.[2]

Classes. As defined by the ICC, Class I carriers have gross operating revenues of at least $3.0 million annually. Class II carriers have annual operating revenues less than $3.0 million but more than $500,000. Class III carriers have revenues under $500,000.

Truckload (TL) or Less-Than-Truckload (LTL). The ICC defines TL shipments as weighing 10,000 pounds or more. LTL shipments weigh less than 10,000 pounds.

FEDERAL DEREGULATION

Common and contract carriers have been regulated since 1935 by the ICC.[3] The regulatory climate established by the Motor Carrier Act of 1935 (1935 MCA) was bolstered by the Reed-Bulwinkle Act of 1948 (RBA). Major changes in this climate are now underway, due to the Motor Carrier Act of 1980 (1980 MCA).

The Motor Carrier Act of 1935

According to the terms of the 1935 MCA, interstate motor carriers had to publish and file with the ICC rates and other charges and allowances. In actual practice, rates were set on a regional basis by the prominent firms in the region. In order to obtain a rate increase, individual truckers had to petition through these regional rate-setting

2. Op. cit., p. 226.
3. *Moody's Transportation Manual,* 1980 Edition, p. 45.

boards. The ICC generally granted rate hikes of less than what had been requested. The rates were allowed based on a target rate of return which the ICC felt the trucking firms should be satisfied with, assuming effective and efficient management.

The ICC was also the final arbiter of which trucking firms could enter the business under the provisions of the 1935 MCA. The entering firm had to prove two things to the ICC:

1. It had to prove that it had the financial reserves to survive in the business. It had to show that it was ready, willing, and able to serve.
2. The entering firm had to prove that there was a definite need for its unique services in the target region. Further, it had to prove that it would not seriously endanger or harm the competitive position of the trucking firms already operating in the region.

It was this latter provision that effectively restricted extensive competition in the trucking industry. Very few entering firms could hope to compete with large regional truckers, for if their proposed operations were in any way sizeable, they would easily be found to have a potentially detrimental effect on the existing competition.

Another provision of the 1935 MCA pertained to contract carriers. They could only contract at any time with a maximum of eight shippers.

In summary, the major effects of the 1935 MCA were collective rate setting and restricted entry. Antitrust pressure on collective rate setting was eased by the RBA.

The Reed-Bulwinkle Act of 1948

The RBA, in effect, legitimized the collective rate-setting activity of the trucking industry as set forth in the 1935 MCA. The RBA permitted common carriers to engage in collective rate-making practices under agreements approved by the ICC. Parties to approved agreements were thus relieved from antitrust prosecution.

The RBA was passed by Congress over then-president Truman's veto. His veto message stated in part:

> Power to control transportation rates is power to influence the success or failure of other businesses. Legislation furthering the exercise of this power by private groups would clearly be contrary to the public interest.[4]

Truman failed in his veto attempt. However, the echoes of his message were brought back to life in the provisions of the 1980 MCA.

The Motor Carrier Act of 1980

The 1980 MCA, which is the culmination of a rare collaboration between President Jimmy Carter and Senator Ted Kennedy, is significantly changing the regulatory climate facing the trucking industry. Its major thrust is in the areas of rate setting, entry requirements, and contract carrier operations.

The 1980 MCA phases out regional rate boards by 1984 while at the same time changing their current role from final arbiter to adviser. In the interim period, trucking firms can adjust rates within a "Zone of Reasonableness" — which equates to a 5 percent maximum rate increase and a 20 percent maximum decrease. Also, at the point in time in 1984 when the regional rate boards cease to exist, the RBA will be negated. This means that after 1984, any collective rate setting will be subject to the antitrust laws.

---

4. *Congressional Digest*, p. 256.

Entry to the trucking industry is eased by the 1980 MCA. The prospective entering company no longer has to prove that it will not be a competitive detriment to established trucking companies in the area. All the prospective entrant need do now is prove that it is financially capable, and that it has the proper asset base and mix to compete successfully.

Under the 1935 MCA, common carriers were prohibited from hauling such goods exempt from ICC regulation as raw agricultural commodities. This meant that many trucks made their return trip—the backhaul—empty. This led to nonproductive costs for fuel, wear and tear, and wages.

Most of these backhaul restrictions have been eliminated by the 1980 MCA. Common carriers are no longer faced with the high probability of empty backhauls. It thus becomes imperative to have an effective LTL network to find a suitable backhaul shipment. In fact, in most cases the benefit of such a network outweighs its cost when overall operation efficiency is calculated.

Finally, restrictions are eased on contract carriers. They are no longer limited to contracts with only eight shippers. This easing of restrictions will permit contract carriers to make significant inroads to the common carriers' TL business. All that is needed is a truck to haul the cargo. Fixed assets, such as terminals, buildings, and warehouses are not necessarily required. This fits the operating structure of most contract carriers.

On the other hand, it is unlikely that contract carriers will move in on common carriers' LTL business. LTL requires much more capital equipment to establish local, regional, and national networks. Contract carriers do not have the financial reserve base to compete in this market segment.

In summary, the purpose of the 1980 MCA is to let trucking rates be set in a fair, competitive atmosphere, and to permit new trucking firms to enter competition with established companies. As President Carter put it on the day he signed the Act, "This Act will bring the trucking industry into the free market system where it belongs. It will encourage new truckers and expansion of existing firms."[5]

Industry Reaction

The reaction of the trucking industry to the 1980 MCA has been less rapturous than Carter's. The industry perceives the Act, which is commonly referred to as trucking deregulation, as the latest in a series of adversities to beset it over the past two years. Diesel fuel costs have practically doubled from early 1979 to the present. The 11-day Teamster's strike in April 1979 caused a total shutdown of the industry, and the resultant wage settlement raised trucking expenses considerably. The economic recession that developed in the spring of 1980 had a depressing effect on the industry, with tonnage 30 percent below what it was in 1979.

The 1980 MCA, according to the trucking industry, heightens the adverse effects of the events of 1979 and 1980 just mentioned. The industry feels that deregulation will further cripple an industry already staggering from the effects of a significant recession in the economy to which it is so closely bound.

Trucking executives fear that deregulation will result in decreased competition rather than in increased competition. Deregulation is occurring at a time when many formerly healthy trucking companies, including two of the largest Class I carriers, McLean and Transcon Freightlines, are showing operating losses for fiscal 1980.[6]

In some cases, the problems are terminal. On July 23, 1980, Wilson Freight Company of Cincinnati, the nation's seventeenth largest common carrier, filed for protection from creditors under Chapter 11 of the Bankruptcy Act. The April Teamster's strike

---

5. "Motor Carrier Act of 1980 signed by President Carter at White House," *Traffic World*, July 7, 1980, p. 67.

6. "Trucking Industry Shaken," *Traffic World*, August 11, 1980, p. 16.

and a 30 percent drop in tonnage from 1979, due largely to the recession, caused Wilson's demise. "The economy just killed us," said John E. Shane, Wilson's president.[7]

Arthur Imperatone, president of A. P. A. Transport Corporation of Bergen, New Jersey, summarized the industry's concerns:

> The law [deregulation] doesn't change the intrinsic problems of the trucking industry. The cost of LTL is still very high, and that cost—coupled with the present market—could mean a regrouping of the industry into fewer, stronger carriers. Marginal carriers are going to find it hard to survive.[8]

New trucking firms, it is believed, will take advantage of the lowered entry barriers, and chip away at the established common carrier's market. Contract and private carriers may also take some of this market. The established companies may attempt to fall back on the lower-margin LTL operations, and engage in rate cutting to weed out the marginal companies. As one carrier's vice president of marketing puts it: "Rate cutting makes no sense unless someone is put out of business. Then the survivors share that traffic. I guess that's what everyone is banking on."[9]

The rate-cutting process is already beginning. Overnite Transportation of Richmond, Virginia, another of the largest Class I common carriers, applied to the ICC on September 5, 1980, for a 10 percent across-the-board reduction in LTL rates. Fifty smaller trucking companies filed with Overnite. Most of these companies are also located in the South.[10]

If Mr. Imperatone is correct, the rate war may put small and marginal trucking firms out of business. After the industry shakeout, it is believed that rates may rise substantially, and that the industry could settle into a more oligopolistic equilibrium than existed before deregulation.

STATE REGULATIONS

The federal government permits a 40-ton maximum weight for loaded trucks. But 10 states and the District of Columbia have laws that do not permit such a high maximum weight. Their argument is that so much weight causes excessive damage to roadways. Truckers counter this by asserting that the 40-ton trucks yield a net fuel savings, and even a total cost savings, over their lighter counterparts. Yellow Freight System, the largest Class I carrier, estimated that it could have saved $4.0 million in fuel costs alone in 1981 if all states had the 40-ton weight limit.[11]

Some states set limits shorter than most on truck length and combination. These restrictions are generally regarded by the trucking industry as more detrimental to their operations. Seventeen states ban the 65-foot-long double trailer combination. The maximum single vehicle length in these states is 45 feet. It is argued by these states that the shorter combination length offers important safety advantages.

The trucking industry has made some headway with respect to these restrictions over the past three years. State courts in Wisconsin (1978) and Iowa (1979) have declared the length restrictions unconstitutional, thus permitting truckers to use the double-trailer vehicles in those two states. The basis of the court rulings was that the states did not adequately prove their case that a safety danger existed. These rulings—especially the one in Iowa—are proving beneficial to trucking firms. Transcon maintains

---

7. "A Steep Downgrade for Truckers," *Business Week*, August 11, 1980, p. 28.

8. D. Davis, "Less Than a Truckload of Regulations," *Distribution*, January, 1981, p. 41.

9. Ibid.

10. R. D. Maggnelt, "Overnite, 50 Smaller Truckers to File for 10% Cut in LTL, AQ Class Rates," *Traffic World*, September 1, 1980, p. 18.

11. *Annual Report*, Yellow Freight System, 1980, p. 5.

they saved $90,000 in fuel costs in Iowa during 1980 because they no longer had to route their double trailers around the state on long, east-west hauls out of Chicago.[12]

The trucking industry is now actively working with the various trucking associations to secure both double trailer and vehicle gross weight legislation on a state-by-state basis. The industry hopes that the advantages of reduced fuel consumption and increased productivity will be sufficiently persuasive to effect the desired changes in these states. These efforts should pay off soon because on March 23, 1981, the United States Supreme Court ruled it was unconstitutional for states to have length and weight restrictions which could not be proved as beneficial to the public.

LABOR RELATIONS

The International Brotherhood of Teamsters has 1.8 million members, of whom 300,000 are employed in the trucking industry as truck drivers and warehouse workers. The average pay of Teamster truck drivers went up 150 percent between 1970 and 1979 due to large wage settlements won by the union in successive three-year contract negotiations.

The most recent settlement took place in April 1979. The terms of the settlement, agreed on after an 11-day strike of selected trucking firms, countered by a lockout by the trucking industry, called for a 14 percent increase in wages and fringe benefits in 1980, followed by further increases of 11 percent in 1981 and 9 percent in 1982.

Many insiders believe that any Teamster strategy for the 1982 contract negotiations based on wage and benefit increases in double digits will bear a very heavy risk factor of accelerated layoffs as a direct consequence. Industry experts, such as Roger Lieb, a professor of transportation at Northeastern University in Boston, predict that the union could lose 10 to 15 percent of its trucking industry members by the mid-1980s, and Teamster insiders agree.[13]

Teamster truckers are under job pressure from the current depressed state of the economy. In 1980, with trucking tonnage down 30 percent, 20 percent of the union's 300,000 drivers and warehouse workers were laid off.

Another source of job pressure comes directly from trucking deregulation. Since contract carriers are no longer limited to a maximum number of eight shippers with which they can contract, these carriers are making incursions into the common carrier's TL business. And since most contract carrier drivers are nonunion, while most common carrier drivers are unionized, this movement represents a net loss of jobs for drivers.

A third source of job pressure will come about if the LTL segment of the trucking industry retrenches, as a result of deregulation. According to this scenario, the strongest LTL carriers will service the most profitable routes, bid down the rates, and force marginal operators to merge with them or go out of business. Then the acquiring companies will halt duplicate runs and close redundant terminals, eliminating teamster jobs.

Thus, there is significant external pressure on the Teamsters to change their bargaining tactics in 1982 by going for a more moderate wage and benefit settlement, which would tend to reduce layoffs. Moderate wage settlements would mean less operating expense for truckers, a lessened probability of business failures, and a higher employment level for Teamster truckers.

Internal political factions within the Teamsters are also impacting its bargaining stance for 1982. Dissident factions within the union—notably the 10,000 member "Teamsters for a Democratic Union"—want to tighten up the union's grievance procedure and stop the trucking industry from introducing production standards. A sudden inability to gain big wage packages could focus the attention of union bargaining on these issues instead.

---

12. *Annual Report,* Transcon Freightlines, 1980, p. 9.
13. "Reregulation Weakens the Teamsters' Clout," *Traffic World,* September 15, 1980, p. 4.

The Teamsters, therefore, may find themselves in a weakened bargaining position for the next go-round in 1982. Since deregulation, the days when the Teamsters could gain large wage increases because they knew that the trucking firms would get ICC approval to pass the costs on to the shipper seem to be over. Big wage settlements may no longer be the overriding goal of the Teamsters in contract negotiations. Since factions with differing goals and aspirations are becoming more vocal, the union is no longer a monolithic structure. The tenor of negotiations in 1982 will tell much about the future choices of the Teamsters and the trucking industry.

NOTES

1. A Class I carrier is one regulated by the Interstate Commerce Commission (ICC), which has annual revenues of at least $3.0 million. Class I carriers are the largest trucking firms.

2. "Lift Controls on Trucking?" *U. S. News and World Report,* August 20, 1979, p. 57.

3. *Annual Report,* McLean Trucking Company, 1980, p. 24.

4. Interviews were conducted with the following McLean executives: E. M. Robins, director of advertising and public relations; Jay Niendorhf, dictrict manager/Texas & Louisiana; Frank Groves, terminal manager/Carrollton; and Lynn Perucca, sales manager/Carrollton.

5. *Annual Report,* p. 4.

6. *Handling and Shipping Management,* January, 1981, p. 52.

7. *Annual Report,* p. 17.

8. See n. 7 above.

9. *The Shareholder* (report to McLean stockholders), February 5, 1981, p. 2.

10. "Trucking and Transport Leasing Industry," *Value Line Investment Survey,* January 12, 1981, p. 278.

11. *Forbes,* March 30, 1981, p. 117.

12. *Annual Report,* p. 22.

13. *Time,* July 14, 1980, p. 15.

14. *Forbes,* October 27, 1980, p. 25.

15. *Handling and Shipping Management,* p. 53.

Case 1-2

A Takeover that Failed: American Express Bids for McGraw-Hill*

The American Express Company (Amex), a financial and travel conglomerate "with a hoard of cash,"[1] wanted to diversify into different and profitable businesses in which to use its excess funds. Competition in credit card services was becoming fierce with the expansion of Visa, Master Charge, and Diners' Club; Amex dominance of the traveler's check market was also threatened. *Business Week* suggested that Amex "look for additional products for its affluent market, or find other businesses that fit [its] specialized mold."[2] After unsuccessful offers during the mid-1970s to Book-of-the-Month Club, Walt Disney Productions, and Philadelphia Life Insurance Company, Amex turned to the publishing house of McGraw-Hill whose 1977 sales amounted to $659 million. It was perhaps a fitting target: McGraw-Hill owned *Business Week*.

During the latter part of the 1970s, takeovers were a primary growth vehicle used by large corporations, and especially by conglomerates. There had been 80 acquisitions in 1978 costing $100 million or more, compared to 41 such acquisitions in 1977. According to *Newsweek*:

> The latest take-over craze took hold [in 1974] when a battered stock market gave birth to the theory that it was cheaper to buy a new company than to expand internally. As the takeovers continue to pile up, many critics wonder if the acquisitions are not siphoning cash from expenditures on new plants that would create jobs. ... Shareholders aren't arguing: to smooth the way for their deals, acquiring companies typically offer 40 to 50 per cent above market value for the stock they want. ... [In 1978] investors paid $2 billion in premiums over pre-offering market prices.[3]

This trend had aroused Federal Trade Commission (FTC) interest because of the potential impact such takeovers could have on market competition. With a suitor the size of Amex, the acquisition was of even greater interest—still further heightened because of an ongoing study by the FTC on the question of concentration of ownership in the media industries.

---

*This case was prepared by George Greanias and Duane Windsor, Rice University, with the intention of providing a basis for class discussion rather than illustrating either effective or ineffective management of a business situation.

AMEX MAKES AN OFFER

The Bid

Amex chairman James D. Robinson III made the offer along with Roger Morley, Amex president and a McGraw-Hill director since 1977. They approached McGraw-Hill chairman Harold McGraw, Jr. with an offer of $34 per share of McGraw-Hill stock. Morley gave McGraw a letter of resignation from the McGraw-Hill board of directors when the offer was made. At the time, the company's stock was selling for $24 on the New York Stock Exchange; book value was $13 a share. Amex would acquire all outstanding stock; the bid totalled $830 million, to be tendered either in straight cash, or cash and Amex stock if McGraw-Hill stockholders preferred. McGraw-Hill would be run as an independent subsidiary with its existing management left intact. Harold McGraw made no immediate reply to the offer. An overture made in June 1978 had been declined.

While the Amex offer apparently was unexpected by Harold McGraw, Robinson believed it had been cordially received. He reported that, "The reception was so damn friendly that we called our investment bankers and told them it was practically a shoo-in." McGraw saw the meeting differently, saying his reaction was one of "shock."[4] McGraw faced a difficult personal struggle to convince his board of directors that the offer should be rejected. He promptly hired the investment banking firm of Morgan Stanley and Attorney Martin Lipton.[5] Both were well known for defense in hostile takeovers. Morgan Stanley specialized in locating "white knights" (firms which agree to act as suitors in a friendly merger arranged to prevent a hostile takeover).

Because a takeover battle then seemed imminent, Amex hired Attorney Joseph H. Flom, "noted for skillful merger tactics."[6] According to *Time*, this move was "in part so that McGraw-Hill could not get him [Flom] first."[7] Amex also hired two investment banking firms, Lazard Freres and Blyth Eastman Dillon. After Amex's last three futile acquisition attempts, "Robinson [was] determined not to fail again."[8]

The Reaction on Wall Street

At this point, a better offer from Amex was expected, although there was some shareholder sentiment that the initial $34 offer should be accepted. With some 20 percent of McGraw-Hill stock in the hands of the McGraw family, Harold McGraw thought he would have substantial support in a vote against the takeover. Nonetheless, conventional wisdom "on the street" favored Amex. "Wall Streeters expect Amex Co. to win, though it probably will have to raise its bid above $40 a share."[9] Due to the trend toward takeovers, "the odds do not seem good for McGraw-Hill's management. In tender offers over the past ten years, the target company has been acquired 85 percent of the time either by the initial aggressor or by another bidder. Even Lipton ... admits 'cash offers are rarely defeated'."[10]

What did McGraw-Hill shareholders think about the initial Amex offer? Their position was unclear. *Fortune* called the $34 offer "handsomely higher"

Section I   Dynamic Environment of Business Strategy and Policy than McGraw-Hill's preoffer market price of $26;[11] *Time* called the bid price "a fat premium."[12] Many investors agreed and notified McGraw-Hill that the offer was an acceptable one. The impetus towards acceptance was given a boost by disputes within the McGraw family. Harold had forced his cousin, Donald McGraw, out of the company in 1977; Donald was said to be "bitter," and was believed to be "eager to sell his 622,000 McGraw-Hill shares to Amex."[13] Other shareholders apparently preferred to hold out for the potential of a higher offer. "The early betting on Wall Street favors American Express Co. in its bid to take over McGraw-Hill Inc.—but not at $34 a share and not until after a protracted struggle."[14]

The McGraw-Hill Rejection

One week after Amex made its initial offer, a special McGraw-Hill board meeting was held. Morgan Stanley advised the board that the $830 million offer was "inadequate." Attorneys told the directors "that a rejection of the offer would in no way breach their fiduciary responsibilities to stockholders."[15] The board (with Amex president Morley no longer a director) unanimously rejected the offer. Thus, began "one of the most bitter and protracted takeover battles in years."[16]

In defending against the takeover bid, Harold McGraw early began to emphasize the theme of rejecting the offer in order to maintain a free and unfettered press. McGraw told *Business Week*, "I have a strong belief in the preservation of the independence of the educational and business publishing media. What could Amex contribute to McGraw-Hill? Our reputation is so high because all publications are fiercely independent." Senior Amex vice-president C. R. Greenwood disagreed. "There is a commonality between the two companies. Both serve the same up-scale achiever markets. Amex could bring to McGraw-Hill its international marketing capabilities as well as its global network and a new kind of management that blends and puts together leadership services."[17]

McGraw-Hill filed a breach-of-trust suit against Morley alleging violation of his fiduciary duties as a director. According to the suit, Morley had acted as a "Trojan horse." Further, the suit claimed that Morley should not have remained on the board after Amex's overture the previous year had been snubbed; Morley, the complaint alleged, had "conspired to misappropriate" confidential information for use by Amex.

> In one respect, the charges against Morley raised an intriguing question: Did Morley violate his duty as a director of McGraw-Hill—or was he really serving the best interests of the company's stockholders by helping to price Amex's bid of $34 a share, $8 above the prevailing price at the time of the offer?[18]

Setting the tone of the ensuing debate, McGraw called the Amex offer "illegal," "improper," "reckless," and "conspiratorial." Harold McGraw's letter of rejection to Amex's board said that, "The independence and credibility of McGraw-Hill is vital to fulfilling its responsibilities to investors, the academic, educational, and scientific communities, as well as those who rely on the information and advisory services we offer."[19] McGraw said it would be improper for Amex to control *Business Week* and *Standard and Poor's* credit rating service due to conflicts of interest with its existing lines of business. (Amex owned $3.5 billion worth of municipal and state securities which *Standard and Poor* evaluated; Amex ownership would allegedly hamper editorial independence of *Business Week*.)[20]

McGraw-Hill's reply also sought to shift the focus of the battle from itself to Amex. McGraw's letter "took a potshot at Amex's low income tax rate"[21] (due to large holdings of tax-exempt municipal and state securities and its use of "float" from traveler's checks). The letter called Amex "a company which pays virtually no federal income tax on its hundreds of millions of dollars of annual income, operates in a manner that raises serious questions under the banking and securities laws, and pays no interest on the billions of dollars it derives from the issuance of traveler's checks to the public."[22] (Amex had an exemption from the Bank Holding Company Act because its banking activities were based in Singapore.)

McGraw also attacked Amex's use of Morgan Guaranty Bank for financing the acquisition; Morgan Guaranty had been McGraw-Hill's banker for over fifty years. He said, "American Express' conspiratorial approach and lack of integrity is further emphasized by [its] obtaining the financing for acquisition of McGraw-Hill from Morgan Guaranty Trust Company which, for more than fifty years, has been McGraw-Hill's principal, bank."[23] No comment was made regarding the bank's apparent willingness to fund the takeover.

McGraw further cited potential antitrust problems which could arise from the acquisition. Many Amex directors served on boards of McGraw-Hill competitors. The acquisition might also reduce competition between McGraw-Hill and Amex in markets such as bond rating and bond insurance. Further, the takeover attempt could have an impact on proposed antitrust legislation. Due to the large amount of money involved, the case was of possible attraction to the Securities and Exchange Commission (SEC) as a test case. McGraw vowed to initiate defensive action through the SEC, FTC, and Federal Communications Commission (FCC). McGraw ran his letter as a two-page advertisement in both the *New York Times* and *Wall Street Journal* (see Appendix III).

The Amex Response

Robinson's response to Harold McGraw's letter was "a study in calculated cool." He stated, "We were . . . disappointed by the intemperate nature of Mr. McGraw's response."[24] Amex promptly filed a libel suit against McGraw-Hill and McGraw charging that through the public statements and action, they were attempting "to oppose, obstruct, delay, and defeat . . . American Express' right to make" the tender offer. In a letter to McGraw that was released to the press, Robinson wrote, "Harold, I can state without equivocation that the editorial freedom and independence of McGraw-Hill's many activities, which you have fostered and supported so thoroughly and professionally, will be fully maintained after the combination of our business."[25] In reply to McGraw-

Hill's "deliberate attempt to impugn the integrity" of Amex, it cited $52 million in income taxes and $100 million in other taxes paid in 1977.[26]

Not only was Amex's offer rejected, but its business ethics had been questioned and its reputation sullied. "Everyone expected a rejection, but [Harold] McGraw did not just reject it. He rejected it in spades," said Robert Holvit of First Manhattan Corporation.[27] The "extreme bitterness of the counterattack" by McGraw surprised Robinson and Morley. Robinson admitted that editorial freedom is important, but he argued that other diversified companies had found acceptable ways to insulate muscular publishing arms from corporate pressures. Said Robinson, "Don't you think we'd be mindful of our responsibility?"[28] Morley denied misuse of inside information; he had known nothing that was "secret." Morley's responsibility as a director, said Robinson, was to the shareholders. Thus, he had done nothing to violate his obligations to the shareholders or to McGraw-Hill.[29].

Exhibit 1

American Express and McGraw-Hill: Profits and Sales

	1978 Sales (% of total)	1978 Profits (% of total)
American Express:		
International Banking	12.7	9.5
Travel Related Services	24.4	43.4
Insurance Services	62.9	47
McGraw-Hill:		
Financial Services	7	6
Broadcasting	6	14
Construction and Computer Services	16	22
Books and Education Services	41	27
Publications	30	31

	American Express		McGraw-Hill	
	Sales (millions of $)	Profits (millions of $)	Sales (millions of $)	Profits (millions of $)
1978...	4,100.0	308.0	761.2	63.7
1977...	3,400.0	262.1	659.0	51.4
1976...	2,900.0	194.5	590.0	40.5
1975...	2,500.0	165.0	536.0	33.1
1974...	2,100.0	156.8	510.0	30.3
1973...	1,900.0	150.9	470.0	27.8

THE TWO COMPANIES

McGraw-Hill: A Family Business

McGraw-Hill began as a magazine publisher in 1909. Harold McGraw's grandfather, James, built the business into twenty magazines and a growing book trade by the 1920s. His four sons then took over the company; three of them eventually became chairmen. Family feuding and an emphasis on trade journals characterized McGraw-Hill during this period—traits which were still evident a generation later. By 1939 McGraw-Hill was the largest educational publisher in the world. The only chief executive officer outside the family had been Shelton Fisher, Donald McGraw, Sr.'s right-hand man at his retirement in 1968. Donald Sr. had named Fisher C.E.O. because he did not think "the boys" (cousins John, Harold, Jr., and Donald, Jr.) were ready yet for the position.[30]

In 1974 Fisher resigned and Harold McGraw, Jr. became chairman, president, and chief executive officer. This appointment was the result of negotiations among the three cousins, and Donald, Jr. evidently expected to be second in command. Harold refused, so Donald quit rather than be Harold's "damn briefcase carrier." He said, "I guess he thought I'd be playing too much golf and drinking too much at lunch."[31] John also eventually resigned from the company management in 1978, but remained on the board. He described the family feuding: "Let's put it this way. We haven't had Thanksgiving dinner at grandmother's house in a number of years."[32] The impact of these events on the takeover attempt was that Harold could not count on support by all McGraw family shareholders; a proxy battle by Donald was a distinct possibility. Harold held approximately 800,000 shares, while John and Donald jointly held about 600,000. Total family holdings were about 20 percent of total shares of McGraw-Hill stock outstanding.

The history of family control had strongly influenced the company's managerial behavior. While McGraw-Hill had grown steadily during the decade preceding the takeover attempt ($45.5 million pretax income on revenues of $305 million in 1978), Harold McGraw was characterized as being "less than aggressive, and possessive regarding 'his company.'" According to *Fortune*:

> Two major criticisms of Harold McGraw can be made: he has been cautious to the point of paralysis on acquisitions ... [and] he has so flattened the organization chart [that] up to a few months ago, all key executives reported to him, making for agonizingly slow decision-making.[33]

Corporate Underdog. In light of the increase of successful takeovers and the trend toward conglomerate ownership in the publishing industry, McGraw-Hill appeared to be the corporate underdog in the Amex tender offer. Harold McGraw saw the bid as a personal challenge. Since becoming president, he had run the company in an entrepreneurial style. McGraw felt he was fighting not only for editorial freedom, but also for his family inheritance. The McGraws largely viewed the company as their own, despite the fact that fewer and fewer McGraws were working there. McGraw was proud of the history of family ownership and control (although in 1979 his designated successor was Joseph L. Dionne, not a family member). McGraw probably felt that if the takeover was successful, his struggle for control of McGraw-Hill would have been in vain.

The independence of McGraw-Hill, partially due to its control by the McGraws, had influenced the nature of its publications and its relationships with authors. As the nation's largest publisher of textbooks, the firm had developed ties with researchers and research institutions which could arguably be threatened if the publisher were part of a conglomerate. Historically, McGraw-Hill had presented a wide range of trade journals. Because of the relatively low contribution margins of such publications, there was concern that due to the conglomerate preoccupation with the "bottom line," trade journals would likely be dropped after a successful takeover. Moreover, it was believed by many that the relationship of McGraw-Hill and independent authors would be radically altered. The Authors Guild (see Appendix IV) stated:

> Authors exist in a symbiotic relationship with publishers. ... the fate of McGraw-Hill, in its struggle to preserve its independence, affects all American authors and all major independent book publishing companies. The conglomeration of American book publishing obviously is harming individual authors: placing them in a weaker bargaining position vis-a-vis these giant corporations; reducing their opportunities to be published; and subjecting them to unfair contractual and business practices.[34]

The Company Position. McGraw-Hill was attractive to Amex for several reasons (see Appendix I for financial statements). McGraw had let $93 million accumulate in cash and short-term investments, which invited acquisition. Moreover, McGraw-Hill owned four television stations, financial services,

Exhibit 2

Segment Reporting for McGraw-Hill (In thousands of dollars)

	1978		1977	
	Operating revenue	Operating profit	Operating revenue	Operating profit
Books and education services	$305,321	$ 45,506	$278,418	$ 35,360
Publications	232,032	43,581	196,192	34,853
Information systems	124,982	25,171	96,761	24,420
Financial services	53,715	8,390	50,605	8,170
Broadcasting operations	45,151	19,619	37,048	14,502
Total operating segments	$761,201	$142,267	$659,024	$117,305
General corporate expense . . .	————	(7,478)	————	(7,106)
Interest expense	————	(2,956)	————	(3,079)
Corporate assets	————	————	————	————
Investment in Rock-McGraw, Inc.	————	————	————	————
Total Company	$761,201	$131,833	$659,024	$107,120

construction and computer services, publishing services (some sixty periodicals), and books and education services. (McGraw-Hill was organized into six operating companies: McGraw-Hill Book Company, Information Systems Company, Publications Company, International Book Company, Broadcasting Company, Inc., and Standard & Poor's Corporation.) Amex projected that it could use its direct mail network to profitably distribute McGraw-Hill publications and other products. The takeover would smooth out the earnings pattern of Amex, but some analysts argued that Amex's "good business fit" argument was superficial. Analyst Herbert Goodfriend of Loeb Rhoades Hornblower said, "Let's face it, it's a straight diversification," according to another analyst, "I can see it now: *Business Week*—don't leave home without it."[35]

The trend in the publishing industry had been decidedly toward conglomerate ownership during the early 1970s. The trade book division of McGraw-Hill competed with ten other major publishers; together, these eleven publishers dominated the trade book market. Seven were owned by conglomerates. Formerly independent textbook publishers had been acquired by Litton Industries, Xerox, ITT, Raytheon, and Time, Inc.[36]

Subsequent to the Amex takeover offer, the Authors Guild asked the Federal Trade Commission (FTC) and Department of Justice to take action to halt this trend. The Guild's letter said, "Since most of the surviving independent firms, like McGraw-Hill, are major textbook publishers, and since many formerly independent textbook firms are now owned by conglomerates, we face the dangerous prospect that textbook publishers in this country could be controlled largely by huge multi-business conglomerates."[37] According to *The Nation*:

> Conglomeratization in publishing is involving larger and larger corporate entities. It may have seemed alarmist last May, when [Leonard C.] Lewin asked ["Publishing Goes Multinational," *The Nation*, May 13, 1978]: "Is it beyond belief that most of the books in the racks a few years hence may be chosen for you, like television programs, by Mobil, Exxon, and the rest?"[38]

Amex: Warring Giant

Amex chairman James D. Robinson III, age 43 at the time of the takeover bid, has been described as "coolly professional,"[39] a deep financial conservative, and a workaholic. Hired away from White Weld investment banking firm in 1970 by former Amex chairman Howard Clark as his successor, "Jimmy Three Sticks" (because of the III after Robinson's name) first ran the American Express International Banking Corporation, and later "travel-related services." In 1975 Robinson was named Amex president; in 1977 he became chairman and chief executive officer.[40]

Roger H. Morley, age 47 during the merger attempt, had succeeded Robinson as Amex president. Both Morley and Robinson were engineers and Harvard Business School graduates. Preferring to function as a team, they emphasized planning and budgeting and were reputed to want "everything that can be, reduced to numbers." Robinson called their approach "no-surprise management." Two of their major priorities were synchronization of the activities of various divisions and growth through acquisitions. Morley had said, "We want to start pawing the ground with our best energy."[41] As a member of the McGraw-Hill board, Morley saw a company he thought ripe for an offer.

Diversification through acquisition or internal growth was essential to maintain Amex's record of annual growth in operating profits. Annual sales had increased from $3.4 billion in 1977 to $4.1 billion in 1978, with net profit increasing from $262.1 million to $308 million. In 1978, 43.4 percent of profits came from travel-related services (traveler's checks, cards, and the travel agency), 47 percent from insurance services, and 9.5 percent from international banking services. By investing the approximately $2.1 billion annual "float" from unredeemed traveler's checks along with insurance premiums, Amex in 1979 held a $3.5 billion portfolio of state and local government bonds. Because municipals are tax exempt, the bonds contributed $210 million tax free to annual income in 1979. Increased competition threatened the base of Amex's profits, and a decline in market share was imminent (see Appendix II for financial statements).

The Company Position. During the late 1960s, Amex's major rivals in the "travel and entertainment" segment of the credit card market were Carte Blanche and Diners' Club. "Practically dormant" in the 1960s, these two competitors had come alive in the 1970s.[42] In the middle-income segment, competition from Visa and Master Charge increased. Further, Visa and Master Charge aggressively sought the high-income, expense account segment which had traditionally gone to Amex. As more companies began to enter the traveler's check market, Amex saw its market share narrow and the prospects for growth decline. In 1968 Amex had had $1.3 billion of credit card billings—about one-third of the market. In 1978 Amex credit card billings had risen to $12.4 billion, but because the total credit card market had grown to about $71 billion of billings, the company's market share had dropped to 17.5 percent.[43]

Amex appeared most threatened by Visa and Master Charge, because banks that belonged to the two associations could offer not only the credit cards, but also their traveler's checks. Amex had traditionally sold its checks through these same banks. Amex had not been successful in marketing its card in Europe; except in England, credit cards and credit in general were met with distrust. The travel agency was a loss leader for its other travel services, and Amex did not compete aggressively in that business.

Fireman's Fund, the insurance company owned by Amex, contributed almost half of total profits in 1978. However, the sharply cyclical profit pattern inherent in the property and casualty business meant that the contribution margin from Fireman's could reasonably be expected to fluctuate greatly. In order to maintain profits when the property and casualty business was in a trough, Amex needed to diversify into less cyclical or seasonal areas of business. (Amex's emphasis on smooth earnings had resulted in several cases of creative use of generally accepted accounting principles.)

The American Express International Banking Corporation contributed least to Amex profit. The bank was very small, and earnings had grown only 8 percent from 1977 to 1978. Return on assets had been about 0.6 percent, while other Amex operations ranged from 16 to 20 percent. As the fastest growing but least profitable operation, the bank had been unable to compete with the international giants. It had been caught in an international margin squeeze in 1978, and had had severe personnel problems. The bank was the only business area in which Amex was not operating well.[44]

Amex is organized into a complicated set of subsidiaries. Under American Express Company itself in New York are financial and investment activities handled by W. H. Morton & Co. Division (tax-exempt securities) and American Express Credit Corporation (CREDCO), which purchases card member receivables. Travel Related Services (1978 assets of $4.47 billion) contained the Card Division, Traveler's Cheque and Money Order Divisions, Travel Division, American Express Publishing Corporation (*Travel & Leisure* magazine), and Payments Systems, Inc. American Express International Banking Corporation of Connecticut (AEIBC, 1978 assets of $5.43 billion) owns banks operat-

Exhibit 3

Segment Reporting for American Express
(In millions of dollars)

	1978	1977	1976
Revenues from operations:			
Travel Related Services	$ 993.3	$ 792.2	$ 687.8
International Banking Services	515.5	380.6	326.2
Insurance Services	2,564.9	2,252.7	1,911.5
Other	10.8	20.7	23.4
Total	$ 4,084.5	$ 3,446.2	$ 2,948.9
Pre-tax operating income:			
Travel Related Services	$ 207.7	$ 179.3	$ 157.5
International Banking Services	53.9	41.4	33.7
Insurance Services	162.4	129.1	38.3
	424.0	349.8	229.5
Other and general corporate expenses	(53.0)	(45.3)	(33.0)
Total	$ 371.0	$ 304.5	$ 196.5
Net income:			
Travel Related Services	$ 144.9	$ 129.4	$ 110.2
International Banking Services	31.8	25.9	21.8
Insurance Services	156.8	127.5	75.3
	333.5	282.8	207.3
Other and general corporate expenses	(25.5)	(20.7)	(12.8)
Total	$ 308.0	$ 262.1	$ 194.5

ing in various countries (Germany, Italy, Denmark, Switzerland, England, Hong Kong), a development company (Cayman Islands and Lebanon), and American Express International Finance Corporation (Netherlands Antilles). Fireman's Fund Insurance Company (San Francisco, 1978 assets of $4.63 billion), includes the American Insurance Companies, Falcon Customer Services, Inc., FAMEX, Inc., The Excess and Special Risk Market, Inc., and a variety of other related subsidiaries. Also affiliated with Amex are Export Credit Corporation, Amex Minerals, and Realty Management Company.

The Search for Acquisitions. Unable to maintain record growth levels in its profitable markets, Amex began searching for an acquisition candidate. It had resources sufficient to make a large takeover; moreover, Amex could offer cash if needed. An early target, Philadelphia Life Insurance Company, would have enlarged Amex's highly profitable insurance operations. Another target was Walt Disney Productions, a significant departure from any of Amex's current operations. A bid for Book-of-the-Month Club indicated Robinson's interest in coupling book distribution with Amex's extensive direct-mail operations. These attempts failed.

After informal offers had been rejected by these firms, Amex began considering McGraw-Hill. McGraw-Hill was in excellent financial shape; it controlled a range of businesses (from publishing to broadcasting); higher profits could be earned in capital-intensive publishing than in securities; other conglomerates had made successful acquisitions in the field; and the acquisition would be a diversification which could smooth Amex's pattern of earnings. Amex vice president C. R. Greenwood said, "They have management, potential growth, and reputation."[45] Further, Amex believed that one third of McGraw-Hill's future business might come from abroad; McGraw-Hill could use Amex's international marketing services and worldwide communications system. In the words of one securities analyst, "[McGraw-Hill] management has carved out a special niche, but has done nothing with a great franchise. There are underutilized assets, lots of cash ($64.1 million) and little debt."[46] Before approaching McGraw-Hill, Amex had "conducted an extensive study of possible acquisition targets throughout the publishing industry including Dow Jones and Co. (publisher of the *Wall Street Journal*). A source close to the situation declined to discuss why McGraw-Hill was selected as the target but stressed that 'this wasn't any rash jump by American Express.' "[47]

Nevertheless, the bid to acquire McGraw-Hill was variously called "a surprise offer," "an out-of-the-blue bid," and "unexpected offer." Perhaps one reason for the surprise was that the acquisition would have been very large, and one that only a giant such as Amex could make. Further, the history of family management meant that Harold McGraw's reaction was not unexpected. The acquisition would be subject to scrutiny by not only the SEC, but also the FCC, FTC, and Department of Justice. Yet there had been signs of Amex's interest before the formal offer. Apparently while a McGraw-Hill director, "Morley had earlier dropped some hints of Amex's interest, but they were so subtle that [Harold] McGraw may have failed to pick them up."[48]

THE TAKEOVER BATTLE

Rejection of the First Bid

Wall Street did not believe that Amex's original bid of $34 per share was an absolutely final offer. While substantially above the market price, the offer was thought to be sufficiently low that Amex could meet any price hike made by McGraw-Hill. Even pushed into the $40 per share range, the acquisition was considered by analysts to be a good one—certainly one which Amex could afford. The initial bid was evidence that Amex had grown in "sophistication" in takeover strategy, because more than purely economic decisions were involved. One analyst said:

> Egos are involved and you've got to go through a certain ritual dance. If you drop the top offer you can imagine on the table, you don't leave the target company's directors any battles to win for their shareholders. These are both white shoes companies and the aim is to come out of this thing with their shoes still white.[49]

The McGraw-Hill board's rejection of the $34 bid was taken by the financial community as neither unexpected nor unusual. The rejection was logical whether or not McGraw-Hill planned eventually to accept Amex as a suitor. Harold McGraw's position was influenced by pride of ownership, and his initial response was predictably negative. The other directors considered McGraw's opinions and the advice of the investment bankers and lawyers hired by McGraw-Hill after the initial bid. By rejecting the first bid, McGraw-Hill gave other potential suitors the opportunity to make better offers; Amex would have to consider raising its bid to halt other tenders and "white knights." The board's unanimity was a strategic coup for Harold McGraw, since at least one family director (John McGraw) was not totally in sympathy with him. Moreover, several shareholders, both small and large (notably Donald McGraw) had made it known that they would be happy to sell at the "right price."

What made the rejection unusual was Harold McGraw's vehemence and bitterness. He clearly viewed the takeover attempt as a personal battle. After the board's rejection he said, "This is one of the proudest moments of my life."[50] McGraw claimed that Amex "lacks the integrity, corporate morality, and sensitivity . . . essential to McGraw-Hill." Further, the offer was "illegal, unsolicited and improper."[51] The strategy planned by McGraw was to attack Amex in the press, in court (with the breach-of-trust suit), and through government channels. McGraw-Hill was the underdog, and McGraw may have believed that his only chance lay in a bitterly defensive reaction. By raising the emotional issues of corporate ethics and editorial independence, McGraw was able to shift the nature of the battle from economic to moral; this strategy was effective both with the government and with shareholders. That McGraw left himself no face-saving "way out" made clear his complete lack of ambivalence regarding the Amex offer.

Exhibit 4 **McGraw-Hill Board of Directors**

Harold W. McGraw, Jr., chairman and president, McGraw-Hill, Inc.

Vernon R. Alden, chairman, Massachusetts Foreign Business Council

Kay Knight Clarke, director of corporate development, Arthur D. Little, Inc.

Daniel F. Crowley, executive vice president for finance, McGraw-Hill, Inc.

Peter O. Lawson-Johnson, chairman, Anglo Company Ltd.

William J. McGill, president, Columbia University

John L. McGraw, private business ventures

Gordon W. McKinley, senior vice president for economics and financial planning, McGraw-Hill, Inc.

Alan J. Pifer, president, Carnegie Corporation of New York

Louis Putze, consultant, Rockwell International Corporation

Howard S. Tuthill, partner, Cummings & Lockwood

James E. Webb, attorney-at-law

George R. Webster, consulting engineer

At the April 24, 1979, annual meeting, all directors were reelected. William T. Seawell, chairman and chief executive officer of Pan American World Airways, replaced Roger H. Morley at that time.

The day after the McGraw-Hill board rejected the offer, a shareholder filed a class-action suit against the firm in New York State Court. The suit claimed that the board had violated its fiduciary duty to the shareholders because it had refused to negotiate with Amex for the "highest price available;" instead, the board had rejected the offer out of hand and hired a law firm known for "defensive tactics." On behalf of all McGraw-Hill shareholders, the plaintiff shareholder asked for compensatory damages in an unspecified amount from the company and the board. New York attorney Abraham Pomerantz, a specialist in class action suits said, "There are squeals all over America from frustrated shareholders of McGraw-Hill. My telephone has been ringing all morning with calls from people who want to join the [lawsuit] parade."[52]

Amex Countermoves

Amex countered McGraw's charges with a libel suit, which charged McGraw-Hill with "publicly disseminating false and misleading statements designed to induce McGraw-Hill shareholders to reject American Express' tender offer."[53] Amex also filed details of its tender offer with the SEC and New York State's attorney general (under the New York Security Takeover Act). The terms included a price of $34 per share; the filings did not prevent Amex from increasing its bid price or offering cash plus securities.

According to the filings, if Amex varied "the terms of its offer before the expiration date by increasing the consideration to be paid for shares [Amex] would pay such increased amount for all shares purchased pursuant to the offer, whether or not such shares had been tendered or purchased prior to such variation in the terms of the offer. . . . The offer, if made, would be made only in compliance with applicable law. Until such time, American Express [reserved] the right to amend, modify, or revoke the offer."[54] With the state thus set for a higher bid, Amex filed early to get the twenty-day waiting period (after the New York filing) underway. (Under New York law, a tender offer could not be made until twenty days after the filing; the state attorney general had fifteen days after the filing to call a public hearing, after which the attorney general could order additional terms. The offer could start only after compliance with such terms. The hearing had to be held within forty days from the filing. Within thirty days after the hearing the attorney general had to determine whether the company had complied with his terms—potentially a grand total of seventy days of delay.)[55]

On January 29, 1979, Amex sent its "better bid" in a letter to the McGraw-Hill board. The new bid was for $40 per share, totaling almost $1 billion in cash. The earlier offer was withdrawn. The letter disagreed with the "scorched earth" policy "apparently being pursued" by McGraw-Hill, and emphasized that the new Amex offer was "conditioned on receipt within a reasonable period of time of a response from a majority of the board of directors of McGraw-Hill, containing either a recommendation that our proposal be accepted or an agreement not to oppose it by propaganda, lobbying, litigation or otherwise." Robinson repeated his guarantee to operate McGraw-Hill as an "independent subsidiary with appropriate mutual board representation." Further, he rejected the "Trojan horse" charges made by McGraw against Morley. Another significant point was the mention of a January 26 telegram from Donald McGraw to Harold McGraw stating his wish to make his own decision concerning the offer.[56]

Rejection of the Second Bid

On January 31, 1979, the McGraw-Hill board again rejected Amex's offer. As a sweetener to disgruntled stockholders, a 28 percent increase in dividends, from $0.25 to $0.32 per quarter, was declared. Harold McGraw also announced a 24 percent increase in annual profits for 1978, to a record $63.7 million.[57] The meeting was described as "tense." The directors got legal advice as to whether they had an obligation to allow shareholders to vote on tender offers. Lipton delivered an opinion that directors do not have such an obligation.[58] McGraw stressed his previous arguments, that editorial independence (especially for *Standard and Poor's* and *Business Week*) would be undermined; further, he charged Morley with "a serious breach of trust" by having served as a McGraw-Hill director.[59]

The directors in their rejection said that "it would be imprudent to sell or merge at a time and under conditions dictated by American Express acting in its own self interest." (Of this argument, *Fortune* said, "It was not made clear whose interest American Express *should* be acting in.")[60] McGraw wrote to shareholders, "There were four basic and insurmountable obstacles to the American Express proposal: It wasn't the right price. It wasn't the right time. It wasn't the right partner. It wasn't legally proper."[61] In reply to Harold's last charge, Donald called it "a ploy that Harold is using to pass by the stockholders because he does not want to sell at any price."[62] While analysts appeared to view the editorial independence issue as a smoke screen, the Authors Guild and McGraw-Hill employees seemed to take it as an issue worth the fight.

Not all shareholders accepted McGraw's arguments. Several more class-action suits (for a total of seven) were filed (including one in federal court by "small" shareholder Harry Lewis); another was threatened by Donald McGraw. The Lewis suit claimed as damages the difference between the pre-offer price of $26 and the offer of $40 (or $14 per share), for a total of $341.6 million.[63] Donald McGraw's threatened suit turned out to be only a passing thing. On January 26 Donald had sent Harold McGraw a telegram urging him to change his position on the takeover; earlier, Donald had said, "I would join a class-action suit with Max Geffen [another large shareholder] . . . the institutions that hold McGraw-Hill stock will join us."[64] Though Donald's suit never materialized, the situation seemed ripe for a proxy fight. (As for the other lawsuits, all of those filed before and after this event were eventually consolidated, as noted below.)

Amex announced that its offer would remain open until March 1, hoping that shareholder pressure would become so intense that the McGraw-Hill board would be forced to reconsider the offer. Robinson said, "You have to know when to close your pocketbook. Everything has a value, and you're crazy to get railroaded and let emotions run away with good judgment." Morley commented, "We're not the type of people to lay out $800 million for a property that has suffered from a scorched earth policy. . . . We're out of the market." Robinson said the second offer was contingent on a friendly reception because "an extended fight would have burned up the resources of McGraw-Hill. If we prevailed, what would we have left?"[65]

McGRAW-HILL'S SECOND FRONT

Congressional Reaction

Despite the concern voiced by Morley and Robinson for McGraw-Hill as a company, a more probable reason for their loss of battle spirit was noise from the nation's capital. Lipton had sparked the interest of Representative Henry Reuss (Democrat-Wisconsin), who chaired the House Banking Committee.

"When it appeared that Reuss's concerns might threaten American Express' exemption from the Bank Holding Company Act, which permits it to operate a variety of businesses, American Express went into panic," an insider said. "Suddenly they were faced with losing their whole business, or most of it, because of one lousy merger."[66] McGraw-Hill also suggested, through document requests, that Amex could be accused of violating U.S. antiboycott laws in its foreign banking activities; for Amex the Arab boycott issue was volatile and very sensitive due to the international nature of its banking activities and exposure to U.S. banking regulation.

SEC

Elsewhere in Washington, the SEC was informally considering whether McGraw's "Trojan horse" charge against Morley was justified. If Morley had given secret McGraw-Hill information to Amex during the planning of the offer, he had done so in violation of U.S. securities laws. If McGraw's charges had not been accurate, he in turn, however, could be judged guilty of making false statements. Due to a lack of case law, however, the area was considered "murky" by the SEC.[67]

FTC

The FTC also voiced "serious concerns" about the merger, and notified both parties that it was examining the proposed acquisition. Initially, Amex had filed under the Hart-Scott-Rodino Antitrust Improvement Act. McGraw-Hill tried to terminate that filing, citing the board's rejection of Amex's second offer. The FTC rejected this request because Amex had not withdrawn the offer or the filing with the FTC. The FTC requested more information, which Amex said was "routine." While McGraw-Hill actively sought federal intervention, Amex was not anxious to deal with the agencies, often sources of costly delays and objections.[68]

In a letter to Amex, the FTC outlines four issues of particular concern (see Appendix V). First was the potential conflict of interest resulting from the control of a financial information publisher by a large financial firm. Second was the potential reciprocity between a bond-rating firm and a firm which underwrote and distributed bonds, held bonds, and insured bond issuers. Third was the possible entrenchment of Amex in some markets due to lower advertising costs in McGraw-Hill publications or, conversely, the entrenchment of McGraw-Hill due to low-cost access to Amex membership lists. Fourth was the possible decrease in competition between McGraw-Hill and Amex in bond rating, bond insurance, and other bond marketing services. The FTC felt that "such a conflict, if it exists, may be inherent in the merger, and that efforts to insulate the publishing operations may not be successful."[69] Section 7 of the Clayton Act forbids any corporation engaged in commerce to acquire the shares of a competing corporation, Section 5 of the Federal Trade Commission Act provides "that unfair methods of competition in commerce are hereby declared unlawful."

FCC

FCC interest stemmed from McGraw-Hill's ownership of four television stations. (Prior FCC approval is required before broadcast licenses may be transferred.) McGraw-Hill asked the FCC to prohibit Amex from tendering an offer without prior FCC approval on an application for license transferral. Amex said it would seek dismissal of the request because it would comply with communications laws; normally approval of transfers takes "a substantial period," said Amex, even without an extraordinary request like that made by McGraw-Hill. Amex planned to ask the FCC's approval on a plan to allow the offer "within a relatively short time."[70] The FCC posed a significant hurdle; during hostile takeovers, it probably would not permit the television stations to be held in a trust pending approval of the applications (as planned by Amex). Indeed, the obstacle was so formidable that in the past some companies had acquired television stations to discourage takeover attempts.

Canada

Amex also had to seek approval from the Canadian government's Foreign Investment Review Agency. Prior approval would be needed before McGraw-Hill's extensive Canadian operations (mainly a large book publishing company) could be transferred.[71] This approval was a smaller hurdle than those posed by the U.S. government. (The need for approvals from the FCC and Canadian government would become academic when the McGraw-Hill board took no further action on the offer.)

Media Concentration

The Amex takeover bid also raised other significant legal issues. For example, the proposed acquisition related directly to the antitrust question raised by the trend toward increased media concentration. In the past, the FTC had not attacked acquisitions of newspaper publishers by large holding companies, so that a majority of local newspapers had come to be controlled by a few such firms. Further, there had been an increase in the joint holding of television and radio stations by one company, and a corresponding decrease in "local ownership." (The FCC had the sole authority to issue licenses for broadcasting and to approve their transfer; the FTC and Department of Justice were interested in the effects of concentration on competition within the industry.) In book publishing, acquisitions by conglomerates had been rapid and successful during the decade preceding the Amex bid. But these acquisitions had spawned relatively few antitrust suits. Due to the lack of case law regarding media concentration, the FTC was not certain that such mergers could be reached under existing laws.

But now there were signs that the FTC might regard the Amex bid as a test case. Both Amex and McGraw-Hill were large and the money involved was substantial. The offer had stimulated a good deal of public attention; publishers and broadcasters, regardless of size, were concerned. Perhaps sensing the possibility of FTC action, McGraw-Hill together with the Authors Guild (among other interest groups), lobbied for FTC action. The FTC might be induced to make the Amex bid a test case if it could be persuaded, first, that such a suit could be successful and, second, that if successful, the case would set a useful precedent. Amex's size, diverse operations, and profitability made it a vulnerable target. Amex was sensitive in a variety of areas which would ease the FTC's job in court. However, the FTC had been looking for a case in which the acquired firm was dominant in a clearly defined market; McGraw-Hill did not fit this criterion well.[72]

The Authors Guild wrote the FTC and Department of Justice to encourage such action: "With serious antitrust and First Amendment issues at stake, the Commission or Antitrust Division should test the application of Section 7 [of the Clayton Act] to this acquisition, the latest and largest in a continuing trend to book publishing concentration and conglomeration that has swallowed up many formerly independent major companies. Section 7 was intended to protect the First Amendment-based, social and cultural, as well as economic, interests threatened by this acquisition, and was not merely intended to regulate the market shares of merging corporations." The Guild found the merger not only harmful to McGraw-Hill's authors and clients, but also to the future of all independent publishers. Inaction by the government, argued the Guild, would effectively sanction the seizure of independent publishers by conglomerates.[73]

Despite the outcome, the merger attracted both administrative and legislative attention. For this reason, one Wall Street analyst said, "The timing of the American Express deal stinks."[74] The FTC voiced its "serious concerns" with the merger, but was "apparently helpless to stop an Amex-McGraw-Hill merger on traditional grounds, [and] saw it as further evidence that rules may be needed to keep media companies out of the hands of industrial giants. And on Capitol Hill, the prospect of an Amex-McGraw-Hill alliance fueled a push for legislation that would curtail what Congressional trust busters saw as a disturbing trend toward giant conglomerate mergers."[75]

The FTC could attack such a merger on several grounds. One would be from the "bigness is bad" standpoint, in an effort to set a precedent against big mergers in general. An attack on conglomerate control of the media was likewise a possibility, since the FTC had voiced concern over media concentration. Less attractive was any assault on the potential entrenchment of Amex and McGraw-Hill in their current markets; because such arguments would be specific to the operations of the two firms, it is unlikely that the case law established would be widely applicable. If the FTC were truly seeking a landmark case, the most attractive legal theories were those of undue size and media concentration.

The FTC attitude toward mergers was not shared by the financial community. While the federal government generally viewed conglomerate mergers as dangerous, Wall Street favored takeovers as an economic means of expansion. In the works at the time was Senator Edward Kennedy's no-fault monopoly bill, which proposed to make size alone a basis for disallowing proposed mergers, as well as for breaking up existing enterprises.[76] Other legislative attacks came through congressional committee hearings and investigations, such as the examination of Amex by the House Banking Committee, an indirect but effective way to discourage the merger. Although Amex held banks overseas, its business was not really that of a bank holding company; its exemption from the Bank Holding Company Act therefore seemed rational and legal. The Act restricted the activities of bank holding companies such that if subject to it, Amex would lose both of its most profitable businesses. Amex was reluctant to deal with Congress or regulatory agencies in excess of the required filings and hearings for fear of having to relitigate decisions essential to its successful continuation as an economic enterprise.

While Harold McGraw had raised the issue of editorial independence, a more probable impact of conglomerate ownership would be on the product line. The Authors Guild maintained that there would be less variety and depth offered in both trade books and textbooks, with decisions based more on financial than artistic criteria. The Guild argued that while in purely economic terms this approach might be an efficient way to make publishing decisions, the FTC should find it socially harmful. Further, the potential conflicts of interest due to the diversity inherent in conglomerate structure were cited as a significant concern. The FTC itself apparently believed that insulating operations such as publishing would be difficult, or impossible.

OTHER CONSIDERATIONS

Director Obligations

The Amex offer also raised the issue of the obligations of directors to stockholders. Many McGraw-Hill stockholders felt that they should be given the opportunity to decide for themselves whether to accept the Amex offer (and the $14 per share premium). McGraw-Hill retained outside counsel Wachtell, Lipton, Rosen, and Katz to advise the board; other lawyers did not agree with the advice given, although the board's rejection relied heavily on the legal opinion. One dissenter said, "Such decisions belong to the people who own the corporation—the shareholders—and not to management, which has a vested interest. [In a class-action] they'll have a hell of a good lawsuit."[77] (Few such suits had in the past been successful, however.)

McGraw-Hill directors maintained that probable intervention by government agencies made consummation of the merger uncertain. Marshall Field's rejection of Carter Hawley Hale Stores and Gerber Products' rejection of Anderson Clayton were cited in support of this position. Yet neither of those prior acquisition attempts was an overwhelming precedent. The Marshall Field merger would have posed significant antitrust problems if consummated. Gerber shareholders had dropped their suit because Anderson Clayton was delayed by the courts. However, the McGraw-Hill case included similar elements, and the directors believed they had sufficient latitude to reject the bid.[78]

The McGraw-Hill board was comprised predominantly of outsiders. According to Harold McGraw, it was "a board which had nothing to gain by rejecting the offer."[79] (McGraw-Hill held only $10 million in liability insurance for directors and officers; total liability would have been $290 million.) The vote was unanimous, despite the ownership by several directors (such as John McGraw) of substantial amounts of stock. Whether the vote against the offer was selfish or disinterested, the large shareholders voted with the outside directors.

At the first annual meeting following the takeover attempt, a shareholder asked Harold McGraw why the decision had not been put to a shareholder vote. He replied:

> It's important to note that the illegalities surrounding the offer would not have made the $40 possible. And those legal problems would not have gone away despite a vote of our shareholders in favor. This is why the law sets up the Board of Directors and gives them clear fiduciary obligations to weigh all aspects of an issue and make the complex decisions that have to be made. ... This was a Board decision. It had to be made. There are more things in life than price, and the Board felt that those factors outweighed the price factor. I would hope and believe that our stockholders will have the $40 before we're through. But not through merger.[80]

Donald McGraw said, "I don't think Harold would be interested if American Express offered $100 a share. He wants the independence."[81] Although there was talk of a proxy fight, this fight never materialized; Donald refused, saying it would take too much time and money.[82]

Conflict of Interest

Morley's dual roles as Amex president and McGraw-Hill director put him in a sensitive position. "Morley may be tainted for the rest of his life," said a partner in a Wall Street firm.[83] According to Robinson, "We've bent over backwards to do this properly, legally and morally. I wish he had never gotten within 10 miles of that place."[84] Morley was in a no-win position. As Amex president, he could be accused of not having done a better job in gauging the reception the offer would receive. As a McGraw-Hill director, he was obligated not to use proprietary information against the firm. For McGraw-Hill, his duty was to bargain for a high premium; for Amex, he should have sought the easiest possible terms.

Morley himself professed no confusion on the nature of his fiduciary responsibilities, and to whom they were owed. "I'm clear on what the responsibilities of directors are," he said. "They're to the company and to the shareholders, not to management."[85] At the next shareholder's meeting after the takeover bid, a shareholder asked Harold McGraw:

> It's felt at McGraw-Hill that Roger Morley did not properly exercise his fiduciary responsibility to McGraw-Hill and stockholders, and that, in effect, the McGraw-Hill board did. Yet it seems to me that Mr. Morley elicited a bid of $40 a share for McGraw-Hill and the Board's actions have driven it back down to $26. Could you explain that?[86]

Harold McGraw replied:

You're basing the entire matter on price. Mr. Morley has a clear fiduciary responsibility which he did not maintain when he was involved with both companies. When you are working for Amex and you're trying to acquire somebody, your job is to buy low. When you're representing McGraw-Hill and under consideration to be acquired, your requirement is to sell high.[87]

McGraw-Hill dropped its breach-of-trust suit against Morley after Amex let its proposed offer expire. Even after the acquisition attempt ended, it remained unclear why Morley had not resigned from the McGraw-Hill board when Amex began considering the takeover.

The State of the Law

While courts generally have been reluctant to grant shareholders damages against management and directors in derivative or class-action suits, directors have been held to the fiduciary duties of care and loyalty. Under New York state law, "directors and officers shall discharge the duties of their respective positions in good faith and with that degree of diligence, care, and skill which the ordinarily prudent man would exercise under similar circumstances in like positions."[88] Directors may rely on professionals for expertise in specific areas (such as attorneys, accountants, and investment bankers); courts have yet to establish the degree to which reliance on such advice is a defense against shareholder action. In this takeover attempt, it was argued that McGraw-Hill had hired "experts" which it knew would advise the board to reject Amex offers. Attorney Martin Lipton and investment banking firm Morgan Stanley were known for their skill in fighting takeovers, and were apparently hired by McGraw-Hill for that purpose.[89] The McGraw-Hill board apparently was not relying on objective advice; moreover, McGraw-Hill shareholders paid for the legal services (about $3.4 million before taxes, $1.7 million after taxes).[90]

Harold McGraw claimed the board considered the price too low or "inadequate" on the advice of Morgan Stanley. One shareholder's attorney replied, "I don't understand how directors can sit down and arrogantly ignore what they are doing to the stockholders. Two plus two is four, and $40 is more than $26. It's simple arithmetic."[91] Disgruntled stockholders felt that the decision on the offer should be put to a shareholder vote by the board. Attorneys advised the board that this method was not the directors' obligation, although no case law has been established on this issue.

Was Harold McGraw fulfilling his duty of care to shareholders (of which he was one), or was his motivation primarily one of company control? Donald McGraw said, "It's not freedom of the press Harold's protecting. It's his own empire."[92] Whether a truthful charge, it would have been a difficult one to support in court. Harold McGraw was careful not to say that McGraw-Hill would not be sold at any price, and he maintained that the board would carefully consider all offers. It is difficult to imagine a suitor approaching McGraw-Hill with a higher premium, and there are few companies which could even merely match Amex's offer.

The duty of loyalty to which directors are held put Morley in a no-win situation; in fulfilling his obligation to either firm, he allegedly would violate his duty to the other. McGraw's "Trojan horse" charge was clearly one to which Morley was vulnerable. Morley argued that the takeover would be to the benefit of both firms' shareholders, and that for this reason he had been able to be loyal to each. The FTC did not pursue its investigation of the charges after the offer expired, and McGraw-Hill dropped its suit. Case law relating to director loyalty primarily concerns conflicts of interest in contracts and financial matters; since there are no precedents for a director in Morley's situation, the legal issue is as yet unresolved.

THE AFTERMATH

Although clothed in theory with ultimate power over corporate affairs, shareholders have little practical recourse against management actions with which they disagree. Due to the large holdings of the McGraw family, a proxy fight would have been extremely difficult without the support of at least part of the family. When Donald declined, management no longer considered the potential of a proxy fight a real threat. At the annual meeting in April 1979, an uncontested slate of directors was approved; the vote reflected no shareholder protest. (However, seven class-actions suits had been filed by March 1979. These were consolidated, and as of the start of 1981, the suit had not yet been settled.) Amex had left its offer open for almost two months, hoping that shareholders pressure would force the board to accept the Amex offer. But the shareholders had proved too weak to do so, mainly because in the end the McGraw family had stayed together. Had the board split or Donald dissented, the shareholders would have been more effective. Instead, the takeover defense cost them $3.4 million. One shareholder said, "I am very, very angry indeed that [McGraw-Hill] spent 6.9¢ per share of my money to lose me another $14."[93]

For his ferocious defense of McGraw-Hill, Harold McGraw was christened an "unlikely hero."[94] Morley and Robinson lost some respect after four merger attempts failed. Robinson was called "young and naive" by *Business Week*; Morley was also scarred by the battle.[95] An analyst suggested that Robinson might lose his job and that Morley might never get a chance to succeed him.[96] Both companies had spent large amounts of managerial time and money on negotiations and legal battles.

Despite the furor generated by the takeover attempt, neither Amex nor McGraw-Hill themselves seemed afterwards to have been much affected by the imbroglio. Both sought additional acquisitions, and McGraw-Hill acquired three companies during the first quarter of 1979.[97] Both firms had relatively good years in terms of profits and stock price, despite higher than usual legal expenditures. McGraw-Hill stock did not climb to the $40 predicted by Harold McGraw during the year; Amex stock performed satisfactorily.[98]

McGraw-Hill, Inc.
Consolidated Balance Sheets
December 31, 1978, 1977, and 1976 (in thousands of dollars)

	1978	1977	1976
Revenues:			
Operating revenue	$761,201	$659,024	$589,764
Other income—net	10,513	8,322	6,134
Total income	$771,714	$667,346	$595,898
Expenses:			
Operating	$367,885	$319,864	$294,578
Selling, general, and administrative	269,040	237,283	212,919
Interest	2,956	3,079	3,347
Total expenses	$639,881	$560,226	$510,844
Income before taxes on income and minority interests	$131,833	$107,120	$ 85,054
Provision for taxes on income	67,530	55,210	43,826
Minority interests in earnings of subsidiaries	642	518	765
Net operating income	$ 63,661	$ 51,392	$ 40,463
Retained income at beginning of year	260,680	228,934	204,334
Net income	$324,341	$280,326	$244,797
Dividends declared:			
Preference stock — $1.20 per share	$ 234	$ 536	$ 1,013
Common stock — $1.00 per share in 1978 and $0.80 in 1977	24,368	19,110	14,850
Dividends	$ 24,602	$ 19,646	$ 15,863
Retained income at end of year	$299,739	$260,680	$228,934
Earnings per common share and common equivalent share	$ 2.57	$ 2.08	$ 1.64

(Appendix I continued on next page.)

APPENDIX I (Continued)

McGraw-Hill, Inc.
Consolidated Statements of Income and Retained Income
December 31, 1978, 1977, and 1976 (in thousands of dollars)

	1978	1977	1976
Assets			
Current Assets:			
Cash (includes certificates of deposit: 1978-$44,958,000; 1977-$35,501,000)	$ 52,320	$ 52,591	$ 21,734
Short-term investments—at cost, which approximates market	40,777	30,483	24,010
Accounts receivable (net of allowance for doubtful accounts: 1978-$30,455; 1977-$25,810)	155,043	130,808	122,148
Inventories:			
Finished goods	71,083	62,976	62,595
Work-in-process	19,561	17,701	18,342
Paper and other materials	14,607	14,057	10,961
Prepaid and other current assets	9,470	8,406	7,294
Total current assets	$362,861	$317,022	$267,084
Investments and other assets:			
Investments in Rock-McGraw, Inc.—at equity	$ 30,276	$ 30,053	$ 29,873
Other investments, including joint ventures	6,400	5,972	5,283
Advances to authors (net of reserve)	5,936	4,772	3,574
Other—at cost (net of reserve)	13,645	12,455	10,201
Total investments and other assets	$ 56,257	$ 53,252	$ 48,931
Property and equipment—at cost:			
Land	$ 5,144	$ 5,038	$ 4,599
Buildings and leasehold improvements	93,534	87,917	82,986
Furniture and equipment	58,587	44,604	38,937
Total property and equipment	$157,265	$137,559	$126,522
Less accumulated depreciation and amortization	61,083	52,693	46,245
Net property and equipment	$ 96,182	$ 84,866	$ 80,277
Goodwill:			
Goodwill and other intangible assets—at cost, less amortization	$100,269	$ 94,680	$ 85,748
Total Assets	$615,569	$549,820	$482,040

Liabilities and Shareholders' Equity

Current Liabilities:		
Notes payable	$ 4,062	$ 3,637
Current portion of long-term debt	6,847	6,973
Accounts payable	40,671	25,360
Accrued royalties	16,815	14,576
Accrued compensation	19,840	9,784
Accrued contributions to retirement plans	12,978	20,805
Accrued taxes:		
Currently payable	39,160	26,295
Deferred	10,924	10,704
Unearned revenue	41,437	31,135
Other current liabilities	12,446	–
Total current liabilities	$205,180	$149,269
Other Liabilities:		
Long-term debt	$ 29,814	$ 41,159
Deferred income taxes	17,493	13,548
Other noncurrent liabilities	20,537	7,433
Total other liabilities	$ 67,844	$ 62,140
Total liabilities	$273,024	$211,409
Shareholders' Equity:		
$1.20 preference stock	$ 1,330	$ 7,950
Common stock	25,268	24,175
Additional paid-in capital	22,443	16,789
Retained income	299,739	228,934
Total shareholders' equity	$348,780	$277,848
Less common stock in treasury—at cost	6,235	7,217
Total shareholders' equity	$342,545	$270,631
Total Liabilities and Shareholders' Equity	$615,569	$482,040

American Express Company
Consolidated Balance Sheets

APPENDIX II   **December 31, 1978, 1977, and 1976 (in thousands of dollars)**

	1978	1977	1976
Assets			
Cash	$ 844.4	$ 673.6	$ 542.1
Time deposits	891.0	858.4	821.3
Investment securities—at cost:			
U.S. Government obligations	$ 395.0	$ 406.2	$ 375.6
U.S. Government agencies' obligations	40.0	47.3	53.1
State and municipal obligations	3,808.0	3,167.3	2,457.3
Other bonds and obligations	735.2	720.1	710.4
Preferred stocks	47.4	47.5	43.4
Total (market value in parentheses)	$ 5,025.6 (4,635.6)	$ 4,388.4 (4,396.0)	$ 3,639.8
Investment securities—at lower of aggregate—cost or market:			
Preferred stocks	$ 99.3	$ 111.3	$ 95.3
Common stocks	72.2	65.7	56.1
Total	$ 171.5	$ 177.0	$ 151.4
Investment securities—at market:			
Preferred stocks	$ 49.5	$ 49.2	$ 44.8
Common stocks	563.3	507.1	505.5
Total	$ 612.8	$ 556.3	$ 550.3
Loans and discounts, less reserves (1978, $74.8; 1977, $59.9)	$ 3,320.2	$ 2,571.1	$ 2,073.3
Accounts receivable and accrued interest, less reserves (1978, $170.8; 1977, $146.1)	2,716.8	2,164.0	1,753.7
Land, buildings and equipment—at cost, less accumulated depreciation (1978, $102.6; 1977, $86.5)	284.8	262.6	239.2
Prepaid policy acquisition expenses	166.4	153.0	129.8
Other assets	636.3	486.4	467.2
Total Assets	$ 14,669.8	$ 12,290.8	$ 10,368.1

Liabilities and Shareholders' Equity

Liabilities:			
Traveler's checks outstanding	$ 2,104.8	$ 1,859.3	$ 1,716.4
Customers' deposits and credit balances held by subsidiaries	4,192.4	3,755.0	3,024.0
Reserves for:			
Property-liability losses and loss expenses	2,124.5	1,723.3	1,363.3
Unearned premiums	875.3	792.2	672.5
Life and disability policies	183.9	147.3	130.4
Money orders and drafts outstanding	323.7	174.9	139.7
Short-term debt and commercial paper	1,116.8	776.2	554.9
Long-term debt	479.2	329.5	304.3
Accounts payable	785.4	333.1	471.1
Deferred income taxes	65.5	61.4	117.3
Other liabilities	843.7	670.4	620.3
Total liabilities	**$ 13,095.2**	**$ 10,922.6**	**$ 9,114.3**
Shareholders' equity:			
Preferred stock, issuable in series—authorized, 20,000,000 shares of $1.66 at 2/3 par value: (Series $2.00 convertible preferred authorized and issued, 540,000 shares in 1978 and 570,000 shares in 1977, stated at mandatory redemption value of $50.00 per share)	$ 27.0	$ 28.5	$ 30.0
Common stock—authorized 100,000,000 shares of $0.60 par value (issued and outstanding, 71,283,613 shares in 1978 and 71,214,012 shares in 1977)	42.8	42.8	42.9
Capital surplus	202.3	199.9	200.8
Net unrealized gains on equity securities carried at market	87.0	77.9	115.5
Retained earnings	1,215.5	1,019.1	864.5
Total shareholders' equity	**$ 1,574.6**	**$ 1,368.2**	**$ 1,253.8**
Total Liabilities and Shareholders' Equity	**$ 14,669.8**	**$ 12,290.8**	**$ 10,368.1**

(Appendix II continued on next page.)

American Express Company
Consolidated Statements of Income
December 31, 1978, 1977, and 1976 (in millions of dollars)

	1978	1977	1976
Revenues:			
Commissions and fees	$ 911.9	$ 738.3	$ 642.9
Interest and dividends	758.6	579.4	496.2
Property-liability and life insurance premiums	2,342.2	2,080.3	1,771.4
Other	71.8	48.2	38.4
Total revenues	$4,084.5	$3,446.2	$2,948.9
Expenses:			
Provisions for losses:			
Insurance....................................	$1,397.4	$1,254.6	$1,141.9
Banking, credit, financial paper and other	126.9	108.0	100.0
Salaries and employee benefits...................	583.6	471.9	420.6
Interest..	367.9	248.9	274.7
Commissions and brokerage	355.2	311.0	208.0
Occupancy and equipment	145.3	125.1	104.7
Advertising and promotion	126.9	83.8	65.7
Taxes other than income taxes	120.0	100.6	85.8
Claims adjustment services	115.7	130.1	89.7
Telephone, telegraph and postage	83.3	74.4	63.2
Cost of financial paper, forms and other printed matter..	51.2	45.3	35.5
Other	240.1	188.0	162.5
Total expenses	$3,713.5	$3,141.7	$2,752.3
Pretax operating income........................	$ 371.0	$ 304.5	196.5
Less income tax provision	63.0	52.1	16.9
Net operating income...........................	$ 308.0	$ 252.4	$ 179.6
Gains on sales of investment securities after income tax provision of $4.0	———	9.7	14.9
Net income	$ 308.0..	$ 262.1	$ 194.5
Net income per share	$ 4.31	$ 3.65	$ 2.70

Harold McGraw's Letter to Amex
Wall Street Journal, **January 18, 1979, p. 29**
A REPLY TO AN "UNCONSCIONABLE" ACTION

To the Board of Directors
American Express Company:

The McGraw-Hill Board of Directors has unanimously instructed me to categorically reject your request to discuss the illegal, improper, unsolicited, and surprising American Express proposal to take over McGraw-Hill.

Further, the McGraw-Hill Board upon the advice of independent legal counsel has directed management to vigorously protect the integrity and vital interests of this company against any takeover attempt you may launch.

You should understand that there are several significant and fundamental reasons that dictate this determination.

1. The independence and credibility of McGraw-Hill is vital to fulfilling its responsibilities to investors, the academic, educational, and scientific communities, as well as those who rely on the information and advisory services we offer.

It would be improper, inappropriate, and in direct violation of this responsibility to entrust McGraw-Hill's sensitive public interest activities (including Business Week and the Standard & Poor's credit rating services) to a company that pays virtually no federal income taxes on its hundreds of millions of dollars of annual income, operates in a manner that raises serious questions under the banking and securities laws, and pays no interest on the billions of dollars it derives from the issuance of traveler's checks to the public.

One dramatic illustration of the potential for serious conflict of interest is the fact that, as a major investor in securities, American Express holds more than $3 billion in state and municipal securities and underwrites and insures additional state and municipal securities—securities that must be independently rated by McGraw-Hill's Standard & Poor's division!

The background and manner of your proposal demonstrates that American Express lacks the integrity, corporate morality, and sensitivity to professional responsibility essential to the McGraw-Hill publishing, broadcasting, and credit rating services relied upon by many people.

Frankly, this surprises us. Such insensitivity and lack of integrity and corporate morality is inconsistent with the reputation many American Express directors have enjoyed over the years. Perhaps it can be explained as impulsive, precipitous, and immature actions taken by younger members of management before the more experienced members of your board had ample opportunity to fully consider this reckless proposal and all of its implications to each company.

Mr. Roger H. Morley, President of American Express, was a director of McGraw-Hill when you formulated and made your proposal. He clearly violated his fiduciary duties to McGraw-Hill and the stockholders of McGraw-Hill by misappropriating confidential information and conspiring with American Express, the members of the Board of Directors of American Express, and others to acquire McGraw-Hill at a price in a manner and at a time that would be most beneficial to American Express, but to the detriment of McGraw-Hill's stockholders.

This breach of trust and conspiracy to subvert the interests of McGraw-Hill and its stockholders was initiated in the spring of 1978 by your Chairman, Mr. James D. Robinson, III. In seeking to solicit our interest in a merger with American Express, Mr. Robinson gave me his absolute word and assurance that if we were not interested in pursuing the matter, nothing further would be done. It was not in McGraw-Hill's best interest and so I made it clear that we were not interested in pursuing it. Yet, as recent events have shown, American Express continued in its plan and preparation. In light of this, Mr. Morley's remaining on the McGraw-Hill Board of Directors for several months following the rejection of Mr. Robinson's approach and our being assured that it would be dropped was insidious. The obvious conflict of interest created by your secret plan to pursue an acquisition of McGraw-Hill while Mr. Morley remained a director is an unprecedented breach of trust.

American Express' conspiratorial approach and lack of integrity is further emphasized by your obtaining the financing for acquisition of McGraw-Hill from Morgan Guaranty Trust Company which, for more than 50 years, has been McGraw-Hill's principal bank—a fact well known to your Mr. Morley. Any company that would use its financial power to cause a bank to violate its relationship with a client lacks the integrity and morality essential to the business of McGraw-Hill.

2. Any combination of American Express and McGraw-Hill would be illegal.

The McGraw-Hill Board of Directors was advised by two independent law firms, White & Case and Wachtell, Lipton, Rosen & Katz, that, in their opinion, your acquisition of McGraw-Hill would raise serious issues under the antitrust laws and can be expected to result in litigation by the government to the detriment of both companies and their stockholders.

In addition, counsel has advised that the prior approval of the Federal Communications Commission and other regulatory agencies is required before American Express could acquire McGraw-Hill, and that any attempt by American Express to do so without such approval would be illegal.

Counsel also has advised that because many of American Express' directors are apparently directors of corporations which are competitors of McGraw-Hill, should American Express acquire McGraw-Hill, there could be multiple violations of United States Anti-Trust Laws and the Federal Communications Act (1934). For example,

- Howard L. Clark is a director of Xerox Corp., which is an educational publisher and also provides information systems.

- Henry H. Henley, Jr. is a director of General Electric Co., which owns and operates radio and TV stations.

- Vernon E. Jordan, Jr. is also a director of Xerox.

- William McChesney Martin, Jr. is a director of Dow Jones & Co., which is publisher of The Wall Street Journal and Barron's and which also owns Richard D. Irwin, publisher of college textbooks.

- William W. Scranton is a director of The New York Times Company which in addition to newspapers, operates radio and TV stations and publishes consumer magazines and books.

The McGraw-Hill Board of Directors believes that the long-run interests of the stockholders of McGraw-Hill would best be served by McGraw-Hill remaining an independent company, and that a takeover of McGraw-Hill would have major adverse impact on the businesses and future profitability of McGraw-Hill.

Accordingly, the McGraw-Hill Board of Directors has instructed and authorized management and legal counsel to prepare and undertake all appropriate actions, including litigation, to protect McGraw-Hill against any improper attempts to take over McGraw-Hill or interfere with its normal business operations.

The McGraw-Hill Board of Directors also has authorized a lawsuit against American Express, Mr. Morley, each other director of American Express, and every other person or entity participating with American Express and Mr. Morley in this conspiratorial breach of his fiduciary duty to McGraw-Hill's stockholders to recover the hundreds of millions of dollars of damages resulting from this wrongful conduct.

To permit American Express' unconscionable actions to succeed would jeopardize the underlying basis for public confidence in American Express as well as McGraw-Hill. For our part, we intend to spare absolutely no effort in protecting McGraw-Hill.

Very truly yours,

Harold W. McGraw, Jr.
Chairman and President
McGraw-Hill, Inc.

January 24, 1979

The Honorable Michael Pertschuk, Chairman
Federal Trade Commission
Pennsylvania Avenue at 6th Street
Washington, D.C. 20530

The Honorable John Shenefield
Assistant Attorney General
Antitrust Division
Department of Justice
Washington, D.C. 20530

Re: American Express Company—McGraw-Hill, Inc.

Dear Chairman Pertschuk and
  Assistant Attorney General Shenefield:

The Authors Guild urges that the Antitrust Division or
Federal Trade Commission take immediate action to prevent the
American Express Company from acquiring McGraw-Hill, Inc.
This takeover, we believe, would violate Section 7 of the Clayton
Act and further weaken the First Amendment marketplace of
ideas, which is entitled to the fullest protection of the antitrust
laws.

With serious antitrust and First Amendment issues at stake,
the Commission or Antitrust Division should test the
application of Section 7 to this acquisition, the latest and
largest in a continuing trend to book-publishing concentration
and conglomeration that has swallowed up many formerly
independent major companies. Section 7 was intended to protect
the First Amendment-based, social and cultural, as well as the
economic, interests threatened by this acquisition, and was not
merely intended to regulate the market shares of merging
corporations.

If inaction by the Commission and Antitrust Division
permits American Express to seize McGraw-Hill, then other
large independent publicly-owned publishing companies are
equally vulnerable to conglomerate takeovers. Since most of
these surviving independent firms, like McGraw-Hill, are major
textbook publishers, and since many formerly-independent
textbook firms are now owned by conglomerates, we face the
dangerous prospect that textbook publishing in this country
could be controlled largely by huge multi-business
conglomerates.

Section 7 Consequences of
the Threatened Acquisition

Since the antitrust consequences of the threatened McGraw-
Hill takeover are apparent to the Commission and Antitrust

Division, we make only brief comment on those involving book publishing:

1. A primary purpose of Section 7 is to preserve independent companies. The takeover would destroy the independence of McGraw-Hill, one of the few major competitors in college textbook publishing and financial publishing.

2. The takeover would continue and stimulate the trend to concentration and conglomeration in every relevant line of book publishing commerce. In textbook publishing, for example, the threat is grave. Independent publishers exposed to conglomerate takeovers include such major publicly-owned firms as Prentice-Hill; John Wiley & Sons; Houghton Mifflin; Macmillan; Scott, Foresman; and Harcourt Brace Jovanovich. Houghton Mifflin recently beat off one such effort at great expense. Harcourt Brace Jovanovich is now struggling to prevent a takeover. Already, many formerly-independent textbook publishers have been acquired by conglomerates such as Litton Industries, Raytheon, Xerox, ITT and Time, Inc.

3. American Express has huge cash resources, derived from its insurance, banking and credit card operations, and the interest-free "float" from traveler's checks. This "deep pocket" would give American Express a great advantage over McGraw-Hill's competitors and also could deter other companies from entering its markets.

4. American Express' enormous direct-mail sales operation, including books, would give it a substantial competitive advantage over other publishers who sell in the mail order market. "Of course, we (American Express) would hope to use our card list of 8.6 million subscribers around the globe who would want to buy McGraw-Hill books through our marketing setup." (N.Y. Times, January 14, 1979; p. 51) Whatever Section 7 label (product extension, vertical integration, etc.) is applied, the teaching of several Supreme Court opinions is that this aspect of the American Express takeover would violate the Section.

5. The McGraw-Hill trade book (i.e., general interest book) division is one of the few independent publishing operations capable of offering some competition to the ten major publishers (seven conglomerate-owned) who dominate the trade book market through their superior promotion, sales and distribution facilities. As you are aware: innumerable small publishers do not even distribute in the national trade book market; so-called imprint publishers are prominent editors who are financed and controlled by major publishing firms; and several modest-sized publishers can distribute their books in the national market only through the few major firms that dominate the distribution process. If McGraw-Hill is acquired by a huge financial conglomerate, whose predominant interest is the "bottom line," there is a substantial threat that its trade book division, which is not as profitable as textbook or financial publishing, would be eliminated. This further would restrict competition in the

trade book market. Thus Bobbs-Merrill, a 150 year old formerly-independent firm now owned by ITT, announced last August it was discontinuing the publication of fiction.

6. The interaction of McGraw-Hill's business periodicals and financial rating services and various American Express operations would raise other antitrust questions.

The Threat to Major Independent Publishers

1. As we have noted, if inaction by the Antitrust Division or Federal Trade Commission permits American Express to capture McGraw-Hill, several other publicly-held independent publishing companies face the increasing threat of involuntary takeover by conglomerates. That risk is magnified because conglomerates are aided in their campaigns to seize independent companies by loans from large commercial banks. Apparently such bank loans will help finance the American Express takeover of McGraw-Hill.* (N.Y. Times January 12, 1979; p. D-1)

2. Should American Express succeed, remaining privately-held independent publishers, and publicly-owned firms, will be deterred from securing needed financing through the public sale of securities—deterred by the threat of involuntary takeovers. Given the estate tax consequences that can cripple the operation of privately-held companies, lax enforcement of Section 7 inexorably drives these companies into "friendly" mergers with conglomerates or large publishing complexes. Indeed, more than one major independent publisher that could have "gone public" has been driven by this dilemma into a conglomerate merger.

The Threat to the First Amendment
Marketplace of Ideas

We believe that a principal reason action should be taken under Section 7 to block the acquisition of McGraw-Hill by American Express is that this takeover would further weaken the First Amendment marketplace of ideas. The Supreme Court has emphasized that the First Amendment "provides powerful reasons" for applying the antitrust laws to protect its "marketplace of ideas." That First Amendment marketplace, the Court has told us, requires "diverse," "antagonistic," and "uninhibited" sources of information and opinion. The essential foundation for these First Amendment qualities is independent ownership of publishing and other media enterprises. The surrender of a major publishing firm's independence to a conglomerate master creates a grave threat to these First Amendment qualities and the marketplace of ideas—whether

---

*We believe it is hardly in the public interest that huge commercial banks, using their depositors' money, should thus dictate who shall own publishing companies or other independent corporations. We believe that such concerted action by banks and acquisitor-corporations raise other legal issues which should be carefully scrutinized by the Federal Trade Commission and the Antitrust Division.

conglomerate control is exercised brazenly or subtly, directly or indirectly, now or in the future.

The First Amendment and Section 7 have a common purpose in preventing acquisitions that destroy the independence of significant publishing companies. Action under Section 7 is even more urgently needed when, as here, an acquisition constitutes an enormous advance in a well-established trend to conglomeration, and a potent stimulus to more conglomeration that will further jeopardize the marketplace of ideas. A U.S. textbook publishing market dominated by conglomerate-owned publishing firms is not the marketplace of ideas envisioned by the First Amendment or Section 7. But if the American Express takeover of McGraw-Hill is not blocked, textbook publishing will have taken a giant step in that direction.

Prior Authors Guild statements have discussed the threats that conglomeration and concentration pose to the First Amendment marketplace of ideas. The following considerations are of particular relevance to the threatened McGraw-Hill takeover:

1. "The press," said Justice Douglas, "has a preferred position in our constitutional scheme not to enable it to make money . . . but to bring fulfillment to the public's right to know." (Quoted by Daniel Schorr, N.Y. Times, January 16, 1979; p. A-15) In book publishing, editorial decisions that meet the company's First Amendment obligations are not always profitable decisions. For example: some sections of a textbook that are relevant and educationally sound may antagonize interest groups or public officials. Publishing these sections would reduce sales; deleting them would assuredly produce larger sales and greater profits. Similar dilemmas arise in deciding whether to publish, or continue printing, valuable textbooks that appeal to modest or limited audiences.

2. Independent publishing companies are not eleemosynary institutions, but their independence gives them greater strength to fulfill their First Amendment obligations in critical situations. Their managements are not answerable to the management of a conglomerate master. Conglomerate owners of publishing houses, as one prominent publishing official informs us, "are interested only in the bottom line"—i.e., "overall profit and loss figures." Conglomeration does not stimulate diversity and other First Amendment qualities.

3. Conglomerate ownership of a book publisher also exposes its editorial decisions to outside pressures. Not only may opponents of a textbook refuse to buy it, they may also boycott other goods or services sold by the conglomerate. And opponents of the conglomerate's policies in other areas may boycott its subsidiary's books. These pressures might well produce censorship by the conglomerate owner or self-censorship by its subsidiary publisher.

4. It is more than conceivable that some prospective books may be rejected (or substantially revised) in light of their possible adverse impact on the conglomerate's other interests or on officials, customers, consumers or financial institutions involved in more important areas of its operations. (A memorandum from the Editor-in-Chief of McGraw-Hill's BUSINESS WEEK magazine effectively summarizes the possible threats to the editorial independence of that magazine, arising from other business operations and interests of American Express.)

5. Written assurances from a conglomerate of continued editorial independence can hardly protect against these grave threats to the First Amendment, which are inherent in the conglomerate acquisition of a strong independent publishing firm. We know from recent experience that conglomerates fire presidents of publishing companies as they do other officers and employees. Written assurances are subject to interpretation. They are not binding forever, if legally binding at all. And they cannot counteract the overwhelming impact of the conglomerate's "bottom line."

Authors exist in a symbiotic relationship with publishers. Neither individual authors nor the Authors Guild see eye to eye with McGraw-Hill or other major publishers on many issues. But the fate of McGraw-Hill, in its struggle to preserve its independence, affects all American authors and all major independent book publishing companies. The conglomeration of American book publishing obviously is harming individual authors: placing them in a weaker bargaining position vis-a-vis these giant corporations; reducing their opportunities to be published; and subjecting them to unfair contractual and business practices. But even more disturbing to authors is the danger to the "marketplace of ideas"—which is at once the indispensable instrument of the First Amendment and the commercial system which communicates their works to the reading public. The trend to conglomeration and concentration already has sorely weakened that marketplace of ideas. If American Express is permitted to capture control of McGraw-Hill, that indispensable structure will be further weakened. And inevitably, other major independent publishers will be absorbed by conglomerate takeovers.

Because of these grave dangers to the marketplace of ideas, and to the public it should serve, The Authors Guild believes that the Federal Trade Commission or Antitrust Division must act, under Section 7, to prevent American Express Company from seizing control of McGraw-Hill, Inc.

Sincerely,

The Authors Guild, Inc.

John Brooks, President   Roger Angell, Vice President

John Hersey, Chairman   Irwin Karp, Chairman
Contract Committee

cc: Hon. David A. Clanton   The Members of the
    Hon. Paul Rand Dixon   Committee on The
    Hon. Elizabeth Hanford Dole   Judiciary, U.S. Senate
    Hon. Robert Pitosky
      Federal Trade   The Members of the
      Commission   Committee on The
                                         Judiciary, U.S. House
    Hon. Griffin B. Bell   of Representatives
    Attorney General

APPENDIX V   **The FTC Writes to American Express**

February 12, 1979

David M. Herschberg, Esquire
General Counsel
American Express Company
American Express Plaza
New York, New York 10004

                    Re: <u>Proposed Acquisition by American Express
                         Company of McGraw-Hill, Inc.</u>

Dear Mr. Herschberg:

   This letter will confirm that American Express' filing under
the Hart-Scott-Rodino Act will remain in effect unless it is
withdrawn by American Express. This information was, as you
are probably already aware, communicated earlier to Mr. Sutton
Keany, Counsel for American Express, by Barry Reingold of the
Premerger Notification Office.

   At this time, it appears to us that the proposed acquisition of
McGraw-Hill by American Express raises serious concerns
under Section 7 of the Clayton Act and Section 5 of the Federal
Trade Commission Act. We have identified the most significant
issues which we now see regarding this proposed acquisition,
and we would like to invite you to provide written factual and
legal comments on them. It is our understanding that McGraw-
Hill does plan to submit such comments. The issues on which
we would like you to focus are:

1. The conflict of interest that may result from the control of a leading publisher of financial information and business news by a large and diversified financial corporation. For example, as a result of the acquisition of McGraw-Hill, American Express might gain an unfair advantage from advance notice of material to be published. In addition, selection of material for publication might be affected by American Express' interests. It is our feeling that such a conflict, if it exists, may be inherent in the merger, and that efforts to insulate the publishing operations may not be successful.

2. The potential for reciprocity that may result from the acquisition of a leading bond rating firm by a firm that is a leading underwriter and distributor of state and municipal bonds, a leading holder of such securities, and a leading provider of insurance services to the issuers of the bonds.

3. The possible lessening of competition between McGraw-Hill and American Express in the provision of bond rating, bond insurance and other services which improve the marketability of state and municipal bonds.

4. The possible entrenchment of American Express in various markets through access to substantially lower advertising rates in McGraw-Hill publications. A similar concern is that the acquisition may entrench McGraw-Hill in various markets through low cost access to American Express' membership lists.

Please feel free, in addition, to discuss any other matters which you feel are relevant.

Your comments, together with the information to be produced in response to our request for additional information under the Hart-Scott-Rodino Act, will be of considerable assistance in assessing the validity and significance of our concerns. We would therefore appreciate your advising us by February 19, 1979, of your proposed schedule both for responding to our second request for information, and for submitting written comments on our concerns.

Very truly yours,

Daniel C. Schwartz
Deputy Director
Bureau of Competition

NOTES

1. *Time,* January 22, 1979, p. 54.
2. *Business Week,* December 19, 1979, p. 58.
3. *Newsweek,* February 12, 1979, p. 67.
4. See n. 3 above.
5. *Time,* January 29, 1979, p. 44.
6. *Business Week,* January 22, 1979, p. 98.
7. *Time,* January 22, 1979, p. 54.
8. *Business Week,* January 22, 1979, p. 98.
9. *Time,* January 22, 1979, p. 54.
10. *Time,* January 29, 1979, p. 44.
11. *Fortune,* February 26, 1979, p. 15.
12. *Time,* January 22, 1979, p. 54.
13. *Newsweek,* February 12, 1979, p. 67.
14. *Wall Street Journal,* January 15, 1979, p. 2.
15. *Newsweek,* February 17, 1979, p. 67.
16. *Newsweek,* January 29, 1979, p. 63.
17. *Business Week,* January 22, 1979, p. 98.
18. *Newsweek,* January 29, 1979, p. 63.
19. *Publisher's Weekly,* January 22, 1979, p. 281.
20. *Newsweek,* January 29, 1979, p. 63.
21. *Newsweek,* February 12, 1979, p. 67.
22. *Publisher's Weekly,* January 22, 1979, p. 281.
23. See n. 22 above.
24. *Newsweek,* January 29, 1979, p. 63.
25. *Publisher's Weekly,* January 22, 1979, p. 281.
26. *Newsweek,* January 29, 1979, p. 63.
27. See n. 26 above.
28. *Fortune,* February 26, 1979, p. 15.
29. See n. 28 above.
30. *Fortune,* May 21, 1979, p. 97.
31. See n. 30 above.
32. *Newsweek,* February 12, 1976, p. 67.
33. *Fortune,* May 21, 1979, p. 97.
34. Letter from The Authors Guild to the Department of Justice and the Federal Trade Commission, January 24, 1979.
35. *Wall Street Journal,* January 15, 1979, p. 2.
36. *Publisher's Weekly,* February 5, 1979, p. 26.
37. Letter from The Authors Guild to the Department of Justice and the Federal Trade Commission, January 24, 1979.
38. *The Nation,* February 10, 1979, p. 133.
39. *Fortune,* February 26, 1979, p. 15.
40. A. F. Ehrbar, "Hazards Down the Track for American Express," *Fortune,* November 6, 1978, p. 95.
41. *Fortune,* November 6, 1978, p. 95.
42. See n. 41 above.
43. See n. 41 above.
44. *Wall Street Journal,* June 16, 1981, p. 12, reported that Amex was considering sale of AEIBC ($6.9 billion in assets on December 31, 1981). At the time, Amex was trying to acquire the large securities firm of Shearson Loeb Rhoades in a $915 million stock swap.
45. *Business Week,* January 22, 1979, p. 98.
46. See n. 45 above.
47. *Wall Street Journal,* January 15, 1979, p. 2.

48. *Time,* January 22, 1979, p. 54.
49. *Wall Street Journal,* January 15, 1979, p. 2.
50. *Newsweek,* February 12, 1979, p. 67.
51. *Newsweek,* January 29, 1979, p. 63.
52. *Time,* February 12, 1979, p. 88.
53. *Time,* January 29, 1979, p. 44.
54. *Wall Street Journal,* January 17, 1979, p. 8.
55. See n. 54 above.
56. *Publisher's Weekly,* February 5, 1979, p. 26.
57. *Time,* February 12, 1979, p. 88.
58. *Business Week,* February 12, 1979, p. 39.
59. *Fortune,* February 26, 1979, p. 15.
60. McGraw-Hill, *Report to Shareholders* (First Quarter, 1979).
61. McGraw-Hill, *Report to Shareholders* (First Quarter, 1979).
62. *Time,* February 12, 1979, p. 88.
63. *Publisher's Weekly,* January 22, 1979, p. 281.
64. *Business Week,* February 12, 1979, p. 39.
65. *Fortune,* May 21, 1979, p. 97.
66. *Newsweek,* February 12, 1979, p. 67.
67. *Newsweek,* February 12, 1979, p. 7.
68. *Wall Street Journal,* February 14, 1979, p. 7.
69. See n. 68 above.
70. *Wall Street Journal,* January 17, 1979, p. 8.
71. *Business Week,* January 22, 1979, p. 98.
72. See n. 71 above.
73. Letter from The Authors Guild to the Department of Justice and the Federal Trade Commission, January 24, 1979.
74. *Newsweek,* February 12, 1979, p. 67.
75. See n. 74 above.
76. A. F. Ehrbar, " 'Bigness' Becomes the Target of the Trustbusters," *Fortune,* March 26, 1979, pp. 34 ff.
77. *Business Week,* February 12, 1979, p. 39.
78. See n. 77 above.
79. McGraw-Hill, *Report to Shareholders* (First Quarter, 1979).
80. See n. 79 above.
81. *Newsweek,* January 29, 1979, p. 63.
82. *Fortune,* May 21, 1979, p. 97.
83. *Newsweek,* February 12, 1979, p. 67.
84. See n. 83 above.
85. *Fortune,* February 26, 1979, p. 15.
86. McGraw-Hill, *Report to Shareholders* (First Quarter, 1979).
87. *Publisher's Weekly,* March 12, 1979, p. 46.
88. *Corporations,* William L. Cary, January, 1976, p. 446.
89. *Time,* January 29, 1979, p. 44.
90. McGraw-Hill, *Report to Shareholders* (First Quarter, 1979).
91. *Newsweek,* February 12, 1979, p. 67.
92. See n. 91 above.
93. McGraw-Hill, *Report to Shareholders* (First Quarter, 1979).
94. *Fortune,* May 21, 1979, p. 15.
95. *Business Week,* February 12, 1979, p. 39.
96. *Newsweek,* February 12, 1979, p. 67.
97. McGraw-Hill acquired Wood & Tower, Inc. (Princeton, N.J.), which provided computer-based cost estimates for new construction and appraisals for existing construction (for the McGraw-Hill Information Systems Company); Pre Test Service, Inc.

(Wallingford, Conn.), which publishes practice examinations for physicians and nurses preparing for qualifying or certifying examinations, together with self-assessment and review books (for the Health Professions Division of the McGraw-Hill Book Company); and BTYE (New Hampshire), the leading magazine in the home computer field (for the McGraw-Hill Publications Company). The firm had also signed a contract to acquire (expected to close in summer 1979) Tratec, Inc. (Los Angeles), which produced and sold audio-visual training programs in marketing management.

98. See Frank H. Easterbrook and Daniel R. Fischel, "The Proper Role of a Target's Management in Responding to a Tender Offer," *Harvard Law Review,* vol. 94 (April 1981), pp. 1161-1204. "Under existing federal and state law, a corporation's managers can resist and often defeat a premium tender offer without liability to either the corporation's shareholders or the unsuccessful tender offeror. Professor Easterbrook and Fischel argue that resistance by a Corporation's managers to premium tender offers, even if it triggers a bidding contract, ultimately decreases shareholder welfare. Shareholders would be better off, the authors claim, were such resistance all but proscribed. ... They conclude by proposing a rule of managerial passivity capable of controlling resistance in actual cases." For a contrary view, see, "The (Happily) Reluctant Brides," *Forbes,* March 17, 1980, p. 126.

Case 1-3

Chrysler Corporation*

On September 20, 1979, an era ended for the Chrysler Corporation. Chrysler's chairman, John J. Ricardo, took an early retirement and turned the reins of power to President Lee A. Iacocca. Lee Iacocca had been hired to fill the vacancy created when Eugene Cafiero was given the post of executive vice chairman. Lee had become available after his brilliant career at Ford had been ended by a dispute with Henry Ford, then the chairman. Ricardo retired not only for health reasons, but also to clear the company of the last ties with a management team that is often blamed for many of the problems with Chrysler.[1]

Chrysler's position was not one which would evoke feelings of envy for Lee Iacocca's task. The company was cash poor, suffering huge operating losses, and facing the prospect of rebuilding its product line in the face of both governmental and market pressures. To understand how Chrysler arrived at the survival condition of 1979, a review of its history, product, and market development is necessary. Walter Chrysler, the founder, was a strong, tough-minded individual. He believed that competitive engineering was the most important aspect of the company. Although his innovations were not always

---

*This case was prepared by Laurence Ondovic, Digital Equipment Corporation, under the supervision of William Naumes, Clark University, with the intention of providing a basis for class discussion rather than illustrating either effective or ineffective management of a business situation. This case was prepared entirely from published sources of information.

successful, as can be illustrated by the famous air-flow design of the late 1930s, he felt that the technological sophistication was necessary, and as such, his product could command a premium price.

The first manager to run the company was L. L. "Tex" Colbert.

L. L. COLBERT 1950-1961

L. L. "Tex" Colbert was involved in the automobile industry since the early 1930s. A lawyer by training, he was on a committee that wrote the automobile industry's code under the National Recovery Administration. At the age of 30 he was a vice president of Dodge. He was a man who, when judged by the executives of the other car companies, had no special talents. His image in Detroit was that of "a man who at times conducts himself with the backslapping joviality of a small-town politician, who occasionally enjoys himself too well at a party. . ."[2] His approach to management can be summarized by the following:

> Management is a business of men and of giving the men the job. You have to analyze the job to be done, get the manpower, and follow-up to see that the job gets done. That's the most important—the follow-up.[3]

The performance of the company under his leadership was erratic. Chrysler's market share peaked in 1953 at about 20 percent of the domestic market. The rules of the game changed in the 1954 model year. While the public was being wooed by the longer, lower, wider cars of their competitors, Chrysler maintained its conservative designs. Ironically, its advertising slogan for 1954 was, "Bigger on the inside, smaller on the outside."[4]

In the midfifties Virgil Exner was given the task of redesigning Chrysler's products. His automobiles became the longest, the widest, the lowest, and had the highest fins of any car on the road. To accomplish this it was necessary to use a two-year model cycle, instead of the traditional three-year cycle. When the 1957 models were introduced, they were well received. The company earned a substantial profit. However, Chrysler's management expected the acceptance to continue for the next two years, so they amortized most of the tooling costs in 1957. They did not plan any major revisions for either 1958 or 1959. The lukewarm reception of the slightly changed 1958 models coupled with the recession of that year, put Chrysler in a precarious position. While Chrysler's balance sheet still looked respectable, it was weak relative to the other carmakers. Not only would the other carmakers be marketing restyled models in 1959, but strong rumors indicated that both General Motors Corporation (GM) and Ford Motor Corporation would be introducing new compact models in 1960.

In 1960 Chrysler introduced the Dodge Dart and the Plymouth Valiant and led the industry in converting to the unitized body construction. This move cost the company approximately $350 million. The Dart was very successful for Chrysler that year. Chrysler sales ran 80 percent ahead of 1959. Strikes, however, by a glass supplier and the steel industry severally depressed

Chrysler's overall performance. This was combined with the heavy write-off on tooling for the new models which kept its earnings to around $1 per share.[5]

Colbert had another problem in the summer of 1960. He had carefully built his management team only to have it ripped apart by a conflict of interest scandal. William Newberg was forced to resign as president after only nine weeks on the job. Another vice president was also directly implicated. Because of subsequent investigations, morale in the company dropped. Others on the team either resigned or were fired.

In 1961 George Love took over as chairman of the board. He selected Lynn Townsend, who had been vice president in charge of operations, to be the president.

GEORGE LOVE/LYNN TOWNSEND 1961-1966

George Love, who was also chairman of Consolidated Coal Co., was a businessman with a wide range of experience. He was responsible for corporate policy concerning strategic management and marketing. Lynn Townsend was given responsibility for the day-to-day operations.

Townsend had been with Chrysler for only four years. He had worked for ten years on the Chrysler account, where he was a full partner at Touche, Ross and Co. He was asked to join Chrysler to set up a profit control system so that the company could compete more effectively.[6]

The main points of his management philosophy were:

1. make a profit on auto sales being written now, not on those that might occur in the future;
2. institute tight cost control procedures, with no room given for sentiment or tradition if these mean lower earnings;
3. use scientific management methods, not seat of the pants intuition;
4. executives either perform or they are gone.

The situation that he inherited in 1961 could at the same time be construed as a disaster and an opportunity. With morale in the company hitting rock bottom, he met little resistance with his reorganization efforts. He began building his team of modern managers. He was a firm believer in having the right man do a job. He was able to select a team in 1961 and keep it in place into 1963. He then instituted another reorganization where he changed his span of control from 14 to 6 staff vice presidents and organized the group vice presidents in line positions.[7]

His primary objective in 1961 was to fit all the pieces together so that they would mesh into a consistently profitable whole. He wanted to create a balanced, flexible system that could expand or contract according to the market pressure. But his bottom-line concern was to sell more cars and make a larger profit from each one.

In order to revitalize the company, Townsend instituted three different operations. First, the dealer force was expanded and strengthened. This included the infusion of nearly $100 million. Second, the entire line of car models was restyled to appeal to the contemporary tastes. Also, the quality was improved to the point where Chrysler could offer the first extended warranty in the industry. Third, the number of models that were offered was expanded so that Chrysler could compete in every segment of the domestic market.

For at least two of these areas, outsiders were brought into the company to head up the tasks. Virgil Boyd was made the vice president and general sales manager. He had been with American Motors Corporation (AMC) before coming to Chrysler. He took the assignment of creating new dealerships and improving the existing ones. He began to monitor the dealers' performance more closely so that deviations from the plan could be quickly identified. By the middle of 1962 his efforts were beginning to pay off, which was evidenced by the higher sales in the 1963 model year.

The other key person that Townsend hired was Elwood Engel, who had been a stylist at Ford. The radical designs of Exner were dumped in favor of simpler and smoother lines similar to those of GM and Ford cars. Engel attempted to build an evolutionary concept so that each year's models were natural extensions of the previous year.

Townsend centralized many functions. The line operations were weakened so that he could maintain tighter control. One area, in particular, that was centralized was production scheduling. The product planning staff analyzed what styles, colors, and models were selling by region. They also used computers to create the production schedules for each variety for each plant. Unlike GM or Ford, who built in response to orders from their dealers, Chrysler scheduled its production based on the results of its computer modeling. This practice was later to be named the "sales bank." This method allowed for an even schedule for production, but at times, especially when the mix was wrong or sales dropped, the company would be burdened with large inventories of finished automobiles. During the period of booming sales, Chrysler was able to maximize the use of its production capacity.

Townsend was a great believer not only in scientific management, but also in computer usage. In the middle 1960s he had the largest computer operation in Detroit. He used his computers to simulate future demand based on historical data, schedule production, and provide huge volumes of reports on daily operations. In at least one instance, he used the simulations to enhance his reputation with the board of directors. They were contemplating a more aggressive expansion policy. However, one of Townsend's computer models indicated a slight downturn in business. On his recommendation the expansion was curtailed. As it turned out, he called the turn perfectly.

In 1962 Townsend instituted the Pentastar which became the corporate logo. Every facet of the company's operations were emblazoned with the design. It was a small tactic that enabled the corporation to project a better picture of the scope of its operations.

From 1964 to 1967 Chrysler allocated $1.7 billion to capital expenditures. Chrysler increased its share of Simca and it bought Rootes of Great Britain. Townsend wanted to compete with GM and Ford on an equal basis. In order to capitalize on the expanding world market, he was forced to buy into operations which often had serious problems. Approximately $500 million of the $1.7 billion was spent on these overseas operations.

Chrysler's performance, despite all of the reorganizations and other turmoil, was good. In fact, many of Townsend's programs were effective cost-cutting mechanisms. In addition to firing employees, which quickly reduced costs, he used computer systems to cut $60 million from Chrysler's average inventory. Another system reduced obsolete material from the end of model runs by 70 percent.

In 1964 Chrysler's sales and its market share were up. But its profits, as a percentage of sales, remained low. The tooling of new models was expensive, in the neighborhood of $300 million per year. Chrysler was in the habit of writing off these expenditures rapidly, which burdened the current year's profits.

With the 1965 model year, Chrysler entered Phase II of its recovery. It now covered 90 percent of the domestic market segments. A young energetic management team was in place. However, it was looking at a marketplace where the traditional segments were beginning to blur. There was a proliferation of models with a corresponding increase in segments. Ford had introduced the Mustang. At that point in time, Townsend was not overly concerned. His goal was to have a balanced product line rather than one hot car.[8] He had every intention of continuing the expansion of both the domestic and foreign operations. Chrysler's diversification programs included recreational vehicles, air conditioning, real estate, and consumer finance.

In 1966 George Love resigned as chairman. Lynn Townsend was elected chief executive officer and chairman of the board. Virgil Boyd was elected to the office of president.

TOWNSEND/BOYD 1966-1970

Boyd was able to continue the momentum that had been generated by the excellent sales year in 1965. Chrysler's sales and market share increased through the 1968 model year. However, a few disappointments clouded the otherwise rosy picture. The European operations continued to be a drag on profits. In 1968 operations abroad yielded less than one-eighth of Chrysler's pretax profits, although they accounted for one-quarter of all Chrysler cars built and one-fifth of its sales.[9] A second soft spot was the lack of any serious challenge to Ford's Mustang. The Plymouth Baracuda was only a reworked Valiant and was never a serious challenge.

Chrysler's management was now a unified team that had been together for over five years. Many of them had occupied various positions during that time to broaden their experience. In addition, Chrysler's compacts had been selling well. All of the key barometers of the company had improved from the rock-bottom days of 1961. Chrysler was planning to increase its production capacity in 1968, which would be used to further its market penetration in the 1970s.

Chrysler had moved aggressivley in the leasing and fleet sales areas by offering discounts and cash rebates. Its price cutting reached the break-even point in many cases. Its market share in these areas had increased almost totally at GM's expense.

Chrysler had not achieved parity with Ford or GM, but it had narrowed the gap significantly. The Chrysler Imperial was the only product which did not make any serious gains in its market segment. In 1968 Chrysler entered the "sporty" or "muscle" car segment. The public acceptance of the Charger far exceeded anyone's expectations.

In 1968 Chrysler's market share climbed to 16.6 percent. Boyd hinted that the corporation was aiming at 20 percent by 1970. This had been and would continue to be one of the company's goals, because 20 percent was the highest that its domestic market share had been since 1953. But even with its expanding share of the domestic market, its earnings hovered between three and four percent of sales.

The 1969 model year exposed some of the increasing vulnerability of the company. Chrysler had become a "me-too" company which followed the market. It anticipated that GM would continue with the rounded look. So for 1969 Chrysler styled its cars accordingly. However, GM's 1969 models were considerably different. Unfortunately for Chrysler, the new GM look was very popular. As a result of this, Chrysler's full-sized cars were out of vogue again. Earnings and earnings per share fell almost 70 percent—to their lowest levels since 1962. Chrysler was forced to restyle for the 1970 model year, an expense which had not been anticipated. Chrysler entered the 1970 model year with a huge backlog of 1969 automobiles.

Another problem that continued to plague Chrysler was the lack of a subcompact car. There had been rumors of a prototype named "25," but it never materialized. Ford introduced the Maverick and continued development on the "Phoenix." GM had the Chevy II and the XP887. But Townsend continued to reject the idea. He had said that "The American automobile industry will never take most of the mini-car import market. A foreign car sells because it is foreign."[10] He was not convinced that there was as much of a market for the under $2000 car as GM and Ford thought.

Chrysler did enter an agreement with Mitsubishi of Japan in which it would get to assemble Valiants in Japan while Chrysler would start importing the Colt. Chrysler also had Simca's models which it could import. But neither of these cars was very well received by the buying public.

The lack of a small car was only the tip of the iceberg which was threatening Chrysler. The conditions of the early 1960s, when Chrysler staged its current recovery, had changed dramatically. At that time, competition consisted of giving longer warranty terms; aggressive selling to taxi, leasing, and car-hire fleets; price competition; choosing better dealers; and a vast upgrading of quality after the shoddiness of the late 1950s. Townsend excelled at all of these. The hard sell of a few models in a fast growing market suited a tight-knit company like Chrysler. But the traditional market segmentation was developing a very large middle price range, which accounted for 69 percent of all domestic automobile sales. It had become a battleground of options and multiple models. While the base price of a new car had dropped by 2 percent over the decade, the average price of a new car was up by 34 percent in the same time period.

Once again, Townsend began cutting costs. In October 1969 he laid off 12,000 of the 140,000 U.S. employees, both white and blue-collar workers. Chrysler delayed its expansion plans at New Stanton, Pennsylvania. All general and administration budgets were cut back to their 1968 levels. As the 1970 model year developed, the automakers saw their sales drop. This fact, following the poor 1969 year, spelled big trouble for Chrysler. They had spent around $450 million on the 1970 models—only to see them sit in the showrooms.

It was with this set of conditions that John J. Ricardo was named as president. Virgil Boyd was appointed to the nominal post of vice chairman of the board of directors.

TOWNSEND/RICARDO 1970-1975

John J. Ricardo has been described as a brusque but articulate, hard-nosed, demanding manager. A minority of the board felt that he was good at executing plans, but his interpersonal skills were weak. They felt that he might alienate the dealers who had become accustomed to Boyd's style.[11]

At the same time, Eugene Cafiero was promoted to fill Ricardo's position as group vice president for U.S. and Canadian operations.

The new management team was looking at a company facing many of the same problems that Townsend faced in 1961. Sales had declined for the last three quarters. Chrysler's products had become too conservative and its range of products too limited. The demand for full-sized cars, which had been Chrysler's bread and butter, had declined 8 percent in two years to about 17 percent of the domestic market. Its aging compacts were selling well, but it had nothing to offer the subcompact buyer except the captive imports.

There were also differences in the current situation, not all of which were positive. Chrysler's cash reserve position was stronger. It also had substantial lines of open credit. However, its foreign operations, which had been acquired during the 1960s, continued to be a financial burden. The total investment was in the neighborhood of $5.8 billion. The long boom in auto sales was over. The market was volatile and complicated by the increased penetration by the imports. The buying public was more finicky. The range of models now included minicars, sporty cars, and specialty cars. The days of the simple low-, medium-, and high-priced cars were over.

Ricardo moved quickly in 1970 to cut costs. By September 1970 he had lopped off $150 million from Chrysler's operation's costs. This included layoffs, terminations, and reorganized functions. He was looking at providing greater economies by switching to common parts and common subassemblies.

Throughout the 1970 model year, the fiasco of the previous year continued to haunt Chrysler. The high inventory levels of the 1969 models at the beginning of the 1970 model year severely dampened the year's sales performance. The situation was further aggravated by a general slump in the automobile industry in 1970.

Chrysler invested $350 million in its 1970 models. It offered the Satellite and two low-priced compacts. But it still did not offer a subcompact model. While this did not affect their current profitability, the delay was definitely risky. If the subcompact market really materialized, Chrysler would be left far behind. Townsend still contended that the buying public was not ready to give up their comfortable large cars for small ones.

Chrysler did expand their imported offerings. It negotiated an agreement with Mitsubishi of Japan which essentially traded the Valiant for the Colt. Chrysler also imported the Cricket from England. But the reception was lukewarm. In addition, the volume of the imports was limited. While Chrysler imported 54,000 Crickets per year, Ford was building 47,000 Pintos per month.

In 1971 the company returned to profitability. This was due in large part to the upswing in the market. These swings in volume graphically pointed out Chrysler's condition. Since the company was highly leveraged, small fluctuations in its sales translated into large losses on the profit and loss statement. Conversely, increases in sales generated very little additional profit. Chrysler netted around 2 cents on every sales dollar. GM was netting 7 cents, while Ford averaged 5 cents. Chrysler was a scaled down imitation of the operations at Ford or GM. It did not have the sales volume to take full advantage of its production capacity.

There were many concerns expressed about the company in the early 1970s. Chrysler's reluctance to lead into new markets was highlighted. It was clearly a "me-too" company which was forced to react to the pressures of the marketplace. Many observers felt that the cost reductions in 1971 may have cut too deeply into the company. Resources in the engineering and product planning departments would be absolutely necessary, if Chrysler was to adequately restructure its product line. By 1973 the sentiment was expressed that Chrysler had lost its identity. It was no longer a full-line producer. Its biggest strength was its compacts, which accounted for 42 percent of its sales. Meanwhile, subcompact cars were accounting for 16 percent of all new cars sold in the domestic market.

Timing, bad luck, and other factors were all working against Chrysler in the early 1970s. It invested $350 million to restyle the 1974 full-sized cars. The project had begun in 1971. Shortly after the 1974 models were introduced, the Arabs began the oil embargo. Late in the 1974 model year, Chrysler was forced to offer rebates to move its huge inventory.

Chrysler's position in the 1975 model year continued to erode. Its market share dropped to 13.5 percent. Its sales were down by 41.7 percent as compared to declines of 34.3 percent at GM and 31.3 at Ford. Chrysler's plans for a subcompact were delayed again. It had $171 million in long-term debt coming due, which would have to be rolled over at a much higher rate of interest. Capital expenditures were trimmed by $75 million.[12] The compact cars, which had long been the stalwarts of the company, were facing stiff competition from the Ford Granada.

In the summer of 1975 Lynn Townsend resigned effective as of October 1, 1975. He had been with the company both in the good and bad times. Now he said it was time to turn the company over to younger men. John Ricardo was promoted to chairman of the board. Eugene Cafiero was elected as president.

JOHN RICARDO/EUGENE CAFIERO 1975-1978

Ricardo and Cafiero were dubbed the "crisis team." The round of congratulatory cocktail parties was bypassed. Chrysler was expected to lose $100 million or more in 1975, which would make its second year of losses. It faced the same set of problems which had plagued it for the last 15 years. Chrysler's basic problem seemed to be that it did not have the products that the buying public wanted when they wanted them. Chrysler made a crucial decision to spend over $700 million to revamp its full-size and intermediate-size cars in 1974 and 1975. But the oil crisis sent whatever buyers there were to smaller cars. The implication of the investment decision was that it did not have the resources to build a subcompact car. Now it had nothing with which to compete with the Vegas, Pintos, and Gremlins.[13]

The Dart and Valiant had gone several years without any major changes. In 1976 Chrysler introduced two luxury compacts, the Aspen and Volare, to help broaden the small car line.

Chrysler was suffering from its rebate program. While it helped to sell cars, it often reduced the profit margins to almost nothing.

In 1976 business improved again. Chrysler's earnings were around $390 million and short-term borrowing had been eliminated—at least for the time being. Ironically, the huge losses of the past two years helped to increase the profits further.

But Chrysler had become a $12 billion marginal producer. Because of its high leverage and low-profit margins, due both to its dependence on compact cars and high unit productions costs, Chrysler fell fast and hard whenever the market fluctuated.

Ricardo's goal was to stop the roller coaster ride. He began by eliminating some of the losing operations that Chrysler was involved with around the world. Rootes lost $150 million between 1975 and 1976. While the British government helped in 1976 with financial aid, the operation still had many problems. Ricardo sold Chrysler Airtemp for $58 million, its empty plant in New Stanton, Pennsylvania to Volkswagen (VW), and liquidated the Big Sky resort in Montana. In a corporate-wide move, he also reinstituted the project to increase standardization of parts. His goal was to reduce Chrysler's parts list from 75,000 to 50,000.

The economic pickup of 1975–1976 definitely helped Chrysler. The Volare and Aspen models sold quite well in that year, as did the Cordoba. Typically, the major product revisions were aimed at the full-sized cars. The introduction of a subcompact model was now targeted to be introduced in the 1978 model year. However, the full impact of the extensive personnel cuts of 1971 and 1974 was now being felt. Having lost so many engineers and designers, it was becoming extremely difficult to make the necessary revisions to their products. Many products were being delivered late to the market. The first models to be built were plagued with problems, ranging from poor fitting parts to severe mechanical problems.

In some respects Chrysler was confronted by bonafide opportunities in late 1976. Cars, in general, were getting smaller. Chrysler led the compact car segment with over a 40 percent share. But to effectively compete, even in 1976, the price tag was $3 billion. If the economy and their sales held up, a good portion of the $3 billion could have been generated from internal cash flows.

Unfortunately Chrysler's sales stumbled again in 1977. Its market share fell to 12.1 percent. In the first quarter of 1978 the losses totaled over $120 million. This level of losses was eliminating any hope for internally financing the new models. Many other forms of credit were also closed to the company. It already had $1.3 billion in long-term debt. Its reputation was poor on Wall Street. Its bonds were dropped to BBB by Standard & Poor's Corp.[14]

While bright spots were few, the sales performance of the Omni/Horizon subcompacts, which were introduced in January 1978, was excellent. These cars quickly jumped to command 18 percent of the subcompact market. In a move to turn the company around in the long run, it was decided to rebuild each plant as the cars which it produced were restyled. The Omni/Horizon plant was running 55 percent ahead of its former capacity. Dealers had a two month backlog of orders for the new subcompacts.

In 1977 GM had changed the rules of the game with the "down-sizing" of its full-sized cars. This further burdened Chrysler, because the new GM products were selling very well and Chrysler did not have the capital to follow GM's lead. Chrysler's products were sliding farther from the kind that the public was buying.

The losses continued. Production and engineering problems only aggravated a bad situation. In the summer of 1978 Eugene Cafiero was given the nominal post of vice chairman of the board. Lee A. Iacocca was brought in to be the president.

RICARDO/IACOCCA 1978-1979

Lee Iacocca was regarded as the "savior" when he came to Chrysler. He had a solid reputation for performance while he was at Ford. Just his presence seemed to boost morale in the organization and bolster confidence in the financial community.

His short-term objective was to keep the company afloat until some changes could be made to the product lines. With the long lead time, from the time that a model is accepted until it is produced, Iacocca could not make any major changes until the 1982 model year.

For the 1979 model year, purely cosmetic changes were planned for most of the products. The full-sized cars were completely redesigned. It was hoped that the New Yorker and the St. Regis would begin to rebuild their market share back up to the 15 percent of the full-sized market segment which had been Chrysler's. But a series of foul-ups early in the model year, such as supply hang-ups and assembly line snags, shut off the supply of full-sized cars until November. Chrysler prepared for the introduction of the new cars with a full scale media blitz. But for the buyers who came to look at them, there was nothing to buy.[15]

As the year continued it was clear that, except for the Omni/Horizon, the rest of Chrysler's product line was in trouble. The compact Volare and Aspen models were down by more than 24 percent. Both GM and Ford were now offering either down-sized or newly designed fuel efficient compact cars. Chrysler's overall market share slipped to 12.4 percent.

In March of 1979, Harold K. Sperlich took over the manufacturing responsibilities from Richard K. Brown. When Brown announced his early retirement, he was promptly replaced by Gar Laux. Both Sperlich and Laux had worked with Iacocca at Ford.

Chrysler's inventory, or sales bank as it was called, was completely out of balance with demand. In the early spring of 1979, Chrysler had over a 100-day supply of unsold cars. They began offering free inventory financing and other incentives to the dealers, along with a cash rebate to the consumer. By June the supply was down to 79 days which, while not acceptable, was a definite improvement.

Another problem surfaced in the Spring of 1979 which was indicative of Chrysler's lack of vertical integration. They had only ordered 300,000 engines from VW for the Omni/Horizon subcompacts. As the model year progressed, it was clear that the demand would be higher, but VW needed its extra capacity for its own production.

Losses from operations continued to mount. Chrysler lost $204 million in the second quarter of 1979. It was obvious that the financing for the needed expansion could never be generated internally. So Chrysler turned to the federal government for assistance.

The initial petition to the government was for aid in the form of either tax refunds or immediate relief from having to meet the costly safety, environmental, and mileage standards on new cars. This proposal was rejected, but G. William Miller, the Secretary of the Treasury, indicated that the government might be willing to support loan guarantees. With these Chrysler could then borrow from private sources who would not consider loaning them money because of the high risk.

Early in September, Ricardo and Iacocca returned to Washington with their request for $1.2 billion in loan guarantees over the next five years. They were looking for $500 million immediately and $700 million in additional loans, if needed.[16] Miller rejected this plan also. He told them to revise the plan and to look for less than $1 billion. They were also required to satisfy the Treasury that they would transform the company into a profitable enterprise.

Chrysler's management had rejected several options which Treasury officials had urged them to consider instead of federal aid. One was to reduce the scope of their operations to become something less than a full-line company. A second was to merge with another firm. The third was to file for bankruptcy.[17] Chrysler's management rejected the proposals because they did not think that it would be profitable to reduce its current range of products of automobiles and trucks. Its current financial position made it an unlikely candidate for a merger. Finally, bankruptcy would have a wide spread effect on the economy and its 30,000 suppliers.

In its plan, Chrysler said that of the $2.1 billion that was needed, it could probably raise $900 million by selling assets and by getting unspecified assistance from the United Auto Workers (UAW) and from state and local governments where Chrysler's facilities are located. The plan projected that Chrysler would become profitable by 1981 and repay the loans by 1985. The plan assumed that the firm's suppliers would continue to accept payments the month after delivery. It also assumed that the various U.S. and foreign banks would continue their existing agreements.

Miller told them to rework the plan. He did not see enough sacrificing by those with the largest stake in the company: the employees, management, the shareholders, and the union.

Shortly after the meeting, John Ricardo announced his retirement, effective September 20, 1979. Lee A. Iacocca became the company's chief executive officer.

NOTES

1. *Business Week,* October 1, 1979, p. 45.
2. *Business Week,* April 30, 1960, p. 137.
3. See n. 2 above.
4. *Fortune,* June 1958, p. 130.
5. *Business Week,* April 30, 1960, p. 131.
6. *Business Week,* October 6, 1962, p. 46.
7. *Business Week,* January 19, 1963, p. 32.
8. *Forbes,* September 15, 1965, p. 19.
9. *Economist,* September 20, 1969, p. 69.
10. *Business Week,* July 5, 1969, p. 48.
11. *Fortune,* April 1970, p. 146.
12. *Financial World,* December 25, 1975, pp. 11–12.
13. *Business Week,* July 21, 1975, p. 16.
14. *Business Week,* May 15, 1978, p. 23.
15. *Business Week,* March 12, 1979, p. 18.
16. *The Boston Globe,* September 16, 1979, p. 67.
17. See n. 16 above.

Chrysler Corporation
Consolidated Profit and Loss Statements
for 1970 to 1978 (in millions)

Exhibit 1

	1978	1977	1976	1975	1974	1973	1972	1971	1970
Sales	$13,618	$13,059	$15,538	$11,598	$10,860	$11,667	$9,641	$7,893	$7,000
Cost of goods sold	$12,640	$11,726	$13,625	$10,618	$9,953	$10,314	$8,407	$6,971	$6,276
General selling and administrative expense	572	453	566	466	485	466	416	370	386
Net sundry expense	262	280	295	233	254	216	191	149	121
Depreciation/special amortization	352	320	402	294	321	371	366	174	177
Interest expense (net)	129	75	130	168	108	32	56	71	47
Taxes on income property	(81)	73	212	26	(78)	203	193	66	(22)
Net income	$ (256)	$ 132	$ 308	$ (207)	$ (183)	$ 65	$ 12	$ 92	$ 15
Dividends	$ 52	$ 54	$ 18	—	$ 79	$ 69	$ 47	$ 30	$ 29

Chrysler Corporation
Consolidated Profit and Loss Statements
for 1960 to 1968 (in millions)

Exhibit 2

	1969	1968	1967	1966	1965	1964	1963	1962	1961	1960
Sales	$7,052	$7,445	$6,213	$5,650	$5,300	$4,287	$3,505	$2,378	$2,127	$3,007
Cost of goods sold	$6,138	$6,122	$5,190	$4,621	$4,269	$3,404	$2,780	$1,927	$1,797	$2,598
General selling and administrative expense	449	429	384	422	372	337	291	229	203	229
Net sundry expense	114	144	121	116	106	72	51	39	33	35
Depreciation	170	162	153	30	102	74	60	56	67	73
Interest expense (net)	32	26	13	9	9	9	10	9	9	9
Taxes on income property	80	272	166	155	104	185	164	61	10	34
Net income	$ 69	$ 290	$ 186	$ 297	$ 338	$ 206	$ 149	$ 57	$ 8	$ 29
Dividends	$ 95	$ 93	$ 92	$ 91	$ 55	$ 28	$ 25	$ 9	$ 9	$ 13

Chrysler Corporation
Consolidated Profit and Loss Statements
for 1951 to 1959 (in millions)

Exhibit 3

	1959	1958	1957	1956	1955	1954	1953	1952	1951
Sales	$ 2,643	$ 2,165	$ 3,565	$ 2,676	$ 3,466	$ 2,072	$ 3,348	$ 2,601	$ 2,547
Cost of goods sold	$ 2,298	$ 1,857	$ 2,910	$ 2,318	$ 2,938	$ 1,826	$ 2,936	$ 2,195	$ 2,256
General selling and administrative expense	238	264	276	217	219	159	144	106	103
Net sundry expense	40	34	46	30	30	23	27	23	20
Depreciation	72	80	89	68	55	50	47	37	26
Interest expense (net)	9	9	8	6	4	1	-	-	-
Taxes on income property	(5)	(39)	132	23	126	3	125	169	79
Net income	$ (9)	$ (40)	$ 104	$ 14	$ 94	$ 10	$ 69	$ 71	$ 63
Dividends	$ 9	$ 13	$ 35	$ 26	$ 35	$ 39	$ 52	$ 52	$ 65

Chrysler Corporation
Consolidated Balance Sheets
for 1970 to 1978 (in millions)

Exhibit 4

	1978	1977	1976	1975	1974	1973	1972	1971	1970
Assets:									
Current assets	$ 3,561	$ 4,153	$ 3,878	$ 3,117	$ 3,697	$ 3,238	$ 2,896	$ 2,411	$ 2,167
Fixed assets	3,420	3,515	3,196	3,150	3,036	2,867	2,601	2,588	2,649
Total assets	$ 6,981	$ 7,668	$ 7,074	$ 6,267	$ 6,733	$ 6,105	$ 5,497	$ 4,999	$ 4,816
Liabilities:									
Current liabilities	$ 2,486	$ 3,090	$ 2,826	$ 2,462	$ 2,709	$ 2,094	$ 1,940	$ 1,648	$ 1,549
Long-term liabilities	1,083	1,120	928	947	875	836	670	698	791
Other	3,412	3,458	3,320	2,858	3,149	3,175	2,887	2,653	2,476
Total liabilities	$ 6,981	$ 7,668	$ 7,074	$ 6,267	$ 6,733	$ 6,105	$ 5,497	$ 4,999	$ 4,816

Chrysler Corporation
Consolidated Balance Sheets
for 1960 to 1969 (in millions)

Exhibit 5

	1969	1968	1967	1966	1965	1964	1963	1962	1961	1960
Assets:										
Current assets	$2,176	$2,210	$1,880	$1,467	$1,480	$1,286	$1,374	$1,007	$893	$802
Fixed assets	2,512	2,188	1,975	1,682	1,454	1,135	750	518	507	567
Total assets	$4,688	$4,398	$3,855	$3,149	$2,934	$2,421	$2,124	$1,525	$1,400	$1,369
Liabilities:										
Current liabilities	$1,644	$1,428	$1,340	$1,022	$961	$901	$818	$445	$386	$371
Long-term liabilities	587	535	360	216	224	242	256	238	250	250
Other	2,457	2,435	2,155	1,911	1,749	1,278	1,050	842	764	748
Total liabilities	$4,688	$4,398	$3,855	$3,149	$2,934	$2,421	$2,124	$1,525	$1,400	$1,369

Chrysler Corporation
Consolidated Balance Sheets
for 1951 to 1959 (in millions)

Exhibit 6

	1959	1958	1957	1956	1955	1954	1953	1952	1951
Assets:									
Current assets	$690	$756	$940	$669	$891	$592	$527	$590	$487
Fixed assets	685	582	557	626	472	443	371	324	271
Total assets	$1,375	$1,338	$1,497	$1,295	$1,363	$1,035	$898	$914	$758
Liabilities:									
Current liabilities	$415	$392	$514	$461	$586	$386	$328	$366	$237
Long-term liabilities	250	250	250	188	125	63	–	–	–
Other	710	696	733	646	652	586	570	548	521
Total liabilities	$1,375	$1,338	$1,497	$1,295	$1,363	$1,035	$898	$914	$758

Exhibit 7

**Chrysler Corporation
Domestic Market Share**

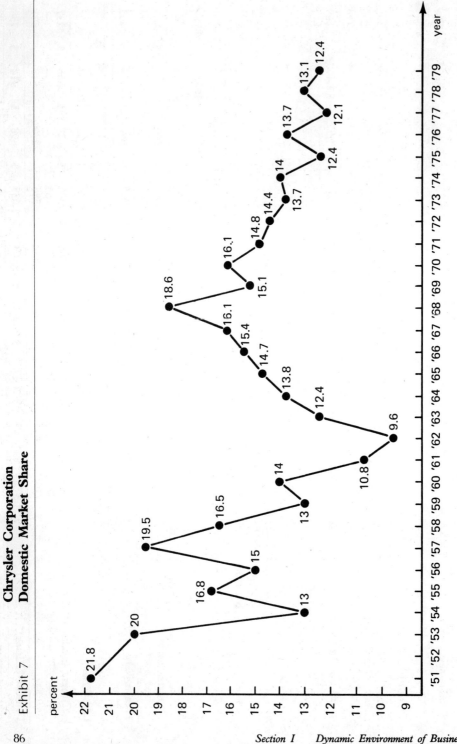

Oximeron Manufacturing Corporation*

The Oximeron Manufacturing Corporation, a large multiproduct machine tools company with annual sales in excess of two billion dollars, employed over 30,000 workers. As with many corporations of this size, pressures to assume socially responsible roles were increasing. Mr. Holcomb, division manager of public affairs, although currently proud of his company's recent involvement in community problems, admitted this was not always the case. He stated:

> Active involvement has not been a traditional characteristic of our firm. Fifteen years ago we felt that action was just money, such as what we gave to the United Fund and educational grants. As late as the late 1960s the firm did not have definite policies or programs to determine when the firm would take specific action in the social area.

Prompted by a community-based Public Affairs Council proposal, the firm developed a policy of community action which included:
1. Aim at causes of problems.
2. Act, not react.
3. Deal with fundamental issues.
4. Look at long-run implications.
5. Incorporate a systems approach.
6. Participate in comprehensive plans of action.
7. Focus on people.
8. Recognize no-policy is *a* policy.

According to Mr. Holcomb, "The company had begun to realize that whatever community problems existed, would eventually become company problems."

A formal process was developed to analyze community problems through a top management committee. Mr. Holcomb indicated the procedure which entailed the following steps in making decisions on specific program involvement.
1. Define the top ten priority community needs by the executive committee consisting of the president and vice presidents.
2. Evaluate corporate capabilities in these areas.
3. Survey community commitment to these areas.
4. Evaluate barriers to success.
5. Calculate probability of successful involvement.

---

*The case was prepared by K. Mark Weaver, University of Alabama, with the intention of providing a basis for class discussion rather than illustrating either effective or ineffective management of a business situation.

The approach was purposely kept low key and focused primarily on corporate/community involvement in solutions—not individual action on the part of the firm or its executives.

In the early 1970s a series of news articles about drug problems prompted Oximeron executives to question whether this condition existed in the community. Planning personnel and other executives addressed the issue and concluded that there were no drug problems at Oximeron. Therefore, drug abuse was not included as one of the "top ten" priority items.

In the late 1970s the community affairs director, Mr. P. James, received a call from the narcotics division of the police department. The call informed him that his 14-year-old son was at the police station, charged with possession of marijuana. This experience prompted Mr. James to begin deeper investigation into the drug problems in the city. According to Mr. James, "It almost always takes a personal experience to get corporations involved in problem areas."

Without official support of the company, he contacted the chief of police, school officials, medical personnel, and social agencies who agreed that a drug problem did exist. Since Mr. James felt that no one at the firm had expertise in this area, he contacted a local agency involved in drug education programs. In addition he recommended to Oximeron's management that the firm grant a $1,500 contribution to drug education programs. Because of his efforts, he was later asked by the drug council to serve on its board of directors as the first industrial representative. Mr. James noted that while his actions weren't normal procedure, "it was for the good of the community."

The initial involvement of Oximeron with the drug education program was through Mr. James' recommendation. Oximeron provided $5,000 for a methadone maintenance program which was supported by the five regional plants. After Mr. James helped these managers identify problem employees, a "domino effect" began within certain parts of the organization. According to Mr. James, some people became "involved." However, upper management didn't really want to know about it. As the domino effect spread, the company became interested in allocating funds and developed an internal guide that addressed drug/alcohol problems inside the company (Exhibit 1).

This led to corporate/community involvement through the United Fund. Mr. James proposed a plan to channel $4,200 of excess employee deductions for the United Fund to a special community panel to deal with drug-related problems. The plan was accepted and led to funding a grant request to the federal government which covered the following five areas:

1. Identification of problems of drugs users.
2. How to approach the problem.
3. What could be done to solve the problem.
4. Type of organization/structure required to deal with the problem.
5. How to minimize program complications.

With Mr. James' support and assistance, the grant was completed and funded for $4 million over an eight-year period. Mr. James stated:

With less than $20,000 we got this city $4 million to deal with its drug problem. According to our sheriff, this will mean $11 million per year savings in losses due to theft (from drug addicts). This also means a savings to the firm and the community in lost wages, etc., which could be as much as another $16 million per year.

However, according to Mr. James, top management in the firm was "passing the buck" as to who was responsible for administering the internal program. A new medical officer was hired who had considerable experience in both drug and alcohol counseling. This appointment, plus Mr. James' continued efforts, led to the establishment of a combined drug/alcohol dependency program. The *new* program included:

1. Corporate social responsibility factors (Exhibit 2).
2. One and one-half day seminars in all U.S. plants.
3. Drug/alcohol problems defined as *medical* problems.
4. Expanded supervisors practices established.
5. Industrial "leadership" in the community.
6. Personnel policies.
7. Identification of problems through job performance.
8. Continued investment in "human assets."

Mr. James pointed out that it was the recognition of economic factors associated with the problem that finally led the way to the new program. He outlined the following economic factors which led to corporate involvement:

1. Sustained job performance

   —lower work quality and quantity
   —absenteeism (on and off the job)
   —irregular working hours
   —time off for minor illness
   —accidents (on and off the job)

2. Employee losses

   —on-the-job experience
   —costs/time involved with training
   —employee replacement/recruiting

3. Medical benefit's costs

4. Company administrative and personnel practices

5. Intangible costs

   —lowered department morale
   —poor decisions and judgment
   —poor customer/public relations
   —misplaced, missent, or damaged stock
   —clerical errors
   —loss of sales

General guidelines of Oximeron's effort in dealing with drug/alcohol programs are presented in Exhibit 3. Specifically their program included recognition of the problems, social responsibility factors, elements for program success, and the set of procedural guidelines for supervisors (Exhibits 4 and 5).

Mr. James was pleased with his company's new stance and said, "We have been late getting started, but I think we are ahead of most firms today, and I think this is a result of taking action when it was needed—even if it meant going around normal procedures."

Mr. James had been chairman of a special committee to evaluate the drug/alcohol program as a vehicle for developing a new planning/decision-making process for future corporate involvement in community affairs. Based on his experience with the implementation of this program, he proposed a review be made by senior management of the priority system for dealing with social issues.

Exhibit 1 **Alcoholism and Drug Dependence**

The company recognizes alcoholism and drug dependence as illnesses which are treatable. It is the company's intent to develop among all employees a realistic understanding of these illnesses to enable and encourage them to seek and take advantage of available treatment resources when needed.

An employee has an alcohol or drug problem of concern to the company if the use of beverage alcohol or psychoactive (mood altering) drugs impairs effectiveness at work.

The company will cooperate with an employee who recognizes that there is an alcohol or drug problem and requests assistance. An employee who makes no effort to get help or fails to cooperate in treatment—and has a continuing job problem—will be subjected to disciplinary action, including discharge.

The primary responsibility for assisting the employee, or initiating other appropriate action, rests with the immediate supervisor. The company desires that no employee with the illness of alcoholism and/or drug dependence have job security or usual promotional opportunities jeopardized by merely requesting assistance through diagnosis and treatment.

Involvement of Medical Officer

Supervisors do not normally have the professional knowledge to diagnose alcoholism and/or drug dependence. Necessary referral to the company medical officer will therefore be based primarily on unsatisfactory job performance. After interview and evaluation, the company medical officer will inform the supervisor of recommendation.

The confidentiality of all communications with reference to the employee and these illnesses will be preserved as privileged medical information and treated in the same manner as any other medical record or information.

New Applicants

Current dependence upon, or misuse of, mood altering drugs or alcohol are valid reasons for rejecting an applicant for employment. (An applicant participating in a recognized methadone maintenance program, and receiving methadone as prescribed, is not necessarily considered a case of misuse or dependence as defined in this section.) When an applicant doesn't admit to such dependence or misuse—but valid evidence exists—the applicant will be subject to the usual company medical practices for job applicants.

On the other hand, the company will give consideration to applications by individuals who have misused alcohol and other mood altering drugs, when (1) it is the opinion of the plant physician that the applicant is physically and mentally acceptable, and (2) the plant physician and employment supervisor concur there is good reason to believe the applicant will not revert to alcoholism or drug dependence or misuse, and will become a dependable employee. Support of the application by reputable community authorities can be helpful in determining the employment decision in such cases.

Employees Returning from Leaves

An employee who has been on a leave of absence (for any reason) is found to be dependent upon or misusing mood altering drugs and/or alcohol, and it can reasonably be assumed that such dependence or misuse will adversely affect job performance, will not be placed on the active roll but continued on medical leave until the medical officer is satisfied the dependence or misuse is under control.

Law Enforcement and In-Plant Discipline

Any knowledge of possession, consumption, or sale of alcohol or illegal mood altering drugs (or the illegal possession or sale of legal mood altering drugs) on company property shall be reported to the officer in charge of security, who will take appropriate action.

Possession, consumption, or sale of alcohol or illegal mood altering drugs on company property will subject an employee to immediate discharge. (Limited sale or consumption of low-alcohol beverages are permitted in some locations outside the United States as a part of long-established local custom.)

Community Involvement

The community constitutes the environment that, in effect, encourages or discourages these problems. Therefore, it is desirable that managers encourage strong community efforts in education, law enforcement, effective judicial processes, treatment, and rehabilitation in connection with alcoholism and drug misuse.

Union Involvement

At some plant locations, the problem of alcoholism and drug dependence has received combined company and union attention through formation of joint committees. Their objective is to work constructively to combat the problems of alcoholism and drug dependence by whatever means deemed appropriate. Where such joint committees do not exist and management recognizes the merit of such a committee in combating the problem, discussion with the union on the subject is encouraged.

Exhibit 2   **Social Responsibility Factors**

---

1. Returning employee to community as a productive employable person.

2. Returning employee to role as a family member and provider.

3. Returning employee to the community as an active and responsible citizen with the resultant effect on the economy of that community as a consumer of goods and services and as a taxpayer.

4. Reducing the costs for welfare benefits needed to provide for the employee if that person had deteriorated to the point where he/she could no longer be employed.

5. Reducing caseloads of other social and helping agencies and the associated costs.

6. Removing the alcoholic person from the highways and roads where over 50 percent of the fatalities are alcohol related.

7. Reducing the court costs, costs of incarceration, and police costs for apprehension and disposition of arrests for drunkenness.

8. Stimulating the interest of others in the development of these programs through our interest as a major multinational corporation.

9. Creating positive attitudinal change through our interest and support toward the illness of alcoholism by removing bias and stigma in various communities where our facilities and dealers exist.

10. Assisting other nations through this interest and support where our employees work in the true spirit of multinational concern for one another.

11. Sharing our experiences and expertise with other companies, involved agencies, and public bodies by promoting the understanding and awareness of the illness of alcoholism and drug dependence.

Exhibit 3   **Elements Necessary for Program Success**

1. Interest, support, endorsement, and encouragement of corporate officers and medical officer.

2. Determine current procedures and practices of administering and resolving behavioral/medical problems in the company.

3. Written policy or procedures outlining company's program, goals, and intent.

4. Clear definition of the alcohol and drug dependence problem.

5. Education and training program for supervisory personnel.

6. Development of working relationships with all appropriate treatment programs and community resources, both public and private.

7. Foster the principle of individualized, continuing treatment, including other members of the family where indicated.

8. Development of a working relationship with the unions to promote their cooperation and support.

9. Appointment of administrator for the program.

10. Treatment costs covered by company employee medical benefits plan.

Exhibit 4   **Procedural Guidelines for Supervisors**

The immediate supervisor is usually in the most favorable position to assist the employee with a behavioral medical problem. Early identification of the problem should be of major concern to the supervisor. The supervisor is encouraged to *document* substandard job performance in a fair and consistent manner within the *customary* company administrative procedures. An attempt to diagnose the illnesses of alcoholism and/or drug dependence is discouraged. Final diagnosis of any illness is the responsibility of the medical officer, assisted by his/her staff.

The supervisor is in a unique position to motivate the employee to seek the assistance needed. Failure to recognize job performance impairment lessens the chances of recovery from alcoholism and/or drug dependence if this is revealed in the final diagnosis. There should be no attempt to conceal the impaired job performance or intentional oversight where there is evidence of a problem on the job. The following indicators of impaired job performance are some of the job deterioration factors that could be documented:

- Half-day or day absenteeism

- Tardiness

- More unusual excuses for absences

- Leaving work early

- Increase in scrap and lower work quality

- Leaving post temporarily

- Lower quantity of work

- Increase in minor illnesses

- Neglecting details formerly attended to

- Making mistakes or errors in judgment

- Avoiding boss or associates

- More intolerant of fellow workers

- Accidents on the job

- Lost time accidents off the job

- Sleeping on the job

- Cycling of work performance

Procedures

1. Employee is informed that job performance is unsatisfactory. Supervisor follows usual company personnel practices in a discussion with employee in reference to his/her work, using a firm and constructive approach.

2. If the job performance remains substandard and the usual corrective action procedures and personnel practices fail to correct job deterioration within a set period of time, the employee is referred to the plant medical officer. If the employee refuses to see the medical officer, he/she is subject to the usual company practices if his/her job performance remains substandard.

3. An evaluation of the employee's health status is completed by the medical officer. If alcoholism and/or drug dependency is *not* eliminated as a cause of poor job performance, the staff advisor discusses: (a) the role of staff advisor in employee assistance program, (b) company policy on alcoholism and drug abuse, and (c) secures necessary background information (fact sheet on drinking and/or drug history).

4. A plan for rehabilitation is established and documented. If the employee does not accept the suggested plan, and substandard work performance continues, he/she is subject to usual administrative corrective action. If the employee indicates cooperation, the medical officer initiates the appropriate referrals. The supervisor is informed of the action taken.

5. The employee must cooperate in the total rehabilitation effort during pretreatment, treatment, and posttreatment.

6. The medical officer will develop follow-up mechanisms to provide the proper level of support for the employee's recovery subsequent to return from leave. The employee is expected to cooperate with this plan.

7. If at any time the supervisor determines an employee is unfit for work, the employee is referred to the medical officer for evaluation and disposition. The employee must obtain a return-to-work pass from the medical officer.

8. An employee with an alcohol and/or drug problem can make a self-referral to the medical officer without supervisory involvement. The usual confidential manner will be followed.

Exhibit 5   **Procedural Guidelines in Outline Format**

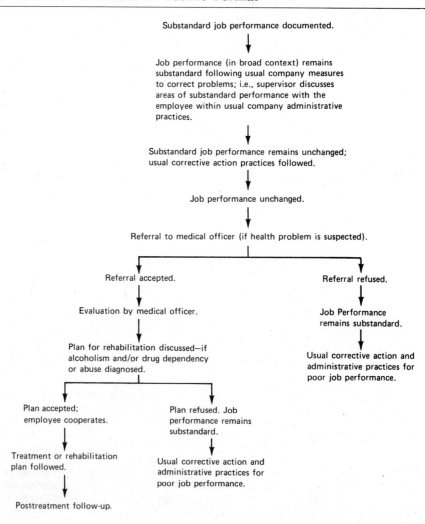

Case 1–5

Braniff International Corporation*

In late 1978, Harding L. Lawrence, then chairman and chief executive of Braniff International, was reviewing his expansion plan for the company. He was particularly overjoyed by the plan's promise that his company, then the nation's seventh largest air carrier, would become a giant in the industry within the months ahead. In no way could he have imagined the kind of situation the Dallas-based carrier would shortly face. Just one year into the expansion program Braniff saw its record profits of $45 million in 1978 turn into a $44.3 million loss in 1979 and another $131 million loss in 1980. Lawrence resigned under tremendous pressure in January 1981. He was succeeded by Vice Chairman John J. Casey who named Howard D. Putnam as president and chief operating officer in late September 1981. The two have since been working on a new marketing concept and the restructuring of Braniff's debt. Taking into consideration the company's current financial position and the overall recession in the economy, industrial experts speculated about the chances of the Dallas-based carrier's survival.

HISTORY AND BACKGROUND

The history of Braniff International began with the founding in 1928 of Airways by Thomas E. Braniff. The small carrier started with one single-engine, four-passenger Stinson Detroiter servicing Oklahoma City and Tulsa once every day. By 1929 the little plane was flying three round trips daily between the two cities. Between 1929 and 1941, Braniff purchased 28 airliners of various sizes. During the Second World War Braniff moved over six and one-half million pounds of top priority cargo for Uncle Sam. It also trained military pilots in instrument flying and held schools for army mechanics and radio operators. The end of the war brought a tremendous boom in civil air transportation, both nationally and internationally. Braniff had the foresight to apply for routes to Latin America as early as 1943. The economically and socially important task of tying the western hemisphere together could only be accomplished effectively through air transportation. Early pioneers of Braniff Airways realized the prominent part American carriers would play in gaining new markets for U.S. products as well as opening markets for foreign producers in the U.S. The opening of Braniff International routes in 1948 offered tremendous potential in industrial and recreational possibilities. With the extension and development of domestic routes, Braniff International became

*This case was prepared by Sexton Adams, Don Powell, and Fred Williams of North Texas State University, and Adelaide Griffin of Texas Woman's University, with the intention of providing a basis for class discussion rather than illustrating either effective or ineffective management of a business situation.

one of the ten largest international air carriers. In an interchange agreement with Pan American Airlines, Braniff provided service to London and Frankfurt, Germany. Braniff also had a contract with the U.S. government to carry military personnel and material to and from the Far East. Braniff's operations since 1946 had become global in nature.

Braniff had built for itself a reputation for innovation in the industry, particularly under Harding Lawrence who took over direction of the carrier in 1965. Braniff International was the first airline to retire its piston engine aircraft; it was also the first airline to utilize jet assist take-off systems at high altitude airports. In 1966 Braniff inaugurated the world's first Boeing B-727 "Quick Change" convertible tri-jet. The B-727 QC could be converted from a passenger/cargo configuration in 30 minutes, which greatly improved aircraft utilization. Moreover, Braniff earned its uniqueness from its brightly colored aircraft and the substitution of Pucci fashions for more conventional hostess uniforms.

DEREGULATION

In his campaign for presidency in 1976, Jimmy Carter made deregulation of the airline industry one of his top legislative priorities. He wasn't able to submit a bill on the matter until 1978, but he quickly appointed Alfred Kahn, an economist and expert on government regulations, to head up the Civil Aeronautics Board (CAB). On October 24, 1978, President Carter signed the bill freeing the airline industry from rigid CAB control. The CAB was scheduled to go out of existence at sunset on January 1, 1985. Under the Airline Deregulation Act of 1978, the CAB's regulatory powers were to be phased out in three steps. Its control over interstate routes would cease at the end of 1981, and its jurisdiction over fares and charter regulation would expire at the close of 1983. The antitrust control over mergers and operations would pass to the Justice Department, authority over federal subsidies to the Department of Transportation, and the Federal Aviation Agency would oversee airline safety and technical matters. These restrictions were insignificant compared to previously rigid CAB authority over rates and routes. The intent of the deregulation law was to promote competition and maintain a high level of safety while protecting small community air service and preventing unreasonable industry concentration. The power to adjust rates up or down also passed from the once autocratic CAB to the carriers themselves. Originally carriers were allowed to raise fares 5 to 10 percent and to lower them as much as 50 percent.

THE EXPANSION PROGRAM

Originally, Braniff's expansion program was strategically sound in that it took full advantage of the Deregulation Act of 1978. It was successful in obtaining new routes and the right to fly to new cities from the CAB. The Act permitted the airlines to apply, on a first-come, first-serve basis, for any of some 1,300 dormant routes that the CAB had previously awarded but which no carriers were currently serving. Braniff had snapped up 437 of the routes and added 49 new routes and 18 cities to its system. It was the biggest route expansion in Braniff's 50-year history. Although the deadline set by Congress to fly new routes was mid-January of 1979, Braniff's executives thought the Christmas rush a good time to become known in new markets. Consequently, they scheduled services over all of their new routes for December 15, 1978. Its new routes included first-time service to eastern cities such as Boston, Cleveland, Pittsburgh, and Philadelphia adding 35 percent to its route miles. However, because the company was rescheduling its fleet, available seats would increase only 11 percent. Most of the new routes would be operated as extensions of existing flights. A plane that arrived in San Antonio in the early evening from the East could continue to Los Angeles, arriving at midnight.

As a result of an interchange agreement with Air France and British Airways to participate in Concorde operations, Braniff inaugurated a Concorde flight between Texas and Washington to London and Paris in January 1979. Later in June it added nonstop service to Amsterdam, Frankfurt, and Brussels. Braniff also began its push into the Transpacific (Far East) service by inaugurating flights to Seoul, Hong Kong, and Singapore the same year. In anticipation of a quick expansion, ten Boeing 727s, with 130 seats each, were delivered in 1978. The company ordered 28 more for delivery during the period 1979 to 1981. Six hundred twenty-seven additional pilots were hired to handle the extra mileage, and the pilots agreed to increase their time in the air each month from 75 to 90 hours. In addition, the company stopped training pilots for other airlines at its Dallas base and began devoting full time to its own flight crew needs. The two flight simulators had been running 20 hours a day as opposed to normal usage of eight hours daily. To a degree the expansion program proved successful, since no other major airline had grown so much so quickly. In just one year Braniff's passenger capacity had expanded by 39 percent. Over a two year period revenues rose by 65 percent to $1.35 billion to make Braniff the sixth largest airline in the United States.

COMPETITORS' ACTIONS IN THE ERA OF DEREGULATION

The furious pace and the strategy underlying Braniff's expansion program were in sharp contrast to what other airlines had been doing since the deregulation. Braniff's competitors had moved with greater caution into new markets and had spent a great amount of time enhancing and integrating their existing route structures. Northwest, for example, entered 18 new markets but only three new cities. United Airlines, whose $3.4 billion of sales in 1978 made it the industry's airborne giant, took only one route out of the grab bag the CAB offered. United elected the strategy of stressing capacity and service. By focusing on logistics, United was ready to accommodate a 17 percent passenger traffic increase in 1978. While other airlines struggled to maintain their existing customer service levels, United's best selling tool, service, remained sharp. As United's Chairman Richard J. Ferris explained, the reason for choosing only one route out of hundreds of dormant routes from CAB was because "the routes would have been unprofitable, unwieldy, and chaotic. We want routes that make sense. Our growth will come with intelligent marketing."[1]

American Airlines, a close competitor of Braniff, had always been a leader in slashing fares since it introduced the "Super Saver" fares in 1973; these cut normal fares 45 percent. In anticipation of increased competition after deregulation, the airline extended its "Super Saver" fares to all of its domestic routes. Thomas Plaskett, American's chief financial officer, explained the move as "merely trying to increase the passenger levels of its existing capacity, planes that would be flying anyway, which made excellent economic sense."[2]

At the same time Delta Airlines was busy fighting a classic confrontation with Eastern Airlines, both of which are Atlanta-based carriers. When airline deregulation was a mere vision, Delta Airlines cautiously opposed it. There was concern that carriers would pull out of small cities, thus reducing potential passengers and damaging its feeder system that pulled small-town passengers into big city airports. Too many airlines would rush to cash in on big city routes. Consequently, negative effects such as the elimination of service to small cities, weaker airlines being forced out of business, and lost employment because of layoffs at carriers troubled by the new system might result.

On the whole, there was wide spread pessimism about the future prospects for the airline business in 1979—a market shift from the exuberant mood of 1978. In 1978 because of the dizzying array of discount fares, air traffic drastically increased. Combined profits of the eleven lines almost doubled to a record of $1.04 billion. According to D. George James, senior vice president for economics and finance at the Air Transport Association, "traffic in 1979 would increase at least 15 percent, not including the effect of the cutoff of Iranian oil supplies on fuel prices."[3] James and other analysts were predicting that industry profits for 1979 would drop sharply to around $700 million. Most of the major airlines were also uneasy with virtual freedom to fly where they chose, and had waited to assess the new look in the marketplace as it unfolded. Faced with this free-for-all, one veteran airline strategist said, "Some carriers have concluded they'll fight their battles in the territory they've already established. They're putting aside resources for defense rather than going overboard on offense the way Braniff has."[4] Another chief officer of a smaller competitor said, "The risk element is awfully high, and they're going to get their comeuppance. We're all waiting to see their first quarter profits."[5]

Airline executives also pointed to those late-night, red-eye departure times in Braniff's new schedule as evidence that Braniff's reach had at last exceeded its grasp. They predicted that Braniff was going to bleed at the bottom line from an unhappy mix of low-load factors, expensive introductory discount fares, and high start-up costs from training personnel and providing new ground facilities. Critics went on to note that Braniff had landed some markets already overpopulated with carriers. Taking its new Seattle-Honolulu route as an example, "It's going to be a long, cool Sunday before that market can support four carriers,"[6] said an airline expert in scheduling.

As for overseas routes, Continental's Robert Six was quick to point out that Braniff was venturing abroad without the marketing muscle it carried in the U.S. In cities where National Airlines had a notable lack of success (Frankfurt and Amsterdam), he thought Braniff could suffer as well. Competitors also argued that the airline would be badly burned by its Concorde service.

BRANIFF UNDER HARDING L. LAWRENCE

The operating philosophy that had emerged during Harding Lawrence's tenure was fundamental. He saw the business traveler, that great constant flow of the air-travel market, as the key to running a profitable airline. To attract him or her, Braniff built schedules around frequent service in narrow-bodied aircraft. The strategy worked; no other carrier had a higher percentage of business travelers (about 70 percent), and few competitors could match the size or the consistency of Braniff's operating margins. Since deregulation, however, Braniff had modified the frequency doctrine to accommodate the increase in new routes. Most of them were served by only one flight a day, and departures were often at inconvenient times—after midnight in several instances. "Our schedule is not the best in the world right now,"[7] conceded John Casey, Braniff's vice chairman.

The reason for such a hasty expansion came from a frustrated desire to grow, as well as the worry that Washington might well "re-regulate" the airline industry if cities complained too loudly about suspended service. In going after new routes, Braniff assumed that the deregulation act might be only a small-window that could slam shut at any moment. "I'm in a big hurry. I don't have much time left to do what I want to do with this airline. I want to get Braniff anchored," said Lawrence. By "anchoring," Lawrence was also getting set for what he and others foresaw as a period of consolidation in the airline industry. The merger moves he predicted in his congressional testimony in 1978, during the debate over deregulation, had already begun in early 1979. Pending combinations between Continental and Western, North Central Airlines and Southern Airways, and the bidding war for National Airlines between Pan Am, Eastern, and Texas International were clear evidence of that. "For those who remain static, there's a question of survival," as Casey had put it.[8]

Lawrence seemed overconfident at times. "If they don't know what I'm doing, they're not looking at the map; they're not studying my history," Lawrence says. "It's all very simple."[9]

Unlike most of its competitors, Braniff had had considerable experience with the rough-and-tumble of the free market in 1979. Along with Texas International, Braniff bitterly fought the incursions of a new intrastate carrier, Southwest Airlines, in its native territory of Texas. Braniff's and T.I.'s hardline tactics prompted a lawsuit which charged the two with conspiring to prevent Southwest from operating in the Dallas-Fort Worth, Houston, and San Antonio markets. Both carriers pleaded nolo contendere in 1978 to the charges, settling for fines of $100,000 apiece.

That kind of aggressiveness explains the super-competitive instincts of Braniff's top managers, as does the story of Lawrence and Richard Ferris of United Airlines:

In October, Ferris bet Lawrence $100 that Braniff could not lease a Boeing 747 in time to start service by the end of the month between Seattle and Honolulu on a route that Pan Am was vacating; there were simply no extra jumbos around. Braniff dug up two that were available on an extremely short-term basis—it leased one 747 from American for three weeks—and flew them on the route until a plane on long-term lease arrived the first week of December. Ferris paid up.[10]

Harding Lawrence was obviously the energizing force behind Braniff's growth. Part promoter, part strategist, he was one for whom it might be said that all the world was both a stage and a map. Lawrence was always out selling Braniff.

Like a number of its larger competitors such as Delta and United, Braniff operated a hub-and-spoke route system. The effect is that of a giant vacuum, sucking in passengers from disparate points and then shooting them out along another spoke. In the Dallas-Fort Worth airport, Braniff had an immensely powerful vacuum. A hub-and-spoke pattern is inherently more elastic than the linear, point-to-point route system of such Braniff competitors as T.W.A. Until February 1977, when it took delivery of four new 727's, Braniff was able to stretch its entire route map by 30 percent without the use of a single additional plane or, perhaps more important, without pulling aircraft out of its major markets to serve new ones. Braniff's objective was to control the flow of traffic as far up and down the system as possible rather than connecting passengers with other carriers. "We've been feeding American and Delta in places like Los Angeles. Why should we feed them if we can feed ourselves,"[11] said John Casey.

The concept of "feed" had a powerful hold on the minds of airline strategists, including those at Braniff. The addition of relatively small amounts of mileage can provide tremendous leverage on a carrier's route structure.

Lawrence saw Braniff's ability in handling the massive expansion program emerging from its operation flexibility. Starting in the 1970s, it began paring down its fleet from seven types of aircraft to three. By 1979 the 104 planes it flew were either 727s (for domestic flights), 747s (for long hauls to Europe and Hawaii), or DC-8s (for Latin America traffic). Each plane operated more efficiently over the distance it flew than any type of aircraft. That was why Lawrence declined to join United and other carriers in purchasing Boeing's new plane, the 767; the old 727 was still cheaper to fly over 550 miles, the average length of one of Braniff's domestic flights. The standardized fleet also gave Braniff more flexibility in training its pilots and manning new routes.

Another Braniff tactic was to buy aircraft regularly, in small quantities, rather than add large chunks of capacity all at once. As the new planes came in, Braniff would sell a few old-timers into the used market. It was an effective means of matching capacity with demand. In 1978 Braniff had planned to sell five 727s; it sold only two as traffic soared. The annual orders to Boeing had resulted in a fleet that, on the average, was the second youngest in the industry (behind Delta's). That meant greater operating efficiencies. Such efficiency, combined with Braniff's traditionally high utilization rates (each plane flies over ten hours per day on the average), gave Braniff break-even factors second only to Northwest's. Furthermore, since the majority of new routes in the expansion program were merely tag-on to its existing system, Braniff needed to cover only the direct operating costs of flying additional mileage. In most cases it could do that even if the plane was only 30 percent full.

Lawrence was brash enough to suggest that Braniff would make some money on its Concorde operations, perhaps $500,000 to $1 million of pretax earnings at the end of 1979, despite the fact that the supersonic jets had been flying from Dallas to Washington with about 65 percent of their seats empty. His confidence stemmed in part from the low-cost contract he negotiated with the French and British governments to operate the plane.

THE BEGINNING OF THE NIGHTMARE

In late June 1979 Harding L. Lawrence suddenly realized that the outcome of Braniff's expansion program was far from his expectation. The company posted a third quarter loss of $10 million. On April 8, 1980, *Standard & Poor's* lowered the rating of Braniff's debentures and notes. Its $11\frac{1}{8}$ percent debenture due in 1987, its 10 percent note due in 1986, and its $9\frac{1}{8}$ percent debenture due in 1987 were lowered from Triple-B minus to Double-B, while its $5\frac{3}{4}$ percent debenture maturing in 1986 maintained a Single-B ranking. For the year 1980, Braniff reported a total net loss of $128.5 million. On January 2, 1981, *Standard & Poor's* again lowered its rating on the company's various notes, certificates, and debentures. The Double-B and the Single-B subordinated debenture was lowered to Triple-C. Exhibits 1 and 2 show the balance sheet and the income statement of Braniff for the years ended 1979 and 1980.

Braniff's heavy losses were caused by some heavy blows beyond its control. First came the soaring fuel prices, with fuel expenses in the third quarter of 1979 exceeding budgeted amounts by $47.7 million. Then the CAB opposed a fare increase on foreign routes making it impossible for the company to recoup the higher fuel costs. To make things worse, the traffic at home softened. These factors caused heavy losses for all the carriers. Braniff, because of its rapid expansion, was more exposed than most others. For example, it needed extra fuel for expansion and was forced to buy it in the spot market, where prices were much higher than under contract.

C. Edward Acker, former Braniff president and chairman of Air Florida noted:

> American Airlines is a big cash flow machine, and it can lose $35 million or so (quarterly) and still survive. But if BI loses that much, pretty soon it's out. It's like you, me, and Bunker Hunt in a poker game—we wouldn't have the staying power to play with him.[12]

Braniff had planned to make an offering of $75 million of preferred stock to the public; but in late 1979, as its losses continued, the offering was called off. Braniff did manage to sell $35 million of preferred stock privately in April 1980 but was forced to call off the planned sale of another $65 million preferred stock because the company failed to meet earnings requirements

Exhibit 1

Braniff International
Balance Sheet (In thousands of dollars)

ASSETS	December 31 1980	1979
Current Assets:		
Cash	$ 19,707	$ 32,007
Marketable securities	92	1,486
Accounts receivable..	133,413	131,988
Inventory of spare parts, materials, supplies	35,047	37,772
Other current assets	9,531	7,788
Total Current assets.......................................	$ 197,790	$ 211,041
Equipment purchase deposits	13,724	30,391
Property and equipment	868,443	863,429
Other assets	27,411	53,040
Total assets..	$1,107,368	$1,157,901
LIABILITIES and SHAREHOLDERS' EQUITY		
Current Liabilities:		
Notes payable...	$ 47,144	$ 66
Current maturities of long-term debt.........................	42,718	23,327
Accounts payable...	96,112	118,420
Current liabilities under capital lease	10,217	10,558
Unearned revenues	51,471	43,002
Dividends payable...	19	1,023
Accrued compensation & retirement benefits	32,303	26,791
Accrued vacation pay..	22,529	21,677
Accrued interest..	15,033	12,588
Other current liabilities	23,486	18,878
Total current liabilities	$ 341,032	$ 276,330
Long-Term Debt, less current maturities:		
Senior debt...	488,600	507,912
Subordinated debt..	95,002	70,286
Other noncurrent liabilities....................................	77,070	90,382
Deferred credits...	4,141	14,374
Redeemable preferred stock	35,343	—
Common stock...	10,010	10,010
Paid-in capital	46,785	46,785
Retained earnings	9,385	141,822
Total liabilities and shareholders' equity.....................	$1,107,368	$1,157,901

included in the private replacement agreement. The failure to raise the $65 million blocked Braniff from using about $220 million of its bank line of credit. Braniff's finances, in the words of one analyst, "are in shambles."

In late 1979, Braniff quietly borrowed $50 million from suppliers to buy Boeing 727's. About $8.5 million was provided by United Technologies Corporation, which made the engines, and the remainder was provided by Boeing. Again in early 1980, Braniff quietly borrowed another $50 million from Boe-

Exhibit 2

Braniff International

Income Statement (In thousands except for per share amounts)

	Year ended December 31	
	1980	**1979**
OPERATING REVENUES		
Airline:		
Passenger..	$1,305,305	$1,200,329
Freight and mail...	84,679	84,559
Charter..	9,119	15,226
Transport related..	31,595	28,213
Other	11,095	8,039
Nonairline subsidiaries.....................................	10,337	9,909
Total operating revenues...............................	$1,452,130	$1,346,275
OPERATING EXPENSES		
Airline:		
Flying and ground operations	$ 600,313	$ 564,841
Aircraft fuel, oil, and taxes	481,128	409,635
Maintenance	133,730	131,691
Nonairline subsidiaries.....................................	2,488	3,271
Sales and advertising	198,906	158,659
Depreciation & amortization, less amounts charged to other		
accounts...	89,296	75,343
General & administrative..................................	53,762	41,273
Total operating expenses...............................	$1,559,623	$1,384,713
OPERATING INCOME (LOSS)	$ (107,493)	$ (38,438)
NONOPERATING EXPENSE (INCOME)		
Interest expense..	$ 92,101	$ 55,919
Interest capitalized	(3,398)	(6,265)
Interest income	(5,344)	(3,809)
Gain on disposal of property and equipment	(79,090)	(1,972)
Unrecoverable preoperating costs	20,329	1,986
Other	3,492	1,667
Total nonoperating expense (loss)......................	$ 28,090	$ 47,526
INCOME (LOSS) BEFORE INCOME TAXES AND		
PREFERRED DIVIDENDS...............................	$ (135,583)	$ (85,964)
PROVISION (CREDIT) FOR INCOME TAXES...............	7,072	37,400
INCOME (LOSS) BEFORE PREFERRED DIVIDENDS OF		
SUBSIDIARY..	$ (128,511)	$ (48,564)
PREFERRED DIVIDENDS OF SUBSIDIARY.................	(2,925)	--
NET INCOME (LOSS).....................................	$ (131,436)	$ (48,564)
NET INCOME (LOSS) PER COMMON SHARE	$ (6.57)	$ (2.43)
WEIGHTED AVERAGE NUMBER OF COMMON SHARES		
OUTSTANDING..	20,019	20,019

Source: Company annual reports, 1980.

ing. In another effort to produce cash, Braniff in May 1980 proposed raising domestic fares by 25 percent, perhaps the biggest across-the-board increase ever tried in the airline industry. However, competitiors would not go along. Braniff dropped its proposal.

AIRLINE ECONOMICS

The airlines used the available seat mile, one passenger flown one mile, rather than a passenger mile flown, as the unit of production since air carrier costs were directly related to the number of seats rather than the number of passengers flown over a given distance. Once an airplane was scheduled on a particular flight, the total cost of that flight varied only slightly with the number of passengers that the plane was carrying. This characteristic of individual flight operation gave rise to the industry view of itself as having an extremely high percentage of fixed costs.

An industry rule of thumb stated that the variable cost of adding an extra passenger to a flight amounted to only 10 percent of the fare paid by that passenger and that the remaining 90 percent passed directly through as a contribution to operating profit. The cost per unit of production was influenced by a variety of factors, including aircraft type and average length of flights. Given this cost per available seat mile, however, an airline's total operating cost was easily computed by multiplying total available seat mile and adding to this the variable cost of 10 percent passenger fares.

Airline costs were, perhaps, less fixed than the industry believed, at least, in the very short run. Over time spans of a year or more, the industry's growth rate and inflation tended to make other fixed available seat mile related costs (such as depreciation and salaries) variable.

While costs were tied closely to available seat miles, the revenue generated on a flight was directly related to the number of passengers carried, how far they were flown, and how much revenue these passengers paid in passenger miles. The third term was commonly called yield per revenue passenger miles.

Given the high proportion of costs that were fixed, profits were very sensitive to the load factor experienced by an airline. Since profitability was so sensitive to the load factor, the industry was concerned with maintaining profitable load factor levels through a policy of restraint in adding capacity. Braniff's operation statistics for the year 1979 and 1980 are shown in Exhibit 3.

RETRENCHING

Unsuccessful in its further attempts to raise cash, Braniff chose to retrench from its expansion program. In August 1980, Braniff gave notice to terminate its lease of a 747 aircraft and offered to sell 10 to 15 of its Boeing 727-200 jets. They sold a 747 jumbo jet, one of the newest jets of Braniff, to Aerolineas Argentinas. In late August 1980 Braniff disclosed the sale of $180 million worth of aircraft, including 15 of its medium range 727's, to American Airlines. The 15 airplanes constituted 21 percent of Braniff's fleet used in domestic routes. By the end of 1980 the operating fleet of the company consisted of the equipment listed in Exhibit 4.

In addition to fleet reduction, several routes were dropped during 1980. In June Braniff dropped its Concorde flight between Dallas-Fort Worth and Washington to London and Paris. The flight had been started in January 1979. On the Pacific, service which had been launched only in the previous two

Exhibit 3

Braniff International
Operating Statistics
(In thousands except for ratios in cents per mile)

	Year Ended December 31	
	1980	**1979**
Revenue plane miles flown:		
Domestic	101,104	131,958
International	32,265	32,151
Percent of schedule passenger miles flown:		
Domestic	99.1%	98.6%
International	98.8%	98.9%
Scheduled revenue passenger miles flown:		
Domestic	7,336,339	9,488,675
International	4,563,568	3,931,664
Scheduled saleable seat miles flown:		
Domestic	13,077,584	17,245,705
International	7,283,171	6,599,751
Passenger load factor:		
Domestic	56.1%	55.0%
International	62.7%	59.6%
Passenger breakeven load factor:		
Domestic	58.9%	58.2%
International	75.2%	63.5%
Average passenger revenue per revenue passenger mile:		
Domestic (cents per mile)	12.4¢	9.5¢
International	8.7¢	7.7¢
Number of revenue passengers carried:		
Domestic	8,818	11,145
International	1,748	1,698
Airmail ton miles flown:		
Domestic	36,041	40,979
International	11,215	7,932
Cargo ton miles flown:		
Domestic	65,084	75,385
International	89,104	67,233

Source: Company annual reports, 1980.

years was dropped. The Los Angeles to Guam and Singapore route was dropped on October 12, 1980. The European routes to Amsterdam and Paris were dropped in October 1980; routes to Brussels and Frankfurt were dropped in January 1981. Braniff discontinued some of its domestic routes as well. Cities granted service during the Deregulation Act but which were discontinued included Birmingham, Cleveland, Milwaukee, Oakland, Pittsburgh, Sacramento, Jacksonville, and West Palm Beach. The cities not part of the Deregulation Act expansion to which service was discontinued were Fort Smith, Shreveport, Little Rock, St. Louis, Detroit, and Colorado Springs.

Exhibit 4

Braniff International Corporation
Flight Equipment

Description	Passenger Capacity	Number	Average Age (yrs.)
Owned Aircraft:			
Boeing 747-200	418	1	2
Boeing 747SP	301	2	1
Boeing 727-100	102/107	10	14
Boeing 727-200	130/134	58	4
Douglas DC-8-62	164	8	13
Total Owned		79	6
Leased Aircraft:			
Boeing 747-100	363/418	2	10
Boeing 747-200	418	2	8
Boeing 747-100	102/107	7	14
Boeing 727-200	130/134	5	11
Douglas DC-8-62	164	2	11
Total Leased		18	12
Total		97	7

MERGING ATTEMPT

On August 5, 1980, Continental Airlines held a preliminary talk on a possible merger with Western and another airline. Braniff was suspected of being the other airline. With the deregulation of the airlines, intensifying competition, and the recession biting into profits, there was growing speculation that mergers between carriers would increase. Neither Western nor Braniff denied the news and rumors died down.

By December 16, 1980, another possible negotiation was in the news, this time between Braniff and Eastern Airlines. Neither Eastern nor Braniff had been doing well financially. In the first nine months of its fiscal year, Eastern lost $34.7 million on revenue of $256 billion. Braniff reported an operational loss of $77.4 million. The sale of some aircrafts reduced that to $51.6 million. Analysts doubted whether an Eastern-Braniff merger would provide any advantages if both carriers were financially weak (Exhibit 5).

Eastern, using its hub at Miami, had been trying to expand southward into Latin America. Acquiring Braniff's Latin American operations would greatly enhance Eastern's expansion plans. Eastern could take over Braniff's routes to Europe. There were advantages that Eastern could gain assuming the merger was not in violation of antitrust laws. On the other hand, the larger Eastern

Exhibit 5   **How Braniff and Eastern Stack Up Financially**

	Sept. 30, 1980 Millions of dollars	Percent change from 1979	Sept. 30, 1979 Millions of dollars
Braniff			
Long-term debt*	$ 700	+24%	$ 565
Stockholders' equity.................	145	−42	251
Operating revenue†	1,127	+13	1,000
Operating income†..................	−77	NM	10
Net income†	−52	NM	7
Eastern			
Long-term debt*	$1,273	+20%	$1,064
Stockholders' equity.................	405	−6	432
Operating revenue†	2,561	+21	2,118
Operating income†..................	−5	NM	87
Net income†	−35	NM	42

*Includes liability on capital leases.
†Nine months
NM = Not meaningful
Reprinted from the December 29, 1980, issue of *Business Week* by special permission, © 1980 by McGraw-Hill, Inc. New York, NY 10020. All rights reserved.

might be able to cushion some of Braniff's financial problems. Though the combination might work in theory, the financial situation might make it impossible.

By the end of January 1981, the Eastern-Braniff merger was abandoned. The negative factors of poor timing, dislocation of personnel, and plans and uncertainties over benefits held final sway with management. In addition, a high combined debt, dealing with the many unions that represented employees of the two airlines, uncertainty whether the Civil Aeronautics Board would award Braniff's South American routes to the merged airlines, degrading efficiencies, added operation costs, and expected layoffs of between 1,000 and 1,500 Eastern employees and an uncertain number of Braniff employees caused the two companies to drop the proposal.

PAY CUT

On November 26, 1980, Braniff chairman Harding Lawrence came up with an idea to cut down the operation expenses. The idea was a volunteer pay cut program by the company's employees. He promised to double whatever they did regarding a paycut in his $300,000 a year salary, but the union voted to reject the program. The union claimed that, according to the company newspaper, the chairman of the board was saying that his company was financially sound.

When John Casey became the president of Braniff in January 1981, he wanted to make the pay cut program work. He acknowledged to the employees that the company was in trouble, and it needed their help to keep it going. By then, employees from the five different unions had become more acquainted with the company's situation. By March 1981, John Casey had suspended his $180,000 yearly salary in order to encourage his 11,500 employees to accept a 10 percent pay cut. Employee acceptance of the proposed pay cut would prove to be critical to Braniff. Braniff creditors had agreed to defer $18 million in principal and interest payments only if Braniff employees agreed to the pay cuts.

Among the five unions (Exhibit 6), Air Transport Dispatchers Association was the first to accept the program. The next day, 4,000 Teamster employees voted to cut their current salaries 10 percent. Although a decisive 79 percent voted to accept the pay cut, the other unions were not convinced that the company was in deep financial trouble. By March 5, 1,380 pilots joined in and, last of all, the machinist's union accepted the plan.

By this move, the company had compromised with its creditors to defer some of its payments to the future. Furthermore, the company could save $2.5 million to $3 million a month with this program.

Exhibit 6

**Braniff International Corporation
Union Structure**

Union	Employees Covered	Number of Employees Covered	Expiration Date of Contract
Association of Flight Attendants	Flight Attendants	1,870	December 31, 1982
International Brotherhood of Teamsters	Clerical and related employees	4,354	August 1, 1981
International Association of Machinists	Mechanics and related employees	1,735	November 30, 1981
	Maintenance technicians and related employees	96	October 31, 1981
Airline Pilots Association	Pilots	1,447	December 1, 1981
Air Transport Dispatchers Association	Dispatchers	47	May 1, 1990

PERSONNEL CHANGES

Harding Lawrence, chairman of Braniff Airlines, announced his resignation on December 31, 1980. Later, in a press conference, he insisted that Braniff was not in deep financial trouble, and he would be playing a major role in the company in the next three or four years. Lawrence had been the chairman and chief executive for more than 15 years, but had come under increasing pressure for Braniff's string of financial losses over the past several quarters and its staggering debt burden. Opponents blamed Lawrence for Braniff's aggressive growth strategy.

Sources speculated that Mr. Lawrence's sudden departure was dictated in the merger talks with Eastern. Other sources said Mr. Lawrence was forced out by the First National Bank of Dallas, which was said to be heavily involved with Braniff financially.

On January 7, 1981, the company named the former vice chairman John J. Casey, chairman and president, replacing Harding Lawrence. Casey said that his immediate plans for Braniff were to revamp its operating structure and to call for accelerating disposal of surplus equipment. Also, action would be taken to revise service patterns. On the international scene, Braniff planned to increase its 747 nonstop service between Dallas-Ft. Worth and London to a daily operation and eliminate scheduled service to Brussels and Frankfurt.

In mid-September 1981, Braniff named Howard D. Putman to be its new president and chief operating officer. Putman was successful in building Southwest Airlines traffic despite mounting competition; and his experience was expected to augment the momentum Braniff had begun in generating its new marketing strategy. Putnam's experience with Southwest and United Airlines gave him the background Braniff needed in its attempt to return to a profitable operation. His objective was to travel the Braniff system and learn about the employees and the operating techniques.

Additional personnel changes included the following. In May 1980, Edson E. "Ted" Bedwith was promoted to the position of vice president of finance. He was dismissed late in March 1981 and was succeeded by Howard P. Swanson, who had been senior vice president of finance and legal advisor of Georgia-Pacific Corporation's Hudson pulp and paper unit. Before that, he was vice president and treasurer of Trans World Airlines for five years. When Putnam became president, he brought with him Mr. Philip Guthrie. Mr. Guthrie was the chief financial officer of Southwest Airlines; he replaced Swanson in mid-September. Exhibit 7 shows the organization chart for Braniff International Corporation at that time.

MARKETING STRATEGY

In late February 1981, Braniff's strategy for recovery was largely based on restructuring its national and domestic system along regional lines to once again develop traditional feed patterns to its longer-haul routes. Also, Braniff hoped to exploit those areas where it believed it had the competitive edge in order to strengthen its South American operation.

Exhibit 7

Braniff International Corporation
Organizational Chart

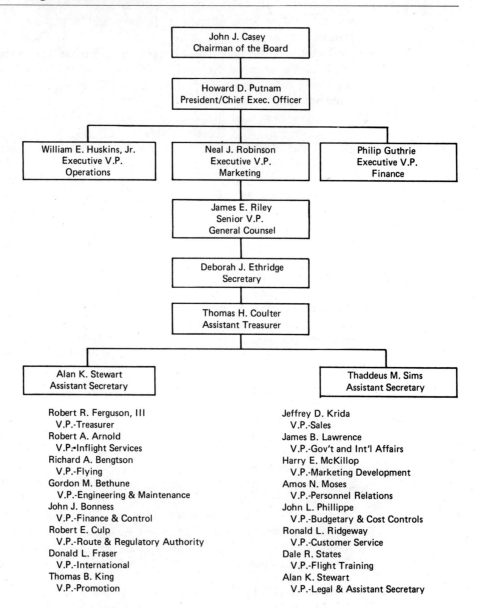

| | John J. Casey |
| Chairman of the Board |

Howard D. Putnam
President/Chief Exec. Officer

William E. Huskins, Jr.
Executive V.P.
Operations

Neal J. Robinson
Executive V.P.
Marketing

Philip Guthrie
Executive V.P.
Finance

James E. Riley
Senior V.P.
General Counsel

Deborah J. Ethridge
Secretary

Thomas H. Coulter
Assistant Treasurer

Alan K. Stewart
Assistant Secretary

Thaddeus M. Sims
Assistant Secretary

Robert R. Ferguson, III
V.P.-Treasurer
Robert A. Arnold
V.P.-Inflight Services
Richard A. Bengtson
V.P.-Flying
Gordon M. Bethune
V.P.-Engineering & Maintenance
John J. Bonness
V.P.-Finance & Control
Robert E. Culp
V.P.-Route & Regulatory Authority
Donald L. Fraser
V.P.-International
Thomas B. King
V.P.-Promotion

Jeffrey D. Krida
V.P.-Sales
James B. Lawrence
V.P.-Gov't and Int'l Affairs
Harry E. McKillop
V.P.-Marketing Development
Amos N. Moses
V.P.-Personnel Relations
John L. Phillippe
V.P.-Budgetary & Cost Controls
Ronald L. Ridgeway
V.P.-Customer Service
Dale R. States
V.P.-Flight Training
Alan K. Stewart
V.P.-Legal & Assistant Secretary

Braniff entered the discount war to build its domestic markets. These had been hard hit by Southwest Airlines and Texas International, as well as other airlines, as they moved in to exploit lucrative sunbelt markets.

Another move on February 21, 1981, was the Good News one-way discount fare of $95 from Dallas-Ft. Worth to Atlanta. On February 28, Braniff also offered a Saturday-Tuesday long weekend, 40 percent discount fare for two adults from Dallas-Ft. Worth to many other cities. Late in August 1981, Braniff introduced another program.

> The program involves eliminating first-class seating, or 12-20 seats, from 33 of its 62 Boeing 727-200's, which will provide a 146-passenger all-coach configuration for those aircraft. Seat pitch of 34-35 inches will be retained. The aircraft can accommodate up to 168 seats with lesser pitch, but Braniff wants to promote seat comfort and other amenities in the all-coach configuration. The one-class aircraft will retain their galleys and offer meals and full beverage service.
>
> Braniff will convert 29 of its 727-200's to 20 first-class and 110 coach seating, and the balance of its 727 fleet, consisting of 17   727-100's, to 12 first-class and 95 coach seating. Nine of its 727-100's have been sold to United Parcel Service, which will be taking delivery of three this month, four next month, and the remainder next February and March.
>
> "The seating changes will result in the airline's adding 240 seats, almost the equivalent of two additional aircraft," a Braniff official said.
>
> The all-coach aircraft will be operated on a two-tier fare structure, with all seats being sold at a 25 percent discount from normal coach fares during off-peak periods, from noon Mondays to noon Wednesdays and all day on Saturdays, and at a 20 percent discount at other times.
>
> The other aircraft, with two classes of seating, will offer a 20 percent fare discount in their coach sections for a limited number of seats if tickets are purchased 14 days in advance. The number of seats will vary, depending on traffic experience in the various schedules.[13]

Braniff also tried to simplify the check-in process by a computer-generated seating chart. The passengers selected their seats, and the agent could forward the seating arrangement to the next station so that personnel there would have details of seats available and their locations.

In September 1981, Braniff gave away free tickets for the media. In announcing its nonstop service between Houston and New York, the airline said it would give two completely free round-trip tickets to any publication, newspaper, radio or television station. Braniff would also offer round-trip tickets from Houston to New York for $278. Free champagne would be furnished to travelers and surprise on-board quiz contests were to be held with round-trip tickets to London as prizes.

In October the company announced its plan to sublease part or all of the building housing its headquarters at Dallas-Ft. Worth Regional Airport and then move the headquarters to Dallas Love Field as a means of further reducing operating costs.

Also in October, Braniff announced that it had begun a new discount fare schedule on its flights from DFW Regional Airport to London and Hawaii. The New "Texas Class" fare would be $300 one way to both London and Hawaii from Dallas-Ft. Worth Regional Airport as opposed to the current fares of $622 for one-way coach to London and $456 for one-way coach to Hawaii. According to Braniff's vice president Sam Coats, the company would also rename the current first class as "World Class" and reduce one-way fare to London from $1,447 to $800 and one-way fare to Hawaii from $657 to $550. The new fares would be effective December 1, 1981. Braniff had daily nonstop Boeing 747 departures to Hawaii and nonstop 747 service four times weekly to London. "We think air fares are too complex," said Putnam. "Braniff is simplifying air fares and eliminating 'small print'."[14] The announcement appeared to mark the final step in Braniff's transformation from a conventional trunk airline into one that resembled a commuter airline. Under the new fare system, regular coach fares would be undercut on similar routes by an average of 45 percent, resulting in an 11 percent decrease in revenue. "Braniff is in a situation where they have to do something to generate customer appeal," said Alfred Norling, an airline analyst. "The new plan certainly looks convenient and simple for the public and for travel agents," he added, "but the question is will Braniff generate enough additional traffic to offset reduced revenue?"[15]

NOTES

1. "United Airlines Flies the Profitable Skies," *Sales and Marketing Management,* January 1979, p. 32.
2. "Cutting Fares is Not the Same as Cutting Your Throat," *Institutional Investor,* May 1978, p. 53.
3. "Braniff's Dizzying Take onto Deregulated Skies," *Fortune,* March 1979, p. 54.
4. See n. 3 above.
5. See n. 3 above.
6. See n. 3 above, p. 53.
7. See n. 3 above, p. 56.
8. See n. 3 above, p. 53.
9. "Sky Wars: The Airlines Enter a New Age," *Dun's Review,* February 1981.
10. See n. 3 above.
11. See n. 3 above.
12. "Rough Weather: Braniff's Cash Shortage is Becoming Desperate," *Wall Street Journal,* July 30, 1980, p. 6.
13. "Braniff Alters Tariffs, Reconfigures Transports," *Aviation Week and Space Technology,* September 7, 1981, p. 36.
14. *Dallas Times Herald,* October 28, 1981.
15. *Wall Street Journal,* November 5, 1981.

POLICY ISSUES IN
HUMAN RESOURCES
MANAGEMENT

The management of the human assets of organizations is often critical to survival. The 1980s have seen even greater concern for "people" interactions and the resulting strategies and policies. The success of firms, such as Hewlett Packard, IBM, Kodak, and others that experts feel are "good places to work," is an indication of attempts to cope with change. Their success is partially attributed to the development of effective management philosophies and policies to make use of human resources.

A basic concern of the successful manager is the integration of the human resources into a system which makes the organization more effective. Organizational effectiveness can mean many things, but most often refers to goal attainment and relates to organizational objectives. Firms must achieve desired results, have the ability to adapt to change, and be able to utilize all resources in the process. The human side of the enterprise is not a separate element, but part of the total system of an organization.

The cases in this section present problems ranging from a very large multinational firm proposing a complete reorganization of a foreign subsidiary to the unique problems of a nonprofit medical facility.

In the *Oilmark Australia Ltd* case a subsidiary of an American oil company is faced with increased local competition, rising prices, and declining profitability. The reaction of the U.S. parent company is to reorganize. The case traces the reorganization process and demonstrates the impact of organization changes on the employees and customers of the firm. Consideration of cultural differences and evaluation of local customs are also potential topics for discussion.

The *Deep Springs Insurance Company* case demonstrates the complexity of developing policies in the human resources area. Managers not only need to know *what* works or doesn't, but *why* a change works or doesn't to develop programs. Management alternatives to increase the chances of success can be explored.

The Corporate Policy case is an example of change implemented without full consideration of employee reactions. Top management felt mobility was important to develop potential managers. Analysis of how such a policy impacts on job performance, group behavior, and the overall manpower planning strategy of the firm are topics for discussion and evaluation.

The *Buena Vista Plant (B)* case concerns a firm experiencing significant technological growth but little growth in the "people" part of the operation. The impact of policies developed prior to expansion is often a significant factor in future growth. The case also offers a chance to consider whether current policies encourage unionization and/or government intervention.

The final case in this section, *Valley Medical Center Laboratories*, a nonprofit organization, offers a different view of organizational growth and policy formulation. Growth and custom have created an organization with two separate but overlapping lines of authority and responsibility. Confusion and conflict are the obvious results in the "gray" areas of decision making. Developing policies which are effective for both administrative and medical functions is also a challenging task for the analyst.

Case 2-1

Oilmark Australia Ltd*

Oilmark Australia Ltd, a subsidiary of an overseas corporation, had been well established in the Australian petroleum market for many years. However, it was faced with increasing competitive pressures, rising costs, and declining profitability. These problems were not unique to the Australian situation. In fact, they had begun to affect the parent company a few years earlier and it had gone through a major reorganization in an attempt to improve its performance. Oilmark Australia was strongly encouraged to follow suit, using the parent organization's approach as a guide and retaining the same consulting firm for assistance.

REORGANIZATION OF THE PARENT COMPANY

Increasing competition, together with the expanding scope and complexity of the petroleum market, had convinced senior management that the maintenance of the corporation's competitive position and continued profitability depended on its ability to serve customers' needs better than rival companies could. Based on an analysis of the market, a consulting firm recommended that a new marketing approach be developed.

The new approach was "customer-oriented" and concentrated on types of customers, in order to learn their requirements and to satisfy these better than competitors were able to do. The analysis showed that customers fell into two main categories: those who use the products themselves and those who resell them to other customers. Within these groups, further differences were identified. Those who purchased and consumed products included transport fleets, industrial concerns, government agencies, marine operators, and aviation enterprises. Customers who resold the products included service-station dealers and rural agents. Agents were either distributors, who purchased products and resold them, or consignment agents, who sold products for Oilmark on a commission basis.

---

*This case was prepared with the intention of providing a basis for class discussion rather than illustrating either effective or ineffective management of a business situation. Reprinted with permission from *Administrative Analysis: Text and Cases*, by John W. Hunt, Gary E. Popp, and Leland V. Entrekin. Sydney: McGraw-Hill Book Company, 1977.

The knowledge and skills necessary for Oilmark people to work effectively in these different marketing fields varied considerably. For example, a sales representative working with service stations needed an understanding of market area analysis, point-of-sale promotion, new business development, and basic bookkeeping. His job was to keep the businesses of his dealers economically viable and to increase sales through his retail outlets. In contrast, the representative who sold direct to industrial and commercial customers required skills in negotiating contracts and a thorough understanding of the industries in which his customers were operating, which often included considerable technical knowledge. Oilmark accepted the recommendation that its marketing division should be organized into departments where these different specialized capabilities could be developed.

The result was a structure based on two departments, Commercial and Resale. Within Resale, the department was further divided into retail sales (service stations), wholesale sales (direct purchase distributors and consignment agents) and a real estate group concerned with the acquisition and development of new sites. The Commercial Department was divided into industrial and transport accounts, with a number of smaller groups dealing with government, aviation, and marine business. This organization structure was implemented at both head office and field levels.

The first objective of the new structure was more effective marketing. However, the company also wanted to become more efficient. It was decided that Oilmark must be streamlined by reducing manpower and obtaining greater output from the personnel who remained in the company.

In effect, two distinct departments—Resale and Commercial—were created, with the manager of each reporting to a General Sales Manager. These arrangements were established at both field and head office levels. More supervisory positions were created in the field because management believed that in the former structure, supervisors had too many sales representatives to control. As a result, in the past, higher-level management had become too involved in detail and did not have enough time to concentrate on longer-range strategy and planning. In the new structure, there would be more supervisors in the field and they would have more authority to make decisions. In order to effect the manpower reductions, work-load studies were carried out and resulted in fewer sales representatives with larger territories to cover.

The next task was implementation of the new organization structure. Meetings were held with senior managers to explain the new structure and were aimed primarily at "protecting employee morale and preventing misinterpretation arising from gossip." To accomplish the same aim on a broader level, a booklet was produced, which explained the new organization in simple terms and indicated what management expected the reorganization to achieve. This was distributed to all Oilmark employees.

Following the initial meetings with senior managers, a task force was formed and given responsibility for bringing the new structure into existence. Its role was to explain the philosophy behind the reorganization and the operation of the new structure, which included developing a timetable for the implementation, ensuring that the best possible appointments were made to positions in the new structure, and achieving the reorganization with the least amount of confusion and interference with current business.

The task force worked with branch managers, who were asked to prepare proposals for restructuring their branches. One branch was selected for a pilot study. The purpose of this was to learn more about operating the structure before putting it into effect on a company-wide basis. The results were reviewed and the task force visited each branch to discuss plans for implementing the new structure. Implementation became the responsibility of each branch manager. Attention then turned to the head office, where meetings were held to explain to staff how their work was to relate to the new field organization.

Up to this point, Oilmark had concentrated on careful planning at top and senior management levels. Now it was necessary to ensure that all the employees in the areas affected by the reorganization understood what the change was meant to accomplish and were committed to making it succeed. This was regarded as a long-term issue, but the initial reactions of employees were vital to future success. In each branch, meetings with sales representatives and supervisors were held. The task force leader listed the objectives of those meetings as:

1. To communicate that the reorganization has been accomplished.
2. To dispel individual uncertainty, lift morale, and enliven *esprit de corps*.
3. To build a determination that the Oilmark group will be highly competitive, will expand, and will prosper.
4. To explain how the new organization will function and who will do what.
5. To establish marketing assignments for the coming year and direct the organization to the first job at hand.
6. To have the sales group go back to the field, confident in their leadership and with an understanding of how to succeed in their jobs.

Letters were sent to branch managers, informing them as to what the basic content and format of the meetings should be. However, they were also encouraged to give their meetings a local flavor to increase the appeal to employees in each branch.

Top management at the Oilmark Corporation were convinced that they had chosen the right direction in which to develop their marketing organization, not only in the parent company but in their overseas subsidiaries as well. Two years later, Oilmark Australia commenced its reorganization.

REORGANIZATION OF OILMARK AUSTRALIA

The objectives of Oilmark Australia's reorganization followed those of the parent company—to improve marketing effectiveness through specialization and to increase efficiency by reducing costs. All the documentation on how the parent company had planned and implemented the reorganization was sent to the Managing Director of Oilmark Australia and he was advised to retain the same consulting firm for assistance.

Prior to the reorganization, Oilmark Australia's marketing activities were decentralized on a geographic basis into branches corresponding to state boundaries. This was also true for credit, accounting and personnel activities (Exhibit 1).

Oilmark Australia Ltd

Exhibit 1 **Marketing Structure before the Reorganization—1972**

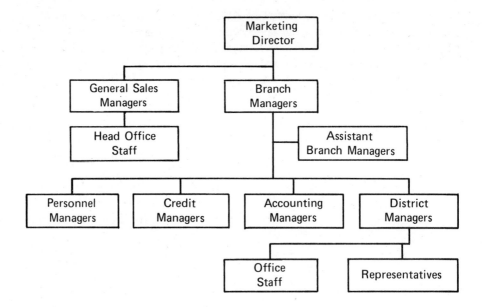

The new organization followed the pattern set by the parent company in dividing the sales department into Resale and Commercial. This was done at both head office and field levels, so that the organization of staff work at head office related clearly to the specialization of the sales force in the field (Exhibit 2). The boundaries of resale branches continued to correspond to those of the States. However, based on work-load studies, the geographical areas of some commercial branches expanded across State boundaries. For example, activities in Victoria and Tasmania were merged into the one branch. Within resale and commercial branches, work-load studies were used also as a basis for reducing the number of sales territories and representatives. At the same time, the number of sales supervisors (area managers) was increased in order to narrow the span of supervision. However, the Australian reorganization went further than that of the parent company, in that nonselling activities were removed from practically every branch and centralized in the head office. Also, prior to

Exhibit 2

Oilmark Australia
Marketing Structure after the Reorganization—1974

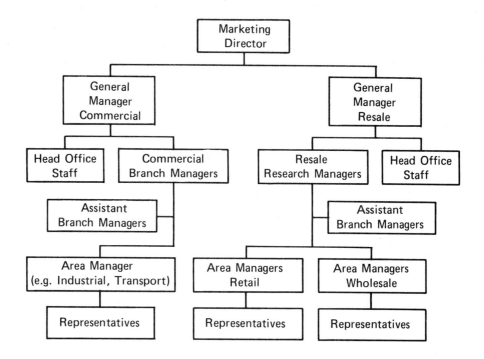

the reorganization, district managers had marketing assistants and office staff. In most cases, after the reorganization, the area managers had neither office staff nor offices. For these managers, now called area managers, their cars were their offices.

The new structure was tested in one resale branch for a period of 18 months, while the rest of the organization carried on as before. Information about the new structure was restricted, because management did not want its competitors to find out. However, some information did leak out to other Oilmark branches. In particular, many employees suspected that there would be fewer jobs in the new organization and began to look for new jobs. As in the parent company, the intention of the pilot study was to get some idea of the effectiveness of the new structure and to experiment with new work-loads for salespeople in the field. At this stage, management decided not to touch the nonselling functions. These were left in the branch. Although management intended to centralize them in the final reorganization, it did not anticipate any difficulties in doing so. For the purpose of the pilot study, it wanted to concentrate on the salespeople, because they were the central target of the change.

When the pilot study period came to an end, the branch manager reported enthusiastically that sales were up, communications were greatly improved and it would be possible to reduce the number of salespeople. The company intended to pay generous preretirement allowances to those employees whom it did not wish to retain. He expressed appreciation that he had been allowed to select his own key personnel to assist in the reorganization, as he was well pleased with their performances. The new structure would work. He said:

> We will cut out the deadwood and the scorers and give Oilmark a lean and hungry look that will scare the hell out of our competitors.

The Managing Director and the Marketing Director, both Australians, were impressed. They had done what the parent company had asked of them and would carry the cost reductions even further. Perhaps, in the future, the parent company would not be so eager to fill the top places in Oilmark Australia with its own people. It had always been a battle in the past for Australians to get on the Board, but things might be different from now on.

EMPLOYEE REACTIONS TO THE REORGANIZATION

At the beginning of the next year, the reorganization was announced to the sales supervisors and representatives. New sales territories were established on the basis of work-load formulas. Representatives generally found that their new territories were larger and they would have new responsibilities apart from selling. Nonsales staff had been moved back to the head office and the representatives were now responsible for preparing their own capital budget proposals, keeping marketing statistics, and initiating credit arrangements for customers.

Although the work loads of the sales representatives had increased, initial reactions generally were favorable. For the past few months, everyone had been worried about keeping his/her job. The unlucky ones got "the golden handshake" and, for the rest, the suspense was over. The new structure looked good. It was cleaner and their marketing proposals would not have to go through so many "post offices" as before. Most of them enjoyed the life of a sales representative and worked hard to get results. They expected that there would be fewer frustrations than before. However, as they began working in the new way, several problems developed. In the light of what management hoped to accomplish by the reorganization, one problem was particularly serious.

The salespeople worked to achieve their sales targets by improving the performance of distributors with whom the company had contacts and by direct efforts to secure new customers. In all dealings, the representative relied heavily on the credit department with respect to any financial transactions that were made. Thus, in order to appoint a new distributor or make alterations to an existing distributorship, approval of the financial arrangements had to come from the area credit officer who reported to a superior in the credit department. This credit officer's decisions could affect customer relations, since he possessed authority to veto or alter terms of payment, including the right to issue instructions that customers whose payments were in arrears must pay cash on delivery. Moreover, although the credit officers usually consulted the relevant representatives before contacting customers, they could contact customers directly, sending copies of the communications to the representatives.

Hence, close cooperation between the representative and the credit officer was essential. The direct and indirect relationships of representatives are shown in Exhibit 3.

Exhibit 3

Oilmark Australia Ltd
Direct and Indirect Relationships of Representatives

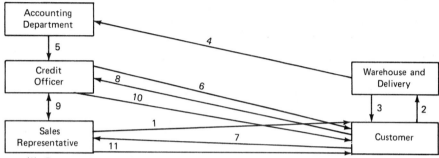

(1) Representative secures business.
(2) Customer places order.
(3) Delivery.
(4) Warehouse sends invoice to accounting department.
(5) Accounting sends details of purchase to credit department.
(6) Credit department sends statement to customer.
(7) If the statement is queried or the customer, for some other reason does not pay his account, he contacts the representative.
(8) In the circumstances outlined in (7), the customer may alternatively contact the credit officer.
(9) Then the credit officer and the representative attempt to resolve the problem.
(10, 11) Both the credit officer and the representative may contact the customer during this process.

The same relationship existed prior to the reorganization, but then the credit officers had been located in the branches. If difficulties arose with respect to an account, the credit officer and the salespeople would get together to sort out the problem. Also, they could spend more time on each problem as the territories and number of customers were smaller for each representative. After the reorganization, distances often prohibited such forms of contact and so written communications had to be used more often. Credit officers began to complain that salespeople were taking too long in attending to problems. The salespeople argued that they did not always have time to get onto credit problems right away. Often, as credit officers began to increase the frequency of direct contacts with customers, the first a salesperson would hear of difficulty was when an irate customer got in touch and threatened to take his or her business elsewhere. Unfortunately, frequently the threats were carried out. The salespeople complained that the credit officers did not understand local conditions and were too rough with customers and distributors. The credit officers would reply that they had little choice in the matter, particularly when they were not getting much cooperation from the salespeople themselves.

About a year later, the company installed a new computer. In June, the old one was returned to the supplier and the new one began operation immediately. On the first run, everything was confused and the information printed out was nonsensical. For three months after that, the company had no accurate idea of the amount it owed to distributors as commission or the amount that was owed by its customers. When the trouble was finally cleared up, the company discovered it was in a tight liquidity position.

Pressure was applied to expedite the collection of payments. The sales and credit people tried to work together to improve the situation. Credit managers visited the branches to discuss collection problems with the salespeople. For a time, relations between the two departments improved. The credit officers showed a sincere desire to understand the problems that were being encountered in the field and the salespeople tried to give prompt attention to credit problems. However, each time a dispute between credit officer and salesperson occurred, it took some time for amicable relations to be restored. As the year drew to a close, salespeople became more concerned with getting orders, while the pressure from credit officers to improve the collection situation became more intense.

One day in December, Ken Johnson, wholesale representative for central Victoria, was sitting in an office at the company depot trying to catch up on his paperwork. Fred Jones, the retail representative in the town, stormed in.

> "Those credit bastards have refused to supply my biggest dealer because he didn't have enough cash to pay for his last delivery! How was the poor bloke supposed to make any money last week while the operations crowd were tearing up his driveway?"

Ken sighed, thinking of his own problems, and wondered:

> How long would it be before they put the boots into old Tom Harris? Tom tried hard, but his agency was going downhill fast. How did the company ever approve his application for an agency? He only had a few hundred dollars when he started. They're keen enough to get these blokes into the business and then make it difficult for them to stay in business. But I suppose the company is right. It has to make a profit.

Ken went back to his paperwork. The telephone rang and as he answered, he heard the following. "What are your Melbourne blokes trying to do to me?", yelled Harris.

> "I dropped 2000 litres of heating oil off at Mr. O'Connor's two weeks ago. Now they say I didn't get his signature and he's queried the amount on the invoice. So I have to pay. He was fifteen kilometres down the paddock when I delivered. If I chase every farmer for a signature I'll never sell anything."

Ken tried to calm Harris down, saying he would put through a long-distance call to Melbourne immediately.

He got through to Mr. Richards in credit.

> "What's all this about sticking Tom Harris with O'Connor's heating oil bill? Tom can't get a customer's signature every time and O'Connor only queried the invoice. He hasn't said he won't pay."

Richards was cool.

Section II   Policy Issues in Human Resources Management

"That's the company policy. We're trying to protect the company's financial position, but we can't do that unless everyone sticks to the rules. If you can't control your agents and customers, then we have to do it from this end."

Later that day, Ken Johnson wrote a letter to the Credit Manager of the company in which he related the events about Harris and O'Connor. The last paragraph began:

"If it is Oilmark Australia's policy to get out of the farm petroleum market, then this is just the perfect way to do it . . . ."

Case 2-2

Deep Springs Insurance Company*

THE PROGRAM

The enrichment project officially began October 1, 1973, and terminated October 1, 1974. The reasons why management turned to this intervention technique are complex, but initially they were attempting to alleviate a number of problems among clerical employees, including lower than desired productivity, high turnover and absenteeism, and generally poor morale. Top management felt certain that job enrichment could solve these problems.

The idea of a job enrichment program germinated early in 1971 when the director of work measurement conducted an on-site inspection of a program among keypunch operators in a competing company. In his report to the senior vice president of administrative services, he indicated that in his opinion the idea of job enrichment based on Herzberg's theory of motivation was not a gimmick and could have application in their own company. Soon after, a search began for a suitable site.

One of the early proponents of job enrichment was the director of the company's Deep Springs office. Orginally he proposed to conduct a program in the home office data input departments and/or Deep Springs keypunch operations. However, in June 1972 he was actively promoting the possibilities of a broader project encompassing all of Deep Springs operations. While top man-

*This case was prepared by Paul J. Champagne, Old Dominion University, with the intention of providing a basis for class discussion rather than illustrating either effective or ineffective management of a business situation. Reprinted with permission from *Application of Decision Sciences in Organizations: A Case Approach* by Joseph C. Latona and K. Mark Weaver with the cooperation of the American Institute for Decision Sciences, Atlanta, Georgia, 1980.

agement gave this proposal serious consideration, by the end of 1972 it was decided that a more limited program should be conducted. To that end, an attitude survey was administered in the spring of 1973 to all Deep Springs clerical employees. The survey was designed to measure employees' attitudes toward ten major aspects of their jobs: (1) advancement; (2) responsibility; (3) work load; (4) job content; (5) salary; (6) supervision; (7) communication; (8) working conditions; (9) training; and (10) management. The results identified three problem areas: job content, responsibility, and communication. It was decided that a job enrichment program would effectively address itself to these issues.

The coding services department was chosen to participate in the program for several reasons. Attitude survey scores from this department were decidedly negative on all three problem areas. Moreover, in coding services, no other major problems were identified through the survey, and there were enough task functions to make enrichment possible. After discussions with local area administrators and the superintendent of the department, a final "go" decision was made.

Early in May 1973, a four-day, off-site workshop was conducted to provide a better understanding of the principles of job enrichment. Participants included all first-line supervisors and their assistants, Deep Springs management, organizational development personnel, and an outside consultant. Upon the recommendation of the consultant, worker participation was rejected on the basis that (1) it was management's prerogative to restructure jobs, (2) it would be awkward for supervisors and subordinates to jointly plan changes in subordinates' jobs, and (3) the expectations of the subordinates might be unrealistic and the actual changes, therefore, disappointing. Workshop members began to apply the principles of Herzberg's motivation-hygiene theory, working out ways of translating responsibility, achievement, recognition and growth into work-related items. During "green lighting" or brainstorming sessions, supervisors contributed ideas for improvement of subordinates' jobs without criticism or comment. During "red lighting" sessions, priority items based on what had to be done first were listed, including possible barriers within management's control and possible steps to overcome them. Subgroups composed of pairs of supervisors and assistant supervisors then selected those items they wished to implement in their units.

At the conclusion of the red lighting and implementation sessions, five items were recommended: (1) coders would take turns handing out work; (2) individual coders would begin requisitioning materials directly from filing units; (3) coders were to become experts in their own areas of responsibility; (4) branch offices would be assigned to coders; and (5) coders would begin reviewing their own error sheets returned by the branch offices. Following the workshop, the supervisory teams met with internal and external consultants every two weeks through the early summer of 1973 to plan the implementation.

Early on, the problem of possible loss of earnings under the company's existing wage incentive plan was discussed by management. Under wage incentive, every job was studied, using time and motion techniques, to determine efficient work cycle times. When an employee produced at a rate equal to 70 percent of maximum possible efficiency, a bonus was added to her base salary. For some this amounted to $40 or more per week.

The basic problem was that enrichment training time would not count toward the weekly bonus. Therefore, employees participating in a job enrichment program involving extensive retraining would be penalized. A number of possible solutions were suggested, including dropping the wage incentive and increasing base salary. It was finally decided to deal with the problem by: (1) lengthening the overall training time to minimize time off measurement, and (2) giving participating employees a bonus equal to the amount lost under the wage incentive during training. Each trainee was compensated for the time off measurement with a single payment of $20 to $40. While this amount was small, it was sufficient to induce 55 percent of the coding services employees to participate in the program. Until this solution was proposed, only 28 percent of the eligible employees had volunteered for the program.

Once retraining was completed, jobs were retimed so that each participating employee's weekly wage incentive bonus would remain at about the same level as it had been prior to retraining. No attempt was made to reclassify the "larger" jobs, (i.e., increase the weekly base pay) since management did not perceive the issue of money as a possible source of trouble.

Most job enrichment programs involve some anticipated changes in the job time cycle; not so here. Under enrichment, coders were expected to handle an entire unit of work, including correction of errors, but no change was made in the wage incentive time standards. For example, if an auto-liability coder performed all the 44 separate tasks required on one unit of work, the time standard for 100 percent efficiency was 33.42 minutes. During the enrichment program this did not change; 100 percent efficiency was still 33.42 minutes. The only difference was that participating coders were required to know and (if necessary) perform each and every task in a unit of work, while nonparticipating coders were not. Participating coders were also accountable for errors made by the branch office or keypunch. If an error was detected in in-coming work, the coders would contact the branch office by telephone, teletype, or memo. When an error was detected by the company computer, the coder was expected to pull the file, reconcile the error, and see that it was processed correctly by the keypunch operators. All of this took time and required that the coders work harder and faster than before in order to stay within the wage incentive time standards.

On October 1, 1973, the program was officially launched using the training schedule devised during the workshop. Membership was strictly voluntary, but everyone was encouraged to participate. The program was presented by management as a method for increasing employee interest and job satisfaction. All those who participated in the program were female high school graduates (average age, 22).

Coding services was composed of three basic units: special multiperil, loss, and auto liability, with each responsible for coding premium or loss evidence on all types of casualty insurance; i.e., marine, fire, auto, personal liability, and so forth. The information coded related to the billing, accounting, and statistical experience of the branch offices. This information was then forwarded to the keypunch department for input into the company's computer system.

Prior to job enrichment, work was distributed to individuals without regard to the branch office that initiated it. Under the program, task modules were established—providing complexity, completeness, discretion, and feedback for a unit of work. After employees had been retrained, all work forwarded from branch offices was assigned to specific individuals, requiring them to perform all tasks and functions necessary to process the work. This created continuing individual accountability for a whole unit of work and clearly associated individual workers with particular branch offices.

At about the same time that job enrichment was getting under way, a number of other changes were being implemented which affected the entire Deep Springs staff. Late in 1973 and early 1974, a number of steps were taken in an effort to deal with a variety of other problems identified by the 1973 attitude survey. For example, carpeting was installed, employees were given better explanations of the company bonus plan, job classifications in a number of departments were revised, improved vending machines were installed in the lunchrooms, restroom facilities were improved, open posting of jobs was begun, greater effort was made to open communication channels between supervisors and subordinates, and a modified flexitime program was instituted. Since management was attempting to deal with several pervasive problems, no incongruity was seen between these changes and the ongoing job enrichment program.

By the early part of 1974, 41 out of 75 eligible employees had opted for and were performing enriched jobs. In March 1974, a follow-up attitude survey was conducted focusing on the same issues as its predecessor. To management's surprise and dismay, there was little or no change in employee attitudes. Responsibility, job content, and communication were still reacted to negatively. The results were particularly disappointing in coding services, in view of the ongoing job enrichment program. Management had expected that enrichment would improve employee attitudes, and when it did not, faith began to wane in its ability to produce the desired outcomes.

The final evaluation at the end of one year's operation of the program indicated some reduction in turnover and absenteeism. The productivity figures were less conclusive, however. While the situation in coding services had improved, the rest of the Deep Springs staff showed even greater gains. Based on these findings, management labeled the program a failure and decided to discontinue all job enrichment activity. The results of the program were not sufficiently impressive to justify to management the cost of job enrichment.

Even though plans for future programs in other areas of the company were shelved, branch coders were allowed to choose whether or not to retain the enriched jobs. The attrition in the program as a result of these choices is indicated in Exhibit 1. Among the three units, special multiperil chose as a group to continue under the program; in auto liability and loss, only 4 employees out of 28 chose to remain in the program and were still in it as of January 1976.

Exhibit 1

Deep Springs Insurance Company
Employees Who Opted to Retain Enriched Jobs
after Completion of the Trial Program

Unit	Number eligible for program	Number opting for and participating in program	Number opting to remain in program 3 months after end of program	Number opting to remain in program 1 year and 3 months after end of program	Percent remaining in program 1 year and 3 months after end of program
Auto-Liability Coding	31	23	9	3	13%
Loss Coding	31	5	2	1	20%
Special Multiperil[1] Coding	13	13	13	13	100%
Total	75	41	24	17[2]	41%

[1] Special multiperil coders decided as a group to retain enriched jobs.

[2] The attrition from the program was not the result of turnover; two employees initially in the program quit the company in the spring of 1975, while two others quit in the spring of 1976. All had opted not to retain the enriched jobs before quitting.

THE RESULTS OF JOB ENRICHMENT

Absenteeism

During the program, absenteeism among participating employees showed marked improvement, as shown in Exhibit 2.

From October 1, 1974, average absenteeism in the enriched group dropped 2.2 days per year, while among nonparticipating personnel it increased 2.9 days. During this same period, the overall Deep Springs staff also experienced some improvement, but only .6 of a day.

According to the three unit supervisors in coding services, job enrichment had its most noticeable impact on absenteeism. When an enriched employee was absent for any period of time, her work was distributed to other members of the unit. This had an impact on the absent employee since errors made by someone else could interfere with the ongoing relationship established between the coder and her branch offices. Errors or delays, though made by someone else, were nevertheless the responsibility of the employee assigned to the branch. Rather than have to deal with problems created by others, employees apparently made a greater effort to be present.

Turnover

It can be seen in Exhibit 3 that turnover among participating employees was also reduced. Turnover in the enriched group was reduced by 50 percent

Exhibit 2

Deep Springs Insurance Company
Annual Absenteeism[1]

Coding Services	October 1, 1972 through October 1, 1973 (before enrichment)	October 1, 1973 through October 1, 1974 (during enrichment)
Enriched Job Participants (n=41)	5.6	3.4
Nonenriched Job Participants (n=34)	7.0	9.9
Deep Springs Clerical Staff (Exclusive of Coding Services) (n=400)	7.8	7.2

[1]The average number of days absent per employee: the total number of absences in a year among the employees in a department divided by the average number of employees in that department.

Exhibit 3

Deep Springs Insurance Company
Annual Turnover[1]

Coding Services	October 1, 1972 through October 1, 1973 (before enrichment)	October 1, 1973 through October 1, 1974 (during enrichment)
Enriched Job Participants (n=41)	72.4%	32.6%
Nonenriched Job Participants (n=34)	72.4%	43.1%
Deep Springs Clerical Staff (Exclusive of Coding Services) (n=400)	67.1%	29.6%

[1]The percentage of employee turnover per year: the total number of quits in a year divided by the total number of employees in the appropriate units.

from the previous year. In addition, among employees on enriched tasks, turnover was 10 percent less than among other personnel in coding services. However, this gain was overshadowed by the overall improvement in the Deep Springs office where turnover was 3 percent less than among the enriched group. To management, it appeared that better results had been obtained without job enrichment.

Even though absenteeism had improved dramatically, turnover made a stronger impression on management. It was apparently viewed as much more important in terms of the company's operations.

Productivity

Management expected job enrichment to have a dramatic impact on productivity, but as Exhibit 4 indicates, the results of the program were inconclusive. Productivity through the third quarter of 1974 among enriched employees was 14.8 percent higher than the nonenriched group, but the overall trend in coding services was downward. From January 1, 1974, through October 1, 1974, productivity in the enriched group had dropped 2 percent (97.3 to 95.3). During the fourth quarter of 1974 this trend was reversed slightly. The enriched group increased to 97.5 percent by the end of 1974. During the first three quarters of 1974 productivity among the nonenriched employees declined from 88 percent to 81.1 percent, a drop of approximately 7 percent, and the fourth quarter of 1974 had been almost stable.

Even though the overall experience of the enriched group was better than that of the nonenriched employees in coding services, the lack of a clear trend was disturbing to management. It was particularly so in comparison with the rest of the Deep Springs staff where productivity through the third quarter of 1974 had been almost stable.

When third quarter productivity for enriched employees was examined by unit, only special multiperil coding showed any improvement. Loss coding was down slightly as was auto-liability coding. Even though productivity among nonenriched employees in loss and auto liability was also down, this offered management little solace. The productivity trends further reinforced management's growing skepticism about the utility of job enrichment.

Exit Interviews

Shortly after the formal end of the program on October 1, 1974, company organizational development personnel conducted interviews with 28 employees selected at random from among those involved in job enrichment. The results appear in Exhibit 5, which show that 82 percent of those interviewed felt the enriched tasks to be more interesting, but a large majority (79 percent) also felt participants should be paid more. Bonus making ability during enrichment was a major problem for 71 percent of these employees.

While these data reveal the basic problem encountered by management, comments made by the employees interviewed indicated even more forcefully

Exhibit 4

Deep Springs Insurance Company
Productive Efficiency in 1974 by Unit[1]

Unit		1st Quarter 1974	2nd Quarter 1974	3rd Quarter 1974	4th Quarter 1974
Loss Coding	Enriched (n=5)	94.8%	89.8%	94.0%	100.8%
	Nonenriched (n=26-28)	98.8	90.0	92.5	89.0
Auto-Liability Coding	Enriched (n=23-24)	97.7	97.0	91.7	94.0
	Nonenriched (n=7-8)	95.8	86.8	69.7	73.6
Special Multiperil Coding	Enriched (n=13-18)	99.4	95.5	100.1	97.8
	Nonenriched (n=0)	—	—	—	—
Total Coding Services	Enriched (n=41-48)	97.3	94.1	95.3	97.5
	Nonenriched (n=33-34)	88.0	88.5	81.1	80.0
Total Deep Springs Clerical Staff (Exclusive of Coding Services) (n=400)		94.0	96.0	93.0	unknown[2]

[1]Productivity was measured by how effectively a unit of employees utilized its time: the unit's average efficiency (i.e., how much work it processed in a given period of time) multiplied by the average percentage of time on measurement (i.e., the amount of time the employees engaged in measured work. This excludes lunch breaks, rest breaks, training time, etc.).

[2]The utilization for the fourth quarter of 1974 was not computed for the total Deep Springs clerical staff by the company.

the primary reason for their continuing discontent. The one item of greatest concern to the coders performing enriched tasks was the problem of lost bonus money during the program.

Comments such as the following were common:

"I like the idea of branch coding, but thank goodness I don't depend on the bonus money."

"I like branch coding, but because you get such a variety of work, it is very hard to make your efficiency. I think the rates (basic job classification) should be raised."

Exhibit 5

Deep Springs Insurance Company
Follow-up Interviews with Randomly Selected
Participants in the Enrichment Program[1]

Response	Percentage Agreeing (Total n = 28)
1. The job was more interesting and enjoyable.	82
2. Should be paid more.	79
a. Job classification should be raised.	29
b. Bonus making ability was a major problem.	71
c. The job should be retimed.	54

[1]Content analysis of interviews with 28 of the 59 participants in job enrichment.
Source: Interviews conducted by home office organizational development personnel.

"I don't like branch coding, because without my bonus money my base pay is nothing. I find myself becoming very disgusted and not even caring about my work. You work harder now and have nothing to show for it."

"I like branch coding because of the variety of work, but I find I have nowhere near the efficiency I used to. If someone offered me a job that paid about the same as my base pay right now, I'd take it. Before, I never would because of my greater bonus money. But now, I'd jump at the chance."

"I like branch coding because I like the variety of work . . . (but) I also think we do a lot of work for our pay—I mean, I really work harder now than I did when I was a regular coder."

Within the individual units, employee reaction to job enrichment was much the same. For example, special multiperil branch coders felt the training was good, but the training payment was too low to adequately compensate for lost bonus earnings.

In response to "How do you feel about the changes?" all four people interviewed in special multiperil coding responded that they were generally more satisfied with the enriched job. They liked having responsibility for particular clients. Most (3 of 4) felt they had more control over the work. All mentioned the increased task variety of the enriched job as a favorable feature. Their major gripes centered around the loss of bonus money which accompanied job redesign. They felt they should be paid a higher base salary since it was definitely harder to earn the same bonus on the new job.

Auto-liability branch coders felt that their training payments had been inadequate when compared to the bonus they could have made on the old job during the same time period. Four of the coders interviewed in this unit were making significantly less bonus money than they had on the old job. The problem was not due to the intrusion of extra jobs into their work by the supervisors, but rather was seen as the need for adequate retiming of work standards to allow for the numerous new tasks involved. As one of the employees put it,

"They [management] didn't look at the whole picture before putting it in [job enrichment]." Or as another stated, "It's more mental work for less money."

The comments from loss coding were much the same. One coder, for example, said that her bonus had slipped from aproximately $40 to $13 per week. This eventually caused her to drop out of the program since, as she put it, "I'm working here for money."

Conclusions and Recommendations

Of all the data gathered during this program, the exit interviews are the most revealing. They point out dramatically the basic problem encountered by management in implementing job enrichment. While many of the coders liked the new tasks, most simply felt that they were not being paid in proportion to their increased duties.

The need to institute new pay practices would seem to be one of the basic requirements for successful job enrichment (Lawler, 1977). Organizations are complex, interrelated systems. If changes are made in the nature of tasks, then changes are required in other areas also. Unfortunately, Deep Springs management made no attempt to do so. They did not compensate for increased responsibilities by providing larger paychecks.

Interestingly enough, the unit supervisors in special multiperil, loss, and auto-liability coding were aware of a problem with pay early in the program. As the supervisor of loss coding put it, "People who depended on the weekly bonus just did not want to retrain. Those who went into the program right away were the people who did not need the few extra bucks a week." Top management, while they made an effort to provide for lost bonus earnings during retraining, failed to consider a long-term solution to these kinds of concerns. Providing pay was not reduced, they were convinced that the greater interest of enriched work would be reward enough.

NOTES

1. Robert N. Ford, *Motivation Through the Work Itself* (New York: American Management Association, Inc., 1969).

2. Frederick Herzberg, *Work and the Nature of Man* (Cleveland: World Publishing Company, 1966).

3. Carl D. Jacobs, "Job Enrichment of Field Technical Representatives—Xerox Corporation," *The Quality of Working Life*, eds. Louis E. Davis and Albert S. Cherns (New York: The Free Press, 1975).

4. Robert Janson, "A Job Enrichment Trial in Data Processing—in an Insurance Company," *The Quality of Working Life*, eds. Louis E. Davis and Albert S. Cherns (New York: The Free Press, 1975).

5. Edward E. Lawler III, "New Approaches to Pay Administration," *Perspectives on Behavior in Organizations*, eds. J. Richard Hackman, Edward E. Lawler III, and Lyman W. Porter (New York: McGraw-Hill Book Company, 1977).

6. Abraham Maslow, *Motivation and Personality* (New York: Harper, 1954).

7. Earl D. Weed, "Job Enrichment: Cleaning up at Texas Instruments," *New Perspectives in Job Enrichment*, ed. John H. Maher (New York: Van Nostrand Reinhold Company, 1971).

Case 2-3

The Corporate Policy*

Sands Manufacturing Company, a 50-year-old company, had grown from a small manufacturing concern to a leader in its industry with a complete line of material handling equipment. Over the years some engineers had become product experts of unquestioned caliber. The company found, however, that these experts were not able to easily adapt when transferred to new job situations. This had hurt Sands because of the tremendous growth and resulting need for older, experienced engineers to assume supervisory roles in new product areas. To give these personnel a broader background and experience in new job situations, the vice president of engineering had instituted a policy to encourage engineering personnel to be more mobile within the company's various branches of engineering.

John Turner, three years out of college, had been working as a design engineer under Lawrence Conner, supervisor of new products in the product design division. John had done moderately well, but really didn't enjoy design work as much as he thought he would. Instead, he felt he would prefer to "get his hands dirty" in one of the test division labs.

Don Sutter, a project engineer in the test division, had been in the same department since his graduation from college 12 years ago. He had worked his way up from test engineer to his present position and was next in line for promotion to supervisor. The current supervisors, however, did not show any sign of either moving to another area or being promoted to another job. For this reason, Don saw his chance of being promoted to supervisor in his department as very limited. Don felt he should take advantage of the new policy encouraging mobility so he had requested a transfer to a design area.

The request was given considerable attention, and a trade was negotiated between the managers of the test division and the product design division. Don was assigned to work for Lawrence Conner in the new products group. John Turner, formerly a design engineer, was assigned to work as a test engineer in the test division (Exhibits 1, 2, and 3).

John began work in his new capacity and in a few months was quite satisfied with the move. Don, on the other hand, encountered some problems which he hadn't anticipated. Don's new supervisor, Lawrence Conner, was less than happy with the trade since he had spent nearly three years developing

---

*This case was prepared by John T. Wholihan and K. Mark Weaver, University of Alabama, with the intention of providing a basis for class discussion rather than illustrating either effective or ineffective management of a business situation.

133

John Turner as a design engineer. He felt he had gained a highly paid project engineer who had no design experience or knowledge of the design process. Don also felt that his co-workers were not pleased to see another project engineer added to the group.

Lee James, a project engineer himself, felt that he would be the next candidate for promotion to supervisor within the design division. Will Round, senior design engineer, felt that he would soon be promoted to project engineer. After the trade, he felt that this would not occur since there were two project engineers in the group. Both Lee and Will saw Don as a threat to their anticipated promotions and privately vowed to give Don as little help as possible. The other design engineers and drafters also realized Don's design background was limited. They were not anxious to have to work with a weak project engineer and casually let it be known.

Lawrence, not knowing how else to use Don, assigned him to "concept" a new material handling product modeled after one currently on the market. This included contacting the company's marketing and manufacturing groups to solicit their input, doing an extensive review of advertisements and sales brochures of the products currently on the market, and traveling extensively to talk with potential customers. (Contact within the design department was minimal during the concept phase of a design.)

After nearly a year, Don concluded that the new product had great potential and reported this to his supervisor, Mr. Conner. The marketing and manufacturing groups delivered similar reports to their respective divisions and the company product committee decided that a prototype machine should be built.

At this point, Conner would normally assign the project engineer who had worked on the original concept to lead the prototype design effort. In this case, however, he decided that Don really wouldn't be able to handle it. Instead, he assigned Lee James as the project engineer to lead the prototype design effort with Don reporting directly to Lee. Lee, not wanting the project to be slowed down, assigned a menial job to Don and proportioned the rest of the work to the others in the group.

In the following months Don found it harder and harder to accept his situation. He was responsible for an insignificant part of a project which he had originally conceived. Lee never made time to listen to Don's suggestions regarding the overall development of the project. Will Round, the senior design engineer, not only kept back information from Don, but went out of his way to make Don's job more difficult and to discredit Don's design efforts. The design engineers and drafters didn't make things easy for Don.

After two years in the design division, Don felt completely out of place and defeated. He did not receive any cooperation from the rest of the group, only an occasional joke about the quality of his work. He felt he had learned practically nothing as a designer and was frustrated in his attempts to participate as a project engineer. At the same time he saw the test division, where he was once highly regarded, being rearranged and felt that he lost any chance of returning to his former position. Don was confused and wondered why the company approved the transfer.

Exhibit 1

Sands Manufacturing Company
Job Definition, Responsibility, and Relationships

Engineering supervisor: Had first level line responsibility in the engineering department. Reported to general supervisor.

Project engineer: Had responsibility to set up and direct work on engineering projects. No line responsibility. Reported to the engineering supervisor.

Senior design engineer: Had responsibility for major portions of projects. Provided technical assistance to younger engineers. Reported to the engineering supervisor.

Design engineer or *test engineer:* Had responsibility for specific parts or components of a design or for specific tests. Reported to the engineering supervisor.

Drafter or *Technician:* Had responsibility to assist design or test engineers. Reported to the engineering supervisor.

Exhibit 2

Sands Manufacturing Company
Organization Chart for Engineering Department,
Design Division Personnel, and New Products Department

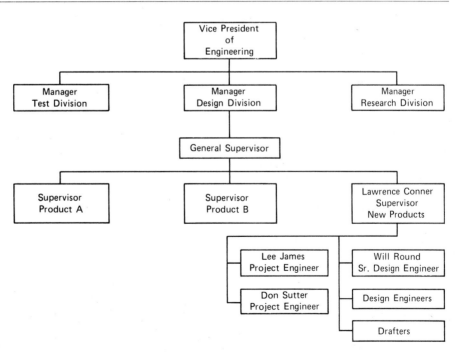

Exhibit 3

Sands Manufacturing Company
Key People in the Case

Lawrence Conner: Supervisor; 55-year-old man; started in the shop at the age of 16; somewhat a Theory X type supervisor; had little chance for advancement himself.

Lee James: Project engineer; 37 years old, worked his way up from drafter; distrustful of college graduates and seldom gave help to anyone.

Don Sutter: Project engineer; 34 years old; college graduate; an upward mobile; had experience in test division only.

Will Round: Senior design engineer; 38 years old; got his degree at night school; rapidly became aware of diminishing chances for promotion.

John Turner: Design engineer; 25 years old; college graduate; worked in design department three years and would have liked a chance at test work.

Case 2-4

Buena Vista Plant*

The Buena Vista Plant had come a long way since the recession of the 1970s. Since Forest Park Corporation's takeover in 1976, the plant had been a beehive of activity. Over the past five-year period the plant's capacity had doubled, production processes had been automated, and the labor force increased to 2,200 workers. The textile plant was one of the largest employers in Plains, Georgia.

The plant's profit picture had improved dramatically since Forest Park acquired the plant. The parent company poured a significant portion of its available resources into the small plant. No longer were foreign and domestic competitors outperforming it. The firm not only maintained its market share but was beginning to increase its market share of the United States textile market.

THE PERSONNEL DEPARTMENT

The personnel department at Buena Vista was quite small. Although the work force it served had increased dramatically, only three people handled all personnel matters. The last person to join the department, John Turner, did so in 1978. As the newest member of the department, John was the most knowledgeable about government regulations, laws, and court cases that impacted personnel activities. Because John was relatively new to the department he had little influence on Al Logan, the personnel director. Al also seemed threatened by the fact that John was completing requirements for a degree in business administration. Much of what John knew about personnel administration was learned in classes at North Carolina A. & T. State University. He had transferred into the personnel office from an assembly-line job in the plant.

Cheryl Giffhorn was, in Al's eyes, the most valuable person in the personnel department. Over the past 14 years she had been his eyes, ears, and right hand "man." As a friend and confidante, she had been absolutely indispensable. Her formal title was that of secretary, but she worked as a personnel paraprofessional. Cheryl had responsibility for prescreening nonexempt and

---

*This case was prepared by George E. Stevens, University of Central Florida, with the intention of providing a basis for class discussion rather than illustrating either effective or ineffective management of a business situation.

hourly applicants, testing, and record keeping related to staffing and employee health. She was deeply involved in preparing a report on the incidence of brown-lung disease (byssinosis), chronic bronchitis, and emphysema; diseases all attributable to exposure to cotton dust. (These diseases were not a problem at the plant but the reports were required by OSHA.)

Al Logan came to the plant in 1957, after studying at Georgia State University and Columbus College. When Al joined the company there was no personnel department. He began his career as a production supervisor. By 1959, the plant employed 250 full-time workers. The plant manager, Angelo Dennis, hand picked Al for the job of personnel director. In the early years, his job as personnel director was easy. He liked working with people. Al saw his job as one of keeping things running smoothly, helping with morale, and solving employee problems. He liked getting out on the shop floor where the people were. Al also liked being chairman of the United Fund drive, a Rotarian, and member of the Chamber of Commerce.

Recently, he found little time for the civic activities that he liked. Each year, like clockwork, he found himself beating back attempts by the Amalgamated Clothing and Textile Workers and other unions to organize the workers. The task was getting harder and more time consuming each year. Recently, Al talked to a consultant who wanted to be paid for telling *him* how to keep unions out. According to Al, his biggest problem was government interference. Every personnel activity seemed to involve some law or government regulation. He knew that he needed to keep up with these new laws on health and safety, equal employment opportunity, pensions, compensation, and labor relations. His duties as personnel director of a larger work force seemed to leave him little time to keep up with recent amendments and court decisions.

One duty that had bugged him the most was his role in grievance procedures. Employees complained about not having any assurance that they would be treated fairly, so a grievance procedure was developed by a committee representing employees at all company levels. The procedure seemed like a good idea at first because it eliminated a complaint workers had and it took away one union bargaining advantage. The problem was that more grievances were being filed and more grievances were going beyond the first and second steps. Grievances at the higher levels required Al's involvement and he resented having to waste his time listening to complaints about wage discrimination, subjective performance evaluations, and being passed over for promotions. A couple of these people had filed complaints with the Equal Employment Opportunity Commission (EEOC) and the Department of Labor.

THE NEW ADDITIONS

In January of 1981, two new lines were opened in the personnel department. Al had authorization to add two new members to the department—one as an assistant personnel director and a second as a personnel assistant. Both jobs were for college educated, trained professionals. Shortly after receipt of the job requisitions a list of internal candidates arrived from headquarters. After examining the list (which included the name of John Turner), Al agreed to examine the records of five candidates for each job. By February he had interviewed the top three candidates. Logan selected Cathie Stango as the new assistant personnel director and Bill Benjamin became the new personnel assistant (Exhibit 1). The heir apparent to the job, John Turner, was not too pleased with Bob's first selection.

Exhibit 1

Buena Vista Plant
Organization Chart for Personnel Department

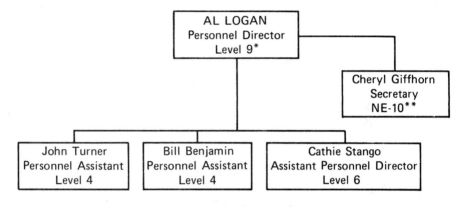

*Level cited here is for exempt job classifications.
**NE cited here is for nonexempt positions.

Cathie Stango had impressive credentials; she had a bachelor's degree from Delaware State College and a MBA from Golden Gate University. She had held a number of personnel positions during her six years with the company. Among her experiences were assignments as assistant personnel director at the Spring Garden Research Facility, undertakings in training, recruiting, and working with the personnel in the EEOC office at headquarters, as well as assignments at the Bristol, Tennessee, and Lexington, Kentucky, plants. Her performance, in all cases, was rated "excellent." Bill Benjamin, the new personnel assistant, had only been with the company two years. He majored in personnel administration at the University of Georgia. He spent his first year in the labor relations department assisting others with collective bargaining. In his second year he worked in the wage and salary department and took on special assignments for the director of employee relations. This was his first plant assignment.

THE TROUBLE WITH CATHIE

It didn't take long for Al to realize that Cathie would be a problem. After only three months on the job, she started causing problems. She was a "know-it-all." Every personnel policy was illegal. Or, she disagreed with it. Al had to stop her from trying to change everything he'd ever written. Cathie fought him about the need to validate the assessment center. She claimed there was adverse impact on blacks. Cathie fought about company policy concerning pregnant women quitting without pay at the end of their second trimester. And, she demanded that the disability policy be written so that pregnancy could be treated the same as any other disability. Well, Al had had enough. They were going to meet and have it out.

THE MEETING

"Mr. Logan? You wanted to talk to me. . . "

"Yes, Cathie, come in and sit down. This conversation is just between us. What I have on my mind needs being said."

"That sounds ominous, what is this all about?"

"Cathie, you have challenged our policies, disagreed with me on the handling of certain grievances, and, in general, made a nuisance of yourself. What you are doing borders on insubordination, and I called you in to verbally reprimand you for your action."

"I am sorry you feel that way, Mr. Logan. My intent was to help you and to help the department. Some of our policies were written ten or more years ago. As John suggested to you, some may not be consistent with current regulations, court decisions, and agency guidelines. For example, the plant policy on disability treats pregnancy differently than it treats other disabilities. In addition, policy here requires pregnant women, regardless of their health or nature of their job, to accept a leave of absence at the end of their second trimester. I don't believe that this policy treats women fairly."

"Cathie, do you know whether the policy is *legal?* If you know about anything that makes the policy illegal then I will make a change, otherwise back off."

"The legality of the policy is questionable at best, although I can't cite a specific regulation or law. But let me mention another problem area. I applaud your development of the textile supervisor assessment center, but my data on selection rates indicates a problem. While 70 percent of the whites participating in the assessment center are picked for promotion, only 52 percent of the black assessees are chosen. I think the EEOC and other agencies would question this difference. Plus, we have not done a validation study."

"You have the answer for everything, Cathie. Actually, I hear you challenging a lot of things, but I don't see anything supporting your position. As for the EEOC, when their representatives schedule a compliance review, then I'll do what they want—within reason. Now, since you have an answer for everything else, what do you think of our decision to fire Jeffrey Clement for moonlighting?"

"To be honest, Mr. Logan, I think you are making a big mistake. I believe there is precedent for firing an employee for holding two full-time jobs. Typically, the employee must make a choice. After reading the supervisor's report, however, I am concerned that the supervisor *thinks* Jeffrey is working two jobs. The supervisor has no proof, and the subordinate refuses to incriminate himself. I don't think we can force the guy, under the threat of discharge, to admit this rule violation."

"Cathie, I think we have a difference of opinion over these policies. Maybe I am too close to them since I had to create them; but I want you to bring me something definitive—court cases, regulations, laws, and so forth—rather than disagreeing openly with me. I have not kept up and I know it. If you show me why change is needed, we'll make the change."

"Okay. Right or wrong, I have charged full speed without documentation or evidence to support my position. All through school and most of my previous jobs I have been pretty independent. I'll work harder at being a better team player."

"Well, Cathie, it's just about time for a shift change. Let's see if we can get to the pop machine before the mad rush makes that impossible. Treat is on the big spender. And, by the way, please call me Al."

Case 2–5

Valley Medical Center Laboratories*

Valley Medical Center (VMC) was a nonprofit organization founded in 1971 with the merger of General Hospital and the Sisters of Mercy Hospital. Valley Medical was an acute, chronic and mental care facility located within the city limits of a medium-sized city. Government regulations limiting the number of beds in a given population had necessitated the merger with another private hospital across town. This merger would decrease the number of hospital beds within the community, and would provide the facilities for a proposed toxicology clinic.

Valley Medical Center Laboratories was an ancillary service of Valley Medical and was located on the third floor of the hospital. The laboratory was a modern, well-equipped department with an annual budget of 3.5 million dollars.

Laboratory services for VMC started with Dr. Brown in 1938. At that time, Mercy and General Hospitals contracted the services of his lab and himself as the resident pathologist. In the years that followed, the laboratory grew in pace with the hospitals and community until Dr. Brown's death in 1959. In 1960 Dr. Smith took over as director of laboratories at Mercy Hospital, and Dr. Williams assumed an equal role at General Hospital. At the time of the merger the laboratories became a department of VMC and were treated as one department even though they were in separate buildings.

ORGANIZATION AND SERVICES OF VMC

At the time of the merger Dr. Davids assumed the role of director of laboratories at Valley Medical Center. He and Dr. Williams formed a corporation as equal partners and contracted their services to VMC. In 1972 the corporation retained the services of Dr. Gates to help reduce the expanding work load and in 1978 made him a full partner. Dr. Davids retained the directorship of the laboratories and delegated the control of some work sections to his colleagues.

Since 1972 the complexity of the laboratory management had grown immensely. Mr. Barry McDonald was appointed laboratory manager in 1971 when the merger occurred, and had since added a staff of seven others to man-

*This case was prepared by Jayanta K. Bandyopadhyay and Richard T. Tarskey, Central Michigan University, with the intention of providing a basis for class discussion rather than illustrating either effective or ineffective management of a business situation.

Exhibit 1

Valley Medical Center Laboratories
Laboratory Administration

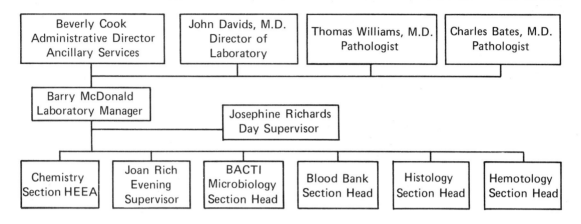

age particular sections (Exhibit 1). Laboratory administration, the policy-making board of the laboratory, included the three pathologists, Barry McDonald, the first shift supervisor, the second shift supervisor, and the five section heads. This group was responsible for the entire operation of the lab, both technical and administrative.

The laboratory had a complex organizational system, somewhat in the form of a matrix (Exhibit 2). Two separate but not so distinct lines of authority existed. The first was medical; anything that concerned the medical welfare of the patient was under the direct control of the pathologist. The other was operations or business and came under the direct control of the laboratory manager.

In the medical aspect, the corporation of Davids, Williams, and Bates had been contracted by the hospital to control the medical areas of the lab. According to Barry McDonald, this was the gray area that created the majority of conflicts for lab operations. According to Dr. Davids, "The medical concern of the patient includes:

  1. type of test used for each request;
  2. accuracy of the test;
  3. precision of the test;
  4. instrumentation used in the performance of the test;
  5. cost of the test;
  6. availability of the test on a routine or emergency basis;

and anything in between." Mr. McDonald stated that this was not the entire story. He felt that he was hampered by all three pathologists making special demands. He stated, "All three have to have their fingers in the pie, and they each want a different kind, that's the problem."

According to the organization chart, Dr. Davids had control of the chemistry and microbiology sections of the lab. Dr. Williams had control of hematol-

Exhibit 2

Valley Medical Center Laboratories
Organizational Chart

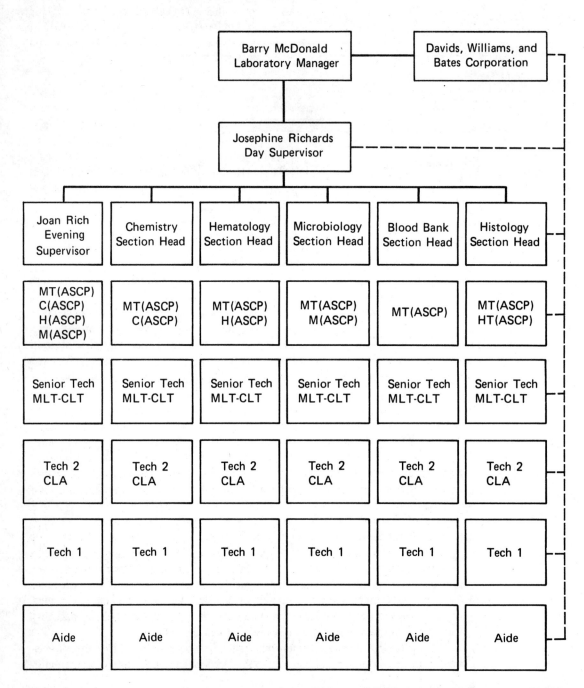

ogy and histology, while Dr. Bates maintained control of the blood bank. Comments concerning these bounds of control somewhat differed from the chart.

Marty K.—a bench tech who worked all sections of the lab stated, "On a given day the control of a specific department may change hands two or three times. A tech doesn't know who to go to; most often I'll go to Dr. Davids if I have a problem. At least I know he'll do something about it."

Greg S.—related, "I work mostly the hematology section of the lab. When we have a problem we are supposed to go to Dr. Williams. This very rarely happens. He gets upset with the smallest things and it's like he doesn't want to be bothered. So we go to Dr. Davids. Then Dr. Williams gets ticked off. I remember once when we received some unknowns from the state to check our quality control. Dr. Williams was too busy to help us with them, so we went to Dr. Davids. A while later Dr. Williams came around and changed some of the answers; Dr. Davids found out, and he had words with Dr. Williams. Then Dr. Davids returned and changed them back and told us not to listen to Dr. Williams. I might add that Dr. Davids was correct."

The crossover of responsibilities by the pathologists was the source of conflicting demands of the pathologists. According to Barry McDonald, "If they would only worry about the sections they were supposed to, my job would be so easy."

The organization of the techs seemed to be more defined (Exhibit 2). The MT (ASCP) was the highest attainable position in the lab. The medical technologist registered by the American Society of Clinical Pathologists was the most sought after requirement of personnel to be hired by the laboratories.

Registration or national certification was not a requirement for all positions within the lab. The lab assistant, lab tech 1, lab tech 2, and senior lab tech positions were open to anyone with a high school education and experience.

The lab assistants' duties included the drawing of blood, making chemical reagents used in the performance of the manual tests, and various other small tasks. The main responsibility of the lab assistant was the early morning collection of blood samples. These assistants worked for all sections and were not assigned to a particular section. Their immediate supervisor on day shift was Josephine Richards, the day shift supervisor. The night shift assistants reported to Joan Rich, the evening supervisor.

Laboratory technicians were required to do the less important, routine tasks in a particular section. These technicians were assigned a particular section for a given day. They only performed tasks relevant to that section and were directly responsible to the section head when on the day shift. On the evening shift, they were accountable to the evening supervisor. Most of the lab techs 1 were lab assistants and were promoted because of seniority.

The category of laboratory technician 2 includes most of the older techs with many years of seniority. Their responsibilities include the performance of some routine tests, instrument maintenance, and quality control. They were not to do any laboratory test that called for an interpretation on the part of the operator. The average person in this classification had very little or no college education and had at least ten years seniority. The CLA (ASCP) falls into this category.

The senior laboratory technician performed most tests in the lab. He worked all sections of the lab and was responsible to the section head on the day shift. On the evening shift, he was under the direct supervision of the evening supervisor. The only duties that the senior tech could not perform were related to the development of new methods and procedures to be used in the lab. The CLT (HEW) and the MLT (ASCP) registeries both fell into this classification on the organization model.

The MT (ASCP) category included categorical specialists also. These specialists were confined to the section in which they were registered. For example, the ASCP also had specialist registeries in chemistry, hematology, microbiology, and histology. These specialists, although not as versatile to the lab as a MT (ASCP), were still very important to the functioning of each section. The educational requirements needed to write these exams included a four-year college degree in the speciality field and two to four years experience in that field. These specialists were needed to work and develop new techniques and procedures designed for better accuracy and efficiency.

Continuing education of the laboratory employees was extremely important and must have kept pace with instrumentation and technical advances of the field. VMC Laboratories seemed to be well aware of this obligation and made every effort to grant special educational leaves of absence.

FINANCIAL AND PRODUCTION ASPECTS

This technical revolution was the reason for the sizable budget the lab operated under. Even though the hospital was a nonprofit organization, the lab operated on a very profitable basis and was the largest money making department in the hospital. The revenues realized from the lab supported many other departments and administrative expenses within the hospital. The budget of $3.5 million was based on approximately $1.5 million for salaries, with the rest being allocated for supplies and education. According to Bert Baker, director of finance, the lab was pretty well self-supporting with some monies being contributed from private donors. These donations ranged from fifty to twenty thousand dollars annually. Unless donations were otherwise requested, they were automatically put in the general fund. The only monies that went to the lab had to be so stipulated at the time of the donation.

The laboratory performed about thirty thousand tests each month. Out of those, about five thousand were for outpatients. In order for the hospital laboratory to receive returns to scale, it had to deal on a volume basis. Many automated instrumentation tests were designed to give lower costs with higher volume. When an emergency test was ordered and could not be run in a "batch," a stat charge was added to the original cost of the test to make up for the inefficiency of doing a single test. Barry McDonald stated that this "stat" charge was being dropped in the near future because many insurance companies would not pay for the charge. He also relayed the fact that these stat charges brought in an additional revenue of approximately ten thousand dollars monthly.

One major point of consideration was the pattern of the work load. There was no way to predict the amount of tests that would be performed daily. Staffing was geared to handle a relevant range in the number of tests. However, this relevant range was quite small and most times the lab was either overstaffed or understaffed. According to Mr. McDonald, "This is a problem that we have been facing since day one. The only cure I can come up with would be to batch more of our tests. But the pathologists won't let us do that because of the medical implications of receiving reports a day late. So we are stuck either way."

There was also a cycle to the daily work load. Morning pickup was done between the hours of 5 a.m. and 7 a.m. About 70 to 80 percent of the day's work was drawn at that time. The lab assistants drew blood during these hours and returned the samples to the lab by 7 a.m. at which time the techs started working. This was quite convenient for the techs because the work was already in the lab when they started work. The remaining 20 to 30 percent of the work was brought up between 11 a.m. and 2 p.m. The majority of the work for the second shift was done between 3 and 7 p.m. Almost all the work that entered the lab after that was emergency situations and could not be predicted.

When considering the work load, the outpatient service also had to be taken into consideration. Mr. McDonald felt this area was the bread and butter of the lab. This was so because the patient came to the hospital during scheduled times. Therefore, the batching of outpatients could be done with great ease and the cost per test was almost cut in half in relation to the cost of the same test done on an inpatient.

The outpatient business of VMC Laboratories was large, even though there was direct competition from another hospital and five private labs in the area. Mr. McDonald stated this was so because the administration really pushed hard for good patient relations. There was also the aspect of cost to consider when dealing with outpatient services. While VMC did not have the lowest cost per test for outpatient services, it did have the shortest turnaround time for most tests. This factor along with moderate pricing maintained the outpatient business.

PERSONNEL AND HUMAN RELATIONS

Within the internal organization of the lab there seemed to be some frustration and resentment on the part of the employees. The following comments were received from a number of workers.

Kathy S.—"There are different rules for different people. There are some people who get special favors and privileges, and that annoys the majority of us."

Barb M.—"Barry will promise you anything just to make you feel better for a little while, but he never delivers. This has happened to a number of people; that's why we lose so many good people."

Kathy N.—"I don't have too many griefs about this place; it's better than my old job. I guess I'm one of their pets, though, because I never question anything. I am a 'yes' person at heart. I have seen other people get the shaft, though. Once they take a disliking to you, forget it. I don't know where the problem is, if its the personnel department or lab management, but there is something that is not par."

Tim M.—"The hospital has been pretty good to me but there is a definite need of good management. Nobody in lab management has any supervisory or management education. They are just old techs with lots of seniority so they got the promotion. Merit means absolutely nothing around here. I've worked here for six years and nobody has ever told me I did a good job; but I get good evaluations, but that's a joke too. They say they are for merit increases, but nobody has ever gotten an increase for merit. Only cost of living. Getting back to the supervision of employees, I remember once when Josephine tried to make a college graduate stand in the corner for making a mistake. That was only about two years ago. Needless to say, that employee told her what she could do with her corner and quit. The lack of management skills goes almost all the way to the top of hospital administration."

Sue C.—"The lab has a lot of possibilities and they have some good people, but they won't be able to keep them with this administration. They don't really care about their people, they think they did you a favor by giving you a job. According to them the only reason people work is for the money. That may be true with some, but not professional people. I want some personal recognition for my work."

The educational background of management personnel was as follows:

Beverly Cook—administrative director of ancillary services — Mrs. Cook had a two-year degree in nursing. She was a registered nurse and had a master's degree from Central Michigan University in health education. She had been with VMC since 1951.

Barry McDonald—laboratory manager — Mr. McDonald had a bachelor of science degree in physics. He initially worked in the chemistry section of the lab and started with VMC in 1956. There was no record of any business education.

Josephine Richards—day supervisor — Mrs. Richards had an associate's degree in medical technology. She received her MT(ASCP) under the old rule of a two-year degree and work experience. While her title stated supervisor, she had not done any benchwork since 1962. She admitted that she had lost her technical expertise, because she had not kept abreast of new developments. She felt she would be better titled as an administrative assistant. She also stated she has never had any managment courses or education.

In an interview with Dr. Davids he stated, "Barry does a good job with the resources available to him. There are some personnel problems that I handle when the need arises, but he pretty well takes care of it." In an interview with Mrs. Cook, she stated, "There are no major problems with the lab; we seem to have a high turnover rate but that has been a problem that has been standard for us. We have good facilities and good people, and our reputation with the doctors is getting better all the time. Overall I am quite pleased with its operation."

Valley Medical Center Laboratories employed about 90 people. Negative comments concerning employee moral came from about 70 percent. Those comments came from employees that averaged about five and one-half years of seniority.

The laboratory and director of finance did not release any financial data that was strictly related to the lab. A copy of the report to the community released in September of 1980 for the fiscal year ending June 30, 1980, included the restricted and unrestricted balance sheets (Exhibits 3 and 4).

Since specific financial data concerning the laboratory was not accessible, it was not possible to analyze the financial conditions of the laboratory. The overall balance sheets were included to highlight the entire operations of the hospital.

In analyzing Valley Medical Center Laboratories there seemed to be two major problems emphasizing poor personnel management. Seventy percent of the employees had negative comments concerning the human relations aspect of their employment. This percentage was almost proof positive that there was room for improvement.

The first major problem of the lab appeared to be a genuine disinterest on the part of the laboratory administration in personnel or human relations. The laboratory administration was oblivious to the fact that there was a humanistic approach to management. This type of management was acceptable in the earlier years of laboratory management when technology and expertise did not necessitate the need for the professional technician. As one employee stated, "They feel they are doing you a favor because they give you a job."

Valley Medical Center Laboratories was well aware of its obligation to the continuing education of its employees. The laboratory manager conveyed the point that this obligation was to the C.A.P. accrediting agency that required this documented program for continuing education, and not the employee. The administration appeared to be only interested in putting results on a report form and not in the person behind the results. This was the reason for the negative comments from tenured employees and the high turnover rate the lab was experiencing.

The second problem was a secondary result of the personnel management problem. This second problem was the lack of sincerity on the part of the manager and supervisors. True concern for their employees was a must, if there was to be sincerity. So it was no surprise to find this superficial type management. A major reason for this lack of motivation seemed to be the appraisal system used by the administration (Exhibit 5).

Exhibit 3

Valley Medical Center Laboratories
Unrestricted Operating Fund
June 30, 1980

ASSETS

Current assets:			
Cash		$ 1,075,828	
Temporary investments		2,300,000	
Accounts receivable:			
Patients	$ 5,944,473		
Facilities fund	31,274		
Other	73,489		
	$ 6,049,236		
Less allowance	350,000	5,699,236	
Inventory		493,440	
Prepaid expense		251,627	
Total current assets			$ 9,820,131
Property, plant, and equipment assets:			
Land	$ 977,754		
Buildings	26,795,265		
Equipment......................................	11,424,383		
Construction in progress	23,926		
	$ 39,221,328		
Less depreciation...........................	8,373,150		
Total property, plant, and			
equipment assets			30,848,178
Other assets:			
Insurance funds	$ 196,325		
Debt retirement	2,342,229		
Goodwill	12,000		
Unamortized bonds...........................	62,181		
Total other assets			2,612,735
Total assets			$ 43,281,044

LIABILITIES AND FUND BALANCE

Liabilities:			
Long-term debt		$ 568,459	
Accounts payable:			
Trade	$ 949,382		
Third party.................................	2,022,381	2,971,763	
Accrued payroll		2,308,974	
Accrued expenses.............................		237,950	
Total current liabilities			$ 6,087,146
Long-term debt			26,645,146
Reserve for insurance claims			124,335
Operating fund balance			10,424,417
Total liabilities and fund balance			$ 43,281,044

Valley Medical Center Laboratories
Restricted Facility Fund

Exhibit 4   **June 30, 1980**

ASSETS

Cash	$ 59,977	
Temporary investments	1,014,358	
Pledges receivable	152,780	
Investments-land	813,465	
Land held for resale	342,300	
Note and interest receivable	41,959	
Total assets		$2,424,839

LIABILITIES

Due to operating fund	$ 31,274	
Land contract payable	47,700	
Reserved for loss on donated assets	160,000	$ 238,974
Fund balance		2,185,865
Total liabilities and fund balance		$2,424,839

This appraisal form was used throughout the hospital for every job classification and position. The appraisal form used by VMC Laboratories showed some very negative characteristics. First, the form was biased toward an average evaluation, due to central tendency, because of only five degrees of performance. Another negative characteristic was that it was very biased, based on personal prejudice. It was also inaccurate because there were no definitions of the terms used in the appraisal. This appraisal did not afford the employee the opportunity to express his personal goals and accomplishments over the past year. In essence, the evaluation form was worthless from the standpoint of employee morale and motivation. This could have been a root cause for the morale and motivation problems in the lab.

Exhibit 5

Valley Medical Center Laboratories
Appraisal Form

Return By __12-1-80__   Job Class. __MT (ASCP)__

Date Returned _____   Effective Date __1-1-81__

Name _____   Date _____

☐ Full Time ☐ Part Time   For the Period _____   45   _____ Year
                                                    worked days

Check <u>ONE</u> column opposite each category that describes most nearly your evaluation of this employee's work.

	OUTSTANDING	GOOD	AVERAGE	BELOW AVERAGE	UNSATISFACTORY
Ability to Learn	☐	☐	☐	☐	☐
Application of Skills	☐	☐	☐	☐	☐
Attendance — Work	☐	☐	☐	☐	☐
Attendance — Hosp. Mtgs.	☐	☐	☐	☐	☐
Attitude	☐	☐	☐	☐	☐
Care of Work Area	☐	☐	☐	☐	☐
Conduct	☐	☐	☐	☐	☐
Cooperation	☐	☐	☐	☐	☐
Dependability	☐	☐	☐	☐	☐
Economy	☐	☐	☐	☐	☐
Judgment	☐	☐	☐	☐	☐
Knowledge of Work	☐	☐	☐	☐	☐
Punctuality	☐	☐	☐	☐	☐
Safety Awareness	☐	☐	☐	☐	☐
Quality of Work	☐	☐	☐	☐	☐
Quantity of Work	☐	☐	☐	☐	☐

POLICY ISSUES IN MARKETING

Marketing, one of the three essential functions of any business, is often a misunderstood pillar of business. In this section several cases are presented that address several relevant marketing issues. The student will be introduced to the concepts of forecasting, personal selling, sales personnel training, advertising, price policies, product definition, product design, and the integration of all of these factors into a coherent, integrated marketing mix.

The first case is *Quick Meal Food Systems Inc.*, a fast-food company trying to decide whether to open another store. Management has been given the responsibility of developing specific operating budgets. The underlying issue, however, really pertains to the essential marketing research preceding operating budgets and promotional campaigns. The case raises several questions. How does one forecast demand? What information is essential in the development of forecasts? Where and how can one obtain necessary information? Once a forecast has been developed, how can it be converted into an effective promotional campaign? These and other issues are raised in the first case and amplified in the second case.

Omni Incorporated presents problems encountered when an outside consultant is employed to develop a sales forecast. In this case, the consultant developed a computer model which produced a forecast for the more than four thousand items in Omni's inventory. Although this effort was monumental and appeared technically sound, the model was about to be scrapped one year after its implementation. A number of questions are raised relative to that impending failure. Was the consultant maladroit in implementation? Were there managerial problems that undermined implementation? Was the model improperly constructed? Had the environment changed significantly? Each of these questions is raised in this case.

Even if marketing forecasts are valid, the marketing problems of an organization do not end here. In the *J. W. Adams Company* case the forecast of industry trends appears valid, but the organization's marketing problems are far from over. The impact of the somewhat bleak forecast on budgeting, advertising policy, and goal setting must be assessed. There are some difficulties in the marketing area and other functional areas of the organization. Viable options or solutions are multifaceted and cannot be determined by looking at the marketing function alone. The dilemma of the J. W. Adams Company is even more interesting in light of current interest rates and new construction.

The *Westinghouse Electric Corporation: Overhead Distribution Transformer Division* case presents the reader with most of the basic elements of the marketing mix. Pricing policy, product definition, promotion, and distribution are all issues discussed in this case. The identification of the *major* problems in this case goes beyond forecasting and advertising. It has been four years since field sales engineers have participated in any sort of formal training program. In addition, the sales force has had an annual turnover of ten percent. The manager is convinced that part of the problem is lack of *product* knowledge by the sales force.

The last case in this section concerns a relatively small business named *Ocala Opportunities Inc.* The case is short, but in spite of its brevity, touches upon all elements of the marketing mix. It also raises the issue of organizational objectives setting for not-for-profit organizations. *Ocala Opportunities Inc.* is a rich case for analysis.

Quick Meal
Food Systems Inc.*

INTRODUCTION

Quick Meal Food Systems Inc. (QM), based in Rocky Mount, North Carolina, opened its doors in 1960. Wilbur Smith, who opened the restaurant, quickly sold his interest for $20,000. As of October 21, 1976, the company owned 328 restaurants and licensed 625. In the summer of 1977 QM had 1,000 stores in operation, both privately and company owned. The 1,000th unit was opened in the summer of 1977 in Davenport, Iowa. The units were directed from the main headquarters in Rocky Mount, North Carolina. QM grossed $214 million in sales in 1977 and $6.4 million in profits. This was a 2.9 percent profit on sales compared with McDonald's profit, which was almost 10 percent for that same year. In 1978 QM expanded to 1,056 stores.

According to *Food Systems News* (August–September, 1977) QM operated in about 70 percent of the U.S. and several foreign countries including El Salvador, Guatemala, and Japan. (Exhibit 1) The company's growth had been outstanding. It was the 25th largest food operation in the U.S. at that time. The U.S. Armed Forces was the number one food operation. Financial data for 1976 is given in Exhibits 2 and 3.

QM and its subsidiaries operated, licensed, and serviced limited-menu, self-service restaurants under the name QM. The QM menu featured popular-priced food, including hamburgers, cheeseburgers, roast beef sandwiches, fish sandwiches, french fried potatoes, apple turnovers, milk shakes and soft drinks.

The Specialty Foods Division processed a varied line of frozen meat and seafood entrees, specialty products, and portion-controlled meat products, which were sold to supermarket chains for home consumption and to institutional distributors.

BACKGROUND

QM was still independent although many competitors, notably Burger King, Jack-in-the-Box, and Taco Bell, were not. QM's major problem has been capital shortage for growth purposes.

---

*This case was prepared by Michael V. Laric, University of Connecticut, with the intention of providing a basis for class discussion rather than illustrating either effective or ineffective management of a business situation. Reprinted with permission from *Application of Decision Sciences in Organizations: A Case Approach* by Joseph C. Latona and K. Mark Weaver with the cooperation of the American Institute for Decision Sciences, Atlanta, Georgia, 1980.

Exhibit 1

Quick Meal Food Systems Inc.
Geographical Distribution*

AREA 1	Company Stores	Licensee Stores
Massachusetts	5	0
Connecticut	17	0
New York	16	1
New Jersey	0	8
Pennsylvania	19	21
Delaware	22	0
Maryland	3	3
West Virginia	1	1
Virginia	18	62
Washington, D.C.	1	0
AREA 2		
North Carolina	57	142
South Carolina	21	70
AREA 3		
Kentucky	11	1
Tennessee	1	35
Georgia	62	22
Florida	5	23
Alabama	5	49
Mississippi	0	10
Louisiana	0	1
AREA 4		
North Dakota	0	7
South Dakota	0	0
Minnesota	1	27
Wisconsin	0	29
Michigan	23	2
Ohio	4	4
Indiana	0	10
Illinois	30	39
Iowa	24	18
Missouri	12	8
Kansas	6	28
Oklahoma	5	8
Arkansas	6	0
Texas	0	1
Arizona	0	10

*Company also has stores in El Salvador (4), Guatemala (1), and Japan (1).

Quick Meal Food Systems Inc.
Consolidated Balance Sheet

Exhibit 2

October 31, 1976 ($000 omitted)

ASSETS	1976	1975
Current assets:		
Cash	$ 6,557	$ 4,282
Receivables (net)	5,342	5,017
Inventories[1]	9,687	9,689
Deferred tax benefits	290	466
Prepayments	1,151	1,066
Total current assets...................	$23,027	$20,520
Net property, etc.[2]	32,625	28,703
Assets leased	3,902	4,372
Investments	—[3]	1,390
Noncurrent receivables	2,274	1,518
Goodwill and intangibles	4,620	4,918
Deferred charges, etc.	369	494
Total assets	$66,817	$61,915

LIABILITIES and STOCKHOLDERS' EQUITY

	1976	1975
Current liabilities:		
Notes, etc. payable	$ 2,312	$ 2,415
Accounts payable	9,473	8,505
Closed stores cost[4]	410	611
Income taxes...........................	1,940	1,747
Total current liabilities.................	$14,135	$13,278
Long-term debt	19,251	20,045
Deferred income taxes	1,787	1,364
Deferred income.........................	261	388
Minority interest	205	172
Closed stores cost[4]	2,148	1,877
Stockholders' equity:		
Common stock[5]	$ 1,714	$ 1,714
Capital surplus	12,100	12,098
Retained earnings........................	15,387	11,168
Reacquired stock[6]	(171)	(189)
Total stockholders' equity	$29,030	$24,791
Total Liabilities and Stockholders' Equity...........................	$66,817	$61,915

[1]Lower cost (fifo) or market.
[2]Depreciation and amortization: 1976, $16,115; 1975, $12,965.
[3]Investment in and advances to a 50 percent owned partnership, at equity in net assets.
[4]Estimated future cost of closed stores.
[5]3,428,390 no par shares.
[6]Shares at cost: 1976, 45,616; 1975, 50,466.

Exhibit 3

Quick Meal Food Systems Inc.
Selected Financial Data
October 31, 1976 ($000 omitted)

	1976	1975
Sales and revenues........................	$188,051	$162,907
Cost of sales	98,668	84,650
Selling, etc. expenses......................	78,527	69,982
Closed store expenses, prov	828	2,308
Income taxes	3,942	1,298
Income continuing operation...............	4,219	1,540
Earnings, common shares.................	$1.25	$0.46
Interest, net..............................	1,867	3,130
Discontinued operations:		
Operating loss...........................	–	26
Disposal loss	–	416
Net income[1].............................	4,219	1,098
Earnings, common shares..................	$1.25	$0.33
Year end shares	3,382,774	3,377,924

[1]After $4,452,916 (1975, $3,960,457) depreciation and amortization.

The current president and chief executive officer, Jack A. Laughery, age 43, was a tough executive who learned the business the hard way. According to *Fortune* (July 17, 1978, p. 16), "Laughery joined a restaurant chain called Sandy's in 1960, and learned the business from the griddle up, flipping hamburgers in St. Paul. He became a vice president of QM when Sandy's merged with the larger chain in 1972. Since becoming C.E.O. three years ago, Laughery has extricated QM from some unprofitable lines of business and has started opening more restaurants in better locations. But to keep growing he needs capital—and that means merger."

QM almost succeeded in trying to merge with Pet, Inc., a $100 million deal. But IC Industries stepped in, and Pet's president and chairman acceded to a $350 million merger. QM was left on the sidelines with just a promise that "good faith" negotiations would continue.

QM's goals were "to provide an above average return to shareholders and to be certain that along with growth ... close and caring relationships" were maintained.

To maintain growth, QM merged with Sandy's, a midwest fast-food chain of 200 units in 1972 and opened units on Interstate 95 in northeastern U.S. in 1974. They had not been successful in penetrating the western United States with their units. (A list of other acquisitions appears in Exhibit 4.) QM had four distribution centers located in Atlanta, Georgia; Independence, Missouri; Mason City, Iowa; and Quakertown, Pennsylvania. QM's products were manufactured by their own factories and the Gol-Pak Company. They were distributed to four areas of the U.S.: (1) the Northeast; (2) North and South Carolina; (3) the Southeast; and (4) the Midwest. (Refer to Exhibit 1 for the exact configuration.)

Exhibit 4

**Subsidiaries and Facilities Maintained by
Quick Meal Food Systems Inc.
(As of October 1976)[1]**

Restaurant Division:

Annapolis, MD
Atlanta, GA
Glastonbury, CT
Kewanee, IL

Mechanicsburg, PA
Rocky Mount, NC
Southfield, MI

Equipment Division:

Kewanee, IL

Rocky Mount, NC

Food Processing & Distribution Division:

Atlanta, GA
Independence, MO
Mason City, IA
Secaucus, NJ

Oneida, NY
Quakertown, PA
Rocky Mount, NC

Fast-Food Division:

Fast Foodmakers, Inc. (Acquired 1969)
Hardee's Restaurants, Inc. (Acquired 1967)

Specialty Foods Division:

Golden Shore Seafoods, Inc. (Acquired 1967)
New Orleans Shrimp Co., Inc. (Acquired 1968)
Gol-Pak Corp. (Acquired 1969)

[1]Based on *Moody's Industrial Manual*, p. 1583.

QM'S ORGANIZATION

The QM organization was led by 21 vice presidents directing over 20,000 employees throughout the system. Next in line were the area executives who supervised regional managers. The regional managers supervised district managers. A district manager directed from five to seven stores and coached the managers in the district.

The store managers were expected to achieve predetermined goals and keep area and corporate staff informed of problems requiring their attention in the district. The store managers also had to plan and execute programs to improve sales, quality of foods, and service. The manager was typically responsible for from 15 to 50 employees and achieving sales and profit goals. He or she also coordinated activities relating to shifts, meeting food standards, unit communications, accident prevention, customer and community relations, and overall operations.

The assistant manager reported to and assisted the unit manager. He or she supervised from 3 to 15 employees and handled recruiting and training of personnel, food production, scheduling, and other tasks necessary to maintain operation of each QM unit.

QM OPENS A NEW STORE

In the fall of 1977 QM's executives were looking into opening a new restaurant next to the campus of the University of Connecticut. The University had over 16,000 students, approximately half of which attended the summer session. The University, located in the town of Storrs, Connecticut, had a population of close to 20,000 people. The per capita income for 1977 was $5,756 with the household income at $19,570 for 1977. The second largest employer in town (after the University with 4,400 employees) was the Mansfield Training School (1,100 employees), a facility for the mentally retarded. Unemployment in 1976 was around 3.5 percent or roughly half the national average. Retail sales (available by county) were $208 million for 1975. Food sales accounted for 30 percent of the above.

Competition existing in fast-food chains included a McDonald's restaurant (7.5 miles away) and another one, which was to open for the fall 1978 semester, about 5 miles away. Several restaurants were available within a two-mile radius from the campus and included two student cafeterias, two luncheonettes, two pizza places, a steak house (about 2.5 miles away), and a restaurant.

QM executives preferred a site which would be adjacent to the campus. The only one available was an underground storage area. QM decided to rent it and began renovating the chosen site with a tentative opening in the fall of 1978 (prior to the beginning of classes at the University). Several data collection efforts were underway to try and assess the existing sales potential and the best ways to build up future sales.

MARKETING RESEARCH DATA FOR NEW RESTAURANTS

Exhibit 5 portrays the local media that was available, categorized into local radio stations and local print media. The advertising rates for each medium and some information about circulation are included. Manager Gary Scutti hired a marketing student to survey the local student population. A copy of the survey questionnaire is presented in Exhibit 6.

The highlights of the brief survey can be summarized as follows: The survey was distributed to 135 students randomly selected. A total of 101 students, consisting of 58 males and 43 females, completed the questionnaires. Sixty persons owned automobiles and kept them on campus. Most were full-time students occasionally working part time. Twenty-two percent had a steady part-time job, earning between $26-40 per week.

Pizza seemed to be preferred by 40 percent of the participants, while 25 percent preferred hamburgers. Twenty-three percent of the students preferred to eat grinders and 13 percent enjoyed eating club sandwiches. None seemed to like hot dogs, part of QM's menu.

When students were asked to rank existing restaurants, 40 percent selected Kathy John's as their first choice while 24 percent chose Subway as their first choice. Both were traditional, full-service restaurants, rather than quick-food outlets.

All the students surveyed preferred FM music on the radio to other media. The station most preferred (and listened to) was WDRC in Hartford (20 percent). Second were both WCCC and WHCN Hartford, each with 17 percent of the samples. Following a close third was WTIC in Hartford with 16 percent. WPLR in New Haven (not listed on Exhibit 5) took fourth place with 10 percent. Five percent listened to WWYZ, a Hartford-Waterbury station, and four students listened to WAQY in Springfield, Massachusetts. WHUS, the local campus radio, was selected by three persons. Unfortunately, this station did not handle commercial broadcasts, although they did engage in sponsorships and public service announcements for the student population.

Students were asked to identify any other newspapers read besides the *Connecticut Daily Campus* (CDC) which is heavily read by all students. Forty-eight percent of the students read the *Hartford Courant* and 15 percent read *The Wall Street Journal*, a required source for some economics and business courses. Fourteen percent read *The New York Times* and 7 percent read the *New York Daily News*.

When students were asked if they had ever eaten at QM before, a majority (73 percent) answered yes. Twenty-seven percent hadn't eaten there before. Sixty-one percent of those who had eaten there said that the food was not as good as other fast-food competitors (such as McDonald's and Burger King). Twenty-eight percent of those who ate at QM previously said it was better than competitors. Thirteen percent felt that only McDonald's was better, whereas Burger King was *NOT* as good.

It was also determined from the survey that 47 percent preferred that QM operate between the hours of 10 a.m. and 3 a.m. Some 25 percent of the respondents preferred it stay open until 12 p.m., while 19 percent indicated their desire to see it open 24 hours a day. It was noted by some that QM could stay open until midnight on weekdays, and later on weekends; for example, until 2 or 3 a.m.

Finally, students were asked for the qualities they were most interested in when patronizing a QM. Many were looking for fast service, fresh and high-quality food at low prices, convenience, room to sit, good social atmosphere, and even cute waitresses!

THE PROBLEM

The newly appointed manager had to propose a specific operating budget for the first two years of operations. Specifically, Mr. Scutti had to propose a media plan and publicity campaigns for the new store. He was not certain whether the data he had available was sufficient and requested the regional manager's help in constructing forecasts and operating plans for the first year.

Exhibit 5

Quick Meal Food Systems Inc.
Local Media Available in the Area for Proposed New Restaurant

RADIO STATIONS AVAILABLE IN THE AREA*

	WCCC, Hartford	WHCN, Hartford	WTIC, Hartford
Dial position:	1290 AM 106.9 FM	106 FM	1080 AM 96.5 FM
Power: (watts)	500 AM 50,000 FM	50,000	15,000 FM 50,000 AM
Period of operation:	24 hrs FM, Day AM	24 hrs	Both 24 hrs
Broadcast format:	Both album-oriented rock	Album-oriented rock	FM-Top 40 Hits AM-Adult contemporary
Sample rates:	1 time–$25.75 6 " –25.75 12 " –25.00	$13-$22.00 depending on frequency and time of day	FM 2 p.m.-midnight, 6 × $20; 6 a.m.-2 p.m., 6× $15; midnight-6 a.m., 6 × $9; AM 6-10 a.m. and 3-7 p.m., 1-12 spots/week, $140; Midday 10-3 p.m., 12 × $85; 8-12 p.m., 12 × $60

	WDRC, Hartford	WXLS, Willimantic	WILI, Willimantic
Dial position:	1360 AM 102.9 FM	98.3 FM	1400 AM
Power: (watts)	5000 AM 15,000 FM	5000	1000 daytime, 250 nights
Period of operation:	24 hrs	24 hrs	24 hrs
Broadcast format:	AM-Top 40 FM-Album-oriented rock	Popular Music	Progressive rock, news on the hour
Sample rates:	$55/minute 5:30-10 a.m. Midday, 10 a.m.-8 p.m. $50; Rest of night-$44	$10.00/60 seconds	Approx. $8/60 seconds depending on the frequency of the broadcast

LOCAL PRINT MEDIA, RATES, AND CIRCULATION

	Connecticut Daily Campus (CDC)	The Chronicle, Willimantic	The Hartford Courant
Circulation:	Monday-Friday	6 days, Monday-Saturday	Daily, mornings
Circulation breakdown:	10,000 distributed on campus, 180 off campus (20,000 readers), AM	10,400 distributed in 15 towns, 5 around Willimantic	Central, Conn. to New Haven to Danielson, Conn. to Mass. line
Page size:	5 column page, 12-16 pp.	8 columns, 18 pp.	7 column page, 90 pp.
Printing method:	Offset	Offset	Offset
Rates per column inch:	$2.05 up to 13" $1.95 13"-31" $1.85 31"-54" $1.75 54"-full page	$2.40	NA
Telephone:	429-9384	423-8466	429-9339

	Stafford Springs Reminder	Gold Mine Shopper (Free)	Broadcasters Shoppers Guide
Circulation:	Weekly, Tuesday	Weekly, Tuesday AM	Weekly
Circulation breakdown:	10,500 in Stafford Springs, Stafford, Tolland, Conn. (not Storrs)	21,700 distributed in 20 towns around Willimantic	28,000 distributed in Willimantic 16 towns
Page size:	4 columns, 8½" × 11" page	4 columns, 30-32 pp.	16 columns, 34-36 pp.
Printing method:	Offset	Offset	Offset
Rates per column inch:	NA	$1.75	$2.00
Telephone:	684-4205	423-8466	456-2211

*WHUS, University of Connecticut, Storrs, Connecticut, operates 24 hours a day but does not accept commercial advertising.

Exhibit 6

Quick Meal Food Systems Inc.
Survey Questionnaire for Area of Proposed New Restaurant

MARKET SURVEY

Hi, I am doing a survey which will determine how the new restaurant near campus can serve your needs. It will only take 2-3 minutes of your time.

Age: _____   SEX: M F   DORM: _____ _____

1. Do you have a car on campus? _____ Yes _____ No

2. Are you employed presently? _____ Yes _____ No

3. Range of weekly take-home pay: (circle)
   a. Less than $10.00   c. $26.00-$40.00
   b. $11.00-$25.00   d. $41.00 or greater

4. What type of food do you prefer? (check)

   a. Pizza _____   b. Grinder _____   c. Hamburger _____
   d. Club Sandwich _____   e. Hot Dog _____

5. If you were out on Saturday night and were hungry, where would you prefer to eat? (Rank 1 for the first choice to 5 as last choice)
   Kathy John's ____ Subway ____ Hardee's ____ Paul's Pizza ____ Husky's ____

6. What radio station do you listen to the most frequently? (check)
   a. WHUS Storrs ____   d. WCCC Hartford ____   g. Other ____
   b. WILI Willimantic ____   e. WHCN Hartford ____
   c. WDRC Hartford ____   f. WTIC Hartford ____

7. What other newspaper publication (other than CDC) do you read? _____
   _____

8. Have you ever eaten at a QM restaurant before?   Yes ____ No ____
   If so, what did you like about it? _____
   Was QM better than McDonald's   Yes ____ No ____
   Was QM better than Burger King? Yes ____ No ____

9. What time would you prefer QM to be open? (check)
   a. 10 a.m.-10 p.m. _____   b. 10 a.m.-3 a.m. _____   c. 10 a.m.-12 p.m. _____
   d. 24 hours daily _____   e. Other times _____

10. What are you most interested in when patronizing QM?
                                                        Thank You.

Case 3-2

Omni Incorporated*

INTRODUCTION

Omni Incorporated, a leading firm in the office supply industry, calls upon its top management each September to render their judgments relative to expected sales for the forthcoming year. These predictions are combined and informally averaged to arrive at an estimate of future sales. Little, if any, effort is made to model or apply advanced quantitative techniques to the sales forecasting process. Once a sales forecast is agreed upon by the executives, Omni's sales force is charged with the responsibility of meeting those goals. This approach to forecasting, often called jury of executive opinion, is common in many industries. Since these predictions are based upon opinion or group judgment rather than empirical evidence or facts, they are frequently quite inaccurate. Omni is no exception in this respect. The company's goals are often either too modest or too ambitious. Overestimation and underestimation create a myriad of problems from cash flow crises to production cycling. As a result and at the insistence of two vice presidents, Omni engaged the services of an outside consultant. This consultant quickly recognized the problem and immediately suggested more sophisticated approaches to forecasting. For several months, the consultant worked on the development of a correlation-regression model. This attempt to "modernize" forecasting techniques at Omni was an ambitious undertaking in the light of the fact that Omni had over 4,000 product items classified into 20 product groups. Almost all of Omni's more than 4,000 products are sold exclusively to retailers and/or wholesalers.

DEVELOPMENT OF THE MODEL

The consultant's research suggested that *GNP, Real GNP, New School Construction, Paper Products and Pulp Sales, U.S. Government Expenditures, State and Local Government Expenditures,* and the *Index of New Business Formation* were leading or coincident indicators for sales at Omni. The resultant

*This case was prepared by Ronald M. Zigli, Appalachian State University, and Eric Pratt, New Mexico State University, with the intention of providing a basis for class discussion rather than illustrating either effective or ineffective management of a business situation. Reprinted with permission from *Application of Decision Sciences in Organization: A Case Approach* by Joseph C. Latona and K. Mark Weaver with the cooperation of the American Institute for Decision Sciences, Atlanta, Georgia, 1980.

model cascaded down through several stages from a very complex algorithm to the naive or simple regression model depending upon the accuracy achieved at each stage or level. This composite model was validated using ten years of data and a post-hoc test of the results. The most complex algorithm was used in cases where items had a correlation coefficient greater than .60. Exponential smoothing was attempted for items that did not meet this minimum requirement. (Basically, exponential smoothing is a technique whereby a new forecast is calculated using the immediately preceding forecast plus a fractional part of the deviation of that forecast from the actual value.) If an item failed to meet the minimum requirements of accuracy using exponential smoothing, the sales forecast was made using simple linear regression with time as the independent variable. Once the forecast for an item was complete, it was aggregated into a product line which was subsequently aggregated into its respective group; and finally, that product group was aggregated into company sales. In general, all aggregated sales forecasts closely approximated actual sales (within 8–11 percent). Exhibits 1 and 2 show a forecast made for product one.

Outliers in some product groups were puzzling to the consultant for a while until it became evident that exogenous but identifiable factors were influencing the exceptionally high sales periods. After some preliminary questions were asked, it came to light that Omni's marketing department instituted sales promotion programs for one or more product items within the affected product line just prior to the unusual peak sales periods. As a result, the consultant incorporated tests including Mean Absolute Deviation to control for this and other contingencies.

Although the consultant made rapid progress in the development of the model, some skepticism was encountered on the part of the company controller, John Bointon, and some other supervisors. John had been with Omni for

Exhibit 1

Product Group 1 (Steel cabinets)
Expressed in units

Model No.	Forecasted Sales	Actual Sales	Percent Variation
B4207	2,000	2,155	8
B7605	1,200	1,303	9
B3315	750	602	20
B7214	900	1,204	34
C1621	2,100	2,551	21
D1210	4,000	4,210	5
F1421	1,700	1,711	1
G8008	825	843	2
L1111	400	406	2
Total	13,875	14,985	8

Exhibit 2

Product Group 1 (Steel cabinets)
Expressed in dollars

Model No.	Forecasted Sales	Actual Sales	Percent Variation
B4207	$ 1,000.00	$ 1,077.50	8
B7605	900.00	977.25	9
B3315	1,010.00	812.70	20
B7214	2,250.00	3,010.00	34
C1621	4,200.00	5,102.00	21
D1210	3,200.00	3,368.00	5
F1421	1,870.00	1,881.00	1
G8008	660.00	674.40	2
L1111	500.00	507.50	2
Total	$15,590.00	$17,410.35	12

12 years and enjoyed a great deal of respect from most of top and middle management. Although John cooperated, he kept claiming that he "was from Missouri" and would believe it when he saw it. On the other hand, Bob Siegel, John's organizational competitor (both reported to George Pritchard, vice president of finance), was most supportive of the consultant's efforts. Bob was a relatively new manager, but he enjoyed the confidence of George Pritchard. Finally, late in the year the consultant was satisfied that the model was working properly and turned it over to top management for implementation.

SCRAPPING THE MODEL

The following year, out of professional curiosity, the consultant inquired about the success of the model. The consultant was astonished to learn that it was about to be scrapped. After weeks of investigation, the consultant learned nothing more than the fact that a pervasive attitude of dissatisfaction existed in the company about the sales forecasting model. By chance alone, the consultant happened to come across Omni's end-of-the-year forecast. Superficially, everything seemed in order. Upon closer examination, however, the consultant noted that several computer runs had been made with varying and different assumptions relative to the decision rules used in the program. Further investigation revealed that the operational version of that forecast was substantially higher than that which the model would have predicted. When the consultant questioned this, John Bointon and others were quick to comment that the model was worthless. John indicated that estimates for many product items were "way off" and completely unusable. For this reason, values were changed, assumptions were varied, and the model was substantially altered in an attempt to develop what John Bointon and others called a "valid" forecast. At this stage, the consultant was at a loss as to how to proceed.

Case 3–3

J. W. Adams Company*

INTRODUCTION AND BACKGROUND

The J. W. Adams Company was founded in April of 1959 by J. W. Adams in an industrialized midwest town of 235,000 persons. The company was engaged in the service and installation of heating and air-conditioning units and was a closed corporation operating in the $1-2 million sales range.

In 1973 the company departmentalized into three departments: (1) service, (2) negotiated sales, and (3) new construction. This system functioned well through 1976, with bids ranging from $30,000 to $200,000.

In 1976 and 1977 the profit margin declined due to three major jobs which proved to be financial losses. These jobs were two university buildings and one building for a local service organization. The firm eliminated bidding on new construction in October of 1978. The company had not recovered from these losses, and at the end of fiscal 1979, service, sales, and new construction were deeply in the red. A realignment resulted with reduction of the work force from 80 to 25 and a reorganization of the firm (see organizational chart Exhibit 1).

The J. W. Adams Company suffered from the effects of several problems, the most pronounced of which, according to Tom Adams, was the company's poor profitability position. Mr. Adams believed that one of the most important (if not "the" most important) reasons for the profit problem was that the company had no viable financial feedback system. Actual and estimated job cost comparisons suffered due to this feedback deficiency. Adams had all but given up on establishing a system by which he could receive this critical information on cash flow.

---

*This case was prepared by Joseph C. Latona, The University of Akron, with the intention of providing a basis for class discussion rather than illustrating either effective or ineffective management of a business situation. Reprinted with permission from *Application of Decision Sciences in Organizations: A Case Approach* by Joseph C. Latona and K. Mark Weaver with the cooperation of the American Institute for Decision Sciences, Atlanta, Georgia, 1980.

J. W. Adams Company
Exhibit 1   ## Organizational Chart

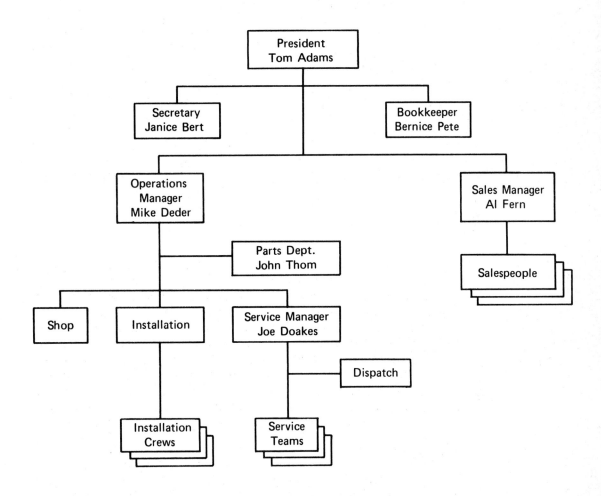

MARKETING

From a marketing viewpoint, however, an even more critical problem existed for the company, affecting not only short-term, but long-term operations, and quite possibly its very survival in the industry. Projected sales for the year 1980 indicated a $300,000 drop from the previous year of $1 million. Ninety percent of these sales were estimated to be primarily repeat business. The service department was expected to produce $600,000 in revenue, which represented a very slight increase from the previous year.

The type of work the company handled was confined to the designing, remodeling, and servicing of small commercial and industrial stuctures. The residential operations had been turned over entirely to the newly incorporated Adams Service Company which was responsible for remodeling work in the residential markets.

Most all sales, aside from service, were negotiated sales. Bidding on new construction proved disastrous for the company and contributed much to the company's problem. According to Adams, "If we can't get the markup, then we don't take the job." The company, however, operated on the basis of breaking even.

With regard to sales, Mr. Adams was aware of the problem but at the same time believed in a low-key kind of promotion:

> We are limited in sales at the present time. The company has no sales program as such. In fact, we've never had a marketing program; we're not even sure what marketing is. Overall, we've been guilty of some "wishy-washy" thinking in the sales department in the last two years. I don't like the local newspaper. Newspaper advertising never got us any notice. Radio promotion always got us attention but no business. Home-builder shows have value, but take too much time, although we have received 30-40 bona fide leads. Pen and pencil sets with our name on them used to be popular, but if I'd consider anything now it would be handout material, such as brochures. Right now, the best advertising we have is our name painted on the sides of our trucks.

Judging from Mr. Adams' statement, it seemed apparent that the lack of sales was a direct result of the company's perfunctory marketing program. In addition to the ineffective promotional campaign, the advertising budget for the 1980-1981 period had allotted $8,000 for sales and $2,000 for service—a drop from the previous year's total of $20,000. This budget figure appeared to have been arbitrarily set, and the dollar deduction from the previous year seemed to be based primarily on Mr. Adams' opinion that advertising was ineffectual for the industry.

PERSONNEL-ORGANIZATION

Tom Adams, 45 years of age, had been with the company since 1961 and assumed the presidency in 1976. He held a degree in electrical engineering from Cleveland State University. Mike Deder was the operations manager in charge of the shop and installation. Deder was 36. Joe Doakes was the service manager and reported to Deder. Doakes was 38. Al Fern was the sales manager and was responsible for generating sales for both the Adams Service Company and the J. W. Adams Company. Fern was 47. John Thom was the manager of the parts department and reported to Deder. Thom was 27. Bernice Pete was the bookkeeper-payroll clerk. The secretary was Janice Bert.

The remaining personnel were distributed in the following manner: (1) five in installation, (2) five in the shop, (3) one in parts, (4) twelve in service, and (5) one in the office. Also, the sole salesperson was concentrating on residential sales for the Adams Service Company, due to the inability to sell industrial accounts. The average age of nonsalary personnel was 34.8 years, with ages ranging from 18-56. Only two employees were scheduled for retirement in the next ten years. No current management personnel were due for immediate retirement (within the next ten years).

Mr. Adams characterized his sales staff, consisting of a sales manager and one new salesperson, as follows:

> Al Fern, the sales manager, has been with us ten years. Although he lacks polish, he gets sales. Right now, Al can only devote 20-25 percent of his time to actual sales managing. Tim Bach, the new salesperson, has potential, but needs to settle down. He's working primarily in the residential section now, since he doesn't know how to get an "in" with the commercial market yet.

Al Fern, in turn, stated his views on the company and its promotional activities:

> The bulk of our business is in new construction for small office and manufacturing buildings. We'll negotiate sales for both large and small jobs in the commercial and industrial field. Advertising for us is a sore point. The brochure we had made up we didn't use because it doesn't reflect our real image. It might appeal to someone who's very artistic, but it wouldn't appeal to our clientele. Our newspaper advertising has been sporadic, and home shows don't pay off. We have no way of tying any sale to a show.

The radio promotions once used by the company had been assigned to an FM station operating out of a suburb. Though Mr. Fern was unaware of any research involved in choosing the morning hour promo-coverage, he felt certain that the radio station itself made the time-slot decision.

The company issued a new commission policy in March 1980, with regard to wages and salaries for the sales personnel. Some of the more important points were:

1. Maximum commission on each sale shall be established at the time of quote.

2. Commission paid, in dollars, will depend on the actual results of the installation when compared to estimate. A reduction, equal to the percentage over estimate, will result, except that no commission will be paid for jobs with a gross profit of less than 23 percent unless previously authorized by the sales manager or company officer.

3. For sales-estimators who do not receive fringe benefits other than transportation, a split of 50-50 on profit over 30 percent will be paid. These people will not be eligible for company profit sharing.

4. Sales personnel receiving fringe benefits will be eligible for the company profit-sharing program.

5. Weekly draw of salespeople will be set at approximately $250, depending on sales record.

Mr. Fern felt that competition had not been a significant factor for the company. When asked, however, why the residential segment of the company had failed, Mr. Fern remarked, "Our advertising for residential was a complete flop all the way." The main reason for the failure, though, he attributed to the fact that J. W. Adams was known primarily for its commercial and industrial work. "Other companies who specialize in residential got the jobs because a lot of people didn't know we even did residential. We still receive calls on the residential jobs but refer them immediately to Adams Service." Mr. Fern summed up the company's line of thought in deciding to shift residential to Adams Service: "We finally came to the conclusion that you just can't sell commercial and residential out of one operation."

Neither Mr. Adams nor Mr. Fern indicated any plans to introduce the new company to the public via a promotional campaign. Business was generated solely by word-of-mouth and the efforts of the salesperson, Tim Bach.

Mr. Fern commented, too, on the company's operations and what he felt were the sales department's major problems:

> I don't want to go back to bidding on new construction. We should stay away from those large jobs in order to maintain our reputation. Sales are slow in coming because of economic conditions. People are price buyers right now rather than quality buyers. Our immediate problem is a lack of orders, but the real problem is the lack of personnel. I think we need one or two dedicated people who could bring in the business. We already have 40 percent of the good customers in the area through repeat business. Eventually the company could support four good people, but right now we just don't have the money.

An HPAC survey of the $4.3 billion market showed actual estimated values (Exhibit 2). Overall, Exhibit 2 estimated a limited growth situation for the industry. Industrial plants, as indicated were expected to be flat in 1981, while multiple dwellings were expected to suffer the greatest decrease.

INDUSTRY TRENDS

The following is a brief review of industry background, trends, and projections for the years 1979 and 1980. For the building industry as a whole, privately-financed housing starts in 1979 amounted to 1.74 million dwelling units, down from 2.02 million in 1978. Total investment in all types of new construction for 1979 was reported at 229.0 billion, or 11.7 percent greater than in 1978. Privately-financed residential construction amounted to $99 billion, and industrial construction reached $15 billion in 1979. The dollar figure for commercial projects amounted to $24.9 billion, and all publicly-financed construction last year totaled $49.0 billion.

According to the *Value Line Investment Survey:*[1]

> Mortgage commitment rates for conventional home mortgages have jumped over two percentage points since August 1980 to around 15%, where they

Exhibit 2

ARI Data for Installed Value of Nonresidential Air Conditioning for 1970 through 1979 together with HPAC estimates for 1980 and 1981

Year	Total Millions of dollars	Field engineered systems		Unitary systems	
		Millions of dollars	Percent	Millions of dollars	Percent
1970	3122.8	2136.0	68.4	986.8	31.6
1971	3215.9	2120.1	65.9	1095.8	34.1
1972	3297.8	1945.3	59.0	1352.5	41.0
1973	3538.8	1968.5	55.6	1570.3	44.4
1974	3560.0	2082.5	58.5	1477.5	41.5
1975	3472.7	2308.5	66.5	1164.2	33.5
1976	3352.3	1915.2	57.1	1437.1	42.9
1977	3511.6	1969.9	56.1	1541.7	43.9
1978	3654.4	2066.9	56.6	1587.5	43.4
1979	4393.0	2447.2	55.7	1945.8	44.3
1980*	4835.0	3000.0	62.0	1835.0	38.0
1981*	5000.0	3000.0	60.0	2000.0	40.0

*HPAC estimates.

are currently. Although mortgage rate increases initially meet with strong resistance, higher mortgage rates do come to be accepted... housing starts dropped sharply in 1974-75 in conjunction with the recession and an increase in mortgage rates to 9%. Rates remained at this level for the next two years and were accepted by increasing numbers of homebuyers. Housing starts increased from 1.1-1.2 million in 1975 to around 2 million in 1977 and 1978. Then the effective mortgage commitment rates began to rise rapidly—from about 10.5% in January 1979 to more than 16% in May 1980. These increases, in conjunction with the 1980 recession, forced housing starts below the 1 million level in mid-1980. Note, though, starts in the latter part of 1980 recovered to around 1.5 million despite interest rate levels higher than any in the previous decade.

We're projecting that the bank prime lending rate (the one charged most credit-worthy customers for short-term loans) will subside from 20% currently to around 15% in the last half of this year. Mortgage rates will be far stickier, in our opinion. With lenders burnt by highly volatile interest rates over the past year, we think mortgage rates for a conventional 80% loan won't descend much below 14%. Part of the reason for the sharp drop in housing starts last year (from 1.74 million in 1979 to about 1.3 million) was that homebuyers were waiting for mortgage rates to fall. We think in 1981 homebuyers will realize that rates are not likely to drop sharply over the next few years, and will step up their purchase plans—as they did in 1975-77 when rates stabilized. This, combined with a projected modest decrease in mortgage rates in the latter part of the year, will allow 1981 housing starts to rise to an estimated 1.5–1.6 million, about 20% above the prior-year level. We project that housing starts next year will continue to expand to 1.8–1.9 million as mortgage rates descend modestly further.

Over the 3- to 5-year period, we think Americans will become more used to paying a higher proportion of income for housing. The payment for a 25-year, 80% mortgage on the median-priced new single-family home required about 18% of median family income in 1965. That percentage rose to almost 30% in 1979. Last year such a home cost an estimated 32% of median family income. We expect home ownership to continue to be part of the American dream over this decade despite the far greater mortgage burden. Strong demand will emanate from the large number of people born in the baby boom of the 1950s, who will be reaching homebuying age. The 25-34 age group, which has accounted for almost half of new, single-family home purchases, will increase from 35 million in 1979 to 40 million by 1985, according to U.S. Census Bureau projections. The 35-44 group, according to their projections, will expand by almost 6 million persons to 31 million over this time period. Indeed, the National Association of Home Builders has estimated demand for new homes at an average 2.3 million units annually for this decade. However, the population push on housing demand will be mitigated by the inability of many families to qualify for a mortgage on a new home, resulting in our estimate of 1.8-1.9 million starts for the 1983-85 period.

Although the American dream of owning a home will persist, we think it will be modified. We expect cheaper-to-build and maintain multi-unit structures will comprise a larger percentage of housing production 3 to 5 years hence. In fact, this trend is already in place. Multi-unit starts rose from 29% of total conventional starts in 1978 to 32% in 1979 to 35% in 1980. One of the main reasons for housing starts remaining near the 1.5 million level in December 1980 was a 9.1% increase in multi-unit starts from the previous month. Single-family starts fell 6.4%. Another expected characteristic of housing 3 to 5 years hence: homes will be smaller, to ease the cost burden. Also, Southern and urban, rather than rural, construction will expand more quickly due to obvious fuel savings. Remodeling outlays will swell as many homeowners decide to upgrade their old home rather than assume an expensive new mortgage.

Expectations for the air conditioning and heating market in particular are provided by some of the leaders in the industry.

Mr. Bob Korte, editor, *Heating/Piping/Air Conditioning,* stated:[2]

A year ago, with the final figures not yet available, we confidently estimated that the nonresidential air conditioning market in 1979 had surpassed the $4 billion mark in terms of installed value for the first time in history. It did indeed, by a substantial margin, and the rise has continued throughout 1980. We now estimate that in 1981, only two years later, the nonresidential air conditioning market, fueled by both the health of the industry and continuing inflation, will reach the $5 billion level in installed value.

What about 1981? Economists seem to agree that we are in a recovery period, but they also tend to use words such as *wobbly* and *shaky* to describe that recovery. The consensus seems to be that nonresidential construction will be up from 3 to 7 percent in terms of dollars, but flat or down as much as 5 percent in terms of square feet. They, as we, feel that strength in nonresidential construction will come in the second half. The residential construction market seems to be up for grabs. Until recently, everyone was confident of vigorous activity in this area in 1981, but as interest rates climb once again, that confidence has faded rapidly.

Our estimates for the nonresidential air conditioning market for 1981 . . . reflect our belief that the field engineered segment will be flat in comparison with 1980. Shipments and bookings remain strong at present but (lagging construction activity) will tail off later in the year. Unitary systems, we feel, will show enough strength throughout the year to bring the total to the $5 billion level.

Possibly overriding these prognostications will be the effects of a new administration and new faces in Congress. The events of last November have generated an aura of optimism within our industry, and if that optimism is warranted—if government does indeed restrict its regulatory activities and if it provides necessary incentives—the air conditioning industry could be on the threshold of tremendous growth. In particular, the retrofit and replacement market, now strong but nowhere near its mammoth potential, could be unleashed to achieve the vital goal of energy conservation.

Mr. Melvin L. Meyer, president, Cleaver-Brooks Division of Aqua-Chem, Inc. in Milwaukee, Wisconsin, believed:[3]

All indications promise the decade of the 1980s to be one of excitement and challenge in our industry of heat generation and energy utilization. The realization of this has been slow to occur because of both internal and external factors in this industry. These have left the industry sluggish throughout most of the initial year of the decade but should ease throughout 1981.

Internally, the industry has been re-evaluating its role and its contribution to society. The days of cheap heat are gone, and a new consciousness has been evolving to provide our product of heat at the lowest practical cost—and that cost includes expenditures of all resources.

Coupled with this has been the external influence of the general economy. The severe slowing in 1980 substantially suppressed demand. Even though evidence of recovery is emerging, tangible effects are not anticipated until mid-1981. Even then, the residuals of high inflation and tight money, and a general "wait and see" attitude, may tend to dampen demand for heating equipment below its potential.

Interpretation of these influences for 1981, however, suggests modest improvement for the industry's products. Certainly select segments of the market will continue their current rapid growth while others poise for the cyclical recovery.

Overlooking this rather conservative outlook for 1981, however, are several factors and trends that may dramatically alter eventuality.

Certainly one is the effect of a new occupant in the White House and a new contingent on Capitol Hill.

The new conservative political wave views business more favorably, and this could result in incentive programs and funding to boost all forms of construction and capital investment by business. Industry and private and public institutions have been seeking new ways to make plants and buildings more energy efficient and reduce the cost of energy use. Incentives for capital improvements would almost surely add impetus to this trend, resulting in greater demand for new boilers and other heating equipment. The new Administration has also vowed to reduce federal bureaucracy and particularly to align the efforts of the Environmental Protection Agency and the Department of Energy. Such an achievement could only help to remove some of the strangling regulations that slow and add tremendous cost to every project.

ACCOUNTING-FINANCE

In the past five years, the J. W. Adams Company had spent a total of $78,103 in legal and auditing fees.

The company has never employed an accountant or finance person. Financial records were handled by a Mrs. Rule, who was more of a bookkeeper with experience than an accountant with knowledge to analyze. As for her system, Tom Adams stated that she was the only one who knew how it worked. She retired in 1978, at which time Adams took over.

Adams stated that he had no faith in the statements. Since the Adams Company was a closed corporation, they did not normally require audited statements, although they were required for some of the loans the company had received.

When asked why he did not hire an accountant, Mr. Adams stated, "No money."

The company employed a production manager, a sales manager, a person to take care of inventory, and a president but no accounting or finance manager. Adams also handled the firm's financial matters along with being a general manager. There was no mention of time sheets being placed in the folders. Cost sheets, a summary of time and material, were kept. Partial billings were completed at the end of the month with production supplying job summaries to insure proper billing. When the job was completed, the cost sheets were summarized, and a final bill was sent out. No analysis of the job was performed other than for billing purposes.

Sixty-seven percent of Adams' funds in 1979-80 came from decreasing trade receivables and increasing trade payables (Exhibit 3).

Since 1975, nearly $100,000 in unapplied labor costs had been recorded in the sales department alone. The service department had recorded almost $4,000 in the same period. Unapplied materials for the same period were nearly $60,000. Since this did not include 1979, the average per year was $16,963 for labor and $9,912 for materials. These figures indicated a need for improving the collection and assignment of material and labor costs (Exhibit 4).

Adams' collection procedure was as follows:

1. List accounts over 30 days.
2. Call by person who deals with particular customer.
3. Repeat calls.

Exhibit 3

J. W. Adams Company
Comparative Balance Sheets

ASSETS	1979	1980
Cash	$ 3,157	$ 12,136
Trade A/R	281,576	234,432
Current installments: Land contract	7,337	7,337
Notes and A/R employees	11,948	14,724
Federal income tax refund: Receivable.......	7,486	—
Inventories.............................	89,068	101,250
Prepaid expenses	5,226	8,104
Deposits	264	7,556
Marketable securities......................	5,888	5,888
Property and equipment....................	38,716	36,306
Cash value—officer life insurance............	6,525	7,756
Leased equipment	6,401	14,603
Land contract	86,233	78,797
Workman's compensation premium..........	9,856	—
Stock subscription: Receivable	4,035	3,052
Unamortized lease costs	—	10,425
Total assets	$563,716	$542,366

LIABILITIES AND STOCKHOLDERS' EQUITY	1979	1980
Notes and mortages payable	$141,693	$ 85,238
Trade A/P...............................	163,273	216,592
Customer advanced payments...............	925	—
Officer advance...........................	118	—
Union dues and funds	13,462	6,001
Accrued interest	1,612	3,225
Accrued payroll	19,654	—
Accrued payroll taxes	15,791	8,174
Accrued sales taxes	2,489	(574)
Accrued property taxes....................	—	3,000
Accrued welfare, pension, and industry funds	—	1,933
Deposits on leased equipment...............	500	5,136
Notes and mortgages payable	61,139	161,925
Capital stock	136,934	136,934
Retained earnings.........................	6,126	6,001
Profit to date	—	(91,219)
Total liabilities and stockholders' equity	$563,716	$542,366

4. Reluctantly turn over to collection agency (charge of 25 percent on all collected accounts).

Adams had also indicated a policy of finance charges. This was a very good idea because it induced customers to pay on time and avoid the extra charge. The only problem was that their bookkeeping machine could not compute the charge. Therefore, it was done by hand. Bills sent out did not contain the charges, since there was no time to compute them.

Exhibit 4

J. W. Adams Company
Unapplied Labor and Material Costs

	Service Department	Sales Department
1975 unapplied labor	$22,933	$2,867
unapplied materials	2,046	–
1976 unapplied labor	27,596	4,212
unapplied materials	307	7,622
1977 unapplied labor	20,995	9,232
unapplied materials	419	–
1978 unapplied labor	18,437	30,920
unapplied materials	542	419
1979 (not recorded in financial statements)		
1980 unapplied labor	8,000	4,000
unapplied materials	500	200

Source: Financial Statements.

Tom Adams indicated his plans to reduce inventories to around $20,000, yet in the 1979-80 fiscal year they increased by $12,181 (Exhibit 3). There was no system of inventory control.

According to Adams, the lag between payments and receipts was an industry-wide problem. Materials for a job had to be purchased in advance and payment was not received until the job was completed. A job could last as long as a year or more, and consequently, could tie up cash for extended periods of time. This problem was somewhat alleviated by escalation clauses in the contracts, which provided for partial billing of delivered materials.

NOTES

1. "Building Industry," *Value Line Investment Survey,* February 6, 1981.
2. Bob Korte, Editor, "Air Conditioning Market: On to New Record Levels," *Heating/Piping/Air Conditioning,* January 1981, p. 151.
3. Melvin L. Meyer, "Factors at Work Could Make 1981 Great for Heating," *Heating/Piping/Air Conditioning,* January 1981, p. 152.

Case 3-4

Westinghouse Electric Corporation: Overhead Distribution Transformer Division*

Bob Ray, the marketing manager for the Overhead Distribution Transformer Division (OHDT) of Westinghouse Electric Corporation, was concerned about his field sales engineers. It had been four years since OHDT had initiated any sort of formal training program directed at the field sales force. Company information revealed that the sales force had an annual turnover of ten percent. His concern for newer salespersons' depth of training was paralleled by his conviction that the veteran sales engineers would benefit from more exposure to product knowledge, especially in light of recent innovations. Interpretation of direct and indirect feedback revealed that both groups were reaching for more depth in product knowledge.

THE WESTINGHOUSE ELECTRIC CORPORATION

Westinghouse was the world's oldest and second largest manufacturer of electrical apparatus and appliances. Founded by inventor George Westinghouse in 1886, the corporation marketed some 300,000 variations of about 8,000 highly diversified basic products ranging from a simple piece of copper wire to a complex commercial nuclear power plant. The firm employed over 145,000 men and women in laboratories, manufacturing plants, sales offices, and distribution centers from coast to coast and around the world. Over 1,800 of its scientists and engineers were actively engaged in research and development activities. The corporation had more than 160,000 stockholders.

Because of its size and the diversity required to serve a variety of markets, Westinghouse was organized into four companies operating within the corporation. The companies were: Power Systems; Industry and Defense; Consumer Products; and Broadcasting, Learning and Leisure Time.

Each company was headed by a president, who had full responsibility for designing, building, and selling the company's products and services throughout the world. Each company had its own staff of specialists in certain fields. It also could draw on corporate resources for additional specialized support in fields such as marketing, manufacturing, engineering, design, research, personnel and public affairs, finance, and law.

*This case was prepared by Norman A. P. Govoni, Babson College, Richard R. Still, California Polytechnic State University, and Kent Mitchell, University of Georgia, with the intention of providing a basis for class discussion rather than illustrating either effective or ineffective management of a business situation. Reprinted with permission from *Application of Decision Sciences in Organizations: A Case Approach* by Joseph C. Latona and K. Mark Weaver with the cooperation of the American Institute for Decision Sciences, Atlanta, Georgia, 1980.

The basic organizational unit of the company was the division, each with its own line of products and services. Each division, in turn, was grouped with a number of other divisions with related products and services, such as major appliances, construction products, or power generation equipment.

Combined sales before taxes were $5.1 billion. The Power Systems Company was the leading contributor to income after taxes with a 43 percent contribution. The Power Systems Company was divided into two main areas: the Power Generation Group and the Transmission and Distribution Division located in Athens, Georgia.

OVERHEAD DISTRIBUTION TRANSFORMER DIVISION (OHDT)

OHDT considered itself first in facilities, developments, and service; and rightfully so, for it had led the nation in overhead distribution transformer sales since 1971 with a fairly consistent market share of about 23 percent. Industry sales were projected to be nearly $900 million by the early 1980s.

Since 1958, all Westinghouse overhead distribution transformers were designed and manufactured in the Athens plant. The previous manufacturing site was in Sharon, Pennsylvania. OHDT was particularly proud of its engineering leadership. In the past few years, Westinghouse had expanded its staff and facility in a time when others were cutting back. Bob Ray was instrumental in making this crucial marketing decision and was later honored with the Corporation's highest award, "The Order of Merit," an award given to three employees each year. In the capacity over demand ratio, the company had been 131 percent, 85 percent, and 88 percent respectively, for the past three years.

COMPETITION

Westinghouse had been recognized for several decades as the primary innovator in the distribution transformer industry. Four other companies, each of which had active R & D facilities, were considered major innovators: General Electric, RTE, Allis-Chalmers, and McGraw-Edison. Other strong companies among the 29 national competitors were Wagner, Kuhlman, and Colt.

The Westinghouse product was generally ranked tops in its field, representing true value for dollar investment. Some competitors, though, had been successful in promoting a less expensive product.

THE CUSTOMER AND PRICING

The electric utility companies were the consumers for distribution transformers, and they were divided into three major classes: investor-owned utilities, rural electric cooperatives, and municipalities. There were approximately 300 investor-owned utilities which accounted for about 80 percent of consumption. The co-ops and municipalities numbered about 920 and 2,000, respectively, and together accounted for the remaining 20 percent. With the increasing migration of families and industries to metropolitan outskirts, the co-ops were expected to represent a considerably larger share of consumption in the years to come. There were about 33 million overhead distribution transformers across the nation. Sales in this market represented about 60 percent change-outs (i.e, replacements in an area where power consumption had increased) and 40 percent new development units.

In pricing, the major utilities negotiated year-long purchasing commitments during November-December of each year. Fierce price competition was prevalent among the investor-owned utilities and large discounts off list prices were normally expected. Pricing for the co-ops and municipalities was more stable with smaller discounts from list being offered. The method of negotiation was small orders throughout the year for the smaller utilities and the sealed bid method for the publicly-owned companies.

PROMOTION

Westinghouse advertised its electrical transmission, generation, and distribution equipment in leading electrical trade journals. Additionally, it was a member of the National Electrical Manufacturers Association (NEMA), which set standards for the industry. NEMA issued monthly reports to its members which included total market volume and member market share information. Distribution was by a field sales force selling direct to customers.

MARKETING MANAGEMENT

The marketing department of OHDT consisted of a marketing manager, a marketing services manager, and four area sales managers who were assisted by a staff of their own. The sales areas were divided geographically. Almost all personnel in the marketing department had an engineering background, which was considered a must in this complex field. The department had ultimate responsibility for success of its product. They were particularly proud that Westinghouse had been number one in market share of transformer sales each year since 1971.

The marketing department had been located in Athens since 1968, when it moved down from Sharon, Pennsylvania. Exhibit 1 shows where the marketing department fitted into the organization of the Athens firm.

THE FIELD SALES FORCE

Overhead distribution transformers were sold through two of the four Westinghouse companies: the Power Systems company and the Industry and Defense company. Each company had its own sales network, as shown in Exhibit 2.

There were over 300 Westinghouse corporate field sales engineers, district managers, and zone managers located throughout the country handling OHDT accounts. In addition to being loaded with OHDT products, the salespeople were responsible for other Westinghouse utility products. For example, they represented the Electrical Relay Division, Circuit Breaker Divison, and the Electric Meter Division, each of which was managed through other corporate channels. The field sales engineers, in serving several product divisions, reported to district managers for product loading.

Exhibit 1

Westinghouse Electric Corporation
Marketing Department—Athens, Georgia

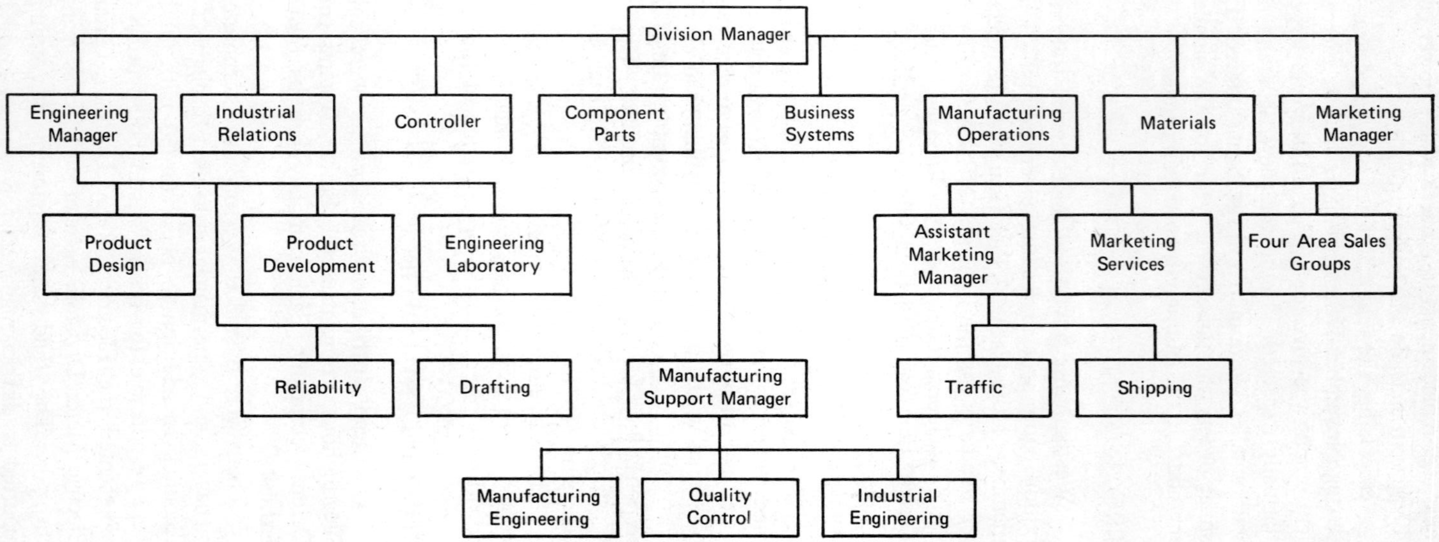

Exhibit 2

**Westinghouse Electric Corporation
Sales Organization Chart**

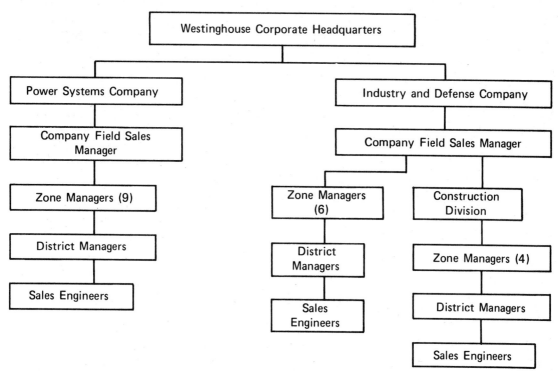

The area sales managers and their staffs (of OHDT) served the field sales engineers by taking and expediting product orders, answering product questions, and collecting feedback. Additionally, they traveled into the field to hold training seminars and to assist salespeople on important sales. Bob Ray often got involved in following through with especially important customers.

TRAINING A FIELD SALES ENGINEER

Westinghouse sales engineers were required to have a Bachelor of Science in Engineering. When brought into the corporation, the new recruit was first sent to Pittsburgh for a basic three-week orientation to the Westinghouse company. The recruit was then assigned to a corporate "graduate studies program" which lasted from three to twelve months, depending on his or her skills. Upon completion, he or she was assigned to the field as an assistant sales engineer to serve a training tenure which lasted anywhere from six to twenty-four months, again depending on individual requirements. During this period, the person would travel for a two-week period visiting the various manufacturing plants he or she would later serve. Each plant gave the future salesperson a two-day training and orientation seminar. Ideally, the sales engineers were supposed to return to these parent manufacturing divisions annually for refresher training. Additionally, they would attend district or zone training seminars held by representatives of the parent divisions.

A sales engineer, depending on experience and length of service to Westinghouse, drew a base salary averaging about $35,000 a year, not including bonus. The number of calls and the type of customer was established according to ability, experience, and product loading. It took, on the average, about $500,000 worth of sales to support a sales engineer in the field.

THOUGHTS OF AN OHDT AREA SALES MANAGER

Marvin Jones was one of the four area sales managers for the OHDT division. Prior to his present assignment, he was a field sales engineer for over 12 years. Reflecting on his days in the field, he remembered quite well the difficulties involved in attending training seminars held by the various divisions. Salespeople recognized that training was essential, that effective selling required sound training, and that a person's potential (not to mention the quota) really could not be realized without training. However, getting a salesperson to a training seminar was a difficult task, because when there was a sale to be made, there wasn't time for training. The training, as important as it was, would have to wait. At least this was the common thing when attendance at refresher training was more or less left to the individual sales engineer.

THE NEED TO TRAIN

Bob Ray was very concerned about the field sales force's depth of knowledge about overhead distribution transformers, especially in light of fairly recent innovations (a trend which would be expected to continue). He knew Westinghouse had become the leading producer of transformers, but he attributed this more to excellent engineering, excessive demand, and the expertise of his department. As questions were coming in to the area sales managers at a slightly higher than normal rate, he pinpointed the problem to training. He also knew that the economy might be expected to take a slight decline. With the growing threat that demand might slacken in the months to come, he felt that competition would really start getting rough. In addition, he realized that an unprepared sales force might not fare so well when the time came to give more in-depth and high quality sales presentations. And it had been a while since Athens had initiated a formal training program. The previous program, which was considered a success, consisted of a campaign to inform the sales force about the overhead distribution transformer, and, as a gimmick, miniature transformer parts were sent to the salespeople. Unfortunately, a salesperson's time was an extremely valuable commodity, and Bob Ray knew it. Training in any organization was one of the most difficult tasks to pull off effectively, even when the trainees were geographically close to management; but the Westinghouse field sales force, scattered across the nation, was another matter. Making the training task even more burdensome was the fact that these sales engineers had more than just the OHDT account to worry about. It was realized that Athens would have to compete for both time and attention.

FROM IDEAS TO ACTION

With the facts on the table, Bob Ray called on Larry Deal, who headed Marketing Services, and his assistant, Glynn Hodges, who at that time was involved with marketing communications. Hodges was sent to Pittsburgh a few times to work jointly with Earl Swartz, the corporate contact to the ad agency used by Westinghouse. By June, Hodges had the layout completed for the proposed solution to the training problem—a training campaign to be called "The Problem Solvers." Bob Ray liked it. It was estimated that the campaign would ultimately cost about $20,000 representing a large slice of the OHDT marketing budget. Exhibit 3 gives an idea of the estimated costs.

Exhibit 3

Westinghouse Overhead Distribution Transformers "The Problem Solvers"—Promotion

General

This document summarizes various elements of the "Problem Solver" promotion. The costs are based on quotations from suppliers who have seen initially prepared layouts.

Puzzles

Five puzzles will be purchased directly from supplier by Westinghouse.

Shipping Boxes for Puzzles

Four hundred each of five different size boxes plus one 6-by-6-inch envelope (for crossword puzzle and brochure mailing), each to be printed in two colors using the same "Problem Solver" design. (Suggestion: each box to have a different color on the design.)

Delivery time: six weeks from receipt of order.

Cost: including converting boxes, design preparation, color plates and printing - $2,500

Crossword Puzzle

To be completed by salesperson and submitted with photo to get personalized jigsaw puzzle prize.

Timing: Six weeks from receipt of words and clues from Westinghouse. Puzzles to be printed in simple 4-page format and inserted in envelope along with cover letter and brochure.

Cost: $800

Jigsaw Puzzle

One 11-by-14-inch puzzle will be sent to every salesperon submitting photo along with completed crossword puzzle. Photos will be held and sent in bulk to puzzle manufacturer, who will then send completed puzzle directly to each salesperson along with the original photo.

Timing: four weeks delivery from receipt of photographs.

Cost: $1,300

Cover Letters

Total of five (one for each puzzle mailing), 400 copies of each.

Cost: including artwork for masthead, copy editing, typesetting, and printing $600

Brochures

One brochure will accompany each of the five puzzle mailings. Each brochure will focus on one aspect of the overhead transformers. The cover will have a full color cover of the puzzle being sent; inside pages will be black and white and use existing line art.

Cost: including photos, typesetting, tissue layout and key art, copy editing, and production supervision for five 20-page booklets $12,000

Total Cost: up to $20,000

ABOUT "THE PROBLEM SOLVERS" CAMPAIGN

An overview of "The Problem Solvers" appears in Exhibit 4, which contains the following: background, program objectives, program implementation, elements of the program (Stages 1 and 2), and a summary of elements and timing.

Exhibit 4

Westinghouse Overhead Distribution Transformers
An Overview of "The Problem Solvers"

Background

The total market for overhead distribution transformers is very good. For Westinghouse, it is excellent.

While Athens is producing at full capacity and the current problem is meeting demand, there still remain several conditions with which Athens must cope if it is to achieve its long-range potential:

1. Many Westinghouse and agent salespeople do not understand the advantages of Westinghouse transformers.

2. There are competitors who manufacture and sell transformers at a cheaper price. These transformers are inferior to those at Westinghouse. The Westinghouse story, which must be communicated through sales personnel to customers, is a *value* story.

3. The present sales boom cannot be expected to continue indefinitely, and the sales force must be prepared to conduct tougher, more effective sales presentations.

Program Objectives

The object of this program is to make Westinghouse and agent sales personnel more effective representatives for Athens by showing them why Westinghouse is the value leader and by giving them the information and tools needed to make more effective presentations.

By accomplishing these objectives, the sales representatives will become more confident of their abilities—and the Westinghouse line. This growing confidence will, in turn, create even greater success.

Program Implementation

This is a two-stage program. The Stage 1 phase, the most important, is directed to the Westinghouse sales force and includes: an explanation of the program, a summary of the transformer market (and the profit contribution made by Westinghouse transformers), and detailed instruction on transformers (using the theme, "The Problem Solvers") along with unique mailings.

The Stage 2 phase is the person-to-person contact between salespeople and customers. Having been effectively indoctrinated into the advantages of Westinghouse transformers, the salespeople are now supplied with effective sales presentation material, which will make contact between sales representatives and customers more productive for the Athens division.

Elements of Program—*Stage 1*

1. Cover letter No. 1 from Mr. Meierkord (general manager, OHDT) or Mr. Ray spelling out the theme "The Problem Solvers," and the purpose of the program.

2. Instruction brochure No. 1 on Cover and Bushing Assembly along with puzzle.

3. Cover letter No. 2 from Meierkord or Ray.

4. Instruction brochure No. 2 on Tank Assembly along with puzzle.

5. Cover letter No. 3 from Meierkord or Ray.

6. Instruction brochure on Core & Coil Assembly along with puzzle.

7. Cover letter No. 4 from Meierkord or Ray. Letter to state that crossword puzzle answers are found in instruction booklet. If salesperson returns completed crossword puzzle along with any photograph of his or her choice, Athens will return a custom-made jigsaw puzzle made out of the photo.

8. Instruction brochure No. 4 on CSP (completely self-protected transformer) features along with crossword puzzle. Crossword puzzle will contain such clues as:

   CSP Transformers (OUTLAST) conventional types by 60 percent.

   CSP arresters (LOWER) discharge voltage on high surge currents.

   After overload trips breaker, breaker can be reset to (TEN) percent more capacity.

Elements of Program—*Stage 2*

After salespeople have studied the four bulletins, they are now better prepared to make more effective presentations to their customers. To help them in their calls, they will be furnished with the following:

1. Cover letter (No. 5) again from Meierkord or Ray, reiterating the profitability of transformers, that they are great "Problem Solvers," and that the salespeople (the ultimate "Problem Solvers") are now well prepared to communicate to their customers why Westinghouse transformers are truly the tops in the field. Cover letter will dwell on the importance of customer presentations, preparation, and follow-through.

2. Flip chart presentation entitled "Westinghouse Distribution Transformers: 'The Problem Solver.'" The presentation will summarize the most important "Features/ Functions/Benefits" from the four technical bulletins. The presentation will be designed in a horizontal format so that the pages are adaptable for photographic slide or strip film reproduction.

3. Customer booklet to be prepared using same text and artwork from the presentation flip chart. Booklet will be left with the customer as a reminder of what was presented and as a source document for later reference.

4. Capabilities brochure, about to be produced, can be an added ingredient to the presentation. While it emphasizes Athens' manufacturing capability — as opposed to the engineering emphasis of the presentation — the booklet is prestigious and will reflect Westinghouse distribution transformers as being a value line.

If not used as part of the presentation, the capabilities brochure would make an impressive mailing to the customer along with a "thank you" letter for listening to the presentation.

Summary—Elements and Timing

Stage 1

First Mailing:	Cover Letter No. 1 (Program Summary)
	Bulletin No. 1 Cover and Bushing
	Puzzle No. 1 (Adult Game)
	Master Crossword Puzzle

Second Mailing:	Cover Letter No. 2
	Bulletin No. 2 Tank Assembly
(Two months later)	Puzzle No. 2

Third Mailing:	Cover Letter No. 3
	Bulletin No. 3 Core and Coil Assembly
(Two months later)	Puzzle No. 3

Fourth Mailing:	Cover Letter No. 4
	Bulletin No. 4 CSP Features
(Two months later)	Puzzle No. 4

Stage 2

Fifth Mailing:	Cover Letter No. 5 (Customer Presentations)
	Flip Chart Presentation
(Two months later)	Presentation Summary for Customer
	Athens Capability Brochure
	Puzzle No. 5

To catch the salesperson's attention, the proposed campaign would consist of expensive and eye-catching adult games which emphasized puzzle problems. The games would cost from $4 - $5 each; a good example was a three-dimensional tic-tac-toe game made of three clear plastic decks mounted on top of each other. Each player was represented by either clear blue or yellow marbles about an inch in diameter each. The game could be won horizontally, vertically, or diagonally.

Along with the mailing of each game would be a cover letter and an information bulletin emphasizing a particular feature of the overhead distribution transformer. As the salesperson read each information bulletin, he or she would fill in "clues" to a master crossword puzzle. When the mailings were completed, the salesperson would send in the completed crossword puzzle and picture of himself or herself (along with the rest of the family if desired) to the marketing department in Athens. Athens would have the picture made into a jigsaw puzzle and return it to the participant a few weeks later.

THE MARKETING SERVICES DIVISION—A SPECIAL PROJECT

Larry Deal's Marketing Services Division had been assigned the responsibility of supporting the ad agency by providing the technical information necessary for turning "The Problem Solvers" idea into a manageable campaign. Brian Kennedy, assigned to marketing communications, and assistant Jody Unsler had been asked to design the instruction brochures and crossword puzzle. Also, coordination with Earl Swartz had resulted in the initial selection of a container for the adult games. The container was a cardboard box with a design of jigsaw puzzle parts; each part had a letter on it with the total spelling being "The Problem Solvers." Kennedy put in some long hours working on the instruction brochures. In explaining the various components of the transformer, he had decided to set a conversational sales presentation scene between a Westinghouse salesperson and a purchasing agent. The salesperson, who was "Mr. Problem Solver" or "Ms. Problem Solver," was smoothly answering the questions asked by a purchasing agent, who was appropriately labeled "Mr. A. Gent" or "Ms. A. Lady."

EARLY NOVEMBER

One morning in early November, Bob Ray was relaxing at his desk sipping a cup of coffee. He was thinking about "The Problem Solvers" campaign. Things were moving along pretty well. At the present rate he would be able to meet the January 15 target date for the first mailing. He knew $20,000 was a lot of money for OHDT to spend on a training campaign of this type, but he was confident in the overall idea and felt it was the best way to reach such a broad and isolated target. However, a few decisions remained. There was some question about the two-month interval between each of the five mailings. He definitely wanted the sales force ready for November-December when the big utilities would negotiate year-long contracts for the following year. In a way he wanted the campaign to last a good while, as it represented a big chunk of the budget, but he wondered whether the field sales force's attention would be held over such a period. Another thought entered his mind about the effectiveness of the campaign's feedback mechanism. He remembered Glynn Hodges said he anticipated a 65 percent response. Another point that was undefined in the campaign was what stand OHDT should take on the future newcomers to the field sales force. Since the previous campaign, the new people learned through OJT (on-the-job-training) and sales materials, as well as picking up what they could from OHDT bulletins. However, this provided only short-range coverage and would break down in the long run, or when making sales got tough. This had been one of the factors contributing to the present situation.

With those thoughts in mind, Bob Ray decided to call a division head meeting that afternoon.

Case 3–5

Ocala Opportunities Inc.*

Steven Arrowood, executive director of Ocala Opportunities Inc., was pondering a problem which he felt would influence the future direction of his organization. How could Ocala Opportunities develop, either alone or in cooperation with other organizations, a product (and a marketing strategy for this product) which would provide a continual source of work for his "clients" and a continual source of revenue for his organization?

BACKGROUND

Ocala Opportunities Inc., established since 1973, was located in the city of Tuelo, population 9,000. Its "clients," who were physically and/or mentally handicapped workers being served by or utilizing the services of a social agency, were drawn from Ocala County, where Tuelo was located, or from the adjoining counties of Birch and Sewell (with a total population of 56,000). The primary task of Ocala Opportunities Inc. was to provide a "sheltered workshop" for these physically and/or mentally handicapped persons. It was begun with a federal grant from the Developmental Disability Services and facilities Act, which provided funds for three employees but no equipment. Since the grant was received in midyear, unused salary monies provided funds for two used vehicles. Funds from this original grant ended after a two-year "start-up" period. Since 1975 Ocala Opportunities had generated funding and services by "tapping existing agencies" such as the county recreation department, county commissioners, and local mental health agencies. In addition, it had received a $20,000 vocational rehabilitation grant for supplies, two new vehicles, other equipment, and a work adjustment coordinator's salary. A second grant from the office of Health, Education, and Welfare Rural Transit Division enabled Ocala Opportunities to purchase two additional outfitted vans for handicapped persons.

ORGANIZATION

The staff of Ocala Opportunities consisted of three persons: Steven Arrowood, executive director; Lottie Clark, vocational rehabilitation counselor; and Muriel Haven, adult developmental activity program (ADAP) counselor.

*This case was prepared by W. Daniel Rountree and Ronald M. Zigli, Appalachian State University, with the intention of providing a basis for class discussion rather than illustrating either effective or ineffective management of a business situation. Copyright 1976 by W. Daniel Rountree and Ronald M. Zigli. Distributed by the Intercollegiate Case Clearing House, Boston, Massachusetts. All rights reserved to the contributors.

In addition, there was a secretary-bookkeeper, and two vocational rehabilitation aides. A twelve-person board of directors served as the governing body. Only one person on the board was a business person; all the others had some association with mental health or social welfare organizations.

Ocala Opportunities worked closely with other social agencies in the three-county area they served. Clients desiring to be a part of the sheltered workshop came into the program through referral from a vocational rehabilitation agency or other agencies which provided Ocala with social, medical, and psychological background information. Once clients became a part of the Ocala program, they went immediately into a 30-day period of evaluation to determine their abilities, talents, interests, and weaknesses. During the period of evaluation, vocational evaluators worked with the clients in different work settings and gave them a series of tests to decide which program area the client should enter. After the evaluation period, clients went into one of two program areas: (1) work adjustment services, a short-term program which prepared persons for entry into the community work force, or (2) the adult developmental activity program, which was for an undefined period of time in which minimally productive persons spent a half day in work activities, and a half day in educational activities.

Funding for these activities was provided as follows: (1) from vocational rehabilitation funds—$11.00 per day for a vocational evaluator and $7.50 per day for someone working in work adjustment services, and (2) $125 per month from state title XX funds for a person working in the adult developmental activity program. These funds covered client transportation, meals, administrative costs, shop operations and equipment, and operating expenses. There were 32 vocational rehabilitation and adult developmental activity program clients at Ocala, and the actual cost of care had been calculated at $250 per person/per month.

CLIENT ACTIVITIES

Activities of clients at Ocala Opportunities depended upon whether they were in the work adjustment program or in ADAP. In work adjustment training, clients would be placed in serving, clothing construction sewing, woodworking, or janitorial work. Some of the specific products they produced, in entirety or partially, included wooden plaques, display racks, pillows, dolls, woven chair bottoms, light-switch assemblies, sock repair, and electronic resistor sleeve assemblies. ADAP clients spent a half day in educational programs learning simple skills. The other half day was spent in work similar to work adjustment clients—on primarily craft items such as baskets, chair bottoms, weaving, or simple assembly tasks.

Both work adjustment and ADAP clients received a check at the end of each two weeks. The pay varied but was not less than $1.00 per day. Pay scales were based on production (piece) rates; thus, wages could be adjusted upward, depending on how well they worked in the areas in which they were placed. Any pay received at the workshop was considered a fee received while in training, not wages paid in employment. Clients worked Mondays through Fridays 12 months a year. They worked from 8 a.m. to 3 p.m. with 30 minutes for lunch and a morning and afternoon break of 15 minutes each.

THE SITUATION AT OCALA

The situation at Ocala was very favorable, but it could deteriorate very quickly unless action was taken and improvements made. Clients at Ocala were busy with items being produced in their own workshop and with subcontracting work for local industries. Subcontracting work had been sporadic and was a "feast or famine" situation. At times the workshop was loaded with rush jobs, and at other times there was no work. Among the subcontracting work was: electronic resistor sleeve assemblies for a local electronics firm, light-switch assemblies for a local electric contractor, wooden display racks for a local producer of jewelry products, and sock repair for a local manufacturer. All of these subcontracts were "one-shot deals" and might not be renewed. Payment to Ocala from the firms was on a piece rate and was approximately the same wages workers in the local plants received, but it did not include payment to Ocala for their overhead expenses.

Ocala Opportunities was housed in a building 150-by-30-feet in total floor area. The contract (work) area constituted approximately one-half of this space. There was a completely equipped kitchen and a woodworking shop completely equipped with basic power tools. Ocala had free access to by-products from local branch plants of furniture companies, electronics and electrical companies, hosiery and lingerie mills, a leather goods manufacturer, a shoe company, nurseries and florists, and a dairy. There were no facilities for pickup or delivery except using one of the vans. The operating budget for Ocala's shop was $100,000.

There was no guaranteed market for the items produced by the clients. Ocala had been permitted to use a log cabin with 300 sq. feet of floor space for $75 a month rent. This cabin was located within the grounds of a local tourist attraction and carried a large sign advertising "Ocala Oddities" crafted by Ocala natives. Approximately $1,000 in net profit had been generated in the two and one-half month tourist season "Ocala Oddities" had been open. No other retail outlet in the three-county area sold products made by Ocala Opportunities clients.

Faced with the uncertainty of continuing subcontracts from local manufacturers, the uncertainty of continuing grant money, and the minimal revenue generated from "Ocala Oddities," Steven Arrowood felt he must very quickly come up with a product which could be produced by minimally skilled persons that would have a continuing market and would provide continuous revenues for his organization. If this objective was met, Ocala Opportunities could become self-sufficient and could provide work with dignity for its clients.

SECTION **IV**

POLICY ISSUES IN PRODUCTION AND OPERATIONS MANAGEMENT

Production or operations management for an organization is a major functional area for any enterprise. Generally issues in this functional area focus on organizational efficiency of the production of goods or rendering of a service. Significant improvements in the efficiency of the production/operations function in organizations began when the scientific method was applied to scientific management by Frederick W. Taylor in the early 1900s. Later, refinements lead to the evolution of management science and operations research. The cases presented in this section highlight some common problems found in both manufacturing and service industries. Although the situations portrayed are not exhaustive, they are representative of the problems faced in production and operation facilities.

This section begins with cases that present situations which are most amenable to resolution using engineering, shop floor, and scientific management solutions. Then cases are introduced that become progressively more complex relative to the quantitative methods necessary for problem solution.

Croydon Incorporated is a manufacturing firm situated in Mishawaka, Indiana. The reader is introduced to scheduling, inventory control, reorder point, records keeping, and shop floor problems indigenous to a manufacturing environment. This case is primarily descriptive, not quantitative, and requires the reader to analyze problems in a production planning framework. Inventory control is one important issue in the problem environment.

Inventory control is addressed again in *Redskin Auto Parts*. This time, the reader is called upon to consider alternative inventory control models and propose a specific design for a computerized inventory control system. The next case, *Southwest University Recruiting Office,* carries the evaluation and design of management information systems one step further. The importance of an accurate, timely, up-to-date information system is addressed; and the problems and procedures for an analysis of information needs by multiple users are presented. This case focuses on user information needs, decision points, and priority systems. Touched upon are such things as the feasibility study, systems design requirements, and other relevant topics. Depending upon the level of sophistication and background of the reader, different types and levels of analysis can be anticipated.

The next case focuses on some problems in a service firm. *International Correspondence Alternatives of a World Class Bank* concerns a proposed firm designed to provide a courier service for an international bank. A feasibility study is called for in this case. Top management has requested an evaluation of the cost effectiveness of implementing a courier service for overseas transportation of documents of bank transactions. A chronology of transaction data is presented, and the reader is challenged to build an analytical or simulation model to assess the effectiveness of such a service.

The last case in this section is entitled *Armco, Inc.: The Bubble Policy* and focuses on the application of the linear programming model to an environmental protection agency air pollution problem. The impact of legislation on Armco and the use of the linear programming model to solve such a problem constitute an interesting application of quantitative methods to a production problem.

Case 4–1

Croydon Incorporated*

In early 1979 Larry Caldwell, materials manager at Croydon, Incorporated, discussed with Hank Thompson the problems the plant had been experiencing in manufacturing:

> The mechanism that is used in the breakers gives us all sorts of trouble, Hank. It has been bugging us for years, as a matter of fact. Sure, the mech's are made on time so the assembly of the breakers is not delayed. But the price we pay for it is a constant expediting mode with hot tags all over the place.

Hank Thompson, originally an industrial engineer with many years experience in manufacturing, had become more and more interested in production planning over the years. He was now working under Larry, who encouraged his active interest in his job. Hank had participated in several courses and seminars in production management during the last year. Hank's reply was:

> I know, Larry. I've been following the production of the mechanisms for two months now, and it is close to chaos now and then. There are too many runs of just a few parts to satisfy the needs from final assembly. The numerous teardowns of jobs already set up are disruptive and inefficient. I made a little study last week of all the parts that go into the mech. Believe it or not, 42 percent of them had an inventory balance of zero. Most of these parts were already ordered, though, with due dates ranging from months in the past to months in the future.

THE PRODUCT

The Croydon plant was situated in Mishawaka, Indiana. It had been in operation since 1961 and had been expanded twice since that time. It employed 116 people, 78 of whom were working in the factory. Croydon's annual sales were around $18 million. The plant's main product line was stationary circuit breakers for utility customers and heavy industry.

*This case was prepared by Urban Wemmerlov, University of Wisconsin, with the intention of providing a basis for class discussion rather than illustrating either effective or ineffective management of a business situation. Reprinted with permission from *Application of Decision Sciences in Organizations: A Case Approach* by Joseph C. Latona and K. Mark Weaver with the cooperation of the American Institute for Decision Sciences, Atlanta, Georgia, 1980.

The circuit breaker, of which there were three different models, was a three-pole, AC heavy-duty fault protector designed for substation or pole-top installation on 25 or 34.5 kilovolt grounded distribution systems. The basic function of the breaker was to protect circuitry from the damaging power surge created by a short in the system. When equipped with appropriate transformers and relays, the breakers could sense an overload condition. An overload could be created by such events as a tree falling on a power line or a momentary flashover. The surge of power created by the fault could be immediately sensed, and the breaker would open. After an adjustable time, the breaker would automatically reclose the circuit to which it was connected. If the overload condition still existed, the breaker would again open up. The breaker could be set to cycle up to four times before it stopped in an opened position. If this was the case, the place where the breaker was installed had to be visited by repair personnel to determine the prevailing cause of the overload. The actual closing and opening of the circuit was done by three rods (one for each pole) that connected or cut off the current while moving up and down. The mechanical movements of the rods were done with the help of a shaft, driven by a mechanism usually just called "the mech."

MANUFACTURING

The stationary circuit breakers were manufactured and assembled in a separate area of the plant. There was one manufacturing section feeding two assembly sections, with each area managed by a supervisor. There was also a stockroom where the approximately 600 parts making up the breakers were stored. This layout, where better than 95 percent of the feeder section's capacity was devoted exclusively to circuit breakers, was set up in 1975. The creation of this "integrated line," as it was called, was an attempt to better control the manufacturing of the breakers and to alleviate the problems with stock-outs in the final assembly. With this arrangement, the number of stock-outs had actually gone down, but several other problems were still remaining.

PRODUCTION PLANNING

The production of the circuit breakers was basically a make-parts-to-stock/assemble-to-order type of operation, even if some parts were purchased, manufactured, or subassembled directly for final assembly. The build schedule for the breakers was specified in the management load plan. The load plan was decided upon after negotiations between representatives from the marketing, manufacturing, and production control departments and was revised every month. It was made up from breakers that were sold and to be delivered within the next 20 weeks. In the past the demand for substation circuit breakers had been relatively stable. The targeted production rate for all three models was currently 40 units per week.

The mech was made up exclusively of parts and subassemblies which were stock items. Each mech consisted of approximately 50 purchased and 75 manufactured parts. About 50 parts were used in the final assembly operation. The mech itself was not a stock item, and there were no stocked parts between the mech and the final breaker. Every week accepted customer orders due 21 weeks or more from the current week (combined lead time was 20 weeks) were exploded to produce computer printed order documents for the nonstocked items. The horizon actually available to final assembly was the current week plus the next four weeks. Because of the stable demand in the past, the shop papers representing each customer order were not transferred to the final assembler. Instead, the assembler knew it was expected that 40 mechanisms per week should be made.

FINAL ASSEMBLY OF THE MECHANISM

The final assembler had a rack with all parts necessary to assemble a mech next to the work station. The integrated line had one material handler, whose task was to make sure that these racks were filled with enough parts to let the assembly operation run smoothly. If the stockroom happened to be out of a part that was needed for assembly, but this part was under fabrication in the shop, the material coordinator was notified. The material coordinator's job was to act as a link between production control and the stockroom and to provide manufacturing with the material it needed. It was also the responsibility of the material coordinator to hand out shop packages to the supervisor when orders were due for release. In situations where assembly had a chance of being starved because of a missing part in the stockroom, the material coordinator could see that this part bypassed the stockroom. The part would then go directly from fabrication to the final assembly area. A special simultaneous receipt/issue form would be filled out by the coordinator and sent to the stockroom. This information would then be passed on to production control.

INVENTORY CONTROL

All parts in the mechanism were controlled by a computerized reorder point system. Manufacturing and purchasing orders for parts were activated when a disbursement of an item lowered the inventory position (on hand and on order) below the reorder point. Every day the stockroom personnel sent information about inventory transactions to production control. These transactions were keyed in at a CRT terminal and processed during the night. For items that had to be ordered, a punched card and a history report were produced the next day. A planner had to sign the card in order to approve the suggested order but could override the system by changing the order quantity and/or the due date for the order. After approval, the processing of the punched card triggered the overnight printing of either a purchasing requisition or a shop package. The latter consisted of manufacturing information sheets (Exhibit 1), operations reporting cards (Exhibit 2), and drawings. The information sheet was principally a two-level bill of material; that is, it listed the parts that made up the item on order. If any of these parts were not stocked, reference to the next lower level and its manufacturing information sheet were given. Order quantities were determined by the computer, based on

Croydon Incorporated
Manufacturing Information Sheet

Exhibit 1

SF319651	00202	1	C	6932A	A42C	A42C	S-2	053179	EBP
ORDER NUMBER	ASSIGN. ITEM	QUANTITY	TYPE	PROD. CODE	MFG. SECT.	DEL. TO	FIN. DEL. TO	MI WRITTEN DATE	WRITER

3877A50G01	04	ASSY LEAD
PART IDENTIFICATION	SUB	PART NAME

BMP
DATA SOURCE

	PRIORITY

LINE	PART-IDENT	SUB	PART-NAME	PLLNO	QTY-ONE	MTL-FROM	ORD-QTY	C-PG
01	3001074H05	07	CLAMP	08	1	C59	1-1	
02	3877A49H01	02	PIPE	02	1	A42C	1	
03	44791EM00P M		PIPE PVC	01	1	BOS	4-5	
			36.500 OF 1.00 SCHED 40 PVC XPIPE					
04	3877A47H01	03	BRKT	07	2	C59	2-1	
05	3877A50H01	04	ABBY FRAME	01		REF	1	
06	3877A50H09	04	LEAD	09	1	A42C	1	
07	62111FN4ML M		CABLE INSUL	09	1	C59	8-5	
			85.000 OF 7-.0612 WHITE CABLE XLEAD					
08	70100FL01S E	07	BOLT HEX	03	4	C39	-1	
09	70210EP61b E	01	NUT HEX	04	4	C59	-1	
10	70510F61OM E	02	WSHR LOCK	06	4	C59	-1	

Exhibit 2

Croydon Incorporated
Operations Reporting Card (Paycard)

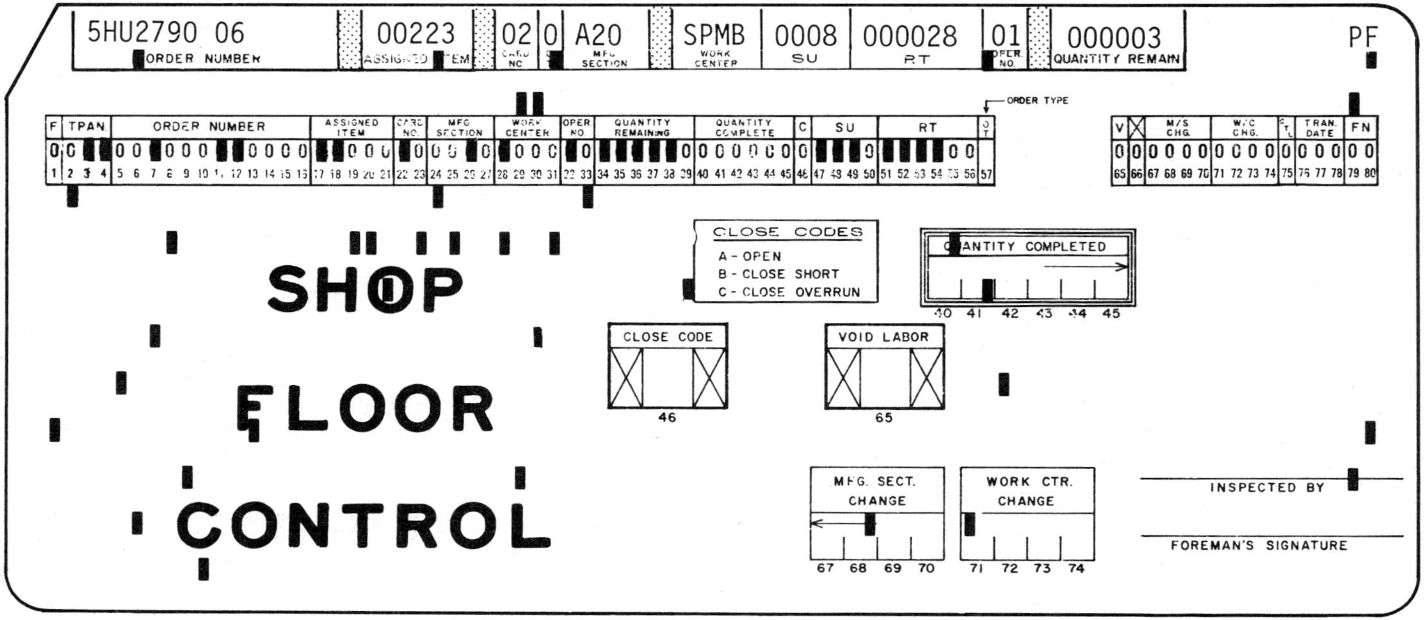

such factors as machine setup or changeover costs, inventory holding costs, and average demand. The demand for a part was recalculated every month using an exponential smoothing model. The average demand could, upon request, also be based on known future demand if this occurred within a prespecified review period. In these cases, the historical average demand and the known future demand were weighted together. A change in the demand estimate would also lead to change of order quantity. Other parameters, such as the reorder point or the safety stock, were reexamined daily by the computer system. On request, the system could produce an extensive report listing all kinds of data; for example, number of days since last stock-out, number of days a current stock-out had lasted, average requirement per time period, average released lot size, and so forth. This report was also automatically produced whenever a reorder point was passed (Exhibit 3). If a purchasing order was issued, the calculated lot sizes often were subject to additional constraints. For example, an economic order quantity involving a purchased part frequently had to be changed to meet minimum vendor deliveries. Price breaks offered by the supplier could be another reason why the planner modified the lot size.

The inventory records were often misleading in that material being stored in the shop, but not being worked on, was not accounted for. For example, if a certain part had an average weekly demand of 40 units, the materials handler could withdraw 240 units because of the part's relatively small size. This would save the materials handler and the person driving the forklift several trips to the stockroom. Such a withdrawal could trigger the ordering of a new lot of 300 parts with a lead time of three weeks. When the inventory later was replenished, assuming on-time delivery, there would still be three weeks supply at the assembly station.

SHOP FLOOR CONTROL

The operations reporting cards in the shop package were also called "paycards." The reason for this was that each supervisor's performance evaluation was based on a weekly productivity index (Exhibit 4). The index was computed by dividing the number of standard hours that was performed by the shop personnel belonging to the supervisor's section, and the actual number of elapsed worker hours. Each paycard, representing one operation, had the number of standard hours for this operation printed on it. The supervisor was supposed to turn in a paycard once an operation had been completed. This would update the status of the job. Every week a list of completions was printed, listing in order number sequence the operations within each order that were completed up to this point. Since the paycards also affected the supervisor's performance ratings, the procedure ensured a very accurate report in that the supervisor always turned in all cards. Larry Caldwell had, however, over the years come to suspect that the supervisors "banked" the paycards to a certain extent. If a supervisor had more standard hours than usual one week, some of the paycards could be held over until a period of low productivity. The name "paycard" was a bit misleading, as the supervisors were on a straight salary.

To help the supervisor sequence the jobs through the feeder section, an exception report was produced that indicated which jobs were more than 48 hours overdue. The jobs were listed in the order of descending lateness. The due date was given to an order based on the lead time and the day of its release. This report was, however, not very often used by the supervisor in the feeder section. Instead, the actual priorities set were communicated by the assembly supervisors and tied directly to the final assembly of the mechanism. This meant that parts that were needed in assembly were scheduled first. Often, this need was detected the very same day, which made immediate expediting necessary.

Parts that were set up and running were often torn down so that a small batch of parts could be run to cover the final assembly needs. The management had special difficulties with parts that were leaving the plant for a subcontracted job. Small batches of material were often sent by cab for heat treatment at a company 50 miles away. Sometimes a part could leave the plant twice before all operations were completed. These parts seemed to be out of stock most often.

SOME RECENT FINDINGS

Hank Thompson reported to Larry Caldwell about the findings he had come up with during the last month.

> Listen to this, Larry. I have found out that Craig, the material coordinator, often forgets, or neglects to tell anyone in the stockroom that he has taken some parts directly to the final assembly area. I also found out, as you suspected, that the supervisors bank the paycards. In most cases this means that they turn in all cards for one job at the same time. Because we have separate systems for production control and inventory, an order can actually have arrived in the stockroom and updated the inventory records kept by production control, while at the same time the order would be listed as open since the paycards have not been turned in.

Larry sighed.

> Yeah, I guess that separate information processing procedures really mess things up. We've got to look into that. We should maybe go for a computerized on-line system with terminals in the stockroom.

Larry got carried away thinking about future possibilities. He was already outlining the new system in his mind, when Hank called him back to reality.

> Well, Larry, that's not all. Get a load of this. When a part leaves the plant to go for heat treatment, and this is the last operation, the supervisor often hands in the paycards before the batch is back in the plant. Can you see the consequences of this, Larry? Now, if . . .

Here, Larry interrupted him.

Croydon Incorporated
ROP History Report

Exhibit 3

BL S-7-D   S T O C K   S T A T U S   R E P O R T   DATE 1019   LEDGER UD   SHEET 1

203C221G02 6 1   LED/RVP   DESCRIPTION   GROUND BOARD

DWG NO STK B40	QUAN CODE 1	ACCOUNT TYPE 1	UNIT OF MEAS PCS
SOURCE CLASS 4B	MFG SECT B40	STOREROOM C69	BIN LOC A 291
REVIEW PERIOD 40	LEAD TIME 30	UNIT COST 35.724	MO SINCE LST ISS 0
REORD COST 15.00	MATL TYPE 73476	MIN DAYS SUPL 21	RAW AMI 6
ORDER CODE 1	ORDER QUAN 15	MAX DAYS SUPL 126	FACTRD AMI 6
REORD CODE 7	REOR POINT 38	UNIT OF REQN 1	B.O.H. 29
LST INV DATE 065-79	DATE LST ISS 098-79	MIN REQN UNIT 1	ISS MTD 35
AVG DMD SIZE 8	STD DEV DMD 8	MAX REQN UNIT 999	RECPT MTD 55
DMD INTERVAL 13.38	D.L.R.W. 096-79	INV ADJ CR 0	SCRAP MTD 0
STK OUT MTD 0	E-FTR{LIM} 1.01	INV ADJ DB 0	FL-STK-BAL 0
USAGE TREND 0	E-FTR{UNLIM} 1.01	INV COMP MTD 0	REC QTD 0
FORECAST DEV 0	CURR STKOUT DAY 0	INV COMP QTD 0	SCRAP QTD 0
CUM FOR DEV 0	ALPHA FACTOR 0.200	INV ADJ MTD 0	STKOUT FREQ 5
MAN ORD ADD QTD 3	UNIT ADDED 45	PRIM SPEC 716	SEC SPEC 000000
ORD CANC QTD 2	UNIT CANC 30	NEXT REQN NO 6	SQ ISS 625
M.S.L.O. 0	S-I M.A.B. 45	S-I EXCESS 45	S-I PRIORITY CD 0
MOS CLO OUT 0	S-I B.O.H. 13	QTD ASN 44	ASN X LTD 1320

RUN CTR 2491   QTD ASN CTR 2   MEAN AVG DEV 6

DUG SUB   MI TRAN CODE   MI LINE NO   USAGE ASN 61

JAN	4	FEB	1	MAR		APRIL	4
MAY	9	JUNE	12	JULY		AUG	5
SEPT	11	OCT	2	NOV		DEC	9

REQN	ORIG	ENT	COMP		CL	OC	RES	EP	ET	T-DT	T-QTY	ORDERED	RECEIVED	BAL-DUE
EE	0738	0738	0509	0879	C	7	0	0	0	0869	15		15	15
FF	0939	0939	0669	0989	C	7	0	0	0	1019	20		20	20
GG	1039	1039	0729	0979	C	7	0	0	0	1019	20		20	20

REQN	ORIG	ENT	COMP		CL	OC	RES	EP	ET	T-DT	T-QTY	ORDERED	RECEIVED	BAL-DUE
05	1069	1269	0969	0969	A	7	0	1	0		20		20	20

DATE	CLASS	ORDER	ITEM	DEL-TO	QUANTITY	ENT-DT	PC-ISS-DT
1029	R	5CN321931		B40	3	0549	
1049	R	3KC114161		B40	1	0599	
1069	R	5CN321932		B40	5	0549	
1119	R	5FW358181B		B40	10	0709	
1139	R	5IN304002X		B40	2	0589	
1329	R	3CG575352		B40	2	0669	
1329	R	50M510841		B40	2	0909	
1339	R	3CG575351		B40	1	0669	
1359	R	5FW358181C		B40	1	0709	
1439	R	5WI481731		B40	10	0749	
1619	R	5WI482301		B40	3	0759	

NORMAL ASMT QUAN WITHIN CD + RP
ABNORMAL ASMT QUAN WITHIN CD + RP
OVERDUE ASSIGNMENTS   35

END OF REPORT

Exhibit 4

Croydon Incorporated
Performance Report

MEASURED DAYWORK SUMMARY OF PERFORMANCE

SEC	PEOPLE	HOURS FOR WEEK		YEAR TO DATE		MANAG'T PERFORMANCE			RATIO
		ELAP	EARN	ELAP	EARN	WEEK	4 WEEK	YEAR	GOAL
B30*	18	710	300	11356	5219	42.3	47.4	46.0	70
B40*	22	942	692	16455	11712	73.5	68.0	71.2	75
C44	4	142	67	2629	1658	47.2	61.8	63.1	80
E50*	30	1143	833	19215	14946	72.9	72.3	77.8	78
BKR	74	2937	1892	49655	33535	64.4	64.7	67.5	76

*B30 and B40 are the two assembly sections. E50 is the major feeder section.

I'll be darned! Of course, if you go to the stockroom and want a part, but the stockroom is empty, they might tell you not to worry because there should be an open order. If you then get in touch with production control they tell you that this order has already been completed. This confusion might lead to a new order being released before the open order comes in. Inaccurate inventory records is just one of our problems with the mech. Hank, I want you to lead a task force consisting of Bruce, who knows the reorder point system well; Phil, the design engineer; and yourself. You should meet every week until the mech production runs smoothly. I will sit in on the meetings as often as I can.

Case 4–2

Redskin Auto Parts*

INTRODUCTION

Frank Snider, the owner/manager of Redskin Auto Parts, was faced with a dilemma. He had been in the auto parts business for over ten years and had done very well without the use of computers or sophisticated inventory control systems. However, in recent years his major competition was coming from large chains of auto parts stores with a computer terminal in every outlet. He was concerned that he might need to modernize in order to stay in business.

Redskin Auto Parts was a fairly large retail auto parts store located in Oxford, Ohio. The company carried a wide variety of items including engine parts for foreign and domestic cars, brake repair parts, muffler systems, oil and other lubricants, mechanics tools, and various auto accessories. The company purchased these parts directly from the manufacturer or from wholesalers. Its customers included service stations, repair shops, and a large fraction of individual customers from all over Butler County. It was well established in the community and had a stated policy "if we don't have the part you want in stock, we will have it for you within 24 hours." This policy required that whenever a customer desired a part Redskin did not have in stock, someone had to call around to other dealers in Hamilton or Cincinnati to locate the part. Then a special run had to be made to get the part, often paying a premium price. It was estimated that each time an item was "back ordered" this way, it cost about $10 in time, phone bills, and transportation to pick it up.

Frank was somewhat concerned that his back orders (and possibly his lost sales) had been increasing in recent years. He did not wish to change his 24-hour service policy, but he was willing to increase his inventory slightly or reallocate it in such a way as to reduce the number of back orders required. He wanted to know how to control his inventory more efficiently and whether or not computerization would be helpful.

STAFF

Frank Snider employed seven people: a secretary who typed purchase orders, kept financial files, and maintained a list of suppliers, a price list, and a

---

*This case was prepared by Donald L. Byrkett, Miami University, Oxford, Ohio, with the intention of providing a basis for class discussion rather than illustrating either effective or ineffective management of a business situation.

file of outstanding purchase orders; two counter persons who handled walk-in customers; three delivery persons who handled orders (called in and subsequently delivered) from service stations and repair shops; and one inventory clerk who reviewed inventory and suggested orders, unloaded and checked incoming orders, and restocked the shelves.

The secretary was paid $10,000 per year, and the other six people were each paid $14,000 per year. Frank normally spent his time helping out on the counter, expediting late orders, reviewing new purchase orders, and locating parts for the special runs.

INVENTORY SYSTEM

The inventory of Redskin Auto Parts consisted of about 8,000 stock keeping units. Of these 8,000 items, about 3,000 were inexpensive items that were reviewed on a quarterly basis and ordered in large quantities (examples include bolts, washers, fuses, and clamps). The remaining 5,000 items were reviewed once a week. This was accomplished by the inventory clerk on a rotating basis; for example, on Monday domestic engine parts were reviewed, on Tuesday, foreign engine parts, and so forth. Each item had a target level that was established by Frank Snider based on his ten years of experience as manager of the store.

The clerk recorded the target level and the stock level for each item. The purchase order file was then checked to see if there were any outstanding orders for this item, and this information was recorded. The suggested order quantity was computed by subtracting the stock level and the outstanding orders from the target level. Some items had to be ordered in certain size quantities; for example, oil had to be ordered by the case (12 quarts per case) and spark plugs had to be ordered in sets (4, 6, or 8 depending on the application). The order quantity was adjusted to the nearest appropriate units.

Frank Snider reviewed this list and made adjustments as his experience would indicate. Sometimes he upped the order quantity in anticipation of a promotion, or sometimes he adjusted the target level due to a large number of recent shortages. The list was then turned over to the secretary who typed the orders and sent them to the appropriate vendors. The lead time varied according to the vendor (there were approximately 100 vendors) but was in the range of 7-21 days.

As shipments came in, the inventory clerk checked to make sure the proper number of items were received and placed these items on the shelf. The corrected invoice was given to the secretary, who made the payment to the vendor and removed the appropriate purchase order from the pending file.

DEMAND PATTERNS

Demand for most items was fairly constant throughout the year. However, Frank had a few items that were definitely seasonal; for example, antifreeze. For these items he maintained a summer target level (March 1 to August 31) and a winter target level (September 1 to February 28).

SHORTAGES

As mentioned earlier, it was the policy of Redskin Auto Parts to obtain any shortage item for the customer within 24 hours. However, some customers did not wish to wait for 24 hours and went somewhere else. This was particularly true of customers desiring items such as oil, accessories, tools, and basic tune-ups items. Generally customers requiring specific, more difficult to find engine parts took advantage of the 24-hour service. No records were kept on the lost sales, but Frank estimated 5 percent of his potential sales were lost due to shortages.

SAMPLE DATA

Five items had been selected as representative of the inventory system. Current characteristics of these items are listed in Exhibit 1. Actual demand data was not available for these items; but by searching through purchase orders for the last 52 weeks, the number of units ordered was available, and by searching through back-order forms the number of units obtained on 24-hour request was available. This data is summarized in Exhibit 2. Similar data was available for all items inventoried.

Exhibit 1

Redskin Auto Parts
Item Characteristics

Description	Target Level	Lead Time	Ordering Units	Back Ordered?	Purchase Cost	Selling Price
ITEM A: 10W-40 Quaker State Oil	520 qts.	7 days	Cases = 12 qts.	No	$5.00/case	$.75/qt.
ITEM B: VW Points #198723	35 units	7 days	Units	Yes	$.93/unit	$1.79/unit
ITEM C: Pinto Carburetor #XYZ248	15 units	14 days	Units	Yes	$15.75/unit	$23.85/unit
ITEM D: Outside Rearview Mirror A16	20 units	21 days	Units	No	$5.22/unit	$9.95/unit
ITEM E: Prestone Antifreeze	100 gals. (Winter) 40 gals. (Summer)	7 days	Cases = 4 gals.	No	$7.50/case	$2.99/gal.

Exhibit 2

Redskin Auto Parts
Demand History
Quantity Ordered (Back Ordered)

Week	Item A (cases)	Item B (units)	Item C (units)	Item D (units)	Item E (cases)
1	17	9	5	2	5
2	13	9	6	9	4
3	13	7	4	5	4
4	21	10	6 (2)	1	3
5	17	11	5	3	3
6	13	11	5 (1)	1	6
7	10	1	1	4	2
8	18	8	1	4	1
9	17	10	2	3	1
10	17	13	1	7	1
11	21	6	1	5	1
12	15	11	1	6	1
13	24	8	5	3	1
14	11	5	1	6	1
15	21	20	2	1	1
16	21	13	4	1	1
17	17	7	7	6	1
18	12	12	5	2	1
19	18	8	4	12	1
20	12	10	3	1	4
21	14	13	1	6	5
22	21	5	6	2	6
23	19	9	1	7	4
24	13	14	2	1	4
25	20	9	6	6	2
26	17	11	6	7	1
27	14	10	4	7	6
28	11	17	6	1	2
29	16	12	6 (1)	6	6
30	12	16	2	6	2
31	14	4	2	5	6
32	17	12	8	4	2
33	12	17	6 (1)	4	7
34	14	7	2 (1)	1	4
35	18	8	2	1	22
36	16	3	6	1	4
37	11	1	8 (1)	2	12
38	20	13	2	2	10
39	19	12	1	3	10
40	18	1	1	1	15
41	16	11	2	7	6
42	13	5	6	10	7
43	23	4	8	3	5
44	21	8	2 (1)	1	9
45	17	2	6	3	9
46	9	6	6	1	5
47	13	15	4 (2)	2	6
48	18	1	3	5	4
49	12	1	5	2	9
50	12	18	8 (1)	4	6
51	20	8	1	1	10
52	18	14	1	4	5

Case 4-3

Southwest University
Recruiting Office*

BACKGROUND

Southwest University always felt a definite responsibility for proper professional placement of its graduates. To this end a recruitment office was established to maintain active contact with prospective employers of graduating students and alumni. While the faculty also shared the responsibility for student placement, university policy was to channel all job interviews through the recruiting office.

The recruitment office was first opened in 1959 and operated with eight interview rooms and a staff of three people. As the university grew, people were added to the staff; but new and larger office space did not become available until in 1977. At that time the recruitment office was given space for 24 interview rooms, a library, office space, and a waiting room.

Since 1974 Southwest University had doubled its enrollment and continued to grow. Enrollment was expected to level off near 30,000 students by 1982. Four hundred companies interviewed twice a year for an average of three days, and as a result, the recruitment office was operating near capacity. The 24 interview rooms were often filled throughout the day during the prime interviewing months, and the volume of paperwork generated had become a major problem.

The suggestion was made that some type of information system was needed to improve scheduling efficiency and to aid in information storage and handling.

OBJECTIVES OF THE RECRUITMENT OFFICE

The recruitment office was established to maintain active contact with prospective employers of graduating students and alumni. It operated under three divisions: (1) on-campus recruitment, (2) educational placement, and (3) alumni placement.

*This case was prepared by August W. Smith, Thomas F. Urban, and Daniel P. Dunlap, all of Texas A & M University, with the intention of providing a basis for class discussion rather than illustrating either effective or ineffective management of a business situation. Reprinted with permission from *Application of Decision Sciences in Organizations: A Case Approach* by Joseph C. Latona and K. Mark Weaver with the cooperation of the American Institute for Decision Sciences, Atlanta, Georgia, 1980.

1. The on-campus recruitment division arranged interviews between prospective employers and graduating students and provided a number of other related student services.
2. The educational placement division was designed to meet the needs of those graduates and faculty seeking positions in the field of education.
3. The alumni placement division was designed to meet the needs of former students who had job experience.

The office also provided advice and assistance on preparing credentials for submission to prospective employers and the proper approach in seeking a job.

DESCRIPTION OF THE SYSTEM

On-campus recruitment division procedures for prospective employers and students were as follows:
1. Prospective employers could request interviews one year to one month in advance. This could be done by phone or letter.

   If the request was made by phone, a staff member checked the schedule to see what days and times were available; and if possible, a date was set.

   If the request was made by letter, a staff member checked the schedule to see if the requested dates were available. If not, a letter was sent to the company indicating that the dates were filled. The company might attempt to schedule again by phone or mail.

   Once a date for interviews was set, the recruitment office sent the prospective employer a confirmation letter and an information packet. From data included in the information packet concerning degrees offered and the estimated number of students to be interviewed, the company recruiter estimated the number of students to be interviewed by major and degree. The prospective employer completed the schedule provided in the information packet (Exhibit 1) and returned it to the recruitment office at least one month prior to the first scheduled date.

   The recruitment office received the schedule and made the following copies and distribution:

   a. deans of appropriate colleges — one copy.
   b. heads of appropriate departments — one copy.
   c. front desk of recruitment office — four copies.

   Interested students signed up at the recruitment office for interviews two weeks prior to the scheduled interview date. If seven or more students signed up for a given day over the 14 interviews available, then the recruitment office called the company to ask if a second interviewer could be sent. If four or less students signed up for interviews on a given day, the recruitment office notified the company of this.

   The company interviewer checked in with the recruitment office on the interview date and received a copy of the schedule and was asked to

Exhibit 1

Southwest University Recruiting Office
Interview Arrangement and Schedule Form

Southwest University Recruiting Office

INTERVIEW ARRANGEMENT AND SCHEDULE FORM

PLEASE NOTE:
(1) PLEASE SEND ALL CORPORATE INTERVIEW LITERATURE FOR PLACEMENT LIBRARY TO ADDRESS AT LEFT.
(2) COMPLETE AND RETURN <u>30</u> DAYS PRIOR TO INTERVIEW DATE. USE SEPARATE FORM FOR EACH SCHEDULE AND INTERVIEW DATE DESIRED. RETAIN FOURTH COPY FOR COMPANY RECORDS. PERSON RESPONSIBLE FOR THIS INTERVIEW ARRANGEMENT PLEASE SIGN BELOW.

SIGNED:

COMPANY NAME AND ADDRESS	PHONE	NAMES OF INTERVIEWERS

INTERVIEW DATE:

CHECK (x) AS APPLICABLE:
□ EQUAL OPPORTUNITY EMPLOYER
□ U.S. CITIZENSHIP OR PERMANENT VISA REQUIRED
□ LITERATURE SENT 30 DAYS PRIOR TO INTERVIEW DATE

WILL INTERVIEW: □ DECEMBER GRADS 19___   □ MAY AND SUMMER GRADS

WILL INTERVIEW FOR SUMMER WORK: □ FRESHMEN   □ SOPHOMORES   □ JUNIORS   □ SENIORS   □ GRADUATES

DEGREES DESIRED	PERMANENT B	M	D	SUM-MER	DEGREES DESIRED	PERMANENT B	M	D	SUM-MER
AGRICULTURE					ENGINEERING				
ARCHITECTURE & ENVIRONMENTAL DESIGN									
					LIBERAL ARTS				
BUSINESS ADMINISTRATION									
					SCIENCES				
EDUCATION									
					OTHER				
GEOSCIENCES									

POSITIONS AVAILABLE OR REMARKS. (ATTACH ADDITIONAL SHEETS IF NECESSARY)

TIME	NAME	DEGREE COURSE YEAR	TIME	NAME	DEGREE COURSE YEAR
8:30			1:30		
9:00			2:00		
9:30			2:30		
10:00			3:00		
10:30			3:30		
11:00			4:00		
11:30			4:30		

STUDENT: PLEASE USE PENCIL ONLY.

Case 4-3   Southwest University Recruiting Office

fill out a current address card. A room number was then assigned to the interviewer.

The recruitment office processed and mailed company requests for official grade transcripts.

Carbon copies of all letters sent to students by employers were received and filed at the recruitment office.

Files on students hired were deactivated; but no workable solution existed for feedback of this information.

2. Students interested in interviewing first registered with the recruitment office by completing a registration and resume form (Exhibit 2). The student made several copies of the form, turned one in to the recruitment office, and retained the rest. The recruitment office then began a file on the student.

The recruitment office sent a letter to each of the personal references listed on the student's form requesting a reference letter. When returned, these references were placed in the student's file.

After registering with the recruitment office, the student checked the tentative schedule for companies with which he/she wished to interview. The schedules were made available for the first time for sign up at 1:00 p.m. on the date that was two weeks in advance of the recruiting date. One copy of the student's resume form was left with the prospective employer's schedule.

It was then up to the student to remember to be at the interview. The student was asked to call the recruitment office if he/she was unable to make it to the interview. If a student canceled an interview, the recruitment office contacted a student on the standby list to come in for that time.

A student that received correspondence from a company was asked to confirm if a copy was also sent to the recruitment office. The student was also asked to notify the recruitment office once an offer was accepted.

The recruitment office would keep a student's file active up to five years after graduation. Three active files were maintained by the office: a file cataloged by name, a file by major, and a file by degree. Files no longer active were not destroyed but were stored.

The educational placement division accounted for approximately five percent of the services performed by the recruitment office. The division actually consisted of only one employee who was responsible for its operation. The employee equally divided time between the educational placement division and helping with on-campus recruitment. The facility was primarily used by members of the university faculty who were looking for other teaching positions and other universities who were in need of teachers. The recruitment office simply attempted to match the two requirements.

Exhibit 2

Southwest University Recruiting Office
Registration and Resume Form

Personal Data

NAME	Last	First	Middle	For Office use only

HOME ADDRESS (Street, City, State) | HOME PHONE

UNIV. ADDRESS (Street, City, State) | UNIV. PHONE | U S CITIZEN YES ☐ NO ☐ | if "No," Type of Visa

PHYSICAL LIMITATIONS (Job Related Only) | FOREIGN LANGUAGES

Type of Work

TYPE OF WORK DESIRED 1st Choice   2nd Choice | DATE AVAILABLE

WORK LOCATION RESTRICTIONS (if any) | Social Security No.

College or Univ. Information

NAME AND LOCATION OF COLLEGES ATTENDED	DATES FROM	TO	DEGREE	GRADUATION DATE	COURSE OF STUDY (1) Major (2) Minor	GRADE PT. AVE (1) Overall (2) Major	GRADE BASIS	CLASS RANK QUARTILE
					1 ------- 2	1 --- 2	A=	
					1 ------- 2	1 --- 2	A=	
					1 ------- 2	1 --- 2	A=	

THESIS AND DISSERTATION TITLE(S)

NAME OF ADVISOR(S)

HONORS, PROFESSIONAL SOCIETIES, FRATERNITIES, AND ACTIVITIES (Give Positions Held)

Employment Information

% COLLEGE EXPENSES EARNED | HOW EARNED (Name of scholarship, if any)

SIGNIFICANT WORK EXPERIENCE (Names and Addresses of Employers)	DESCRIPTION OF WORK	HOURS PER WEEK	DATES EMPLOYED FROM	TO

Military

PRESENT SELECTIVE SERVICE STATUS | ANTICIPATED MILITARY DUTY Branch | From | To

PREVIOUS SERVICE

Branch	From	To	Rank	Experience

General Information

REFERENCES (Names and addresses- Preferably Faculty and Business-Approx. Four)--Please notify references of your intent to use their names prior to listing.

OTHER INFORMATION (Community Activities, Hobbies, and Interests, etc.)

(Alumni Only) MINIMUM SALARY EXPECTED $
Use other side to relate additional information that may help employers understand your background, academic training, experience, or special interests.

I have been informed that my personal and scholastic records are confidential under provisions of the 1974 Family Educational Rights and Privacy Act. However, to facilitate placement assistance provided to me, I authorize Southwest University to release them to prospective employers.

SIGNATURE

DATE

The alumni placement division accounted for an additional five percent of the recruitment office's services by attempting to place past graduates of Southwest University who were once again in the job market with companies who were looking for employees with experience.

The procedure for utilizing the services of the alumni placement division was simple. Companies in need of people with specific job experience contacted the recruitment office by phone or mail. The recruitment office maintained a list of jobs and then placed them in categories according to the job description (i.e., mechanical engineer, accountant, management). Companies were asked to keep the recruitment office informed as to the current status of job openings.

Alumni could contact the recruitment office and request to be placed on their mailing list. Once every month a list of available jobs was mailed. It was the responsibility of the alumnus to contact the company he or she was interested in and set up an interview. The alumnus was asked to notify the recruitment office when the job listings were no longer to be mailed.

One recruitment office employee maintained two sets of files for the alumni placement division. The files consisted of alumni names and personal information and of companies with job openings. The peak work load for this recruitment office employee occurred near the end of the month when the mailing list was prepared. During the rest of the month the employee helped with on-campus recruitment (Exhibit 3).

Exhibit 3

Southwest University Recruiting Office
Employee Allocation Chart (Figures in Percent)

	Dept. Mgmt.	Student Counseling	Employer Scheduling	Student Scheduling	Secretarial Support	Educational Division	Alumni Division
Director	30	40	10	10		5	5
Employee No. 1		10		80	10		
Employee No. 2		10		80	10		
Employee No. 3			90		10		
Employee No. 4				40	10	50	
Employee No. 5				40	10		50

CONSIDERATIONS FOR A NEW SYSTEM

Due to the increased enrollment, the work load for all three divisions of the recruitment office had been steadily growing during the peak months (Exhibit 4). The following were immediate problem areas:

Exhibit 4

Southwest University Recruiting Office
Primary Months for Conducting Interviews

Months	Percent of Employers Interviewing
January	18
February	71
March	47
April	8
May	3
June	—
July	—
August	—
September	24
October	68
November	47
December	8

1. The 1 p.m. sign-up time had become almost unmanageable. Most students had to wait in long lines; and many, especially those with 1 p.m. classes, were unable to get on the schedules.
2. Maintaining and updating the three active files was an increasing burden each year.
3. Storage space for the inactive files was becoming scarce.
4. A low percentage of students notified the recruitment office once they had taken a job. That kept their files active and prevented the office from making an accurate estimate of their effectiveness in placing students.

In hope of better understanding the current situation, questionnaires were prepared and given to company recruiters and on-campus students. The results are listed below:

1. Recruiter questionnaire results.
   a. Prospective employers seem to be locked into their recruiting cycle by competition, student participation, and type of work (i.e., teaching, civil service).
   b. Approximately 50 percent of all interviewers questioned either did not know or were unwilling to divulge the type and number of jobs for which they were interviewing.
   c. The following suggestions were made by the companies questioned:
      1) Insure students receive company literature prior to the interview.
      2) Have the company interview package available the day *before* the first interview.

2. Student questionnaire results.
    a. A significant number of students were not familiar with the services provided by the recruitment office.
    b. Students were dissatisfied with the 1 p.m. sign-up time due to the overcrowding.
    c. Seventy percent of the students questioned felt they should know the number and types of jobs available for the company interviewing.

The university administration was sufficiently concerned about the situation to authorize a study of a new information system. Funds for the project were not a severe constraint, although the administration wanted the least expensive and most efficient alternative.

The university data processing facility operated as a centralized data processing facility providing data processing services for academic research and administrative efforts of the university. Batch processing, on-line inquiry and update, and all combinations in between were available. The system 2000 general-purpose data base management system was available at the facility.

The approximate costs for the university data processing service were as follows:

1. CRT and printer — $300 per month
2. Computer time and related items — $500 per month
3. Programming and file maintenance — $300 per month

VENDOR SELECTION CRITERIA

All three proposals were to be evaluated equally based on the following criteria with its appropriate weighting in percent:

1. Chance of failure or risk level — 30 percent
2. Operating and maintenance costs — 25 percent
3. Percentage of user needs met — 25 percent
4. Time to implement the system — 20 percent

IMPLEMENTATION REQUIREMENTS

In addition to the selection criteria above, the committee felt obligated to place certain additional requirements on implementation of the system. These are listed below.

1. The accumulation of inactive files must be stored in an efficient manner.
2. The long sign-up lines at 1 p.m. each day should be eliminated in a way equitable to all students.
3. The scheduling of students and companies was to be automated without loss of documentation.
4. The possibility of implementing a "performance" record for the office that would include the percentage of students acquiring employment and the types of jobs offered by companies was to be investigated.

PROPOSALS

Southwest University Data Processing Facility

The university data processing facility located on campus near the recruitment office provided the university a list of alternatives for implementation of an information system. These are presented below in the order of increasing complexity.

1. At the close of each day's operation a batch update of the necessary files using the forms completed that day by employers, office staff, faculty, and students would be performed. The makeup and content of those files would be made up as a result of a study by a systems analyst and recruitment office personnel. Management of the files would be accomplished with the System 2000 general purpose data base management system.

   A complete printout of desired files would be made following the batch update. Printouts could be sorted on several key works, such as name, degree, and major for the student files, and company, or date for the schedules. This too would be determined following a system analysis.

   The cost of such a service would be approximately:

   $300 per month — computer time
   $300 per month — programming and file maintenance

2. The data processing facility had the capability of placing up to 5 CRT displays in the recruitment office. The displays could be used then in addition to the daily computer output, in full or part, as a simple inquiry system. A batch update would be made each day. The cost breakdown of this alternative was as follows:

   $300 per month — programming and file maintenance
   $150 per month — for each CRT used
   $400 per month — computer time

3. The third alternative was to install CRT displays for the purpose of an inquiry and on-line update. A printer would also be installed, if desired, for printout of any file such as a particular company's list of scheduled interviews. This list of interviews could include blanks where times were open in the schedule. This on-line system would have a cost breakdown as follows:

   $150 per month — for each CRT desired
   $700 per month — computer time (average)
   $150 per month — printer
   $400 per month — programming and file maintenance

The priority on the system had not been determined, but of course, time sharing of the computer was necessary, and some delay was to be expected for all on-line uses.

Minicomputer

The second proposal came from the member of the executive committee. The possibility of installing a minicomputer with data base management capability was to be investigated. The location of the system should be ideally at the recruitment office itself. The committee member could provide no cost figures but seemed confident both Hewlett-Packard, Digital Equipment, and possibly other companies made systems capable of meeting the system requirements.

Brigstown Data Management

A company located in a city 90 miles from Southwest University had suggested an on-line service they were sure would meet all the recruitment office requirements. The company itself operated an IBM system 310 Model 135 computer with state-of-the-art auxiliary equipment. A sister company in the area provided "shadow" backup in case of a breakdown. The data base was managed by the IBM Data Language/1 DOS/VS.

What the company proposed was similar to services they were currently providing to an airline and a savings and loan. Implementation would require one CRT, two special typewriters and a high-speed printer. The company schedules would be prepared on special forms that fit in the on-line typewriters. A student's name would be typed onto the form and into the files at the same time. The CRT was available for on-line inquiry and update of the files. The line printer was available for output of student files and company schedules on demand. Reports would be prepared as required as well as appropriate mailer master copies. Student files would automatically be printed out when deactivated in a form suitable for microfilming. The cost for these services was estimated as follows:

Equipment rental:
$200 per month — 1 CRT
$400 per month — 1 line printer
$1,000 per month — 2 on-line typewriters
$500 per month — computer time (est.)
$900 per month — programming and file maintenance

It was further pointed out that the special on-line typewriters did not, at that time, exist. The time of production of the machines was expected to take one year from the time of a written contract.

Case 4–4

International Correspondence Alternatives of a World-Class Bank*

Within the collection service division of this world-class bank, the major portion of the incoming international correspondence was negotiable instruments and their supporting documents. The bank processed these transactions by updating the accounts involved and advised the customer of the processing. At times, customers would inquire as to the status of their transaction before receipt of this advice. Since a large staff was necessary to handle such inquiries, bank management was interested in knowing the cost benefit of using a courier service to deliver these transactions and advices.

BACKGROUND

All international correspondence items were transported worldwide by postal service. The cost involved depended upon the weight of the items and their destinations. Each shipment passed through a series of handling agents such as the U.S. Postal Service, the airlines, and the overseas post offices, none of which had control of the shipment for its entire journey. The delivery time for this service varied according to the country of origin/destination, the distance, and the overall operating conditions of the post offices and other carriers involved.

COURIER SERVICE

Bank management was considering the use of a courier service as an alternative to the above system. The cost of this service depended not only upon the weight of the items being transported and the origin/destination, but also on the frequency of deliveries between any two locations. The courier service method followed a simpler, more direct route than the postal method. A courier would pick up the outgoing item at an origin, accompany it by plane, and deliver it directly to the destination where a signed receipt would be issued. This service was offered to most countries with guaranteed delivery times. A courier service was expected to expedite delivery time, thereby improving customer service in general and decreasing the float (the interest lost on unavailable funds) for the bank.

*This case was prepared by Kurt J. Engemann, Iona College, and Michael Vesoniarakis, Chase Manhattan Bank, with the intention of providing a basis for class discussion rather than illustrating either effective or ineffective management for a business situation. Reprinted with permission from *Application of Decision Sciences in Organizations: A Case Approach* by Joseph C. Latona and K. Mark Weaver with the cooperation of the American Institute for Decision Sciences, Atlanta, Georgia, 1980.

THE STUDY'S OBJECTIVE

Bank management had requested that the operations research department study this situation. The objective of this study was to evaluate the cost-effectiveness of implementing a courier service for overseas transportation of these transactions.

The span of the operations research study would include analyzing the effect of the courier services implementation upon the volume of customers' inquiries. Customers sometimes would inquire, by phone or cable, as to the status of their transactions prior to their receiving an advising document from the bank indicating completion of processing. It was hypothesized that a customer's impatience would grow directly as the time span between the date the customer sent the transaction to the bank and the date on which the customer received the bank's advising document. If this time span reached the customer's "impatience threshold," the customer would send an inquiry to the bank.

Such inquiries were costly to the bank because it was necessary to maintain a large staff to respond to the customers. If the delivery times could be decreased, less customers would reach their "impatience thresholds," resulting in fewer inquiries and thereby requiring a smaller staff.

CHRONOLOGY OF A TRANSACTION AND CORRESPONDING DATA

In order to address this part of the study, a sufficiently large random sample over the previous year's transaction data was taken. Each transaction case contained the following dates which are chronologically represented in Exhibit 1:

A— Date the customer mailed the transaction to the bank.

B— Receipt date of the transaction at the bank and the bank's processing began.

C— Date the bank finished processing the transaction, credited the appropriate accounts, and mailed out the advice to the customer.

D— Date on which the customer grew impatient of not receiving the bank's advice of the transaction being completed and sent an inquiry to the bank. (Not all transactions had associated inquiries.)

The receiving date of the advice by the customer was unknown (labeled E in Exhibit 1).

The data on all mailing and processing times are given in Exhibits 2 and 3. Exhibit 2 shows the relative frequency for sampled mailing times, and Exhibit 3 shows the relative frequency for sampled processing times.

From the status related inquiry data, Exhibit 4 was compiled. This shows the relative frequency for the number of days until the customers reached their "impatience threshold."

No significant correlation was found between the random variables represented in these exhibits. Also, it can be assumed that the mailing time of the advice was the same as the mailing time of the transaction to the bank. (On the average, this should be true.) Daily transaction volume was approximately 2,000.

Exhibit 1   **Chronology of a Transaction**

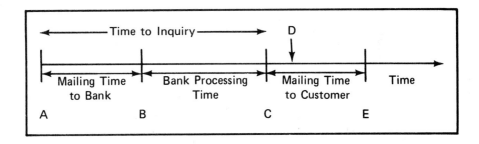

Exhibit 2   **Relative Frequency of Mailing Time**

Number of Days	Relative Frequency	Number of Days	Relative Frequency
1	.007	11	.094
2	.009	12	.101
3	.012	13	.116
4	.006	14	.118
5	.016	15	.050
6	.026	16	.057
7	.049	17	.053
8	.058	18	.053
9	.062	19	.029
10	.068	20	.016

Exhibit 3

Relative Frequency of Processing Time

Number of Days	Relative Frequency	Number of Days	Relative Frequency
1	.058	6	.147
2	.062	7	.073
3	.169	8	.073
4	.169	9	.056
5	.148	10	.045

Exhibit 4

Relative Frequency of "Impatience Threshold"

Number of Days	Relative Frequency	Number of Days	Relative Frequency
1	.015	11	.028
2	.016	12	.027
3	.021	13	.026
4	.043	14	.025
5	.094	15	.021
6	.136	16	.018
7	.259	17	.016
8	.145	18	.014
9	.050	19	.008
10	.031	20	.007

Case 4–5

Armco Inc.:
The Bubble Policy*

MIDDLETOWN, OHIO, OCTOBER 10, 1979

Bruce Steiner, senior project engineer at Armco, got back from lunch and found a pile of paper left for him by John Barker, director of environmental engineering. Steiner knew that Barker had spent a good deal of time in the past year promoting the new "bubble" method of determining air pollution emissions compliance for industrial plants. The bubble method restricted the total pollution output of a plant (as if it were under a bubble) rather than the pollution from each individual point source (smokestacks, vents, etc.). According to Barker, this new method promised both capital spending reductions and energy savings to industry while giving the same pollution emissions performance, since industry would be left to meet a goal in the most cost-effective way.

Steiner saw that the first item on the pile was a copy of a recent article in *Fortune* which summarized the state of affairs with the bubble policy.[1]

As Steiner finished the article, Barker stopped by and brought him up to date:

> I've been trying to come up with some hard data on the comparative costs of the bubble method and to get some way of showing how industry could use the method—both to get other industries on the bandwagon and to convince the EPA that the bubble policy is good for everyone. So I took advantage of an opportunity to get an MBA student at the University of Virginia to work up a simplified linear program modeling steelmaking here at Middletown. Since we know how much air pollution each process puts out, we ought to be able to add the "bubble" to the model. For a first cut, air-borne particulates can be put in, but the model ought to be flexible enough to add other pollutants later. The LP model and the basic data you need are right here. I'm hoping we'll be able to put some price on the value of adding pollution equipment as opposed to changing our production in some way. The EPA is after us right now to install $14 million worth of hoods and baghouses on our furnaces, but I wonder if we could achieve the same particulate reduction more cheaply. What I'd like you to

*This case was prepared by W. K. Sessoms under the supervision of Samuel E. Bodily and H. Landis Gable, Colgate Darden Graduate Business School, with the intention of providing a basis for class discussion rather than illustrating either effective or ineffective management of a business situation. Copyright by the Colgate Darden Graduate Business School, sponsors of the University of Virginia, Charlottesville, Virginia, 1982.

do is check out the feasibility of using LP in arguing for the bubble method and in making operational and capital spending decisions if the bubble method is approved.

ARMCO INC.

Armco is a fully integrated steel producer. In 1978 it had eight plants in the U.S. and was the country's fifth largest steelmaker in tonnage and third largest in sales. Armco, since its founding in 1901, has led the industry in product and methods innovations, starting with the integrated mill itself and including electrical steels, continuous flat rolling, commercial development of taconite ores, development of many grades of stainless steel, and large-scale direct reduction furnaces, to mention only a few advances.

Armco had also led the industry in both sensitivity to environmental questions and in actions to alleviate pollution. By the end of 1978, Armco had spent over $300 million on pollution control, 85 percent before being required by state or federal authorities. Armco claimed to have stopped 95 percent of its process pollution emissions. A 1977 report on pollution in the steel industry placed Armco's performance first, with the other six major firms "tied for last."[2]

In 1979 Armco was engaged in several projects to control windblown fugitive dust, a pollutant not yet recognized and controlled by law. Barker stated, however, that these "nonprocess" sources accounted for 61 percent of all "total plant" particulate emissions, as measured by EPA developed and approved methods. Projects under way in late 1979 included: paving of dirt roads, cleaning of paved roads, busing of employees from central parking lots to reduce the creation of dust, and planting of over 5,000 trees and shrubs in and around the mill complex to cover bare areas.

THE CLEAN AIR ACT AND THE ENVIRONMENTAL PROTECTION AGENCY

The Clean Air Act (CAA) of 1970 required the Environmental Protection Agency (EPA) to establish and enforce air quality goals (the EPA is also responsible for control of water pollution and solid wastes). The EPA set up National Ambient Air Quality Standards (NAAQS) for six airborne pollutants: sulfur oxides (SO_x), nitrogen dioxide, carbon monoxide, photochemicals, hydrocarbons, and particulates. These standards postulated "threshold levels" beyond which ambient pollutants were damaging to health and welfare. States were given the primary responsibility to develop and implement programs to achieve these standards. In the attempt to bring regions or firms into compliance, emission rate standards were also set "stack-by-stack" for most industrial processes. In most cases the state specified what equipment had to be installed and where. Also, 247 "air-quality control regions" were established and classed either as "clean" or as "nonattainment" regions. "Nonattainment" meant that the NAAQS for at least one pollutant were not met.

The EPA's first task was to bring nonattainment regions into compliance. On the one hand, existing sources had to be cleaned up or shut down, and on the other hand, the EPA proposed to effectively shut off industrial growth in nonattainment regions by refusing to issue emissions permits for *new* sources of pollution until all NAAQS were met. Compliance was easier said than done, however. By the 1975 deadline set in the CAA, 160 of the 247 regions still violated the NAAQS for one or more pollutants. Often, emissions improvements as stipulated stack-by-stack seemed to be more costly than industry could bear and survive. Industries such as steel, however, were often crucial to local economies. As Barker had commented,

> This policy forces the installation of capital and energy intensive control devices on each and every source without regard to the source's relative contribution to the ambient air quality and without regard to ratios of cost and benefit per ton on pollutant captured.

Also, some industry observers felt that the drain pollution equipment placed on capital investment funds partly explained the United States steel industry's poor international performance. Therefore, under pressure from industry and local governments as well as the environmental movement, the EPA had by 1979 evolved compromise policies.

The EPA's first step was the creation of the "offset" policy in late 1976. "Offsets" allow firms to trade pollution "rights" within nonattainment regions. A firm may *add* a pollution source if it reduces pollution by a greater amount somewhere within the air-quality control region, either by buying controls from another firm, by adding controls to its own operations, or by shutting down one of its present sources to name a few possibilities. One category of pollution could not be traded for another: SO_x could only be traded for SO_x, for instance. By 1977 firms could "bank" excess pollution reductions, and a market in pollution "rights" developed, though it was far from clear how a price per ton of pollutant could be set in such a thin market without some idea of the value of an offset to a firm.

The "bubble policy," which the EPA had officially proposed on January 18, 1979, was a conceptual relative of the offsets policy. Like the offsets policy, the bubble policy was concerned with the new effect of pollution sources rather than with regulating each point source of pollution. Regulations were so tightly written, however, that options to trade one source for another remained limited. Approval procedures for industry's compliance plans prepared under the bubble policy by state, local, and federal officials remained complex. Industry faced a risk that a bubble plan prepared in good faith would be rejected. Rejection involved retroactive noncompliance fines as well as the cost of installing mandated stack-by-stack equipment. For this reason, industry had made few commitments to bubble policy compliance plans.

THE MIDDLETOWN PLANT AND STEELMAKING

Armco's corporate headquarters and its original and still largest plant are in Middletown, Ohio, not far from the family home in Cincinnati of Armco's founder, George M. Verity. The Middletown plant had been the focus in 1965–1972 of what has been called the U.S.'s last great steel industry project, Project 600 (for $600 million). Much of the plant had been rebuilt or modernized. It is an integrated mill, receiving coal, iron ore, limestone, and steel scrap and producing various semifinished sheet steel products.

A simplified flow diagram for the prefinishing processes at Middletown is shown in Exhibit 1 (the finishing processes produce few air pollutants). Although not explicit in the diagram, each stage of the process may actually have several production units (there are six open hearth furnaces, for instance). Process capacities and 1978 tonnages of inputs and intermediate outputs are included on the flow diagram. Blast furnace and coke oven by-product gases were used in the plant and gave energy credits. Scrap and other material such as iron-rich flue dust were also recycled within the plant. Variable costs in 1979 are given in Exhibit 2. Middletown, at this time, had no constraints on demand for its product nor on the supply of raw materials.

Steelmaking has three distinct phases: preparation of raw materials, production of pig iron, and production and finishing of steel. Coke is prepared by heating metallurgical coal and is the primary agent for reducing iron ore. Sinter plants recapture iron from waste materials, but the preparation of sinter requires some ore and limestone. The ore itself is usually pelletized before going to the blast furnace. The blast furnaces produce pig iron (and slag waste). Molten pig iron and scrap steel are combined in the steelmaking furnaces. At Middletown the steel is either cast by a continuous process into slabs or cast into ingots which require subsequent processing before they can be rolled into slabs. Slabs are heated and rolled to form hot rolled carbon steel coils, the basis for all sheet steel products.

THE LINEAR PROGRAMMING MODEL

Mr. Steiner saw that the LP model Barker had left him maximized annual contribution for the part of steel production shown in Exhibit 1, using a transfer price of $350 per ton for hot rolled carbon coils. Exhibit 3 is the matrix and Exhibit 4 is the solution. The input-output numbers in the matrix did not conform exactly to those in the flow diagram, because Armco chose to use industry average data rather than Middletown-specific data for some of the numbers. This did not concern Mr. Steiner, but he did want to be sure that the variables and constraints in the model matched the flow diagram. He was also concerned about some comments pencilled in the margins by Jim Botsko about deficiencies in the objective function:

> I don't believe the LP has all the costs included. Each process takes more than one ton of material in for each ton of output. These extra materials don't get charged because the objective function has only processing costs.

Jim had jotted an example of how he calculated costs added at each process (here for the continuous caster):

Material In ($/ton)	Yield	Material Out ($/ton)	+	Operating Cost	=	Total Cost	Added Cost
$226	94%	$240.43	+	$28.14	=	$268.57	$42.57

Another problem with the model that Jim noted was that the optimal LP solution ran the open hearth (OH) furnace at capacity while leaving excess capacity in the basic oxygen furnace (BOF). Since the OH was older technology and had higher operating costs, it was industry practice to use the newer and cheaper BOF. Mr. Steiner knew he first had to verify the LP before using it to answer questions about pollution emissions.

PARTICULATE EMISSIONS

The Middletown plant was in a nonattainment region for particulate air pollution which was generated in steelmaking in three categories:

1. *Process emissions* could be captured at a point source, such as a smoke-stack.
2. *Process fugitive emissions* were generated by production processes, but were not emitted nor captured at a point. A large part of such emissions occurred when a furnace door was opened or closed during charging. Dust from handling coal or limestone was also significant.
3. *Windblown fugitive emissions* originated as dust from ore piles, roads within the plant, and bare areas.

Process emissions were the first target for pollution control, and by 1979 most feasible particulate emissions controls were in place. The hoods and baghouses proposed by the EPA for Middletown in 1979 were for process fugitives, and in effect evacuated and filtered the air of entire buildings. A 2,000 horsepower electric fan was typical for these devices. Arthur D. Little, Inc. reported in May 1975 that:

> The control of (process) fugitive emissions, when demanded by regulatory agencies, is perhaps the most challenging pollution control problem facing the industry. In many situations, the electric power requirements are so great that more pollutants are produced by the electric generating plants than are removed from the steel plant.[3]

Windblown fugitive emissions were not included in the bubble policy as proposed by the EPA.

Steiner hoped to be able to make additions to the LP model to look at some of the choices they faced with respect to particulate emissions. Among the alternatives were those of adding the proposed equipment, purchasing off-sets or altering production in some way. He wanted to know how much would be saved under the bubble policy for particulates. The particulates produced under optimal production for stack-by-stack constraints had been estimated as shown in Exhibit 5. His first task would be to determine the optimal production plan under the bubble policy. Emissions rate reductions (including process fugitives) for both present controls and proposed controls together with capital costs and operating energy needs are in Exhibit 6.

NOTES

1. "A Brave Experiment in Pollution Control," *Fortune*, February 12, 1979, pp. 120–123.

2. *Environmental Steel Update.* James S. Cannon and Frederick S. Armentrout. Council on Economic Priorities, New York, San Francisco, 1977.

3. *Steel and the Environment: A Cost Impact Analysis.* Arthur D. Little, Inc., May 1975.

Armco Inc.—The Bubble Policy
Prefinishing Process Flows and Annual Capacities(*) (In Millions of Tons)

Exhibit 1

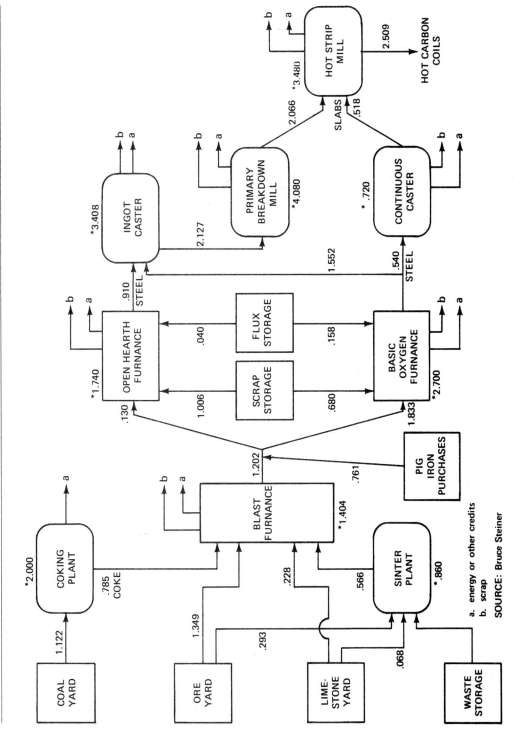

a. energy or other credits
b. scrap

SOURCE: Bruce Steiner

Armco Inc.—The Bubble Policy
Variable Costs/Credits by Process Center
(Dollars per ton of Intermediate Product)

Exhibit 2

Costs	Ore Yard	Coal Yard	Scrap Yard	Sinter Plant	Coke Plant	Blast Furnace	Open Hearth Furnace	Basic Oxygen Furnace	Ingot Casting	Continuous Casting	Primary Breakdown Mill	Hot Strip Mill
Raw Material	34.00	45.00	93.00	2.67[1]	—	2.09*	1.68**	3.36**	—	—	—	—
Labor	1.00	.83	3.32	4.99	7.15	4.82	14.79	7.15	.50	17.95	4.16	6.98
Water	.04	.19	.15	1.47	21.42	42.27	23.55	8.92	—	7.72	5.40	20.84
Power	.60	.74	.79	7.72	4.05	4.17	3.70	5.17	—	1.67	7.14	19.75
Fuel	—	—	—	.04	—	—	.10	.01	—	.02	.05	.08
Maintenance	.56	.83	1.22	1.88	3.57	4.47	9.06	4.19	4.06	4.94	3.01	6.07
Total Costs	36.20	47.59	98.48	18.77	36.19	57.82	52.88	28.80	4.56	32.30	19.76	53.72
Credits												
Scrap	—	—	—	—	—	.93	1.86	1.86	1.86	3.72	17.67	3.72
Energy	—	—	—	—	.23	.13	—	—	—	—	—	—
Other	—	—	—	—	1.63	.03	.06	.13	.34	.44	.45	.41
New Costs	36.20	47.59	98.48	18.77	34.33	56.73	50.96	26.81	2.36	28.14	(1.36)	49.59[2]

1. Limestone costs $11 per ton, flux $42 per ton. Sinter plant "raw materials" are mostly waste products.
2. The transfer price for hot carbon coils is $350 per ton.
* Limestone
** Flux

Figures disguised to protect Armco's proprietary interests. Based on Exhibits 8A and 8B of *Integrated Iron and Steel Industry*, Vol. II. Temple, Barker, and Sloane, Inc.

Armco Inc.—The Bubble Policy
LP Variables and Matrix

Exhibit 3

Objective coefficients (top row, by column): 1: 36.2 | 2: 36.2 | 3: 47.59 | 4: 18.77 | 5: 34.33 | 6: 98.48 | 7: 98.48 | 8: 56.73 | 9: 56.73 | 10: 50.96 | 11: 26.81 | 12: 26.81 | 13: 2.36 | 14: 1.36 | 15: 28.14 | 16: 300.41

		1. Ore to Sinter Plant	2. Ore to Blast Furnace	3. Coal	4. Sinter	5. Coke	6. Scrap to Open Hearth	7. Scrap to Basic Oxygen	8. Pig Iron to Open Hearth	9. Pig Iron to Basic Oxygen	10. Open Hearth to Ingots	11. Basic Oxygen to Ingots	12. Basic Oxygen to C Cast	13. Ingots Cast	14. Primary Breakdown Slabs	15. Continuous Cast Slabs	16. Hot Carbon Coils	RHS
CAPACITIES:																		
A	Sinter Plant				1.0													≤ .860
B	Coke Oven					1.0												≤ 2.000
C	Blast Furnace								1.0	1.0								≤ 1.404
D	Open Hearth Furn										1.0							≤ 1.740
E	Basic Oxygen Furn											1.0	1.0					≤ 2.700
F	Ingot Casting													1.0				≤ 3.408
G	Primary Breakdown														1.0			≤ 4.080
H	Continuous Casting															1.0		≤ .720
I	Hot-Strip Mill																1.0	≤ 3.480
INPUT-OUTPUT:																		
J	Ore-Sinter	-1			.52													= 0
K	Coal-Coke			-1		1.43												= 0
L	Ore-Pig Iron		-1						1.12	1.12								= 0
M	Sinter-Pig Iron				-1				.47	.47								= 0
N	Coke-Pig Iron					-1			.65	.65								= 0
O	OHF: Scrap-Steel						-1				1.08							= 0
P	OHF: Pig Iron-Steel								-1		.14							= 0
Q	BOF: Scrap-Steel							-1				.32	.32					= 0
R	BOF: Pig Iron-Steel									-1		.81	.81					= 0
S	Steel-Ingots										-1	-1		1.02				= 0
T	Ingots-Slabs													-1	1.20			= 0
U	Steel-Cont Cast Slabs												-1			1.06		= 0
V	Slabs-Hot Carbon Coils														-1	-1	1.03	= 0

Exhibit 4

Armco Inc.—The Bubble Policy
LP Solution

**Optimal Solution

$Z = 148.854$

**Decision Variables

1	0.3431	ore to sinter plant
2	1.5725	ore to blast furnace
3	1.3050	coal
4	0.6599	sinter
5	0.9126	coke
6	1.8792	scrap to open-hearth
7	0.4584	scrap to blast furnace
8	0.2436	pig iron to open-hearth
9	1.1604	pig iron to basic oxygen
10	1.7400	open-hearth to ingots
11	0.6694	basic oxygen to ingots
12	0.7632	basic oxygen to continuous caster
13	2.3621	ingots cast
14	1.9685	primary breakdown slabs
15	0.7200	continuous cast slabs
16	2.6102	hot carbon coils

**Slack or Surplus in Constraints

A	0.2001	sinter plant
B	1.0874	coke oven
E	1.2674	basic oxygen furnace
F	1.0459	ingot casting
G	2.1115	primary breakdown
I	0.8698	hot-strip mill

**Shadow Prices for Constraints

C	39.1965	blast furnace
D	48.8667	open-hearth furnace
H	12.2134	continuous caster
J	36.1999	ore-sinter
K	47.5899	coal-coke
L	36.1999	ore-pig iron
M	37.5939	sinter-pig iron
N	102.3836	coke-pig iron
O	98.4800	OHF: scrap-steel
P	220.6888	OHF: pig iron-steel
Q	98.4800	BOF: scrap-steel
R	220.6888	BOF: pig iron-steel
S	237.0815	steel-ingots
T	244.1831	ingots-slabs
U	237.0815	steel-cont. cast slabs
V	291.6598	steel-hot carbon coils

Exhibit 5

Armco Inc.—The Bubble Policy
Particulate Emissions Under 1978 Production and LP Optimum Production[1]

Process Sources	1978 Production (Millions of tons)	Particulate Emissions (Millions of lbs)	LP Production (Millions of tons)	Particulate Emissions (Millions of lbs)[2]
Ore Yard	1.349[3]	.795	1.916	1.130
Coal Yard	1.122	.045	1.305	.052
Sinter Plant	.566	.440	.660	.513
Coke Plant	.785	.984	.913	1.145
Scrap Yard	1.686	.202	2.337	.280
Blast Furnace	1.202	.570	1.404	.665
Open Hearth Furnace	.910	.784	1.740	1.498
Basic Oxygen Furnace	2.092			
	1.056			
	1.433			
	.724			
Ingot Casting	2.127	0	2.362	0
Primary Breakdown	2.066	.322	1.968	.307
Continuous Casting	.518	0	.720	0
Hot Strip Mill	2.509	0	2.610	0
Total		5.198		6.314

Nonprocess Sources				
Misc. Storage Piles	—	.315	—	—
Bare Areas	—	.280	—	—
Unpaved Roads	—	1.260	—	—
Paved Roads	—	6.678	—	—
Other Sources	—	.719	—	—
Total		9.252		

1. Process and process fugitive emissions.
2. Estimated.
3. Emissions occur in storage of ore that goes to the blast furnace (sinter excluded).
Source: Bruce Steiner

Exhibit 6

Armco Inc.—The Bubble Policy
Performance and Costs of
Particulate Emissions Controls

Present Controls

	Particle Emissions Reduction[1] (lbs/Ton)	Annual Operating Cost[2] ($/Ton of Product)	Capital Cost[3] (Millions of 1979 $)
Coke Oven	1.231	.33	$ 82.5
Sinter Plant	11.289	1.00	2.9
Open Hearth Furnace	22.200	1.56	16.9
Basic Oxygen Furnace (A)	.287	{ .10	.6
Basic Oxygen Furnace (B)	23.007		16.9
Primary Breakdown Mill	.039	.02	7.2

Proposed Controls

1. Process

	Particle Emissions Reduction (lbs/Ton)	Annual Operating Cost ($/Ton)	Capital Cost[3] (Millions of 1979 $)	System
Ore Yard	.295	Negligible	$ .1	Spray Equipment
Coal Yard	.040	Negligible	.4	Spray Equipment
Blast Furnace (EPA Proposed)	.333	.97	4.0	Hoods, Baghouses
Open Hearth Furnace (EPA Proposed)	.134	1.29	5.0	Hoods, Baghouses
Basic Oxygen Furnace (EPA Proposed)	.387	2.04	5.0	Hoods, Baghouses

2. Nonprocess

	Annual Particulate Emissions Reduction (Millions of lbs)	Annual Operating Cost	Capital Cost[3] (Millions of 1979 $)	System
Mis. Storage Piles	.158	< $500	.1	Spray Equipment
Bare Areas	.015	< $500	<.1	Seeding and Planting
Unpaved Roads	.374	$300,000	1.525	Pave and Treat Roads
Paved Roads	6.084	$400,000	2.375	Clean & Treat Roads, Reduce Traffic

1. Rate calculated from 1978 performance.
2. Included in the variable costs in Exhibit 3.
3. Armco annualizes capital costs on a 20-year basis.
   Source: Bruce Steiner

POLICY ISSUES IN ACCOUNTING AND FINANCE

Finance is another functional area of any organization. Very often managerial decisions can be evaluated using a variety of accounting and financial measures of success. Each of the cases presented in this section deals with one or more of these accounting or financial measures. The growth and survival of any organization is dependent upon its financial health. Financial planning is essential and must be done continuously.

In the first case, *Wood Stove Works,* the cost structure and cost behavior of an organization are addressed. Different pricing methods are considered and projected income statements are developed. Liquidity, budgeting standard costs, funds flow analysis, and a valid sales forecast are important elements in the analysis of Wood Stove Works. The next case takes the reader one step further in measuring internal efficiency of the organization's financial function. The *Sweet Girl Products Company* uses standard costing and an accompanying variance analysis system. Standard costing seems to be working properly; however, the variance analysis system appears to be unsatisfactory. The reader is asked to assess a proposed new variance system and determine its acceptability by the organization's constituency.

The next three cases are future oriented and focus more on measures of future success and place less emphasis on internal efficiency. In *Contemporary Furniture,* the reader is asked to develop a percent-of-sales forecast (balance sheet projection) along with a cash budget. The reader is also asked to compare and determine how the forecast is related to a cash budget. The *Contemporary Furniture* case presumes that the reader has a basic understanding of regression analysis. The fourth case is *Solvo, Inc.* This case addresses some of the financing difficulties encountered by small firms. Specifically, this case investigates the options for financing growth. The reader is asked to assess the desirability of financing growth through equity, retained earnings, and/or debt. In making this assessment, it is necessary to evaluate each option looking at sources and uses of funds and applying some ratio analyses.

The last case, entitled *Highland Lakes Development, Inc.,* requires an assessment of several projects and their viability relative to a desired return-on-investment. This evaluation takes the form of a benefit-cost analysis. In this section, the reader is introduced to several financial measures of internal efficiency and later presented with cases that look toward assessing future financial performance. Effective financial policies like those in production and marketing are a necessary, but not a sufficient, condition for organizational health and viability.

Case 5–1

Wood Stove Works*

Wood Stove Works, located in central New Hampshire, was formed in 1977 by two partner/owners to manufacture wood burning stoves which they had designed. The owners used all of their savings and remortgaged their homes to raise the necessary capital to start the business.

Background

"If this stove was made by anybody else it would probably cost $50 more," said Charlie Martin, co-owner of Wood Stove Works. "The design and quality of our stove is more efficient than Fisher, Jotul, and All Nighter, the market leaders in our area, and our selling price is about 15 percent under theirs. We have had our stove tested and are very pleased with the results. We are a little disappointed in our 'very good' rating and think we should have gotten an 'excellent' rating, but the tests were conducted in Massachusetts, and considering that fact, we should be pleased with the results."

"We must be doing something right," said Jerry Therrian, the other co-owner. "Our design has been copied already with a few modifications. Fortunately, those modifications made their stoves less attractive. We were approached last fall by a salesman who wanted an exclusive on our stove, but he wanted too much money, and we told him to go pound sand."

"Apparently he worked out a deal with another manufacturer," said Charlie, "copied our basic design, and started selling the stove in December near our price. We have no idea how this will affect our market position, but it has to hurt some."

"We found out that the other manufacturer is getting steel at a lower price from Canada and probably won't be affected by the steel increase," said Jerry. "We've also heard that they have lower operational costs, and their margin on sales is higher than ours. We want to raise our prices, but we're afraid of an adverse affect on our current market position."

"Demand took a nose dive during the middle of January," said Jerry. "We were straight out during December until Christmas and naturally assumed that demand would spill over into the first quarter of 1978. We hired more people and added a second shift, but as soon as mid-January rolled around, our orders fell off and we had to unload our inventory."

"Not only did we unload our inventory, but also our help," said Charlie. "We eliminated our second shift and cut back on our first. Winter is no real

*This case was prepared by Michael A. Kole, University of New Hampshire, with the intention of providing a basis for class discussion rather than illustrating either effective or ineffective management of a business situation. Reprinted with permission from *Application of Decision Sciences in Organizations: A Case Approach* by Joseph C. Latona and K. Mark Weaver with the cooperation of the American Institute for Decision Sciences, Atlanta, Georgia, 1980.

picnic up here. It seems as if we were spending more time pushing vehicles out of snowbanks than producing stoves."

Charlie continued, "We lowered our 1978 sales estimate after the drop in demand throughout the marketplace during the first few months of 1978. To raise cash and keep our business going, we pushed direct sales to individuals at discounts. As a result, the company boosted its first quarter sales well above our projections." (Exhibit 3)

CURRENT DECISION SITUATION

On April 15, 1978, the two owners received their financial statements for the first quarter of the year (Exhibits 1 and 2). Charlie and Jerry were quite

Exhibit 1

Wood Stove Works
Unaudited Balance Sheet
March 31, 1978

ASSETS

Current assets:

Cash	$ 62	
Accounts receivable	12,100	
Inventory	19,825	
Total current assets...................		$31,987

Noncurrent assets:

Machinery/equipment	$ 9,136	
Less accumulated depreciation	1,215	
Total noncurrent assets		7,921
Total assets		$39,908

LIABILITIES and PARTNERSHIP EQUITY

Current liabilities:

Accounts payable	$32,818	
Accrued payroll taxes	1,544	
Equipment loan—current portion	839	
Loan payable...........................	2,500	$37,701

Noncurrent liabilities:

Equipment loan	$ 2,390	
Less current portion (above)............	839	1,551
Total liabilities		$39,252

Partnership equity:

Beginning balance	$ 8,000	
Less withdrawals	(1,570)	
Net loss	(5,774)	$ 656
Total liabilities and partnership equity.......		$39,908

Wood Stove Works
Unaudited Statement of Income and Expense

Exhibit 2   **For the Period January 1, 1978–March 31, 1978**

Revenue:

Sales			$63,645
Less: Sales returns and allowances		$ 802	
Sales discounts		3,000	3,802
Net sales			$59,843

Cost of sales:

Beginning inventory	$ 2,025		
Purchases	55,346		
Freight and subcontracting	932		
Operational supplies	2,393		
Direct labor	14,481		
Total goods available		$75,177	
Less ending inventory		19,825	
Cost of goods sold			55,352
Gross Profit			$ 4,491

Cost of operation:

Payroll taxes	$ 1,120	
Employee benefits	68	
Rent	300	
Repairs (trucks and equipment)	965	
Auto maintenance and travel	2,093	
Electricity (includes heat)	766	
Advertising	600	
Insurance	236	
Consumer testing	750	
Legal and accounting	1,392	
Licenses	50	
Office expense (includes supplies)	835	
Telephone	627	
Bank charges	16	
Interest	42	
Depreciation	405	
Total cost of operation		10,265
Net Profit or loss for period		($ 5,774)

concerned about their financial situation. They scheduled a meeting for April 20, 1978, to make new plans for the coming year. The partners expected sales to increase significantly that summer and to grow dramatically in the fall. They knew that they had to keep the business going through the spring and increase their material purchase early in the summer. The partners also felt that any major changes should be made prior to the summer.

Exhibit 3

Wood Stove Works
Schedule of Units Sold and On Hand
March 31, 1978

	W-118	W-124	W-130	Total
Units sold January-March	67	130	102	299
Dollar amount (at list price)	$11,725	$27,950	$23,970	$63,645
Units on hand March 31, 1978:				
Materials	142	65	84	291
Work in progress.....................	—	—	—	—
Finished goods	—	7	6	13

Sales Estimate for 1978
(Prepared February 20, 1978)

	W-118	W-124	W-130	Fireplace	Total
January-March	45	96	57	—	198
April	28	41	29	—	98
May..........................	21	34	21	—	76
June..........................	21	34	21	—	76
July	35	50	40	40	165
August	45	60	50	31	186
September	100	130	100	66	396
October.......................	125	155	125	81	486
November	125	155	125	81	486
December	45	60	50	31	186
Total........................	590	815	618	330	2,353

MATERIAL COSTS

The owners then provided information about their material costs. All fabricated parts were delivered to the company at a cost of $.295 per pound. Firebrick cost was $.375 each. The price of the door and vent cap was $28.56 for the small and $37.50 for the medium and the large. (This was the price charged at the foundry.) Experience showed that 15 stoves could be welded with one set of oxygen and acetylene tanks at $32 per set. The owners also stated that it took about one pint of paint to finish a stove, and a gallon costs $14.38. Miscellaneous parts, which included rivet washers, the special gas used to bend the door handle, other bits and pieces, the hinges, the wedge, and a knob for the handle averaged at a cost of $2.20 per stove. The cost of welding rod averaged about $1.00 per pound, and it required approximately 6.8, 8.4, and 11.2 pounds of rod in the three sizes of units.

Exhibit 4

Wood Stove Works
Schedule of Workers
March 31, 1978

	Wages per hour	Status
Supervisor	$4.25	full time
Leadman	3.75	full time
Laborer	3.50	full time
Laborer	3.50	full time

Note:
Employee FICA .0605 on first $17,700

State unemployment .0270 on first $6,000

Federal unemployment .0070 on first $6,000

"We really don't have any difficulty with scrap or spoilage because of the nature of our production process," Jerry said. "All of our steel is precut and we just assemble the necessary pieces (Exhibit 5). The only way significant scrap could occur would be if major damage was done to one of the parts early in the process, and such damage would be obvious and unusual."

"They charge us a pretty penny to process and precut the steel," Charlie said. "We are thinking of buying a camagraph and doing the cutting ourselves. That would save us anywhere from three to five cents per pound. But we really don't have the room, and we would need to hire another person full time just to cut the steel."

BUILDING

"We definitely have to move out of here," Charlie added. "I'm not going to spend another winter like the last one in that unheated converted barn. We might have to close down during January and February. In fact, I really don't think that would be a bad idea."

"We are thinking of renting a place in Concord," said Jerry. "The owner of the building is also willing to rent us a truck and forklift and may even include the vehicles in the rental agreement. We are also thinking of buying a building."

LABOR COSTS

The conversation switched to the labor force and the workers (Exhibit 4). "We've really got a good work crew, and if any problems arise, Charlie and I

Exhibit 5

Wood Stove Works
Schedule of Stove Parts

| | | Number of Pounds Per Stove | | |
		W-118	W-124	W-130
F*	Bottom	19.84	29.37	39.36
F	Back	13.03	18.25	20.45
F	Sides (2 pieces)	56.52	91.80	101.73
F	Brick clip (3 pieces)	4.31	5.12	5.94
F	Front top	11.51	13.88	14.61
F	Middle top	22.67	31.88	44.27
F	Rear top and baffle	15.83	25.35	28.49
F	Flue plate	5.95	7.93	8.93
F	Flue	1.08	1.31	1.31
F	Front and rear legs (2 each)	11.59	13.87	13.87
F	Seal (4 pieces)	2.79	3.53	3.53
	Door and vent cap	40.00	54.00	54.00
	Wedge	.30	.30	.30
	Hinges (2 pieces)	.36	.36	.36
F	Handle	.67	.67	.67
F	Ash fender	5.20	5.94	6.32
F	Ash fender edge	1.30	1.40	1.45
	Paint (1 pint)	—	—	—
	Brick (16, 24, and 30 needed respectively for the 118, 124, and 130 stoves)	53.92	80.88	101.10
	Weldment	6.80	8.40	11.20
F	Front (4 pieces)	8.30	12.68	15.22
	Total weight	281.97	406.92	473.11
	Total weight of fabricated parts	180.59	262.98	306.15

*Fabricated part purchased from the steel vendor.

try to iron out the situation," Jerry said. "Since the first of the year we have been recording the times for various steps in the production process. This is done on a card that accompanies a stove through production. The times are recorded by the workers themselves."

"The workers take the times for the job cards from a time clock that displays time in hundredths of an hour instead of minutes," Charlie noted. "We also noticed that workers are often called from their work for tasks such as loading and unloading trucks, making deliveries, and moving materials and equipment around the shop. Sometimes a worker will record the fact that he had to unload a truck, for instance, but he won't note how long it took him to do it. On other occassions, he'll forget altogether to record that he had been pulled off the line. But even with all the commotion that occurs during the winter, I would estimate that the workers only spend about 10 percent of their time away from their work doing other things."

"I'd like to think so," added Charlie. "We should be able to produce a stove in less than the six and one-half worker hours they allowed us when we worked at Fisher."

"I agree," said Jerry, "but we better use our first six month's experience to estimate this year's labor cost. You know we stopped our second shift at the end of January and it wasn't until mid-February that we were down to our current four workers."

OTHER COSTS

An analysis of the overhead costs was then discussed. The owners felt that the following items could reasonably be expected to vary as volume varied during the coming year:

- Office expense (including supplies)
- Electricity (including heat)
- Telephone
- Auto maintenance and travel

The estimated annual costs of the following items were:

Advertising	$2,400
Insurance	950
Legal and professional	3,100
Consumer testing	750
Licenses	50
Bank charges	65
Interest	170

Jerry said the cost of repairing the truck and equipment would increase as they got older due to increasing wear.

Other required expenses or allocations were depreciation on welding equipment and a truck. Salvage value on the truck was estimated at 20 percent with a five-year life. The machinery also had a five-year life, but no salvage value. The owners stated that they really needed an additional truck, and a forklift truck and believed they could get a good deal on such equipment for about $9,000. The owners also hoped to draw $250 each per week for their time and effort.

"I'd just like to mention that we did have a sales manager and a production manager," Charlie concluded. "If we get busy again, I may hire a salesperson on a commission basis, but in the meantime, I will be handling the sales end of the business, while Jerry will be overseeing the production end of the business."

Case 5–2

Sweet Girl Products Company*

The Sweet Girl Products Company produced and marketed ladies wear. The company had many production plants in the United States. In 1976 the company completed the construction of its Alaska plant at McKinley Park, Alaska. The new plant was built to produce a simple dress that fit the needs of the area residents. The company was a decentralized organization; however, the accounting system in each plant was similar to the other and designed by the top management.

BACKGROUND

The firm built the plant in Alaska with a capacity of producing 125,000 dresses a year. However, the planning committee completed a marketing research study which indicated that 96,000 dresses per year would be sold in the five-year planning horizon.

The firm felt that the 125,000-dress capacity would be the most economical way to provide for the seasonal and cyclical variations that were expected to push demand to 125,000 dresses from time to time over the next five years.

THE ACCOUNTING SYSTEM

A standard cost system was installed for product costing and control purposes; however, management was dissatisfied with the overhead variance systems that had been installed.

This case was prepared by Morcos F. Massoud, California State Polytechnic University, with the intention of providing a basis for class discussion rather than illustrating either effective or ineffective management of a business situation. Reprinted with permission from *Application of Decision Sciences in Organizations: A Case Approach* by Joseph C. Latona and K. Mark Weaver with the cooperation of the American Institute for Decision Sciences, Atlanta, Georgia, 1980.

While the plant was in construction, a special task force from corporate headquarters designed the standard cost system for the plant. The design, with the exception of establishing standards, was relatively easy. Sweet Girl Products had been operating standard cost systems in all its plants since 1960. Alaska's system was a duplicate of the system installed throughout the company.

The cost system recognized the following variance accounts:

- Material price
- Material usage
- Labor rate
- Labor efficiency
- Overhead spending
- Overhead efficiency
- Overhead volume

The first report under the system was prepared for May 1977 (Exhibit 1). Overhead variances were reported monthly as shown in this exhibit. The

Sweet Girl Products Company
Overhead Variances (Monthly)
Exhibit 1   **Alaska Plant**

Department: Finishing

Reporting period: May 1 - 31, 1977

Output for the period: Budgeted — 8,000 dresses (8,000 direct labor hours)

Actual — 7,500 dresses (7,400 direct labor hours)

Standard product hours: 1 dress per hour

Flexible budget: $40,000 fixed cost per month plus $3 variable overhead cost per direct labor hour

Cost and Variance Analysis

	Variable Overhead	Fixed Overhead	Total Overhead
Actual	$22,950	$41,000	$63,950
Applied	22,500	37,500	60,000
	$ 450	$ 3,500	$ 3,950*

*Spending variance — $1,750 unfavorable
Efficiency variance — 800 favorable
Volume variance — 3,000 unfavorable

Total variance — $3,950

report was presented to departmental supervisors by Mr. Conners, the plant controller, and Mr. Ash, the plant manager. Both men agreed that a meeting should be called so that reports could be explained to the departmental heads and supervisors. Mr. Conners thought that he should explain the reports in a question and answer period, and that Mr. Ash should be present.

VARIANCES AND CAPACITY

The top management was behind the reporting efforts of the accounting department. Mr. Ash sat back and listened as Mr. Conners explained the meaning of the material, labor, and overhead variances. With respect to the overhead variances, he explained how the overhead rates were developed from the flexible budget equation and the "normal capacity" measure of 96,000 dresses per year.

No questions were asked about the mechanics of the flexible budgeting procedure since accounting personnel worked side-by-side with production supervisors in developing the departmental standards and budgets. However, the supervisors did question the advisability of developing rates from normal capacity. The manager of the finishing department, Mr. Ford, asked, "What does normal capacity mean? Who provided you with the capacity measure?"

Mr. Conners explained that normal capacity represented the average annual sales that the company is expected to make over the five-year planning period. It was used to justify the figure of 96,000 dresses per year or 8,000 dresses per month which was developed by the marketing research staff at corporate headquarters. Mr. Ash asked Mr. Conners to explain the relevance of the normal capacity figure to plant management.

Mr. Conners replied, "Well, Charley, I have to admit that the figure is not relevant to your people. We use normal capacity as our measure of capacity because corporate headquarters in Wisconsin wants it that way. They use the volume variance to judge the effectiveness of corporate planning."

"O.K., Jim," said Mr. Ash, "We can't fight City Hall, but maybe you can develop a way of pleasing headquarters and at the same time meeting our needs. While I have you on the subject of variances, how about explaining the meaning of the spending and efficiency variances."

"I think you and the rest of the group will find these a lot easier to take," replied Mr. Conners. "The spending variance represents how well you have controlled overhead costs in your departments. This follows because it represents the difference between the actual overhead spent and the overhead allowance generated by the flexible budget. Bear in mind the budget allowance is developed from actual hours worked, and so we have isolated efficiency considerations from this figure. The efficiency variance, on the other hand, is a measure of how much labor efficiency has saved or cost us for the period. In other words, when you overrun your time allowance, you do not simply cost the company labor dollars, but you also cost it overhead dollars. For example, when Pete Ford beat his time allowance by 100 hours this month, he not only saved us $400 in labor dollars, but he also saved us $800 in overhead costs.

Well, any other questions on the variances? O.K., then, I would like to say a thing or two about the follow-up procedures. Naturally, we want these reports to assist you in your efforts to control costs in your departments. I think they will, if you take the time to learn the meaning of the variances. I, as well as my whole staff, will be available to answer your questions. Charley Ash and I have agreed that material and labor variances will be issued each Friday around noontime and that the overhead variance reports will be issued once a month on the last Friday of the month. Neither Charley nor I wish to make pencil pushers out of you, and so we are only going to ask for formal explanations of variances if they are unfavorable and if they overrun the allowance by ten percent. My senior staff people will help you prepare these reports. Charley, do you want to add anything?"

"Yes, I do," said Mr. Ash, "I want to thank you for your time. I think we have a better understanding of the reports now. I would also like to add that I do not view these reports as punitive devices. I think we should view these as an important tool for our cost control effort. Although I can't deny that I will review the reports carefully and that I will drop around to find out how each of the sections are doing, no one need fear that the reports are going to be misused against them."

PERFORMANCE EVALUATION AND CONTROLLABLE VARIABLES

The system was used throughout 1977 without any mechanical difficulty. But Ash and the department heads were not happy with it. They thought that the overhead variances should be redesigned so as to be more meaningful. Specifically, the volume variance was not meaningful to them because they had no control over sales, nor did they have responsibility for planning the original capacity of 125,000 dresses. They could only produce in accordance with the schedules released for the month. These schedules were designed around sales achievements and forecasts as well as inventory needs. The efficiency variance also caused a great deal of disenchantment. Production supervisors complained (although only when they overran standard hours in output) that they were being penalized by being charged with the total overhead rate rather than just with the variable rate.

THE NEW SYSTEM

Mr. Conners sympathized with the production supervisors and agreed to discuss the problem with the people at corporate headquarters at the budget meeting in November. Conners thought that he could, without difficulty, get headquarters to accept the following three-variances system:

1. Budget variance — total actual overhead less budgeted overhead at actual hours
2. Efficiency variance — budgeted overhead at actual hours less budgeted overhead at standard hours
3. Volume variance — budgeted overhead at standard hours less standard hours at standard rates

At the November meeting, Mr. Bob Smith, the corporate controller, discussed Alaska's problems with Mr. Conners. He agreed that the overhead variances as defined by the system presently in operation were not as useful to plant management as it should or could be. In fact, he was impressed with Mr. Conners' analysis of the inadequacies of the system.* "Jim, I certainly am glad that you have pointed this out to me. I do not know why this point was not raised before. When we designed the system and procedures back in 1970, the system was ideal. As you probably recall, we were operating near 100 percent capacity in all our shops at that time. It's clear that we had better remind our people that the present procedures are meaningful only if they are operating near full capacity."

"To sum it up, Jim, change your system to fit your needs. We have said many times that our internal accounting and reporting systems have to be decentralized to meet local management needs. However, we can't very well decentralize the basic financial data required for our published statements. Go ahead and do what you have to do with the internal system, but give my office volume variance and produce cost data based on normal capacity."

With the green light, Mr. Conners came back to Alaska and discussed the proposed system with Charley Ash. Ash was impressed with the proposal since he thought it had overcome all the disadvantages of the current system.

Under the new system (1) capacity variances would be measured from scheduled production and thus only report plant management's failure to meet their operating plan, and (2) efficiency variances would be based on variable costs, the only costs that departmental managers had control over in the short run.

Throughout 1978 Alaska's plant management worked with the new overhead variances. Mr. Conners realized the success of the change and began to ready a paper for corporate office review. When the rough draft was completed, he forwarded it to Mr. Smith for comments. After reviewing the report, Smith called Mr. Conners in for an informal meeting with himself and Dick Leer, assistant corporate controller.

The meeting probed the possibility of breaking up the difference between the volume variance reported at the plant level and that reported to corporate management into one or more meaningful components.

Smith and Leer thought that if meaningful components could be defined and assigned to individuals or functions, the Sweet Girl's products would achieve a significant step forward in their attempt to control capacity utilization. All agreed that if the variances were to be meaningful, they would have to be defined around the actual work responsibilities of the function contributing to capacity utilization and that variances would have to measure revenue lost (that is, opportunity cost) by the company as a result of the idle capacity. They also agreed that sales, production, and planning were the functions that could be assigned responsibility for the capacity variance, but they were unsure as to how the assignment should be made.

---

*Mr. Conners planned to define scheduled hours as the hours scheduled in the production budget for the coming period rather than work with a normal capacity notion.

Case 5-3

Contemporary Furniture*

BACKGROUND INFORMATION

As owner and general manager of Contemporary Furniture, Robert Gruenwald was proud that the opening of his third retail outlet was accomplished in late October 1977 for only $11,000 in cash. This amount included all deposits, furnishings, and inventory. This third store was in a shopping center in Grandview, a Kansas City, Missouri, suburb. The other two stores were in Kansas City, Kansas, and in Merriam, Kansas. Since most purchases of the chrome furniture and furnishings products came from younger, affluent buyers, per capita income for the areas surrounding the various stores was important. Exhibit 1 shows "per capita" income for various areas in the Kansas City metropolitan area.

Contemporary Furniture both manufactured and retailed chrome furniture in addition to selling furnishings purchased from other suppliers. The manufacturing and storage area for items not currently on retail display was handled in an 1,800 square foot facility in an industrial area of Kansas City, Kansas. Manufacturing involved sizing, cutting, and assembling parts into finished products. Certain components were purchased ready-to-assemble, such as molded plastic bars. Most significant furniture pieces were delivered to customers where glass components, if any, were put in place. A $300 standard design table required a normal manufacturing time of about two to three hours; customer designed furniture required a longer manufacturing time. The flexibility of modern chrome furniture permitted the customer to design pieces for specific locations, functions, and so forth.

FINANCIAL SITUATION

Operating results had been erratic since the business opened in March 1974. Profits had ranged from $5,000 (1976) down to recent large losses. Gruenwald believed that the new outlet would produce sales equal to the other two outlets in a very short period of time. With the fixed costs of the manu-

*This case was prepared by Brian Belt, University of Missouri-Kansas City, and Frank Keller, University of Houston at Clear Lake City, with the intention of providing a basis for class discussion rather than illustrating either effective or ineffective management of a business situation. Reprinted with permission from *Application of Decision Sciences in Organizations: A Case Approach* by Joseph C. Latona and K. Mark Weaver with the cooperation of the American Institute for Decision Sciences, Atlanta, Georgia, 1980.

Exhibit 1

**Kansas City Metropolitan Area:
Population and Per Capita Income by
County and Selected Cities**

Area	1975 Population	1974 Per Capita Income (In dollars)
Kansas City Metropolitan Area	1,278,400	5,073
Leavenworth County (Kansas)	55,400	4,134
Johnson County (Kansas).	238,300	6,639
Leawood.	11,400	9,844
Prairie Village.	26,600	7,525
Overland Park	81,000	6,759
Merriam	11,500	6,143
Shawnee	22,700	5,376
Wyandotte County (Kansas)	177,600	4,221
Kansas City, Kansas	168,200	4,220
Jackson County (Missouri)	634,600	4,816
Raytown.	33,000	5,914
Independence	111,500	4,970
Grandview	22,200	5,051
Kansas City, Missouri (part).	403,200	4,666
Clay County (Missouri)	133,200	4,958
North Kansas City	5,000	5,968
Kansas City, Missouri (part).	56,600	4,921
Liberty	15,000	4,738
Platte County (Missouri)	39,300	5,297

facturing facility as well as the general administrative fixed expenses, Gruen-wald felt the additional sales would help solve the recent profit problems. Since the new store had opened in the first week of November 1977, the store was able to participate in the heavy Christmas sales period. Exhibit 2 shows sales per store for Contemporary Furniture since inception. Monthly sales adjustment (MSA) values are shown to indicate seasonality of sales.

Mr. Gruenwald believed that sales would be 50 percent higher in 1978 than in 1977 due primarily to the new store opening. Now that the new store was open he felt that November and December 1977 sales would be about $50,000 to $60,000. Gruenwald had learned of a technique called the "percent of sales" forecast which would help to forecast how much surplus would be generated for the next year. He had heard of this technique at a seminar for small business owners but had never attempted to use it. Exhibit 3 provides balance sheet items for September 30, 1977, as well as the two fiscal years

Exhibit 2

**Contemporary Furniture
Sales Per Store Since Inception***

	1974	1975	1976	1977	Monthly Sales Adjustment**
January	——	3,000	5,500	7,800	.75
February	——	1,600	6,500	9,300	.76
March	——	1,600	7,000	9,200	.76
April	3,800	9,400	9,000	8,700	1.19
May	6,000	3,500	10,100	8,800	1.07
June	7,400	1,800	8,500	7,500	.97
July	4,800	7,000	8,600	10,300	1.10
August	4,800	5,500	11,000	11,400	1.12
September	6,400	8,500	7,700	8,700	1.13
October	3,000	9,900	7,700	7,900	.96
November	3,800	8,400	12,500	——	1.05
December	3,800	9,400	12,500	——	1.14

*Store No. 1 opened March 1974; Store No. 2 opened May 1975; and Store No. 3 opened November 1977.

**Monthly Sales Adjustment (MSA) is value to multiply regression-calculated monthly sales value to obtain estimated monthly sales.

Regression equation:

$$Y = 143X + 3970$$

where: Y = monthly sales per store for any month since 3/74

X = number of months since 3/74

which ended March 31, 1977 and 1976; these balance sheet items vary rather directly with sales levels.

Gruenwald felt the need for some type of cash budget to indicate when the projected surpluses would be available. Mr. Gruenwald had negotiated a $55,000 note payable with Kansas City Metropolitan State Bank; the 180-day note matured on April 19, 1978, and Gruenwald wanted to be sure he could repay the obligation, or renegotiate on a timely basis. Further, Gruenwald wanted to open a fourth Contemporary Furniture retail outlet in either Raytown, Missouri, or North Kansas City as soon as $15,000 was available after paying off the Kansas City Metropolitan State Bank note. Due to the need for beginning lease negotiations as soon as possible, Gruenwald needed to know when the cash would be available.

Although the regression equation indicated a 1978 average sales-per-store of $11,400, the owner felt safer with an $11,000 average sales-per-store for calendar year 1978. Exhibit 4 illustrates income statement accounts for the fiscal periods March 31, 1976, March 31, 1977, and September 30, 1977. Purchased goods represented essentially all of the cost of goods sold (COGS) and were ordered, on the average, approximately one month in advance of sales and were paid two months thereafter. All other expenses can be assumed to have been paid in the month of the sale. Most noncommercial sales throughout the year were cash or credit card transactions; for these sales, cash could be considered received at the time of the sales. Some noncommercial sales were "layaway"; these occurred on a highly seasonal (that is, Christmas) basis (see Exhibit 3). Most commercial sales were "net 30" and were paid on a timely basis; however, the fluctuations in the relatively large, commercial sales could cause accounts receivable to fluctuate substantially (see Exhibit 3).

Exhibit 3

Contemporary Furniture
Selected Balance Sheet Accounts

	September 30, 1977	Percent of Sales	March 31, 1977	Percent of Sales	March 31, 1976	Percent of Sales
Assets						
Cash and savings account	$ 3,152	1.39	$ 3,547	1.54	$ 3,333	2.11
Accounts receivable*	29,866	13.15	9,348	4.06	8,000	5.06
Inventory	14,964	6.59	23,538	10.22	20,637	13.06
Liabilities						
Accounts payable	24,256	10.68	14,154	6.15	8,959	5.67
Accruals	2,338	1.03	2,550	1.11	2,416	1.53
Annualized sales	227,102		230,314		157,998	
Profit margin (profit ÷ sales)	−14.77		−1.25		+2.98	

*Include "layaway on order" but not "due from officers."

Exhibit 4

Contemporary Furniture
Income Statements for Fiscal Years Ending 1976,
1977, and First Half of Fiscal Year to be Ended in 1978

	Fiscal Period Ending		
	March 31, 1976 (12 months)	March 31, 1977 (12 months)	September 30, 1977 (6 months)
Sales	$ 157,998	$ 230,314	$ 113,551
Less: Cost of goods sold (including freight)	85,999	130,122	64,751
Delivery	1,510	2,424	2,265
Wages and wage taxes	27,349	57,645	31,123
Rent	12,191	11,616	10,137
Utilities, telephone	4,004	4,802	3,320
Insurance, licenses, other taxes	2,200	2,730	1,989
Supplies, services, miscellaneous	10,022	7,893	5,786
Advertising	7,190	10,904	7,921
Interest	2,195	4,318	2,598
Depreciation	630	749	434
Net Profit*	$ 4,708	($ 2,889)	($ 16,773)

*Contemporary Furniture is taxed as a "Sub-Chapter S" corporation and tax liabilities are not shown here.

Case 5–4

Solvo, Inc.*

HISTORY OF SOLVO

Solvo, Inc., a petro-chemical processor of automotive specialties, was founded by Frank Solvo in 1970. The company processed such items as antifreeze, windshield washer solvent, and engine degreaser. Other production included the packaging of charcoal lighter fluid, motor oil, and transmission fluid.

Operations began in Frank Solvo's garage on a part-time basis and included the processing of a limited line and amount of automotive specialties. These products were distributed locally to gas stations, auto repair garages, and a few warehouse distributors. Solvo established a reputable name through quality products and excellent service which resulted in increased demand for their products. By 1978, with the increasing sales volume and increased expectations, the business was incorporated. Expansion into 13 states east of the Mississippi River followed.

Frank Solvo held the position of president and Sam Edgar, Solvo's son-in-law, was vice president and general manager. In 1980 Solvo maintained a payroll of 36 full- and part-time employees (Exhibit 1) and witnessed an exceptional gain in sales and income. Sales in the years 1978, 1979, and 1980 were as follows (Exhibit 3):

	1978	1979	1980
Sales	$133,679.38	$184,838.81	$854,964.58

Over 80 percent of sales were in the categories of antifreeze and windshield washer fluid.

Solvo sold its products exclusively to large retailers who handled bulk items. Mr. Solvo felt that product loyalty was nil, and therefore, price and bulk were the major problems his firm faced.

---

*This case was prepared by Joseph C. Latona, The University of Akron, with the intention of providing a basis for class discussion rather than illustrating either effective or ineffective management of a business situation. Reprinted with permission from *Application of Decision Sciences in Organizations: A Case Approach* by Joseph C. Latona and K. Mark Weaver with the cooperation of the American Institute for Decision Sciences, Atlanta, Georgia, 1980.

Solvo projected sales to reach $1 million in the near future. The financial position of Solvo, Inc., until 1980, had not been sound (Exhibits 2, 4, and 5). Since incorporation in 1978, the firm had difficulty acquiring funds needed for expansion. When funds had been obtained, growth was too rapid, resulting in losses or very small profits. With increased sales, the facility Solvo occupied in 1974 was being expanded to provide for larger expected sales.

Frank Solvo controlled 90 percent of the nonmarketed stock and the remaining 10 percent was owned by a salesperson working for the company. Solvo was reluctant to dilute the amount of his controlling interest and, therefore, tended to resist the issuing of new stock or the sale of stock to obtain more funds.

There was considerable concern regarding the increasing dominance of big business in the industry. Procurement of raw materials had been and could continue to be a problem. If the larger companies exerted influence over Solvo's suppliers, Solvo felt raw material procurement could become very difficult.

There had been no dividend policy in the past. The president received a bonus in lieu of a dividend because of tax advantages.

Depreciation was computed on a straight-line basis for all depreciable assets. Some problems with the collection of accounts receivable had occurred in the past and could continue in the future. Two new personnel, an office worker and an assistant for the president, were to be hired.

Solvo's increasing accrued payroll taxes and income taxes could cause difficulties in the future. By prolonging the payment of these liabilities the possibility of not having enough cash, when they were due, increased.

PRODUCTION

The production operations at Solvo were, for the most part, semiautomatic. The machines used in the operations were designed to handle two specific functions, filling and capping the product containers (though capping was done in some processing lines manually). The plant was specifically designed to manufacture liquid products; therefore, an elaborate system of pipes were found overhead throughout the production area. These pipes and hoses connected storage and mixing tanks to the filling machines along the production lines. The liquid levels in the large tanks were maintained by a perpetual inventory system. When eight to ten thousand gallons of chemical had been pumped out of the tanks, they were immediately refilled.

There were five production operations or lines available in the plant to handle the variety of products produced. Normally only two lines operated at one time, although management felt that three lines could be run efficiently.

Six to eight people were utilized per production line. The employees were stationed along the line to primarily handle the following tasks:
1. unpacking of empty containers
2. placing empty containers on conveyor belts

3. labeling containers
4. checking containers for proper fluid levels
5. capping containers
6. checking that caps are fitted correctly and are on tight
7. boxing assembly for finished product
8. packaging finished product
9. stapling
10. stacking boxes

When a skid load was finished and products were ready, a forklift truck removed the skid to the storage area.

The plant operated at 80 percent capacity when working full time. Frank Solvo defined full time as operating two lines during the day and two at night. One supervisor was responsible for both production lines.

One production line was fully automatic; it was self-designed by Mr. Solvo. The machine was used in manufacturing windshield solvent, Solvo's leading sales item. The machine had the capacity to fill and cap up to 100 one-gallon containers per minute. Operating at this speed, it would be possible to produce a large semitrailer load in 45 minutes. This machine was usually gauged at 40 one-gallon containers a minute for maximum efficiency.

Because of present plant storage facilities and production planning, no finished product inventory was kept. Finished products were kept no longer than 56 hours, with a majority shipped the day of production. On the average, five semitrailer loads were sent out per day. During the heavy selling months of Fall, they tried to ship more if the trucks were available.

FINANCIAL PROBLEMS OF SOLVO

The major financial problem facing Solvo, Inc. was the increased funds that would be needed for future growth. The debt ratio was 79.5 percent with current liabilities accounting for 47.1 percent of the 79.5 percent. All assets of the firm had been pledged as collateral for present loans outstanding. Additional funding would require higher interest loans (the present interest was above average), and the note payable to the president would most likely be subordinated. It appeared that the greatest need for funds would not be for plant or equipment, but rather for increases in inventory, accounts receivable, wages, and vehicles. If they continued to finance through debt, their inventory had to turn over more than it had, and the collection of accounts receivable had to remain at their average 48-day collections. Although the use of financial leverage did increase the return to shareholders, it also increased the risk of the business in meeting their fixed costs.

A local bank informed Mr. Solvo that a possible $50,000–$100,000 loan would be possible if a plant were to be built (building pledged and note to president subordinated) or equipment purchased. However, some of Mr. Solvo's personal assets might be required as collateral.

Also of concern to Mr. Solvo was the absence of a dividend policy. If income continued to rise, the tax advantages of giving a large bonus to the president might be eliminated.

Since there were no formalized budgets, a growth in sales would further complicate Solvo's understanding of its cash flow position. Short-term loans might be needed to finance material purchases and accounts receivable during the peak processing period until receivables could be collected.

A final concern was the present value of Solvo's undervalued assets.

The following were three of the options available to Solvo for financing future growth:

1. Issue new stock
2. Equity financing
3. Debt financing

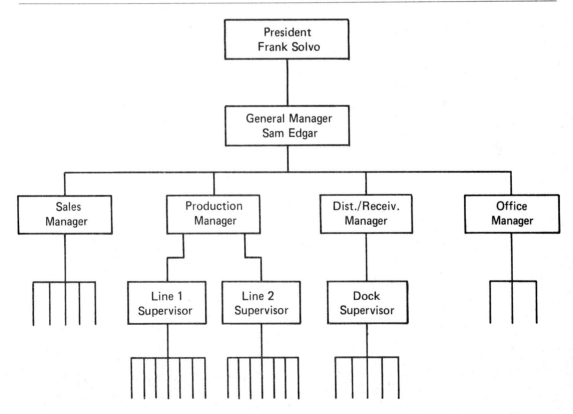

Exhibit 1

Solvo, Inc.
Organizational Chart

Exhibit 2

Solvo, Inc.
Balance Sheet as of October 31, 1978
(Sole Proprietorship)

ASSETS

Current assets:
Cash in bank—Regular .... $ 459.10
Cash in bank—General 33.35
Cash in bank—Farmers Bank 7.16
Accounts receivable 45,951.11
Inventory 37,896.29
    Total current assets .... $ 84,347.01

Plant assets:
Office equipment .... $ 855.96
  Less allowance for depreciation ...... 192.77 $ 663.19
Vehicles $7,803.44
  Less allowance for depreciation 3,595.62   4,207.82
Equipment $3,756.65
  Less allowance for depreciation 1,144.32   2,612.33
    Total plant assets 7,483.34

Other assets:
Deposit—Workmen's Compensation .... $ 200.00
Prepaid interest 616.89
    Total other assets 816.89

Total assets .... $ 92,647.24

LIABILITIES

Current liabilities:
Accounts payable .... $ 42,474.97
Withheld taxes 443.06
Notes payable—current portion 16,168.18
    Total current liabilities .... $ 59,086.21

Long-term liabilities:
Small Business Administration .... $ 34,743.46
First National Bank—factored accounts   22,835.86
American National Bank 1,093.16
Automation Leasing 335.92
American Bank of Commerce 2,330.51
First National Bank 918.06
Note payable 5,000.00
Note payable 587.51
  Less current portion .... (16,168.18)
    Total long-term liabilities 51,676.30
Total liabilities .... $ 110,762.51

(Continued on next page.)

CAPITAL

Frank Solvo, Capital (deficit)..........	$(29,994.70)	
Net profit/loss	11,879.43	
Total capital		(18,115.27)
Total Liabilities and Capital		$ 92,647.24

Exhibit 3

Solvo, Inc.
Comparative Income Statement
For Years Ended October 31, 1980, 1979, and 1978 (Unaudited)

	1980		1979		1978	
	Amount	Percent of Sales*	Amount	Percent of Sales*	Amount	Percent of Sales*
Operating revenue:						
Sales:						
Reconditioning	—	—	—	—	$ 2,165.55	1.6
Pro products	—	—	—	—	17,165.88	12.8
Chemicals—consumer	—	—	—	—	80,788.67	60.4
Chemicals—industrial	—	—	—	—	9.60	—
Miscellaneous products	$ 3,957.43	.5	—	—	—	—
Solvo products	726,365.77	85.0	$166,606.49	90.1	—	—
Hubcaps	—	—	—	—	15,752.22	11.8
Accessories	5,778.32	.7	10,384.73	5.6	14,186.23	10.6
Wholesale bulk	110,649.93	12.9	7,847.59	4.2	—	—
Wheelcovers	5,206.57	.6	—	—	—	—
Other	3,006.56	.4	—	—	3,611.23	2.7
Total sales	$854,964.58	100.00	$184,838.81	100.0	$133,679.38	100.0
Cost of goods sold:						
Purchases	$607,081.44	71.0	$121,386.44	65.7	$ 91,217.30	68.2
Freight	798.45	.1	629.48	.3	541.34	.4
Inventory adjustment	—	—	—	—	(22,515.39)	(16.8)
Cost of goods sold	$607,879.89	71.1	$122,015.92	66.0	$ 69,243.25	51.8
Gross profit on sales	$247,084.69	28.9	$ 62,822.89	33.9	$ 64,436.13	48.2

Operating expenses:	$		$		$	
Advertising expense	178.65	—	127.08	—	400.08	.3
Bad debts expense	176.11	—	—	—	40.00	—
Commissions expense	60,808.78	7.1	1,505.00	.8	229.20	—
Depreciation expense	7,084.33	.8	2,948.00	1.6	2,538.85	1.9
Gas and oil expense	2,023.08	.2	—	—	—	—
Insurance expense	3,702.01	.4	2,777.31	1.5	3,096.45	2.3
Legal and accounting expense	3,583.25	.4	2,135.75	1.2	1,238.75	.9
Maintenance and repairs expense	1,439.50	.2	927.24	.5	1,177.01	.9
Miscellaneous expense	4,523.37	.5	(561.66)	(.3)	554.71	.4
Office supplies expense	2,822.84	.3	1,276.60	.7	869.94	.7
Rent expense—building	3,720.00	.4	2,828.16	1.5	3,704.25	2.8
Rent expense—equipment	1,750.15	.2	2,015.64	1.0	965.21	.7
Salary expense	34,303.27	4.0	15,171.67	8.2	13,698.33	10.2
Salary expense—officers	30,000.00	3.5	8,364.02	4.5	7,140.00	5.3
Shop supplies expense	10,196.76	1.2	298.73	.2	572.45	.4
Subcontracted services expense	870.50	.1	1,116.17	.6	3,086.75	2.3
Taxes—payroll	3,370.66	.4	683.89	.4	1,497.47	1.1
Taxes—other	4,289.15	.5	1,549.73	.8	448.95	.3
Travel and entertainment expense	5,890.87	.7	3,491.85	1.9	1,658.10	1.2
Truck expense	27,550.53	3.2	12,770.56	6.9	5,398.26	4.0
Utilities expense	4,170.49	.5	3,622.32	2.0	2,570.13	1.9
Total operating expenses	$212,454.30	24.8	$ 63,048.06	34.1	50,884.89	38.1
Income from operations	$ 34,630.39	4.1	$ (225.17)	.1	$ 13,551.24	10.52
Other income	—	—	$ 1,115.16	.6	$ 263.42	.2
Other expenses:						
Interest expense	4,863.28	.6	3,135.96	1.7	2,494.33	1.9
Net addition (subtraction)	$ (4,863.28)	(.6)	$ (2,020.80)	(1.1)	$ (2,230.91)	(1.7)
Net income	$ 29,767.11	3.4	$ (2,245.97)	(1.2)	$ 11,320.33	8.5

*Percentage totals may not equal sum of parts because of rounding.

Exhibit 4

Solvo, Inc.
Statement of Financial Condition, February 28, 1981 (Unaudited)

ASSETS

Current assets:		
Cash on hand.........................	$ 400.00	
*Cash in banks (overdrawn)............	(18,810.74)	
Accounts receivable—trade.............	151,538.91	
Inventory............................	40,949.52	
Total current assets		$ 174,077.69
Plant assets:		
Building $1,926.30		
Less allowance for depreciation...... 1,366.41	$ 10,559.89	
Office equipment.................... $1,462.80		
Less allowance for depreciation...... 558.44	904.36	
Vehicles $1,016.84		
Less allowance for depreciation...... 8,633.34	22,383.50	
Equipment—shop $2,796.65		
Less allowance for depreciation...... 3,479.51	9,317.14	
Total plant assets		43,164.89
Other assets:		
Workmen's Compensation deposit......	$ 200.00	
Deferred interest expense	15,565.96	
Prepaid taxes	60.00	
Total other assets		15,825.96
Total assets..........................		$ 233,068.54

LIABILITIES AND STOCKHOLDERS' EQUITY

Current liabilities:		
Accounts payable—trade...............	$ 32,597.15	
Accrued and withheld payroll taxes	12,000.66	
Accrued taxes........................	1,330.00	
Notes payable.......................	37,585.24	
Current portion of long-term liabilities	26,378.48	
Total current liabilities		$ 109,891.53
Long-term liabilities:		
Small Business Administration Loan—		
First National Bank	$ 74,562.00	
Equipment loans payable:		
First National Bank	9,272.89	
American Bank of Commerce	167.06	
Less current portion above........	(26,378.48)	
Total long—term liabilities		57,623.47
Other liabilities		
Note payable—officer		17,940.74
Total liabilities.........................		$ 185,455.74
Common stock—5,000 shares par $1.00 ...	$ 5,000.00	
Retained earnings October 31, 1980...... $ 520.57		
Net earnings—four months ending		
February 28, 1981 .... 42,860.18		
Dividends paid....................... (200.00)		
Officer's life insurance............... (567.96)		
Net retained earnings February 28, 1981	42,612.79	
Total stockholders' equity.............		$ 47,612.79
Total liabilities and stockholders' equity ..		$ 233,068.53

*Bonus of $19,310.00 paid to President Solvo.

Exhibit 5

Solvo, Inc.
Income Statement (Unaudited)
For Four Months Ended February 28, 1981

	Amount	Percent of Sales*
Operating revenue:		
Sales:		
Miscellaneous products	$ 936.59	.3
Solvo products	280,237.80	99.3
Wheelcovers	320.98	.1
Accessories	320.08	.1
Other	157.71	—
Total sales	$281,973.16	100.0
Cost of goods sold:		
Purchases, chemicals, etc	$ 77,399.48	27.0
Bottles and cartons	92,258.91	33.0
Labels......................................	4,495.65	1.6
Drums and skids	731.04	.3
Burfords	2,826.74	1.0
Freight.....................................	1,711.06	.6
Cost of goods sold	$179,422.88	63.6
Gross profit on sales	$102,550.28	36.3
Operating expenses:		
Advertising expense	$ 191.76	.1
Commissions expense	6,117.42	2.2
Depreciation expense	2,677.66	.9
Discounts allowed	590.93	.2
Gas and oil expense	3,094.60	1.1
Insurance expense	1,354.78	.5
Interest expense	4,290.97	1.5
Legal and accounting expense	722.50	.3
Maintenance and repairs expense	1,189.33	.4
Miscellaneous expense	140.69	—
Office supplies expense	1,770.31	.6
Rent expense—building	780.00	.3
Rent expense—equipment	1,513.96	.5
Salary expense	24,442.08	8.7
Shop supplies expense	1,287.18	.5
Taxes—payroll	4,844.51	1.7
Taxes—other	2,386.26	.8
Travel expense..............................	2,982.59	1.1
Truck expense	(2,400.28)	(.9)
Utilities expense	1,712.84	.6
Total operating expense........................	$ 59,690.09	21.2
Net income	$ 42,860.19	15.2

*Percentage totals may not equal sum of parts because of rounding.

Highland Lakes Development, Inc.*

INTRODUCTION AND BACKGROUND

Ralph Smith and David Baker had been friends since college days. Upon graduation they both moved to Houston, Texas, where they had been successful in land development in a rapidly growing area. For the past 15 years they had spent a week each year with their families in the Highland Lakes area near Austin, Texas, in central Texas. Six lakes are connected by the Colorado River. Although dams were constructed in the 1930s for flood control and irrigation purposes, the areas around them had become popular recreational areas in more recent decades. In recent years a major resort facility had been developed for playing world championship tennis. Adjoining areas were beginning to boom, and there was considerable room for accommodating different land needs and recreational life-styles. Fresh water fishing was good year around, and water sports were popular practically year around. Deer and other wildlife were hunted in the entire area.

The central Texas Highland Lakes area had become a major scenic and recreational area attracting many sports groups, civic organizations and conventions. Several major highways linked the area to the major cities of San Antonio, Houston, and Dallas, all within several hours of travel time, which permitted weekend excursions and short trips from heavily populated areas of the state to the Highland Lakes area.

The rolling hills, colorful valleys, and changing scenic views at various times of the year made the area an artist's or nature lover's delight. Much of the area remained virgin land untouched by developers. Developers coming into the area were building natural-looking structures which complemented the landscape. Both Smith and Baker appreciated the beauty of the area and wanted to maintain this beauty in any resort or recreational development. Why not have the best of natural beauty and modern facilities to keep people relaxed and totally tranquil? This was the view they shared.

FINANCING THE VENTURE

In March 1977 a tract of land overlooking Lake Travis became available for sale by an area rancher, who was quite elderly and in failing health. The land nearby (also for sale) included a peninsula of the lake with boat docks, 15 cabins, and a small restaurant. Smith and Baker recognized the value of the two properties for developing a major resort. Remodeling of the cabins and

---

*This case was prepared by August William Smith and Thomas Urban, both of Texas A & M University, with the intention of providing a basis for class discussion rather than illustrating either effective or ineffective management of a business situation.

restaurant could be undertaken in the short run with more extensive development of the adjoining tract over a longer period. To accomplish their plans they would set up a corporation called Highland Lakes Development, Inc. It would take about a $300,000 down payment to purchase the peninsula, its existing cabins and restaurant, and the adjoining tract of land. An additional loan of $1.2 million to cover the $400,000 balance to the landowners and $800,000 for building and remodeling would also be needed. Area bankers indicated they could foresee no problems in providing the loan amount for a period of 20 years at 14 percent interest.

ORGANIZATION OF FACILITIES

To highlight changes, the name was changed from Lake Lodges to Highland Lakes Resort to emphasize the new "image" and ownership. One billboard indicated plans for tennis courts, a new lodge house and a 9- or 18-hole golf course designed by a well-known golfer. Eventually, some of the land would have room for other recreational facilities, townhouses, and perhaps condominiums. The restaurant was to be remodeled into a first-rate delicatessen type shop with a larger resort restaurant to be built on the hillside within five years. Some of the residents nearby felt the new owners were trying to do too much too soon.

As remodeling moved well underway, Smith and Baker hoped to open the restaurant on or before the July 4th weekend in 1977. This would attract a number of area people and vacationers and acquaint them with this new resort development. Hopefully, the lodge house would also open by the July 4th weekend to accommodate a limited number of guests. The original 9-hole golf course and small pro shop would open in August, and they would start taking reservations in late July. Golf carts would not arrive until the Spring of 1978 because of delays in placing the order. Some canoes, small fishing boats, and motors would be available for rent by the July 4th weekend. This equipment and a limited number of tennis courts would provide the main recreational alternatives for guests during the opening. Shortly thereafter golfing would begin, and other recreational alternatives might be added in the near future.

SALES AND ADVERTISING

For the initial opening, advertising would be handled entirely by the owners. They planned to run ads in area newspapers and in those of larger cities, such as Dallas, Houston, and San Antonio. Small brochures and mailers would also be sent to recreational-type groups, sport associations (such as the local bass club), sports stores, and other interested persons. Based on the limited, initial facilities, it was felt that these advertising and promotion plans would be sufficient.

THE MANAGEMENT PHASE

Smith and Baker decided to hire a general manager, Michael Jones, a business graduate from a nearby university, who had worked for the state parks

and wildlife group for two years following graduation. He would be hired at
$20,000 a year base salary to start in July 1977. Jones was aggressive, extro-
verted, and liked fishing, hunting, and working in an outdoor environment. A
second individual, Mark Rogers, would be hired to handle boat rentals and the
golf course and tennis courts when they opened, and to supervise grounds.
Jones would supervise all operations, but especially the restaurant and lodge
house. The owners met with these new managers to discuss tentative rates,
likely income and expenses during 1977, and assumptions underlying these
estimates. The rates and pro forma income and expense statement are given in
Exhibits 1 and 2.

Exhibit 1

Highland Lakes Development, Inc.
Suggested Rates 1977*

Rooms

    Lodge House - $30.00 per day/single person
      (10 rooms) $40.00 per day/double occupancy

    Separate Cabins- $50.00 per day/double occupancy
      (7 units) $60.00 per day/above double occupancy

                $200.00 per week/double occupancy
                $250.00 per week/above double occupancy

(Average income - full occupancy = $760/day)
(90% occupancy July-August, 50% occupancy remainder of year)

Boats and Motors

Use of private boat dock to put in boat - $4.00

Canoes (6)   -$ 6.00/day

Boats 16' Long (6)   -$15.00/day

Motors-Below 35hp (4)   -$ 8.00/day
      35hp or larger (4)   -$12.00/day

Gasoline $1.50 per gallon

(Averages $200/day in July-August; $60/day remainder of year)

Golf and Tennis

If staying there - Golf green fee   -$5.00
            - Tennis court reserved -$3.00/hr

If not staying there Rates double
Rates increase $2.00 on the weekend

(Average July-August revenues - golf $50/day; Tennis $25/day; remainder of year
about 50% of peaks)

*These rates appear to be competitive with other lodges and resorts in the nearby area.

Exhibit 2

Highland Lakes Development, Inc.
Pro Forma Income and Expense Statement
First Year 1977

	July-August	September-December	Totals
Restaurant			
Revenues	$24,000	$18,000	
Fixed expenses*	12,000	14,000	
Variable expenses**	3,000	2,000	
Net income	$ 9,000	$ 2,000	$11,000
Lodge			
Revenues	$20,500	$18,500	
Fixed expenses	9,000	12,000	
Variable expenses	2,000	1,500	
Net income	$ 9,500	$ 5,000	14,500
Cabins			
Revenues	$21,000	$19,500	
Fixed expenses	8,000	13,000	
Variable expenses	4,000	2,000	
Net income	$ 9,000	$ 4,500	13,500
Boats, Motors, Gas, and Supplies			
Revenues	$13,000	$ 7,200	
Fixed expenses	5,200	6,000	
Variable expenses	1,500	1,200	
Net income	$ 6,300	–	6,300
Golf and Pro Shop			
Revenues	$ 4,700	$ 3,500	
Fixed expenses	2,400	2,400	
Variable expenses	200	300	
Net income	$ 2,100	$ 800	2,900
Tennis Courts			
Revenues	$ 1,600	$ 800	
Fixed expenses	600	300	
Variable expenses	100	200	
Net income	$ 900	$ 300	1,200
Total net income			$49,400

*Mortgage, salaries, supplies, etc.
**Extras, promotions, tune-ups, cleaning, fertilizer, etc.

FUTURE PROJECTS AND INVESTMENT ALTERNATIVES

The owners were considering the following development projects as separate alternatives for the next several years. They wanted to undertake those developments which would best insure greater use of the resort consistent with their overall objectives and favorable return on investment. These alternatives were:

1. Expand the present lodge to double its present capacity during 1978 at an added cost of about $150,000 to be paid back in ten years. This would increase overall resort revenues about $30,000 a year over the next four years and $15,000 over the subsequent six years.
2. Add a heated indoor swimming pool at the existing lodge for about $40,000 total cost during 1978. This would encourage greater use of other facilities and increase occupancy during the winter at about $10,000 a year over the next ten years.
3. Expand the golf course to 18 holes during 1978 at an approximate cost of $50,000. This would enhance the resort grounds and lead to estimated benefits of $13,000 a year for the next five years and $8,000 a year for the subsequent five years.
4. Expand present limited tennis courts at a cost of $30,000 divided over the years 1978 and 1979. This would enhance greater resort use by $8,000 a year over the next ten years. Less maintenance is required for tennis courts than for a golf course. Also, additional total usage of facilities may be enhanced.
5. Double the present number of boats and motors and improve the dock facilities. This would likely double revenues and help overcome the present shortage. Cost would be about $90,000, but resort revenues would increase by $23,000 a year for the next ten years. More individuals would have access to other lake recreational events as well. Boaters not staying at this resort would be encouraged to temporarily dock and eat at the restaurant or use other facilities.
6. Add horse stables at a cost of $80,000 divided over 1978 and 1979. This addition would promote greater year around use of the resort and lead to at least $15,000 in increased revenues over the next 6 years and about $10,000 over the subsequent 4 years.

Each of the development projects and investment alternatives had particular merits. Yet, the owners did not want to overextend themselves until the resort was better established. As a result, Smith and Baker had imposed the following limits on capital they planned to invest in the resort during 1978 and 1979.

Maximum investment in 1978 $80,000
Maximum investment in 1978-79 $160,000

POLICY ISSUES IN INTERNATIONAL BUSINESS

The need for exposure to the area of international business is a direct result of the "shrinking" world in which organizations exist. Management must understand how international trade developed and where it is going. Developing an international perspective can be viewed as an integrative activity which combines the traditional functional fields discussed in the previous sections with the need to develop strategies and policies in dealing with unfamiliar customs, languages, markets, economic systems, and regulations.

The cases in this section point out the opportunities and constraints which arise when a firm is trying to make the decision to enter international markets or is experiencing problems in existing foreign operations.

Managers will recognize the potential extensions of their domestic business but must carefully examine the modifications required in foreign operations. The cases in this section point out the difficulties and potential gains for small and large firms. The cases dealing in products or markets unfamiliar to the analyst may require more outside reading or research.

The *Hustler, Inc.* case is an example of a small emerging firm with adequate sales potential in the United States. Its reaction to foreign inquiries is typical of many smaller firms. The establishment of a growth strategy which considers world markets and the policy decisions arising from the action can be developed. The case presents a complete range of functional issues that must be considered before expansion plans can be finalized.

Analysts may also want to consider factors in market alternatives which minimize foreign competition in the future and take advantage of foreign investment incentives.

Normally the first phase of internationalizing a firm's operations is to direct exports to a market, while establishing branch offices in other countries is often a second step in this process. The *Tidewater Imports, Inc.* case demonstrates one of the potential problems a firm may encounter in foreign branches. What would appear to be a simple question, "What should we pay people?" is shown to entail more complex policies than the firm expected. Determination of compensation policies for foreign assignments may be a critical factor in success of the venture.

The *W. H. Mosse Company* case demonstrates the task ahead of a common small company in deciding to export. Consideration of the United Kingdom because of its similarities (but obvious differences, also) is a logical first step. Expansion in continental Europe offers the first real implications of international marketing development for a small company. The case provides a broad sweep of the strategic issues involved in this process. Problems ranging from how firms get information related to issues to complex legal issues are available for analysis.

The *Motor Vehicle Manufacturers Pty Ltd* case presents a complex situation in the automobile industry in Australia. Changes in government policy were seen as a threat to the entire industry. In addition, changes in the product, market, competition, and overall demand in the industry presented major challenges to the firm's long-run strategy for survival. The case can be viewed in a restrospective fashion to consider parallels with the future of the United States market. The forecasts for the 1974 to 1983 period provide an opportunity to review the case in an historical fashion.

The last case in this section is *Compañia Empacadora de la Puerco,* a foreign company that creates a serious dilemma for an American firm. A change in *Compañia Empacadora de la Puerco's* government contributes and further complicates the problem. Government regulation, product quality, competition for foreign trade, and litigation are some of the relevant issues in this case.

Case 6–1

Hustler, Inc.*

INTRODUCTION

Hustler, Inc., an Arkansas corporation, is a leading manufacturer of the Hustler recreational vehicle. The company was actively engaged in the marketing of the machine in the United States and exporting it to foreign countries.

The rapid development of the Hustler as a recreational and versatile utility machine had placed demands upon production that couldn't be met unless an expansion program was initiated. The depressed economy seemed to be righting itself, which further made the anticipated expansion timely. Before this depressed period, leisure-time product companies were selling at some of the highest profit-to-earnings ratios of any securities.

The full expansion program envisioned by Hustler management included the following steps:

1. Maintain at least one month's component supply at all times to act as a buffer for any unanticipated business interruptions such as labor strikes, freight interruptions, and material shortages. This would also permit production scheduling to be more in line with demand.
2. Take advantage of volume discounts and thereby lower unit cost of production.
3. Take advantage of recently abandoned programs by other manufacturers who had made bargains of components available for cash purchases at good savings. (For the most part, these manufacturers anticipated another snowmobile boom. Individual company burdens and costs did not allow them to pioneer a market as well as a company of the size of Hustler which had single product concentration effort.)
4. Increase production to allow development of distributors in the far West and New England states.
5. Greatly expand export to foreign countries.
6. Have a ready inventory. (The projection was to retail 75 machines in October and November from the plant to area hunters giving a high unit profit on these "house" sales.)
7. Develop and finalize the "Mini-Hustler" for their own marketing program. (A large, highly profitable contract was available to Hustler for

*This case was prepared by Wayne H. Goff, Texas Eastern University, with the intention of providing a basis for class discussion rather than illustrating either effective or ineffective management of a business situation. Reprinted from *Application of Decision Sciences in Organizations: A Case Approach* by Joseph C. Latona and K. Mark Weaver with the cooperation and permission of the American Institute for Decision Sciences, Atlanta, Georgia, 1980.

building private label machines of this nature. Three meetings had already been held between Hustler and one of the leading merchandising firms in the United States.)

8. Develop other recreational and utility vehicle products such as golf carts and electric factory personnel carriers.

HISTORY

Hustler began business in June 1969. Prior to this time a working partnership had been in effect since November 1968. This primarily was a research and development period in which the product was brought to a saleable state.

In early fall of 1969 the first Hustlers were sold. This machine was far superior to any of the competition at that time. Over 150 machines were sold with this basic design. Owners of these machines are still some of the most satisfied recreational vehicle owners in the United States. Almost a year later, with the company's expectations even higher, management decided to change from the original design to an even more efficient drive train requiring less maintenance. The new design also included an increase in horsepower by 20 percent. This was accomplished at no extra cost by improved production methods.

On its fifth anniversary of business, Hustler was one of the most respected names in the industry. Though small in contribution to overall sales statistics, the company enjoyed national recognition and admiration of all fellow manufacturers. In its first two years of existence, the Hustler recorded the greatest number of wins per entry in competition in the National Recreational Vehicle Association sanctioned rallies held throughout the country. Owner referral sales were running several times higher with Hustler than with any other recreational vehicle.

THE INDUSTRY

Industry forecasts shown in Exhibit 1 were derived from each manufacturer's estimates of high, low, and average industry production for the five years beginning with 1972.

Hustler, Inc.

Exhibit 1   **Industry Production Estimates (Units)**

	1972	1973	1974	1975	1976
High	50,000	100,000	200,000	350,000	500,000
Average	18,235	30,135	50,261	73,916	97,000
Low	5,000	7,500	9,680	10,650	11,720

These average figures, coupled with the fact that Hustler was one of the six leading producers, would tend to assure adequate sales.

Another factor that could have increased sales was the realization of the expected reduction or elimination of the Canadian import tax. This 17 percent tax applied to machines shipped into Canada for resale from the United States.

MARKET POTENTIAL

As in any new industry, market surveys and sales sampling figures must always be accepted cautiously. It had been company policy to temper its enthusiasm and discount these fantastic figures with a little skepticism.

Estimates as high as a total sales volume of 250,000 units by 1973 were commonplace in the manufacturers' circles. Hustler chose to use a composite forecast of Rockwell engine, Borg-Warner gear, NRVA, and Recreatives Division of W. R. Grace, which suggested 15,000 in 1971; 20,000 in 1972; and 35,000 in 1973. The company found these figures more than enough to excite its dreams of a solid business future.

PROFIT OUTLOOK

Although the profit picture in the first year was negative, a monthly profit was established in November 1970. Since that time, January 1971 was the only month that a new profit from operations had not been enjoyed. During this time, capital was not available for a constant supply of components.

In November 1970 a new design was proven and marketed for the first time, with the same high standards employed in the previous model. A decision to job out many production items was made in a move to concentrate more effort in assembly and marketing. It was hoped that efficiency and profit could be increased by concentrating the limited manpower to these two important areas.

Exhibit 2 displays the most accurate figure available to show the potential of this company using today's actual component parts costs.

Exhibit 3 reflects quantity parts prices known to be available and the new body material after tooling costs of some $3,500.

Exhibit 4 displays Hustler's balance sheet as of March 31, 1971.

PLANT EMPLOYMENT

Plant employment at that time was six. To accomplish the goals of production listed on the pro forma, it had to be increased to eight. Production efficiency continued to increase due to improved assembly procedures.

Workmen of the area were from Arkansas farm family stock and represented a high level of intelligence and personal initiative. Coupled with this fact was the material advantage of the company location in an area where a constant supply of reasonably priced labor was available. The average wage paid at Hustler was $2.70 an hour. To the extent possible, the company had followed the practice of keeping its employee payroll to a minimum. Other benefits included central location to the market resulting in minimum freight costs.

The company was entertaining the idea of a 4-day-40-hour workweek, which would permit a second crew to prepare the week's production for shipping.

FOREIGN LICENSEE AGREEMENTS

Hustler had been approached by no less than 15 foreign manufacturers for licenses to build Hustlers in their respective countries. These included Australia, India, Germany, Belgium, France, and others. These requests had come from legitimate manufacturers primarily engaged in agriculture type products. Such offers have been courteously ignored. A potential continuous revenue for this company could be developed in this area. The internal problem of lack of working capital had not permitted proper attention to these opportunities.

Hustler, Inc.
Monthly Pro Forma State of Income (Based on actual parts cost)

Exhibit 2

	Wholesale Units	Estimated per Unit	Accessories Estimated per Unit	Total Units	Total Accessories	Total	Percent of Sales
Sales	40	$1,322	$200	$52,880	$8,000	$60,880	100
Cost of production:							
Component parts	40	$ 822	$150	$32,880	$6,000	$38,880	
Labor	40	70	—	2,800	—	2,800	
Freight	40	40	—	1,600	—	1,600	
Commissions expense	40	30	—	1,200	—	1,200	
Total cost of production		$ 962	$150	$38,480	$6,000	$44,480	73
Gross Profit		$ 360	$ 50	$14,400	$2,000	$16,400	27
Fixed expenses:							
Salaries—office						$ 873	
Telephone						275	
Rent						300	
Utilities						80	
Office supplies						80	
Auto lease and expense						230	
Insurance						101	
Plant supplies						230	
Legal and accounting						50	
Interest						500	
Payroll taxes						225	
Officer's bonus						600	
Maintenance						160	
Advertising						90	
Dues and subscriptions						47	
Variable expenses:							
Travel and sales promotion						125	
Miscellaneous						10	
Total expenses						$ 3,976	7
Net income						$12,424	20

Hustler, Inc.
Monthly Pro Forma Statement of Income (Based on projected parts cost)

Exhibit 3

	Wholesale Units	Estimated per Unit	Accessories Estimated per Unit	Total Units	Total Accessories	Total	Percent of Sales
Sales....................	40	$1,322	$200	$52,880	$8,000	$60,880	100
Cost of production:							
Component parts........	40	$ 697	$150	$27,880	$6,000	$33,880	
Labor..................	40	70	—	2,800	—	2,800	
Freight................	40	30	—	1,200	—	1,200	
Commissions expense.....	40	30	—	1,200	—	1,200	
Total cost of production..		$ 827	$150	$33,080	$6,000	$39,080	64
Gross Profit...........		$ 495	$ 50	$19,800	$2,000	$21,800	36
Fixed expenses:							
Salaries—office						$ 873	
Telephone						275	
Rent						300	
Utilities						80	
Office supplies						80	
Auto lease and expense						230	
Insurance						101	
Plant supplies						230	
Legal and accounting						50	
Interest						500	
Payroll taxes						225	
Officer's bonus						600	
Maintenance						160	
Advertising						90	
Dues and subscriptions						47	
Variable expenses:							
Travel and sales promotion						125	
Miscellaneous						10	
Total expenses.........						$ 3,976	7
Net income............						$17,824	29

Exhibit 4

Hustler, Inc.
Balance Sheet, March 31, 1971 (Unaudited)

ASSETS

Current assets:

Cash on hand		$ 50.00	
Accounts receivable		34,274.91	
Advances to salesmen		1,962.94	
Inventories		54,993.15	
Prepaid expenses		1,598.79	
Total current assets			$ 92,879.79

Other assets:

Organization expense, in process of amortization		$25,618.63	
Franchise—NRVA		200.00	
			25,818.63

Improvements, furniture, and equipment:

Plant equipment	$ 5,330.88		
Leasehold improvements	4,387.49		
Office furniture and equipment	2,999.33		
Autos and trucks	3,080.00		
Molds	5,970.00	$21,767.60	
Less accumulated depreciation		3,013.98	
Total improvements, furniture and equipment			18,753.72
Total assets			$137,452.14

LIABILITIES

Current liabilities:

Bank overdraft		$ 4,931.57	
Accounts payable—trade		44,324.99	
Portion of long-term notes due in one year		20,004.00	
Payroll taxes withheld and accrued		965.49	
Sales tax payable		12.42	
Customer deposits		5,244.19	
Total current liabilities			$ 75,482.66

Noncurrent liabilities:

Note payable—secured by inventory, accounts receivable, furniture and fixtures and endorsements payable—$1625.00 per month at 8½ percent	$ 51,299.36		
Less portion due one year	19,500.00	$31,799.36	
Note payable—secured by office furniture	$ 2,484.00		
Less portion due within one year	1,104.00	1,380.00	
Total noncurrent liabilities			33,179.36
Total liabilities			$108,662.02

STOCKHOLDERS' EQUITY

Capital stock—500 shares par value $1.00	$ 500.00		
Additional capital contributed	54,066.04	$54,566.04	
Retained earnings deficit		(25,775.92)	
Total stockholders' equity			28,790.12
Total liabilities and stockholders' equity			$137,452.14

Case 6–2

Tidewater Imports, Inc.*

The headquarters of Tidewater Imports, Inc. was in Norfolk, Virginia, and the firm had branch offices in Naples, Italy; Osaka, Japan; and London, England. The overseas branches were opened by managers sent from the Norfolk headquarters; most were looking for the "experience" of living in another country after having handled imports from that country. It was Tidewater's practice to base salary on what the manager had been paid in Norfolk and simply convert this to currency of the country where the branch was located at the current exchange rate. Contracts were for three years. With the expansion of the branches, Tidewater hired several Englishmen for positions in its Naples and Osaka offices.

Although business was good, there seemed to be an increasing number of complaints about salary inequalities. The president of Tidewater asked the personnel director to look into the problem and to propose a policy to reduce the number of complaints. The personnel director reviewed the letters on file and talked with several of those in the branches. The following are examples of what were found:

Bill Zadd (American accountant in Naples):

"We like it here in Italy—the sun, the water, the 'good life.' But I'm not sure we can afford it much longer. Sure, some things are cheaper here, but we have to give up a lot, too. Here we live in a small, old apartment with plumbing that doesn't work most of the time. It is nothing like the new, spacious split-level we had back in Virginia Beach. Here we really can't afford the household appliances.

"We like the fresh fruits and vegetables, but the time and effort it takes to prepare meals makes us long for the 'quick and easy' foods of the supermarket. Before we came here we thought anyone with a maid was really living, but here our maid is a necessity. Without her, my wife would spend all of her time shopping and preparing meals, not to mention handling all the bills and fixing the things that go wrong. Also, she prevents us from having to pay the inflated

---

*This case was prepared by Sam C. Holliday, Old Dominion Univeristy, with the intention of providing a basis for class discussion rather than illustrating either effective or ineffective management of a business situation.

'rich American' prices we would be charged if we were the ones doing the shopping.

"At first we tried sending our children to local schools, but that didn't work out. So we decided to send them to school in England, and that's not cheap.

"To top it off, I learned that Italians with training and experience similar to mine are getting paid twice as much as I do by the big Italian companies.

"All in all, what I thought was a great salary when I accepted the three-year contract just doesn't seem to be so great now. Besides, I get paid in lira, and its value relative to the U.S. dollar has dropped 14 percent over the past three years. I'm actually working for a lot less now than I was when I came over here!"

Joan Billings (American secretary in London):

"I don't regret having taken this job, but it does cost me a pretty penny. My chance to live in London is something I'll always value, but I'm coming home at the end of this year. I just can't afford to stay. I know we complain about prices and taxes in the States, but you wouldn't believe what it's like here. Everything I used to buy back home costs twice as much here as in Virginia. All winter I froze in my flat because of the lack of heat. And TAXES! As a secretary, I don't have a big salary, but would you believe that taxes take more than 50 percent of what I get paid. I read in the papers that the British pound has improved with respect to the U.S. dollar, so I guess I'm lucky to be paid in pounds. Frankly, however, it doesn't seem to balance out.

"Unless Tidewater increases my salary to cover the taxes, it won't be worthwhile for me to stay here."

Jack Smith (A citizen of the United Kingdom, working in Japan for Tidewater Imports as a trade specialist):

"I'd like to be moved to the headquarters in Norfolk. The taxes are too high in England, so I don't want to go home; however, after twenty years in the Far East, I'd like to live someplace where I'm not a foreigner. Canada, Australia, or the States would all be fine, but I would like to stay with Tidewater.

"When I accepted my contract from Tidewater, I made a mistake in not taking my pay in pounds. I chose not to take my pay in pounds because the pound had been dropping in value for so long that I never thought it would make a comeback. I thought that the yen would continue to increase in value. However, it hasn't worked out that way.

"Of course, all of my years in the Far East mean that I know not only the Japanese market, but the rest of this part of the world. I think I could be of value back in the States handling exports to the whole Far East. My Japanese assistant knows this end of the work, and I believe a Japanese national gets along better here."

Management was considering the following factors in salary for Tidewater overseas personnel:

1. Should all employees be paid in local currency?
2. Should salary be based on the salary level of an individual's home country, or on the local salary level?
3. How do you compensate for differences in the official exchange rate and the "black market" rate?
4. In countries with tight exchange controls (requiring earnings in local currency to be spent locally) should you pay part of the salary in the individual's home country currency?
5. How do you compensate for "hardship"?
6. How do you provide equity with others in a country with similar skills and experience?
7. How do you calculate "cost of living" adjustments?
8. How do you provide for fluctuations in the exchange rates?

Exchange rates for the past three years showed that the following changes had occurred in the U.S. cent in relation to a unit in each of the three foreign currencies used in countries where Tidewater had branches:

	1981	1978	Change	Percent Change
Yen	.4916	.41603	+ .0756	+ 18
Pound	235.55	193.96	+ 141.59	+ 72
Lira	.0997	.11619	− .01649	− 14

The personnel director did not know how much to weigh the changes in relation to the other factors he considered.

The W. H. Mosse Company*

In October 1974 Jim Furlong, marketing director of what was then known as Davis-Mosse Company, was planning a visit to the SIAL International Food Fair in Paris which was due to take place during the following month. His company had arranged to make a presentation there of their bread mix product range. Knowing that he would meet many food buyers from all over Europe, Mr. Furlong hoped to further explore the possibility of expanding the company's exporting activities. They already had successfully exported the product range to the United Kingdom (U.K.), but the company was less successful in the Netherlands where they introduced the bread mixes on a trial basis after the previous ANUGA Food Fair during 1973. Most of the present exporting activity had its origins in a series of meetings held during April and May of 1969 when the Mosse Company, as it was known then, sat down to formulate a development plan and marketing strategy for the company. The bread mix products had now been on the Irish market for almost four years and had achieved a satisfactory level of acceptance. The company was, however, facing a number of difficulties on the domestic market. An indifferent future potential for the bread mix product range forced the company to consider whether it should become more involved in exporting, and if so, there was the decision of selecting new markets which would yield the highest promise of success. Alternatively, the company could choose to concentrate on the Irish and U.K. markets where it had already gained considerable experience. The decisions taken with respect to these issues would, to a large extent, determine the future of the bread mix program, and to a lesser extent they would determine the overall development of the company.

HISTORICAL BACKGROUND

In 1973 the Mosse Company merged with the company of S. and A. G. Davis Ltd., Enniscorthy, County Wexford. Both parties had considered the continued rationalization in the flour milling industry and Ireland's entry into the E.E.C. (January 1, 1973) along with its considerable competitive and other ramifications for the small Irish miller. Davis was somewhat the larger of the two firms and had been concentrating on feed compounding and flour milling. The merger resulted in a number of benefits to both parties. The overlap of Davis Ltd. and Mosse Company operations in the southeast was eliminated. The new group could now buy their foreign wheat requirements in bulk without having to rely on intermediary handlers. In addition, the merger resulted in

---

*This case was prepared by M. F. Bradley, University College, Dublin, Ireland, with the intention of providing a basis for class discussion rather than illustrating either effective or ineffective management of a business situation.

production being centralized in Enniscorthy where there was sufficient capacity to mill the total requirements for a declining total market. The merger also gave the new group a greater share of the quantity of flour marketed under the quota system on the domestic market. Finally, the merger provided additional support both in terms of financial backup and personnel to the growing exporting operation of the Mosse Company.

SALES PERFORMANCE OF BREAD MIXES IN THE DOMESTIC MARKET

Since its launch in 1971 the company sold in excess of 150,000 cases of its bread mix on the Irish market. Total revenue for this period was estimated at just under £330,000. Before launching the product the marketing director stated that he would be happy if sales reached 10,000 in kilos of bread mix per week. The actual sales record was 39,375 cases in 1971-72, rising to 39,736 cases in the following year, but falling off to 34,487 cases in 1974. Average wholesale prices were £1.79 per case in 1971-72 rising to £3.00 in 1974. During 1973-74 the company did not promote the product at all due to severe price control measures imposed on the industry by the National Prices Commission. The company believed that this was the main reason why sales in these latter two years were not as favorable as the earlier experience. Like retail flour sales, a pronounced seasonal pattern also occurs in the sale of bread mix products. Approximately 60 to 65 percent of sales occurred in the six-month period October to March each year. This had an effect on promotional campaigns and, to a lesser extent, on distribution. In terms of market share, the Mosse product had 85 percent of the Irish market in 1971-72. The balance was held by Howards. Odlums entered the market with a bread mix product during 1972-73 and Ranks introduced a competitive product in 1974. The Davis-Mosse Company believed that these trends, combined with the absence of promotional expenditure in recent years, accounted for the decline in market share for their products (Exhibit 1).

THE UNITED KINGDOM MARKET

For any Irish company and especially any small Irish company, the U.K. tends to become the market in which any export aspirations are first tested. The case of access due to geographical proximity and the lack of any complexity—as regards tariffs, quotas, import licences, and health regulations—which tends to typify international marketing activities, makes the U.K. market a particularly attractive one for Irish companies. As a Coras Trachtala (CTT) adviser pointed out, trade is simplified by the common language and currency, and these, along with other similarities, often lure Irish companies into viewing the U.K. as a larger version of the Irish market. Consequently, the tendency is often to merely extend marketing strategy to cope with size.

In the case of the Mosse Company, the U.K. market offered a further attraction in that Irish food exporters had established wide acceptance among

Exhibit 1

**Bread Mix Sales, Prices,
and Market Shares—Ireland 1971-1974**

	1971-72	1972-73	1973-74
Unit Sales (Cases)			
October-March	25,594	23,842	23,659
April-September	13,781	15,894	12,739
Total for the year	39,375	39,736	36,398
Wholesale prices			
Pounds per case*	1.79	2.03	2.07
Retail prices			
Pence per kilo pack	13-14	14.5-15.5	15-16
Market shares			
Mosse (percent)	85	50	48

*Case contained 16 × 1 kilo packs.

U.K. consumers since extensive marketing efforts had begun in the early 1960s for Kerrygold butter and the Irish beef. The company's management was of the opinion that Irish and English eating habits were not too different, and the main problems it would have in establishing a substantial export trade would be with distribution and supply. At the same time, however, the Mosse Company was aware that there were some significant regional variations in dietary content and tastes which would have to be investigated.

During the Spring and Summer of 1971 as the new bread mix product was being tested in the southeast of Ireland, the Mosse Company availed of an opportunity to distribute a number of cases of the bread mix through a contact a company director had in the north. This type of product would be reasonably similar in both countries. As a result of the experiment, U.K. consumer reaction to the product was considered favorable.

In addition to the initial favorable acceptance of Mosse's Brown Soda Bread Mix on the U.K. market, the company also had considerable data on the U.K. bread market in general, which indicated that exporting in a serious capacity to the U.K. could result in an attractive payoff. A number of recent trends in the U.K. bread market which held some promise for Mosse's management included the shift in consumption towards brown and specialty breads and the increasing emphasis on traditional methods of preparing foods.

Thus Stanley Mosse and Jim Furlong, although they had little or no experience in international marketing or involvement with the U.K. market, were quite confident about the future of the Mosse brown soda bread mixes in this very attractive potential export market.

United Kingdom Market for Bread

The U.K. market for bread in 1973 had been estimated to be in the region of 2.64 million tons. In 1956, with a population of some four million less, consumption was in the order of 3.77 million tons per year. In terms of retail value the market had grown due to inflation and the added value such as the convenience provided by the sliced loaf and the growth of the more expensive specialty products (slimming breads). While the bread market in 1973 was worth £446m at retail prices which was effectively double the 1956 value, the percentage of food expenditure spent on bread during the past number of years had remained rather constant until 1973 when the share dropped somewhat.

The consumption of brown bread had remained steady for a considerable number of years in the British market. The "other" category tended to decline somewhat during the early 1960s, but more recently the interest in products to assist dieters had given this section a renewed lease on life. The effect had been a downturn in the consumption of ordinary white bread (Exhibit 2).

Exhibit 2 **Bread Consumption, Prices, and Expenditure—United Kingdom 1960-1973**

Year	Ounces Per Capita of Weekly Bread Consumption in Home	Pence Per Capita of Weekly Bread Expenditure in Home	Percent Share in Food Expenditure	Pence Per Pound of Bread*	Value of Consumption by Bread Types		
					Percent White	Percent Brown	Percent Other
1960	45	9	6.2	2.9	73	8	19
1964	42	11	6.4	3.5	78	9	13
1968	38	12	6.5	4.5	77	9	14
1971	36	14	6.2	5.4	75	9	16
1972	34	15	6.2	5.8	74	9	17
1973	33	16	5.7	6.2	73	9	18

*Large, wrapped, white loaf
Source: National Food Survey (U.K.)

The U.K. Bakery Industry

The U.K. bakery industry was highly competitive as indicated by its innovative marketing. The industry was dominated by three very large firms which followed a policy of matching competitive actions.

The big three of the bakery trade controlled two-thirds of all production through their 200 plants, a further 100 or so large bakeries had most of the remainder; however, some 5,000 family bakers still existed and shared approximately five percent of the market. The three major companies were Ranks Hovis McDougall, Associated British Foods, and Spillers French. As in Ireland, rationalization also occurred in Britain taking the form of a complex series of integrations involving flour milling, baking, retail outlets, and the animal feeds products which result from the milling process.

An innovation in the bread market had been the arrival of the part-baked loaf. The housewife bought a semifinished refrigerated product then baked it in an oven for 20 minutes. The idea behind the development was to combine the freshness of newly baked bread with the convenience of buying a mass produced brand. Ranks "Take and Bake" was first in the field followed very quickly by Spillers "Homebake." After an initial enthusiastic response, sales of these products fell to much less than one percent of the wrapped bread market. At the time it was judged that the products were relatively expensive and not very convenient.

In the market for bread, slimming breads were a special case. The aim of the producers of slimming bread was to provide bread which contained fewer calories on a slice-for-slice basis. This was done by reducing the starch content, adding protein, or simply by making the slices thinner. The forerunners of modern slimming breads were the Energen starch-reduced rolls. Since then the market had expanded considerably. Total sales of slimming breads in 1972 were £16 million, in 1973 sales reached £21 million, and it was estimated that in 1974 sales were approximately £23 million.

Total advertising expenditure on bread increased from £2.5 million in 1969 to £3.5 million in 1973. This compared with £238,000 spent by the industry in advertising in 1955 when most of the expenditure was by Hovis Limited. In 1968 the bulk of the advertising was through the medium of television, which then accounted for over 90 percent of the total. Before 1968 most advertising concentrated on the standard loaf of each of the major companies in the market. The leading bakeries engaged in the promotion of branded bread products primarily to maintain their bargaining position with retailers, especially the larger food chains. In addition, by continued reminders to consumers of existing known brand names, brand advertising was designed to discourage the larger supermarket chains from integrating into baking. Few of the bakeries believed in competitive advertising as a means of increasing sales. Nevertheless, with the specialist-type breads, considerable sums were being successfully spent on advertising.

Approximately one-third of press and television advertising went on slimming bread. Nimble regularly spent more than £500,000 annually on advertising, followed closely by Slimcea. However, the ratio of advertising to sales was low at approximately .77 percent. This was compared with a ratio of two percent for 1935.

"The Big Three" in the baking industry in the United Kingdom had one or more interests in the principal forms of bread distribution. Spillers French supplied their co-op partners and the Lyons outlets, Ranks controlled distribution companies such as Marchi Zeller, and ABF had bakers' shops such as Tip Top and the Fine Fare supermarket chain.

In May 1974 the British Market Research Bureau interviewed 964 housewives to investigate where bread was being bought and the type of bread purchased. It was evident that the introduction of the wrapped loaf and the element of convenience combined with improved keeping qualities had strengthened the hand of the grocer over the traditional bread roundsman. The grocer/supermarket was dominant in the retail selling of bread and this was particularly true in the northern part of the country. Bread was frequently sold in the supermarkets in this part of the country as a cut-price item to attract people into stores. Class and age differences were not, however, as pronounced.

There were a number of pronounced differences among the types of bread purchased by the British housewife. In the survey housewives were asked the type of bread purchased by them in the previous week. As the data referred to buying occasions and not to quantities bought, the data somewhat overstated the picture with respect to brown and speciality breads which were normally sold in small loaves. Families with children were heavy purchasers of the wrapped white loaf. Brown bread was purchased more frequently by housewives without children than those with children.

United Kingdom Market for Mosse's Bread Mix

Supported by the reaction of the press and trade at the reception in CTT's London office during the summer of 1971, the Mosse Company decided in November 1972 to commission more detailed research of the United Kingdom market. The information already available on the bread market was of a general nature, and the company felt that it should have some reaction to its bread mix from the marketplace.

Having identified the urban consumer as their primary target—just as they had done in the Irish market—Jim Furlong and Stanley Mosse were naturally most interested in the north of England where they had had most involvement so far and, of course, in the massive marketplace of urban England and the city of London. (It was estimated at this time that 70 percent of the grocery buying power was concentrated in the greater London area.) Manchester was identified as the most important representative of the company's involvement in the former area, and so London and Manchester were identified as the two areas which should be investigated at this stage.

A marketing research firm was commissioned to examine the London and Manchester markets. With respect to the London research, a two-stage program was adopted. Discussion groups were held with three groups of ten housewives—each to investigate attitudes towards the brown bread mix in terms of preparation, taste, appearance, and overall acceptability as a product. Secondary objectives included those of examining in depth the reactions to packaging, mixing instructions, name, pricing, and promotional concepts. Each of the three London groups belonged to the ABCI social classes. At the time the housewives were recruited to take part in the discussion groups, each was given a half-kilo pack of the product in a plain bag with no identification of the firm and asked to prepare it according to supplied instructions before coming to the session.

In addition to the discussion groups, a number of placement tests were carried out on the product. Fifty housewives from the London suburbs were invited to try a "blind" half-kilo pack of Mosse's Brown Soda Bread Mix.

These housewives were asked to complete a questionnaire after they tried the product. As an incentive to complete the questionnaires, the housewives were offered either 25p in cash or 25p worth of the product. Of the 50 housewives selected, 40 had returned completed questionnaires by the deadline set by the research company. The principal results of this research as reported by the research company are found in Exhibit 3.

Exhibit 3	**Research Findings by U.K. Product and Placement Test of Mosse's Brown Soda Bread Mix**

The Product:

1. This type of brown bread was unfamiliar to the majority of London housewives who took part in the groups or placement tests.

2. About two-thirds of the participating housewives found the end product acceptable, including one-third who were enthusiastic.

3. Flavor and texture of the bread were the major determinants of product acceptance. The enthusiasts described it as "nutty," "wholesome," "tasty," and "chunky." The critics reported it as "stodgy," "tasteless," and "did not rise properly."

4. Whether they liked the bread or not, most housewives found it easy and quick to prepare—although a number did not follow the instructions on the pack.

5. The bread mix was perceived as a flour-type product and was not seen as a cake mix. Housewives in the groups and placement tests would expect to find the product in their grocery stores alongside either the flour or bread.

Presentation and Labeling:

1. The ordinary flour-type pack was very favorably received. Housewives were adamant that a cake-mix-type pack would be most unsuitable.

2. Considerable difficulty arose over the name "Brown Soda Bread Mix." For United Kingdom housewives this title was misleading. The researchers suggested titles such as "traditional," "old fashioned," "country" or "homemade."

3. The necessity to use the term "soda bread" also gave rise to difficulties. Many housewives, especially the younger ones associated "soda" more with washing than baking.

Price and Pack Size:

1. Most of the housewives tended to price the product low. The average price estimated by the housewives in the product test who were most favorably disposed towards the bread mix was 8p to 9p for the half-kilo size. The ideas of price were partly based on the price of flour and more particularly on the known level of $10^1/_2$p for the standard loaf.

2. The enthusiastic housewives rejected the idea of paying 23p to 25p for a kilo pack. There was little interest in the kilo pack anyway since the product was viewed as a specialty bread rather than an everyday product.

Differences between London and Manchester:

1. The Manchester group, unlike the London groups, was more inclined to identify the product as a health food on the one hand and to position it with cake mixes in the local grocery store, because they viewed it more as a convenience food.

2. While a flour-type pack was preferred to a carton, there was a strong suggestion that the relatively subtle coloring and style of the existing Mosse pack would be less effective in the northern part of the country.

3. Because of price, many of the Manchester housewives viewed the product as an occasional purchase only—as a treat or a standby product.

Conclusions of Research Firm:

1. Since there was very little consumer interest in any easy to prepare bread mix, the success of Mosse Brown Soda Bread Mix would depend almost entirely upon the acceptability of the end product.

2. In a promotional program there was a need to concentrate on projecting the desirable taste and texture of the product. The fact that it was easy and quick to make was an ancillary benefit.

3. The proposed retail price would inhibit both trial and subsequent frequency of purchase. Hence, it would be necessary to convince potential buyers of the inherent quality of the product.

U.K. Market Launch of Mosse's Bread Mix

At this stage Jim Furlong considered that his company had enough information to continue marketing in the United Kingdom. Consumer and trade reaction to both the brown and the recently introduced white bread mix had been proving favorable. The Mosse management faced the decision of how it should put a full-scale marketing program into operation in the United Kingdom.

Advertising Campaign. Since so much of U.K. grocery purchasing power was concentrated within the London region, a launch in that area in the Autumn of 1973 was preferred by the company as an alternative to the originally planned north of England launch. It was suggested to Mosse that a viable TV campaign in the London area would generate consumer demand and facilitate a valuable merchandising function. A London based advertising agency made a number of recommendations for a London TV campaign which might be carried out during September-October 1973 (Exhibit 4).

The basic difference between Schedule I and Schedule II (Exhibit 4) was that the former would use 30-second exposures concentrating on daytime coverage while the latter would use a core of 30-second exposures across the board coverage backed up by high frequency, 15-second messages within "dealer support spots." The additional expenditure indicated in the third

Exhibit 4

Proposal for London Region TV Campaign
Relative Effectiveness

	Schedule I	Schedule II	Schedule III
Air-time costs	£10,500	£10,500	£13,500
Number of spots	23	21	25
Housewife T.V.R.	260	333	418
Estimated coverage	72%	79%	83%
Average frequency	3.6	4.2	5.0

schedule would secure an additional 30-second peak spot and at least one more prime, off peak and two more "dealer support spots."

Distribution. The selection of an appropriate channel of distribution provided the Mosse Company with one of the most important and most difficult problems in developing this, their first export market. Having decided on aiming their market efforts at the potentially huge London market, they identified a number of alternative arrangements from which they could select their eventual channel of distribution. The main alternatives open to the company were to channel the soda bread mix products through a food broker, *or* secondly through an ordinary distributor *or* thirdly, direct to specialty stores.

As food brokers are specialists, they would offer a service to both buyers and sellers of food items which involved basically bringing together parties to arrange a trading relationship, but they can and do offer much more as "specialists" in this particular field. In return for a commission, a food broker would offer Mosse Company the timesaving facility of introducing them to a number of interested buyers, and as an executive pointed out to Jim Furlong, the broker would have as great an interest in encouraging actual trade between the parties, since commissions are normally paid only on the occurrence of a transaction. The broker could also offer specialized market advice and customer profiles. As the soda bread mix products did not comprise that great a proportion of the overall Davis-Mosse production operation, the timesaving possibility was very attractive to Jim Furlong who had overall marketing responsibility for the company.

Finding a suitable distributor in the London area proved a formidable task. With the help of CTT an extensive search was undertaken to identify suitable candidates. Eventually Jim Furlong, in liaison with the London office of CTT, was able to single out, after a process of preliminary search and interviews of interested distributors, one particularly attractive candidate. Waissel's Limited of London distributed to most of the food stores large and small in the southeast of England. In addition to this essential feature, Jim Furlong admired the outlook and approach of the company. He said at the time, "What we want is a distributor who aggressively goes after the food store business, and Waissels, in the person of Sidney Waissel, the managing director, offers just that." Furthermore, Waissels was an established food distributor and Sidney Waissel had developed a wide range of important contacts in the retailing end of the industry over the years. Since Mosses was most interested in establishing maximum volume in turnover terms, such contacts were particularly attractive. (Sidney Waissel had mentioned Woolworths and Safeways, among other outlets, to Jim Furlong as being on his list of close contacts.)

The other main alternative opening to Mosses was the specialty store. Howards, of Crookstown, Cork, who had preceded Mosses into the Irish bread mix market had already begun to market its soda bread mix products through the specialty store chain of Fortrum and Mason. The products were offered in attractive "high-class" box packs, obviously aimed at a rather up-market range of consumer. As Mosses was designing a new pack for the U.K. market, the notion of matching Howard's strategy did not particularly concern Jim Furlong. Although in the long term volume prospects were perhaps limited, the specialty stores did offer the prospect of higher margins. Under the "specialty" heading could also be included the possibility of supplying delicatessens, health food stores, and the like which were at this time becoming very significant in terms of food retailing in cosmopolitan London.

Before Mosses had made its final decision as to distribution channel, Waissels came up with the idea of running an introductory program for Mosses. As a preliminary offering, Sidney Waissel arranged for a week-long-in-store demonstration/market test of the brown soda bread mix in each of ten Woolworth stores located throughout England. The in-store promotion was held during the week commencing May 22, 1973. Sidney Waissel considered the demonstration to have been very successful and in a follow-up letter to Mosses stated that ". . . store managers were well pleased, and considering that we were introducing from cold the brown soda bread mix only, the results, in our opinion, were more than satisfactory. The average of all ten branches was 23 cases." Jim Furlong was favorably impressed.

Costs and Pricing. While recognizing that costs would vary depending on the distribution channel selected, Mosses estimated that, for 1973–74 at least, the average ex-mill price f.o.b. Enniscorthy would be in the region of £2.01 per case. They also estimated that for a wholesaler or distributor who provided a transport and storage service and who bought full container loads of the soda bread mix products, the average margin expected would be 50 percent on the ex-mill cost. The retailer in turn, would be expecting to add a margin of about 33 percent on this wholesale price. On this basis, the estimated retail price of bread mix was in the region of 12.5p per pound.

As it continued to explore the United Kingdom market, Mosses came to realize that while there were strong similarities between that market and the Irish market for its soda bread mix products, there were also considerable differences between the two markets. In particular, it was clear from the research that the company had commissioned, that tastes were definitely different. Jim

Furlong and Stanley Mosse believed that the U.K. consumer was more willing to try new products than was a typical Irish consumer. However, Mosses did recognize that the U.K. consumer would have to be educated in the use of the soda bread mix products since they were relatively new to the market.

Other differences which were realized by the company included the more stringent food labeling regulations in the United Kingdom. Labeling regulations were very detailed and strict observance was maintained. Since bread in the U.K. was typically a yeast-type product, all breads not based on yeast had to carry this information on the pack. Hence, a soda bread would have to contain the word "soda" in the product name. A summary of the labeling regulations in operation at the time follow:

1. The product name must be approved by the appropriate authorities.
2. The product weight, country of origin, name of manufacturer must be specified on the package.
3. Product ingredients must be specified on the pack in a separate box. Ingredients must be listed in a descending order by weight.

Nevertheless, despite these problems, Stanley Mosse and Jim Furlong were still confident that with the right marketing they could achieve their objective of developing an export market which would in the long run provide maximum returns in terms of revenue and profits. As Stanley Mosse said to the press, "Being a small company has its advantages in that we, for example, because of our size, can cope with any problems which arise, quickly and effectively." A further incentive to develop the U.K. market in the short term in order to reap longer term benefits, was the wide range of aids that CTT, the Irish Exports Promotions Board, and the Industrial Development Authority (IDA) were offering to Irish firms (Appendix I).

With the aid of such incentives, Jim Furlong believed that the company could expect, depending on wholesale and retail margins for the soda bread mix products, to break even or perhaps make a small profit on its first year's trade in an international market.

CONTINENTAL EUROPEAN MARKETS

In close liaison with CTT executives, Jim Furlong was able to identify the major potential export markets outside the U.K. Although one contact with a Dallas, Texas, mail-order firm later proved that there was an opening in the U.S. market (cases of soda bread mix were exported unmodified and the Dallas firm placed Mosses in its Christmas catalog) and although there was a possibility of manufacturing under license in Australia, it was to the continental European markets that Mosses looked upon with most interest. Eventually, having attended various trade fairs—both the larger ones such as ANUGA (Cologne) and SIAL (Paris) and some smaller local ones—and having analyzed each of the potential markets with the help of CTT, Jim Furlong was able to short-list his target markets. Germany, France, Netherlands, and Belgium comprised this list.

Fresh from their experiences in the U.K. market, it was clearly evident to the Mosse management that widely different distribution systems could be obtained in each of the continental European markets of interest to the company, and that all such differences would have to be identified and closely studied before actual marketing could begin. With the geographic situation of Ireland vis-a-vis the continent of Europe, Mosses was aware, too, that in examining such markets there was a relatively high investment in terms of both costs and management time.

Jim Furlong proceeded with this examination of the selected markets by arranging visits to each. The fact that CTT had an office in all of the relevant countries was of great benefit to him. Furlong later recalled that the visits "proved invaluable in assessing the practical potential of these markets." He discovered that not alone did the relative importance of retail outlets from bread and flour products vary throughout continental Europe but purchasing habits of consumers also varied considerably. In taking such differences into account in practical terms, Mosses again called on the services of CTT. With their help, Jim Furlong was able to identify viable segments of the markets and also to develop profiles on distribution networks in each market.

From his experience in the U.K. market, Jim Furlong had come to the conclusion that in export marketing the personality of a company's distributor or agent was of utmost importance. He had made a mental note to look for, on the positive side, signs of friendliness, interest, and determination and on the negative side any signs of apathy or feintness of interest in assessing potential distributors or agents for Mosse's products.

Having made several visits to the Continent and having obtained data from a number of sources, particularly the individual CTT offices in the respective countries on his short list, Jim Furlong was able to set out summary analyses of all he had learned on the potential markets. For each country his approach was to develop a "country profile," summarizing the relevant factual data on the particular country and then setting out the specific market details available to him. (Comparative data on European countries is included in Appendix II.)

Germany.

Furlong's "country profile" is set out as follows: "The country's climate provides colder winters and hotter summers than are common to Ireland. It becomes more continental as one travels southward. While German is spoken throughout the country, there are quite varying regional dialects. CTT recommends that although many German businessmen speak English, trade literature and all correspondence should be in German. The country's standard of living is considerably higher than in Ireland, and as in all six E.C.C. countries, the metric system has been in operation for years. Although agriculture is shadowed somewhat by the performance of industry, Germany produces significant amounts of cereals, the main categories being rye and wheat. At the same time, however, food imports are high, and Ireland exports a considerable amount of meat to Germany. The currency used, the deutsche mark, is relatively strong compared to sterling. There are three cities in Germany with populations in excess of one million (West Berlin, Hamburg, and Munich) and five approaching one million (Cologne, Dortmund, Dusseldorf, Essen and Frankfurt)."

A major potential problem which occupied much of the Mosse management's consideration of the German market concerned food regulations. These regulations were very intricate and varied according to region; and Mosse's realized that this would make it necessary for the company to prepare to meet with a whole range of restrictions on their exports to that market. This problem was compounded by the fact that the wrap-over style pack in use on the Irish and U.K. markets would not be acceptable in Germany. With these problems in mind, Mosses proceeded to examine the German market in more detail.

Bread Production. It had been estimated that approximately 200 varieties of bread were produced in Germany. Retail sales of bread had been placed at an annual value of DM8,000 million, of which 75 percent was accounted for by artisan output and the remainder by industrial bread. The number of artisan bakers in 1974 was estimated by EIU to be about 35,000 and that of industrial producers at below 300. Bread production had increased substantially in Germany during the period 1971–1974 (Exhibit 5).

Exhibit 5

Production of Bakery Products Germany 1971–1974

Product	1971	1972	1973	1974 (est.)
Bread (000's tons)	889	929	932	978
(DM million)	1,144	1,241	1,328	1,467
Rolls (000's tons)	92	90	99	98
(DM million)	150	149	165	174
Pastry (000's tons)	91	106	102	105
(DM million)	322	374	379	399

Source: EIU: Marketing in Europe, No. 152.

Bread in Germany is noted for its regional varieties. Very few German bread manufacturers had been able to achieve more than a regional penetration. However, mergers and takeovers had been taking place, thereby reducing the number of independent suppliers. By the end of 1971, 94 companies, representing approximately 30 percent of the total number and employing about 70 percent of the total bakery workers, accounted for more than 70 percent of the total output of bread and related products.

Bread Consumption. As with other western countries the consumption of bread in Germany, during the past number of years had shown a pronounced downward trend. Annual per capita consumption of bread and related products was estimated to have contracted from 96 kilograms in 1950 to approximately 65 kilograms in 1971. Eighty-two percent of all bread sold was accounted for by whole loaves and the remaining 18 percent was sold as sliced bread.

Bread Distribution. Bread and related products had been estimated to make up about 6 percent of the total supermarket food sales and 4.5 percent of turnover in general food outlets. The main channel for the consumer market, which distributed about 80 percent of industrial baked bread, was the direct delivery from producers to retailers (95 percent); whereas wholesalers who concentrated on special type breads handled only 5 percent of the sales. It was estimated that between 1970 and 1974 the share of all bread sold through bakeries and pastry shops fell from 64.5 percent of the total to 59 percent, while the share being sold through general food stores increased accordingly (Exhibit 6).

Exhibit 6

Distribution Outlet for Retail Sales of Bread, Germany 1970–1974

Retail Outlet	1970	1974 (est.)
	Percent	
Bakeries and pastry shops	64.5	59.0
General food stores	35.5	41.0
— Voluntary chains	16.4	17.0
— Retailers Buying Association	6.7	7.0
— Food multiples	5.7	8.0
— Others	6.7	9.3

Bread Imports. There had been little foreign trade in German-produced bread. During 1971 approximately 1.1 percent of the total German bread sales were sold abroad. However, German imports of bread had been increasing. In 1971 bread imports were valued at DM28.4 million of which two thirds represented imports of crispbread from Sweden. The switch in German consumption patterns towards more sophisticated and more health oriented eating habits favored the production of special bread varieties. Crispbread had benefited from this trend.

According to Jim Furlong, the typical German housewife was not unlike her Irish counterpart. Rural connections were strong and country goodness was held in high regard. The younger generation was regarded as being very willing to try something new and something different.

As the analysis of the German market proceeded, a number of unexpected opportunities came to Jim Furlong's attention. Furlong learned of a German food chain which was seeking a private label operation to compete with an established and successful national branded soda bread mix product. In this context he did not foresee any difficulty in producing for the private label market while at the same time marketing the company's branded products in Germany. This view was supported by the fact that yeast bread mix under the "Dr. Oetkar" brand name was being produced at this time on the German market, and it was rumored that two more companies, Kraft and Diamonte, were also considering entering the market. The yeast bread mix was produced on the same principle as the soda bread mix but much more time was involved, since strenuous kneading was required and the dough mix had to be allowed to "set" for a while before baking. The resulting bread corresponded to the yeast bread produced by bakers. Furthermore, Furlong had also come into contact with a very friendly and interested food distributor in the Munich area who appeared to have extensive contacts in the retail trade.

Belgium.

Belgium has a temperate climate, quite similar to that of Ireland. The official languages are Flemish and French and since language is a contentious matter in Belgium, diplomacy is always required. English is widely understood at a business level and is generally more acceptable than French in the north of the country (Flemish speaking area). It is better, although not essential, according to CTT sources, to use French rather than English in Brussels and in the south of Belgium. The standard of living is approximate to that in Germany. Agricultural production is extensive, and the country is self-sufficient in sugar, eggs, butter, and meat. The chief crops are oats and wheat. Despite the self-sufficiency in meat, Irish exports are well represented by meat produce. About 36 percent of the population is situated in urban areas, the most important of which are Brussels (1 million) and Antwerp (926,000).

Jim Furlong learned from CTT that distribution methods varied with the product, but that generally speaking, manufacturers had found it best to sell consumer goods through a distributor carrying stocks. Furthermore, the services of wholesalers and manufacturer's agents were extensively used in the distribution of consumer goods, although at the same time, in addition to department and chain stores, a number of important retailers bought direct from manufacturers and importers. Many importers employed travelers to visit retailers regularly.

Bread Production and Consumption. No statistics on the production of bread in Belgium existed, but it was estimated that in 1974 annual bread consumption was running at approximately 680,000 tons per year. However, bread consumption was reported to be falling at an annual rate of between two and three percent. The varieties of bread which may be sold in Belgium, the weight, and the price were defined by law. In recent years there had been a growing preference for improved varieties of bread (pain ameliore) which in 1974 was expected to account for about half of the bread sales. It was expected that bread consumption in Belgium would continue to decline by about two percent per year. However, industrial bakers were expected to expand their operations at the expense of the artisan bakers.

Bread Distribution. Bread was usually sold wrapped. It was estimated in 1974 that 90 percent of bread sold was in sliced form. There was a tendency for purchasers to prefer smaller loaves, as younger consumers preferred fresh bread, in contrast to older generations who liked bread to be a day old before eating.

Approximately 60 percent of all bread was retailed through some 7,000 retail bakeries. Some retail bakers also distributed door-to-door. A survey of distribution patterns carried out in 1973 had shown that 38 percent of purchases were made at a bakery, 39 percent of purchases were from a door-to-door service, 12 percent of purchases were made from general grocery stores, seven percent from supermarkets and four percent from department stores. The market is highly competitive, and the larger retail outlets tended to rely on a number of suppliers, switching to the baker offering the best margins. For these reasons they supplied and sought to avoid being dependent on one retailer for more than 15 percent of sales.

Bread Prices. Retail bread prices in mid-1974 ranged from BF11 for a 500 gram household loaf to BF18.5 for a 400 gram loaf of brown bread (Exhibit 7).

Exhibit 7   **Retail Bread Prices (Sliced)**
Belgium, May 1974

Bread Type	Size (gram)	Price (BF)
Household bread	500	11.00
Improved bread	450	11.00
Wholemeal bread	600	17.00
Brown/mixed bread........................	—	18.50

Source: EIU store checks.

Bread Imports. Imports of bread into Belgium were of minor importance. German varieties were the most popular among imported breads. The principal varieties included crispbread and unleavened bread.

France

Jim Furlong's "country profile" was as follows: "The climate is not unlike that of Germany, and the same approach to language should be adopted. A very high standard of living is enjoyed, and the proportion of income being spent on food and clothing is declining. Agricultural output is very significant with a rapidly increasing cereal production concentrated on wheat. Irish exports to France consist mainly of agricultural products; however, beef, veal, and skim milk head the list. The French franc is not quite as strong against sterling as the deutsche mark. A third of the population (some 50 million) is aged 20 or less, and the main centers are Paris (9 million), Lyon (1 million), Lille-Roubaux — Tourcoing (1.3 million) and Marseilles (1 million). Paris is the principal marketing and distribution center, and about half the nation's business is done there."

Furlong was also aware that a considerable amount of cereals were imported into Ireland from France and that his contacts in the Irish milling industry would in turn have many contacts in that industry in France.

Bread Production and Consumption. As in the case of Belgium, there were no official figures for bread production in France. However, estimates of three million tons per year had been made. Bread consumption continued to decline, having fallen by three kilograms per capita to 196 kilograms between 1970 and 1971.

Bread Distribution. The market for presliced and packed bread in the early 1970s was expanding at about 25 percent per year. Turnover in this type of bread was estimated to have reached FF100 million in 1972, which represented 1.5 percent of the overall bread market—assessed to be worth FF6,800 million in that year. About 70 percent of presliced loaves were bought in self-service outlets as against 20 percent in grocery stores and 10 percent in bakeries.

Bread Imports. France was a net importer of bread, and the position in 1973 showed imports exceeding exports by FF82 million in value and by 25,000 tons in volume. The U.K. bakeries had been attempting to gain a substantial foothold in this market. In the autumn of 1973 Rank-Hovis McDougall acquired 80 percent of the capital of a leading French bakery group with an annual turnover of approximately FF45 million, and this enabled them to achieve penetration through the so-called "boulangerie ring," which was behind most anticompetition moves in the French bakery industry.

As in Germany, food regulations posed a difficult obstacle for Irish exporters. In France, however, the problem was of a rather different nature. The French regulations contained clauses which made it difficult to sell a soda-based product on the market. This brought a different problem to light for the Mosse management as regarded French culture in terms of bread-baking traditions—bread produced in France normally used yeast as the raising agent. Besides this, Mosse's was aware that the French operated a number of nontariff barriers to imports which could be applied on the smallest of technicalities and which, as many Irish exporters had discovered, could delay access into the French market for months or even years.

Netherlands

The Netherlands has a marine climate with cool summers and mild winters similar to those in Ireland. While Dutch is the national language, English is widely spoken, and at most business meetings the services of an interpreter are unnecessary. As in France, a high standard of living is enjoyed. Dutch agriculture is highly productive, but cereal production is minimal. Irish exports are mainly agricultural; however, they concentrate on beef and dairy produce. The currency, the guilder, is relatively strong against sterling. The population, in an area half the size of Ireland, is approaching 14 million. The largest cities are Amsterdam, Rotterdam (both 1 million), and The Hague (700,000). Amsterdam is the principal financial, commercial, and cultural center.

The CTT executive advising Furlong on the Dutch market pointed out that while substantial business was done directly with importers, it was nevertheless advisable to appoint an agent. Given the small area of the country and the excellent transport system which existed there, it was obvious that nationwide distribution of any product could be handled with ease. Having made a number of preliminary visits to the Netherlands, Jim Furlong began to believe that there was a significant market potential for both the brown and the white soda bread mix products.

Consumption

Per capita consumption of bread in the Netherlands contracted from 61.5 kilograms in 1960 to 46.9 kilograms in 1971. However, there was evidence that this downward trend had leveled off in recent years. Expenditure on bakery products in current money terms had risen substantially during the period 1969-1973 (Exhibit 8).

Dutch Home Baking

A feature of the Netherlands market which appeared of particular relevance to the marketing of food to be prepared in the home was the type of baking facilities available in the home. Traditionally, the Dutch have used cooking

Exhibit 8

**Consumer Expenditure on Bakery Products
The Netherlands, 1969–1973**

Bakery Products	1969	1970	1971	1972	1973
			Fl. million		
Bread..................................	894	923	994	1,095	1,194
Cakes..................................	36	37	39	N.A.*	N.A.
Biscuits.................................	59	59	63	N.A.	N.A.
Industrial pastry.........................	415	464	500	N.A.	N.A.

*Not available
Source: EIU *Marketing in Europe*, No. 149.

facilities which required the preparation of bread type products on the top of the cooker as opposed to in an oven. However, the younger generation was beginning to buy cookers with ovens as opposed to their older counterparts who preferred the cooker without the oven included (Exhibit 9).

Exhibit 9

Sales of Gas Cookers (000's)
The Netherlands, 1971-1974

Gas Cookers	1971	1972	1973	1974 (est.)
With ovens	102	106	113	150
Without ovens	189	206	204	225

Source: EIU Marketing in Europe, No. 151.

Retailing

The major food retailers in the Netherlands were the large multiples: Albert Heijn Supermart N.V. (Ahold Group) had 637 branches and operated 403 supermarkets; Simon de Wit was associated with Albert Heijn and had 182 supermarkets while De Gruyter had over 500 stores, 386 of which were self-service shops and 60 were supermarkets; Edah N.V. had 300 branches, including 50 supermarkets. Consequently, it was clear to Jim Furlong that Mosses needed an agent or distributor who had extensive contacts among these major retailer organizations.

Mosse's management had met a large Dutch food distributor at the 1973 Anuga Fair, and sometime after, they decided to contact him. A number of meetings were held to discuss marketing details, and through these Jim Furlong had been impressed by the size of the distributor's operation as well as the personality of its managing director. Mosses agreed to appoint the distributor to market the soda bread mix products in the Netherlands for an initial period of six months. However, it soon became apparent to Jim Furlong that the venture was not as promising as had appeared to be the case earlier in that the Dutch distributor displayed a marked lack of interest in the Mosse products. The agreements had now expired and the relationship was not renewed.

Aids to Irish Exporters

There are a number of aids available to Irish firms involved in export marketing. Among the more important are the tax relief obtainable on earnings accrued to the firm from overseas sales and the various government grants which are, in the main, channeled through CTT, the Irish Exports Promotion Board. A brief outline of the support given under these headings is presented below.

Export Tax Relief

The following is a summary of the relief from taxation on profits made on the export operations of Irish companies taken from Leaflet No. 4 published by the Revenue Commissioners.

This relief is granted to companies (whether or not registered or managed or controlled in the State). The relief is, broadly speaking, confined to profits arising from the sale of goods which have been manufactured in the State and exported by the company claiming the relief. Where the company is not the manufacturer of the goods exported, relief may be claimed by it only where the goods exported are sold by wholesalers. Relief may also be claimed, subject to conditions, in respect to profits arising from the rendering to nonresidents of certain services, such as design and planning services in connection with foreign engineering projects and the processing of materials belonging to a nonresident.

The profits which are attributable to exports are wholly relieved of income tax and corporation profits tax for a continuous period not exceeding fifteen years and are relieved at gradually reducing rates for the succeeding period of not more than four consecutive years. The reducing rates are 80 percent for the first of these four years and 75 percent, 50 percent, and 35 percent for the second, third, and fourth years respectively. In no case may relief be given for any year or period ending after April 5, 1990.

A measure of unilateral relief from double taxation is granted to a company which derives dividends or interest from the investment in a foreign subsidiary of profits which have been relieved from tax under the exports relief provisions. Unilateral relief is confined to dividends or interest arising in countries with which comprehensive double taxation agreements are not in force.

Incentive Grants Scheme

In discharging its function as a promoter of Irish exports, Coras Trachtala (CTT), the Irish Exports Promotions Board, provides a range of incentive grants to be availed of by exporters. The principal grants include demonstrations, support for advertising and promotion, fairs, exhibitions, design and consultancy, and marketing research.

Advertising and Promotion

Grants may be made to exporting firms in the context of total export marketing plans towards the cost of new advertising/promotional campaigns in overseas market areas. For North America the maximum grant payable is £16,000. Elsewhere the maximum grant payable is £8,000 per product per market.

Fairs, Exhibitions, and Demonstrations

Grants may be made to exporting companies towards the cost of undertaking approved fair or exhibition participation, or demonstration, subject to a number of conditions. The maximum grant allowed is 50 percent of approved direct costs incurred. Entertainment costs may not be included. The maximum grant is £1,000 for any one project in Europe and £1,500 elsewhere. The maximum grant for each company is £5,000 in Europe or £7,500 elsewhere.

Design and Consultancy

Grants may be made to manufacturing companies towards the cost of engaging designers to survey their design needs and recommend future design policy or to design an individual product or range of products. The maximum grant payable is 50 percent of the designer's or consultant's fees and expenses, but the grant does not exceed £2,000.

Marketing Research

In the context of a marketing plan grants may be made to exporting firms towards the cost of undertaking formalized professional marketing research and consultancy in overseas market areas. Grants may be for 50 percent of direct costs subject to a maximum of £5,000.

Production Grants

Various Industrial Development Authority new machinery grants were in operation at this time.

POPULATION IN SELECTED MARKETS, 1971

Market	Percent Under Age 15	Percent from Age 15 to 64	Percent from Age 65 and over	Total in Thousands
Ireland	31.2	57.8	11.0	2,950
United Kingdom	24.0	63.2	12.8	55,811
Germany	22.4	63.7	13.9	60,651
France	24.8	62.3	12.9	51,005
Italy	24.4	64.6	11.0	53,748
Netherlands	27.2	62.6	10.2	13,120
Belgium	22.8	63.6	13.6	9,745
Luxembourg	20.9	66.5	12.6	331
Denmark	23.2	64.5	12.3	4,950

Source: Eurostat—*Basic Statistics of the Community,* 1971.

SELECTED MEASURES OF LIVING STANDARDS

Market	Grain as flour[a]	Meat[a]	Passenger Cars[b]	Television Sets[c]	Telephones[c]
	kg/capita/year		Per 1,000 population		
Ireland	90.5	83.6	139	170	103
United Kingdom	71.5	72.3	222	293	269
Germany (FR)	66.0	87.2	253	272	226
France	76.2	96.0	256	214	171
Italy	129.0	57.3	210	180	174
Netherlands	63.4	65.7	212	233	259
Belgium	78.4	82.7	223	209	210
Luxembourg	78.4	82.7	289	207	324
Denmark	70.1	62.5	231	277	342

[a]1970–1971
[b]January 1, 1972
[c]January 1, 1971

Source: Eurostat—*Basic Statistics of the Community,* 1972.

SELECTED GROCERY STATISTICS, 1971

Country	Average Number of People per Grocer	Average Annual per Capita Grocery Expenditure by Pounds	Average Annual Turnover per Grocer by Pounds
Ireland	227	38	9,000
Britain	488	67	33,000
Germany (FR)	341	99	34,000
France	367	82	30,000
Italy	276	21	6,000
Netherlands	741	61	45,000
Belgium Luxembourg	273	72	19,000

Source: Nielsen—*Marketing in Europe,* 1972.

Case 6–4

Motor Vehicle
Manufacturers Pty Ltd*

In 1974 the senior management of Motor Vehicle Manufacturers Pty Ltd (MVM) was faced with a set of complex and enigmatic problems. The solutions to these problems would have far-reaching and long-term consequences for its operations in Australia and for its 14,000 employees. There were three major decision areas contributing to these problems. The first area related to the company's decisions for products, markets, and production processes. The second related to the structure and dynamics of what was, without doubt, the most competitive automobile industry in the world. In the Australian car market, there existed a larger number of different makes and models of passenger cars than in any other significant car market in the world. The annual sales volume of most of these models was extremely small and distribution was very costly, since dealerships and markets were widely scattered over the 7.8 million square kilometers of Australia. The third problem area was related to government policy on the future of the motor industry in Australia.

In the past, there existed a "Government Plan for the Industry," which specified the degree of local content desired by the government for cars manufactured or assembled in Australia. The tariffs imposed on imported cars and components were consistent with the objectives of this plan. The new labor administration, which came into government in December 1972, requested the then Tariff Board (later renamed the Industries Assistance Commission) to instigate a full inquiry into the motor industry in Australia and to make recommendations to the Australian government on the future of the industry. The Industries Assistance Commission (IAC) concluded its investigation and made its recommendations to the government in 1974. The IAC was critical of the industry, claiming that there were too many engine and chassis plants in Australia in view of the smallness of the market. It also believed there were too many makes and models being manufactured or assembled.

The Commission's recommendations for a reduction in tariffs on imported cars and components, if adopted, would force the manufacturers to close down their manufacturing operations in Australia and concentrate on selling built-up imported cars and locally assembled, rather than manufactured cars. The gov-

---
*This case was prepared with the intention of providing a basis for class discussion rather than illustrating either effective or ineffective management of a business situation. Reprinted with permission from *Administrative Analysis: Text and Cases*, by John W. Hunt, Gary E. Popp, and Leland V. Entrekin. Sydney: McGraw-Hill Book Company, 1977.

ernment's decision would affect the future of several hundred million dollars worth of plant and equipment, as well as the jobs of tens of thousands of employees.

THE AUSTRALIAN AUTOMOBILE INDUSTRY

The automobile industry in Australia comprised four manufacturers and two assemblers. Production facilities were heavily concentrated in Melbourne, Sydney, and Adelaide, with only minor assembly and subassembly plants in other cities. Typically, a manufacturer would buy most of its parts and components from hundreds of local suppliers. All of the manufacturers were affiliates of multinational corporations and, consequently, the Australian company would also buy many parts from other affiliates of the enterprise, located throughout the world. The manufacturer would normally make its own stampings for body panels and do the body welding operations inside the assembly plant. Most manufacturers produced their own engines and one company made its own automatic transmissions.

Generally, however, the industry revolved around the assembly of vehicles from Australian-made and imported parts, using locally manufactured bodies, chassis, and engines. Some product lines were simply assembled from imported, completely knocked down (CKD) kits.

THE QUESTION OF FUTURE GROWTH

Industry sales had grown strongly in the past ten years (Exhibit 1), reflecting strong growth in personal incomes, population, and output of the economy (Exhibit 2).

Exhibit 1 **Passenger Vehicle Industry Growth Rates**

| | | Growth of Park* | | Scrappage | | | New Car Sales | |
| | Park* Jan. 1 (× 10³) | Units (× 10³) | Percent Park* | Units (× 10³) | Percent Park* | Units (× 10³) | Percent Change from Previous Year | Imports as Percent of Sales |
Year								
1964....	2500	209	8.4	124	5.0	333	8.1	6.7
1965....	2709	187	6.9	145	5.4	332	(0.3)	8.0
1966....	2896	165	5.7	142	4.9	307	(7.5)	6.9
1967....	3061	181	5.9	155	5.1	336	9.5	9.7
1968....	3242	203	6.3	166	5.1	369	9.8	13.4
1969....	3445	231	6.7	169	4.9	400	8.4	9.5
1970....	3676	223	6.1	188	5.1	411	2.8	10.3
1971....	3899	219	5.6	197	5.1	416	1.2	12.4
1972....	4118	191	4.6	214	5.2	405	(2.6)	8.0
1973....	4309	231	5.4	228	5.3	459	13.3	14.0

* Park refers to the number of vehicles on the register.

Exhibit 2

Selected Economic Growth Indicators—Australia

Year	Disposable Personal Income (× 10³)	Year over Year Percent Increase	Population at Dec. 31 (× 10³)	Year over Year Percent Increase
1964....	13113	—	11168	1.98
1965....	13906	6	11390	1.99
1966....	14725	5.9	11604	1.88
1967....	15851	7.6	11817	1.84
1968....	16885	6.5	12044	1.91
1969....	18549	9.9	12307	2.19
1970....	20560	10.8	12631	2.63
1971....	23353	13.6	12829	1.56
1972....	25917	11.0	13029	1.56
1973....	30210	16.6	13198	1.3

Year	Seasonally Adjusted Average Weekly Earnings Per Employed Male Unit Dec.	Year over Year Percent Increase	Gross Domestic Product in Constant Prices (× 10³)	Year over Year Percent Increase
1964....	$55.20	6.8	20297	6.6
1965....	57.50	4.2	21298	4.9
1966....	61.20	6.4	21898	2.8
1967....	64.90	6.0	23190	5.9
1968....	69.80	7.6	24682	6.4
1969....	75.10	7.6	26450	7.2
1970....	82.00	9.2	27375	3.5
1971....	91.80	12.0	28558	4.3
1972....	100.10	9.0	29649	3.8
1973....	115.20	15.1	31737	7.0

Despite the strong growth in vehicle ownership since the 1950s, there were now signs of a change in this trend (Exhibit 3). Industry analysts were concerned that the slowdown in new demand, coupled with the reduced population growth, indicated that the industry's growth years were coming to an end. Certainly, the growth of the two-car family had steadily reduced the number of persons per car over many years (Exhibit 4), but industry observers believed it would be more difficult to reduce the number of persons per car in the future than it had been in the past. In 1973, the figure was 2.9 persons per car compared to 2.0 in the United States.

THE QUESTION OF MARKET SEGMENTATION

An analysis of market demand patterns revealed certain interesting trends. Until World War II, the market had been dominated by the small cars, principally the British models such as Austin and Morris. Then the American manufacturers greatly expanded their facilities in Australia, tending to concentrate

Exhibit 3   **Replacement Demand and New Demand—Passenger Vehicles**

Year	Park* Jan. 1 ($\times 10^3$)	New Registrations ($\times 10^3$)	Replacement Demand + (scrappage) ($\times 10^3$)	Replacement Demand as Percent of New Registrations	New Demand ($\times 10^3$)	New Demand as Percent of New Registrations
1964....	2500	333	124	37.2	209	62.8
1965....	2709	332	145	43.7	187	56.3
1966....	2896	307	142	46.3	165	53.7
1967....	3061	336	155	46.1	181	53.9
1968....	3242	369	166	45.0	203	55.0
1969....	3445	400	169	42.3	231	57.7
1970....	3676	411	188	45.7	223	54.3
1971....	3899	416	197	47.4	219	52.6
1972....	4118	405	214	52.8	191	47.2
1973....	4309	459	228	49.7	231	50.3

* Park refers to number of vehicles on register.
+ Assumes that every car scrapped is replaced.

Exhibit 4   **Persons Per Car—Australia, December 31**

Year	Persons Per Car
1963	4.38
1964	4.12
1965	3.93
1966	3.79
1967	3.64
1968	3.50
1969	3.35
1970	3.24
1971	3.12
1972	3.02
1973	2.91

on the slightly larger, family-sized car. Over the years, this type of vehicle had increased in size, comfort, and safety features. Not surprisingly, this segment of the market had increased dramatically, at the expense of the small-car segment. In the 1960s, however, the trend was reversed and, in 1973, the number of small cars registered actually exceeded the volume of registrations for medium-sized family cars (Exhibit 5). There were many factors related to this swing back to smaller cars:

1. Increased urban traffic congestion and parking problems.
2. Growing consumer concern with fuel economy and overall operating costs of motor vehicles (Exhibit 6).

Type of Car	Percent of Passenger-Car Registrations							
	1966	**1967**	**1968**	**1969**	**1970**	**1971**	**1972**	**1973**
Small light (e.g. Mini, Honda, Escort)	12.3	15.4	17.0	16.3	16.4	18.2	19.1	21.3
Large light (e.g. Corona, Datsun 180B)	16.6	17.3	18.3	20.3	23.6	23.1	24.8	25.6
Total small cars.........................	28.9	32.7	35.3	36.6	40.0	41.3	43.9	46.9
Medium (e.g. Holden, Valiant)	—	62.5	59.2	57.3	53.9	52.8	49.0	46.3
Upper medium (e.g. Volvo, Statesman, Fairlane).................................	—	2.3	3.3	4.3	4.5	4.3	5.6	5.1
Luxury/specialty (e.g. Jaguar, Lincoln, MG, Jensen, Rolls Royce, Aston Martin).........	2.5	2.5	2.2	1.8	1.6	1.6	1.5	1.7
Total passenger-car registrations	100	100	100	100	100	100	100	100

3. An increase in the number of women owning and driving cars and therefore making the original purchase decision.

4. An increase in the size of the "youth" age groups, together with greater affluence and a preference for smaller cars.

5. Spectacular growth of the Japanese car industry and its success in promoting the popularity of a lower-priced, higher-value motoring package.

6. An increase in the price of six-cylinder family cars and an increase in the package size.

7. Changing consumer attitudes towards the role of the motor car in modern society. It is viewed less as a status symbol and more as a transport medium, as well as an expense burden of growing significance.

8. Competition from other consumer durables and luxury goods, such as pleasure boats, holiday homes, caravans and recreation vehicles, cheaper and more attractive overseas packages, sporting and other recreation goods and, more recently, color television.

The big question being asked in the industry concerned just how much further this segmentation shift would move. Some observers believed that there would always be a strong demand for an Australian family-sized car, even if to a lesser extent than in the 1960s. Other analysts warned that rising petrol prices and costs of ownership would push consumers much further towards the smaller cars.

Exhibit 6   **Selected Costs of Purchase and Operation of Passenger Cars**

Australian Government Sales Tax Rates—New Motor Vehicles

Period from:	Rate (%)
August 1, 1930	2.5
July 11, 1931	6
October 26, 1933	5
September 11, 1936	4
September 22, 1938	5
September 9, 1939	6
May 3, 1940	8.33
November 22, 1940	10
May 1, 1942	12.5
November 15, 1946	10
September 8, 1949	8.33
October 13, 1950	10
September 27, 1951	20
September 10, 1953	16.66
March 15, 1956	30
November 16, 1960	40
February 22, 1961	30
February 7, 1962	22.5
August 12, 1964	25
August 14, 1968	25
August 19, 1970	27.5

Rate of Increase in Petrol Prices—Melbourne Area

Year	Percent Increase on Previous Year
1966	5.9
1967	3.1
1968	3.0
1969	2.5
1970	10.3
1971	6.4
1972	Nil
1973	10.1

(Continued on next page.)

Year	Consumer Price Index (Dec. qtr)	Percent Increase Dec. to Dec.	Motoring Price Index*	Percent Increase Dec. to Dec.	Motoring Goods†	Percent Increase Dec. to Dec.	Motoring Services and Charges‡	Percent Increase Dec. to Dec.
	Price Changes for Motor Cars and Servicing Compared with Changes in General Level of Prices							
1964....	93.7	4.0	94.9	—	97.4	—	89.2	—
1965....	97.4	4.0	98.2	3.5	99.4	2.1	95.2	6.7
1966....	99.7	2.4	99.9	1.7	100.1	0.7	99.5	4.5
1967....	103.0	3.3	102.2	2.3	101.7	1.6	103.5	4.0
1968....	105.7	2.6	108.0	5.7	103.6	1.9	118.3	14.3
1969....	108.7	2.8	110.2	2.0	105.1	1.5	122.4	3.5
1970....	114.0	4.9	115.7	5.0	110.2	4.9	128.9	5.3
1971....	122.2	7.2	122.4	5.8	114.6	4.0	141.5	9.8
1972....	127.7	4.5	128.1	4.7	117.5	2.5	154.5	9.2
1973....	144.6	13.2	137.5	7.3	126.1	7.3	165.9	7.4
1974....	168.1	16.3	163.9	19.2	144.7	14.8	222.3	34.0

* A subindex of the Consumer Price Index, it is a composite of the indexes for motoring goods and motoring services and charges.
† A subindex of the Consumer Price Index, it includes the motor car, petrol, oil, tires, tubes, tire retreading and battery.
‡ A subindex of the Consumer Price Index, it includes lubrication, repairs, registration fee, third-party insurance and driver's licence.

THE QUESTION OF IMPORTS

Japanese cars comprised, on the average, about 90 percent of the volume of cars imported into Australia. Approximately 50 percent of the Japanese cars sold in Australia were imported fully built up, while 50 percent were assembled locally from imported kits and locally available parts.

The recession, which partly resulted from the energy crisis, caused a slump in car sales in Japan's principal markets (i.e. Japan, United States, and Western Europe). In seeking to dispose of huge unsold stocks of cars, the Japanese viewed Australia as a lucrative market. Being relatively untouched by the energy crisis, Australia was one of the few countries that, in 1974, enjoyed buoyant economic conditions and a booming demand for cars. Furthermore, the Australian government had reduced tariffs by 25 percent on imported goods in July 1973 and this, coupled with three revaluations of the Australian dollar, created very favorable conditions for the Japanese manufacturers to accelerate their car exports to Australia. This they did (Exhibit 7).

Exhibit 7

Japanese Imports into Australia—
Built-up New Passenger Cars

Year	Volume
1968	36199
1969	26617
1970	26694
1971	42324
1972	28140
1973	57289
1974	127828

These imports were almost all small cars. The effect was not only to increase the Japanese share of the small-car market segments, but also to increase the size of these segments in relation to the total passenger-car market (Exhibit 5). Concern was expressed over the unemployment that these imports were creating in Australia. At one stage, union action prevented the unloading of foreign cars from ships in Melbourne and Sydney. Industry observers wondered how long it would take the Australian government to impose quotas on foreign car imports.

THE COMPANY

Motor Vehicle Manufacturers Pty Ltd (MVM) was the Australian affiliate of a United States company that ranked as one of the three largest multinational corporations in the world. The parent company derived some 36 percent of its sales from outside the United States and about 40 percent of its total assets were located abroad.

PRODUCTS AND MARKETS

The Australian company manufactured and assembled a wide range of passenger and commercial vehicles, which competed in all segments of the market. Its performance in these segments had varied over the years between wide extremes (Exhibit 8). Its shares of the total passenger-car market had fluctuated in recent years between 20 percent and 27 percent.

MVM had competed aggressively and successfully in the medium, upper-medium, and luxury-car market segments. Its position in the small end of the market, however, had been progressively eroded away by strong Japanese competition.

While many departments within the company closely watched the market trends and believed that economic and market forces would continue to expand small-car demand, the company as a whole placed great importance on the medium-sized car. The reason was fundamentally a financial one. The fact was that little, if any, profit was made on any cars smaller than the medium range.

Exhibit 8

Motor Vehicle Manufacturers Pty Ltd
Market Segment Penetration by Product Line*

Type	1968	1969	1970	1971	1972	1973
Gnat (small light)	—	—	12.4	10.5	13.0	8.6
Cavalier (large light)	24.3	26.0	19.6	19.7	24.6	20.3
Viking (medium)	20.8	22.9	25.0	26.5	33.2	29.4
Executive (upper medium)	72.2	49.3	53.9	47.6	51.3	37.8
Elite (luxury)	9.8	4.7	11.6	8.7	9.5	16.9

* For each product, the figure shown represents that product's share (percent) of its relevant market segment—for example, in 1971, the Gnat enjoyed a 10.5 percent share of the small—light segment. Thus the data are *not* shares of the total passenger-car market.

The Gnat contributed little to profitability. In a recent year, Gnat sales (units) comprised 9.3 percent of the company's passenger-car sales volume. Economic profit per unit was negligible ($100-$150) and usually it was, in fact, a loss. The Cavalier comprised 20 percent of sales volume, with very small economic profits per unit ($150-$300). The family-sized car, the Viking, comprised 59 percent of sales volume and returned a reasonable profit per unit ($500-$900). The Executive comprised 9.7 percent of sales volume and economic profit per unit was $1200-$1600. The Elite comprised 2 percent of sales volume and economic profit per unit was about $2500.

Thus, it can be seen that the small cars contributed neither the volume nor the profit per unit. The medium cars combined a reasonable profit with a large volume and hence were known as the "bread-and-butter line." The upper-medium and luxury lines combined a small volume with a large profit per unit. For these reasons, MVM had resisted the move into small cars. To MVM, the move to smaller cars portended a shift to smaller profits. Since it supplied one-quarter of the market, MVM could, to some extent, impose its will on that market. Thus MVM dealers would "encourage" the would-be Cavalier buyer to "trade up" to a Viking.

MVM's profitability was squeezed by several other factors, which were related to the pattern of its principal markets. One major market comprised sales to federal, state, and municipal governments and public instrumentalities. This type of sale was by tender and all manufacturers usually engaged in highly competitive bidding. Profits were low and losses were common on such sales. Another major market consisted of exports. The company had been encouraged by successive federal governments to build export markets. Only the government's export subsidy made such sales profitable. In the 1973 federal budget, it was announced that the subsidy would cease from June 30, 1974. A third major market was sales to company fleets. Taxi, cigarette, rent-a-car, food, and other companies ordered large volumes of cars. Again, competition resulted in losses or low profits. So it was the fourth market, that is, the private consumer, which was the basis for company profitability.

It was difficult for MVM employees to know which markets to pursue from time to time. In periods of buoyant demand, government, fleet, and export sales would take second place behind the more profitable dealer private sales. Nevertheless, the company believed it should show some interest in the less profitable markets at such times, since it might need the volume for plant throughput, scale economies, and employment levels when the economy moved into a recession. A manufacturer who ignored government buyers, when private business generally was brisk, might discover that he had been forgotten as a source of supply to government, when private demand was slack. MVM employees were sometimes confused over the changing priorities of these submarkets from time to time.

ORGANIZATION AND LABOR RELATIONS

MVM was functionally organized in six divisions (Exhibit 9). The managing director, Duncan Faulkner, reported to the president of Motor Vehicle Manufacturers Asia/Pacific, a company whose offices were also located in Melbourne. This was a "paper" company, which coordinated the operations of all affiliates of the multinational in the Asia and Pacific region. The president of this "paper" company, in turn, reported to the vice-president of International Automotive Operations, in Detroit.

Val Erskine, marketing director, was an Australian who had left a senior sales management position at a competing company three years earlier. He held no academic or professional qualifications. Erskine was known for his aggressive and overbearing disposition and was regarded as the second most powerful executive in the company. It was rumored that he would soon retire.

Keith Halliday, director of research and development, had come from the British affiliate of the multinational five years earlier. He had a B.B. from Birmingham, England, and a Ph.D. from Purdue, a well-known American engineering school. He had a quiet, reserved personality and tended to be ineffective at board meetings, always taking a defensive approach. It was rumored that he would soon take up a position in the Brazilian affiliate.

Karl Jorgensen, director of finance, was a German who had arrived a year earlier from the South African affiliate. He was a graduate in finance and business administration from a reputable American university. As an analyst of financial matters, he was not a detail man, preferring to take a global, overall view of situations. His predecessor had had an eye for detail and had regularly amazed his younger managers and analysts with his ability to pick up an error on a huge page of figures at first glance. Jorgensen was unfamiliar with the Australian economic, political, and financial environment. Until he familiarized himself with the local situation, he was forced to rely on the advice of his managers. About the time Jorgensen arrived in Australia, the new Australian labor government had established a Prices Justification Tribunal. One of Jorgensen's responsibilities was to give testimony before the Tribunal, in support of price increase applications by MVM. On two occasions, lack of knowledge of local conditions had proved an embarrassment to Jorgensen. He had a tendency, as one manager put it, "to rush in where angels fear to tread." His pro-

Motor Vehicle Manufacturers Pty Ltd
Company Organization

Exhibit 9

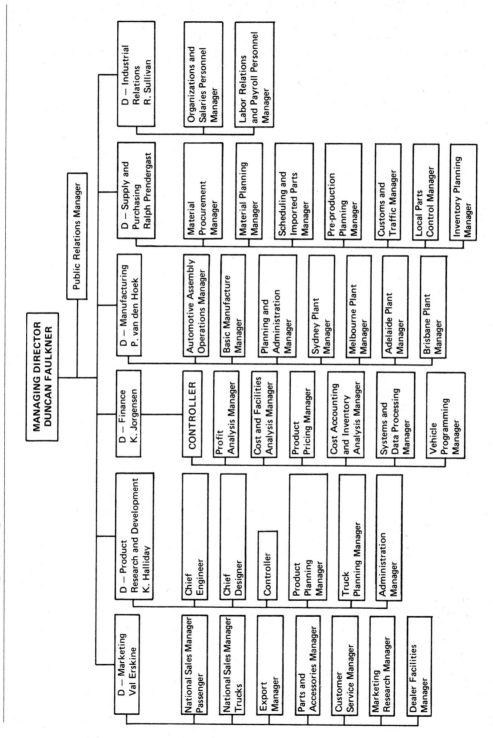

pensity to make outlandish suggestions at board meetings, with the managing director having to restrain him, caused some uneasiness within the finance office.

Pieter van den Hoek, director of manufacturing, was an Australian engineer who had been with the company for thirty years. This was unusual at MVM. He was responsible for the largest and most diverse division of the company. Operations were extensive and geographically dispersed. A nonaggressive person, van den Hoek was unable to defend the manufacturing division when it came under attack from Val Erskine at board meetings. Economic, marketing and financial matters were unfamiliar to van den Hoek, who tended to view all problems in terms of engineering and manufacturing. It had recently been decided to appoint van den Hoek to a newly created position entitled "coordinator, special studies." The move had been deferred, pending the location of a suitable successor.

Ralph Prendergast, director of supply and purchasing, was an Australian who had worked for twenty years in the purchasing area of the steel industry. He came to MVM ten years earlier as manager of preproduction planning and, after five years, he was appointed director. One of his major responsibilities was to go to Japan regularly to buy steel. The company used very little Australian steel, and Prendergast would frequently make steel purchases worth several million dollars from Japanese producers.

Ken Sullivan, director of industrial relations, was an ex-British army major. He had little industrial or business experience. He privately admitted to being "a bit of an elitist" and was a strong believer in discipline, authority, and the right of management to manage. He had been known to remark ruefully that "the British workers are getting out of control" and was afraid that the situation would be repeated in Australia. Through several damaging strikes, he had faithfully maintained a tough and unyielding company stance. His office was not renowned for its adeptness in building a spirit of company loyalty among salaried employees. Hourly employees, of whom 90 percent were non-English-speaking migrants of some 25 nationalities, were hired and fired, or lost through attrition to such an extent that MVM had one of the highest rates of labor turnover in Australia. Little attempt was made to introduce new salaried employees to the company.

One young analyst remarked, "I've always wanted to see the inside of a car assembly plant. But in this place they won't let you into the plant. I could work here in this office for 40 years, massaging numbers that I'm told represent cars and trucks and never ever see a real live car. I'm assured that we do actually make cars down the road there in the plant."

A young assembly-line worker commented, "All day, every day, I fit rear parking lights to the cars as they move along the line. I wish just once they'd let me have a go at fitting front parking lights."

MANUFACTURING

Manufacturing was a complex and frustrating process in the automobile industry. MVM procured parts and components from hundreds of local suppliers, as well as importing many parts from other MVM-affiliated companies in the United States, Britain, France, New Zealand, Canada, and the Philippines. If a local supplier went on strike and could not supply parts for a week or several weeks, possibly several thousand vehicle orders would be held up. If the supplier made clocks, all cars with clocks ordered as an option would be held up. If the supplier made a part common to many cars (e.g. automatic transmissions), then much of MVM's assembly options would be disrupted. When the supplier finally went back to work, it would be many weeks, or possibly months, before he was able to clear his backlog of orders.

During the 1973-74 period, there was not a single day when one or more of MVM's suppliers was not on strike. The result of these interruptions to supply was that MVM rarely met its production schedules. The more options ordered by the customer for his car, the greater the likelihood of production delays due to parts shortages. Customers thus became wary about ordering options. MVM's profit margin on options was considerably higher than its margin on the base vehicle.

Imported parts also posed a problem. The lead time for procuring parts from Europe and North America was four months. If the Australian company estimated that it would require 500 trucks from the British affiliate to sell in Australia in the month of July, the Australian company needed to cable its order to Britain in January. The British affiliate would incorporate the Australian order into its production schedules for February, then pack and ship the boxes. The boxes would spend up to three months on the water, arriving at Port Melbourne in late May. Assuming that customs clearance could be expedited, the boxes would be in-plant for assembly in June. Wholesaling and distribution of the finished product to dealers would occur in July. This timing assumed that the British affiliate was able to supply the trucks, that shipping space was available when required, and that the ship encountered no port strikes or other delays on its voyage to Australia. These events, however, were common. Furthermore, when the boxes finally arrived, it was frequently discovered that some parts were missing and these would have to be airfreighted from Britain at considerable expense.

The long lead times reduced the company's ability to react to market changes. For example, if there was a slump in demand for cars, the company would immediately cut its assembly operations and reduce its orders for parts. Delivery of local parts would ease back almost immediately. Imported parts, however, would continue to arrive at the previous high levels for another five months. This was because the Australian affiliate was committed to accept any parts that had been shipped out of the overseas plant. The result was rapidly increasing inventories of parts in Australia. These inventories would typically take many months to work down.

Another manufacturing problem was that of short production runs and parts complexity. MVM's Melbourne plant assembled most of the cars in the company's range. Thus, at any one time on the assembly line, there was a bewildering variety of vehicles. First, there were the various product lines, such as the Cavalier, Viking, Executive, and Elite. Secondly, each product line offered several body styles, such as sedan, wagon, hardtop, utility, and van. Some body styles were available with two doors or four doors. Thirdly, each product line offered several series types, such as standard, 600, deluxe, and sports. The higher the series, the more luxurious the finish, with certain parts becoming standard equipment instead of optional as on the lower series vehicles. Due to these many variations, MVM's plant in Melbourne was the most complex automobile assembly plant in the world. Not only did the assembly workers have to change their operations for each car coming along the line, but the plant had to maintain inventories for the large number of unique parts. In order to compete successfully in the Australian car market, MVM's strategy had been oriented towards offering the customer a large number of options and option combinations. There were, in all, some 4,500 options and option combinations available (Exhibit 10).

Each option required unique parts procurement and introduced further complexity into the assembly process. Each combination of options added more complexity—for example, if a tape player was ordered on a Viking four-door standard sedan, it made a difference whether or not air conditioning was also ordered. Several different parts would be unique to each combination. For each of the 4,500 options and combinations, individual forecasting of future demand had to be undertaken every month. Based on these forecasts, separate orders would be placed on suppliers and inventories maintained in the plant. The forecasting had to be done manually for each item every month, although the company was in the process of computerizing this task.

Some options were in little demand. As an example, one engine type was specified by only 10 percent of all buyers ordering the Viking Riviera sedan. The Riviera sedan, in turn, amounted to only 1.9 percent of total Viking passenger car sales, the latter being 65,660 units in 1972. Nevertheless, in order to support this demand, MVM manufactured the engine, maintained in-plant inventories, and required dealers to maintain inventories of parts unique to this engine. New options or the availability of existing options in new combinations were added to the range from time to time as a marketing tactic. Few low-usage options were ever dropped from the range.

Due to the small size of the Australian car market, MVM, like its competitors, did not follow the United States strategy of launching completely new models every year. Typically, an investment of $50 million to $80 million would be required to research, design, and develop a totally new major product. About 12 to 18 months after the introduction of a completely new product, the company would introduce what was known as a "minor face-lift." This "new" model would normally involve no major changes to the previous model. It comprised a new "skin;" that is, minor styling and feature changes to the body of the car. There might also be some minor changes to the dashboard, front grille, and headlights. Some new paint colors and options would be added to the existing range. The purpose of the minor face-lift was twofold. First, it was an attempt to freshen up the "old" model and boost sales by promoting the face-lifted product as a new model. Second, the face-lifted model would incorporate hundreds of minor improvements and refinements resulting from dealer and customer feedback on the initial model. It was hence a chance to "get the bugs out" of the old model.

Exhibit 10

Motor Vehicle Manufacturers Pty Ltd
Selected Options and Option Combinations

Viking Options	Combinations
Power disc brakes	Passenger, 6-cylinder manual
	Passenger, 6-cylinder automatic
	Commercial, 6-cylinder manual
	Commercial, 6-cylinder automatic
	Passenger, 300 Cubic Inch Displacement (C.I.D.) manual
	Passenger, 300 C.I.D. automatic
	Commercial, 300 C.I.D. manual
	Commercial, 300 C.I.D. automatic
Radial ply tires	Four-door sedan, 6 cylinder
	Four-door sedan, 8 cylinder
	Wagon, 6 cylinder
	Wagon, 8 cylinder
	Utility
	Two-door hardtop, 6 cylinder
	Two-door hardtop, 8 cylinder
Vinyl roof	Four door, brown
	Four door, blue
	Four door, green
	Four door, black
	Four door, beige
	Two door, brown
	Two door, blue
	Two door, green
	Two door, black
	Two door, beige
Tape player	Standard, 600 and Riviera, excluding air conditioning
	Deluxe, excluding air conditioning
	Sports, excluding air conditioning
	Four-door standard, 600 and Riviera, with air conditioning
	Four-door Deluxe, with air conditioning
	Sports, with air conditioning
	Standard and 600 wagons, with air conditioning
	Deluxe wagon, with air conditioning
	Two-door Deluxe, excluding air conditioning
	Two-door Deluxe, with air conditioning
	8 cylinder

Perhaps 18 months after the introduction of the minor-face-lifted product the company would introduce either a medium-face-lifted or major-face-lifted model. This would comprise more or less substantial changes to the body, dashboard, grille, headlights, and interior. It also included mechanical alterations — for example, changes to the braking system, transmission, suspension, engine, and so forth. The purpose was to gain all the sales and marketing benefits of a new model without having to make the large investment required for a completely new model. Thus the company would run a completely new product for five or six years, long enough to recover the original high development costs and make a reasonable contribution to profits.

Due to the large number of parts in a motor vehicle and the need to reduce large inventories of these parts, the company aimed for maximum commonality of components between product lines. Thus the Viking engines were also fitted to the Cavalier and Executive. Many other components and options (such as tires, brakes, transmissions, dashboard, steering wheels, headlights, parking lights, and radios) were interchangeable between product lines. The advantages included smaller inventories of parts in the plant and at dealerships, simplification of the procurement function, reduced parts obsolescence when models were discontinued or "run out," simplification of assembly operations, and economies in tooling and development.

FUTURE COMPANY STRATEGY

Since Japanese small cars had achieved spectacular success in the Australian market, the large American manufacturers were anxious to share in that success. These companies made arrangements with Japanese manufacturers whereby the American company would assemble the Japanese cars in Australia and market them through their existing distribution networks. Two such manufacturers had concluded arrangements with Japanese companies and had been most successful in selling Australian-assembled Japanese cars. Since the American manufacturer lacked comparable products in its range, this arrangement provided a quick means for penetrating the small-car market. The Japanese supplier of the knocked-down vehicles also benefited, because knocked-down vehicles entered Australia under lower tariff barriers than did fully assembled imports. Furthermore, knocked-down vehicles would not be affected by any import quotas that might be imposed by the Australian government on imported cars. The Japanese manufacturer thus had access to the comprehensive distribution networks, dealerships, and promotional expertise of the American manufacturers in Australia. MVM had no such arrangement. It continued to manufacture and assemble a traditional company small car developed by the British affiliate. Buyers of Japanese small cars frequently commented that MVM small cars were too expensive, offered less value in terms of quality, standard equipment, extra safety and comfort features, and were mechanically less reliable than Japanese cars.

MVM's future product/market strategy involved the assembly of a small car from the German affiliate, which, it was hoped, would enable MVM to recapture its share of the small-car market. The company insisted that Australians would continue to buy large family cars. Consequently, there were plans to introduce new Viking and Executive models in 1976. There would be some rationalization of the range, however, so that there would be only three series types for the Viking, instead of the present five (Standard, 600, Riviera, Deluxe, and Sports).

Company market and economic research indicated that Australia was about to experience a boom in recreation-related and leisure-time industries, similar to that which occurred in the United States and Canada. Many of the company's trucks and passenger-derivative commercial vehicles (vans) were easily converted into camper and holiday units for individuals, couples, or entire families. Several such products had been designed and exhibited at the Royal Show in Melbourne and at exhibitions and motor shows in other cities. When these products went on sale, the customer response was overwhelming and sales were beyond the company's expectations. Future plans aimed at further developing this market.

Based on historical data, MVM's finance office developed a ten-year plan of anticipated industry growth (Exhibit 11). It was considered to be a reasonable forecast of likely future demand patterns.

Exhibit 11

Motor Vehicle Manufacturers Pty Ltd
Ten-Year Plan, Passenger Vehicle Industry Growth Rates

Year	Park* Jan. 1 ($\times 10^3$)	Growth of Park*		Scrappage		New Car Sales		
		Units ($\times 10^3$)	Percent Park*	Units ($\times 10^3$)	Percent Park*	Units ($\times 10^3$)	Percent Change from Previous Years	Imports as Percent of Sales
1974....	4540	234	5.2	245	5.4	479	4.4	12.0
1975....	4774	237	5.0	263	5.5	500	4.4	12.0
1976....	5011	241	4.8	281	5.6	522	4.4	12.0
1977....	5252	246	4.7	299	5.7	545	4.4	12.0
1978....	5498	250	4.5	319	5.8	569	4.4	12.0
1979....	5748	255	4.4	339	5.9	594	4.4	12.0
1980....	6003	260	4.3	360	6.0	620	4.4	12.0
1981....	6263	265	4.2	382	6.1	647	4.4	12.0
1982....	6528	271	4.2	405	6.2	676	4.4	12.0
1983....	6799	278	4.1	428	6.3	706	4.4	12.0

*Park refers to number of vehicles on register.

The finance office made certain assumptions regarding future economic activity. These included:

1. Population would continue to grow at 2 percent per annum over the ten-year planning period.
2. Disposable personal income would increase at an annual average rate of 14 percent.
3. Average weekly earnings would grow at a 9 percent annual average rate.
4. Gross domestic product would grow at a 5 percent annual average rate in real terms.

MVM's forecasts for market saturation are presented in Exhibit 12.

Exhibit 12

Motor Vehicle Manufacturers Pty Ltd
Ten-Year Plan Replacement Demand and New Demand
(Passenger Vehicles)

Year	Park* Jan. 1 ($\times 10^3$)	New Registrations ($\times 10^3$)	Replacement Demand ($\times 10^3$)	Replacement Demand as Percent of New Registrations	New Demand ($\times 10^3$)	New Demand as Percent of New Registrations
1974....	4,540	479	245	51.1	234	48.9
1975....	4,774	500	263	52.6	237	47.4
1976....	5,011	522	281	53.8	241	46.2
1977....	5,252	545	299	54.9	246	45.1
1978....	5,498	569	319	56.1	250	43.9
1979....	5,748	594	339	57.1	255	42.9
1980....	6,003	620	360	58.1	260	41.9
1981....	6,263	647	382	59.0	265	41.0
1982....	6,528	676	405	59.9	271	40.1
1983....	6,799	706	428	60.6	278	39.4

*Park refers to number of vehicles on register.

The reduction in the number of persons per car implied in these forecasts is shown in Exhibit 13.

Exhibit 13

Motor Vehicle Manufacturers Pty Ltd
Persons Per Car, Forecast 1974 to 1983

Year	Population (Dec. 31) (000)	Park* (Dec. 3) (000)	Persons per Car (Dec. 31)
1974....	13 462	4774	2.8
1975....	13 732	5011	2.7
1976....	14 007	5252	2.7
1977....	14 288	5498	2.6
1978....	14 574	5748	2.5
1979....	14 866	6003	2.5
1980....	15 164	6263	2.4
1981....	15 468	6528	2.4
1982....	15 778	6799	2.3
1983....	16 094	7077	2.3

*Park refers to number of vehicles on register.

The company's assumptions for future changes in market segmentation are presented in Exhibit 14.

Exhibit 14

Motor Vehicle Manufacturers Pty Ltd—Ten-Year Plan
Australian Passenger-Car Market Segmentation Forecasts

Type	Percent of Australian Passenger-Car Market									
	1974	1975	1976	1977	1978	1979	1980	1981	1982	1983
Small Light..............	22.0	19.5	19.0	19.2	19.4	19.8	20.0	20.5	21.0	21.0
Large Light..............	26.5	26.0	26.5	27.5	29.0	30.0	31.0	31.5	32.0	32.0
Total Small Cars........	48.5	45.5	45.5	46.7	48.4	49.8	51.0	52.0	53.0	53.0
Medium	43.5	46.2	45.8	44.6	42.6	40.9	39.6	38.5	37.4	37.4
Upper Medium	6.0	6.2	6.5	6.5	6.7	6.9	7.0	7.0	7.1	7.1
Luxury/Specialty	2.0	2.1	2.2	2.2	2.3	2.4	2.4	2.5	2.5	2.5
Total Passenger-Car Registrations	100.0	100.0	100.0	100.0	100.0	100.0	100.0	100.0	100.0	100.0

In association with MVM's marketing office, the finance office developed projected market shares by product line (Exhibit 15).

Exhibit 15

Motor Vehicle Manufacturers Pty Ltd
Projected Market Shares by Product Line*

Type	1974	1975	1976	1977	1978	1979	1980	1981	1982	1983
Gnat	7.0	8.0	10.0	12.0	12.0	12.0	12.0	12.0	12.0	12.0
Cavalier	18.0	19.0	21.0	23.0	23.0	23.0	23.0	23.0	23.0	23.0
Viking.......	33.0	34.0	34.0	34.0	34.0	34.0	34.0	34.0	34.0	34.0
Executive	40.0	43.0	46.0	46.0	46.0	46.0	46.0	46.0	46.0	46.0
Elite†	32.0	40.0	40.0	40.0	40.0	40.0	40.0	40.0	40.0	40.0

* For each product, the figure presented represents that product's share of its relevant market segment, and *not* its share of the total passenger-car market.

† The large increase in the share of this segment is explained in terms of new product actions. In 1973, MVM introduced a new Australian-designed and Australian-developed luxury car, whose market share was confidently expected to greatly exceed the historical shares of previous Elite models. Previous models were American-designed and manufactured in Australia in much smaller volumes than was envisaged for the 1973 model Elite.

In November 1974 the managing director of MVM Pty Ltd, Duncan Faulkner, left Melbourne on an international flight bound for Detroit. He carried with him three suitcases containing the 1975 budget of MVM. In presenting the budget to the central staff at world headquarters, he would explain that the Australian affiliate was in a sound position to expand sales, market share, and profits as soon as the economy recovered late in 1975 or early in 1976. The company's planned new product actions would recapture lost market shares and assist in the restoration of profitability . . . the future suggested exciting possibilities . . . expansion of the assembly plant was needed, because . . . the Australian company had performed better than many other affiliates in 1974 . . .

Two weeks after Faulkner's departure, Leyland Australia announced that it would cease production of its new P76 medium passenger car, close its Zetland plant in Sydney, and retrench several thousand workers. The company would cease most of its manufacturing activities in Australia and concentrate on selling fully built-up imported cars. Leyland blamed the flood of imports for its predicament.

Two weeks after the Leyland shock, one of the largest manufacturers of motor vehicles announced its plan to retrench three thousand plant workers by Christmas. The company blamed high levels of car imports for its loss of sales volume.

Case 6–5

Compañia Empacadora
de la Puerco*

INTRODUCTION

U.S. Pork Packers, Inc. (USPPI), was a U.S. pork packing company with its head offices in Chicago. Most of its business was derived from the wholesale of pork in the United States to restaurants, hospitals, schools, and other institutions. The remainder of its sales were from the export of pork from the U.S. to other countries.

USPPI got about 40 percent of its pork from the U.S. and the rest was from sources in Canada, Australia, Costa Rica, Nicaragua, and Honduras. As its sales had been growing steadily since 1970 when the company first began its operations, USPPI was always looking for new sources of pork—especially at lower prices.

BUSINESS NEGOTIATIONS

In October 1981 Mr. Graham, vice president of production at USPPI, was approached by two businessmen, Senors Hernandez and Garcia from Guatador, who were interested in becoming suppliers for USPPI. (See Exhibits 1–5 for related economic statistics on Guatador.) Hernandez and Garcia, through their company Compañia Empacadora de la Puerco (CEP), ran a modern slaughterhouse facility located in El Cuerton on the Pacific Coast of Guatador. They were looking for a steady buyer for their pork, as well as someone who would be willing to finance the purchase of special refrigeration equipment for the plant. They thought that an agreement with USPPI would be beneficial to both parties.

At the request of the president of USPPI, Mr. Graham went to the slaughterhouse to check out the facility and, if it looked good and met USPPI's specifications, to enter into negotiations with CEP.

In January 1982 a contract was signed between USPPI and CEP. Under the terms of the contract, CEP agreed to sell exclusively to USPPI all pork processed by CEP at the El Cuerton facility. This pork was to be cut in tradi-

---

*This case was prepared by Martha G. Kirchner under the supervision of Fairborz Ghadar, George Washington University, with the intention of providing a basis for class discussion rather than illustrating either effective or ineffective management of a business situation.

Exhibit 1

Gross Domestic Product
by Economic Activity: Guatador (in million pesos)

	1977	1978	1979	1980	1981	1982
Agriculture and livestock	3,615.7	3,464.2	4,032.4	5,024.0	5,172.1	5,605.5
Forestry and logging	69.5	89.6	124.7	119.7	123.7	108.6
Hunting and fishing	122.2	132.1	160.8	167.9	181.8	154.3
Mining and quarrying ...	88.2	57.8	52.3	58.4	67.3	101.6
Manufacturing	3,194.1	3,640.6	3,980.1	4,463.9	4,660.5	5,040.8
Electricity and water.....	142.5	258.7	357.2	459.0	447.7	508.9
Construction	930.9	893.7	1,019.1	1,048.1	635.2	228.3
Wholesale and retail trade	3,480.6	3,547.8	4,302.8	5,674.3	5,239.6	3,293.8
Transport and communications	892.2	896.8	1,043.5	1,388.8	1,177.7	1,000.6
Finance and insurance ...	471.0	455.5	575.1	645.7	617.0	540.2
Owner-occupied dwellings	824.3	910.7	1,037.6	1,189.7	1,124.2	741.7
Public administration	884.0	1,050.0	1,253.4	1,400.8	1,601.2	1,642.8
Other services..........	1,039.8	1,078.6	1,204.4	1,564.0	1,133.8	877.0
Total..................	15,755.0	16,476.1	19,143.4	23,204.3	22,181.8	19,844.1

Exhibit 2

Direction of Trade: Guatador
Imports (in million of U.S. dollars)

	1976	1977	1978	1979	1980	1981	1982
WORLD	483.73	829.40	764.79	787.44	1,127.74	877.96	700.05
INDUSTRIAL COUNTRIES	292.53	495.29	446.11	437.78	664.07	495.31	243.99
United States	166.57	264.90	248.24	243.65	325.20	275.65	163.12
OIL EXPORTING COUNTRIES	25.08	41.54	95.10	84.78	128.12	101.64	162.62
NON-OIL DEVELOPING COUNTRIES	165.38	284.58	220.91	262.64	332.04	277.91	290.03
Africa	.11	.28	.16	.19	2.20	2.61	.04
Asia......................	3.62	6.97	5.47	5.35	13.76	7.38	2.19
Europe	.25	2.08	7.38	1.68	3.22	3.59	4.80
Middle East	.32	.54	.88	.32	.32	.42	1.30
Western Hemisphere........	161.08	274.71	207.02	255.16	312.54	263.91	281.61
USSR/CHINA/E.EUROPE	.74	7.99	2.67	2.24	3.50	3.10	3.41

Exhibit 3

Direction of Trade: Guatador
Exports (in million of U.S. dollars)

	1976	1977	1978	1979	1980	1981	1982
WORLD	411.21	501.84	495.57	803.58	942.36	956.00	1,011.55
INDUSTRIAL COUNTRIES	278.15	328.90	366.47	534.22	612.89	603.45	664.17
United States	139.81	109.09	155.40	249.08	223.55	238.73	337.70
OIL EXPORTING COUNTRIES	.10	7.03	3.16	5.16	19.00	4.07	2.29
NON-OIL DEVELOPING COUNTRIES	126.13	196.52	183.93	251.52	279.22	294.32	285.51
Africa	.31	10.36	6.02	3.71	3.01	—	.97
Asia	24.47	28.87	31.03	55.92	49.86	68.56	30.88
Europe	2.73	12.60	4.21	.93	10.86	.93	2.79
Middle East	—	—	.02	—	.04	.02	.04
Western Hemisphere	98.62	144.69	142.65	190.96	215.45	224.81	250.83
USSR/CHINA/E. EUROPE	6.83	39.41	.65	12.68	31.25	54.16	59.58

Exhibit 4

Breakdown of Pork Imports
into the United States

IMPORTED BY THE UNITED STATES FROM WORLDWIDE SOURCES

	Quantity (lbs.)	Value (dollars)
1980	1,174,000,000	1,878,400,000
1981	1,431,000,000	2,289,600,000
1982	1,515,000,000	2,343,000,000
1983	1,373,000,000	2,196,800,000
1984	1,155,000,000	1,848,000,000

IMPORTED BY THE UNITED STATES FROM GUATADOR

	Quantity (lbs.)	Value (dollars)
1980	51,260,283	82,016,453
1981	67,978,316	108,770,000
1982	74,415,739	119,070,000
1983	45,919,352	73,470,963
1984	19,069,311	30,510,898

Exhibit 5

Balance of Payments Statistics: Guatador (in millions of SDRs)

	1978	1979	1980	1981	1982	1983	1984
Current account	−55.3	−213.9	−152.4	−34.0	−155.4	−19.9	124.3
Merchandise: exports f.o.b.	233.5	316.8	308.8	469.3	545.3	516.0	476.7
Merchandise: imports f.o.b.......	−274.7	−450.5	−397.1	−420.1	−603.1	−441.9	−301.0
Trade balance...............	−41.2	−133.7	−88.3	49.2	−57.8	74.1	175.7
Other goods/services: credit	37.1	55.4	68.3	76.1	82.8	68.6	52.0
Other goods/services: debit......	−99.4	−148.5	−146.1	−167.4	−190.0	−170.2	−159.3
Total goods/services..........	−103.5	−226.8	−166.1	−42.1	−165.0	−27.5	68.4
Private unrequited transfers	23.1	2.8	3.4	.9	.6	.1	1.0
Total, excl. unofficial transfers	−80.4	−224.0	−162.7	−41.2	−164.4	−27.4	69.4
Official unrequited transfers	25.1	10.1	10.3	7.2	9.0	7.5	54.9
Direct investment and other long-term capital	94.0	144.3	125.5	26.1	178.7	63.5	29.9
Direct investment	11.1	11.5	9.0	11.2	8.6	5.6	2.2
Portfolio investment	−	−	−	−	−	−	−
Other long-term capital	82.9	132.8	116.5	14.9	170.1	57.9	27.7
Other short-term capital	12.6	56.0	38.1	−11.4	−17.7	−149.8	−199.5
Net errors and omissions........	−1.3	−9.6	−1.1	.7	−3.4	−7.4	−7.4
Counterpart items	−7.7	−1.8	4.2	−2.0	−5.6	−4.6	2.0
Exceptional financing	−	−	21.3	12.2	2.2	44.0	56.8
Liabilities constituting foreign authorities reserves	3.1	−.2	−1.1	8.3	4.8	−8.7	4.1
Total change in reserves	−45.4	25.2	−34.5	.1	−3.6	82.9	−10.2
Monetary gold	−.2	−.1	−	−	−.4	−.1	−.4
SDRs	.5	−.1	1.2	1.1	−.3	−.5	4.3
Reserve position in fund	−	−	−	−	−	−	−
Foreign exchange assets......................	−23.1	11.1	−19.7	−22.9	3.8	83.8	−56.5
Other claims................	−26.5	16.4	−21.4	28.7	−	−.3	.9
Use of fund credit	3.9	−2.1	5.4	−6.8	−6.7	−	41.5
Conversion rate: Guatadoran peso to SDR	8.3449	8.4344	8.5310	8.1120	8.2033	8.7969	11.9578

tional cuts (loin chops, crown roasts, etc.), individually wrapped, packed, and frozen in 50-pound cartons. The pork had to meet U.S. Department of Agriculture (USDA) standard specifications, and had to be accepted for import by the USDA with a duty of four cents per pound. CEP was to ship the pork to San Diego on transportation provided by USPPI no more than 15 days after processing. CEP would also be responsible for storing and loading the pork onto USPPI boats, paying any export taxes due to Guatador, and permitting USPPI inspectors to visit the facility periodically. CEP would be liable for any rejections by USDA and agreed to replace any rejected pork or to reimburse the purchase price of the pork (less transportation costs).

USPPI agreed to buy all CEP's pork produced and processed under USDA specification and import quotas for a price of eight cents less per pound than the price for Australian pork as quoted in the latest *Yellow Sheet of National Provisioner Daily Market Service.*

The contract was valid for five years and had an extension clause for three additional years. The contract could be terminated by either party at the end of the first five years. Production under the contract was to begin June 15, 1982.

In addition to the above contract, a secured loan agreement was signed between USPPI and Hernandez and Garcia wherein USPPI would loan Hernandez and Garcia $450,000 for five years at an interest rate of one percent above the prime on the unpaid balance as charged by the United Bank of Chicago. Hernandez and Garcia were to repay the loan in five installments. The first fifth, plus accrued interest, was due after the first full year, the second fifth after the second full year, and so forth until the entire loan and interest were paid by the end of the fifth year.

Hernandez and Garcia pledged 5,000 shares of CEP stock as collateral and agreed not to sell or issue new shares without prior approval of USPPI. They also agreed to carry a casualty insurance policy on the facility for at least $900,000 until the loan was repaid. If Hernandez or Garcia failed in any way to carry out the terms of the agreement, USPPI retained the right to call the loan due, keep the 5,000 shares of CEP stock, and/or exercise any other legal rights according to the laws of the state of Illinois, or the Republic of Guatador, or any international law.

USDA AND THE JUNTA

On January 15, 1983, a USDA newsletter announced that four pork packaging plants in Guatador, including the one at El Cuerton, had been removed from its list of approved exporting facilities because department officials had not been able to inspect the plants since October 1982 due to civil unrest. (In order for a foreign pork packaging plant to retain department certification for export to the U.S., it must be inspected by department inspectors every three months.) The newsletter went on to state that pork which had been processed and packed prior to January 15 would be subject to "normal" department inspection upon arrival at U.S. ports. No pork processed later than that date would be permitted in the U.S.

On December 28, 1982, a shipment of 8,750 cartons of pork from the El Cuerton plant (worth $700,000) that had been processed on December 20, 1982, was rejected by the USDA in San Diego for containing levels of DDT in excess of permitted tolerances. USPPI advised CEP of the problem by telex and were assured that the pork would be replaced. USPPI could have shipped the pork out of the U.S. and sold it overseas. However, this alternative was highly unattractive due to the double transportation costs; USPPI would exercise this option only as a last resort. On February 2, 1983, a junta overthrew the ruling Gomez family and all communication with Guatador was cut. USPPI did not hear anything else from CEP or about CEP until it was advised by the American Embassy in Los Bravas that CEP's facility at El Cuerton had been confiscated by the junta through Revolutionary Decrees Nos. 6, 29, and 56 in March 1983 (Appendix 1). Although CEP's owners, Hernandez and Garcia, had no direct relationship to the Gomez family, their plant was confiscated as a "preventative" measure.

USPPI advised Lloyds of London of the confiscation and submitted a claim to them for $389,730. At the same time in an effort to protect their investment and realizing that their chances of having the 8,750 cartons of pork replaced or the price refunded were slim, USPPI protested the method of sampling used in the rejection of the pork by the USDA and requested that the pork be retested. The USDA refused to split up the 8,750 cartons (which were still in San Diego at the AB Cold Storage Warehouse), and insisted that if one of the 150 randomly selected samples failed inspection, the entire shipment would fail inspection (Appendix 2).

In August 1983 the Department of Agriculture finally agreed to retest the pork in lots based on slaughter date rather than treat the entire 8,750 cartons as one lot. Of the 8,750 cartons retested, 6,830 (worth $546,400) were accepted leaving only 1,920 cartons still rejected.

Throughout this period, USPPI had repeatedly tried to contact CEP but to no avail. They were also unsuccessful in getting any response from the Compañia Nacional de la Puerco (CNP), the Guatadorian governmental agency in charge of the export of all pork commodities, about the rejected pork or concerning their request for adequate, prompt, and effective compensation as required by the 1953 Treaty of Friendship, Commerce and Navigation between the U.S. and Guatador for the equipment that had been confiscated. Intervention by the U.S. Embassy on their behalf also proved fruitless.

In November 1983 the fighting in Guatador had ceased and USDA inspectors were once again able to go in and inspect the facilities at El Cuerton. Processing was resumed on November 5, 1983, but the facility at El Cuerton, now under the direction of CNP, refused to sell pork under the terms of the contract to USPPI. Instead, they were selling it to another American pork packer—E & W Pork, Inc. (E&W). USPPI was advised by its local office in San Diego that E&W had bought 1,500 cartons of pork from CNP and was expecting it to arrive in San Diego from Guatador on November 15.

USPPI filed suit in San Diego against CEP and CNP and requested a temporary restraining order against E&W. USPPI's attorneys had hoped that the 1,500 cartons of pork that E&W had purchased from CNP could be used to help offset the pork that still needed replacing. The District Court in San Diego denied the request citing that no relationship had been established between CEP and CNP, and therefore E&W was the legal owner of the pork having purchased it from CNP.

In January 1984 USPPI discovered that 9,500 cartons of pork belonging to CNP was being held at a cold storage facility in Los Angeles and was to be loaded onto a freighter for shipment outside of the U.S. USPPI's attorneys filed another suit against CEP and CNP and requested that the 9,500 cartons be attached. This time they won. CNP had already had the cartons loaded onto the boat when the court ruled in favor of USPPI. Backed by U.S. marshals and a court order, Mr. Graham had the pork off-loaded and placed in another cold storage facility.

Within twelve hours of the court-approved action, representatives of CNP were in contact with USPPI protesting the attachment. They expressed a desire to meet immediately to discuss the matter. The Guatadorian Ministry of Justice also contacted USPPI and explained the procedures to be followed for the adjudication of their newly recognized claims against CEP. USPPI was told they would have to deal with the Ministry of Finance, the Ministry of Agriculture, and the Ministry of Foreign Trade.

A meeting was set for February 10 in Los Bravas with Mr. Graham leading the USPPI team. He felt positive about the forthcoming meeting—after all, CNP pork valued at more than the amount of their total claim was being held under a court order in the United States. The U.S. had been Guatador's largest trading partner prior to the junta, and the new government was finding that it was more beneficial to settle claims with U.S. companies than to risk losing U.S. foreign aid and future markets.

APPENDIX I · **Revolutionary Decrees**

Excerpt from Revolutionary Decree No. 6

"The Junta for the national reconstruction of the Republic of Guatador hereby decrees that:
—the attorney general is to immediately proceed with the intervention, requisition and confiscation of all properties of the Gomez family."

Excerpt from Revolutionary Decree No. 29

"The Junta for the national reconstruction of the Republic of Guatador hereby decrees that:
—the powers conferred on the attorney general by Decree No. 6 includes preventative intervention."

Excerpt from Revolutionary Decree No. 56

"The Junta for the national reconstruction of the Republic of Guatador hereby:
—establishes through the Foreign Trade Ministry, Compania Nacional de la Puerco (CNP), to oversee and handle all export of commodities, including pork."

An internal memorandum of the U.S. Department of Agriculture dated January 28, 1983, stated that 1.5 million pounds of pork produced and shipped prior to January 15, 1983, were being held in San Diego and that another 1.3 million pounds of pork were in transit. Due to the political unrest and the previous violations history of three of the four pork packaging facilities in Guatador, *all* pork from Guatador would be tested at a rate that "departs from our standard testing procedures." The basis for the new sampling procedures was based on the fact that during 1982, in 968 random samples of U.S. pork, ten had levels of DDT that exceeded the tolerance. Therefore, the U.S. violation rate was 0.48 percent of 1.8 percent with 95 percent confidence. Using the upper limit of 1.8 percent, 150 samples would be needed to detect a 1.8 percent violation rate with the same level of confidence. Therefore, 150 samples would be taken from each packaging plant.

COMPREHENSIVE CASES IN STRATEGY AND POLICY FORMULATION AND IMPLEMENTATION

The formulation and implementation of corporate strategy and policy is a highly complex process that can be studied through the use of comprehensive cases. Comprehensive cases for our purpose are those which require the analyst to consider more than one functional answer in a solution and to examine the interaction between fields.

This final section presents a series of such cases designed to challenge case analysts. No functional classification of the cases is provided. The cases may have a primary focus in a given functional area but still require consideration of a broad range of issues and functional fields. The cases are listed alphabetically and are not in any order of difficulty or scope. This lack of "guidance" is deliberate in order to assist the analyst in developing skill and competency in evaluating situations without any "leads" toward a desired solution. The use of comprehensive cases offers a wide range of approaches to problem analysis.

Case 7–1

Allied Chemical Corporation*

Allied Chemical is a large, diversified chemical manufacturing firm headquartered in Morristown, New Jersey, with manufacturing and processing plants located worldwide. Allied Chemical operations comprises of six business segments:

1. Energy Products and Services—production includes liquified petroleum gases (LPG), liquified natural gases (LNG), residue gas, crude oil, and ethylene.
2. Inorganic Chemicals—production includes resins, hydrochloric, hydrofluoric and nitric acids, soda and sodium by-products, and soda ash.
3. Organic Chemicals—production includes resins used in paints, enamels, and other coatings, and textiles.
4. Agricultural Chemicals—includes ammonia-based products used primarily for the manufacture and application of fertilizers.
5. Fibers—production includes nylon, rayon and other products.
6. Other—production includes coal and coke operations, automotive safety restraints, paving materials, and packaging films.

The year 1979 was one of strong contrasts in performance among Allied's business segments. The energy products and services operations made a significant gain in sales and earnings. The fibers operations also did well. However, these strong performances were offset by lower margins in many of the chemical product lines, substantially higher losses in coal and coke, and a significant loss in agricultural chemicals.

Allied's former chairman and chief executive officer, John T. Connor, retired under a mandatory retirement program on November 30, 1979. The question of management succession had been under active consideration of the nominating and review committee of the board of directors. The committee recommended E. L. Hennessey, Jr., as president and chief executive officer. In a discussion, Mr. Hennessey said:

> The economic environment in 1980 will be a challenging one, with much of American industry caught in a profit squeeze between rising costs and competitive and governmental pressures to keep prices down. To deal with the economic uncertainties, Allied has not only moved aggressively to correct loss situations, but has cut costs and trimmed spending plans wherever possible without damaging long-range growth prospects. And Allied continues to believe our growth will pay off in improved earnings for our stockholders over the next few years.

---

*This case was prepared by Sexton Adams, North Texas State University, Adelaide Griffin, Texas Woman's University, and Don Powell, North Texas State University, with the intention of providing a basis for class discussion rather than illustrating either effective or ineffective management of a business situation.

However, Allied, along with other large chemical firms, was having problems in maintaining performance, as shown in Exhibit 1.

Allied Chemical Profitability

Exhibit 1 — **(In millions of dollars, except per share amounts)**

	1979	1978	1977	1976
Sales and operating revenues	4,332	3,268	2,922	2,630
Net income	11	120	135	126
Net income per share common	0.20	4.25	4.93	4.52

Source: Allied Chemical Annual Report, 1980, Allied Chemical Corporation, Morristown, New Jersey.

While sales continued to increase, net income continued to decline. Allied, along with other large chemical firms, was facing hardships including foreign competition, foreign taxes, governmental regulations, and environmental costs that would only add to the cost-profit squeeze.

HISTORY

Allied Chemical Corporation was incorporated in New York on December 17, 1920, to consolidate the control of The Barrett Co., General Chemical Co., National Aniline and Chemical Co., Semet-Solvay Co., and the Solvay Process Co. It was called Allied Chemical and Dye Corporation and later changed to Allied Chemical Corporation in 1958. In 1979 Allied operated over 200 plants, research laboratories, mines, quarries, and other facilities throughout the United States, Canada, and Europe. Allied operated these in an effort to reduce shipping costs, as most chemicals were shipped in bulk quantities. It also operated research and development laboratories in close proximity to manufacturing facilities.

The corporation was expanding its oil and gas operations and, as of December 31, 1979, held leases or other interests in producing oil and gas properties in: (1) the United States, (2) British sector of the North Sea, (3) Canada, (4) Argentina, and (5) Indonesia. It also had interests in or rights to conduct exploratory activities on undeveloped acreage in: (1) the United States, (2) Canada, (3) British and West German sectors of the North Sea, (4) Brazil, (5) Italy, (6) Indonesia, (7) Australia, (8) Tunisia, (9) Bahrain, (10) Jamaica, and (11) onshore and offshore Spain.

ORGANIZATION

With the November 30, 1979, retirement of chairman and chief executive officer, John T. Connor, and the nomination and election of president and chief executive officer, E. L. Hennessey, Jr., much of the time and energy of the board of directors had been diverted away from the task of managing the firm. However, with the nomination and election process completed, the board would be able to direct all attention to managing the company. The company had a 15-member board of directors that included ten external members and five internal members. The board of directors as of December 31, 1979, was as follows:

E. L. Hennessey, Jr., chairman and chief executive officer.

John T. Connor, former chairman and chief executive officer.

Joseph B. Collinson, chairman and chief executive officer, Textrom, Inc., diversified manufacturing company.

John P. Fishwick, president and chief executive officer, Norfolk and Western Railway.

E. Burke Giblin, chairman of the executive committee, Warner-Lambert Company.

Robert T. Mulcahy, former president, Allied Chemical Corporation.

Robert T. Perkins, retired chairman of the executive committee, Metropolitan Life Insurance Company.

Robert R. Shinn, president and chief executive officer, Citibank and Citicorp.

Alexander B. Trowbridge, vice-chairman, Allied Chemical.

Brian D. Forrow, vice-president and general counsel, Allied Chemical.

Roger H. Morley, president, American Express Company.

Charles W. Nichols, private investor.

John D. Glover, chairman of the board, Cambridge Research Institute Inc., business consultants.

Helen S. Meyner, director, Prudential Insurance Co. of America.

Stanley P. Porter, retired partner of Arthur Young & Co.

In a discussion, President and Chief Executive Officer E. L. Hennessey, Jr., said:

> We plan to continue our strategy of redeveloping assets in those businesses we believe have the best future growth potential for Allied Chemical. We will continue to divest ourselves of operations which are marginal in profitability or which for other reasons do not fit into our long-range plans.

Allied Chemical was divided into seven divisions in the six major business segments. Each division was directed by a division president who was responsible for the day-to-day operations of his division as well as communicating with the board of directors. (Exhibit 2)

MARKETING

Allied had seen the oil and gas operations grow dramatically in sales and operating income as production continued to grow. The fibers business made

Allied Chemical Corporation
Partial Organizational Chart

Exhibit 2

```
                          ┌─────────────────────┐
                          │ Chairman of the Board│
                          └──────────┬──────────┘
                                     │
                          ┌─────────────────────┐
                          │  Board of Directors │
                          └──────────┬──────────┘
                                     │
                          ┌─────────────────────┐
                          │      President      │
                          └──────────┬──────────┘
                                     │
   ┌─────────────┬─────────────┬────┴────────┬──────────────┬──────────────┐
   │             │             │             │              │              │
┌──────────┐ ┌──────────┐ ┌──────────┐ ┌──────────────┐ ┌──────────┐ ┌──────────┐
│ Energy   │ │Inorganic │ │ Organic  │ │ Agricultural │ │Fibers and│ │  Other   │
│Products  │ │Chemicals │ │Chemicals │ │  Chemicals   │ │ Plastics │ │          │
│and       │ │          │ │          │ │              │ │          │ │          │
│Services  │ │          │ │          │ │              │ │          │ │          │
└────┬─────┘ └────┬─────┘ └────┬─────┘ └──────┬───────┘ └────┬─────┘ └────┬─────┘
     │            │            │              │              │            │
┌─────────┐ ┌──────────┐ ┌──────────┐ ┌──────────────┐ ┌──────────┐ ┌──────────┬──────────┐
│James E  │ │Frederick │ │A. Clark  │ │Garvin C.     │ │R. Thomas │ │Edgar S.  │Karl W.   │
│McCallum │ │L.McDonald│ │Johnson   │ │Matthison     │ │Cummings  │ │Brower    │Dickerman │
│President│ │President │ │President │ │President     │ │President │ │President │President │
│         │ │          │ │          │ │              │ │          │ │          │Semet-    │
│         │ │          │ │          │ │              │ │          │ │          │Solvay    │
│         │ │          │ │          │ │              │ │          │ │          │Div.      │
└────┬────┘ └────┬─────┘ └────┬─────┘ └──────┬───────┘ └────┬─────┘ └──────────┴────┬─────┘
     │           │            │              │              │                        │
┌─────────┐ ┌──────────┐ ┌──────────┐ ┌──────────────┐ ┌──────────┐           ┌──────────┐
│produces │ │produces  │ │produces  │ │produces      │ │produces  │           │coal &    │
│natural  │ │acids     │ │resins and│ │fertilizers   │ │nylon,yarn│           │coke      │
│gas and  │ │          │ │textiles  │ │and by-       │ │and rayon │           │operations│
│crude oil│ │          │ │          │ │products      │ │          │           │paving    │
│         │ │          │ │          │ │              │ │          │           │materials │
└─────────┘ └──────────┘ └──────────┘ └──────────────┘ └──────────┘           └──────────┘
```

significant gains in sales and earnings as 1979 sales were essentially at capacity, and work was started to increase capacity at two major production facilities. However, earnings of many of Allied's chemical businesses suffered because of industry overcapacity, which kept processing below levels needed to cover rising production and overhead costs (Exhibit 3).

Exhibit 3

Allied Chemical Corporation
Net Sales and Income by Products Group
(In millions of dollars)

	1979		1978		1977		1976	
	Total Sales	Operating Income	Total Sales	Operating Income	Total Sales	Operating Income	Total Sales	Operating Income
Energy products and services	1,369	392	948	307	676	193	461	31
Inorganic chemicals ...	775	22	657	66	623	80	573	91
Organic chemicals	725	6	537	15	529	31	573	63
Agricultural chemicals	155	—	162	(31)	180	—	185	38
Fibers and plastics ...	940	120	497	85	441	63	380	60
Other	368	24	467	(41)	474	(37)	458	2
Total	4,332	564	3,268	401	2,923	330	2,630	285

Source: Allied Chemical Corporation Annual Report, 1979.

CHEMICAL INDUSTRY OUTLOOK

Tightening supply conditions sparked by the Iranian oil curtailment created unusually strong demand for U.S. manufactured petrochemicals, plastics, fibers, and other products through much of 1979. The demand would lead to increased profits which would provide enough momentum to allow chemical firms to report a creditable profit performance for 1980. Sales of chemicals and allied products were forecast to rise to $145 billion in 1979, up from $130 billion in 1978, and with estimated sales of $160 billion in 1980 (Exhibit 4).

However, major challenges and opportunities faced the chemical industry as it faced a new decade. Mr. Hennessey, Jr., chief executive officer of Allied Chemical Corporation, believed the industry had some major concerns, including:

> ... (1) the tendency for state-controlled nations to subsidize their chemical industries and seek markets for their output at any price, (2) the looming

Exhibit 4

Chemical Industry Sales
(In billions of dollars)

Year	Industry Sales	Allied Chemical Sales	Allied's Percent of Industry Sales
1969	48.3	1.316	2.73
1970	49.3	1.248	2.53
1971	51.9	1.325	2.55
1972	57.4	1.501	2.61
1973	65.0	1.664	2.56
1974	83.7	2.215	2.65
1975	89.7	2.333	2.60
1976	104.0	2.629	2.53
1977	118.1	2.922	2.48
1978	130.0	3.268	2.51
1979	145.0	4.332	2.99
1980 (est.)	160.0	5.4	3.4

Source: "Chemicals, Current Analysis," *Standard & Poor's Industry Surveys,* July 3, 1980.

development of a petrochemical industry by OPEC nations in the second half of the decade and the effect this will have on U.S. companies and the world markets, and (3) the ongoing takeover of U.S. companies by foreigners through purchases of outstanding stock.

CHEMICAL INDUSTRY PROFITS

"Earnings for most of the large chemical firms should be up about three percent in 1980, and miscellaneous chemicals should have an earnings increase of about five percent," according to John Baker of Dow Chemical. In a conversation, Mr. E. L. Hennessey, Jr., of Allied Chemical said:

With competition increasing domestically and with more firms trying to capture a larger share of the export market before it shrinks, a moderation or possibly a reversal of recent price increases will be necessary. Prices for all chemicals and related products have risen at a fifteen percent annual rate compared to twenty percent for the previous year. On the other hand, manufacturers are faced with an unrelenting climb in raw material costs, energy, and labor costs which should cause profits to decline for the industry. For 1979, the return on sales for the chemical industry was 6.8 percent and should be about 6.3 percent in 1980, and slower price increases should be seen as demand will remain soft through 1980.

CHEMICAL INDUSTRY PRODUCTION

An early projection of 1980 domestic production of chemicals and related products (on a dollar-value basis) called for stable growth of about 12 percent compared to the 1973-1978 average of 15 percent. The area most likely to show gains was industrial chemicals, aided by strong demand from foreign countries arising from lower cost for U.S. manufacturers. Other sectors that were expected to do better than average were cosmetics, pharmaceuticals, and industrial inorganic chemicals.

RESEARCH AND DEVELOPMENT

In the 1960s, U.S. industry spent close to three percent of sales for research and development, but spent only 1.87 percent in 1978. A substantial portion of the decline in those years may be attributable to the 1974 tax code revision, which redefined research and development outlays. Generally, research and development costs were limited to those expenses that involved the technological aspects of product and process development and that extended knowledge of physical sciences useful in commercial production. Specifically excluded were costs pertaining to routine product improvement, market research, test marketing, seasonal style changes, quality control, and engineering follow-through in production. Also excluded were legal costs related to patents and costs associated with their sale or development outlays as shown in Exhibit 5.

Exhibit 5

**Research and Development Outlays
(as a percentage of total sales)**

	1979	1978
Office equipment	5.70	5.65
Health care	4.25	4.30
Leisure time	4.20	4.50
Aerospace	2.75	2.70
Automobile	2.60	2.50
Electronics	2.55	2.45
Chemicals	2.45	2.55
Machinery	1.90	2.05
Rubber fabricating	1.65	1.70
Home furnishings	1.60	1.70
Allied Chemical Corp.	1.87	1.77
Composite average (all industries)	1.83	1.87

Source: "R & D Costs," *Standard & Poor's Industry Surveys,* September 6, 1980.

FINANCIAL

According to *Chemical Week* magazine, earnings of the six leading chemical companies were expected to have flat-to-moderate growth in 1980, after an 11 percent increase in 1979, and an 18 percent increase in 1978. The chemical industry enjoyed strong market conditions in 1979, but these conditions were expected to weaken in 1980 as the economy slumped. Excess capacity hampered the implementation of adequate price relief and squeezed profit margins. The tight supply conditions that prevailed in 1979 created a seller's market and enabled producers to institute long-awaited price increases.

Capital spending was expected to increase 13 percent in 1980, which would only keep up with the inflation rate at that time. Expenditures for investments in new plants and equipment were expected to remain under ten percent for the third year in succession. A review of industry capital spending as a percent of sales is presented in Exhibit 6.

Exhibit 6

Capital Spending as a Percent of Sales

Year	Percent
1969	10.9
1970	11.6
1971	10.6
1972	8.9
1973	9.9
1974	11.9
1975	12.8
1976	12.7
1977	11.6
1978	9.8
1979	9.8
1980 (Projected)	13.0

Source: "Chemicals, Current Analysis," *Standard & Poor's Industry Surveys,* September 6, 1980.

In mid-1979 the Treasury Department announced that chemical companies would be allowed to reduce to seven-and-one-half years (from nine years) the shortest period over which chemical companies could depreciate their equipment. The new rules encouraged greater spending for new plant expansion.

Industry profitability, measured as a return on stockholder's equity, remained strong at approximately 13 percent. The dividend pay-out ratio was expected to rise in the next few years due to an endless quest for growth capital. It appeared that industry executives must continue to pay out an increasing percentage of earnings as dividends in order to obtain growth capital.

An added capital expense for the chemical industry would be in the area of environmental protection. Additional stringent laws and regulations continued to drive environmental costs upward. This was evidenced in environmental spending at Allied Chemical as shown in Exhibit 7.

ENVIRONMENTAL POLLUTION AND OTHER LEGAL DIFFICULTIES

Kepone

Kepone is a chlorinated organic compound similar to DDT. Allied Chemical produced the pesticide from 1966 to 1973 at its Hopewell, Virginia, chemi-

Exhibit 7

Allied Chemical Corporation
Environmental Costs (In millions of dollars)

Year	Expense	Percentage of Sales
1975	27	1.15
1976	29	1.10
1977	35	1.20
1978	72	2.20
1979	101	3.10

Source: Allied Chemical Corporation Annual Report, 1980.

cal plant. In 1973 Virgil Hundtofte and William Moore, former employees of Allied, formed Life Science Products Company. Life Science Products Company had a total process contract with Allied to produce Kepone solely for Allied until it was closed on July 24, 1975, by the Virginia Department of Health. Seventy of the plant's 150 employees showed symptoms of Kepone poisoning including tremors, slurring of speech, chest and joint pains. Disposal of Kepone by Allied, followed by Life Science Products Company, contaminated a large portion of the James River. According to the U.S. Attorney's Office at Richmond, Allied and Life Science actually dumped Kepone into the river. In December of 1975 the river was closed to fishing because of the poison being traced to fish caught from the James.

On October 6, 1976, Federal Judge Robert R. Merhige, Jr. fined Allied Chemical Corporation $13,375,000 for its part in polluting the James River with Kepone. Judge Merhige was quoted as saying, "I hope that the size of the fine will deter employees of other companies from polluting the environment." Besides the employees of Life Science suffering from various nerve disorders, the fishermen on the James lost their means to a livelihood by authorities banning the sale of fish caught from the James. Claims of the employees and the fishermen totaled around $200 million in civil suits against Allied. Life Science Products was imposed a fine of $3.8 million. William Moore and Virgil Hundtofte were fined $25,000 each. After the pronounced sentence, Allied's John T. Connor, who was chairman at the time, stated, "We are pleased that the court has found Allied Chemical not guilty of charges of aiding and abetting Life Science Products Company and conspiring with it to break the law." However, Allied pleaded nolo contendere to 940 counts of pumping chemicals into the river. Of the 940 counts, 144 were dismissed against Allied. Connor pointed out that only 312 of the counts involved Kepone and 628 covered two low toxic, biodegradable chemicals, TAIC and THEIC.

Allied was not only being held responsible for polluting the James River by toxic chemicals, but it was held responsible for dredging about 100 miles of the James. Approximately 100 miles of the James was closed to commercial fishing by state health authorities. The estimated cost to Allied of dredging the

James was about half a billion dollars. Problems existed after dredging the James, such as what to do with the contaminated soil containing Kepone.

Allied had run into problems with solutions to the disposal of the contaminated soil. Allied was planning to dispose of around 100,000 pounds of soil and equipment contaminated with Kepone by burying it in a 16-story deep missile silo in Idaho. However, the state of Idaho rejected the idea of burying the soil in the abandoned silo near Boise. Burning the Kepone stored in barrels turned out to be a nonworkable solution because of the dangerous gases that would be released into the atmosphere. One of the gases released by burning Kepone was a deadly type of gas similar to arsenic gas fumes. The negative results of the burning had put a damper on Allied's plan of using a mobile incinerator for use in disposing of contaminated material in Hopewell. Plans of continued action for disposing of the Kepone contaminated by Allied included finding locations where the material could be safely buried and disposing of the liquid material by chemical type reactions which would leave a safe residue.

Allied set up an original fund of $8 million to help problems caused by its Hopewell, Virginia, Kepone-making operations. The Virginia Environmental Endowment of $8 million, according to Allied, was to "alleviate the effects of Kepone on the environment and on those whose livelihoods have been impaired by it." The endowment was a separate independent organization whose board of directors was appointed by Judge Robert R. Merhige, Jr. The endowment's board would, according to Allied, "fund scientific research projects to implement remedial efforts and other scientific programs and measures (including financial and economic assistance in the form of loans or such) as the board of directors in its sole discretion shall deem appropriate." Allied conceded that the net financial drain to the corporation would probably be around $4 million rather than $8 million because the endowment was considered a charitable contribution. Judge Merhige pointed out, however, that the endowment did not affect civil suits against Allied by former plant workers claiming injury from unsafe plant conditions at Hopewell or civil suits against Allied by James River watermen for loss of income due to the closing of the river to all commercial fishing. Allied hoped that by creating the endowment, it could express its sincerity on alleviating problems caused by Kepone pollution.

Before leaving the discussion of the Kepone related circumstances, it should be pointed out that in the court proceeding, Allied Chemical experts stated that Environmental Protection Agency levels for action of Kepone pollution could quadruple without changing the safety factor recommended by the Environmental Protection Agency's own experts. Allied Chemical experts also suggested that raising the action level for fish from 0.1 parts per million to at least 0.4 parts per million would be more realistic and consistent with data and would alleviate some of the economic hardship caused by "unnecessarily severe levels." Allied Chemical experts also claimed that the action level for Kepone had been set at a level far more severe than other chemicals which were of far greater potential danger to the environment.

Armco Suit

Allied supplied blast furnace coke and cokeoven gas to Armco's steel production plant at Ashland, Kentucky. Armco filed a suit against Allied for $32 million for Allied's failure to deliver coke and cokeoven gas as specified in a contract to Armco's plant. The suit also asked for $185 million for damages that would occur through 1982. Allied denied breach of contract because of certain contingencies within the contract. These contingencies relieved performance by either party because of equipment failures, labor problems, and failure of supply materials. Allied also claimed that Armco caused operational problems at Allied's Ashland plant by supplying coal of inferior quality. All of Allied's output went to Armco; likewise, Armco furnished all of the coal used by Allied. Coke battery damage and excessive demurrage was claimed against Armco by Allied as a result of the inferior coal. After court proceedings, lasting most of 1979, Allied was found guilty of charges leveled by Armco. Allied was held responsible to Armco for an initial $34 million but not long-term damages amounting to $185 million from 1978 through 1980. Allied appealed the verdict; however, the appeal was not successful as other court proceedings arrived at the same verdict. Allied paid the fine and suspended coke business transactions involved with Armco.

ALLIED OPERATIONAL STRATEGIES

Plant Modifications

Semet-Solvay was a division of Allied that managed the company's coal and coke operation. In 1977 Allied spent $45 million to rehabilitate a foundry coke plant in Detroit, Michigan. The division's president said, "Rehabilitation of our foundry coke battery in Detroit will serve not only to increase the facility's capacity but also should serve to end concerns among area residents that the plant is a source of environmental contamination." The project brought the screening capacity to 700,000 tons annually. Not only did this action by Allied improve environmental conditions, it also included improvements in coal preheating, coal preparation, and by-product recovery from operations. Allied was the largest producer of coke in the United States. Operations by Allied's management to revitalize older plants in terms of environmental safety and energy savings was an attempted strategy to meet environmental expectations along with decreasing long-run cost of operations.

Energy Endeavors

Allied's first phase of oil and gas exploration development in the North Sea was Piper Field during 1976. Allied owned 20 percent interest. This 20 percent cost to Allied was $250 million. John T. Connor, Allied Chemical's former chairman said, "Allied's commitment to participate heavily in the development of oil and gas in the North Sea was made over five years ago and has had a high priority among its capital spending programs and strategy planning efforts." Allied also owned 20 percent interest in the Claymore Field located in the North Sea. In late 1980 production of 250,000 barrels per day from the Piper Field and 170,000 barrels of oil from the Claymore Field would reach peak levels for both fields. Mr. Connor stated, "When the two fields reach peak production levels, Allied Chemical will experience substantially increased cash flows. In addition, the flow of crude will provide a raw material backup for Allied's expanding petrochemicals-based operations." The United Kingdom's energy corporation, British National Oil Corporation, had the option to buy up to 51 percent of the crude oil and natural gas derived from the Piper and Claymore Fields. Connor pointed out that this arrangement protected the legitimate interest of the United Kingdom. Allied's participation in the North Sea represented the company's largest single endeavor among its oil and gas operations.

Although the North Sea ventures were the largest for Allied in gas and oil, other ventures such as the Salou field in the Mediterranean Sea off the coast of Tarragona, Spain, held significant promise of 15 million barrels. Allied's Union Texas/Espana division was involved not only in the Salou field off Spain but also areas around the Bay of Biscay north of Spain. In Indonesia, Allied Chemical and its partners had natural gas production wells in the Bodak Field in East Kalimantan. Allied's position and strategy involving energy could best be summarized by Mr. Connor's statement, "Clearly, the cash flows derived from the company's participation in these ventures will be most impressive. Moreover, they serve to vindicate a long-term business strategy of our corporation."

Research and Development in Solar Energy

Allied's shift in strategy to all energy fields could be expressed by research and development into the area of solar energy. Allied's research and development division invented a photochemical diode device which simplified the conversion of sunlight energy into chemical energy. This discovery had been a leading force in the solar energy development and utilization field. The process used small simple wafers that created specific chemical reactions when suspended in a chemical liquid and exposed to sunlight. Allied's Materials Research Center actively pursued practical goals of development for the diode structures. These actions by the Material Research Center developed into high efficiencies for light energy conversion for the solar energy field along with long-term stabilities and low cost to manufacture units for the solar energy conversion industry. Likewise, Allied benefited from the low cost of manufacture and long-term stability of sales of diodes as many energy experts looked to energy from solar conversion for future needs.

Divestments

As shown previously, Allied Chemical's long-term strategies involved concentrating on improving and expanding its energy aspects of business. For the last five years, Allied's strategy had been to divest itself of the unprofitable aspects of its business. For example, in 1977 Allied Chemical sold its organic pigments to Harmon Colors Corporation. The sale included all manufacturing facilities, laboratories, and sales offices which were staffed by approximately 325 employees. By this type of divesture, Allied completely disengaged itself from the organic pigments business. The organic pigments area of the business had turned out to be unprofitable from 1974 to 1977. Allied's divestment of unprofitable business segments from 1977, along with energy expansion, reversed a declining shift in earnings per share.

By divestment and expansion of its participation in oil and gas, Allied's profits from continuing operations more than tripled in 1980 as compared to 1979. Other chemical firms showed a significant drop in earnings as can be seen from Exhibit 8.

Exhibit 8   **Third Quarter Net Income**

| | 1980 | | 1979 | | |
	Millions of Dollars	**Per Share**	**Millions of Dollars**	**Per Share**	**Percent Change**
Allied	$ 66.2	$1.80	$(123.7)	$(4.35)	
Celanese	$ 21	$1.43	$ 37.	$ 2.47	−43
Dow	$160.5	$ .88	$ 198.4	$ 1.09	−19
Rohm & Haas	$ 22.6	$1.75	$ 29.2	$ 2.26	−14

Source: Wall Street Journal, October 17, 1980.

The $123.7 million dollar loss of Allied in the third quarter of 1979 was a net loss after nonrecurring, after-tax charges of $163.2 million to cover losses connected with the divestiture of several operations and other one-time costs.

All four companies had small sales increases for the third quarter with Allied having the largest of six percent from $1.25 billion to $1.32 billion. Celanese's sales rose one percent from $778 million to $785 million as Dow's sales increased four percent from $2.43 billion to $2.52 billion. Rohm and Haas's sales were up three percent from $391.9 million to $403.8 million. As is depicted in the Exhibit 9, except for Allied, the net income of all three chemical companies first nine months of 1980, as compared to 1979, had a negative change.

Exhibit 9   **Nine Months Net Income**

| | 1980 | | 1979 | | |
	Millions of Dollars	**Per Share**	**Millions of Dollars**	**Per Share**	**Percent Change**
Allied	$207.5	$5.88	$ (56.6)	$(2.00)	
Celanese	$ 82	$5.51	$114	$ 7.67	−28
Dow	$562.2	$3.09	$589.6	$ 3.25	− 5
Rohm & Haas	$ 76.7	$5.95	$ 84.6	$ 6.56	− 9.3

Source: Wall Street Journal, October 17, 1980.

Rohm and Haas chairman, Vincent L. Gregory, Jr., attributed the company's nine-month drop in earnings to a drop in volume of shipments. G. J. Williams, Dow's financial vice president, said, "The third quarter was a definite turnaround in the U.S. in virtually all parts of the economy." However, Williams said that business activity outside the U.S., particularly key European markets, had slowed drastically therefore causing Rohm and Haas and Dow to reduce operations in order to reduce inventory. All companies emphasized a drastic decline in demand for chemicals with an improvement in fibers demand. As an example of industry conditions, Celanese fiber profits were up 36 percent. However, profits from the chemicals business were down 62 percent with profits from plastics and specialties off 70 percent. Edward L. Hennessey, Jr., Allied's current president and chief executive officer, attributed Allied's higher earnings to sales in fibers and the oil and gas industry. Hennessey expressed his opinion that problems faced in the chemical industry because of poor economic conditions demonstrated the need for large corporations such as Allied to diversify and not depend on one specific industry for survival. Hennessey said that the reason for chemical and plastic sales decline was due to poor economic conditions worldwide and especially the auto industry recession. Hennessey stated that the most important aspect of the third quarter results for Allied was that 90 percent of Allied's profit from operations came from its oil and gas enterprises. He also pointed out the direct link of profitability to oil and gas operations through Allied's third quarter reports. Allied's oil and gas endeavors accounted for 32 percent of sales while chemicals accounted for 24 percent. However, 90 percent of Allied's third quarter operation profits was from oil and gas.

Future Operations.   Allied Chemical had been in a state of transformation for five years (Exhibits 10-14). This transformation had involved divestiture of certain operations and a strategy of concentrating in areas of oil and gas. In the third quarter of 1980, Allied's financial strength was improving on the background of its oil and gas operations. The move to divest of unprofitable businesses and acquire business strength in oil and gas was turning out to be the successful corporate strategy for Allied. Likewise, W. R. Grace was a chemical company that reported a third quarter 1980 net income of $68 million. This was up from $44.5 million during three quarters of 1979. John Spelling, Grace's chief financial officer, explained that Grace's oil and gas operations and its oil field service business helped push the natural resources segment earnings up 15 percent in the quarter from the same time in 1979. As a result of the U.S. auto industry's decline in production, the demand for chemicals and plastics was drastically reduced. Likewise, because of a slowdown in the economy of the U.S. along with a slowdown of key European markets, the chemical industries demand had become a great deal less.

Chemical companies had also faced costly capital expenditures to upgrade plants to meet environmental protection agency requirements. For example, Allied was bearing the cost of clean-up and lawsuits stemming from Kepone pollution and the resulting negative public relations. Chemical companies faced difficult times with capital intensive plants producing below capacity because of falling demand for chemicals. Existence of slowing down economies in the U.S. and foreign vital markets did not show a promising increase in demand for chemicals. However, the oil and gas industry would continue to be of prime importance with the energy crisis that faced the world.

Exhibit 10

**Allied Chemical Corporation
Financial Report**

	1979	1978	1977	1976	1975	1974
Net sales (billions)...................................	4.33	3.27	2.92	2.63	2.33	2.22
Net income (millions)................................	11	120	135	117	116	144
Net income (as a percent of sales)	0.25	3.7	4.6	4.4	5.0	6.5
Cash dividend per share	2.00	1.85	1.80	1.80	1.80	1.53
Property, plant, and equipment additions (in millions)	475	502	465	352	314	306
Rate of return on Stockholders' equity (percent)	0.86	9.7	11.8	11.2	11.6	15.8
Rate of return on total capital........................	0.64	7.2	8.4	8.0	8.6	10.8

Source: Allied's 1979 annual financial statement.

Exhibit 11

**Allied Chemical Corporation
Geographical Operations (In millions of dollars)**

	Year	United States	Canada and Europe	Other	Total
Net sales	1979	3,306	712	314	4,332
	1978	2,606	500	162	3,268
	1977	2,530	351	.42	2,923
Net income	1979	(100)	75	36	11
	1978	7	76	37	120
	1977	54	59	22	135
Assets	1979	3,062	825	322	4,209
	1978	2,544	629	164	3,228
	1977	2,430	544	96	2,872

Source: Allied's 1979 annual financial statement.

Allied Chemical Corporation
Consolidated Earning Statement (Year ending December 31)
(In millions of dollars, except times interest earned and earning per share)

Exhibit 12

Year	Sales and Operating Revenue	Operating Income	Depreciation, Amortization, and Depletion	Income Taxes	Fixed Charges	Times Interest Earned	Net Income	Earnings per Share	Dividends per Share
1970	1,249	191	120	14	28	2.36	43	1.56	1.00
1971	1,326	207	119	19	29	2.59	52	1.88	1.10
1972	1,500	231	117	31	30	3.06	65	2.38	1.20
1973	1,665	271	109	54	29	4.30	95	22.9	1.29
1974	2,216	363	115	82	28	6.32	144	3.26	1.53
1975	2,333	352	129	73	40	3.88	116	5.17	1.80
1976	2,630	368	136	63	45	3.80	126	4.52	1.80
1977	2,923	446	164	104	55	3.50	135	4.93	1.80
1978	3,268	534	203	148	69	2.75	120	4.25	1.85
1979	4,332	921	225	385	102	2.73	.11	0.20	2.00

Source: Allied's 1979 annual financial statement.

Exhibit 13

Allied Chemical Corporation
Financial and Operating Data

	1979	1978	1977	1976	1975	1974	1973	1972
Current assets/current liabilities	1.21	1.43	1.69	1.96	2.14	1.93	2.43	2.81
Percent cash and securities to current assets	7.79	7.22	5.22	7.53	12.24	11.34	19.67	17.33
Percent inventory to current assets	37.28	36.02	39.53	44.83	43.28	44.86	35.52	34.23
Capitalization:								
Percent long-term debt	43.67	36.81	33.63	32.26	32.66	26.78	29.09	32.25
Percent common stock and equity	56.33	63.19	66.37	67.74	67.34	73.22	70.91	62.75
Sales/inventory	7.19	9.79	9.03	7.89	7.68	7.70	7.34	7.31
Sales/receivables	5.73	6.56	6.71	7.74	7.86	8.21	6.06	5.32
Percent net income to total assets	0.26	3.72	4.71	4.64	4.97	6.97	4.83	3.62

Allied Chemical Corporation
Comparative Consolidated Balance Sheet, As of December 31
(In thousands of dollars)

Exhibit 14

ASSETS	1978	1977	1976	1975	1974	1973	1972
Cash	21,260	11,248	22,262	26,858	17,293	20,033	29,856
Short term secur. & time deposits	45,646	31,472	33,701	59,121	55,497	105,604	74,034
Accts. & notes receiv., net	498,209	435,759	339,838	296,991	269,838	274,537	281,990
Inventories	333,701	323,615	333,247	303,941	287,919	226,855	205,194
Other current assets	27,678	16,589	14,321	15,376	11,298	11,654	8,457
Total current assets	926,494	818,683	743,369	702,287	641,845	638,683	599,531
Marketable securities, cost	3,096	3,396	3,538	3,640	3,728	3,861	3,956
Investments & advances, cost	165,316	134,649	128,612	133,263	113,284	88,881	80,511
Property, plant & equipment cost	3,739,889	3,450,819	3,129,926	2,901,046	2,703,504	2,500,660	2,381,385
Less: Res. for depreciation, etc.	1,698,480	1,641,446	1,587,589	1,534,056	1,494,220	1,455,727	1,391,037
Net property account	2,041,409	1,809,373	1,542,337	1,366,990	1,209,284	1,044,933	990,348
Goodwill, patents, licenses & def. chgs.	91,634	106,061	109,703	122,026	91,903	85,034	84,051
Total	3,227,949	2,872,162	2,527,559	2,328,206	2,060,044	1,861,392	1,758,397
LIABILITIES							
Accounts payable & accr. liab.	438,770	388,643	313,214	266,919	254,143	218,589	182,365
Notes & loans payable	47,995	33,176	32,272	25,047	12,411	16,087	8,965
Taxes accrued	144,738	52,963	22,051	24,190	53,148	28,067	22,410
Interest accrued	15,328	10,662	11,309	10,814	7,818	—	—
Long-term debt due in one year	—	—	—	—	4,726	—	—
Total current liabilities	646,831	485,444	378,846	326,970	332,246	262,743	213,740

Long-term debt	741,008	606,612	527,615	503,523	354,071	354,228	383,856
Res. for pensions & contingencies	67,549	70,292	71,109	48,787	61,887	74,086	84,900
Deferred income	46,386	37,369	37,721	26,994	27,894	18,985	19,086
Deferred income tax	247,852	252,197	200,596	170,365	130,544	106,914	91,170
Cap. lease obligations	205,999	222,939	203,672	213,366	184,977	180,860	159,178
Common stock (par $9)	375,464	365,932	364,305	364,305	364,305	364,305	364,305
Retained earnings	910,450	846,804	763,508	696,692	631,159	530,117	475,852
Total stockholders' equity	1,285,914	1,212,736	1,127,813	1,060,997	995,464	894,422	840,137
Less: Treasury stock	13,590	15,427	19,813	22,796	27,039	30,846	33,690
Net stockholders' equity	1,272,324	1,197,309	1,108,000	1,038,201	968,425	863,576	806,467
Total	3,227,949	2,872,162	2,527,559	2,328,206	2,060,044	1,861,392	1,758,397
Net current assets	279,663	333,239	364,523	375,317	309,599	375,940	385,791
PROPERTY ACCOUNT— ANALYSIS							
Additions at cost	502,040	464,638	351,613	313,319	302,217	193,812	147,462
Retirements or sales	212,966	143,749	122,733	116,099	101,116	74,535	113,512
Other additions	—	—	—	322	6,641	—	—
DEPR. & DEPL. RES.— ANALYSIS							
Additions chgd. to income	202,975	164,307	145,049	136,899	123,276	116,469	123,993
Retire renewals chgd. to res.	145,941	110,450	91,516	97,013	84,783	51,779	76,411
Other additions	—	—	—	—	1,685	—	—
Other deductions	—	—	—	—	—	16,666	16,947

Source: Taken from reports to Securities and Exchange Commission.

Case 7–2

Bell Helicopter Textron*

INTRODUCTION

The ten o'clock news began with an exciting story about a high rise fire in Las Vegas. The camera zoomed in so close you could see the fright on the faces of the panicking people. You may have thought to yourself "How can they possibly get such close-up pictures of the people on the top of a burning high rise?" Better yet, how could they get the people out of the rooms and down to safety? Many were rescued from the roof of the hotel when lifted off by helicopter. Perhaps those rescued owed their lives to Bell Helicopter Textron's JetRanger rescue unit manufactured by the Fort Worth, Texas, based company.

Bell Helicopter Textron was the largest division of the Textron conglomerate. The corporation was built on the principle of balanced corporate diversification and quality products by adhering to three important priorities: people development, internal profit growth, and new initiatives. This dedication to growth and initiation had led to the creation of five major operating groups within the company: aerospace, consumer, industrial, metal products, and creative capital. Each operating division was provided with the capital and planning assistance to meet demonstrated needs for growth. This business structure in Textron combined the enthusiasm and quick response of moderate-sized enterprises with the planning and financial resources of a large corporation.

Bell Helicopter Textron produced and sold not only the commercial models seen in news stories or at corporate headquarters, but they also were one of the largest suppliers of military aircraft. Expansion of their main facilities in Fort Worth to over three million square feet was an indication the company expected further growth in sales in the future.

CORPORATE HISTORY

Bell Aircraft Corporation was founded on July 10, 1935, in Buffalo, New York, by the late Lawrence D. Bell. However, it was not until 1941 that work first began on the helicopter. Bell's first attempt at designing and developing a

*This case was prepared by Adelaide Griffin, Texas Woman's University, and Sexton Adams and Don Powell, North Texas State University, with the intention of providing a basis for class discussion rather than illustrating either effective or ineffective management of a business situation.

helicopter received rapid recognition from the public and the government. In fact it only took five years from the start of the first unit until the development of the first production airship for the U.S. Army on December 31, 1946. The overwhelming acceptance and demand by the Army and exciting stories of marooned shipwreck victim rescues by helicopters provided tremendous growth and development for Bell. The growth continued with the support of new army contracts and the opening of navy contracts until Bell rolled out the 1000th unit in April, 1953.

Bell continued this growth and attracted the attention of Textron, Inc. of Providence, Rhode Island, in 1960 which led to the purchase of Bell. Under the control of Textron, Bell continued its tremendous growth. The company consistently added both commercial and military units to its product line that set the standards for the industry.

This growth and standard of excellence had continued into the 1980s. February 1, 1980, marked the introduction of the Model 222. This unit had been specifically designed with the offshore oil market in mind. It combined a large seating capacity with high speeds to meet this specialized need.

The company's steady growth in the commercial market had given the earnings picture a needed boost. Bell delivered a record 783 commercial helicopters in 1980 which amounted to a 30 percent increase over 1979.[1] A former employee of Bell indicated that Bell had placed increased emphasis on the commercial market and felt that this area of sales would become the most important in the future.

MANAGEMENT

Corporate management at Bell had been under constant change during the period covering 1975 to 1981.[2] This volatility in the management ranks had led to key personnel losses to many of Bell's competitors. James F. Atkins, however, had held the position of president since 1972.[3] He had been very active in the dynamic growth of Bell and its expansion into international sales markets. Mr. Atkins joined Bell in 1940 when he made the move to Fort Worth to become controller of Bell's new helicopter division.

Following Textron's purchase of Bell in 1960, Atkins became executive vice president. (See Exhibit 1 for organizational chart.) He had played an active role in the helicopter industry by holding positions in the National Aeronautic Association, American Helicopter Association of America, and the American Institute of Aeronautics and Astronautics. He served on the board of directors of Southern Methodist University Foundation for Science and Engineering and as a director of First National Bank of Fort Worth.

The second man in command at Bell was appointed executive vice president in March, 1981. Jack Horner joined Bell in 1974 as vice president-operations and was promoted to senior vice president in 1977. Horner was a graduate of Yale University with a B.S. in Industrial Administration. His helicopter industry experience covered a quarter of a century.

Horner was commissioned a lieutenant in the U.S. Marines in 1951. He won four air medals in Korea as an infantry officer and aerial observer. After

Exhibit 1

Bell Helicopter Textron Organizational Chart

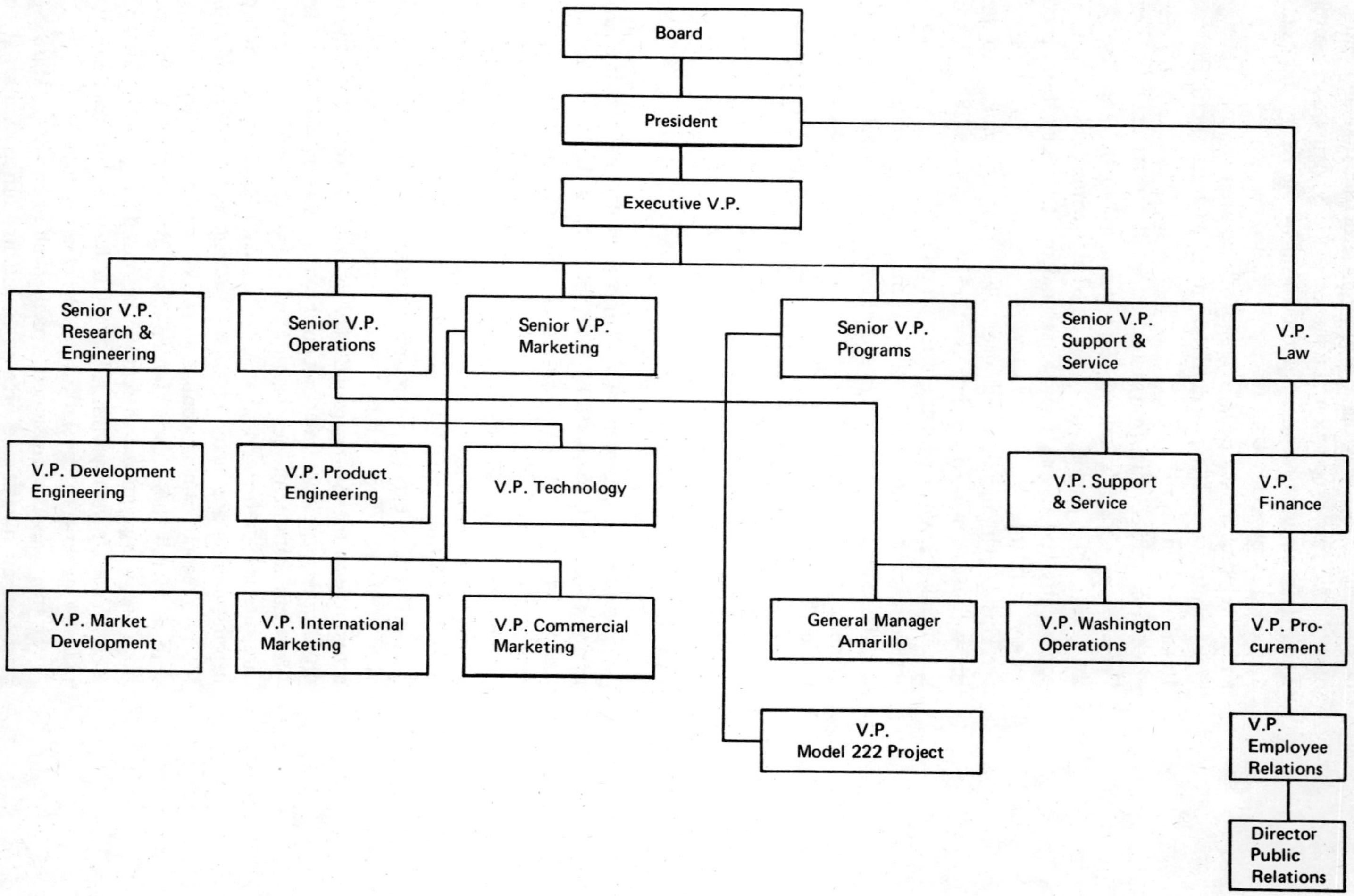

his release from active duty with the rank of Captain in 1956, he completed pilot training in both helicopter and fixed wing.

Promoted to fill the void left by Horner as senior vice president-marketing was Dwayne K. Jose. Mr. Atkins and Mr. Jose had total responsibility for the company's worldwide marketing programs, including those in the United States and foreign governments and all commercial business.

"Dwayne brings to his new position 21 years of marketing experience with Bell, both in commercial and international marketplaces," said Atkins at a company meeting. "His greatest accomplishment has been in building the U.S. commercial market for Bell and our industry."[4]

Jose had joined Bell in 1960 as commercial sales manager. He held a B.S. degree from Iowa State College.

Third in line at Bell was Mr. Robert R. Lynn. Mr. Lynn was senior vice president-research and engineering. He began his career with the organization in 1950 at Bell Aircraft Corporation in Buffalo, New York. In 1951 he was transferred to the newly established Fort Worth division of Bell.

During his association with the company he had served in such important capacities as chief of research and development, director of test and evaluation, and director of design engineering. Lynn was appointed vice president-research and engineering in 1974 and was elevated to senior vice president in 1977.

A native of Charleston, West Virginia, he received his B.S. in mechanical engineering and his M.S. in Aeronautical Engineering from Princeton University.

Richard K. (Dick) May, senior vice president-operations, had over 30 years of experience with leading aircraft manufacturers and all phases of production engineering and manufacturing. May joined Bell in 1972 as manager-manufacturing engineering. Prior to his association with Bell he had served as chief manufacturing engineering-research and fabrication for General Dynamics. May began his aviation career with Rohr Aircraft in 1941 as a tool designer, followed by a three-year tenure with Douglas Aircraft Corporation in Tulsa in the same field.

From 1951 to 1955, May was general supervisor of tool design at Lockheed Aircraft, Marietta, Georgia. He returned to General Dynamics in Fort Worth in 1955 where he became chief of manufacturing research and fabrication. He attended both the University of Nebraska and Texas Christian University.

Charles R. Rudnig was senior vice president-medium helicopters at Bell Helicopter Textron. The medium helicopter programs included the 205, 212, 214, 214ST, and 412 models.

Rudnig served as president of Bell Operations Corporation from January 1976 to November 1979. Bell Operations Corporation was formed in November 1975 to carry out a long-term coproduction and joint-venture agreement with the government of Iran. Prior to the BOC appointment, he served as vice president of program management at Bell Helicopter Textron beginning in 1971.

Rudnig earned a B.S. degree in engineering from Iowa State University and had pursued graduate studies at Ohio State University and Massachusetts Institute of Technology.

Bell had established a pattern in the past and continued to manage the company with a strong leadership group at the top coordinating all of the company actions. The nature of the military business carried out by Bell required a well-coordinated company to enable it to submit bids for the new products. Bell's swing to the commercial market had caused many of the top management personnel to be shifted into new positions. Those individuals who were previously concerned with working with the government and securing government contracts took on a new role of presenting their product to the commercial market.

Bell had also encountered problems in its relations with union employees. The company's shift from military contracts to short-run contracts had created a surplus of workers. Approximately 150 people were laid off in January 1981, and by July of 1981 a total of 1,500 people had been terminated.[5]

BELL COMMERCIAL MODELS[6]

Bell Helicopter Textron's commercial helicopters encompassed a versatile assortment of rotary-wing products.

The 18-seat 214ST SuperTransport was Bell's newest addition to the market. Its engines offered outstanding hot-day, high-altitude performance with 3,250 takeoff horsepower. This newest helicopter was ideal for the long-range offshore crew change mission, with its range of more than 400 nautical miles. The aircraft was also certified for use under instrument flight rules (IFR). This was an extremely important requirement because, for example, companies on oil rigs had to operate around the clock. Additionally, the helicopter had a gross weight of 17,200 pounds and an internal useful load of approximately 7,500 pounds.

The Model 222 began customer service in February 1980. It was expected to capture a significant share of the rotary-wing and fixed-wing (airplane) markets. Designed for fast, quiet, and comfortable executive travel, this aircraft seated up to ten passengers, and had a range of up to 330 nautical miles. Its two 615 shaft horsepower (shp) Lycoming LTS-101-650C-2 engines were the most advanced in their power class. This helicopter was particularly unusual for it possessed a retractable wheel landing gear. The normal skid-type landing gear was fixed in place.

Bell was known for its characteristic two-bladed helicopters. This was changing for both commercial and military models. The Model 412 was the advanced technology, four-bladed, commercial variant of the twin-engined Model 212. (Since June 1980, Bell's 212 had been powered by Canadian Pratt and Whitney's improved PT6T-3 "Twin Pac" engines. The Model 212 had also been IFR certified.) The 412 was faster, smoother, and quieter than the 15-seat aircraft. A kit to convert existing 212s to the four-bladed configuration was being developed. In addition to a 25 percent increase in speed (up to 25 knots), this helicopter offered a 40 percent reduction in vibration too. The 412 had a transmission takeoff rating of 1,308 shp, compared with 1,290 shp for the 212, and a gross weight of 11,600 pounds compared to 11,200 pounds (based on preliminary design criteria). The 412 received Federal Aviation Administration (FAA) certification in January 1981. Comparison between some of Bell's helicopters are shown in Exhibit 2.

Bell's seven-passenger LongRanger II incorporated advanced 500 shp Allison 250-C28B turboshaft engines which offered additional power from earlier types. This helicopter maintained many proven features that the firm developed for the widely accepted Model 206L, including the Noda-Matric™ transmission suspension system for unexcelled ride smoothness. The aircraft received FAA certification for single pilot IFR operations in December 1978.

JetRanger III, a five-seat aircraft, was the latest and most powerful of this series. It was flown all over the world, as were so many other Bell helicopters. It provided more speed and power with one 420 shp Allison 250-C20B engine

Exhibit 2

Bell Helicopter Textron
Comparisons of Helicopters

Name	Seats	Powerplant(s)	Speed (KTS) (At Sea Level)	Range (NM)	Price (In dollars)
JetRanger III	5	Allison 250-C20B, 420 shp	118	300	277,500
LongRanger II	7	Allison 250-C28B, 500 shp	113	300	445,000
205A-1	15	Lyc. T531-13B 1,400 shp	110	270	895,000
212 Twin.....................	15	2 P&W PT6T-3, 900 shp	100	226	1,175,000
222	8-10	2 Lyc. LTS-101-650C-2, 615 shp	130	330	1,195,000
412	15	2 P&W PT6T 3B, 900 shp each	123	243	1,650,000
214B Biglifter..................	16	Lyc. T550-8D, 2,930 shp	140	172	1,800,000
214 B-1	16	Lyc. T550-8D, 2,930 shp	140	178	1,800,000
214ST........................	18-19	2 GE CT 7-2 1,625 shp each	142	403	3,650,000

Source: AOPA Pilot, Vol. 24, No. 3, (Washington, D.C., 1981), pp. 74, 80.

which offered a 20-horsepower increase over the JetRanger II. It also had increased high altitude hover ceilings plus greater speed, at altitude, on hot days.

The 16-passenger 214B Biglifter could lift more than 7,000 pounds. Powered by a single 2,930 shp Lycoming T550-8D turbine engine, this helicopter was an outstanding performer of the petroleum industry, the construction industry, and forestry assignments.

Bell's 15-place Model 205A-1 was a design offspring of the remarkable "Huey" military helicopter. It was a design that had proved its reliability on thousands of jobs covering millions of flight hours. For transporting people, hauling cargo, or as a two-ton aerial crane, this was the original "do-everything" helicopter.[7]

BELL MILITARY MODELS[8]

Bell Helicopter manufactured a diversified line of military aircraft. The utility transports had a "U" prefix, the antiarmor aircraft were designated with an "A" prefix, and observation helicopters began with an "O." Military helicopters included the UH-1H Iroquois (Huey) and the AH-1S Huey Cobra.

Bell was at work on production and modification contracts that would upgrade U.S. Army and Marine Corps armed helicopters. The Army had awarded Bell production contracts for the AH-1S. This was an improved version of the Huey Cobra. Bell developed the AH-1G, Huey Cobra, for the Army in 1966 to satisfy urgent combat needs in Vietnam. A total purchase of 297 AH-1S units had been planned by the Army. A contract called for the AH-1S to be delivered to the National Guard starting in the spring of 1981. (A ceremony in April signified that beginning.) Bell had also delivered 57 AH-1T twin-engine SeaCobras, to the U.S. Marines. Both helicopters offered improved engines and dynamics, increased performance, and lower maintenance requirements. The AH-1S was equipped with the tube-launched, optically-tracked, wire-guided (TOW) missile system, and a Lycoming T53-L-703 engine. The AH-1S was rated at 1,800 shp and used an uprated drive train. It incorporated additional operational and maintenance improvements, making it the Army's most modern, antiarmor helicopter.

The AH-1T incorporated features of the AH-1S airframe, Model 412 dynamics, and an upgraded engine. With its maximum useful load of 5,392 pounds (fuel and ordnance), the AH-1T offered an improved payload over the AH-1J's 2,523 pounds. Maximum gross weight of the AH-1T was 14,000 pounds, compared to the AH-1J's 10,000 pounds. It was powered by a Pratt and Whitney T400-WV-402 twin-turbine engine.

In addition to these production contracts, Bell had modified 290 AH-1G Huey Cobras to the AH-1S configuration. Bell had programmed additional 384 AH-1Ss for conversion to the modernized AH-1S in fiscal year 1981-82 timeframe. Bell was also flight testing a four-bladed AH-1S Cobra, which had reached speeds of 170 knots. It utilized the advanced rotor system designed for the firm's Model 412.

Bell had produced more than 1,700 attack (antiarmor) helicopters and was the only manufacturer in the free world to build production helicopters dedicated to the gunship role.

Bell planned to submit a proposal for a near-term Scout helicopter to the U.S. Army. The firm was proposing modification of existing OH-58 aircraft in the inventory with systems as a quick and reasonable cost means of meeting the requirement for a near-term Scout. The Army was considering modification of five existing Bell or Hughes light observation helicopters as prototypes and a program converting 200 to 720 aircraft to the new configuration. Hughes was Bell's only competitor in the Army's Helicopter Improvement Program (AHIP).[9]

Another major Bell project had been the development of two XV-15 NASA/Army/Navy tilt rotor research aircraft. It was designed to take off and land vertically like a helicopter, and fly horizontally like an airplane. One of the aircraft had attained a true airspeed of 301 knots (346 miles per hour) in level flight. When Bell completed its contract portion of XV-15 flight tests, the second craft was shipped to NASA's Dryden Flight Research Center at Edwards Air Force Base for envelope expansion and proof of concept flight tests. The first aircraft was being refurbished by Bell personnel at the NASA/Ames research center, Moffett Field, California. Throughout 1981, both aircraft were involved in a comprehensive evaluation program at NASA/Ames. The program assessed potential applications in military and civil transport requirements. This included flight operations on aircraft carriers and offshore oil platforms.

FINANCIAL PERFORMANCE

Bell Helicopter was the flagship division of Textron, according to the president's speech at the Helicopter Association of America's annual convention. The percent of sales of helicopters to total sales of Textron had been declining. In 1975 sales were 30 percent and declined to 22 percent in 1979 of Textron's sales. The growth in helicopter sales in this time period was 15 percent, while Textron's sales growth was 38 percent. This growth performance was confounded with Textron's growth strategy of acquisitions.

In 1978 Textron had cash and short-term investments of $171 million. A $75 million long-term borrowing in 1977 contributed to this liquidity. Advanced payments on large helicopter contracts also contributed to this liquidity. However, Bell's Iranian contracts were terminated and had a negative impact on this liquidity. By year-end 1979, cash and short-term investments were $30 million, and short-term borrowings were $64 million.

In December 1980, $75 million of 8½ percent notes were at maturity, while earlier in 1980 Textron issued $85.4 million of 7 3/4 percent Subordinate Debentures due 2005. During 1980, Textron and its unconsolidated finance subsidiary expanded their combined lines of credit for both short-term and revolving debt from $310 million to $445 million. Twenty-six million dollars were used at year-end 1980.

It was anticipated that cash flows from operation plus the unused portion of existing credit lines would be ample to accommodate the needs of Textron during 1981. The same case would be applicable to Bell.

The income statement and statements of financial position for Bell Helicopter are shown in Exhibits 3 and 4.

Textron, Inc.

Exhibit 3   **Consolidated Statement of Income**

	1980	1979	1978
Sales	$ 3,376.7	$ 3,095.4	$ 2,932.4
Costs and expenses:			
Cost of sales	2,507.9	2,295.3	2,216.4
Selling and administrative expense	475.9	427.2	378.1
Depreciation	64.9	56.9	48.4
	$ 3,048.7	$ 2,779.4	$ 2,642.9
Operating income	$ 328.0	$ 316.0	$ 289.5
Interest income	8.8	11.2	19.9
Interest expense	(40.9)	(31.4)	(26.6)
Income from continuing operations before income taxes	$ 295.9	$ 295.8	$ 282.8
Income taxes	126.5	130.7	126.2
Income from continuing operations	$ 169.4	$ 165.1	$ 156.6
Discontinued operation, net of income taxes:			
Income (loss) from operations	$ (13.3)	$ 4.7	$ 11.5
Estimated (loss) on disposals	(70.0)	—	—
	$ (83.3)	$ 4.7	$ 11.5
Net Income	$ 86.1	$ 169.8	$ 168.1

Textron Inc.

Exhibit 4   **Consolidated Balance Sheet (In millions)**

Assets	1980	1979	1978
Current assets:			
Cash	$ 15.5	$ 23.0	$ 16.6
Short-term investments, at cost (approximates market)	5.3	6.9	154.6
Accounts receivable (less allowances of $13.2 and $16.2)	532.1	538.4	534.3
Inventories:			
Finished goods	262.6	258.4	229.0

Work in process (less progress payments of $131.8 and $106.5)	494.7	456.3	320.0
Raw materials and supplies	131.5	152.4	140.5
Deferred income taxes	30.7	24.9	32.0
Prepaid expenses	13.4	13.4	14.0
Net assets of discontinued operations, less reserve for loss on disposals	98.0	–	–
Total current assets	$ 1,583.8	$ 1,473.7	$ 1,441.0
Investment in unconsolidated Co	41.1	35.7	32.4
Other investments	84.6	86.0	81.4
Property, Plant, and Equipment—at cost:			
Land and buildings	221.4	236.4	224.0
Machinery and equipment	703.2	737.7	659.4
Less accumulated depreciation	(518.6)	(561.2)	(516.9)
Cost in excess of net assets of companies acquired, less amortization	44.4	38.1	34.6
Other assets	27.5	32.8	34.9
Total assets	$ 2,187.4	$ 2,079.2	$ 1,990.8

Liabilities and Stockholders' Equity

Current liabilities:			
Short-term debt	$ 83.3	$ 64.0	$ 27.7
Current maturities of long-term debt	5.5	81.9	7.4
Accounts payable	250.7	176.4	185.4
Federal income taxes	72.7	42.8	59.0
Other current liabilities	283.3	341.4	368.1
Total current liabilities	$ 695.5	$ 706.5	$ 647.6
Long-term debt	$ 301.6	$ 222.9	$ 290.4
Deferred investment tax credits	18.1	16.9	14.0
Other liabilities	18.4	13.9	20.1
Total liabilities	$ 1,033.6	$ 960.2	$ 972.1
Stockholders' Equity:			
Capital stock:			
Preferred stock, 15,000,000 shares authorized:			
$2.08 cumulative convertible preferred stock, Series A (liquidation value $125.8)	$ 59.4	$ 69.1	$ 72.2
$1.40 convertible preferred dividend stock, Series B (preferred only as dividends)	16.7	22.1	39.9
Common stock, 25¢ par value (authorized 75,000,000 shares)	8.7	8.5	8.1
Capital surplus	120.6	105.8	85.2
Retained earnings	983.0	947.5	846.2
Less cost of treasury shares	(34.6)	(34.0)	(32.9)
Total stockholders' equity	$ 1,153.8	$ 1,119.0	$ 1,018.7
Total liabilities and stockholder's equity	$ 2,187.4	$ 2,079.2	$ 1,990.8

MARKETING AND DISTRIBUTION

Bell built helicopters for the commercial (nonmilitary) and military market. There is hardly anyone alive today over the age of 15 years who has not seen a Bell UH-1 "Huey" assault helicopter or an AH-1G "Cobra" gunship on the television evening news in the late 60s and early 70s. Today Bell does not depend on military sales, although it still has OH-58 (Light Observation Helicopter) and AH-1S (Cobra gunship) as well as some work on UH-1H (assault helicopters) and spare parts for all of these.

Bell competed in the mid 70s to build the Army's replacement aircraft for the AH-1 but lost to Hughes Aircraft. Another large military contract was missed by Bell in 1979 when a $214.7 million contract for 90 U.S. Coast Guard helicopters went to Aerospatiale Helicopter Corporation, a subsidiary of Aerospatiale. Bell's bid was $215.8 million, one-half of one percent bidding difference. Bell protested to the Senate Finance Committee, asking them to consider the fairness of the award in the light of whether the true cost of design and development were included in Aerospatiale's bid. Bell also wanted consideration given to the possible adverse effects to "military base capability and damage to commercial competitive structures."[10]

Bell filed a motion in U.S. District Court in late 1979 but got no relief. The Coast Guard evaluated the Aerospatiale SA366 "significantly superior" to the Bell 222 in design quality emphasizing greater range capability.[11]

The bulk of Bell's business is now commercial and no small part of that is from the offshore oil industry in Texas and other parts of the Gulf Coast. For instance, in 1978 Bell accounted for over 86 percent of the market in this area.[12] An official in one of Bell's rival companies said, "These oil company presidents are particular about what helicopters their employees ride in. We attempt to appeal to the executives."[13]

Bell used the direct sales marketing technique. Concerning direct sales, Jim Atkins remarked in February 1980,

> In the year 1979, for the first time, we broke the $200 million mark. Our 1979 sales were 60 percent higher than our 1978 sales. That was quite an impressive task for us to accomplish in that year. We started out the year, and I think at this conference last year, we announced that we were forming three new sales divisions, giving Dwayne Jose and his people eight divisions in the U.S. and Canada. The success of these divisions and the effect on sales in their areas has been great and has proven to us the concept of direct selling.[14]

During the 70s Bell distributed through the established aircraft dealer organization of Atlantic Aviation. This proved to be unsatisfactory to Bell and the company was convinced that their method of direct selling was best.

Demonstrator helicopters were flown by expert pilots to the sales regions and were demonstrated to prospective customers. In some cases, orders were taken for future delivery while in others, the "demonstrator" aircraft was sold. The Regional Sales Divisions were:

Mountain Division	Aurora, Colorado
Great Lakes Division	Chicago, Illinois
Central Division	Fort Worth, Texas
Eastern Division	Montgomeryville, Pennsylvania (Phila.)
Southeast Division	Tucker, Georgia (Atlanta)
Western Division	Van Nuys, California (L.A.)
Canada East	Ottawa, Ontario
Canada West	Calgary, Alberta

International sales were, however, sometimes conducted through fixed/wing aircraft manufacturers/distributors in the customer's country. These sales were conducted in different ways in different countries. The type of sale, through a national company after approval by the State Department, or direct to the customer after approval, was determined by a complex set of "rules." These "rules" had evolved over the years as a result of laws and various agreements between countries.

Bell boasted of an outstanding reputation for support after the sale both technically and logistically as indicated by Mr. Atkins,

> You recognize we have approximately 130 service centers throughout the United States, and they serve a good position in performing maintenance for their corporate users around the United States. We want to continue to develop our service centers and right now we have many FBO's (Fixed Base Operators—at airports) that are service centers for Bell products. We're going to continue to develop that, but as far as the sale of the vehicle, it's our present intention to stay with direct selling. We think there's a lot of technical expertise involved in the sale of a helicopter. We think we have that and it's difficult to spread it among many other people. We think probably that we can sell at a lesser cost than a dealer network might sell it. And, taking these things into consideration and with the fact we have made the kind of progress that we think is reasonable to make in the commercial market, I think we'll stay with direct selling.[15]

Also overseas there were full-time Bell people available in Australia and Germany for "After Hours Support." This provided a support facility in all of Bell's major markets.

More recently Jim Atkins had more to say regarding Bell's reputation for service,

> I believe that we have the reputation around the world as being number one in product support .... To re-emphasize and to expand our product support this year we intend to create a new division of the company under a senior officer of the company. He will have total profit and loss responsibility and he will have responsibility for training, for technical services, for logistics and for technical publications. Everything that happens after the sale will be his responsibility ... We have leadership in this field, and it's a leadership we're not going to give up.[16]

Bell's market extended to 163 countries with 103 of those countries already using their products. In 1980 international sales exceeded $300 million (U.S. and Canada) and military sales were approximately $275 million[17] (Exhibit 5).

Exhibit 5

Bell Helicopter Textron
Financial Information—Product Groups (In millions)

	1980		1979		1978		1977		1976	
Trade sales-continuing operations										
Aerospace-Helicopters........	$ 894	(27%)	$ 758	(24%)	$ 903	(31%)	$ 817	(32%)	$ 801	(34%)
Other	235	(7%)	176	(6%)	180	(6%)	150	(6%)	167	(7%)
Total Aerospace.............	1,129	(34%)	934	(30%)	1,083	(37%)	967	(38%)	968	(41%)
Consumer	889	(26%)	861	(28%)	683	(23%)	542	(22%)	489	(21%)
Industrial...................	602	(18%)	599	(19%)	567	(19%)	525	(21%)	473	(20%)
Metal product..............	757	(22%)	701	(23%)	599	(21%)	484	(19%)	432	(18%)
Totals...................	$3,377	(100%)	$3,095	(100%)	$2,932	(100%)	$2,518	(100%)	$2,362	(100%)

Bell had been building helicopters for Iran since the mid-1970s and had entered a helicopter coproduction program. Bell was also engaged in the training of Iranian helicopter pilots and mechanics in Iran. This was done "under foreign military sales contracts with the U.S. Government . . ." which included "the establishment of logistical systems and operational overhaul facilities."

The coproduction contract was terminated by the Government of Iran in December of 1978 because of "force majeure" events. These included "civil unrest, political, and economic instability."

The full cost of the termination had not yet been determined, but it was believed "that such cost is fully covered by amounts received under the advance funding provisions of the contract." The costs of the pilot and mechanic training and systems and facilities development contract termination were expected to be covered by reimbursement "under the terms of the contracts." Furthermore, Textron "believes it is entitled to reimbursement for certain costs absorbed during 1978 and to profits to the date of termination, for which it will make a claim to the Government of Iran."[18]

In spite of this setback in 1979 which resulted in a 16 percent decline in overall sales, an increase in commercial sales resulted in a 12 percent increase in income which lessened the shock of the loss of the Iranian contracts.[19]

OPERATIONS AND PRODUCTION

Bell Helicopter had all its manufacturing facilities at Fort Worth, Texas, with the exception of one plant located at Amarillo, Texas. Bell employed approximately 9,500 people in Texas. The Fort Worth plant was on 1,160 acres and had an enclosed space of 2,600,000 sq. ft.

Although Bell was capable of producing practically all of the helicopter components, except engines, "it has followed a policy of subcontracting a portion of such components."[20] Their machine shop was around 400,000 sq. ft. in area which housed machine tools valued at over $50 million. Bell felt that it was the best shop of its type in the Southwest, maybe the entire U.S. Jack Horner commented,

Exhibit 6

Textron's Sales over the Past Five Years

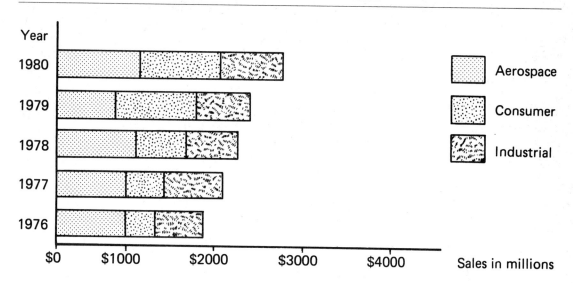

We have a machine shop which is about 400,000 square feet. Probably to replace it in the open market today would take a couple hundred million dollars, if you look at the machine tools in it.[21]

In addition to production in the continental U.S., overseas Bell helicopters were built under license by Construzioni Aeronauticle Biovanni Agusta of Milan, Italy, and Mitsue & Co., Ltd. of Tokyo, Japan.

At the beginning of 1980, Bell produced 75 to 80 aircraft per month of eight different models. In 1981 production ran about 66 JetRangers and Long-Rangers per month with about six 212/412s per month for an annual total of 800 aircraft. Bell proudly pointed out that this production was completely based on "small programs." The Vietnam War saw more Bell helicopters than any other in use in combat from start to finish. Bell had apparently broken itself from any reliance it might have developed on the government contract.

There had been delays in deliveries of the company's new Model 222 due to holdups in production of the Lycoming engine that powered the aircraft. Avco Lycoming's LTS 101 engine was experiencing production problems which in turn impacted adversely on Bell's production. Lycoming officials claimed they made "extensive managerial changes . . . in an effort to correct the engine production delays. Additional production capacity is being provided at a cost in the double digit millions."[22]

Robert Ames, executive vice president for the Aerospace Group, Textron, said,

Textron is in aerospace through Bell Aerospace and Bell Helicopter. Bell Helicopter is our flagship division. It is the most important division in Textron, therefore, gets a great deal of attention, a great deal of support . . . . I think what's significant about all of that is that we have accepted the transition to a private commercial business rather than a military venture and we've done it with total support of Jim (Atkins).[23]

Mr. Atkins remarked, "We want to have a good mix of business for the future. The days of being 95 percent U.S. Government were pretty risky ... To maintain a 70-80 production rate many problems have to be solved. The majority of the contracts are for two to five ships for many different applications: corporate, medvac, police, etc." Jim Atkins noted, "to produce seven or eight different models in those 80 ships, we have plenty of production problems."[24] He went on to explain some of the production problems when asked if the problems were with engines or shortage of capability,

> "No, it goes basically back to raw materials, and especially specialty materials, high specialty steels, high specialty aluminums. It goes to forgings; it goes to castings; it goes to bearings. If we could conquer the specialty steels and aluminums plus the castings, forgings and bearings, I think we'd have it made ... large aluminum corporations ... returns on their investment is not high enough .... In the forging-casting area, of course, the OSHA regulations put a lot of people out of business. It's pretty hard to get people to invest in that area at this point ... If we don't have forgings, we find a way to cut a part from bar, and the capability that we have inhouse is really the only reason that we're building 75 ships a month."[25]

FUTURE

Bell conducted a long-range forecast in 1980 that projected $1.5 billion in total annual sales by 1984. As has been pointed out, the company broke the $300 million mark in commercial sales in 1980 for the first time. Commercial sales were considered to be all sales that were not U.S. or Canadian government business in the U.S. and Canada. Exhibit 7 shows the steady increase expected by Bell over the next five years covering 1980 through 1984.

Bell was aggressively planning ahead and was spending considerable research and development money. In 1979 $60 million was spent on R&D. A key long-term project was the XV-15 tilt-rotor research aircraft. This program arose from a joint contract with U.S. Army Research and Technology Laboratories (AVRADCOM) and NASA for two test aircraft. The vertical take-off and landing (VTOL) aircraft had drawn attention from all the military services and each service had expressed interest in the versatile aircraft. The combination of versatilities of the "land anywhere" helicopter with the speed and efficiency of the fixed-wing aircraft was highly desirable for military applications. The engine nacelles were tilted to turn the propellor into helicopter rotors for hovering flight. The XV-15 had been flown at speeds over 300 miles per hour. Jim Atkins stated his feelings about the R&D costs and initial production costs of the SV-15,

> ... to me the first customer has to be the United States Government. They are the only people who have enough money to invest in a program of this type. So, to me, it's likely that it could even be a three service program, where they might undertake a major development aimed at the requirements of perhaps the three services. I would see that a development to the production of a tilt rotor type vehicle would be a ten-year period.[26]

Exhibit 7 **Bell Helicopter Sales Forecast**

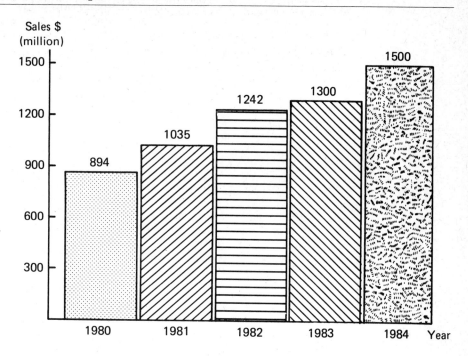

Sales $ (million)

| 1980 | 1981 | 1982 | 1983 | 1984 |
| 894 | 1035 | 1242 | 1300 | 1500 |

Year

Bell had conducted design studies on a 30-passenger helicopter, its largest so far. Designated the D-236 and designed for the offshore oil industry application, the aircraft had not attracted any contracts so far. This aircraft would allow Bell to increase its market share of the offshore business which was already over 85 percent. Sikorsky and Aerospatiale were the other major competitors and were withholding their market share through the larger helicopters.

CONCLUSION

Bell Helicopter faced many problems in several aspects of its business. However, there seemed to be in place a shift in Textron's corporate strategy which could resolve many of these problems. In the past, Textron had a hands-off policy on its divisions by allowing them to formulate separate long-range strategic plans. Thus, corporate strategy consisted of the consolidation of the five-year plans of the divisions. This "bottoms up" approach of planning was being replaced by the "top down" method. The shift now was that the Textron corporate office would play a much larger role in the preparation of these strategic plans. Corporate office would be setting policies with which the divisions must comply. They would set standards of profit performance, and return on shareholders' investment.

In view of this change in corporate policy, Bell faced a new challenge in the future. Not only was the marketing shift swinging from the military to the commercial market, but the way in which company policy was dictated was also changing. With the increased pressure to produce up-to-date models and at a reasonable price by competitors such as Aerospatiale and Sikorsky, Bell had to either rise up and meet the challenge or give way to the law of competition.

NOTES

1. *Bell Helicopter Highlights*, published by Bell Helicopter, 1981.
2. All biography information taken from biography releases, 1981.
3. Unnamed source, Aerospatiale, Inc., 1981.
4. *Bell Helicopter News*, Vol. 29, No. 10, February 27, 1981.
5. Unnamed source, Aerospatiale, Inc. 1981.
6. "Bell Commercial Models," Bell Helicopter Textron Public Relations Release.
7. "Information Processing Careers at B.H.T.," Bell Helicopter Textron brochure.
8. "Bell Military Models," Bell Helicopter Textron Public Relations Release.
9. "Manufacturer to Propose Scout Helicopter," *Aviation Week and Space Technology*, (March 2, 1981), p. 63.
10. "Compact Damper, Noda-matic, ®" *Rotorways*, Vol. 9, No. 1, May 1980.
11. "The Offshore Transportation Industry," *Rotorways*, Vol. 8, No. 3, June 1979.
12. See n. 11 above.
13. "Textron Protests Coast Guard Award," *Aviation Week and Space Technology*, July 23, 1979, p. 57.
14. From a press conference held by James F. Atkins, president, Bell Helicopter Textron, on February 10, 1980, during the Helicopter Association of America's annual meeting.
15. "After Hours Support," *Rotor Breeze*, November 1980.
16. James F. Atkins, "Our 10,000 People Keep Us on Top," *Bell Helicopter News*, Vol. 29, No. 9, February 13, 1981.
17. See n. 16 above.
18. "Textron, Inc.," *Moody's Industrial Manual*, 1980.
19. "Textron," Annual Report 1979, February 6, 1980.
20. "Textron, Inc.," *Moody's Industrial Manual*, 1980.
21. James F. Atkins, "Our 10,000 People Keep Us on Top," *Bell Helicopter News*, Vol. 29, No. 9, February 13, 1981.
22. "Bell Paces Textron's 1980 Sales Increases," *Bell Helicopter News*, Vol. 29, No. 10, February 27, 1981.
23. James F. Atkins, "Our 10,000 People Keep Us on Top," *Bell Helicopter News*, Vol. 29, No. 9, February 13, 1981.
24. From a press conference held by James F. Atkins, president, Bell Helicopter Textron, on February 10, 1980, during the Helicopter Association of America's annual meeting.
25. See n. 24 above.
26. See n. 24 above.
27. "Civil Helicopter Growth Seen Through 1986," *Aviation Week and Space Technology*, March 9, 1981, pp. 240–45.

Case 7–3

Capital Carpets*

INTRODUCTION

"We are the Cadillac of the carpet industry. We make the finest quality carpets and use the best materials available. Latest industry projections, however, show only a slight growth for the quality portion of the carpet market. This information has prompted me to ask Bob Hartley, general manager of production, and John Prince, general manager of marketing, to assess the possibility of expanding our product line." These words were stated by Charles D. Parker, president of Capital Carpets, at the January 1975 board meeting (Exhibit 1).

Capital had been using the name "Capital Carpets" and a logo in which that name appeared in a rectangle. The logo, which also included a shuttle and a stylized end-view of carpeting, had been registered in the name of Capital-Materials Carpet Company; the name "Capital" was not registered as a trademark until March 1974. Since then all carpets have borne the Capital symbol.

BACKGROUND

Capital Carpets established its first sales office in Atlanta, Georgia, in 1908. In 1975 Capital operated three manufacturing facilities—a spinning plant and a tufting plant, both in Savannah, Georgia, and a weaving plant in Atlanta. Capital's line included tufted and woven carpets made of both wool and synthetic fibers. Woven patterned and figured designs, patterned after oriental carpets, were Capital's specialty. The company had 1,570 employees. Its ten sales offices were located in the United States: New York, Boston, Atlanta, Pittsburgh, Chicago, Savannah, Cleveland, St. Louis, Detroit, and San Francisco.

Capital's sales for the fiscal year ending March 31, 1974, were $34 million, on which it earned a profit of $1,641,571, equivalent to $0.80 per share. Capital's assets totaled $27,584,194 (Exhibits 2, 3, and 4).

THE CAPITAL SITUATION

The overall image that Capital's management was trying to achieve was that of a high-grade manufacturing operation with a good name for quality

---

*This case was prepared by Anthony M. Akel, C.W. Post Center, Long Island University, with the intention of providing a basis for class discussion rather than illustrating either effective or ineffective management of a business situation. Reprinted with permission from *Application of Decision Sciences in Organizations: A Case Approach* by Joseph C. Latona and K. Mark Weaver with the cooperation of the American Institute for Decision Sciences, Atlanta, Georgia, 1980.

Exhibit 1

Capital Carpets
Corporate Organization Chart, March 1, 1974

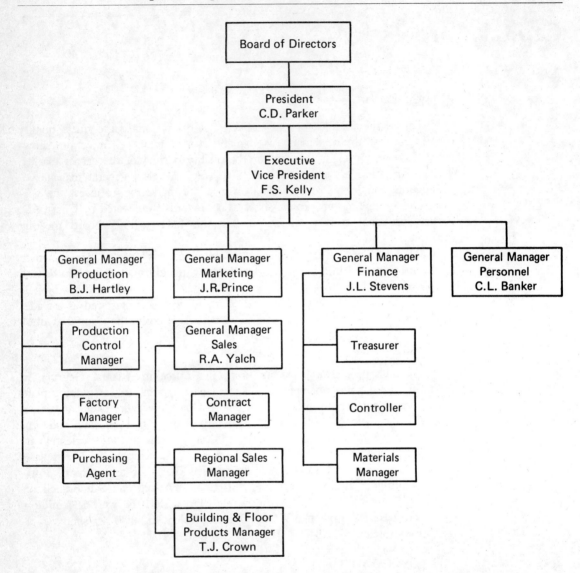

products in the carpet trade. Its name, however, was not well known to retail consumers because the company had not concentrated on that market.

Capital had achieved a good growth record and its sales had doubled between 1970 and 1974. Carpet production was 50 percent in wool compared to the industry average of 15 percent. Capital used synthetics in tufted carpets, but was limited to stock-dyed fibers because of a lack of piece-dyeing equipment.

Exhibit 2

Capital Carpets
Balance Sheet—March 31, 1974

ASSETS

Current assets:

Cash	$ 876,815	
Accounts receivable	4,322,437	
Inventories, at the lower of cost or market:		
Finished goods	5,127,383	
Work in process	2,414,814	
Raw materials and supplies	713,112	
Prepaid expenses and other current assets	225,949	
Total current assets		$13,680,510
Plant and equipment:		
Land	$ 1,705,634	
Buildings	4,991,059	
Equipment	9,443,445	
Plant additions in progress	834,590	
	$16,974,728	
Less accumulated depreciation	3,071,044	
Net plant and equipment		13,903,684
Total assets		$27,584,194

LIABILITIES and NET WORTH

Current liabilities:

Accounts payable	$ 1,525,514	
Federal income tax	1,775,843	
Accrued liabilities	1,729,884	
Current portion of long-term debt	235,105	
Total current liabilities		$ 5,266,346
Long-term debts		4,629,900
Other liabilities		215,521
Total liabilities		$10,111,767
Net worth:		
Preferred stock	$ 927,845	
Common stock	1,871,145	
Capital surplus	2,332,423	
Earned surplus	12,341,014	
Total net worth		17,472,427
Total liabilities and net worth		$27,584,194

Capital's equipment included several 60-year-old gripper looms which were the only remaining ones in the United States. The Capital management proposed to retain its present equipment, but to emphasize tufting. Management planned to expand product lines which were versatile and full since Capital's specialties—floral and abstract patterns—were no longer popular at retail.

Exhibit 3

Capital Carpets
Income Statement—March 31, 1974

Net sales		$34,241,538
Operating costs and expenses:		
Cost of sales...	$24,385,013	
Depreciation	784,806	
Warehouse, shipping, selling, and administrative expenses	5,324,214	30,494,033
Operating income		$ 3,747,505
Other expenses:		
Interest on long-term debt	$297,197	
Other interest	32,894	$ 330,091
Income taxes...		1,775,843
Total other expenses		2,105,934
Net earnings		$ 1,641,571
Dividends paid ($.20 per share in 1974)......................		$ (558,125)
Amount added to reinvested earnings		$ 1,083,446
Reinvested earnings...		11,257,568
Capital stock...		2,798,990
Capital surplus		2,332,423
Shareowners' equity		$17,472,427
Net earnings per share.......................................		$ .81

Exhibit 4

Capital Carpets
Five-Year Summary

Year Ended June 30th	Sales	Net Income	Earnings	Cash Dividends	Common Stock Price Range
1974	$34,241	$1,641	$.81	$.20	9-½—6
1973	30,356	1,275	.57	.10	12—7
1972	28,560	1,845	.86	0	22—15
1971	24,665	1,760	.82	0	20—8
1970	18,938	1,285	.63	0	12—3-½

Commenting about the manufacturing facilities and organization of Capital, B. J. Hartley, general manager of production, stated:

> The Atlanta plant, devoted primarily to weaving, contains much equipment which is old and slow. . . . The spinning plant at Savannah, while operated efficiently, is burdened with slow equipment . . . The tufting plant at Savannah is new and the installed equipment is modern; however, it is apparent to even a casual observer that the operators have much to learn about efficient output. The organization of Capital is weak in the areas of planning, scheduling, training, preventive maintenance, industrial engineering, and overall supervision.

Capital's distribution consisted of sales which were one-third to wholesalers, one-third to retail contract market, and one-third to private retailers. Thirty-three percent of its sales were direct contract sales (and 70 percent contract in terms of end-users) compared to the industry average of 20 percent. Competitors believed that Capital built up considerable ill will among wholesalers by its pricing tactics of underbidding wholesalers for attractive contract jobs. This practice left only less desirable business for wholesalers.

Capital's management proposed to retain its strong position in the contract field, build its wholesale business by revising its pricing policies, and increase its retail business by increasing advertising expenditures. Capital did almost no advertising, spending $19,000 in 1973 and nothing in 1974. Management proposed to budget $800,000 for 1975 in line with its new program of expansion.

CAPITAL'S MARKET POSITION

The development of Capital's market position began in the 1950s when most carpeting was woven (versus tufted) and the main fiber was wool (versus synthetics). Capital's lines consisted of wool friezes and plushes, both manufactured on Velvet looms; wool floral and abstract designs, made on Wilton looms; and wool orientals and specialties, manufactured on gripper Axminster looms. Capital sales through retailers were concentrated heavily on the wool friezes and the domestic Orientals. At the time, contract carpeting was primarily for hotels and fashionable restaurants, and the demand was not great.

In the late 1950s the carpet industry experienced the beginning of a very strong growth trend. The tufting process and man-made fibers, coupled with their relatively low price, caused retail markets to expand. The institutional and commercial markets also expanded. These markets were traditionally higher quality, higher priced carpet markets.

As the retail demand moved away from high-quality wool woven carpeting, Capital concentrated upon the contract market. To achieve growth, Capital adopted a strategy of out-servicing and out-pricing its competitors in the contract field. Capital's facilities enabled the company to offer speedy delivery and small production runs; this resulted in very low margins in a field which was generally less profitable than the retail field. As the dual market trend continued, Capital came to be isolated in the contract field while its competitors, who had moved into tufting early, were able to sell to all segments of the market. Capital's entry into tufting was limited and late (Exhibit 5).

Exhibit 5

Capital Carpets
Production (in hundred yards), July 12, 1974

Year	Tufted	Woven	Total	Percent Growth	Percent of Industry
1962		540	540		4
1963		603	603	12	4
1964		488	488	−18	3
1965		498	498	2	2
1966	50	619	669	34	3
1967	89	620	709	6	2
1968	180	491	671	−5	2
1969	240	610	850	27	3
1970	550	654	1,204	42	4
1971	1,100	500	1,600	33	3
1972	1,600	400	2,000	25	2
1973	1,950	300	2,250	13	2
1974	2,300	200	2,500	11	3

THE CARPET INDUSTRY—COMPETITION AND MANUFACTURING

The rug and carpet industry had always been considered highly competitive. The 1972 census reports showed that there were over 150 individual companies with 250 plants manufacturing carpet and scatter rugs in the United States. Compared with 1958, the number of companies manufacturing tufted carpets increased 30 percent, while the number of woven carpet manufacturers declined by 25 percent. The number of carpet looms in place declined from 3,234 in 1958 to approximately 1,500 in 1972. Thus, competition existed not only among different companies producing the same type of rugs, but also among different types of rugs and carpets.

Major producers were said to account for some 40 percent to 50 percent of the industry total. Mohasco was the leader; including Firth, acquired in 1962, its sales were estimated to account for about 11 percent. As a result of the acquisition of Lees by Burlington Industries in early 1960, it was not feasible to accurately estimate the company's share of total industry sales. However, it was believed that Lees probably accounted for about 10 percent. Bigelow-San-ford, 94 percent owned by Sperry and Hutchinson, was next in importance, accounting for about 9 percent. Other important producers included Coronet, a fast-growing concern almost wholly engaged in tufted carpeting, Masland (C.H.) & Sons, Roxbury Carpet, and Armstrong Cork (through its acquisition of E & B Carpet). E. T. Barwick Mills and Magee Carpet, both privately owned, were also important in the industry.

Historically, all carpeting had been of woven construction, and most of it was woven from wool. In woven carpeting the pile and backing yarns were alternately raised and lowered while the shuttle, flying across the loom, bound the yarn with jute or cotton thread. The most common types of woven carpeting were Velvet, Wilton, or Axminster. Velvet was used mostly for solid colors. Wilton was woven on a Jacquard loom, which used a series of perforated cards similar to player-piano rolls. These rolls regulated the feeding of different colors of yarn into the loom and made possible the introduction of intricate patterns having great clarity. Axminster was woven on a special carpet loom, which allowed an almost unlimited combination of design and color. The changing of patterns on all types of carpet construction was a slow, expensive process. The weaving was also slow; sometimes only ten or twelve linear feet were produced in a working day. Woven carpets were relatively high priced, and their sale was usually limited to prestige installations.

The tufted method of producing carpeting, first introduced in 1949, was relatively new. In tufting, the machine acted as a mammoth sewing machine, with hundreds of needles aligned across the width of the machine. A yarn threaded through each needle eye was pierced through the backing fabric. As the needle was retracted, a loop (the tuft) was formed and held by the backing fabric. A heavy coating of latex was later applied to the back of the fabric to anchor the tufts permanently into place. Whereas weaving machines fabricated the entire carpet, including the backing and pile, tufting construction concerned only the pile. The backing was prefabricated. Electronic control in both the yarn feed and the needle action permitted the creation of pattern textures. While any fiber could be tufted, most tufted carpets were made from synthetics (Exhibit 6). Tufting was a speedy production process compared to weaving, and quality tufted carpets sold at prices which were considerably below those of woven carpets. In the relatively short period of its existence, tufted carpeting had taken over 80 percent of the United States market, and other markets were undergoing the same experience.

Until the advent of the broadloom tufted carpet machines in the late 1940s, tufted output was limited to such items as small scatter rugs and bath mats. With the development of this machine, which does not require a large capital outlay or much skilled labor, tufted broadloom square yard volume increased more than fifty times from the early 1950s, when tufted data were first available, to 1974.

Total domestic broadloom shipments increased steadily from 64.7 million square yards (90 percent woven) in 1951 to over 400 million (preliminary) in 1974 (approximately 10 percent woven and knitted). As these figures indicate, the entire postwar gain is attributable to the tufted process, with shipments of

Exhibit 6   **Carpet Fiber Chart***

FIBER	PLUS QUALITIES	MINUS QUALITIES	CLEANABILITY
Wool	Excellent durability; springy and crush-resistant; adaptable to styling; flame resistant.	Must be mothproofed; can be damaged by alkaline detergents; waste or reprocessed wool is a poor choice.	Needs cleaning less frequently than synthetics but is more difficult to clean.
Acrylic *trade names:* Acrilan, Creslan, Orlon, Sayelle, Zefran, Zefkrome	Takes color well; springy and crush-resistant; good soil resistance; resists mildew and sun.	Not very fire resistant; generates static electricity; may pill.	Cleans very well.
Modacrylics *trade names:* Verel, Dynel, Elura	Used in blends for flame resistance; very durable; usable in high-pile rugs.	Lacks good resilience; pills and shreds easily.	Cleans very well.
Nylon *trade names:* Anso, Antron, Cadon, Caprolan, Cumuloft, Enkalure, Enkaloft.	Exceptional durability; springy and crush-resistant; non-allergenic; now affected by mildew.	Soils easily in bright colors; pills in staple loop pile; Some static electricity; fiber melts; cool to touch; buy virgin not waste nylon.	Excellent cleanability.
Polyester *trade names:* Avlin, Dacron, Fortrel, Encron, Kodel, Trevira	Excellent durability and crush resistance, not affected by moths or mildew.	Cool to touch; some pilling and static electricity.	Excellent.
Olefin *trade names:* Vectra, Herculon, Marvess, Polycrest	Good durability; good soil resistance; non-allergenic, lightweight.	Fiber melts in lower grades; likely to crush.	When stains set in, they are difficult to remove.
Polypropylene	Very good wearing; good resistance to crushing and soiling; outstanding resistance to stains.	Poor flame resistance; crushes easily.	Excellent.
Cotton	Soft, excellent durability; not subject to moths or mildew.	Fiber and color can be destroyed by lye or bleach.	Small rugs can be machine washed, carpet shampooed successfully.
Rayon	Takes color well; is soft; good chemical resistance; not affected by moths.	In less dense pile, has poor flame resistance; crushes; poor durability and soil resistance.	As cleanable as cotton.

*Jan Brown, *Buy it Right—A Shoppers Guide to Home Furnishings*, Consumers Services Division, Career Institute, Mundelein, Illinois, 2nd Ed., pp. 166–167.

woven rugs and carpets in 1974 less than in the 1950s. Tufted was able to achieve its rapid penetration of the market primarily because it was much cheaper to manufacture.

CAPITAL'S AXMINSTER LINE

Capital had the only gripper Axminster operation in the U.S. From a production scheduling standpoint, this permitted them to plan shorter runs, and with respect to the appearance of the carpeting, they were able to produce a more clearly defined pattern. However, the gripper looms were sixty years old and the production rate was only 18 linear inches an hour. A full working day was required to shift from one pattern to another. Until Capital added tufted carpeting to its line, the Axminster looms produced Capital's only significant retail line—the domestic Oriental collection and a collection of modern shag designs. Capital offered a wide range of patterns and sizes in its domestic Orientals.

CAPITAL'S ENTRY IN TUFTING

Although the carpeting industry adopted tufting of synthetic fibers as early as 1950, Capital responded to the trend in 1964, when it built a tufting mill and introduced acrylic and nylon fibers to its weaving operations. Tufting produced carpeting much faster than weaving machines and therefore at lower production cost. With synthetics, less yarn was required per square yard because synthetics had greater bulking capabilities. Since 80 percent of the cost of the carpet was in the yarn, the use of synthetics brought about further cost reductions which quickly reduced the retail price of carpeting.

Capital's first tufting plant had three tufters, a scroll machine, a cutpile machine and a seven-roll loop machine. It was limited capacity production, but it permitted Capital to offer a diversified line.

DYEING OPERATIONS

Capital had equipment to blend, card, and spin raw wool, and could skein-dye a minimum run of 1,100 pounds which, in terms of 45 to 48 ounce cloth, would be approximately 250 square yards, or two full rolls. This could be doubled by using dual kettles operating under the same dye-lot for 2,200 pounds. However, in stock dyeing (yarn being dyed before blending, carding, and spinning), Capital was limited to a 5,000 pound minimum. Stock dyeing did not restrict them to one-yard count as did skein dyeing, but committed them to a longer run of one color.

When considering its frieze patterns, Capital had to think in terms of minimum 5,000 pound runs because, in addition to dyeing their frieze yarn, they heat-set it in their stock-dye kettles. To offset production run commitments, it offered frieze in several widths, which caused inventory problems. Capital also made proprietary lines for large-volume accounts, such as chain department stores and mail-order houses.

SYNTHETICS

When Capital entered the tufting field, difficulties in fiber procurement were encountered. In the acrylic field the company started with DuPont Orlon, which had to be spun and stock-dyed by an outside commission spinner and dyer, since Capital did not have sufficient capacity to handle its own spinning of man-made fibers. Also, Orlon was considered by the trade to be of lower quality than Acrilan.

In the summer of 1966, Capital was successful in negotiating a contract with Chemstrand. This enabled Capital to use the Acrilan fiber. In the nylon field Capital resorted to buying from a continuous filament nylon producer in Holland. This producer could supply Capital with solution-dyed material. Capital did not have facilities to do piece-dyeing and thus paid a high price for yarn.

Capital introduced one line made from staple nylon, which was purchased from DuPont and spun and stock-dyed by Capital. This was Capital's Cosmic line, which became one of its most successful sellers and one of its most profitable items.

By 1974 Capital had ten running tufted lines, of which five were considered to be poorly colored, poorly styled, and considerably overpriced. This was primarily due to yarn source. When using solution-dyed continuous filament nylon, creels had to be changed after every color run. This created inventory problems and resulted in higher costs. Capital was at the mercy of the commission spinner and dyer as far as the preparation of acrylic yarn was concerned, and it was at the mercy of its raw material supplier as far as solution-dyed continuous filament nylon was concerned. Capital did not have the same capability for yarn preparation and dyeing on man-made fibers as it had for wool.

In the winter of 1974 the Capital product assortment, including both weaving and tufting, included 44 percent wool, 40 percent acrylic, and 16 percent nylon. The comparable assortment for the total U.S. carpet industry was 16 percent wool, 25 percent acrylic, 50 percent nylon, and 8 percent in other fibers. Due to Capital's inability to piece-dye, it did not have products in the continuous filament nylon lines, which were the most popular ones. Competition gained footholds in the retail market with tufted products that replaced Capital's wool twist with tufted synthetic fiber twists. Acrylics required stronger heat-set than was possible by stock-dyeing and required an autoclave. Competitors obtained these, but Capital did not. Acrylic twist yarns produced a cloth which had very much the appearance of wool, but was considerably lower priced. Competitive tufted plush products, in both nylon and acrylics, were making inroads into the woven wool velvet market and Capital, due to its lack of facilities, found itself at a disadvantage.

MARKETING PROGRAM

Traditionally Capital's sales department had been told by manufacturing what products to sell. Prices had been determined by the accounting department. Top Capital management had compiled a sales budget each year, and the sales department was charged with meeting this budget. John Prince, general manager of marketing, was aware that Richard Yalch, general sales manager, was unhappy with the way the sales budget was determined. Yalch claimed that his organization was not given enough flexibility and that effective selling techniques and effective training programs cost more than he was getting. His argument bothered Charles Parker; however, Jay Stevens, general manager of finance, pointed out that Capital had been doing well with the present method and that sales departments in many firms perennially asked for more dollars.

The Capital sales effort was characterized by opportunistic attempts to grasp at anything which would bring immediate sales. Since other carpet manufacturers were turning to wholesalers, Capital tried it on a limited basis, but, at the same time, Capital sold direct to any retailer who was willing to buy from them. Many times Capital sold carpeting to retailers at prices which were as low or lower than prices to wholesalers.

Richard Yalch slanted his efforts toward woven carpet and contract work. He felt the carpet business could not afford the luxury of a wholesaler's margin. Capital's salesmen were considered to be knowledgeable carpet men, but they were strongly oriented toward the contract field. Thus, Capital had a strong contract operation. All carpeting business other than private home installations was considered contract business. This business typically included office buildings, banks, stores, schools, auditoriums, clubs, hotels, mortuaries, motels, churches, and apartment houses. While retail carpet sales had followed the trend toward synthetics, contract merchandise had not followed the trend to nearly the same extent. Tufted synthetics were gaining a larger percentage of the growing contract market, but most of this gain was at the expense of installations which had formerly used hard-surfaced materials. Most public space area customers were still choosing woven fabrics of close construction in Velvet, Wilton, and Axminster weaves. Wool was still the predominant fiber. Professional buyers showed less inclination to experiment with new materials and constructions than did retail customers.

Contract carpeting was sold by the manufacturer to several distinct classifications of customers:

1. *Large department store contract divisions.* These consisted of all larger jobs where the credit was secure.
2. *Contract houses who specialized in contract but often did retail business.* These also did the larger jobs, but they included apartment houses, and so forth, where the credit risk was often vague.
3. *Direct retail accounts which were often solicited and accounted for a small amount of contract business on the side.* These were typically small local jobs, where personal acquaintance with the customer was important.
4. *Distributors who took jobs in their dealers' localities on the basis of personal connections, mutual church or club memberships, and so forth.* Political connections accounted for a significant portion of this business.

The Capital management believed that contract carpet selling was a special field. In it the manufacturer's salesman had to pick a fabric designed for the purpose, and at the same time one which acquired the business for Capital. Typical contract carpetings were constructed to withstand heavy usage in public areas, and they were more expensive than retail carpeting. This called for technical manufacturing knowledge on the part of the salesman. Furthermore, most large jobs were put out on the basis of open tender, which required that the salesman produce complete technical specifications. The manufacturer's salesman was also required to give advice on installation and maintenance. Careful cultivation of customer relations was required so that if Capital was underbid on an open tender job, there might be a second opportunity to price the job—perhaps in a less expensive fabric, a mill second, or a discontinued line.

In the spring of 1974 the Capital headquarters management was in the process of making firm its policy attitudes with respect to the future composition of its business. At the time, measured in terms of the ultimate consumer, the Capital business was 70 percent contract and 30 percent other, with some six accounts generating 70 percent of Capital sales. On this contract base it was the intention to build two businesses—wholesale and retail.

It was the stated aim of the Capital management that it intended to be especially solicitous to preserve the contract heart of its business, and that this was to be the source from which the wholesale-retail business was to be spawned. The sales management suggested that the following tactics might aid in keeping the contract business:

1. Determine to remain price-competitive.
2. Keep Capital men imbued with the idea that the company intended to become even stronger in its contract position.
3. Specialize in contract sales management, with Capital men becoming the experts.
4. Bring Capital's contract know-how to bear on the U.S. carpet business via:
   a. technical information;
   b. installation;
   c. job organization;
   d. contract leads and their pursuit;
   e. the ABC approach;
   f. job finance;
   g. soliciting specifiers (such as architects) versus end users;
   h. catering to decorators, color consultants;
   i. providing specifiers with miniature sample sets, and so forth.
   j. concentrated follow-up on lost jobs to discover the reason for the job loss.
5. Develop products and techniques unique to Capital.
6. Develop tight technical specifications.
7. Build up for Capital a reputation as the innovator, the pacesetter.

DISTRIBUTION

Changing the Capital distribution pattern would be slow for a number of reasons. The initial tufting capacity would not support an immediate all-out effort. It was believed that the Capital color line would need reworking; the present colors were "hard" and considered to be poorly correlated, and some commercially dyed yarns lacked color control. Sixty-five percent of Capital's business was in Chicago and Detroit. Sixty-five retail accounts there now sold Capital carpets, and all of them, at times, bought directly from Capital. Wholesalers there also handled the Capital line, but their relationship with Capital was a tenuous one. Management believed that changing these relationships would require delicate diplomacy.

Capital had 13 wholesale stocks across the country. After considerable investigation, it was concluded that it would be in the best interests to have the wholesaler establish selected distribution at retail. Since most retailers sold from samples, it was essential that they purchase sample books. It was felt that one wholesaler would be in a better position to offer semiexclusivity to a retailer who would purchase and display the new "Capital Carpets" sample books. Of the 13 distributor stocks, 8 of them were carrying competing lines. The distributor organization was revamped so that there were 11 wholesale stocks.

For each wholesaler, Capital set up an exclusive territory based on the trading areas normally covered by the wholesaler. A "suggested zone selling price" was established for each wholesaler, based on his landed cost, which would return a gross profit on full rolls of 16 percent, and on cut quantities of 24.5 percent. This margin was arrived at after discussing with all Capital wholesalers the margins which they were earning on their carpet lines. It was felt that if the margins originally set up were not attractive, Capital would not be able to set up the wholesaler organization it desired. The original margins set up were high by United States standards.

As part of the new arrangement the wholesaler would participate in contract business and his dealers would be bidding against the large contract houses who would be buying direct from Capital. Considering that every contract job was priced differently, depending upon its size and the carpet construction involved, wholesalers were expected to earn gross margins of 5 percent to 10 percent on this portion of their business.

Since the new wholesalers would represent the Capital line exclusively in their territories, it was expected that it would be possible for them to be somewhat flexible in their pricing. This would be especially true in the instance of those retail accounts which had previously purchased directly from Capital at prices which had been lower than the wholesaler's cost. The intention was that they would be serviced in the interim by the wholesaler at prices which would be between the retailer's old buying price and the new "suggested wholesaler selling price."

Capital did not arrange a volume rebate program for its wholesalers, but the intention was to give consideration to this at a later date, after a proper product line had been established. If a volume rebate program was to be adopted, the gross margin available would undoubtedly require reduction.

Consideration had been given to offering a two percent cash discount to the wholesalers, but it was decided not to do so because this would mean increasing factory prices by two percent, and very little would be gained. It was not normal practice for wholesalers to give a cash discount to retail dealers.

EXPANSION

On April 3, 1974, Mr. J. R. Prince wrote the following memorandum to Mr. F. S. Kelly, executive vice president:

> Capital is a very strong contract business and weak in distribution through wholesalers and retailers. Therefore, if we expand, we plan to make as few changes as possible in the duties and responsibilities of our sales organization. Our present salespeople will continue to report to their present sales manager, who will be spending a good portion of time in Chicago, the new district office, rather than Atlanta. The sales manager will not be moving to Chicago, however. The new Capital sales force will be moving into the other nine offices throughout the country and the present office district managers will continue to assume responsibility for establishing wholesale distribution, with the help of new Capital sales representatives on a stewardship or functional arrangement. We will not set up new divisions, or bring the marketing function to a different location. . . . The key is our ten district managers will be involved in the wholesaling sense.

At a May 1, 1974, meeting, Mr. Kelly suggested to Mr. Prince that selling and administration expenses in the event of expansion would increase considerably. Assuming Capital sales at a level of $50 million, the following estimate was made of the additional personnel required for marketing and administration:

5	commodity managers
5	field sales managers
50	salespersons
25	secretarial and clerical for sales
5	assistants in the bureau of merchandising
25	order department
5	installation instructors
120	total marketing

Specific amounts were estimated for Capital advertising, samples, and wholesalers' convention (Exhibit 7).

Exhibit 7   **Capital Carpets**

PART I

The total expansion program at Capital has been broken into three parts as follows:

Project	Amount	Recovery Period	Added Profit Avg.-5 Yrs.	Return On Added Capital Avg.-5 Yrs.
Tufter, Piece Dyeing, and Building	$ 675,000	1.5 Yrs.	$ 651,000	20.5%
Yarn Preparation, Stock Dyeing, and Building ..	1,082,000	3.0 Yrs.	1,281,000	30.1
Autoclave...................................	58,000	1.0 Yrs.	155,000	30.4
	$1,815,000		$2,087,000	26.8%

PART II

Expansion Funds

Funds needed for a cut-pile tufter and piece-dyeing equipment.

Items	Estimated Cost
One cut-pile tufter	$ 98,100
Two 15′ dye becks	86,000
One sample unit	1,200
Vacuum extracting equipment	38,200
Twelve wet carts	12,000
One 1,500 lb. scale	2,500
Storage racks	4,500
Piece-dyeing installation costs	40,000
Manufacturing building—18,000 sq. ft.	266,000
Warehouse building—7,500 sq. ft.	89,500
Warehouse roll racks	15,000
Contingency for building	12,500
Contingency for machinery items....................................	10,000
Total new capital required..	$675,500

The building costs shown above are specific for the manufacturing area required for piece dyeing, and one-half of the costs for additional warehouse space included in the total building project.

This project is a combination cost reduction and expanded capacity job based on the following economic assumptions:

Capacity

The cut-pile tufter will enable us to produce an additional 200,000 square yards of tufted carpet per year. At our present average mix of nylon and acrilan, this will produce $2,260,000 per year in additional net sales and $550,000 of gross margin.

The addition of piece-dyeing equipment will increase nylon sales and margin as shown below:

Year	Sq. Yds. (000)	Sales Amount (000)	Gross Margin
1975	1,000	$2,000	$333
1976	1,300	2,800	500
1977	1,500	3,000	684
1978	1,500	3,000	684
1979	1,500	3,000	684

PART III

Cost Reduction

Piece dyeing will enable us to eliminate the need for commission dyers, and we will substitute continuous filament nylon for staple. This will result in direct cost saving of 26 cents per pound for nylon. As a result of longer production runs using neutral color fiber, we also expect to improve manufacturing margins by 2 percent in 1975 and 1976, and 3 percent thereafter. The net manufacturing savings will accrue as follows:

Year	Direct Cost Savings .26/lb. (000)	Prod. Efficiency (000)	Added Mfg. Expense (000)	Net Savings (000)
1975	$143	$44	$(70)	$117
1976	208	64	(80)	192
1977	286	132	(85)	333
1978	286	132	(85)	333
1979	286	132	(85)	333
Average	$242	$101	$(81)	$262

Selling, Administrative and Interest Expenses

We have made provision for increased selling and administrative expenses at 4.5 percent of additional net sales. Interest costs are 6 percent of the capital funds, or $40,500 per year.

PART IV

Capital Employed

Capital requirements for accounts receivable, inventories, and property plant and equipment are detailed below. We do not expect to increase cash or miscellaneous assets as a result of this project.

Year	Accounts Receivable (45 Days) (000)	Inventory (000)	P.P. & E. (000)	Total Increase (000)
1975	$258	$609	451	$1,318
1976	307	669	423	1,399
1977	408	889	395	1,692
1978	408	889	367	1,664
1979	408	889	339	1,636
Average	$358	$789	395	$1,542

Based on the foregoing assumptions *additional* sales, net profit, capital and ROCE for the 1975-1979 period are as follows:

Year	Net Sales (000)	Net Profits (000)	Capital Emp. (000)	ROCE
1975	$7,060	$463	$3,018	15.3%
1976	7,460	582	3,099	18.7
1977	8,260	737	3,292	22.5
1978	8,260	373	3,264	22.9
1979	8,260	373	3,236	23.4
Average	$7,860	$506	$3,182	20.5%

Recovery Period

We will recover our fixed capital expenditures of $675,500 in 1.5 years. This employs the average method over the five-year period. Calculated on the specific method, our recovery period will be 2.1 years.

In light of the proposal made by Mr. F. S. Kelly, Charles D. Parker, president of Capital, announced that the Capital Carpet marketing organization was being restructured to enable Capital to maintain its strong position in the contract field.

Effective July 1, 1974, Mr. Thomas J. Crown, the assistant manager, building and floor products division, was appointed general sales manager of Capital Carpets. Mr. Crown had had 16 years of experience in field sales and marketing management. He was to be responsible for all the marketing operations of Capital and would personally direct the field sales functions at the wholesale and retail levels.

On the same date Mr. B. L. Burns became manager, contract sales, reporting to Mr. Crown. Mr. Burns, who had been managing Capital's contract sales, was henceforth to devote his full time to the contract business, emphasizing the forthcoming new tufted contract lines.

In October 1974, B. J. Hartley suggested that a 72,000 square foot addition to the Savannah, Georgia, tufting plant would be advantageous. The new plant would adjoin the existing building and would house piece-dyeing facilities, spinning equipment, and added warehousing. An additional tufting machine would also be installed in the existing Savannah plant. The building, if begun in February 1975, would be completed by March 1976. An autoclave to heat-set a hard twist would be installed in October and an additional two cards and spinning frames would be installed in December. The enlarged facilities would permit Capital to process all of their carpets from bulk fiber to the finished carpet with less dependence on outside spinners and dyers.

THE DECISION

In December 1974 the Capital management made an exhaustive analysis of its line with a view of revamping it. They wished to continue with Capital's traditional wool, nylon, and Acrilan, with which Capital was familiar and which involved little risk; however, they also wanted to have a line that was long and complete enough to match any competitor's. Management realized that their line was short and incomplete, but they questioned how fast the transition to a long line should be made.

There were competitors who were doing a considerably larger volume and could support a long line on a profitable basis. The Capital management, however, was inclined to believe that what was economic for these established competitors was not necessarily economic for Capital, considering its incomplete and limited production facilities, market image, inexperience with man-made fibers, and one-sided market orientation. The Capital management was inclined toward building up the line as soon as feasible since industry projections for 1975 were favorable. Shipments of carpets and rugs were estimated to rise some 14 percent for the first half of 1975 over the corresponding period of a year earlier. Dollar volume was expected to rise at an even greater rate. Dollar rise was attributed to upgraded product mixes and higher unit prices. Dollar volume was estimated to rise to $3.2 billion or more. Greater utilization of plant and an improved industry-wide inventory position were cited as reasons why manufacturer's profit margins should be widened in the first half of 1975 and profitability should be at least maintained in the final six months despite price limitations. Thus, another record earnings year was in prospect for 1975 for most carpet and rug producers and further progress tentatively was projected for 1976 if raw materials availability did not become critical.

Case 7–4

Compo, Inc.*

Compo was an independent data service center, serving primarily small businesses, and was established in 1970 by Robert Adams. It had grown to some 35 employees and sales of $622,000. Other top management officers included Donald Bannie, vice president of operations, and Richard Bond, vice president of sales and programming (Exhibit 1).

SALES HISTORY

1978	$328,130
1979	$463,750
1980	$579,317
1981	$622,965

Sales figures for 1982 were difficult to estimate, but management felt that Compo would show growth comparable to previous years. A target goal of $1,000,000 in sales by 1985 had been set, and management felt this goal would be met.

SERVICE MIX

The types of information-processing services offered by Compo were custom-designed programs and packaged, ready-to-run programs. Compo was primarily a customhouse, with 90 percent of sales in this area. Packaged programs, totaling ten percent of sales, were the basic accounting functions of payroll, accounts receivable, accounts payable, inventory, and general ledger. Other functions for managerial control were incorporated into the custom programs as dictated by the needs of various customers.

Compo was, and wished to remain a customhouse, dedicated to start-to-finish data service for each customer. The tailoring of a program to the unique requirements of each customer was more costly and time-consuming than packaged programs, but management preferred the custom work and felt that this market could support its sales goal of $1 million by 1985.

---

*This case was prepared by Joseph C. Latona, The University of Akron, with the intention of providing a basis for class discussion rather than illustrating either effective or ineffective management of a business situation. Reprinted with permission from *Application of Decision Sciences in Organizations: A Case Approach* by Joseph C. Latona and K. Mark Weaver with the cooperation of the American Institute for Decision Sciences, Atlanta, Georgia, 1980.

Compo, Inc.
Organizational Chart

Exhibit 1

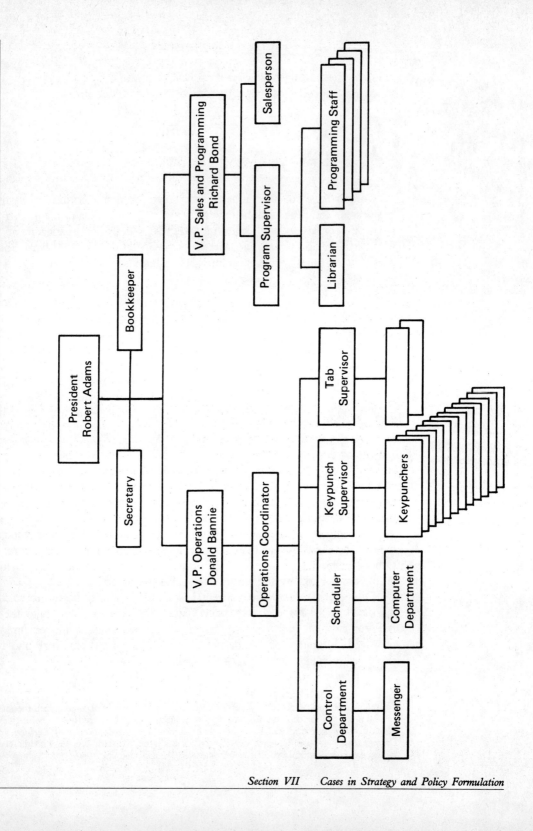

Overall, the operations at Compo were considered successful, if measured by sales growth, facility expansion, and reputation earned. The only negative aspects of the firm were the seeming lack of directed expansion plans, strategy and goals, and the threat of minicomputers and microcomputers.

CUSTOMERS, MARKETS

Compo serviced accounts in the Middletown, Dayton, and Springfield, Ohio, areas. The accounts covered a wide range of business and industry: banks, manufacturers, retailers, churches, doctors, transportation lines, governmental agencies, and various small businesses.

Within the basic market area, Mr. Bannie estimated that there were close to 20,000 businesses. He had calculated the market potential in the following manner:

	20,000	businesses
less	18,000	with fewer than 20 employees, and consequently, too small to require data processing services
	2,000	
less	250	which were large enough to have in-house processing equipment
	1,750	potential customers

Of these 1,750 potentials, Compo serviced roughly 110, and appeared to have about a 6 percent share of the market. Figures were unavailable as to how many service companies were competing, but Mr. Bannie had estimated the number to be around 25; so this market share looked reasonable, since an average share would be approximately 4 percent. Extending this further, if Compo commanded 6 percent of the market, with sales of $623,000, then the total market potential would be in the neighborhood of $10 million. If Compo expected sales of $1 million, it must capture a full 10 percent of the market. These figures were computed with 1981 sales figures, and if the growth trend continued, $1 million sales could be attained with possibly 8 percent or 9 percent of the market.

FUNCTIONS OF SERVICES PROVIDED

Number of functions provided per customer	Approximate percentage of total
1	35
2-5	40
6-10	13
over 10	12
	100

There were 35 to 40 or more payroll packages, some of which were included in the above figures.

PROMOTION, ADVERTISING

In the past several years, Compo had spent very little on advertising or promotion. Direct mail was most often employed, but a minimal return had made even these ventures only sparingly successful. There had been some print advertising and participation in trade shows and exhibits.

In the past four years, Compo had expended $755, $3,128, $1,166, and $746 on advertising. This ranged from a high of .67 percent of sales to a low of .12 percent of sales.

COMPETITION

The chief competitors of Compo were, in order of importance, (1) minicomputers and microcomputers, (2) service bureaus with large parent companies, (3) independent service bureaus, and (4) banks. The basic means of competition was price (services offered were similar). Quality, dependability, and reliability were essential factors in maintaining customers, and Compo's image in these areas was excellent.

SELLING

Compo had no formal sales organization. It had been mentioned often by both Mr. Bannie and Mr. Bond that in such an organization where service was the product, everyone in the company was a salesperson, capable of obtaining leads, making initial telephone contacts, answering questions, and solving problems of customers.

The formal sales efforts were headed by Richard Bond. His efforts were aided by one "official" salesperson. Since 98 percent of all leads were obtained in referrals, the selling function, to a large degree, consisted of following up on cases where either Mr. Bannie or Mr. Bond had had initial contact, or it consisted of updating current customers' services and accounts and suggesting expanded programs or services for them.

Again, since the referral system was almost wholly used, there were, and could be, no quotas set for call, telephone contacts, and so forth. No formal sales strategy was implemented.

PRODUCTION

Compo, Inc. was organized to accept data input from its customers and prepare information in a form acceptable to the customer. Information was produced by comparing, summarizing, grouping, classifying, associating, reducing, or otherwise processing data into a meaningful form. Information necessarily involved the relationship of data with other data. The object of every data processing system is information (Appendix I). The system to deliver information to the customer is given below:

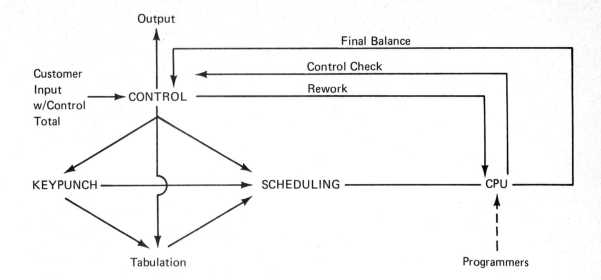

The customer transmitted the data with control totals. The control group was responsible for routing input to the system and output to the customer. This group was responsible for providing the information to the customer given the data. It had the option, depending on the form of the input, of routing the input to the keypunch area for coding, or to the tabulation department for preparation and "massaging" of the data, or directly to the scheduler for processing. Once the data was processed by the computer, the control group verified that the control total obtained from the central processing unit operator (CPU operator) matched the total given by the customer. The job might be reworked or the customer might be called. Once the balance was achieved, control sent the job to a courier if it was to be delivered or held it for pickup. Tabulation might have assisted in packaging a job. Control also logged each job for the time spent in processing.

The tabulation group (tab) sorted, collated, or tabulated data as needed. It also packaged jobs if needed. The trend was to employ alternative types of input where the tabulation group would not be required.

The keypunch operators were responsible for transforming data input in raw form into data acceptable to the computer. This raw data was coded onto a keypunch card, and these keypunch cards were verified for accuracy.

The computer or CPU group was responsible for processing the data. This group logged the CPU time that was spent on each job. At its disposal was an IBM 360/30 computer with 60K core capacity and a 360 enhancer, four 2311 disc drives, two 2403 tape drives, one card reader, and one 2403 printer.

The programming group was responsible for the software, or programs, which were the instructions to operate the computer. These programs were used repetitively if operable and in no need of revision. This group was not directly involved in data processing each time.

The simplified flow diagram represented Compo's data system. In the discussion of the system with the general manager, it became evident that the system was quite satisfactory. Apparently input and output data contained few errors and those that occurred were easily remedied. Reports were seldom late or inadequate; no mention of customer complaints about the quality or timeliness of the service was made.

Little apparent problem was being experienced with the hardware. The 60K core of the computer with the enhancer seemed more than sufficient for the operation; in fact, it more than doubled one competitor in the Dayton, Middletown, and Springfield area.

The work waiting to be processed appeared to have been substantially reduced. This might have been due to the batch processing advantages of the enhancer or simply more efficient programming, or more efficient scheduling. In viewing the system, no major problems were evident. The future markets appeared to be Compo's long-range challenge. The question was, would Compo's system be able to meet the demands placed on it in the future as a result of growth, reorganization, or new technology (particularly the minicomputer and microcomputer)? New methods of handling or transmitting data might render methods obsolete, or new equipment might perform more accurately, faster, and at less cost. Fundamentally, the customer might demand a different service, that is, developing software and serving the microcomputer. Industry changes and the company goal of nearly doubling sales surpassing $1,000,000 within the next five years was the challenge of Compo's long-range policies.

The first industry trend evident for the service bureau was growth. Nationally the growth of user data processing expenditures would grow from over $50 billion in 1978 to approximately $80 billion in 1984, an annual rate of 16 percent. The data services market would grow 20 percent annually, from approximately $8.4 billion in 1978 to $13.9 billion in 1984. Within data services, network information services and software products would grow the fastest at annual rates of 27 percent. Just behind these, facilities management would grow annually at 25 percent. Support services would grow at ten percent.

Compo, Inc. had to determine if it wished to remain primarily a customhouse, begin moves toward "packaged" systems sales, or sell and service microcomputers (Appendix I).

FINANCE AND ACCOUNTING

Comparative balance sheets and income statements for the 1977–1981 years are shown in Exhibits 2 and 3, respectively. Generally, they revealed that Compo was a growing, prospering company.

The financial area was considered by management to be a key area of the company and integrally related to its overall strategy. Compo's high capital investment required that debt levels of the firm be substantial. For 1982, it was estimated that Compo would spend as much as $200 thousand on equipment and supplies. The importance of the financial area was underscored by the president, Robert Adams:

> Historically, Compo's financing has been on a project-to-project basis. Therefore, investments were dependent upon single customer contracts and it was simply a "go" or "no go" situation which prohibited accurate, long-term capital planning.
>
> Over the next five years our business mix should change markedly. We should become more of a merchant-oriented company serving a variety of industries, businesses, and public sector-type firms. We must now have a more flexible financing capability which will focus on the long term and recognize the changing mix of our business.

Exhibit 2

Compo, Inc.
Comparative Balance Sheets

ASSETS	1977	1978	1979	1980	1981
Current assets:					
Cash on hand and in bank	$ 1,291.99	$ 26.39	$ 151.31	$ 6,144.31	$ 16,879.69
Accounts receivable	76,863.28	98,196.58	84,417.28	106,554.29	103,030.41
Prepaid expense	848.21	1,024.95	1,404.34	1,234.00	28,954.00
Cash value—life insurance	—	9,524.66	9,776.86	11,809.40	—
Total current assets	$ 79,003.48	$108,772.58	$ 95,749.87	$125,742.00	$148,864.10
Fixed assets:					
Fixtures and equipment	$ 34,483.20	$ 34,334.24	$ 55,173.75	$ 61,759.04	$ 71,642.04
Less accumulated depreciation	(24,577.57)	(20,474.14)	(28,989.40)	(34,530.61)	(29,874.26)
Automobile(s)	3,915.84	7,262.69	10,994.66	18,638.66	23,602.38
Less accumulated depreciation	(1,522.78)	(3,876.85)	(5,995.42)	(9,716.06)	(16,121.75)
Leasehold improvements	17,511.22	17,640.18	17,774.05	17,774.05	17,774.05
Less accumulated depreciation	(2,896.43)	(7,654.43)	(6,996.05)	(9,042.53)	(6,685.04)
Sign	426.87	426.87	426.87	426.87	426.87
Less accumulated depreciation	(59.78)	(315.85)	(162.26)	(213.50)	(162.13)
Total fixed assets	$ 27,280.57	$ 27,342.71	$ 42,226.20	$ 45,095.92	$ 60,602.16
Other assets:					
Organization costs	$ 1,191.74	$ 887.54	$ 583.34	$ 279.14	$ —
Worker's compensation deposit	464.00	512.00	626.00	626.00	626.00
Investment	—	—	—	12,272.59	12,272.59
Unamortized goodwill	115,635.40	97,766.96	97,766.96	87,990.26	78,213.56
Total other assets	$117,291.14	$ 99,166.50	$ 98,976.30	$101,167.99	$ 91,112.15
Total assets	$223,575.19	$235,281.79	$236,952.37	$272,005.91	$300,578.41
LIABILITIES					
Current liabilities:					
Due to banks—current	$ 27,000.00	$ 18,000.00	$ 20,937.00	$ 20,937.00	$ 24,000.00
Notes payable	15,000.00	15,000.00	15,000.00	10,436.37	—
Notes payable	24,252.00	—	2,879.88	1,075.84	28,396.80
Accounts payable	24,393.67	28,704.84	17,233.23	17,409.33	23,497.36
Payroll taxes	2,952.57	3,478.54	4,026.12	3,654.19	5,288.62
Worker's compensation accrued	391.20	444.04	474.10	976.54	696.15
Miscellaneous current liabilities	3,260.90	121.82	17,553.17	2,111.28	1,806.14
Total current liabilities	$ 97,250.34	$ 65,749.24	$ 78,103.50	$ 56,600.55	$ 83,685.07

Long-term liabilities:

	1977	1978	1979	1980	1981
Due to banks	$ 23,500.00	$ 90,670.05	$ 67,723.67	$ 45,826.20	$ 18,879.83
Due to individuals	28,696.91	19,186.37	4,186.37	—	—
Due to officers	38.14	1,697.14	4,398.54	15,367.89	12,867.89
Due to IBM for equipment	20,208.90	—	—	—	—
Due on automobile	—	—	1,196.67	—	4,313.40
Total long-term liabilities	$ 72,443.95	$111,553.56	$ 77,505.25	$ 61,194.09	$ 36,061.12
Total liabilities	$169,694.29	$177,302.80	$155,608.75	$117,794.64	$119,746.19

STOCKHOLDERS' EQUITY

	1977	1978	1979	1980	1981
Common stock	$ 22,575.79	$ 22,575.79	$ 24,575.79	$ 25,960.79	$ 29,335.79
Retained earnings	31,305.11	35,403.20	59,267.83	134,750.48	157,996.43
Less Treasury stock	—	—	(2,500.00)	(6,500.00)	(6,500.00)
Total stockholders' equity	$ 53,880.90	$ 57,978.99	$ 81,343.62	$154,211.27	$180,832.22
Total liabilities and stockholders' equity	$223,575.19	$235,281.79	$236,952.37	$272,005.91	$300,578.41
Working capital (CA–CL)	$(18,246.86)	$ 43,023.34	$ 17,646.37	$ 69,141.45	$ 65,179.03

Exhibit 3

Compo, Inc.
Comparative Income Statements

	1977	1978	1979	1980	1981
Revenue from services	$336,043.12	$328,130.74	$463,750.48	$579,316.85	$622,965.01
Less:					
Direct salaries	$105,563.36	$111,960.64	$159,635.37	$185,407.88	$252,804.96
Equipment costs	117,803.46	111,596.55	97,623.62	120,157.76	122,663.24
Production supplies	18,314.14	29,544.44	25,291.44	34,766.59	55,247.97
Occupancy costs	11,582.79	14,497.13	19,389.12	20,919.85	16,918.49
Payroll tax and fringes	10,385.04	10,224.59	17,371.29	25,100.10	35,004.05
Total direct costs	$263,648.79	$277,823.35	$319,310.84	$386,352.18	$482,638.71
Gross profit	$ 72,394.33	$ 50,307.39	$144,439.64	$192,964.67	$140,326.30
Less company overhead	64,632.66	45,890.27	108,817.32	124,642.29	106,637.32
Net income from operations	$ 7,761.67	$ 4,417.12	$ 35,622.32	$ 68,322.38	$ 33,688.98
Other income (expense)	878.26	1,148.11	1,502.36	2,865.47	1,957.64
Net income for the period*	$ 8,639.93	$ 5,565.23	$ 37,124.68	$ 71,187.85	$ 35,646.62

*Net income before taxes: taxes figured on a cash account basis.

"Millionaire Machine?"*

The computer services industry, once the crying stepchild of the matured hardware industry, is attracting attention and money. Big money.

Stock prices are up, the pace of mergers and acquisitions quickens, startup ventures abound, new products find quick success, prominent companies go public. Growth—of markets, revenues, and profits—is the word on everyone's lips.

Dp professionals, company managers, and investors are all enjoying the growth and change. And yet, some observers, particularly those with a financial stake, are not too sure about the industry's future.

They ask: can the astounding growth of software and services, which currently outpaces that of the overall computer industry, continue for long? Or will the business, and stock prices, crash the way they did so spectacularly in the early 70s?

To answer such questions and to make sense of what some seem to think are contradicting signals, a method of analyzing the services market's current state and future potential is needed. In lieu of a crystal ball, the traditional life cycle concept may be applied effectively. Just as humans and other living organisms go through specific periods of birth, growth, maturity, and decline, industries may show similar tendencies.

The industrial revolution created enormous fortunes as capital and labor moved from agriculture to manufacturing. The movement's by-product was a significantly improved standard of living. Similarly, the shift of capital and labor now occurring, from established industries into information industries, is again creating significant fortunes and benefiting the standard of living.

Like the industrial revolution, the information revolution is spawning a whole list of small industries, each composed of many companies. Computer services, a term Wall Street uses to embrace a wide variety of companies whose principal value lies in their computer software, is just one of many businesses in the information industry. Others include computers, telecommunications, peripherals, and semiconductors. The computer services industry itself may be segmented into timesharing, facilities management, turnkey systems, packaged software products, and contract programming.

Capital flowing into these growth areas is fleeing from older industries which offer little growth and a return on equity lower than the inflation rate. By contrast, computer services companies offer growth rates considerably higher than the inflation rate and many times the growth of the economy as a whole. Peter Cunningham, of Input, Inc., estimates industry growth at about 20%, broken down as follows:

	1980 (in $bil.)	1985 (in $bil.)
Processing services	$8.8	$18.8
Software products	2.4	8.7
Professional services	3.4	7.5

The average annual growth rate for each of the three categories is: Processing Services, 17%; Software Products, 29%; and Professional Services, 17%.

Recognizing this substantial growth, Wall Street has poured money into the industry. In 1980, the computer services stocks followed by Alex. Brown & Sons more than doubled on average—performing significantly better than the market as a whole, as shown in Figure 1.

In the early growth stage of the life cycle, computer services companies are enjoying a fast track because of three sources of available growth. First, the market for computer services is rapidly expanding as decreasing costs bring computing within

*Alfred R. Berkeley, "Millionaire Machine?" *Datamation*, August 1981, pp. 20, 21, 22, 27, 31, 32, 34, 36. Reprinted with permission of *Datamation*® magazine, ©Copyright by Technical Publishing Company, a Dun & Bradstreet Company. All rights reserved.

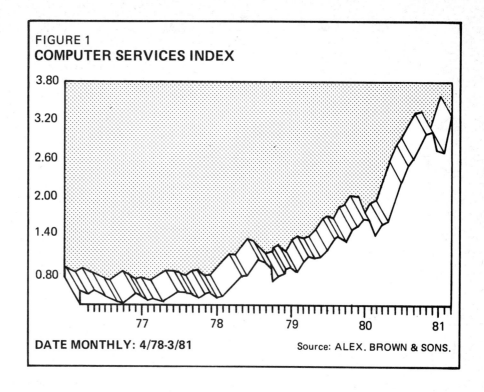

FIGURE 1
COMPUTER SERVICES INDEX

DATE MONTHLY: 4/78-3/81   Source: ALEX. BROWN & SONS.

reach of more and more buyers. Second, not all among those who can afford and want computing use it. Hence, growth is available through additional market penetration. Third, growth is available to any company grabbing market share from competitors.

In mature markets, it is not unusual to find the dominant competitor commanding a 50%, 60%, or 70% share of the market. (General Motors provides a classic example.) No such dominant competitors, however, have yet emerged in computer services. In fact, the very largest competitors command less than 5% of the market.

The unusual growth opportunities have attracted much investment attention because in older industries growth is slow or declining, markets are fully penetrated, and the sole source of growth is someone else's market share. Further computer services growth is leveraged and enhanced by other industries' investments. Importantly, plummeting semiconductor prices bring real benefits to computer users by creating price-elastic markets. Hence the explosive demand for cost-efficient computing.

To investors, the ability to benefit directly from others' advances has important implications (i.e., the closer a producer is to the end user in the manufacturing and distribution chain, the more stable the demand is for its service). Conversely, the more removed a producer becomes from the end user, the more susceptible it is to the accordian effect of inventory and capital spending curtailments up and down the chain of producers. Schematically, raw material is converted to parts, parts to components, components to products, products to systems, and now in this business, systems to networks. To the extent that different providers up and down that chain curtail their inventories, the lower-level producers find the demand for their products violently fluctuating. The earnings of such companies are even more erratic because these companies are often both financially and operationally leveraged. Additionally, as a general rule, the closer the business is to raw materials, the more capital intensive it is, as in the case of computer services:

```
Raw Material + Capital + Labor
Part 1 + Part 2 + ... + Part N
Component 1 + Component 2 + ... + Component N
Product 1 + Product 2 + ... + Product N
System 1 + System 2 + ... + System N
Network 1 + Network 2 + ... + Network N
User
```

Software enters the chain as a product, and computer services such as timesharing and turnkey systems enter at the systems level—relatively close to the end user. Computer services companies add value to "iron" produced by others. One of the reasons that computer services companies are now acquisition targets is that they represent a way for hardware vendors to integrate forward, add additional value, and create complete solutions to users' problems. By entering the chain at a higher level, computer services companies benefit from other participants and investments. This means lower capital intensity, lower labor intensity, and higher operating leverage.

Frank Lautenberg of Automatic Data Processing, Inc., stresses the difference between computers and computing: computers are tools; computing provides solutions. Computing turns data into information and information into insights. Insights provide raw material for knowledge, which is power. The computer services industry turns computers into computing, and provides solutions to significant information problems.

As the demand for computing soars, computer services companies fill the gap between supply and demand. The computer population is increasing faster than the supply of trained programmers, with every new general-purpose computer sold needing 150 to 400 separate programs in a typical business installation—from utilities and programming aids to database management systems and applications. Wall Street is particularly intrigued with this "software multiplier" concept. The marketplace expresses such supply/demand imbalance in its pricing mechanisms; trained computer programmers earn significantly more than the average American worker; even entry-level programmers receive more than the minimum wage. Figure 2 shows educated estimates of programmer and computer populations by G. T. Orwick of Management Science America.

But while a shortage of computer programmers contributes to the growth of computer services, the industry also profits from significant economies of scale. Assembling and distributing specialized computer solutions for a vast customer base is ultimately cheaper than having users acquire requisite skills and facilities on an individual basis. All buyers together, however, pay more than the costs of providing the solution. Thus the industry offers access on terms economical to both buyer and seller. The seller's risk lies in attracting enough customers, while customers are faced with a classic "make or buy" decision. Relevant costs are fully allocated life cycle costs, and economies of scale provided by computer services are large because solutions to significant problems involve complex software. (All the easy programs have been written!)

A buyer can license a database management system for about $100,000; building a similar system might cost $1,000,000, might take several years to implement, and might never work. The decision switches from "whether" to "which?" Since computers require a specialized body of knowledge, since the intricacies of major applications require their own body of knowledge, and since the costs of developing significant solutions can be shared by many users, the economies of scale in computer services are real and permanent. The compelling economics of computer services have given the whole industry a new legitimacy and acceptance.

Computer services companies benefit from selling old products to new customers and new products to old customers. For example, virtually every major hospital in the country uses computers to manage information. Nonetheless, major independent computer services vendors have consistently added new products over the last decade. One of the largest, Shared Medical Systems, now offers 28 different modules. The com-

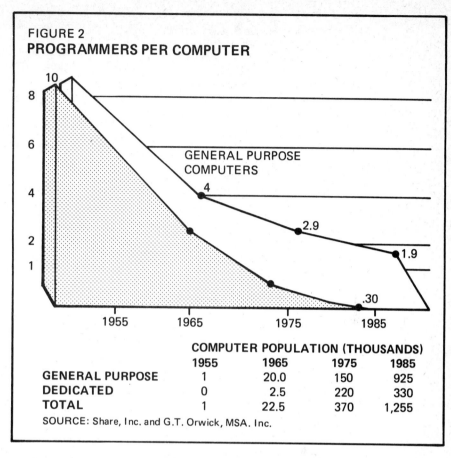

FIGURE 2
PROGRAMMERS PER COMPUTER

GENERAL PURPOSE
COMPUTERS

COMPUTER POPULATION (THOUSANDS)				
	1955	1965	1975	1985
GENERAL PURPOSE	1	20.0	150	925
DEDICATED	0	2.5	220	330
TOTAL	1	22.5	370	1,255

SOURCE: Share, Inc. and G.T. Orwick, MSA. Inc.

pany's average revenues per hospital bed per day have risen to $2.07 from $1.16 over the last six years. This trend has spread to other industries as computerization brings efficiency, discipline, and control to more and more corporate functions.

Life cycle analogies also show that market share changes swiftly. Vendors delivering excellent service at attractive prices before competition arises can usurp and dominate thousands of small individual markets for computer services. Triad Systems, Inc., serving the automotive parts retailer, is a fine example. But winning market share in head-to-head battles with entrenched competitors can be terribly expensive. Acquisition represents a far more fruitful strategy, as Automatic Data Processing, Anacomp, and Tymshare have clearly demonstrated. Dominant competitors in other industries have emerged in the same way. The cumulative investment in product features and marketing have prompted new entrants to tackle potential competitors directly by buying existing participants.

Economic shifts caused by technological advances represent yet another reason for industry growth, perhaps illustrated most dramatically by the shift between hardware and software costs. Plummeting hardware costs contrast sharply with inflating programmer costs. Consider the apocryphal tale of the manufacturer who paid about $5 for the microprocessor and over $100,000 to develop software for it. Conventional wisdom in the industry claims that in the late 1960s hardware costs consumed 80% of the dollar, programming costs consumed 20%. Now the ratio may be reversed. This highlights the compelling economics of buying computer services to a point where the rate of growth for services is faster than the rate of growth for hardware. Additionally, computer services spread high ongoing maintenance costs among many users while developing cost-efficient, universal applications for entire industries.

Trust accounting, for example, is the toughest computer application facing modern banking. Maintaining a trust department typically consumes between 8% and 10% of the bank's data processing assets, although on the average the service produces only between 1% and 2% of the bank's revenues, and often less of the profits. But the trust industry is experiencing wave after wave of significant change. New investment vehicles are entering the market. Traditional holdings, stocks, and bonds are being joined by options, Ginnie Mae pass-throughs, commodities, oil drilling partnerships, financial futures, and even stamps and diamonds. Add to all this increasingly burdensome government reporting requirements for ERISA, IRA and Keogh accounts, and the Comptroller of the Currency.

When the trust department requests software modification or development, however, it's usually queued behind electronic funds transfer, automatic teller machines, and interest bearing checking. The department can hardly afford to wait its turn; here, it may find purchased computer services the better alternative, where companies like SEI will spend almost $2 million this year alone to enhance and maintain its trust accounting software. These costs exceed the revenues of many trust departments and the profits of all but the larger ones, but when life cycle costs are understood, the economics become clear.

In the early stages of any business life cycle, management emphasis is on producing a product that works, on product features, and on performance. But as the business matures, and as competition matches product features and marketing capabilities, capital and marketing strategy become paramount. For computer services, marketing is now key, but capital has not yet become a critical determinant of success. The relative importance of each factor shifts as markets mature. For example, technology changes throughout the life cycle greatly influence service companies' product development, marketing strategy, and financial controls. Products must keep pace with new advancements, so R&D costs remain high.

Similarly, marketing investments remain substantial because of rapid market growth. All participants assume heavy reinvestment spurred by fast growth and fast technological change: professionals must invest time in education and reeducation; managers must forego a percentage of profits for new product development; and shareholders must exchange dividends for corporate reinvestment. Also, some companies use Wall Street's reborn interest in the industry to raise low-cost capital to weather hard times and to make incremental investments and acquisitions. Competitors must follow suit or risk losing market share.

The services industry has moved from selling computer tools to creating customer solutions. To capture new users who might never have considered service contracts, the maturing industry has resorted to product enhancements such as user-friendly access and multiple program and services packaging to make leasing time as economical as possible. A parallel shift from single product, single market strategies to multiple product, multiple market strategies often occurs as growth proceeds.

The shift toward multiple channels of distribution for computer services deserves mention. Increased competition and sophistication in product performance has forced many participants to change the definition of their business. As products evolve from tools to solutions, business formats evolve into distribution modes. A company that entered the business viewing itself as a timesharing firm may grow to view timesharing as just one way to deliver computing solutions to customers.

The shift toward multiple distribution modes is no easy task. While it is an absolute bonanza for the customer to be able to move easily up and down the scale, using as much or as little of an offering as needed at an ever decreasing cost per transaction, the vendor has a vastly different view. There are often heavy initial costs associated with marketing a new product, and the revenues that were repetitive in a timesharing offering may become one-time revenues in a turnkey system or software environment.

Other complications arising from multiple distribution channels involve the sales cycle and the degree of knowledge and expertise required by the vendor's sales force. For example, buying a solution via timesharing is a variable expense, easily canceled on short notice, and any line manager in the buying organization probably has authority to make the purchase decision. A solution in the form of a turnkey minicomputer, however, is probably a capital budgeting item for the buyer, requires advanced planning and rather high-level approval, and cannot be canceled. Furthermore, if a customer's level of usage is high enough to justify a turnkey system, the solution offered is probably rather important to business continuity.

The vendor's sales force requires sophisticated knowledge of the solution and ability to sell at a rather high organizational level. Selling the same solution in the form of a software product for use on the customer's large in-house computers is quite another task. Here, the vendor's sales force must interact with professionals as well as with high-level line managers. At this level of use, the solution probably addresses problems that are core to company survival. It is unlikely that the salesperson who sells the solution via timesharing is the same person who can sell the solution as a software product. The industry is plainly wrestling with these problems now. Nonetheless, the trend is clear: more and more services will be offered via multiple distribution channels.

For new entrants, penetrating established markets has become increasingly difficult and expensive. The trend can clearly be seen in virtually all niches of the market. In the early days of timesharing, it was competitively sufficient to offer raw time on a computer. Once several vendors offered raw time, competition turned to selling specialized software, aggressive competitors invested in interactive capabilities and remote processing.

The cycle continues today with companies vending databases and specialized access programs. Existing competitors have financed these capabilities from earnings over time; a new entrant would have to commit significant capital to play the game.

Emphasis is also shifting from individual products and services to integrated systems. This is part and parcel of the shift to provide complete solutions to users' needs. The trend in financial software products, for instance, is clearly toward offering communicating programs. It used to be sufficient to offer good standalone accounts payable or fixed assets, general ledger, payroll, etc.—each able to interact where appropriate. Competition demands that the vendor satisfy two of his customers' dilemmas—writing and maintaining a solution, and weaving that solution into the overall flow of the enterprise. The customer benefits from this competitive quest for superiority in the market.

Another shift is toward world competition. Decreased telecommunications costs have propelled the timesharing firms into more and more markets. Software product vendors are going international too, drawn by large, untapped markets and compelling economics. American companies are not alone in the move to worldwide competition. The French government, for example, nurtures and protects domestic industry while its companies, like Cap-Gemini, acquire U.S. computer service firms.

Overall, competition has encouraged entrepreneurial management styles and structures to move toward more formalized, more professional arrangements. Owners and managers who have traditionally focused on product performance and personal selling now find themselves in the business of managing people, bankers, and vendors.

Hardware/software cost relationship reversal has led to significant shifts in relations between hardware and software vendors. The hardware industry has tried for years to ignore the computer services industry. Now computer services firms are among their largest customers and among their toughest competitors in selling computing solutions and software. At International Computer Programs Inc.'s annual software awards meeting in San Antonio this year, almost a dozen hardware manufacturers sat at the same podium and virtually begged the assembled software houses to do business with them, through them, and for them. The bait was all sorts of free or low cost hardware, technical support, and promotion.

The hardware vendors, of course, hoped to tap the enormous capital investment and accumulated experience of the software houses. Economically, the ICP meeting may have been a milestone event for the computer services industry. The seesaw is tipping: in the past, vendors sold hardware and gave away software; now, vendors sell hardware and software. In the future, vendors may sell software and give away hardware. Passionate courting of software houses by hardware firms is further prompted by the zero cost hardware concept. Since hardware alone doesn't provide solutions, its pricing moves from value to cost. The only way the hardware vendor can continue to price its products to value is to create value by adding software.

Further evidence of the dramatic shift in value between hardware and software lies in the astounding lineup of bidders for the U.S. Army's so-called "viable" contract. The army is requesting proposals from vendors to automate administrative support at its bases. Traditionally, such proposals would have been submitted by hardware vendors. In this case, the major contractors are Electronic Data Systems and Computer Sciences Corp., each using hardware vendors as subcontractors! One cannot overemphasize the significance of this arrangement as evidence of the shift in power toward software.

As noted, the quest for growth has led the industry through a number of rather obvious shifts: toward solutions rather than tools, toward integrated systems, and toward multiple markets and multiple distribution channels. In sum, the trend is toward "vertical markets." Vertical marketing means the computer services vendor satisfies all computing requirements for a single market. Shared Medical Systems is probably the best known vendor using this approach, meeting virtually any health industry computing need. The vertical approach incorporates complete solutions, hardware, software, integrated interactive programs, and complete backup support. Vertical marketing offers buyers substantially simplified purchase decisions while giving substantial operating leverage and clear competitive advantages to vendors.

Certainly, marriage and divorce are no strangers to the computer services industry, each producing significant impact. The merger and acquisition movement has in fact effectively placed a "safety net" under industry investors in that successful companies are extremely valuable properties. Eyes were opened industrywide and particularly on Wall Street by prices paid for access to the business by well-heeled outsiders. Broadview Associates provides summary figures.

Acquiring firms pay high prices because growth is valuable and acquisition carries much lower risk than starting from scratch. If a company does not perform well, it can probably be sold at a handsome price. Acquisitions accomplish different tasks for different competitors. McGraw-Hill and Dun & Bradstreet entered the business to gain electronic publishing capability for large, valuable databases and another distribution channel or delivery method for ongoing publishing efforts. Automatic Data Processing, Anacomp, and Tymshare are clearly executing growth through acquisitions strategy. Life cycle analysis shows us that the giants of many industries have grown large via acquisitions. It happened in railroads (Pennsylvania Railroad), in tobacco (remember the tobacco trusts), in public utilities, and in textiles (Burlington Industries). Computer hardware manufacturers like Burroughs and CDC acquire software houses to add value to hardware offerings and to move from providing tools to providing solutions.

The aggressive approach to acquisitions reflects participants' sure knowledge that growth does not go on forever and that deals should be struck "before the music stops." Virtually every company in the industry actively seeks acquisitions, much like the larger fish drooling over a smaller prey. Also contributing to the stepped-up pace of mergers and acquisitions is the fact that there are willing sellers as well as willing buyers. Many computer services companies go on the block because entrepreneurs can cash in, finance product growth, and bring in additional marketing and development resources. There are literally thousands of small computer services companies without resources—management, financial, or otherwise—to sustain the battle. Cashing in at today's prices looks awfully good to many of them. Secondly, fast-paced activity is assured as new companies attracted by plummeting computer costs open up still unspoken-for markets.

Larger computer services companies are probably affordable only to very large companies outside the computing industry. Many corporations, Exxon for example, need fast growing businesses to sustain their own growth. Further, antitrust considerations and high prices may restrain the takeover of large computer services companies but that could be acquired by large outsiders. Companies like Shared Medical Systems, National Data Corporation, Comshare, and Quotron Systems fit into this category. Below these are companies representing fair game for insiders and outsiders alike. While outsiders grow by acquiring computer services companies, and industry insiders buy other industry insiders, it seems unlikely that industry insiders will seek industry outsiders. Clearly, the best use of time and money is in this business.

The computer services industry has developed all the trappings of permanence. Professions such as accounting and legal services have honed field specialists, and a whole body of law has emerged for patenting and copyrighting software. The Association of Data Processing Services Organizations has created industry support and represents the industry before government. The press has recognized the industry with specific publications, and academia has responded with more course and degree offerings related to software and services. Finally, Wall Street has focused on computer services as an industry in its own right, no longer an awkward appendage of other companies.

The investment community has taken an extraordinary interest in computer services for several reasons. The services industry as a whole is growing at about 20% per year. Input, Inc., of Palo Alto, Calif., estimates that some parts of the industry are growing faster than 30%, while individual niches and some companies are growing faster than 50% per year. Fast growth is coupled with the potential of enormous size. The industry, earning just over $14 billion in revenues today, is clearly going to be one of the largest industries in the country by the end of the decade. Fast growth and large scale become even more appealing because of the industry's unique financial characteristics. Computer services have been called the "millionaire machine" because it is possible for a smart fellow to develop a useful program and make himself rich. At the industry level, computer services are relatively less capital intensive, have relatively higher operating leverage, and relatively higher output per employee than most industries. Some older, more mature industries may offer better operating leverage, or lower capital intensity, or lower labor intensity, but they do not offer growth or returns on equity greater than the rate of inflation.

Professionals and managers have significant sunk costs—in training and experience, if not in cash—in their industry. Investors have no such constraints. The capital markets are highly liquid, and continued high inflation has put an extraordinarily high premium on companies capable of growing more rapidly than the rate of inflation. Money is pouring out of yesterday's industries into tomorrow's industries, and computer services are major beneficiaries of this shift. Capital is no longer a constraint for promising vendors. With a growing number of computer services companies tapping the public market for funds, more investment vehicles are available, thus enabling investors to spread their risks in this increasingly attractive industry. Computer services accounting practices are particularly attractive to investors. For the most part, revenues reported approximate cash received and expenses reported approximate cash disbursed. Development costs are generally expenses. Most parts of the industry are able to generate a stream of repeat income from their customer base. Timesharing is built around repeat revenue, and turnkey systems and software products usually generate a stream of maintenance revenue. Extensive cash flow finances ongoing product development and enhancement.

Perhaps the most appealing characteristic to investors is the industry's unique technological niche. Many investors feel that computer services represent the most defendable high growth, high technology investment available. With American tax laws and free market policies encouraging sustained foreign competition in virtually all the older industries (steel, textiles, automobiles, etc.) and increasingly in high technology businesses (semiconductors and computers), computer services companies seem uniquely protected by software's intimate association with the workings of American business.

Even generalized software programs incorporate features that require an intimate understanding of our business culture.

Software is not a commodity item. It is still priced to value, and this should continue as its value is continuously enhanced by ongoing development.

As the essence of value in any computer services offering, software occupies a uniquely protected position between the rapidly changing technology of computer hardware and the slowly evolving needs of the end user.

Computer users expect to change hardware as new generations permit more performance at lower prices; they do not expect to change their way of doing business. Hence, while computers come and go in an organization, the software stays on. In economic terms, hardware's life cycle is substantially shorter than software's life cycle as reflected by new generations of hardware remaining software-compatible with older generations. Consider that there are some $95 billion worth of computers installed vs. between $200 billion and $400 billion worth of software installed.

When the old-timer observes the computer services industry of today, he cannot help but remember the same industry of a decade ago. Then, as now, it was a darling of Wall Street. Will it crash into disrepute again? Are there important differences between the industry then and now? In those days, hardware was relatively expensive and software relatively cheap. Back then, computers were used by very large enterprises and by government. Today business computing comes in all shapes and sizes.

In the past, computer services companies capitalized software development costs and reported profits that rarely approximated cash flow. In those days, the whole concept of buying software was new; IBM gave away "bundled" software until 1969. The independent software products industry was truly an infant.

Today the industry has won respectability through proven performance and compelling economics. Large user groups exist and support specific products and services. So strong is this movement that most software and services sales are done by reference base selling.

Times have changed, and so has the industry, but clearly, computer services has earned a vital—and permanent—place in the information revolution.

Case 7–5

Days Inns of America, Inc.*

In February of 1980, Roy B. Burnette, senior vice president of marketing and sales for Days Inns of America, Inc. (DIA), a chain of family-oriented budget motels, commented that DIA had two problems. One involved the phenomenon that what people experienced at one motel, they assumed of all. To a degree, this was desirable because with standardization of quality and service, DIA could ensure that guests would associate the good impression received at one motel with the next in another town. However, one element could not be standardized—room rates. As a result, widely varying rates adversely affected travelers' perceptions of DIA. Management could not legally dictate an across-the-board rate to its franchisees, but it could set "guidelines," indicating a rate 20 percent to 30 percent lower than local competition. "A tourist staying in a Fort Lauderdale Days Inn might pay $40 a night. How do you convince him that, in this area where the going rate is $60 and up, he is getting a real bargain? And how do you convince him that a Days Inn in Macon, Georgia, would not be as expensive?"

The second problem also concerned room rates. Under DIA's system, a one-franchise operation could be sold to a successor. As the franchise changed hands, the capital investment increased because of rising property prices, higher interest rates on loans, refurbishing costs, and other expenses. Consequently, to obtain a reasonable return on investment, the new owner raised prices.

Background

The Days Inns chain of "budget luxury" motels was founded in 1970 by Cecil B. Day, who had made a fortune in the real estate and construction business. By the time he was 35, he "retired," intending to devote his life to his church and family. Shortly afterwards, while traveling with his wife and five children, he became convinced that a market existed for inexpensive, family-oriented, quality roadside motels.

During a trip through New England in 1968, Mr. Day concluded that motel rates were burdensomely high for the average vacationing family. This market segment needed a motel operation positioned in the niche between spartan, cheap motels, and high-priced facilities. Day's target market, therefore, was the traveling, vacationing family. He wanted to provide quality lodging,

---

*This case was prepared by Richard R. Still, California Polytechnic State University, with contributions from two of his graduate students, Courtney Sprague and Thomas D. Hafley of the University of Georgia, with the intention of providing a basis for class discussion rather than illustrating either effective or ineffective management of a business situation.

fair, honest service, and a wholesome family atmosphere. Liquor was prohibited from any Days Inn property, and two Bibles were provided in every room.

Day's first unit, named "8 Days Inn" (because of the eight-dollar room rate) opened at Savannah Beach, Georgia, and startled the competition because its room rate was 40 percent to 50 percent below the competition. By eliminating expensive lobbies and elaborate convention facilities, Days Inn had since kept its prices 20 percent to 30 percent below the competition. As room rates rose with inflation, the "8" was dropped from the logo.

DEVELOPMENT PATTERN

The chain expanded up and down the east coast of the United States, establishing itself along the main arteries from New England to Florida. It gradually expanded westward and into the North Central region of the U.S. In 1975 Days Inns of America, Inc. licensed Canterra Development Corporation to develop "Days Inn" and "Days Lodge" motel-hotels in Canada. As of 1979 there was one operating Days Inn in Cambridge, Ontario, and five more were either planned or under construction in Canada.

The majority of Days Inns—some 60 percent—were franchised, 27 percent were company-owned, and 13 percent were owned by affiliated companies. The total number of motels in the chain was 308, making it the sixth largest motel chain in America. This ranking was in terms of the number of properties owned—thus excluding Best Western (which would normally have been the second largest chain), Budget Hotels, and Friendship Inns. These three chains were really referral systems operating national reservations systems, but not owning motels.

During the oil embargo of 1973–1974, DIA installed gas pumps at all its motels to ensure gas supplies for guests. Guests could plan their itinerary from one Days Inn to the next and be assured that they could get gas each morning to continue their trips.

During the gas shortage of the summer of 1978, DIA lost five percentage points in occupancy rate. The industry lost 20 percentage points. DIA managed incrementally to decrease its room occupancy breakeven point. In 1978 the breakeven point was 60 percent; by 1979 it was 50 percent. "(The company) is now in a stronger financial condition than at any time in its history," said Kenneth Neimann, chief financial officer. "It is now in a position to weather virtually any economic challenge" (Exhibits 1, 2, and 3).

After Mr. Day's 14-month battle with bone cancer and untimely death at the age of 44 in December 1978, Richard Kessler was named chairman of the board. This was a nominal change, as Mr. Kessler had been given complete operational authority over the company years before. Mr. Day, son of a Baptist preacher, was a very religious man and felt the need to spend most of his time and effort directing the religious and charitable activities of the Day Company Foundation, a nonprofit organization that received ten percent of the after-tax profits. During the rapid growth of the motel chain (one room built every 20 minutes from 1971–1975), Kessler and Day held to the philosophy that good, honest, no-frills lodging was what people wanted.

By 1979, Days Inns had expanded as far west as Arizona. It operated in 28 states and Canada and was planning further expansion into Colorado and California. In addition, a Days Inns affiliate, C. B. Day Realty of Florida, was planning to expand further into southeast Florida. According to Tom Prince, president of the affiliate, there was "real room for expansion in that area." The company also was working to saturate the Washington, D.C., area with Days Inns motels by building five more in the Alexandria, Virginia, area (Exhibit 4).

Over the years, the target market changed and expanded to include not only vacationing American families, but vacationing foreigners, traveling business people, truck drivers, and senior citizens. The major thrust of the advertising and facilities' design, however, remained geared toward the middle-income family with two or more children, two or more cars, and two or more weeks of annual vacation.

THE U.S. MOTEL INDUSTRY

Rapid expansion of the interstate highway system, coupled with cheap gasoline prices, encouraged a burgeoning of family vacationing travelers in the 1950s. "Tourist courts" mushroomed, and unlike downtown hotels, they were convenient, informal, and cheap—and the car stayed right outside the front door. Most motels were small, independently owned, and highly variable in quality. "Twenty years ago," said an industry observer, "you'd always go in first and look over the room, because many were kind of sleazy, and the beds were poor. Even if you took the room, you couldn't count on things like the air conditioning working."

Holiday Inns was the first to recognize the unfilled niche between uncertain motel accommodations and expensive hotels. In 1952, the first Holiday Inn opened in Memphis, letting children stay free with parents, and offering ice, a swimming pool, room telephone, and kennel service. The consumer appeal was the chain's assurance that what they knew of one motel, they could assume of all. "You always know there'll be a Coke machine at the end of the hall and a certain standard of housekeeping," said one consumer, "and the rooms always have a work area."

Much standardization grew out of cost control. "There's a conscious effort to standardize," said Roy Burnette, "given maintenance and replacement costs, and the chance to buy in quantity." By the 1970s, there were several competitive chains, each offering standardized accommodations and service. The 1973-75 recession and gas crisis proved a watershed for the industry. Marginal mom-and-pop operations folded by the thousands, and the large chains employed sophisticated marketing techniques in a scramble for the biggest piece of the remaining lodging pie. According to Dan Philip, vice president, market group research and development for Holiday Inns, the marketing trend in the lodging industry was already a cross between a consumer service and a prepackaged good. "The primary commonality," said Philip, "is that the person getting a burger or renting a room en route has very little psychological commitment to the product, so you can have a standardized system of rules for delivering that product, whether it's a Big Mac, a Whopper, or a Holiday Inn room."

The industry's market research began to define, describe, and segment the market. Business travel was confirmed as the most steady segment, even during travel slumps caused by gas shortages, and provided the largest dollar volume. Family vacationers, even in summer, provided a quarter of the total volume. To a great extent, observed industry insiders, the nation was taking shorter pleasure trips, and doing more "destination" travel. The number of women travelers—almost 30 percent of U.S. business travel—was increasing, according to Best Western. More women were also traveling with their children.

By 1979 chains controlled 29 percent of U.S. motel properties and 63 percent of the rooms. In 1978, according to *Standard and Poor*, 52 percent of the lodging industry's business was from business travel, 25 percent from pleasure, and the rest from conventions. Pleasure travel was aided by many factors including increased leisure time, and the coming of age of the post-World War II baby boom. The dollar's weakness in foreign markets encouraged more foreigners to travel in the U.S. and kept more Americans vacationing at home.

Some chains began to court the business segment by locating around airports and metropolitan locations, and providing convention facilities, lounges, and entertainment. Others focused on featuring their operations as destinations in themselves, going into resort properties, and most recently, gambling. In 1979 the *Los Angeles Times* noted that hotels and motels seemed to have gone full circle, from one-story motels on the highway to high-rise hotels clustered around urban centers.

Since the 1973-1974 oil embargo, growth in the number of rooms belonging to chains had been modest (Exhibit 5). Chains were focusing on refurbishing old rooms and "pruning" marginal units from their systems, concentrating on airport and metropolitan locations. Ramada Inns and Howard Johnson reduced the number of motels in their systems. New construction had picked up progressively since it bottomed out in 1975, but construction costs rose rapidly. In 1979 the average cost of constructing a "modest" motel was estimated at $20,000 a room. Because of rising construction and financing costs, industry observers predicted a shortage of rooms by the early 1980s. In order to expand more rapidly, most leading chains franchised extensively; for example, in 1978, out of 1,718 hotels and motels in the Holiday Inns system, 1,488 were franchised.

FRANCHISE OPERATION

DIA's franchise operation presented three important advantages. One advantage was the franchising afforded a wider base of operation, giving the company a chance to cover a larger territory. A second advantage was that the company received from each franchise a minimum initial fee of $15,000 and monthly payments of three percent of gross receipts. This helped fuel the company's own motel development. A third advantage was that franchising helped spread the risk; if a particular franchise lost money, the effect on DIA was minimal.

The main disadvantage was loss of immediate control over each motel's operation. The rates which each franchisee charged for rooms and food was a problem. There was no way management could force a franchisee to charge a rate 20 percent to 30 percent below local competition. Management felt this competitive edge was essential to maintenance of the budget luxury image. The difficulty in getting franchisees to charge the suggested rate was tied to increasing property values. As original owners sold their motels, purchasers had to pay higher prices for land and buildings. New owners had to charge more for the rooms than their predecessors to obtain positive returns on their investments.

DIA offered nonexclusive rights to construct and operate Days Inns Plan facilities. It expected franchisees to obtain debt financing on their own. DIA required the franchisee to contribute equity of not less than 25 percent of the total cost. With a motel of 122 rooms and an average cost of construction of $20,000 per room, this required an investor to have over $600,000 liquidity in the motel operation. On top of this, the contract required the investor to spend at least $6,100 for motel promotion during the two months before and three months after the opening. There was also a stipulation that any rights or options which the investor had on property during the time he was applying for a franchise had to cover a period of 90 days or more. This was to give the executive committee enough time to review thoroughly the application.

The contract was filled with a variety of rules governing quality of service. To maintain the Days Inns "image," no franchisee was "allowed to sell any materials deemed by franchisor to be pornographic," nor "to sell, serve, or apply for any license, permit or authority to sell or serve, alcoholic beverages (nor permit consumption of alcoholic beverages in any restaurant or public building area) on the premises or any other property adjacent or contiguous thereto, which is owned or controlled, directly or indirectly, by Franchisee. . . ."

In 1979 DIA received a total of 75 applications. Forty-six met financial guidelines. Thirty-eight were approved.

DAYS INNS MANAGEMENT

The DIA management team was young—not only in age, but in experience. Kessler was in his early thirties when he became chairman of the board. He surrounded himself with young, capable executives. Quite a few of the top executives were graduates of Georgia Tech—Mr. Kessler's alma mater.

Kessler's executive recruitment was influenced by his deep admiration of Walt Disney Productions. While in Florida developing property through Day Realty of Orlando, Inc., he became familiar with Disney World. He and Day felt that Walt Disney ran a "tight operation," so they hired James B. Murphy (operations manager for Disney), and David B. Workman (head of manpower development of Disney Enterprises). In 1979 Mr. Murphy was senior vice president of Franchise Operations for Days Inns, and Mr. Workman was senior vice-president of employee relations. Other top executives were Robert C. Bush (senior executive vice-president and chief administrative officer), H. Douglas McClain (senior executive vice-president and chief operating officer), William B. Hargett (senior vice-president for franchise sales and development), Roy B. Burnette (senior vice-president for marketing and sales), and Kenneth Niemann (executive vice-president, treasurer, and chief financial officer).

STATUS AS PRIVATELY-HELD CORPORATION

As a privately-held company, DIA did not pursue profit maximization as a publicly-held company might have done. The outstanding stock was owned by 31 executives and motel managers who were interested in spending money on projects such as installation of solar heating panels and expansion of the reservation center—both likely to prove cost effective over a relatively short period. Short-term net income generation had secondary priority.

The owners also leaned toward investing in unique projects with uncertain payback periods. One example was paying a world-renowned painter to give lessons to a talented employee. The company planned to receive royalties from future sale of the employee's art, once he became famous.

A similar dream lay behind the sponsorship of James Tillman, known as "The Voice of Days Inns." Mr. Kessler and other executives recognized Tillman's extraordinary singing ability, so they regularly sponsored him as he performed at community events. In 1979 he opened the 35th Annual National Cherry Blossom Festival Parade in Washington, D.C., by singing the National Anthem. Top management hoped he would get a chance to sing on the Lawrence Welk Show. If he "made it big" in the television and recording industry, DIA would earn enough from royalties to achieve a handsome return on its investment.

RESERVATIONS SYSTEM

DIA's reservation center in 1970 consisted of one telephone and one woman. In 1973 the center expanded to 100 agents, yet it was still operated manually. Reservation agents used bulletin boards and marked an "X" next to a motel location as it was filled to capacity. Rooms could be reserved for two months in advance. If someone wanted a room beyond this time, agents had to refer to a card file.

In 1975 the system was computerized. There were still 100 agents, but each used an on-line terminal to reserve rooms for people calling a toll-free number. This system was leased on a 24-hour-a-day basis from MICOR, Inc., a subsidiary of Ramada Inns. In addition to Days Inns and Ramada Inns, Best Western, Quality Inns, and Americana Motels utilized this reservation system.

The Days Inns Center was located at the company headquarters in Atlanta, and in case the system failed ("went down"), the reservationists still had the card files to fall back upon. In 1979 the center received 3.4 million calls and made 1.8 million reservations. The phone bill exceeded $1 million a year.

Additional demands on the system were expected in the future, so plans had been finalized to expand the facility from 8,000 to 15,000 square feet, and increase the number of agents from 150 to 180 in 1980. It was anticipated that each reservationist at the center would handle approximately 33,750 calls per year.

DAYS INNS' ADVERTISING AND PROMOTION

The overall marketing philosophy of Days Inns was to meet the needs of five audiences. The first was the customers. All advertisements and promotions had to generate new customers, retain existing customers, and attract any dissatisfied customers who had stayed at a Days Inn and were unimpressed. The advertisements of the late 1970s aimed to alter dissatisfied customers' perceptions of the chain, to convince them of the Days Inns' "budget luxury" image, and encourage them to try the motel chain again.

The second audience was the business and financial community. DIA considered it imperative to project a sound financial image to banks, savings and loans, and insurance companies—the places from which the company obtained most of its funding. These financial institutions had to believe that DIA was a good investment.

The third audience included potential investors. The company needed to give potential franchisees the feeling that if they invested their time and money in the "Days Inns Plan," they would receive strong support in nationwide promotions, local cooperative advertising, and motel management expertise.

The fourth audience comprised existing franchisees. Advertisements aimed to keep them happy with the franchise operation, and to reinforce positive perceptions of the company's public relations efforts.

The fifth audience was made up of 10,000 DIA employees. Company advertisements were supposed to make employees feel comfortable with their jobs and the company. Employees who felt proud of what they were doing, it was reasoned, would be better able to express to their customers the value which DIA had to offer.

DIA had its own in-house marketing department. It handled most of the production and placement of promotional material, including copy, layout, and graphic arts. In addition, DIA used a New York advertising agency to place national advertising.

One of the marketing department's largest expenditures, and the most cost effective, was the $1 million spent on outdoor billboards and signs. In the beginning, this was the only advertising the company could afford since it owned or leased the land and could build its own signs. In the late 1970s, this was still a relatively inexpensive yet effective way to let travelers know about the inns. DIA signs, painted bright yellow, and all using the same format and familiar "sunrise in the cupola" logo were easy to see from the highway and were distinctive.

The marketing department utilized radio and television in addition to the billboards, motel signs, newspapers, and magazines. In 1979 the company spent a total of $2.5 million on TV (Channel 17, Atlanta), radio (4,000 spots nationwide), and print media. Radio spots were concentrated along major interstate highways in the early morning and evening. Television spots were broadcast via satellite to stations throughout the United States.

A major "awareness level test" was scheduled for Philadelphia early in 1980. DIA planned to show its television advertisements in Philadelphia while using Pittsburgh as a control area. The plan was to survey the two areas later to determine effectiveness of the ads.

During 1979, DIA spent approximately $30.1 million for replacement of almost everything in the motel rooms. This was the third year of a four-year plan for upgrading every company-owned room. DIA replaced carpet in more than 5,000 rooms, installed new wall vinyl in more than 2,000, and replaced color televisions in 9,500 rooms. The televisions alone cost $2.3 million. Other expenditures were for bedspreads, bedding, draperies, lamps, chairs, vanities, pictures, and air conditioners.

To reduce the impact of energy costs on room prices, DIA installed solar heating panels (funded in part through federal grants) in 11 inns. A solar heating system for one motel cost $10,163 to install. The anticipated payback period was originally set at seven years, but later was cut to four years.

In 1975 DIA directed promotion towards senior citizens, a market segment not previously cultivated by the lodging industry. The "September Days Club" was founded and free membership cards were issued entitling holders to 10 percent discounts on food, gifts, gasoline, and lodging costs at participating motels. The response was tremendous. In 1975, 44 million Americans were over the age of 55. Though the program was originally intended for the month of September only, the time limit was removed, and the club grew from 75,000 members in March 1975 to 100,000 in June 1975 and 800,000 in January 1977.

Membership was no longer free in 1977, and members paid a $3 annual membership fee (or $7.50 for three years, or got a life membership "for both you and your spouse" for $15). In 1979 the annual fee was raised to $5 (for single or couple) and membership dropped to 500,000. In addition to discounts on motel costs, members now could get 25 percent discounts on Hertz Rent-a-Cars, reduced rates at various theme parks and attractions, a four-color magazine called *September Days* which came out four times a year, and participation in conventions sponsored by the club.

The national director of the club, Tom C. Lawler, said that club members were particularly desirable guests. "They take good care of our rooms, they travel most often in pairs, and usually in the spring and fall off-seasons. They tend to eat where they stay and take advantage of their discounts by eating at Days Inns in their hometowns. They are a tremendous market!" By 1977 senior citizens accounted for 15 to 20 percent of total DIA occupancy.

Franchisees in North Carolina were experimenting with an "Inn-credible card" entitling certain businessmen to 10 percent discounts at any North Carolina Days Inn. This was generating higher occupancy levels in participating motels.

DIA at first did not use travel agents and only paid commissions to agents for group bookings of ten or more. This was changed in 1977 when a prepaid voucher system, Travel Agent Nite Chek (TANC), was instituted. Through TANC, agents earned ten percent commissions on rooms booked at any of Days Inns properties. Accordingly, bookings by travel agents increased by about 200 percent in the first year the TANC System was used. With the voucher system, an agent called a special toll-free number (1-800-241-7322) for reservations. The agent then sent in payment (less the ten-percent commission). The TANC voucher was forwarded directly to the Days Inn location, and a copy sent to the agent.

Promotion for the TANC program was low key and accounted for five percent of total occupancy. The company was planning to step up the promotion of TANC. According to Mr. Wright, "We look upon our travel agent customers as a market. Our business from bus tours has increased tremendously because of agent involvement." DIA recently had increased its advertising of TANC and planned to attend more trade shows to work with travel industry personnel. A 32-page directory of locations and rates was made available to agents and customers at no charge. The directory had recently been restructured and made available to the general public through a four-page supplement in the PARADE section of Sunday newspapers, enabling Days Inns to reach more than 18 million homes. In addition, DIA's New York agency placed advertisements in *Time, Newsweek, People, National Geographic, TV Guide, Life,* and *Better Homes and Gardens.*

FUTURE PLANS

Despite shifts in travel patterns of the American public, DIA management reaffirmed its commitment to market the chain to the family, the business traveler, and the senior citizen, while communicating the message of savings, comfort, and convenience. Roy Burnette saw Days Inns occupying the niche in the travel market that chains such as Holiday Inns abandoned when they built expensive high rises, resorts, and casinos. When asked if he saw Days Inns occupying the same niche 10 or 15 years from 1980, he affirmed that he did.

Because of the tight loan situation, the company was slowing down its expansion expectations to three units per year. The vice president for marketing and sales said that the company would be getting away from the open roadside, selling off marginal units and leaving only the "A-1" motels due to the drop in family travel caused by higher gasoline prices. The company also planned to expand into additional metropolitan areas and near airports and resort facilities.

Days Inns of America, Inc.
Consolidated Balance Sheets (Historical Cost) and Statements of Current Values

Exhibit 1

Assets	September 30, 1979 Statement of Current Values	September 30, 1979 Balance Sheet (Historical Cost)	September 30, 1978 Statement of Current Values	September 30, 1978 Balance Sheet (Historical Cost)
Current assets:				
Cash ($60,000 and $86,000 restricted)	$ 136,000	$ 136,000	$ 92,000	$ 92,000
Money market investments	4,030,000	4,030,000	3,003,000	3,003,000
Accounts and notes receivable net of allowance for doubtful accounts of $1,400,000 and $927,000:				
Affiliated companies	479,000	479,000	186,000	186,000
Non-affiliated franchisees	960,000	960,000	1,504,000	1,504,000
Other	1,761,000	1,761,000	816,000	816,000
Retail inventories and supplies	1,842,000	1,842,000	1,484,000	1,484,000
Prepaid expenses	670,000	670,000	637,000	637,000
Total current assets	9,878,000	9,878,000	7,722,000	7,722,000
Property and equipment	101,539,000	65,267,000	81,013,000	56,750,000
Less: Accumulated depreciation		(21,205,000)		(18,984,000)
Accounts and notes receivable:				
Stockholders and affiliated companies	4,669,000	4,669,000	4,821,000	4,821,000
Non-affiliated franchisees and other	504,000	504,000	346,000	346,000
Franchise agreements	18,500,000		15,500,000	
Deferred charges	648,000	648,000	802,000	802,000
Accumulated income tax prepayments	85,000	85,000	127,000	127,000
Other assets	39,000	39,000	58,000	58,000
	$135,862,000	$ 59,885,000	$110,389,000	$ 51,642,000

Liabilities and Stockholders' Equity

Current liabilities:				
Notes payable	$ 2,491,000	$ 2,766,000	$ 3,723,000	$ 3,838,000
Accounts payable	5,449,000	5,449,000	3,078,000	3,078,000
Accrued expenses and other liabilities	2,882,000	2,882,000	2,802,000	2,802,000
Income taxes payable	396,000	396,000	722,000	722,000
Current liabilities excluding deferred income taxes	11,218,000	11,493,000	10,325,000	10,440,000
Deferred income taxes	650,000	650,000		
Total current liabilities	11,868,000	12,143,000	10,325,000	10,440,000
Notes payable, due after one year	32,536,000	35,564,000	30,118,000	31,696,000
Accounts and notes payable to stockholders and affiliated companies, due after one year	3,072,000	3,318,000	3,849,000	3,981,000
Income taxes on realization of estimated current values	23,500,000		17,900,000	
Real estate commissions on realization of estimated current values	3,600,000		2,900,000	
Deferred income and deposits	620,000	620,000	868,000	868,000
Stockholders' equity:				
Common stock, without par value—1,000,000 shares authorized, 341,670 shares issued	59,000	59,000	59,000	59,000
Capital surplus	949,000	949,000	949,000	949,000
Retained earnings	8,931,000	8,931,000	4,590,000	4,590,000
Unrealized appreciation	52,426,000		39,772,000	
	62,365,000	9,939,000	45,370,000	5,598,000
Less: Treasury stock, at cost—33,460 and 19,320 shares	1,699,000	1,699,000	941,000	941,000
Total stockholders' equity	60,666,000	8,240,000	44,429,000	4,657,000
Commitments and contingent liabilities	$135,862,000	$ 59,885,000	$110,389,000	$ 51,642,000

Exhibit 2

Days Inns of America, Inc.
Consolidated Statements of Income

| | For the year ended September 30, | |
	1979	1978
Net revenue:		
Lodging	$ 48,065,000	$44,242,000
Food, gasoline and novelties	44,024,000	36,896,000
Franchise fees—initial	566,000	337,000
—recurring	9,795,000	7,757,000
Rental income	3,921,000	3,766,000
Other income	2,192,000	1,885,000
Proceeds from officer's life insurance	1,000,000	——
	109,563,000	94,883,000
Costs and expenses:		
Cost of food, gasoline and novelties	31,434,000	25,234,000
Selling, general, administrative and		
operating expenses	52,860,000	46,587,000
Rental expense—motel and restaurant leases	10,411,000	10,197,000
Depreciation and amortization	5,222,000	5,309,000
Interest expense, net of interest income		
of $635,000 and $543,000	3,267,000	3,476,000
	103,194,000	90,803,000
Income before provision for income taxes	6,369,000	4,080,000
Provision for income taxes	2,028,000	1,260,000
Net income	$ 4,341,000	$ 2,820,000

Exhibit 3

Days Inns of America, Inc.
Consolidated Statements of Stockholders' Equity

	Common Stock	Treasury Stock	Capital Surplus	Retained Earnings	Total
Balance—September 30, 1977	$59,000	($ 414,000)	$949,000	$1,870,000	$2,464,000
Net income				2,820,000	2,820,000
Purchase of treasury stock		(527,000)			(527,000)
Cash dividends				(100,000)	(100,000)
Balance—September 30, 1978	59,000	(941,000)	949,000	4,590,000	4,657,000
Net income				4,341,000	4,341,000
Purchase of treasury stock		(758,000)			(758,000)
Balance—September 30, 1979	$59,000	($1,699,000)	$949,000	$8,931,000	$8,240,000

Days Inns of America, Inc.
Statements of Forecasted Income and Stockholders' Equity

Exhibit 4

		For the years ending September 30,			
	1980	1981	1982	1983	1984
Net revenue:					
Lodging	$ 50,756,000	$ 54,579,000	$ 58,712,000	$ 63,066,000	$ 67,585,000
Food, gasoline and novelties	50,132,000	56,046,000	62,661,000	69,727,000	77,294,000
Franchise fees—initial	538,000	665,000	792,000	929,000	1,046,000
—recurring	10,907,000	12,506,000	14,230,000	16,247,000	18,758,000
Rental income	4,187,000	3,505,000	1,263,000	1,318,000	1,372,000
Other income	2,378,000	2,556,000	2,769,000	2,995,000	3,219,000
	118,898,000	129,857,000	140,427,000	154,282,000	169,274,000
Costs and expenses					
Cost of food, gasoline and novelties	36,875,000	41,416,000	46,318,000	51,582,000	57,182,000
Selling, general, administrative and operating expenses	55,284,000	60,428,000	66,251,000	72,273,000	78,872,000
Rental expense	9,584,000	9,113,000	—	—	—
Depreciation and amortization	6,097,000	6,089,000	8,896,000	9,626,000	10,356,000
Interest expense net of interest income	3,332,000	3,785,000	9,367,000	9,518,000	9,614,000
	111,172,000	120,831,000	130,832,000	142,999,000	156,024,000
Income before provision for income taxes	7,726,000	9,026,000	9,595,000	11,283,000	13,250,000
Provision for income taxes	3,327,000	3,711,000	3,947,000	4,732,000	5,656,000
Net income	$ 4,399,000	$ 5,315,000	$ 5,648,000	$ 6,551,000	$ 7,594,000
Stockholders' equity	$ 12,388,000	$ 17,703,000	$ 18,128,000	$ 24,679,000	$ 32,273,000
Occupancy	73%	74%	75%	76%	77%
Average room rate	$ 19.00	$ 19.50	$ 20.00	$ 20.50	$ 21.00
Number of franchise motel openings	20	25	30	35	40
Total rooms in chain	45,000	48,400	52,400	57,000	62,200

Food, gas, and novelty sales are forecasted on the basis of revenue per rented room. The average sale per rented room is expected to increase at 5% for food and novelties and 8% for gasoline. Although sales will increase, the cost of food and gasoline will remain constant at 35% and 93%, respectively. Novelty costs will decrease from 67% in 1980 to 60% in 1984, based on improved inventory controls and a modernized marketing concept.

Initial franchise fees from new openings are projected at $22,200 for each complete motel operation, as well as conversions of other motels, ownership transfers and site inspections. Recurring franchise fees were calculated using 1) an increase in total rooms, 2) approximately the same occupancy as company operated units, and 3) a slightly higher average room rate for 1981 through 1983. By 1984, the average room rate for franchise locations is expected to approximate the company average. Recurring franchise royalties from affiliates total $298,000, $306,000, $315,000, $323,000, and $332,000 for 1980 through 1984, respectively, and are estimated

(Continued on next page.)

based on the terms of the amended agreements discussed in Note 2 to the consolidated financial statements.

Rental income includes revenue from leased motels and the operation of an apartment complex converted from a motel during 1978. Total rental income forecasted to be earned from the apartment complex during 1980 is based on an occupancy of approximately 95%. The apartment complex is expected to be sold by March 31, 1980 and therefore, no rental income or related expense is included in the projections for 1981 through 1984. No gain or loss on the sale of the property is included in the 1980 results.

Selling, general, administrative, and operating costs are forecasted to increase 5% to 10% per year. Salaries and wages have been adjusted for expected increases. Beginning in 1981, combined initial advertising and start-up costs of $300,000 a year are included for the expansion properties. Total operating expenses for the five year period are forecasted to increase by a total of approximately 43%.

Beginning in 1982, substantially all lease agreements will be required to be capitalized in accordance with Financial Accounting Standard No. 13—Accounting for Leases (FAS 13). Accordingly, the forecasts for the years 1982, 1983, and 1984 reflect capitalizations of such leases in effect as of September 30, 1979, less any leases expected to be discontinued because of the sale of the property. Capitalization of such leases results in a decrease in net income of $284,000, $185,000, and $2,000 for 1982 through 1984, respectively. The cumulative effect on stockholders' equity at September 30, 1982 is a decrease of $5,223,000. Rental income and expense, depreciation and interest expenses have been appropriately presented in accordance with FAS 13 for 1982 through 1984. If the provisions of FAS 13 had been adopted at September 30, 1979, the effect of capitalizing the company's leases would be to decrease forecasted net income by $318,000 and $251,000 in 1980 and 1981, respectively.

During 1980 and 1981, rental expense is based on lease agreements in existence at September 30, 1979, less any payment on properties expected to be sold, and net of income earned on subleases of $737,000 and $863,000, respectively. For the period from 1982 through 1984, rental expense has been restated in accordance with FAS 13 and the income earned on operating subleases of $924,000, $974,000, and $1,023,000, respectively, is shown in rental income.

Estimates of depreciation reflect a decrease in depreciable assets at leased properties, an increase in replacements and improvements at company operated sites, and the addition of three sites per year beginning in 1981. The estimated cost for replacements and additions is approximately $36,000,000 over the next five years and for new sites is $22,000,000 for 1981 through 1984.

Interest expense is based on loans in effect at September 30, 1979, plus assumed financing at 12% per annum on the new properties. All other interest is based on a constant level of debt with repayments offset by additional financing of capital expenditures. Interest income will increase based on higher levels of cash available for investment.

Provisions for income taxes are calculated using the applicable tax rates, less investment tax credits from property and equipment additions and the construction of new motel properties.

Forecasted stockholders' equity assumes that the only changes arise from: 1) operations, 2) the restatement of lease agreements in accordance with FAS 13 in 1982, and 3) a cash dividend of $251,000 in 1980. No attempt has been made to forecast dividends for 1981 through 1984.

The accounting policies used in the forecasts are those applied in the financial statements for 1979. The consolidated financial statements and accompanying notes for the years ended September 30, 1979 and 1978 should be read in conjunction with the above forecasts.

Exhibit 5

**Worldwide Growth in Number of Rooms
for Selected Hotel Chains (in thousands of units)**

CHAINS	1970	1972	1974	1976	1977	1978	Annual Growth Rate from 1970
Holiday Inns	182.5	222.7	267.0	278.1	279.0	286.5	5.7%
Best Western	NA	80.0	90.0	109.1	141.2	152.7	11.3%
ITT Sheraton	59.6	71.5	90.2	97.2	99.2	102.0	7.5%
Ramada Inns	35.6	60.0	91.6	94.3	95.0	92.5	12.7%
Trust House	46.5	52.7	56.6	76.3	81.5	75.0	7.7%
Hilton Hotels	46.5	47.7	56.7	62.8	62.9	66.7	5.2%
Howard Johnson	39.5	46.8	58.1	59.2	59.2	59.1	5.5%

Source: Service World International

Case 7–6

Gerber Products Company*

Gerber Products is the largest producer of baby foods in the world with domestic food plants located in Fremont, Michigan; Oakland, California; Asheville, North Carolina; and Fort Smith, Arkansas. The company was founded in 1901 as the Fremont Canning Company in Fremont, Michigan. The fledgling company was then involved in a canned food business that served the midwest United States. In 1928 it entered the commercial baby food industry. The company's name was changed to Gerber Products in 1941.

Gerber is primarily engaged in manufacturing, providing, and selling consumer goods and services for preschool children. Its line of baby foods include strained and junior foods, cereals, meat, juices, and various related items. There are approximately 140 varieties of baby food in the Gerber line. In addition to baby foods, other principal products include clothing, vaporizers, humidifiers, nursers, nurser accessories, diaper bags, infant care and safety items, and juvenile furniture. These products are sold nationally for resale to consumers through various retail outlets. The services provided by the company include insurance and child care centers. With the acquisition of CW Transport, Inc. in 1979, Gerber is now also engaged in the trucking business. The company also operates in international markets through subsidiaries, licensees, and exports.

THE BABY FOOD INDUSTRY

In 1979 the baby food market was estimated to be a $524 million industry in the U.S. In recent years Gerber's share of the market has fluctuated between 60–70 percent of the total; the remainder being divided between Beech-Nut and Heinz. The East Coast is regarded as the strongest market for Beech-Nut while Heinz has its strength in the midwest area. Gerber, on the other hand, has fairly uniform strength throughout the country, and its foods are distributed in 95 percent of the major supermarkets in the United States. In recent years the consumption of baby food per baby has been relatively steady. However, the recent increase in the number of births has tended to offset this leveling effect. Furthermore, medical opinion appears to be shifting in

---

*This case was prepared by D. E. Ezell, University of Baltimore, Edmund R. Gray, and B. L. Kedia, Louisiana State University, with the intention of providing a basis for class discussion rather than illustrating either effective or ineffective management of a business situation. The case was prepared with the assistance of, but not necessarily endorsement of Gerber Products Company. The statements made and the conclusions drawn are not necessarily those of the company except where direct quotations are indicated.

favor of earlier introduction of solid foods depending upon baby's weight, appetite, and growth rate, rather than upon age alone (four to six months old rather than six months or older).

A very significant characteristic of the industry is the nature of its market. It loses its current customers after a year (babies outgrow baby food), and then must rely on the future population of babies for continued prosperity. Two other important characteristics of the industry involve competitive factors and demographic changes.

Competitive Factors

The third of the market which Gerber does not control is divided between Heinz and Beech-Nut. In the year 1976-77 Beech-Nut made significant gains in the market primarily through an advertising campaign which stressed that its baby foods contain "no added salt, preservatives, artificial flavors or colors." This "all natural" campaign propelled Beech-Nut into the number two position in the industry. Gerber and Heinz, interestingly, had also significantly reduced the salt and sugar content of their baby foods but did not emphasize this fact in their promotions. Hence, it appears Beech-Nut capitalized on something that had become common practice in the industry.

Even before Beech-Nut's "all natural" blitz, a movement was emerging where more and more mothers were forsaking the "little glass jars," for fresh foods they cooked and strained themselves. This trend was in response to charges made by Ralph Nader, *Consumer Reports*, and others that the nutritional value in prepared baby foods was not all it should be. Although this "antiprocessed" attitude gained acceptance across the country, it was especially prevalent on the Pacific Coast. Statistics show an increase in the antiprocessed attitude from 8 percent in the early 70s to 15 percent in the mid 70s. Obviously, if the "homemade" trend continues, it would result in serious market erosion for commercial baby foods. It has also been suggested that increased consumer resistance may be due to the high prices as well. After the lifting of federal price controls in 1974, Gerber raised its prices 8 percent in May and boosted them another ten percent in October. Consumer response to such price hikes tends to reinforce the "homemade" trend.

Product price clearly is an important competitive factor in the industry. The first price war was initiated by Gerber's competitors in 1959. Although it was limited to California and Florida, it was a cause for concern because during this period Gerber's production costs were increasing and its profitability was declining. Fortunately for Gerber and the industry, the price war was short-lived and none of the producers of commercially prepared baby foods suffered great financial damage.

The next price war did not come for another ten years, but this time it lasted for three years. Again it was started by Gerber's competitors in reaction to the prediction of a continuing drop in both the birth rate and the total number of births in the United States. They felt they needed to get a larger share of the total dollars spent on babies. Gerber's vice president of marketing, Floyd N. Head, explained the action of his competitors as "a simple thing of economics." According to Head, you need so much volume and distribution in this business, and neither Heinz or Beech-Nut command a large market share, so they decided to cut prices in order to gain new customers. As long as the price differential was 1 cent per jar, Gerber was still able to compete effectively and hold its market share. However, when the spread opened up to 1-1/2 cents to 2-1/2 cents per jar, Gerber's market share started eroding, and when the spread hit 3 cents or 4 cents a jar, Gerber had to retaliate. For example, in Detroit, Gerber's local market share tumbled from 65 percent to 30 percent. In retaliation, Gerber lowered its prices and narrowed the margin to 1 cent to 1-1/2 cents a jar. At this point in 1971, price controls were imposed and all three companies were trapped at their "bargain-basement" prices. To make matters worse the industry's costs increased significantly during the price war—meat costs alone nearly doubled during one twelve-month period.

Gerber was hurt by the price war, but its competitors were crippled. When the price controls were lifted in 1974, the price war was over and the wounded producers retreated to rebuild. At this time Swift and Company, which had held 3 percent to 4 percent of the market, withdrew from the industry. Heinz Baby Food profits suffered and Beech-Nut, a subsidiary of the Squibb Corporation, was sold to Baker Laboratories. Surprisingly enough, Gerber showed a profit during the period.

Baby Trends

Perhaps the most important environmental factors affecting the baby food industry are the rate of birth and the number of births per country. It can be said that the birthrate has a ripple effect on almost all industries, but when babies are your principle market, any change in this rate is critical. It is generally accepted that the baby boom of the 50s and 60s in the United States has slowed down. This is the result of such factors as improved birth control methods, abortions, and changing life-styles. The fact that a large number of couples no longer feel the need to formalize their marriage has a depressing effect on the birthrate. Moreover, even among married couples there is a trend toward the wife working and smaller family units.

According to *Current Population Reports*, almost one-half (45 percent) of the women in the age group of 20 to 24 were unmarried in 1979. This level of marriage postponement was in sharp contrast to 28 percent in 1960. Furthermore, the number of unmarried women in the 25 to 29 category approximately doubled between 1970 (10.5 percent) and 1979 (19.6 percent) after showing no change during the 1960s. The divorce rate approximately doubled during the 1970-79 period, rising from 47 divorced persons per 1,000 married persons in 1970 to 92 in 1979. The number of divorces in 1979 (1,170,000) was approximately one-half the number of marriages (2,317,000); the corresponding numbers in 1970 were 708,000 and 2,159,000 respectively. The number of unmarried couples of opposite sex living together increased more than twice in 1979 as compared to 1970 (1,346,000 versus 523,000).

The number of babies born in the U.S. in 1973 dropped to 3.1 million, the lowest level since World War II. The highest level of births occurred through

1956-62 averaging 4.2-4.3 million births per year, and was 3.7 million as recently as 1970. The number of babies born in the U.S. during the four-year period 1973-1976 remained fairly constant averaging 3.15 million births per year. The rate of births per 1,000 population during this period was also fairly constant averaging 14.8 births per 1,000 population. The birthrate increased in 1977 and 1978 when it was 15.3 and was higher still in 1979 when it reached the 15.8 per 1,000 population. Exhibit 1 shows population change for the United States during a ten-year period, from 1970 to 1980.

Exhibit 1

Estimates of the Components of Population Change for the United States: January 1, 1970, to January 1, 1980 (Numbers in thousands. Includes Armed Forces overseas)

Calendar Year	Population at Beginning of Period	Components of Change During Year				
		Total Increase[1]	Natural Increase	Births	Deaths	Net Civilian Immigration
NUMBER						
1980	221,719	—	—	—	—	—
1979	219,699	2,019	1,560	3,468	1,908	460
1978	217,874	1,825	1,403	3,328	1,925	427
1977	216,058	1,816	1,426	3,327	1,900	394
1976	214,446	1,611	1,258	3,168	1,910	353
1975	212,748	1,698	1,251	3,144	1,894	449
1974	211,207	1,541	1,225	3,160	1,935	316
1973	209,711	1,496	1,163	3,137	1,974	331
1972	208,088	1,623	1,293	3,258	1,965	325
1971	206,076	2,012	1,626	3,556	1,930	387
1970	203,849	2,227	1,812	3,739	1,927	438
RATE PER 1,000 MIDYEAR POPULATION						
1979	(X)	9.2	7.1	15.7	8.7	2.1
1978	(X)	8.3	6.4	15.3	8.8	2.0
1977	(X)	8.4	6.6	15.3	8.8	1.8
1976	(X)	7.5	5.8	14.7	8.9	1.6
1975	(X)	8.0	5.9	14.7	8.9	2.1
1974	(X)	7.3	5.8	14.9	9.1	1.5
1973	(X)	7.1	5.5	14.9	9.4	1.6
1972	(X)	7.8	6.2	15.6	9.4	1.6
1971	(X)	9.7	7.9	17.2	9.3	1.9
1970	(X)	10.9	8.8	18.2	9.4	2.1

[1] Includes estimates of overseas admissions into and discharges from the Armed Forces. For 1970, includes error of closure between censuses.

Source: Data consistent with U.S. Bureau of Census, *Current Population*, Series P-25, No. 878. Estimates of births and deaths (with an allowance for deaths of Armed Forces overseas) are from the National Center for Health Statistics. Estimates of net civilian immigration are based partly on data from the Immigration and Naturalization Service.

The fertility rate in 1979 was estimated to be 1,840 children per 1,000 women (implying that 1.84 children per woman were born). The fertility rate has steadily declined from the 1955-59 period, when it was 3,690. It is believed that the declining rates of childbearing reflect changing attitudes about early marriage and childbearing as well as the pursuit of educational and career goals. There was, however, a slight increase in the fertility rate during the period 1977-1979. Exhibit 2 shows the total fertility rate during the period 1920-1979. Exhibit 3 illustrates the total fertility rate as well as changes in numbers of live births in the 1970s.

The increase in births for the years 1977-79 in a proportion greater than the increase in the fertility rate is the result of a large number of women entering the main childbearing ages of 20 to 29. By 1985 there will be 21 million women in that age group, compared with 11 million in 1957. Even at the present low birthrate of 1.8 children per woman, the actual number of births should rise by 500,000 to 3.6 million in 1984. The normal childbearing ages are regarded to be between 15 to 44 years. Exhibit 4 provides a perspective on the present and future age structures of the population. In 1978 the largest aggregation of females were those aged 15 to 24. This group and the category 25 to 29 years were the only age groups in which there were more females in 1978 than are projected for the year 2000. The size of these groups reflects the higher fertility rates of the post-World War II "baby boom," the effects of which can be seen carried through to the year 2000 when they reach ages 35 to 54.

Exhibit 2   **Total Fertility Rate: 1920 to 1979***

Year or Period	Rate	Year or Period	Rate	Year or Period	Rate
1979[1]	1,840	1971	2,275	1955-59	3,690
1978	1,800	1970	2,480	1950-54	3,337
1977	1,826	1969	2,465	1945-49	2,985
1976	1,768	1968	2,477	1940-44	2,523
1975	1,799	1967	2,573	1935-39	2,235
1974	1,857	1966	2,736	1930-34	2,376
1973	1,896	1965	2,928	1925-29	2,840
1972	2,022	1960-64	3,459	1920-24	3,248

*The total fertility rate for a given year shows how many births a group of 1,000 women would have by the end of their childbearing period, if during their entire reproductive period they were to experience the age-specific birthrates for that given year. A fertility rate of 2,000 is necessary for long run replacement of the population in the absence of net migration.

[1] Provisional estimate.

Source: The rate for 1979 is estimated by the Bureau of Census; for 1940 to 1978, National Center for Health Statistics, Vital Statistics of the United States and Monthly Vital Statistics Report (various issues); for 1920-24 to 1935-39, U.S. Bureau of the Census, *Current Population Reports*, Series P-23, No. 36.

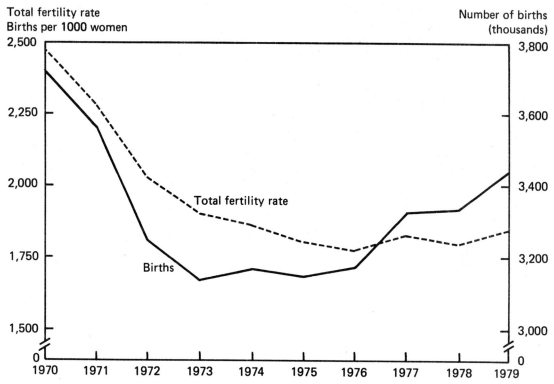

Exhibit 3

**Total Fertility Rate and
Number of Live Births: 1970 to 1979***

SOURCE: U.S. National Center for Health Statistics, *Monthly Vital Statistics Report* (various issues) and unpublished Census Bureau estimates.

DIVERSIFICATION EFFORTS

With the declining birthrate it was felt that Gerber needed to diversify if it was to continue to grow and prosper. In keeping with the slogan that "Babies are our business," the company focused its diversification strategy around the concept of selling more items of merchandise per baby. To facilitate the diversification process, a Gerber venture group was established early in 1974. The group met every Monday morning for the purpose of screening new ideas and forwarding promising proposals to the company's planning committee. The concept of a venture group was abandoned within a year.

The categories that follow represent the major areas of Gerber's diversification.

Exhibit 4

Estimates and Projections of the Population of the United States by Age and Sex: 1970 to 2000 (Numbers in thousands. As of July 1. Total population includes Armed Forces overseas.)

Sex, Year, and Series	All Ages	Under 5 Years	5 to 14 Years	15 to 24 Years	25 to 44 Years	45 to 64 Years	65 Years and over	Median Age
Women:								
1970	104,609	8,406	19,980	18,048	24,599	21,896	11,681	29.3
1975	109,346	7,765	18,497	19,898	27,238	22,711	13,236	30.0
1978	112,046	7,507	17,373	20,511	29,549	22,831	14,276	31.0
1985								
Series I*	122,437	11,161	16,965	19,049	36,036	22,932	16,293	31.9
Series II**	119,514	9,171	16,032					32.7
Series III***	117,564	7,919	15,333					33.2
2000								
Series I	144,746	11,517	24,270	20,972	38,409	30,473	19,105	34.1
Series II	133,790	8,699	19,087	18,018				36.8
Series III	126,714	6,899	15,786	16,042				38.5
Men:								
1970	100,269	8,742	20,754	18,452	23,837	20,079	8,407	26.6
1975	104,213	8,114	19,236	20,346	26,497	20,835	9,184	27.6
1978	106,502	7,855	18,090	20,986	28,771	21,021	9,778	28.5
1985								
Series I	116,441	11,726	17,775	19,468	35,198	21,261	11,012	29.5
Series II	113,366	9,632	16,794					30.3
Series III	111,315	8,315	16,060					30.8
2000								
Series I	138,091	12,121	25,525	21,684	37,385	28,659	12,717	30.8
Series II	126,588	9,153	20,067	18,607				34.1
Series III	119,162	7,259	16,593	16,549				36.0

PERCENT DISTRIBUTION

Women:

1970	100.0	8.0	19.1	17.3	23.5	20.9	11.2	(X)
1975	100.0	7.1	16.9	18.2	24.9	20.8	12.1	(X)
1978	100.0	6.7	15.5	18.3	26.4	20.4	12.7	(X)
1985								
Series I	100.0	9.1	13.9	15.6	29.4	18.7	13.3	(X)
Series II	100.0	7.7	13.4	15.9	30.2	19.2	13.6	(X)
Series III	100.0	6.7	13.0	16.2	30.7	19.5	13.9	(X)
2000								
Series I	100.0	8.0	16.8	14.5	26.5	21.1	13.2	(X)
Series II	100.0	6.5	14.3	13.5	28.7	22.8	14.3	(X)
Series III	100.0	5.4	12.5	12.7	30.3	24.0	15.1	(X)

Men:

1970	100.0	8.7	20.7	18.4	23.8	20.0	8.4	(X)
1975	100.0	7.8	18.5	19.5	25.4	20.0	8.8	(X)
1978	100.0	7.4	17.0	19.7	27.0	19.7	9.2	(X)
1985								
Series I	100.0	10.1	15.3	16.7	30.2	18.3	9.5	(X)
Series II	100.0	8.5	14.8	17.2	31.0	18.8	9.7	(X)
Series III	100.0	7.5	14.4	17.5	31.6	19.1	9.9	(X)
2000								
Series I	100.0	8.8	18.5	15.7	27.1	20.8	9.2	(X)
Series II	100.0	7.2	15.9	14.7	29.5	22.6	10.0	(X)
Series III	100.0	6.1	13.9	13.9	31.4	24.1	10.7	(X)

* Based on women who enter childbearing age and will average 2.7 births/woman.
** Based on women who enter childbearing age and will average 2.1 births/woman.
*** Based on women who enter childbearing age and will average 1.7 births/woman.

Source: U.S. Department of Commerce, Bureau of the Census, Current Population Reports, Series P-25, Nos. 800, 721, and 704.

Special Products

In keeping with the company's philosophy, Gerber has sought to grow through the sale of additional baby products and services (nonfood items) primarily to families with infants and small children. There were approximately 400 different items in the special product line in 1979, which were sold through approximately 50,000 retail outlets (including a small number of company-owned outlet stores) in the United States. The success of special products is attributed to the confidence which parents have in products bearing the Gerber name. During the decade of the eighties, the company plans to become an increasing factor in the total baby needs market by adding new items to, and additional distribution of, special products.

Gerber first entered the infant clothing market in 1960 by acquiring a vinyl pants and bib company. During the year 1979-80, the company was the leader in the submarket of vinyl pants; however, a much larger market exists in disposable diapers. And disposable diapers eliminate the need for rubber pants. In addition to vinyl pants and bibs, the baby wear division produces shirts, training pants, and socks. Gerber has also expanded its clothing line to include children through their preschool years. During 1978-79, new sneakers were introduced in six different patterns in sizes 2 to 8. The sneakers were a part of the Gerber "footwear line" which includes shoes, socks, booties, and "funzie" slippers. A special line of silk-screen-printed shirts in six different patterns was also added during the year.

In 1970 Gerber Products purchased an infant toiletries and accessories company operating under the name of Hankscraft. In 1979-80 Hankscraft was the leader in the sale of humidifiers and vaporizers. During this year, its line of carryall bags, which serve as multipurpose bags as well as the familiar diaper bag, was expanded. In addition four new safety items were introduced—outlet covers, a cabinet lock, door knob covers, and outlet plugs. Hankscraft division also produced nursers and nurser accessories and a number of infant care products.

The Spartan Printing and Graphic Arts Company was acquired in 1971. This division now offers internal and external photographic, design, printing, and advertising services. Additionally, Gerber Metal Products division was organized in the late 70s. This division consists of two units, a container manufacturing plant (acquired in 1971) and a metal lithographic operation (built in 1977) at which flat metal sheets are printed for later use in the manufacturing of containers. This division also serves both internal needs and outside customers.

In 1974-75, Gerber acquired the Walter W. Moyer Company, Inc., a manufacturer of children's underwear and knit apparel. At the time of the takeover, the Moyer Company with plants in Pennsylvania and Arizona, had annual sales between $16 and $17 million. It currently produces a broad line of knitwear garments for sale under the Gerber name as well as for private label distribution. The Health Care division, formed in 1978, distributes and sells an incontinent pant system and a variety of other products designed for use in medical and extended care facilities. In 1979 Gerber opened a subsidiary—

G & M Finishing—for the purpose of bleaching and dyeing knit fabrics. In addition to supplying the needs of the Moyer plant, G & M Finishing has the capacity to provide bleaching and dyeing services to other knit users.

A line of plush stuffed toys are produced by the Atlanta Novelty division (acquired in 1973). The popular Gerber Baby doll is also produced and sold by this division. In the year 1980, Gerber purchased the Reliance Products Corporation of Woodsocket, Rhode Island. Reliance produces a broad line of products for infants including the widely accepted NUK line of nurser bottle nipples and orthodontic exercisers for infants.

Life and Health Care Insurance

Gerber organized a life insurance subsidiary in 1968 to sell low-priced policies to young parents by mail. In 1970 a "child-care" policy, providing hospitalization insurance for children under legal age, was introduced. The unique characteristic of this policy is that the child's parents need not be insured. Gerber considered this to be a natural extension of its business of helping young parents provide for their children. The company is licensed by most states to write and sell life and other types of personal insurance. While the company has used some licensed agents in its insurance business, direct response, including extensive newspaper and television advertising, remains the principle avenue of marketing insurance policies.

The life insurance division was a disappointment through 1975, having lost $858,000 in 1973 and $945,000 in 1974. However, Gerber tightened administrative control over the unit, and profits from the insurance operation amounted to $109,000 in 1976-1977, an increase of $49,000 from the previous period, 1975-1976. The life insurance has since continued to make contributions to the overall performance of the company and experienced the best year in 1980, at which time the company had about one-half billion dollars of insurance in force.

Day Care Centers

Gerber announced the formation of a Children's Centers division in early 1971. The initial nursery schools were established in Villa Park, Illinois; Cleveland, Ohio; and Costa Mesa, California. In 1980 there were 32 such nursery school and day-care centers in seven metropolitan areas of the United States. These centers have encountered some problems, mostly at the local administrative level. The company regards them as a test marketing of the day-care centers concept that will provide experience for determining whether or not to expand. Their performance, to date, has been only marginally profitable. In addition to expecting a major extension of child care activity in the decade of the eighties, the company is planning to operate a Gerber children's center for a private employer.

The Adult Market

Gerber faces a tough challenge in trying to crack the adult market. In hopes of appealing to this market, Gerber developed a "Rediscover Gerber" ad campaign that promoted specialty fruits and desserts, waffle toppings, and "the 60-second parfait." One ad put it, "Next time you're looking for something to eat, baby yourself with the unexpected snack." A Gerber executive acknowledged the challenge of the adult market this way, "Let's face it, people think of baby food as pretty bland stuff." Currently, the firm is planning to reintroduce its "dessert line" and promote it as snack food for young people (particularly teenage girls).

Another attempt to penetrate the adult market was through single-serving adult foods under the "Singles" label introduced in 1974. At that time, about 11.2 million households, out of a total of 63.2 million households, were single-person households. In addition, the number of two-person households accounted for another 18.9 million. Thus, the primary and secondary target markets for these products included nearly half of all households in the United States. This contrasts markedly with the ten percent of U.S. households which have babies.

A number of problems have been encountered with the Singles line. In an interview reported in *Advertising Age*, John C. Suerth, then chairman of Gerber, conceded that in spite of a different jar design and label, the Singles line still gave the appearance of baby food. He also conceded that the word "Singles" was misleading. When the company used the word "Singles" it was thinking in terms of single-serving and not in terms of food for singles. Because of these problems the Singles line did not gain consumer acceptance and was dropped, which resulted in a write down of about $450,000.

Gerber also test marketed three other adult products—a peanut spread, a catsup, and a spaghetti sauce—during the 1974-77 period. These products would put Gerber in competition with such companies as Best Foods, makers of Skippy; Swift Derby Foods, makers of Peter Pan; Procter and Gamble, makers of Jif peanut spread; and Kraft Foods and Borden which also recently entered the peanut butter market. In the catsup and spaghetti sauce market, Gerber would have to compete against companies such as Heinz, Hunt-Wesson, and Del Monte. The test market results led to the abandonment of these products.

C. W. Transport Acquisition

Gerber acquired C. W. Transport, Inc. in August 1979 through a stock transfer. The Wisconsin-based common carrier trucking firm serving 11 states in the midwest and southeast represents Gerber's largest acquisition to date. Company officials plan to integrate the new unit into internal shipping operations and also maintain it as a profit center in its own right.

MARKETING POLICIES

Distribution System

Traditionally, Gerber has marketed its baby food products through grocery stores and supermarkets across the U.S., as well as in 68 foreign countries. As noted earlier, however, grocery outlets are now being asked to sell special products such as vinyl pants, baby and preschool children's clothing, infant toiletries, vaporizers, and other infant accessories — the concept being to build a sort of baby center in the stores. The company has met some resistance in this effort, however. For example, Thriftmart, Inc., a southern California food chain, stocks many Gerber baby food items, but only one nonfood product: plastic pants. According to Thriftmart the traffic just did not warrant carrying other Gerber products.

In recent years in an attempt to increase market penetration, Gerber expanded its channels to include discount houses, drug chains, department stores, and specialty shops for the growing line of nonfood baby products. Moreover in 1979 two divisions, grocery products and special products, were created. A principal reason for the reorganization was the divergent marketing channels utilized by the two product lines. The grocery products division concentrates on food stores while the special products division focuses on mass merchandising, drug outlets, and other segments of Gerber distribution.

A major strength of Gerber's distribution system is a new computerized market information system, covering 50,000 food stores, accounting for about 85 percent to 90 percent of the country's total retail food sales. The system called MARS (market auditing report service) provides instant information relative to various Gerber products in terms of store inventory, shelf space, mix, movement, and turnover compared with competition. The system enables the company to isolate almost any facet of its distribution.

Promotion

Gerber's promotional efforts have been largely directed toward two groups: mothers and pediatricians. The company tries to reach mothers through advertising in baby publications and by direct mail promotions. It also relies on the "word of mouth" advertising by mothers who have used Gerber products.

The direct mail campaign is perhaps Gerber's key promotional tool. The lists used in the campaign are derived from birth records. Three to six weeks after a birth the new mother receives literature and coupons for Gerber baby foods that are redeemable at the local grocery stores. Afterwards, follow-up coupons are sent. The redemption rate of these coupons is around 20 percent.

Promotion to pediatricians takes other forms. Gerber sponsors the *Pediatric Basics*, a respected journal for pediatricians. The company also maintains a professional relations department whose staff calls upon hospitals and doctors to promote Gerber products. Information about new Gerber products and latest findings in infant nutrition is shared with the health professionals who serve new parents throughout the country.

In keeping with its attempts to diversify, in 1972 Gerber shortened its slogan from "Babies are our business . . . our *only* business" to "Babies are our business." The slogan "Gerber prepares foods for the most important person in the world . . . your baby" is also used in various advertisements. The company considers its name a valuable asset. Former chairman Suerth explained it this way, "Everything we're doing is really based on our success in the baby food area. So you better keep the lead dog pretty healthy."

FOREIGN OPERATIONS

Gerber was a late entrant in the overseas market. In 1965 it derived only 7 percent of its total sales from overseas operations. However, since 1974, international sales have ranged between 16 to 20 percent of the consolidated sales. In 1980 Gerber maintained subsidiaries in Canada, Mexico, Venezuela, and Costa Rica. It operated a joint venture in Brazil, and had licensees in Australia, France, Italy, Japan, the Phillipines, and South Africa. In addition, export shipments were made to about 80 countries around the world. Food items constituted most of the overseas sales, although some special products, particularly vinyl waterproof pants, nursers and nurser accessories, and vaporizers were also exported.

Sales and pretax earnings attributable to international operations (foreign subsidiaries, foreign licensees, and exports) as an approximate percentage of consolidated sales, and consolidated pretax earnings for the years 1975-1980 were as follows:

	1975	1976	1977	1978	1979	1980
Sales	17.2%	19.6%	18.2%	16.2%	17.1%	16.9%
Pretax earnings	22.2%	16.9%	2.7%	2.8%	6.9%	7.2%

Increased sales were attained primarily in major Latin American markets despite political uncertainties in much of that part of the world. Subsidiaries in Mexico, Costa Rica, and Venezuela experienced growth in sales volume. However, contribution of international sales to earnings was scverly limited due to increasing costs and stringent price controls in foreign markets. In Venezuela, for example, baby food selling prices have been frozen since limited price increases were permitted in the latter part of the fiscal year 1978.

In 1980 Gerber sold its 82 percent interest in a Venezuelan subsidiary. The Venezuelan company now produces and markets a broad line of Gerber baby foods under a licensing agreement.

Sales and pretax earnings of the Venezuelan company and the rest of the international operations for the years 1978 through 1980 were as follows:

	1978	1979	1980
	(Thousands of Dollars)		
International sales:			
Venezuela	33,182	42,847	45,687
Other	38,628	42,717	56,305
International pretax earnings:			
Venezuela	951	2,990	1,100
Other	482	829	3,241

In spite of the pressures of rising costs, inflation, and price controls, Gerber expects continued growth in the international markets. Improvement in the economic and educational standards, along with the knowledge of nutrition, are regarded as the primary reasons for the increasing demand of Gerber products.

FINANCE

After a steady growth in sales and profit, Gerber was faced with eroding sales and earnings during 1973, 1974 and 1975 (Exhibits 5 and 6). "We got hit with so many things at one time—reduced births, price controls, rising costs, and severe price competition," said Suerth. The company has, however, recovered from the setback. With a minor exception in the year 1977, profits have steadily increased since 1976. In the years 1979 and 1980 profits were at an all-time high. In 1980 Gerber had an equity of nearly $228 million and a long-term debt of only $20 million.

Until the acquisition of C. W. Transport, Inc. in August 1979, the company's operations were divided into two industry segments: (1) sales of food and (2) sales of special products and services. In the year 1980 a third segment, sales from transportation services, was added. The relative contribution of each segment to the consolidated sales for the last six years was as follows (000's omitted):

Year	Food	Special Products and Services	Transportation	Total
1975	283,512	44,627	–	328,139
1976	314,693	57,725	–	372,418
1977	335,412	69,186	–	404,598
1978	364,210	78,868	–	443,078
1979	404,203	94,812	–	499,015
1980	435,838	108,084	58,064	601,986

Net earnings from the new transportation services segment in 1980 were $2,328,000.

In the *Gerber's Annual Report to Stockholders* for the years 1979 and 1980, it was noted that the increases in sales of domestic food in the two preceding years of the report were primarily due to higher selling prices rather than the increases in the sales volume. Furthermore, net earnings for special products and services declined in the last two fiscal years. This was especially true in the petroleum based products.

RESEARCH AND DEVELOPMENT

Gerber research activities are located at the corporate headquarters in Fremont, Michigan. Research efforts primarily concentrate on the development of new foods, product formulations, new processing methods, and improved material usage. In light of ever-increasing knowledge of infant nutrition and frequent feedback provided by practicing pediatricians, product formulas are continuously evaluated and retested. For example, the use of salt was completely discontinued in 1978 and sugar usage was significantly reduced. Studies in packaging and agricultural research are also carried out on a regular basis. Cornucopia Farms, headquartered at Barker, New York, supplies the firm with fresh produce and apple juice and serves as a natural laboratory for the company's agricultural research projects. Charles F. Whitten, professor of pediat-

Exhibit 5

Gerber Products Company
Consolidated Income Account, Years Ended March 31
($000s)

	1969	1970	1971	1972
Net sales	$ 202,180	$ 217,171	$ 261,851	$ 282,601
Other income	1,127	1,365	1,087	1,138
Equity earnings	–	–	–	–
Transport revenue	–	–	–	–
Total	$ 203,307	$ 218,536	$ 262,938	$ 283,739
Cost of sales	$ 116,381	$ 126,306	$ 156,466	$ 170,793
Transport expense	–	–	–	–
Selling expense	55,675	59,669	69,307	73,574
Interest expense	53	–	287	291
Equity in affiliated earnings	–	–	–	cr 30
Income tax	16,620	16,880	18,170	18,699
Minority interest	80	179	214	159
Foreign exchange loss	–	–	–	–
Net profit	$ 14,498	$ 15,502	$ 18,494	$ 20,253
Previous retained earnings	74,292	79,603	85,768	94,212
Common stock dividends	9,187	9,337	10,082	10,883
Pool of interests adjustment	–	–	cr 32	–
Retained earnings	$ 79,603	$ 85,768	$ 94,212	$ 103,582
Earnings per common share	$ 1.75	$ 1.87	$ 2.19	$ 2.40
Number of common shares	8,304,629	8,295,230	8,447,214	8,440,130

rics, Wayne State University School of Medicine and Dena C. Cederquist, professor emeritus, Department of Food Science and Human Nutrition, Michigan State University, are on the Gerber board of directors.

A TAKEOVER BID BY ANDERSON, CLAYTON AND COMPANY

On April 18, 1977, Anderson, Clayton and Company, a Houston-based foods and oil-seeds group, offered to buy all 8.1 million shares of Gerber at $40 a share. In 1976 Anderson, Clayton's return was 11.5 percent on $759 million of sales, while Gerber's was 16.6 percent on $372 million of sales. According to President Guinee of Anderson, Clayton, the acquisition would boost his company's return on equity and increase its stake in the grocery products business. Gerber's stock had sold as low as 8½ in 1974, at 21 in November 1976, and was selling in the mid-30s at the time of the offer. The purchase of 90,000 shares in the open market by Anderson, Clayton was instrumental in boosting stock price.

Gerber executives doggedly resisted the takeover attempt and filed suits in state and federal courts charging: (1) Anderson, Clayton manipulated Gerber's stock price before making the offer, (2) the proposed offer would be in violation of antitrust laws because it would give Anderson, Clayton monopoly

1973	1974	1975	1976	1977	1978	1979	1980
$ 278,473	$ 285,437	$ 328,140	$ 372,418	$ 404,598	$ 443,078	$ 499,016	$ 543,922
823	1,401	1,290	1,651	1,974	2,077	2,217	2,209
–	–	–	–	291	267	208	312
–	–	–	–	–	–	–	58,064
$ 279,296	$ 286,838	$ 329,430	$ 374,069	$ 406,863	$ 445,422	$ 501,441	$ 604,507
$ 176,742	$ 189,818	$ 214,164	$ 236,409	$ 263,569	$ 291,870	$ 336,457	$ 368,790
–	–	–	–	–	–	–	49,558
71,373	73,556	79,664	90,358	95,579	104,895	110,740	126,130
584	1,661	2,321	1,672	1,961	2,636	3,661	6,175
dr 964	dr 1,258	dr 645	dr 135	–	–	–	–
13,980	9,100	16,070	22,281	22,611	22,033	22,798	24,254
234	323	228	325	cr 251	cr 11	321	cr 116
–	–	–	–	1,060	–	–	–
$ 15,419	$ 11,122	$ 16,338	$ 22,889	$ 22,334	$ 23,999	$ 27,464	$ 29,716
103,582	$ 107,648	108,400	116,565	130,508	142,472	155,065	170,261
11,353	10,370	8,173	8,946	10,370	11,406	12,268	13,852
$ 107,648	$ 108,400	$ 116,565	$ 130,508	$ 142,472	$ 155,065	$ 170,261	$ 186,125
$ 1.87	$ 1.35	$ 2.01	$ 2.81	$ 2.75	$ 2.94	$ 3.35	$ 3.34
8,250,800	8,214,680	8,132,803	8,133,201	8,134,014	8,164,278	8,192,264	8,901,151

power in the baby food industry and reduce competition in the salad dressing market, which Gerber had considered entering (Anderson, Clayton held 12 percent of the market with its Seven Seas brand), and (3) Anderson, Clayton had failed to disclose $2.1 million in illegal payments the company had made abroad during the preceding several years.

The situation resulted in legal entanglements and consequent delays. On September 19, Anderson, Clayton withdrew its offer, saying that because of the legal problems, any takeover could not be completed until late 1978 or early 1979. "These delays aren't acceptable," said Mr. Barlow, the Anderson, Clayton chairman.

During the takeover struggle, Gerber stock rose to a high of 39½. On September 19, the day Anderson, Clayton withdrew its offer, the price of Gerber stock dropped from 34 3/8 to 28 1/4. Those who bought a large number of shares, anticipating a successful takeover, lost heavily. In August and September 1977, four class-action suits were filed by stockholders against Gerber alleging violation of the Securities and Exchange Act of 1934 because the company's opposition to tender offer was not in the best interest of the shareholders, but rather in the self-interest of the directors. All four suits were dismissed by the court.

Exhibit 6

Gerber Products Company
Consolidated Balance Sheet, as of March 31
($000s)

ASSETS	1969	1970	1971	1972
Current assets:				
Cash	$ 3,591	$ 3,579	$ 3,877	$ 1,408
Commercial paper	12,079	8,190	—	—
Marketable securities (cost).................	—	—	13,794	3,286
Receivables	14,761	16,672	21,686	23,244
Finished products	34,933	39,880	39,640	47,975
New materials and supplies	7,071	9,605	10,977	12,392
Total current assets.........................	$ 72,435	$ 77,926	$ 89,974	$ 88,305
Property, plant, and equipment (net)	35,800	37,890	43,184	53,250
Investment in consolidated subsidiaries	5,089	5,509	5,527	8,772
Goodwill	1	1	—	—
Miscellaneous receivables......................	1,596	1,990	3,442	2,327
Intangibles..................................	701	854	1,083	867
Total assets	$115,622	$124,170	$143,210	$153,521

LIABILITIES AND STOCKHOLDERS' EQUITY

	1969	1970	1971	1972
Current liabilities:				
Accounts payable..........................	$ 5,492	$ 7,575	$ 18,421	$ 18,837
Notes payable.............................	259	83	1,420	1,701
Accruals	5,905	6,536	—	—
Income tax	3,395	3,849	4,383	3,934
Debt due	414	—	—	—
Total current liabilities......................	$ 15,465	$ 18,043	$ 24,224	$ 24,472
Long-term debt	75	—	1,904	1,808
Deferred credit..............................	550	825	1,816	1,963
Minority interest	452	482	695	1,673
Pension costs	680	583	—	—
Total liabilities	$ 17,222	$ 19,933	$ 28,639	$ 29,916
Common stock (2.50)........................	$ 21,234	$ 21,234	$ 21,234	$ 21,234
Paid-in surplus	3,045	3,045	2,983	2,946
Retained earnings	79,603	85,768	91,895	101,265
Stockholders' equity	$103,882	$110,047	$116,113	$125,446
Less reacquired stock	5,482	5,810	1,542	1,841
Total stockholders' equity	$ 98,400	$104,237	$114,571	$123,605
Total liabilities and stockholders' equity	$115,622	$124,170	$143,210	$153,521

1973	1974	1975	1976	1977	1978	1979	1980
$ 2,861	$ 2,722	$ 4,357	$ 3,045	$ 1,558	$ 2,366	$ 3,254	$ 7,105
—	—	—	—	—	—	—	—
4,557	1,925	1,766	15,522	11,987	9,873	3,475	4,484
25,128	27,939	28,192	30,233	35,815	42,914	53,662	65,733
44,886	46,542	47,571	43,984	49,320	49,713	59,475	62,949
14,395	17,076	21,366	24,844	30,779	30,390	42,571	40,096
$ 91,827	$ 96,204	$ 103,252	$ 117,628	$ 129,459	$ 135,256	$ 162,437	$ 180,367
58,844	62,834	68,523	70,823	80,700	89,820	100,978	129,060
9,311	9,462	10,000	10,572	11,778	12,813	13,455	24,912
—	—	—	—	—	—	—	—
1,921	3,645	3,636	4,729	4,759	6,555	7,376	10,308
767	1,413	1,171	406	431	324	238	8,149
$162,670	$ 173,558	$ 186,582	$ 204,158	$ 227,127	$ 244,768	$ 284,484	$ 352,796
$ 17,423	$ 20,348	$ 19,936	$ 26,996	$ 34,168	$ 33,193	$ 40,132	$ 55,380
10,986	18,562	14,015	1,802	8,317	12,321	24,173	40,262
—	—	—	—	—	—	—	—
2,360	2,388	2,566	6,875	4,860	3,368	4,139	5,492
—	—	—	—	—	—	—	—
$ 30,769	$ 41,298	$ 36,517	$ 35,673	$ 47,345	$ 48,882	$ 68,444	$ 101,134
2,835	3,420	13,244	17,360	15,728	18,112	21,994	19,990
3,250	4,239	4,654	4,666	5,836	6,535	6,855	8,505
2,557	1,337	1,546	1,890	1,675	1,664	1,985	1,906
—	—	—	—	—	—	—	—
$ 39,411	$ 50,294	$ 55,961	$ 59,589	$ 70,584	$ 75,193	$ 99,278	$ 131,535
$ 21,234	$ 21,235	$ 21,234	$ 21,235	$ 21,235	$ 21,235	$ 21,235	$ 22,980
2,946	2,945	2,946	2,942	2,935	2,720	2,549	20,759
105,331	106,083	114,248	128,191	140,155	152,748	167,944	183,808
$129,511	$ 130,263	$ 138,428	$ 152,368	$ 164,325	$ 176,703	191,728	$ 227,547
6,252	6,999	7,807	7,799	7,782	7,128	6,522	6,286
$123,259	$ 123,264	$ 130,621	$ 144,569	$ 156,543	$ 169,575	$ 185,206	$ 221,261
$162,670	$ 173,558	$ 186,582	$ 204,158	$ 227,127	$ 244,768	$ 284,484	$ 352,796

NOTES

"Anderson Clayton Withdraws Gerber Bid," *Financial Times*, September 20, 1977, p. 28.

"Baby Talk," *Forbes*, August 1, 1975, pp. 40–41.

"Bid by Anderson Clayton to Buy Gerber Dropped," *The Wall Street Journal*, September 20, 1977, p. 38.

"But It's Cold Out There," *Forbes*, September 15, 1973, p. 40.

"Conversation with Gerber's John Suerth," *Advertising Age*, 46:29, February 3, 1975.

"Does Father Know Best?" *Forbes*, 121:31–2, March 6, 1978.

Fifty Years of Caring, Gerber Products Company, internal brochure.

Gerber's Annual Report to Stockholders, Gerber Products Company, 1970–1980.

"Gerber Back on the Ad Track," *Advertising Age*, 49:1, March 6, 1978.

"Gerber Finds There is Still Plenty of Profits in Moppets," *Barrons*, 55L34–35, March 3, 1975.

"Gerber Jumps on No-Salt Bandwagon," *Advertising Age*, June 6, 1977, p. 4.

"Gerber Products Says Bid to Settle Walkout at Plant is Rejected," *The Wall Street Journal*, April 4, 1977, p. 20.

"Gerber: Selling More to the Same Mothers is Our Objective Now," *Business Week*, October 16, 1978, pp. 192–195.

"Gerber: Where Have All the Babies Gone?" *Commerical and Financial Chronicle*, 221:3, March 22, 1976.

"Growing Pains in the Baby Market," *Forbes*, December 15, 1959, p. 19.

Koshetz, Herbert. "Gerber Charged With Damaging Its Shareholders," *New York Times*, August 10, 1977, p. d1.

"Lower Birthrate Crimps the Baby Food Market," *Business Week*, July 13, 1974, pp. 44–48.

Moody's Industrial Manual, Gerber Products Company, 1968–1978.

"Nothing Is Too Good For Our Stockholders," *Forbes*, 119:55, May 15, 1977.

"Outlook on the Baby-Food Market," *Business Week*, July 13, 1974, p. 45.

Serrin, William. "How Gerber Foiled a Takeover," *New York Times*, September 2, 1977, p. F1–2.

Standard and Poor's Industrial Manual, Gerber Products Company, 1978.

Standard and Poor's Stock Report, Gerber Products Company, 1978.

"The Bad News in Babyland," *Dun's*, December, 1972, p. 104.

"The Lost Generation Wasn't," *Forbes*, October 1, 1965, pp. 51–2.

U.S. Bureau of Census, *Current Population Reports*, Series P–20, No. 350, May 1980.

"What Population Explosion," *Forbes*, March 1, 1967, pp. 60–61.

Case 7–7

The Management OST System
At Texas Instruments*

BACKGROUND

Since World War II, Texas Instruments Incorporated (TI) has continued to be a strategic developer in electronics and related industries, experiencing growth of about 30 percent compounded each year in net sales billed and net income from 1946 to 1963, and 17 percent from 1963 to the mid 1970s (Exhibit 1). Highlights of TI history are graphed in Exhibit 2. In 1951 TI introduced the first silicon transistor, followed by rapid transistor production, to become the principal supplier of semiconductors to the computer industry when the first solid-state computers were introduced in the late 1950s and early 1960s. The invention and development of the integrated circuit in production in the early 1960s enhanced the design of commercial computers. Further breakthroughs with the introduction of plastic encapsulated circuits in 1966 lowered the production cost of integrated circuits by 50 percent and led to more sophisticated circuits by the early 1970s. TI continued to be an innovator in technology, production, and distribution during this period. With entry into the industrial data terminal market in 1971 based upon development of a semiconductor printing device, TI entered the calculator market with unique experience in integrated circuits, displays, and keyboards.

In the 1970s TI also experienced periods of economic instability based on market shifts and recessions, much like that experienced by other firms in the electronics industry. In recent years planners at TI have experienced the need for understanding ways to capitalize on growth periods, while still maintaining ever-present contingency plans to accommodate market shifts and economic recessions.

LONG-RANGE PLANNING AND GOAL SETTING

Long-range planning and goal setting became especially evident at TI during the early 1970s. This included coordinated efforts to balance research and development, production, and marketing and distribution functions for particular TI businesses; also included were attempts to seize new opportunities, and

---

*This case was prepared by August W. Smith, Texas A & M University, with assistance from Texas Instruments Incorporated, where Smith has served as a consultant. The case was written with the intention of providing a basis for class discussion rather than illustrating either effective or ineffective management of a business situation.

Exhibit 1

Texas Instruments Incorporated
Net Sales Billed and Net Income
(Millions of dollars)

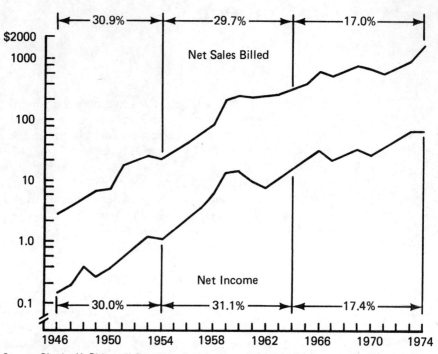

Source: Charles H. Phipps, " Corporate Development: The OST System," (paper presented to the Corporate Growth Association, St. Louis, Missouri, September 9, 1975). p 14.

to maximize worldwide merchandising effectiveness in consumer as well as industrial, military, and government business. Customer problems became opportunities to develop new products and services, even at a time of great Japanese challenge and entrenchment in the electronics industry. At TI one noted during this period that emphasis was on maintaining a basic relationship and equation, where quality (reliability) times performance divided by price equals value. Increasing value was viewed as the way to meet competition aggressively and continuously.

Strategic planning was further stimulated by the increasing complexity of the marketplace in the late 1970s which was also projected for the 1980s. Corporate planners became increasingly aware of new political and economic instabilities, periodic market realignments, new competition, persistent high rates of inflation, a new order of priorities in international markets, and raw material shortages. With this new complex set of challenges, there was an even greater need to produce and market the right " mix" of products in tune with specific users, markets, and environments. Therefore, breakthroughs in technology,

Texas Instruments Incorporated
Highlights of Growth Since 1946
Exhibit 2   ## Net Sales Billed (Millions of dollars)

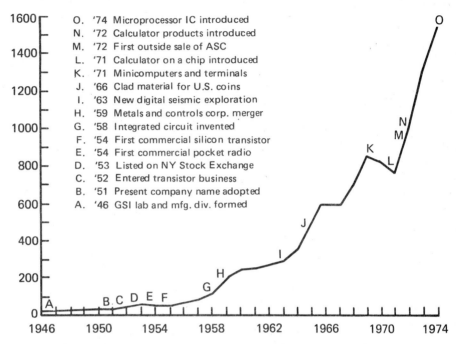

O. '74 Microprocessor IC introduced
N. '72 Calculator products introduced
M. '72 First outside sale of ASC
L. '71 Calculator on a chip introduced
K. '71 Minicomputers and terminals
J. '66 Clad material for U.S. coins
I. '63 New digital seismic exploration
H. '59 Metals and controls corp. merger
G. '58 Integrated circuit invented
F. '54 First commercial silicon transistor
E. '54 First commercial pocket radio
D. '53 Listed on NY Stock Exchange
C. '52 Entered transistor business
B. '51 Present company name adopted
A. '46 GSI lab and mfg. div. formed

Source : Charles H. Phipps, " Corporate Development: The OST System, " (paper presented to the Corporate Growth Association, St. Louis, Missouri, September 9, 1975). p. 14.

production, and marketing methods were clearly required. In turn, this placed greater importance on management's ability and skill in each area of TI business.

By the early 1970s TI had evolved into a technologically-oriented company that was vertically integrated between basic materials and electrical products, components, or subassemblies to equipment groups and service groups with relatively complete lines of products and services to support government, military, industrial, and consumer-user groups. The product and service groups provide the primary basis for departmentation below the president and chief executive officer. Overall corporate objectives are divided into groups to establish specific business objectives. In the 1970s groups ranged from basic materials to components and major equipment, services, and support systems. An organization chart in 1981 indicates major corporate functions and product groups including semiconductor, distributed computing, consumer electronic, materials and electrical, government electronic products, and geophysical exploration services (Exhibit 3). Each product group contributes to particular busi-

Exhibit 3

**Texas Instruments Incorporated
Organization Chart, 1981**

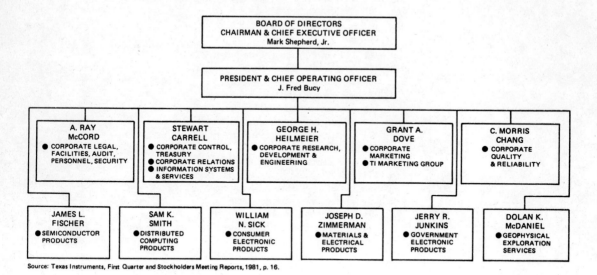

Source: Texas Instruments, First Quarter and Stockholders Meeting Reports, 1981, p. 16.

ness objectives of the organization (Exhibit 4). Each product group may include multiple strategies which contribute to a common business objective.

Strategies are divided into tactical action programs (TAP) at the department level, which provide operational checkpoints and detailed guidelines to insure progress toward given strategies at the product customer center (PCC) level. Strategies are evaluated every 6 to 18 months. A specific individual is responsible for each TAP with definite starting and finishing requirements and resources. At the branch level, each TAP may be further divided into separate work packages which relate specific work activities to an individual coordinator or manager. Thus, there are essentially five levels in the organization structure and goal hierarchy structure of the company: corporate objectives, business objectives, strategies, tactical action programs, and work packages.

THE MANAGEMENT OST SYSTEM

Part of the aggressive growth at TI can be attributed to its management systems which operationalize and continuously review and update specific objectives, strategies, and tactics of the various diverse TI organizational units, operations, and reporting systems. With greater degrees of diversity come added problems in communication, coordination, and control; also, rapid changes in technical breakthroughs, developments and continual innovations in the marketplace, and competition create the need for shorter response time and decentralized decision making in diverse operations spread out around the world. There is a need for on-going, practical, and flexible systems to adequately manage growth and added complexity. Corporate intentions (plans,

Exhibit 4

Texas Instruments Incorporated
Organizational Operating and Strategic Goals

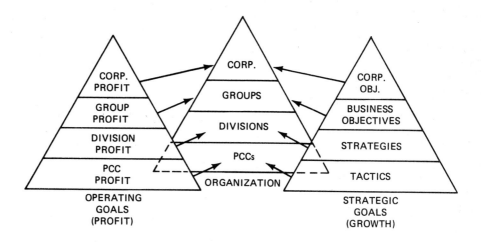

OPERATING
GOALS
(PROFIT)

STRATEGIC
GOALS
(GROWTH)

objectives, and goals) should enhance actions and controls at every level of the organization. Also, relationships between organizational functions and higher and lower levels need to be readily realigned to remain an adaptive forward-moving system.

The system TI specifically developed to coordinate its overall operations, goal hierarchy, and reporting and performance reviews is the OST system. OST stands for obectives, strategies, and tactics as a support overlay to its organization structure. The corporate objective at the executive level identifies overall economic and social purposes and rationale for existence relative to external groups such as shareholders, customers, community, and society at large. Each corporate objective is refined in a set of business objectives which identifies specific boundaries of each business (or economic component) system, and which relate these to technical and market developments evident in the industry. Refining the market and product mix, widening or narrowing technical goals, and overcoming obstacles or reaching out to new opportunities occur at this level. Emphasis is on a horizon of five to ten years (that is, projecting to the end of the current decade). The business objectives provide a broad view of major opportunities as specified in worldwide terms, by industry structure, and major environmental segments for the upcoming decade. Major objectives are defined in terms of financial, market, personnel (or people) resources, and requirements. There were nine business objectives in the mid 1970s.

Strategies are also expressed in worldwide industry and environmental terms but focus more on intermediate goals over the next three to five years. They emphasize potential innovations and interventions and note key resources and key decision points, alternatives, and major milestones to be reached. Strategies provide the linking pins between broad-based business objectives and more detailed tactical, on-going, day-to-day operations to insure progress toward specific business objectives. It is estimated that over 60 strategies could be readily identified at TI in the mid 1970s. Usually strategies are defined in such a way to allow quantitative measurement and comparison, although qualitative (more judgmental) measures may also be evident. Some of the more critical middle-level management decisions involve strategy formulation, implementation, and evaluation. Each strategy usually relates a major segment of business to a given industry representing an alternative market segment that is, electronic subsystems in automobiles, buses, or airplanes.

Finally, tactics focus on individual milestones and responsibilities. Also, specific funding resources and requirements are elaborated in detail and are defined in terms of measurable short-term goals. The funding cycle is tied in with tactical project plans which are also called decision packages in a zero base budgeting (ZBB) approach. The funding cycle covers the forthcoming year. Criteria and measurements vary considerably according to the nature of each tactic. When tactics are approved by the corporate development committee, these tactics or decision packages become tactical action programs (TAP). To prevent the proliferation of TAPs over time and as the company grows, each TAP is evaluated yearly back to a zero base where every budget line item is rejustified in light of current requirements for the coming year.

The practicality of OST is evident in how strategies are tied to particular TAPs. This is where programs are made specific—who, when, what, how, why. Each TAP may involve a variety of work packages and may cross areas of the organization. Each tactical action plan meets the needs of a specific situation and responds to relatively short-term changes in requirements and resource allocations. It is like a field maneuver unit made up of component packages which can quickly shift its plans and controls for individual resources such as budget money, skilled personnel, facilities, and so forth. A TAP is more than just the sum of several work packages; it contributes ultimately to a given strategy. There were over 250 tactical programs in the mid 1970s. The various OST relationships can be illustrated in a matrix format to highlight how each objective, strategy, and tactical action program (TAP) relates to each group, division, and product customer center (PCC) (Exhibit 5). The PCC links specific products or services to specific customers or end-user types. This matrix shows authority relationships. The strategic mode notes a manager's responsibilities worldwide for a major business or product line, whereas his line authority may be quite limited to only direct support for today's product line or to a specific geographic segment. A strategy manager must draw upon the services of other operating entities and gain their cooperation in executing programs. The combined strategic and operating modes mean that managers essentially wear "two hats" at the same time.

MULTIPLE ROLES AND REWARDS

Managers at the strategy and tactical action program levels wear at least "two hats"—by coordinating operations below them and relating operational results to higher level strategies. These managers typically meet once or twice

Exhibit 5

Texas Instruments Incorporated
Strategic and Operating Modes

OBJ	STRAT	TAP	GROUP 1					GROUP 2	
			DIVISION A			DIVISION B		DIVISION	
			PCC 1	PCC 2	PCC 3	PCC 4	PCC 5	PCC 6	PCC 7
1	A	1			X				
		2					X		
		3						X	
		4		X					
	B	5					X		
		6				X			
		7	X						
2	C	8	X						
		9							X

SOURCE: Charles H. Phipps, "Corporate Development: The OST System," (paper presented to the Corporate Growth Association, St. Louis, Missouri, September 9, 1975). p 8.

a month to coordinate lower performance with specific strategy goals. Most of their time, however, is spent on day-to-day operating problems, changes, and cost and profit issues. Time for strategy planning is often limited because of more pressing and readily evident requirements for tactical planning. While it is theoretically good to stress tying long-range strategic plans to short-term tactical plans, the reality is quite often emphasizing feedback tactics rather than "feedforward" strategies. Officially TI managers continue to have a dual responsibility for strategies and tactical operations. This aids in identifying those managers who are more adept at translating between strategies and tactics and who can relate short-term concerns with longer-range concerns. Yet this role shifts because of external environmental realities beyond the control of the individual managers. How quickly technical and economic changes affect this industry and product-customer area determines just how adaptive a manager needs to be. One manager may be highly talented in a rapidly changing product-customer area but may fare only mediocre in the judgment of higher managers, while another less talented manager in a slowly changing product-customer area may appear more totally in control of his area of responsiblility.

The "multiple hats" dilemma and identities of individuals complicate the incentive compensation systems. Managers at each level are asked to identify preferred workers according to individual contributions during the performance period, usually a year. Incentive amounts vary by corporate levels and organizational units. Individuals may be making comparable contributions but yet be in different job grades, with different functions and responsibilities. The top 20 percent is compared at each level up to the division and group levels, where the ratings are merged into an overall framework. Traditionally managers at the strategy level receive much greater rewards than those at the tactical action programs level. This may be rewarding strategy managers differently than tactical managers. Because of the favorable growth in the entire company, virtually every PCC manager on up receives some monetary bonus each year. In addition, there are stock-option plans with various levels of participation to reward those who remain with the company for longer periods of time.

THE STRATEGIC PLANNING CYCLE

The strategic planning cycle begins in the first quarter of each year with a planning conference (Exhibit 6). Over 400 managers with operational responsibilities from all over the world attend, along with corporate officers and board tactical programs and may be reoriented during the course of the year when business objective managers recommend such shifts.

Exhibit 6

**Texas Instruments Incorporated
Strategic Planning Cycle**

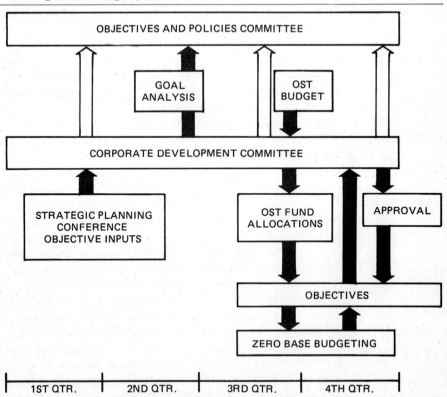

Source: Charles H. Phipps, "Corporate Development: The OST System," (paper presented to the Corporate Growth Association, St. Louis, Missouri, September 9, 1975), p. 16.

members. Each business objective manager assesses opportunities and redefines long-range goals to the group. This position is supported by presentations from key strategy managers who then define their business goals and resource requirements. By the end of the second quarter, plans are drawn up, goals reviewed, and corrective actions determined.

In the third quarter, the corporate OST expenditure level is defined for the upcoming year, and the corporate development committee allocates funds to each of the business objectives based upon their growth opportunities, competitive status, and progress made to date in executing their various plans. In turn, objective and strategy managers define and rank their tactical programs, noting any backlog. After several iterations these are presented to the corporate development committee for approval. Funds may be shifted between objectives and

RESOURCE REVIEW AND CONFLICT RESOLUTION

In any diverse organization individuals are always reviewing their progress or that of their organizational unit relative to others. To obtain a variety of inputs into the OST structure and evaluation, several committees aid in this process by resolving some potential conflicts before they occur. The OST Committee has 13 members, including the president, group vice presidents, and the vice president of corporate development. This committee meets for one or two days about every two or three weeks or as needed. The agenda is predetermined and focuses on a given area, usually one business objective or new opportunity at each session. There is often a diversity of viewpoints initially, but these usually "boil down" to one or two feasible courses of action by the end of the session.

In addition, there is a management committee with nearly the same organizational composition that focuses on operational and administrative issues and allocations and uses of resources in the various strategies and tactical action programs. Note that members of this committee do not relate exclusively to any single objective or strategy and, hence, can be more "open" to the relative merits of various objectives and strategies.

Both the OST committee and management committee make decisions about two budgets—the OST funds and the operating expense funds. There is a separate profit and loss statement for each organizational unit. OST funds are discretionary and allocated using zero-base budgeting whereby previous entitlements do not insure continued equal or increased support in subsequent time periods. Each budget period the managers must indicate how they justify every budget item. The greater the overall profits from previous periods, the greater the funds set aside for OST purposes. At least some OST funds are placed in reserve for contingencies during the year. For example, a given TAP or strategy manager may request additional funds to meet some new requirement or unforeseen problem. Almost every product area has some setbacks every few years, and not all experience continued positive growth every period. Various realignments of OST commitments have been necessary since the early 1970s.

When input requirements and assumptions change, so do processes and output requirements.

OST managers down the chain of command have decentralized authority to commit capital and people resources and adjust them to meet changing goals or constraints. Normally problems are experienced by the TAP manager who then signals this to the attention of the strategy manager, and then, upward to the objective manager to ultimately reach corporate development. The dynamics of this system are much more complex than can be readily explained in two dimensions on an orgainzation chart. There are various interactions and consequences at each level and between levels. Budget forecasts may indicate that shifts are needed at several levels and between components at a given level. While most OST funds are committed to personnel and engineering and development functions, they can be used to rescue any unit in trouble. Normally, the performance of each tactical action program is reviewed monthly in some detail. Any items with significant variation in sales or expenses are likely to receive special attention at least at two levels of the organization. Perhaps it is this continual sharing of basic information between levels which makes OST work with some degree of success in the rapidly changing, high-technology organizational units which make up TI.

SYNERGISTIC IMPACT OF OST PROGRAMS

In addition to the innovative and adaptive management planning and review aspects of OST, this management system provides a "synergistic impact by coupling the capabilities of different business," according to Charles Phipps in "Corporate Developments: The OST System." He further states:

> We strongly believe that the technology developed in one business can often be concurrently coupled with that of other businesses so that the Corporation realizes something more than the individual sums of its many product operations. The OST system provides the means to couple activities, that otherwise would have minimal interaction, together into a single strategic program.

Also relevant is the concern to "boundary span" and "transfer technology" from one organization to another (Exhibit 7). Hopefully the OST provides some added visibility toward removing barriers in specific areas of technology and allows them to transfer ideas between and among those who implement product and market development decisions. But innovation and internal development implementation decisions are not all isolated or ideally achieved in an ultimate sense. Also, they often require considerable interaction and information between different types of individuals who must learn to use this system to better manage their areas of responsibility.

Exhibit 7

Texas Instruments Incorporated
Synergistic Impact of OST Programs

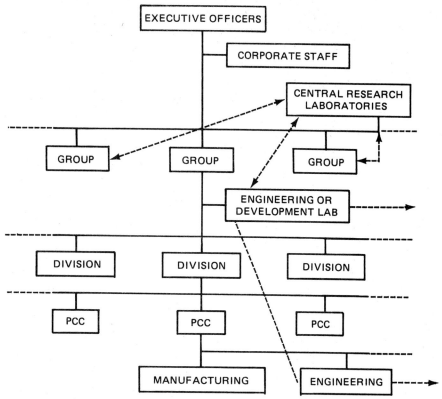

Source: Charles H. Phipps, "Corporate Development: The OST System," (paper presented to the Corporate Growth Association, St. Louis, Missouri, September 9, 1975), p. 10.

NOTES

NOTES